Strategic International Business

Compiled and Edited by:

Jonathan H. Westover, Ph.D.
Utah Valley University

First printed/published in 2014 in the USA
by HCI Press
as part of Leading Innovative Organizations series

Library of Congress Cataloging-in-Publication Data

Strategic International Business / Jonathan H. Westover, editor.
        p. cm. -- (Leading Innovative Organizations series)
ISBN-13: 978-0692308424; ISBN-10: 0692308423 (HCI Press)
1. International Business. 2. Global. 3. Strategy I. Westover, Jonathan H.

Table of Contents

About the Editor

Dr. Jonathan H. Westover is an Associate Professor of Management and Associate Director of the Center for the Study of Ethics at Utah Valley University, specializing in international human resource management, organizational development, and community-engaged experiential learning. He is also a human resource development and performance management consultant. Already a recipient of numerous research, teaching, and service awards and fellowships early in his academic career, Jonathan also recently was named a Fulbright Scholar and was visiting faculty in the MBA program at Belarusian State University (Minsk, Belarus), and he is also a regular visiting faculty member in other graduate business programs in the U.S., UK, France, Poland, and China. Prior to his doctoral studies in the Sociology of Work and Organizations, Comparative International Sociology, and International Political Economy (University of Utah), he received his B.S. in Sociology (Research and Analysis emphasis, Business Management minor, Korean minor) and MPA (emphasis in Human Resource Management) from the Marriott School of Management at Brigham Young University. He also received graduate certificates in demography and higher education teaching during his time at the University of Utah. His ongoing research examines issues of globalization, labor transformation, work quality characteristics, and the determinants of job satisfaction cross-nationally.

Acknowledgements

This text was compiled, edited, and adapted from open source texts at http://www.saylor.org/books and created under a Creative Commons Attribution-NonCommercial ShareAlike 3.0 License without attribution as requested by the work's original creator or licensee. Please contact me for a free copy of the e-text. I would like to thank the many anonymous individuals who contributed their own wisdom and writing to this edited work, particularly those who contributed to the text *International Business*. Of course, this text would not be possible without each of their important contributions. Most of all, I would like to publically thank my wife (Jacque) and my six wonderful children (Sara, Amber, Lia, Kaylie, David, and Brayden) for all of their love and support!

Preface

The overarching logic of the book is intuitive—organized around answers to the what, where, why, and how of international business.

WHAT? Section one introduces what is international business and who has an interest in it. Students will sift through the globalization debate and understanding the impact of ethics on global businesses. Additionally, students will explore the evolution of international trade from past to present, with a focus on how firms and professionals can better understand today's complex global business arena by understanding the impact of political and legal factors. The section concludes with a chapter on understanding how cultures are defined and the impact on business interactions and practices with tangible tips for negotiating across cultures.

WHERE? Section two develops student knowledge about key facets of the global business environment and the key elements of trade and cooperation between nations and global organizations. Today, with increasing numbers of companies of all sizes operating internationally, no business or country can remain an island. Rather, the interconnections between countries, businesses, and institutions are inextricable. Even how we define the world is changing. No longer classified into simple and neat categories, the rapid changes within countries are redefining how global businesses think about developed, developing, and emerging markets. This section addresses the evolving nature of country classifications and helps develop a student's ability to comprehend the rationale of how to analyze a specific country's stage of development—rather than just memorize which countries are emerging. Further, this section provides a unique approach and takes country-related "deep dives" that give greater detail about specific key countries. This section ends with chapters devoted to providing accessible discussions of complex financial concepts within the global monetary system and the global capital markets, including currency and global venture capital.

WHY? Section three develops knowledge about how a student or organization can exploit opportunities in that global environment. Students will learn about the fundamental choices they have in terms of international expansion and why such choices matter. Using different models of internationalization and global market assessment, they will also learn why international business opportunities vary in their promise and complexity. In this section, students also do a deeper dive into the topics of exporting, importing, and global sourcing since these are likely to be the first forms of international business a student will encounter.

HOW? Section four is devoted to strategy and entrepreneurship in a flattening world and how key organizational activities can be managed for global effectiveness. This part of the book shifts gears from the perspective of existing businesses to that of new business possibilities. Our objective is to highlight strategy, entrepreneurship, and strategic and entrepreneurial opportunities in a flat and flattening world. Beyond the basics of international strategy and entrepreneurship, students will be exposed to international human resource management so that they can better understand the global war for talent. They will also develop good fundamental knowledge of international research and development, marketing, distribution, finance, and accounting.

Features

Each chapter contains several staple and innovative features as follows:
- opening cases—cases that are relatively timeless from an international business perspective and current and topical
- sidebars titled "Did You Know"—factoids about international business
- sidebars titled "Amusing Anecdote"—factoids about global marketing snafus and other mistakes coupled with related key international business facts
- sidebars titled "An Eye on Ethics," which provide examples of the ethical issues that arise in international business
- chapter summaries
- end of chapter exercises based on AACSB learning standards—these exercises include review questions, experiential exercises, ethical dilemmas, and exercises related to the opening chapter case
- a closing section titled "Tools in Your Walkabout Kit" with specific and practical tools related to international business

- supplemental support materials by chapter

As you'd expect, our textbook also provides a set of end-of-chapter questions that are mapped to AACSB learning standards, such that the instructor will be able to measure how well students are grasping course content while ensuring alignment with the AACSB guidelines.

We recognize that you have choices on textbooks for your course, but hope that our innovative approach to both essential global business content and technology delivery options will encourage you to join our revolution.

Chapter 1:
Introduction to Strategic International Business

WHAT'S IN IT FOR ME?

1. What is international business?
2. Who has an interest in international business?
3. What forms do international businesses take?
4. What is the globalization debate?
5. What is the relationship between international business and ethics?

This chapter introduces you to the study of international business. After reading a short case study on Google Inc., the Internet search-engine company, you'll begin to learn what makes international business such an essential subject for students around the world. Because international business is a vital ingredient in strategic management and entrepreneurship, this book uses these complementary perspectives to help you understand international business. Managers, entrepreneurs, workers, for-profit and nonprofit organizations, and governments all have a vested interest in understanding and shaping global business practices and trends. Section 1.1 "What Is International Business?" gives you a working definition of international business; Section 1.2 "Who Is Interested in International Business?" helps you see which actors are likely to have a direct and indirect interest in it. You'll then learn about some of the different forms international businesses take; you'll also gain a general understanding of the globalization debate. This debate centers on (1) whether the world is flat, in the sense that all markets are interconnected and competing unfettered with each other, or (2) whether differences across countries and markets are more significant than the commonalities. In fact, some critics negatively describe the "world is flat" perspective as globaloney! What you'll discover from the discussion of this debate is that the world may not be flat in the purest sense, but there are powerful forces, also called flatteners, at work in the world's economies. Section 1.5 "Ethics and International Business" concludes with an introductory discussion of the relationship between international business and ethics.

OPENING CASE: GOOGLE'S STEEP LEARNING CURVE IN CHINA

Of all the changes going on in the world, the Internet is the one development that many people believe makes our world a smaller place—a flat or flattening world, according to

Thomas Friedman, Pulitzer Prize–winning author of The World Is Flat: A Brief History of the Twenty-First Century and The Lexus and the Olive Tree: Understanding Globalization. Because of this flattening effect, Internet businesses should be able to cross borders easily and profitably with little constraint. However, with few exceptions, cross-border business ventures always seem to challenge even the most able of competitors, Internet-based or not. Some new international ventures succeed, while many others fail. But in every venture the managers involved can and do learn something new. Google Inc.'s learning curve in China is a case in point.

In 2006, Google announced the opening of its Chinese-language website amid great fanfare. While Google had access to the Chinese market through Google.com at the time, the new site, Google.cn, gave the company a more powerful, direct vehicle to further penetrate the approximately 94 million households with Internet access in China. As company founders Larry Page and Sergey Brin said at the time, "Unfortunately, access for Chinese users to the Google service outside of China was slow and unreliable, and some content was restricted by complex filtering within each Chinese ISP. Ironically, we were unable to get much public or governmental attention paid to the issue. Although we dislike altering our search results in any way, we ultimately decided that staying out of China simply meant diminishing service and influence there. Building a real operation in China should increase our influence on market practices and certainly will enhance our service to the Chinese people." [1]

A Big Market, Bigger Concerns

Google's move into China gave it access to a very large market, but it also raised some ethical issues. Chinese authorities are notorious for their hardline censorship rules regarding the Internet. They take a firm stance against risqué content and have objected to The Sims computer game, fearing it would corrupt their nation's youth. Any content that was judged as possibly threatening "state security, damaging the nation's glory, disturbing social order, and infringing on other's legitimate rights" was also banned. [2]When asked how working in this kind of environment fit with Google's informal motto of "Don't be evil" and its code-of-conduct aspiration of striving toward the "highest possible standard of ethical business," Google's executives stressed that the license was just to set up a representative office in Beijing and no more than that—although they did concede that Google was keenly interested in the market. As reported to the business press, "For the time being, [we] will be using the [China] office as a base from which to conduct market research and learn more about the market." [3] Google likewise sidestepped the ethical questions by stating it couldn't address the issues until it was fully operational in China and knew exactly what the situation was.

One Year Later

Google appointed Dr. Kai-Fu Lee to lead the company's new China effort. He had grown up in Taiwan, earned BS and PhD degrees from Columbia and Carnegie Mellon, respectively, and was fluent in both English and Mandarin. Before joining Google in 2005, he worked for Apple in California and then for Microsoft in China; he set up Microsoft Research Asia, the company's research-and-development lab in Beijing. When asked by a New York Times reporter about the cultural challenges of doing business in China, Lee responded, "The ideals that we uphold here are really just so important and noble. How to build stuff that users like, and figure out how to make money later. And 'Don't Do Evil' [referring to the motto 'Don't be evil']. All of those things. I think I've always been an idealist in my heart." [4]

Despite Lee's support of Google's utopian motto, the company's conduct in China during its first year seemed less than idealistic. In January, a few months after Lee opened the Beijing office, the company announced it would be introducing a new version of its search engine for the Chinese market. Google's representatives explained that in order to obey China's censorship laws, the company had agreed to remove any websites disapproved of by the Chinese government from the search results it would display. For example, any site that promoted the Falun Gong, a government-banned spiritual movement, would not be displayed. Similarly (and ironically) sites promoting free speech in China would not be displayed, and there would be no mention of the 1989 Tiananmen Square massacre. As one Western reporter noted, "If you search for 'Tibet' or 'Falun Gong' most anywhere in the world on google.com, you'll find thousands of blog entries, news items, and chat rooms on Chinese repression. Do the same search inside China on google.cn, and most, if not all, of these links will be gone. Google will have erased them completely." [5]

Google's decision didn't go over well in the United States. In February 2006, company executives were called into congressional hearings and compared to Nazi collaborators. The company's stock fell, and protesters waved placards outside the company's headquarters in Mountain View, California. Google wasn't the only American technology company to run aground in China during those months, nor was it the worst offender. However, Google's executives were supposed to be different; given their lofty motto, they were supposed to be a cut above the rest. When the company went public in 2004, its founders wrote in the company's official filing for the US Securities and Exchange Commission that Google is "a company that is trustworthy and interested in the public good." Now, politicians and the public were asking how Google could balance that with making nice with a repressive Chinese regime and the Communist Party behind it. [6] One exchange between Rep. Tom Lantos (D-CA) and Google Vice President Elliot Schrage went like this:

Lantos:	You have nothing to be ashamed of?
Schrage:	I am not ashamed of it, and I am not proud of it…We have taken a path, we have begun on a path, we have done a path that…will ultimately benefit all the users in China. If we determined, congressman, as a result of changing circumstances or as a result of the implementation of the Google.cn program that we are not achieving those results then we will assess our performance, our ability to achieve those goals, and whether to remain in the market. [7]

See the video "Google on Operating inside China" at http://news.cnet.com/1606-2-6040114.html. In the video, Schrage, the vice president for corporate communications and public affairs, discusses Google's competitive situation in China. Rep. James Leach (R-IA) subsequently accuses Google of becoming a servant of the Chinese government.

Google Ends Censorship in China

In 2010, Google announced that it was no longer willing to censor search results on its Chinese service. The world's leading search engine said the decision followed a cyber attack that it believes was aimed at gathering information on Chinese human rights activists. [8] Google also cited the Chinese government's restrictions on the Internet in China during 2009. [9] Google's announcement led to speculation whether Google would close its offices in China or would close Google.cn. Human rights activists cheered Google's move, while business pundits speculated on the possibly huge financial costs that would result from losing access to one of the world's largest and fastest-growing consumer markets.

In an announcement provided to the US Securities and Exchange Commission, Google's founders summarized their stance and the motivation for it. Below are excerpts from Google Chief Legal Officer David Drummond's announcement on January 12, 2010. [10]

Like many other well-known organizations, we face cyber attacks of varying degrees on a regular basis. In mid-December, we detected a highly sophisticated and targeted attack on our corporate infrastructure originating from China, resulting in the theft of intellectual property from Google. However, it soon became clear that what at first appeared to be solely a security incident—albeit a significant one—was something quite different.

First, this attack was not just on Google. As part of our investigation, we have discovered that at least twenty other large companies from a wide range of businesses—including the Internet, finance, technology, media, and chemical sectors—have been similarly targeted. We are currently in the process of notifying those companies, and we are also working with the relevant US authorities.

Second, we have evidence to suggest that a primary goal of the attackers was accessing the Gmail accounts of Chinese human rights activists. Based on our investigation to date, we believe their attack did not achieve that objective. Only two Gmail accounts appear to have been accessed, and that activity was limited to account information (such as the date the account was created) and subject line, rather than the content of emails themselves.

Third, as part of this investigation but independent of the attack on Google, we have discovered that the accounts of dozens of US-, China- and Europe-based Gmail users who are advocates of human rights in China appear to have been routinely accessed by third parties. These accounts have not been accessed through any security breach at Google, but most likely via phishing scams or malware placed on the users' computers.

We have taken the unusual step of sharing information about these attacks with a broad audience, not just because of the security and human rights implications of what we have unearthed, but also because this information goes to the heart of a much bigger global debate about freedom of speech. In the last two decades, China's economic reform programs and

its citizens' entrepreneurial flair have lifted hundreds of millions of Chinese people out of poverty. Indeed, this great nation is at the heart of much economic progress and development in the world today.

The decision to review our business operations in China has been incredibly hard, and we know that it will have potentially far-reaching consequences. We want to make clear that this move was driven by our executives in the United States, without the knowledge or involvement of our employees in China who have worked incredibly hard to make Google.cn the success it is today. We are committed to working responsibly to resolve the very difficult issues raised.

The Chinese government's first response to Google's announcement was simply that it was "seeking more information." [11] In the interim, Google "shut down its censored Chinese version and gave mainlanders an uncensored search engine in simplified Chinese, delivered from its servers in Hong Kong." [12] Like most firms that venture out of their home markets, Google's experiences in China and other foreign markets have driven the company to reassess how it does business in countries with distinctly different laws.

OPENING CASE EXERCISES

(AACSB: Ethical Reasoning, Multiculturalism, Reflective Thinking, Analytical Skills)

1. Can Google afford not to do business in China?
2. Which stakeholders would be affected by Google's managers' possible decision to shut down its China operations? How would they be affected? What trade-offs would Google be making?
3. Should Google's managers be surprised by the China predicament?

[1] Larry Page and Sergey Brin, "2005 Founders' Letter," Google Investor Relations, December 31, 2005, accessed October 25, 2010, http://investor.google.com/corporate/2005/founders-letter.html.
[2] John Oates, "Chinese Government Censors Online Games," Register, June 1, 2004, accessed November 12, 2010, http://www.theregister.co.uk/2004/06/01/china_bans_games.
[3] Lucy Sherriff, "Google Goes to China," Register, May 11, 2005, accessed January 25, 2010, http://www.theregister.co.uk/2005/05/11/google_china.
[4] Clive Thompson, "Google's China Problem (and China's Google Problem)," New York Times, April 23, 2006, accessed January 25, 2010, http://www.nytimes.com/2006/04/23/magazine/23google.html.
[5] Clive Thompson, "Google's China Problem (and China's Google Problem)," New York Times, April 23, 2006, accessed January 25, 2010, http://www.nytimes.com/2006/04/23/magazine/23google.html.
[6] Larry Page and Sergey Brin, "2004 Founders' IPO Letter," Google Investor Relations, August 18, 2004, accessed October 25, 2010, http://investor.google.com/corporate/2004/ipo-founders-letter.html.

[7] Declan McCullagh, "Congressman Quizzes Net Companies on Shame," CNET, February 15, 2006, accessed January 25, 2010, http://news.cnet.com/Congressman-quizzes-Net-companies-on-shame/2100-1028_3-6040250.html.

[8] Jessica E. Vascellaro, Jason Dean, and Siobhan Gorman, "Google Warns of China Exit over Hacking," January 13, 2010, accessed November 12, 2010, http://online.wsj.com/article/SB126333757451026659.html#ixzz157TXi4FV.

[9] Tania Branigan, "Google to End Censorship in China over Cyber Attacks," Guardian, January 13, 2010, accessed November 12, 2010, http://www.guardian.co.uk/technology/2010/jan/12/google-china-ends-censorship.

[10] David Drummond, "A New Approach to China," Official Google Blog, January 12, 2010, accessed January 25, 2010, http://googleblog.blogspot.com/2010/01/new-approach-to-china.html.

[11] Tania Branigan, "Google Challenge to China over Censorship," Guardian, January 13, 2010, accessed January 25, 2010, http://www.guardian.co.uk/technology/2010/jan/13/google-china-censorship-battle.

[12] Harry McCracken, "Google's Bold China Move," PCWorld, March 23, 2010, accessed November 12, 2010, http://www.pcworld.com/article/192130/googles_bold_china_move.html

1.1   What Is International Business?

LEARNING OBJECTIVES

1. Know the definition of international business.
2. Comprehend how strategic management is related to international business.
3. Understand how entrepreneurship is related to international business.

The Definition of International Business

As the opening case study on Google suggests, international business relates to any situation where the production or distribution of goods or services crosses country borders. Globalization—the shift toward a more interdependent and integrated global economy—creates greater opportunities for international business. Such globalization can take place in terms of markets, where trade barriers are falling and buyer preferences are changing. It can also be seen in terms of production, where a company can source goods and services easily from other countries. Some managers consider the definition of international business to relate purely to "business," as suggested in the Google case. However, a broader definition of international business may serve you better both personally and professionally in a world that has moved beyond simple industrial production. International business encompasses a full range of cross-border exchanges of goods, services, or resources between two or more nations. These exchanges can go beyond the exchange of money for physical goods to include international transfers of other resources, such as people,

intellectual property (e.g., patents, copyrights, brand trademarks, and data), and contractual assets or liabilities (e.g., the right to use some foreign asset, provide some future service to foreign customers, or execute a complex financial instrument). The entities involved in international business range from large multinational firms with thousands of employees doing business in many countries around the world to a small one-person company acting as an importer or exporter. This broader definition of international business also encompasses for-profit border-crossing transactions as well as transactions motivated by nonfinancial gains (e.g., triple bottom line, corporate social responsibility, and political favor) that affect a business's future.

Strategic Management and Entrepreneurship

A knowledge of both strategic management and entrepreneurship will enhance your understanding of international business. Strategic management is the body of knowledge that answers questions about the development and implementation of good strategies and is mainly concerned with the determinants of firm performance. A strategy, in turn, is the central, integrated, and externally oriented concept of how an organization will achieve its performance objectives. [1] One of the basic tools of strategy is aSWOT (strengths, weaknesses, opportunities, threats) assesment. The SWOT tool helps you take stock of an organization's internal characteristics—its strengths and weaknesses—to formulate an action plan that builds on what it does well while overcoming or working around weaknesses. Similarly, the external part of SWOT—the opportunities and threats—helps you assess those environmental conditions that favor or threaten the organization's strategy. Because strategic management is concerned with organizational performance—be that social, environmental, or economic—your understanding of a company's SWOT will help you better assess how international business factors should be accounted for in the firm's strategy.

Entrepreneurship, in contrast, is defined as the recognition of opportunities (i.e., needs, wants, problems, and challenges) and the use or creation of resources to implement innovative ideas for new, thoughtfully planned ventures. An entrepreneur is a person who engages in entrepreneurship. Entrepreneurship, like strategic management, will help you to think about the opportunities available when you connect new ideas with new markets. For instance, given Google's current global presence, it's difficult to imagine that the company started out slightly more than a decade ago as the entrepreneurial venture of two college students. Google was founded by Larry Page and Sergey Brin, students at Stanford University. It was first incorporated as a privately held company on September 4, 1998. Increasingly, as the Google case study demonstrates, international businesses have an opportunity to create positive social, environmental, and economic values across borders. An entrepreneurial perspective will serve you well in this regard.

Spotlight on International Strategy and Entrepreneurship

Hemali Thakkar and three of her fellow classmates at Harvard found a way to mesh the power of play with electrical power. The foursome invented "a soccer ball with the ability to generate electricity," Thakkar said. [2] Every kick of the ball creates a current that's captured for future use. Fifteen minutes of play lights a lamp for three hours.

Called the sOccket, the soccer ball can bring off-grid electricity to developing countries. Even better, the soccer ball can replace kerosene lamps. Burning kerosene is not only bad for the environment because of carbon dioxide emissions but it's also a health hazard: according to the World Bank, breathing kerosene fumes indoors has the same effects as smoking two packs of cigarettes per day. [3]

How did the idea of sOccket emerge? All four students (Jessica Lin, Jessica Matthews, Julia Silverman, and Hemali Thakkar) had experience with developing countries, so they knew that kids love playing soccer (it's the world's most popular sport). They also knew that most of these kids lived in homes that had no reliable energy. [4]

As of November 2010, the sOccket prototype cost $70 to manufacture, but the team hopes to bring the cost down to $10 when production is scaled up. [5] One ingenious way to bring costs down is to set up facilities where developing-world entrepreneurs assemble and sell the balls themselves.

At this point it's also important to introduce you to the concepts of intrapreneurship and the intrapreneur. Intrapreneurship is a form of entrepreneurship that takes place inside a business that is already in existence. An intrapreneur, in turn, is a person within the established business who takes direct responsibility for turning an idea into a profitable finished product through assertive risk taking and innovation. An entrepreneur is starting a business, while an intrapreneur is developing a new product or service in an already existing business. Thus, the ideas of entrepreneurship can be applied not only in new ventures but

also in the context of existing organizations—even government.

KEY TAKEAWAYS

- International business encompasses a full range of cross-border exchanges of goods, services, or resources between two or more nations. These exchanges can go beyond the exchange of money for physical goods to include international transfers of other resources, such as people, intellectual property (e.g., patents, copyrights, brand trademarks, and data), and contractual assets or liabilities (e.g., the right to use some foreign asset, provide some future service to foreign customers, or execute a complex financial instrument).

- Strategic management is the body of knowledge that answers questions about the development and implementation of good strategies and is mainly concerned with the determinants of firm performance. Because strategic management is concerned with organizational performance, your understanding of a company's SWOT (strengths, weaknesses, opportunities, threats) helps you better assess how international business factors should be accounted for in the firm's strategy.

- Entrepreneurship is the recognition of opportunities (i.e., needs, wants, problems, and challenges) and the use or creation of resources to implement innovative ideas. Entrepreneurship helps you think about the opportunities available when you connect new ideas with new markets.

EXERCISES

(AACSB: Reflective Thinking, Analytical Skills)
1. What is international business?
2. Why is an understanding of strategy management important in the context of international business?
3. Why is an understanding of entrepreneurship important in the context of international business?

[1] {Author's name retracted as requested by the work's original creator or licensee} and William G. Sanders, Strategic Management: A Dynamic Perspective, Concepts and Cases (Upper Saddle River, NJ: Pearson Education, 2007).
[2] "Harnessing the Power of Soccer," interview with Thakkar Hemali by Ike Sriskandarajah, October 20, 2010, accessed November 12, 2010, http://www.loe.org/shows/segments.htm?programID=10-P13-00044&segmentID=5.
[3] Ariel Schwartz, "The SOccket: A Soccer Ball to Replace Kerosene Lamps," Fast Company, January 26, 2010, accessed November 12, 2010, http://www.fastcompany.com/blog/ariel-schwartz/sustainability/soccket-soccer-ball-replace-kerosene-lamps.

[4] Clark Boyd, "SOccket: Soccer Ball by Day, Light by Night," Discovery News, February 18, 2010, accessed November 12, 2010, http://news.discovery.com/tech/soccket-soccer-ball-by-day-light-by-night.html.
[5] Ike Sriskandarajah, "Soccer Ball Brings Off-Grid Electricity Onto the Field," The Atlantic, November 3, 2010, accessed November 12, 2010, http://www.theatlantic.com/technology/archive/2010/11/soccer-ball-brings-off-grid-electricity-onto-the-field/65977.

1.2 Who Is Interested in International Business?
LEARNING OBJECTIVES

1. Know who has an interest in international business.
2. Understand what a stakeholder is and why stakeholder analysis might be important in the study of international business.
3. Recognize that an organization's stakeholders include more than its suppliers and customers.

The Stakeholders

As you now know, *international business* refers to a broad set of entities and activities. But who cares about international business in the first place? To answer this question, let's discuss stakeholders and stakeholder analysis. A stakeholder is an individual or organization whose interests may be affected as the result of what another individual or organization does. [1]Stakeholder analysis is a technique you use to identify and assess the importance of key people, groups of people, or institutions that may significantly influence the success of your activity, project, or business. In the context of what you are learning here, individuals or organizations will have an interest in international business if it affects them in some way—positively or negatively. [2] That is, they have something important at stake as a result of some aspect of international business.

Obviously, Google and its managers need to understand international business because they do business in many countries outside their home country. A little more than half the company's revenues come from outside the United States. [3]Does this mean that international business wouldn't be relevant to Google if it only produced and sold its products in one country? Absolutely not! Factors of international business would still affect Google—through any supplies it buys from foreign suppliers, as well as the possible impact of foreign competitors that threaten to take business from Google in its home markets. Even if these factors were not present, Google could still be affected by price swings—for instance, in the international prices of computer parts, even if they bought those parts from US suppliers. After all, the prices of some of the commodities used to make those parts are determined globally, not locally.

Beyond its involvement in web advertising, which requires massive investments in computer-server farms around the world, Google is increasingly active in other products and services—for example, cell phones and the operating systems they use.

So far, this chapter has covered only how a business and its managers should understand international business, regardless of whether their organization sells or produces products or services across borders. Who else might be an international business stakeholder beyond Google and its management? First, Google is likely to have to pay taxes, right? It probably pays sales taxes in markets where it sells its products, as well as property and payroll taxes in countries where it has production facilities. Each of these governmental stakeholders has an important economic interest in Google. Moreover, in many countries, the government is responsible for protecting the environment. Google's large computer-server farms consume energy and generate waste, and its products (e.g., cell phones) come in disposable packaging, thus impacting the environment in places where they are manufactured and sold.

Beyond the company and governments, other stakeholder groups might include industry associations, trade groups, suppliers, and labor. For instance, you've already learned that Google is an Internet search-engine company, so it could be a member of various computer-related industry associations. Labor is also a stakeholder. This can include not only the people immediately employed by a business like Google but also contract workers or workers who will lose or gain employment opportunities depending on where Google chooses to produce and sell its products and services.

Did You Know?

From our opening case, you've learned a little about how different countries deal with personal privacy. At about the same time Google was experiencing difficulty protecting individuals' privacy in China, its managers in Italy were being convicted of violating consumer-privacy laws. Google executives had been accused of breaking Italian law by allowing a video clip of four boys bullying another child to be posted online. [4] The video had originally been posted by the boys themselves and Google removed the video when Italy's Interior Ministry requested its removal. [5] The three Google executives were absolved of the defamation charges but convicted of privacy violations. [6] Google said that the conviction of its top Italian managers "attacks the 'principles of freedom' of the Internet and poses a serious threat to the web." [7] Following the conviction, several privacy advocates stepped up to speak out in Google's defense—a position quite contrary to their typical stances in Google privacy stories. [8]

KEY TAKEAWAYS

- Beyond yourself, as an international business student and future international business person, you can identify the people and organizations that might have an interest in international business if their interests are affected now or in the future by it. Such international business stakeholders include employees, managers, businesses, governments, and nongovernmental organizations.

- Stakeholder analysis is a technique used to identify and assess the importance of key people, groups of people, or institutions that may significantly influence the success of an activity, project, or business.

EXERCISES

(AACSB: Reflective Thinking, Analytical Skills)

1. What is a stakeholder?
2. Why is stakeholder analysis important in international business?

[1] {Authors' names retracted as requested by the work's original creator or licensee}, Principles of Management (Nyack, NY)

[2] Management Sciences for Health and the United Nations Children's Fund, "Stakeholder Analysis," The Guide to Managing for Quality, 1998, accessed November 21, 2010, http://erc.msh.org/quality/ittools/itstkan.cfm.

[3] "Google Announces First Quarter 2009 Results," Google Investor Relations, April 16, 2009, accessed January 25, 2010, http://investor.google.com/releases/2009Q1 google earnings.html.

[4] "Google Bosses Convicted in Italy," BBC News, February 24, 2010, accessed November 21, 2010, http://news.bbc.co.uk/2/hi/8533695.stm.

[5] J. R. Raphael, "Italy's Google Convictions Set a Dangerous Precedent," PCWorld, February 24, 2010, accessed November 21, 2010, http://www.pcworld.com/article/190191/italys google convictions set a dangerous precedent.html.

[6] Colleen Barry, "Three Google Employees Convicted in Italian Court of Privacy Violations," Associated Press, February 24, 2010, accessed November 21, 2010, http://www.cleveland.com/world/index.ssf/2010/02/three google empl oyees convict.html.

[7] Paul McNamara, "Conviction of Google Execs in Italy Sheer Madness," PCWorld, February 24, 2010, accessed April 5, 2010, http://www.pcworld.com/article/190125/conviction of google execs in italy sheer madness.html.

[8] Jaikumar Vijayan, "Conviction of Google Execs Alarms Privacy Advocates," PCWorld, February 24, 2010, accessed April 5, 2010, http://www.pcworld.com/article/190175/conviction of google execs al arms privacy advocates.html.

1.3 What Forms Do International Businesses Take?
LEARNING OBJECTIVES

1. Know the possible forms that international businesses can take.
2. Understand the differences between exporting, importing, and foreign direct investment.
3. See how governments and nongovernmental organizations can be international businesses.

The Forms of International Business

It probably doesn't surprise you that international businesses can take on a variety of forms. Recognizing that international business, based on our broad definition, spans business, government, and nongovernmental organizations (NGOs), let's start by looking at business.

A business can be a person or organization engaged in commerce with the aim of achieving a profit. Business profit is typically gauged in financial and economic terms. However, some level of sustained financial and economic profits are needed for a business to achieve other sustainable outcomes measured as social or environmental performance. For example, many companies that are for-profit businesses also have a social and environmental mission. Table 1.1 "Sample Three-Part Mission Statement" provides an example of a company with this kind of mission.

On the one hand, while companies such as Ben & Jerry's (part of Unilever) and SC Johnson are very large, it's hard to imagine any business—small or large—that doesn't have international operating concerns. On the other hand, the *international* part of a firm's business can vary considerably, from importing to exporting to having significant operations outside its home country. An importer sells products and services that are sourced from other countries; an exporter, in contrast, sells products and services in foreign countries that are sourced from its home country. Beyond importing and exporting, some organizations maintain offices in other countries; this forms the basis for their level of foreign direct investment. Foreign direct investment means that a firm is investing assets directly into a foreign country's buildings, equipment, or organizations. In some cases, these foreign offices are carbon copies of the parent firm; that is, they have all the value creation and support activities, just in a different country. In other cases, the foreign operations are focused on a small subset of activities tailored to the local market, or those that the entity supplies for operations every place in which the firm operates.

Table 1.1 Sample Three-Part Mission Statement

Social and Environmental Mission	Product Mission	Economic Mission
Part of being a responsible company is working hard to help solve the world's environmental problems and, importantly, also helping those who buy our products to make more responsible choices. [1]	To make, distribute, and sell the finest quality products with a continued commitment to promoting business practices that respect the Earth and the environment. [2]	To create long-term value and capture the greatest opportunity for our stakeholders by delivering sustainable, profitable growth in sales, earnings, and cash flow in a global company built on pride, integrity, and respect. [3]

When a firm makes choices about foreign operations that increase national and local responsiveness, the organization is more able to adapt to national and local market conditions. In contrast, the greater the level of standardization—both within and across markets—the greater the possible level of global efficiency. In many cases, the choice of foreign location generates unique advantages, referred to as location advantages. Location advantages include better access to raw materials, less costly labor, key suppliers, key customers, energy, and natural resources. For instance, Google locates its computer-server farms—the technological backbone of its massive Internet services—close to dams that produce hydroelectric power because it's one of the cheapest sources of electricity. [4] Ultimately, managerial choices regarding the trade-off between *global efficiency* and *local responsiveness* are a function of the firm's strategy and are likely to be a significant determinant of firm performance.

International Forms of Government

Governmental bodies also take on different international forms. Among political scientists, government is generally considered to be the body of people that sets and administers public policy and exercises executive, political, and sovereign power through customs, institutions, and laws within a state, country, or other political unit. Or more simply, government

is the organization, or agency, through which a political unit exercises its authority, controls and administers public policy, and directs and controls the actions of its members or subjects.

Most national governments, for instance, maintain embassies and consulates in foreign countries. National governments also participate in international treaties related to such issues as trade, the environment, or child labor. For example, the North American Free Trade Agreement (NAFTA) is an agreement signed by the governments of the United States, Canada, and Mexico to create a trade bloc in North America to reduce or eliminate tariffs among the member countries and thus facilitate trade. The Kyoto Protocol is an agreement aimed at combating global warming among participating countries. In some cases, such as with the European Community (EC), agreements span trade, the environment, labor, and many other subjects related to business, social, and environmental issues. The Atlanta Agreement, in turn, is an agreement between participating governments and companies to eliminate child labor in the production of soccer balls in Pakistan. [5] Finally, supraorganizations such as the United Nations (UN) or the World Trade Organization (WTO) are practically separate governments themselves, with certain powers over all member countries. [6]

Nongovernmental Organizations

National nongovernmental organizations (NGOs) include any nonprofit, voluntary citizens' groups that are organized on a local, national, or international level. International NGOs (NGOs whose operations cross borders) date back to at least 1839. [7] For example, Rotary International was founded in 1905. It has been estimated that, by 1914, there were 1,083 NGOs. [8]International NGOs were important in the antislavery movement and the movement for women's suffrage, but the phrase "nongovernmental organization" didn't enter the common lexicon until 1945, when the UN was established along with the provisions in Article 71 of Chapter 10 of the UN charter, [9], which granted a consultative role to organizations that are neither governments nor member states.

During the twentieth century, globalization actually fostered the development of NGOs because many problems couldn't be solved within a single nation. In addition, international treaties and organizations, such as the WTO, were perceived by human rights activists as being too centered on the interests of business. Some argued that in an attempt to counterbalance this trend, NGOs were formed to emphasize humanitarian issues, developmental aid, and sustainable development. A prominent example of this is the World Social Forum—a rival convention to the World Economic Forum held every January in Davos, Switzerland.

KEY TAKEAWAYS

- International businesses take on a variety of forms. Importers sell goods and services obtained from other countries, while exporters sell goods and services from their home country abroad.

- Firms can also make choices about the extent and structure of their foreign direct investments, from simply an array of satellite sales offices to integrated production, sales, and distribution centers in foreign countries.

- Government and nongovernmental organizations also comprise international business.

EXERCISES

(AACSB: Reflective Thinking, Analytical Skills)

1. What is the difference between an exporter and an importer?
2. What is a location advantage?
3. How is government considered an international business?

[1] "Investing in People, Investing for the Planet," SC Johnson, accessed November 21, 2010, http://www.scjohnson.com/en/commitment/report/CEO-Letter.aspx.

[2] "Ben & Jerry's," Unilever, accessed November 21, 2010, http://www.unileverusa.com/brands/foodbrands/benandjerrys.

[3] "Our Business Purpose," Amtrak, accessed November 21, 2010, http://www.aramark.com/AboutARAMARK/BusinessPurpose.

[4] Stephanie N. Mehta, "Behold the Server Farm! Glorious Temple of the Information Age! "Fortune, August 1, 2006, accessed April 27, 2010, http://money.cnn.com/magazines/fortune/fortune_archive/2006/08/07/8382587/index.htm.

[5] "Atlanta Agreement," Independent Monitoring Association for Child Labor, accessed November 12, 2010, http://www.imacpak.org/atlanta.htm.

[6] United Nations website, accessed January 20, 2010, http://www.un.org; World Trade Organization website, accessed January 20, 2010, http://www.wto.org.

[7] Steve Charnovitz, "Two Centuries of Participation: NGOs and International Governance," Michigan Journal of International Law 18, no. 183 (Winter 1997): 183–286.

[8] Oliver P. Richmond and Henry F. Carey, eds., Subcontracting Peace: The Challenges of NGO Peacebuilding (Burlington, VT: Ashgate, 2005), 21; United Nations, "Chapter X: The Economic and Social Council," Charter of the United Nations, accessed April 28, 2010, http://www.un.org/en/documents/charter/chapter10.shtml.

[9] United Nations, "Chapter X: The Economic and Social Council," Charter of the United Nations, accessed April 28, 2010, http://www.un.org/en/documents/charter/chapter10.shtml.

1.4 The Globalization Debate
LEARNING OBJECTIVES

1. Understand the flattening world perspective in the globalization debate.
2. Understand the multidomestic perspective in the globalization debate.
3. Know the dimensions of the CAGE analytical framework.

In today's global economy, everyone is accustomed to buying goods from other countries—electronics from Taiwan, vegetables from Mexico, clothing from China, cars from Korea, and skirts from India. Most modern shoppers take the "Made in [a foreign country]" stickers on their products for granted. Long-distance commerce wasn't always this common, although foreign trade—the movement of goods from one geographic region to another—has been a key factor in human affairs since prehistoric times. Thousands of years ago, merchants transported only the most precious items—silk, gold and other precious metals and jewels, spices, porcelains, and medicines—via ancient, extended land and sea trade routes, including the famed Silk Road through central Asia. Moving goods great distances was simply too hard and costly to waste the effort on ordinary products, although people often carted grain and other foods over shorter distances from farms to market towns. [1]

What is the globalization debate? Well, it's not so much a debate as it is a stark difference of opinion on how the internationalization of businesses is affecting countries' cultural, consumer, and national identities—and whether these changes are desirable. For instance, the ubiquity of such food purveyors as Coca-Cola and McDonald's in practically every country reflects the fact that some consumer tastes are converging, though at the likely expense of local beverages and foods. Remember, globalization refers to the shift toward a more interdependent and integrated global economy. This shift is fueled largely by (1) declining trade and investment barriers and (2) new technologies, such as the Internet. The globalization debate surrounds whether and how fast markets are actually merging together.

We Live in a Flat World
The flat-world view is largely credited to Thomas Friedman and his 2005 best seller, *The World Is Flat*. Although the next section provides you with an alternative way of thinking about the world (a multidomestic view), it is nonetheless important to understand the flat-world perspective. Friedman covers the world for the *New York Times*, and his access to important local authorities, corporate executives,

local *Times* bureaus and researchers, the Internet, and a voice recorder enabled him to compile a huge amount of information. Many people consider globalization a modern phenomenon, but according to Friedman, this is its third stage. The first stage of global development, what Friedman calls "Globalization 1.0," started with Columbus's discovery of the New World and ran from 1492 to about 1800. Driven by nationalism and religion, this lengthy stage was characterized by how much industrial power countries could produce and apply.

"Globalization 2.0," from about 1800 to 2000, was disrupted by the Great Depression and both World Wars and was largely shaped by the emerging power of huge, multinational corporations. Globalization 2.0 grew with the European mercantile stock companies as they expanded in search of new markets, cheap labor, and raw materials. It continued with subsequent advances in sea and rail transportation. This period saw the introduction of modern communications and cheaper shipping costs. "Globalization 3.0" began around 2000, with advances in global electronic interconnectivity that allowed individuals to communicate as never before.

In Globalization 1.0, nations dominated global expansion. Globalization 2.0 was driven by the ascension of multinational companies, which pushed global development. In Globalization 3.0, major software advances have allowed an unprecedented number of people worldwide to work together with unlimited potential.

The Mumbai Taxman

What shape will globalization take in the third phase? Friedman asks us to consider the friendly local accountants who do your taxes. They can easily outsource your work via a server to a tax team in Mumbai, India. This increasingly popular outsourcing trend has its benefits. As Friedman notes, in 2003, about 25,000 US tax returns were done in India. [2] By 2004, it was some 100,000 returns, with 400,000 anticipated in 2005. A software program specifically designed to let midsized US tax firms outsource their files enabled this development, giving better job prospects to the 70,000 accounting students who graduate annually in India. At a starting salary of $100 per month, these accountants are completing US returns and competing with US tax preparers.

Chris C. Got It Wrong?

In 1492, Christopher Columbus set sail for India, going west. He had the Niña, the Pinta, and the Santa María. He never did find India, but he called the people he met "Indians" and came home and reported to his king and queen: "The world

is round." I set off for India 512 years later. I knew just which direction I was going in—I went east. I was in Lufthansa business class, and I came home and reported only to my wife and only in a whisper: "The world is flat."

And therein lies a tale of technology and geoeconomics that is fundamentally reshaping our lives—much, much more quickly than many people realize. It all happened while we were sleeping, or rather while we were focused on 9/11, the dot-com bust, and Enron—which even prompted some to wonder whether globalization was over. Actually, just the opposite was true, which is why it's time to wake up and prepare ourselves for this flat world, because others already are, and there is no time to waste. [3]

This job competition is not restricted to accountants. Companies can outsource any service or business that can be broken down to its key components and converted to computerized operations. This includes everything from making restaurant reservations to reporting corporate earnings to reading x-rays. And it doesn't stop at basic services. With the "globalization of innovation," multinationals in India are filing increasing numbers of US patent applications, ranging from aircraft-engine designs to transportation systems and microprocessor chips. Japanese-speaking Chinese nationals in Dailian, China, now answer call-center questions from Japanese consumers. Due to Dailian's location near Japan and Korea, as well as its numerous universities, hospitals, and golf courses, some 2,800 Japanese companies outsource operations there. While many companies are outsourcing to other countries, some are using "home sourcing"—allowing people to work at home. JetBlue uses home sourcing for reservation clerks. Today, about 16 percent of the US workforce works from home. In many ways, outsourcing and home sourcing are related; both allow people to work from anywhere.

How the World Got Flat

Friedman identifies ten major events that helped reshape the modern world and make it flat: [4]

1. **11/9/89: When the walls came down and the windows went up.** The fall of the Berlin Wall ended old-style communism and planned economies. Capitalism ascended.
2. **8/9/95: When Netscape went public.** Internet browsing and e-mail helped propel the Internet by making it commercially viable and user friendly.
3. **Work-flow software: Let's do lunch. Have your application talk to my application.** With more

powerful, easier-to-use software and improved connectivity, more people can share work. Thus, complex projects with more interdependent parts can be worked on collaboratively from anywhere.

4. **Open-sourcing: Self-organizing, collaborative communities.** Providing basic software online for free gives everyone source code, thus accelerating collaboration and software development.

5. **Outsourcing: Y2K.** The Internet lets firms use employees worldwide and send specific work to the most qualified, cheapest labor, wherever it is. Enter India, with educated and talented people who work at a fraction of US or European wages. Indian technicians and software experts built an international reputation during the Y2K millennium event. The feared computer-system breakdown never happened, but the Indian IT industry began handling e-commerce and related businesses worldwide.

6. **Offshoring: Running with gazelles, eating with lions.** When it comes to jobs leaving and factories being built in cheaper places, people think of China, Malaysia, Thailand, Mexico, Ireland, Brazil, and Vietnam. But going offshore isn't just moving part of a manufacturing or service process. It means creating a new business model to make more goods for non-US sale, thus increasing US exports.

7. **Supply-chaining: Eating sushi in Arkansas.** Walmart demonstrates that improved acquisition and distribution can lower costs and make suppliers boost quality.

8. **Insourcing: What the guys in funny brown shorts are really doing.** This kind of service collaboration happens when firms devise new service combinations to improve service. Take United Parcel Service (UPS). The "brown" company delivers packages globally, but it also repairs Toshiba computers and organizes delivery routes for Papa John's pizza. With insourcing, UPS uses its logistics expertise to help clients create new businesses.

9. **Informing: Google, Yahoo!, and MSN Web Search.** Google revolutionized information searching. Its users conduct some one billion searches annually. This search methodology and the wide access to knowledge on the Internet transforms information into a commodity people can use to spawn entirely new businesses.

10. **The steroids: Digital, mobile, personal, and virtual.** Technological advances range from wireless communication to processing, resulting in extremely powerful computing capability and transmission. One new Intel chip processes some 11 million instructions per second (MIPS), compared to 60,000 MIPS in 1971.

These ten factors had powerful roles in making the world smaller, but each worked in isolation until, Freidman writes, the convergence of three more powerful forces: (1) new software and increased public familiarity with the Internet, (2) the incorporation of that knowledge into business and personal communication, and (3) the market influx of billions of people from Asia and the former Soviet Union who want to become more prosperous—fast. Converging, these factors generated their own critical mass. The benefits of each event became greater as it merged with another event. Increased global collaboration by talented people without regard to geographic boundaries, language, or time zones created opportunity for billions of people.

Political allegiances are also shifting. While critics say outsourcing costs US jobs, it can also work the other way. When the state of Indiana bid for a new contract to overhaul its employment claims processing system, a computer firm in India won. The company's bid would have saved Indiana $8 million, but local political forces made the state cancel the contract. In such situations, the line between the exploited and the exploiter becomes blurred.

Corporate nationality is also blurring. Hewlett-Packard (HP) is based in California, but it has employees in 178 countries. HP manufactures parts wherever it's cheapest to do so. Multinationals like HP do what's best for them, not what's best for their home countries. This leads to critical issues about job loss versus the benefits of globalization.

Since the world's flattening can't be stopped, new workers and those facing dislocation should refine their skills and capitalize on new opportunities. One key is to become an expert in a job that can't be delegated offshore. This ranges from local barbers and plumbers to professionals such as surgeons and specialized lawyers.

We Live in a Multidomestic World, Not a Flat One!

International business professor Pankaj Ghemawat takes strong issue with the view that the world is flat and instead espouses a world he characterizes as "semiglobalized" and "multidomestic." If the world were flat, international business and global strategy would be easy. According to Ghemawat, it would be domestic strategy applied to a bigger market. In the semiglobalized world, however, global strategy begins with noticing national differences. [5]

Ghemawat's research suggests that to study "barriers to cross-border economic activity" you will use a "CAGE" analysis. The CAGE framework covers these four factors: [6]

1. **Culture.** Generally, cultural differences between two countries reduce their economic exchange. Culture refers to a people's norms, common beliefs, and practices. Cultural distance refers to differences based in language, norms, national or ethnic identity, levels of trust, tolerance, respect for entrepreneurship and social networks, or other country-specific qualities. Some products have a strong national identification, such as the Molson beer company in Canada (see Molson's "I am Canadian" ad campaign). [7] Conversely, genetically modified foods (GMOs) are commonly accepted in North America but highly disdained in Western Europe. Such cultural distance for GMOs would make it easier to sell GMO corn in the United States but impossible to sell in Germany. Some differences are surprisingly specific (such as the Chinese dislike of dark beverages, which Coca-Cola marketers discovered too late).

2. **Administration.** Bilateral trade flows show that administratively similar countries trade much more with each other. Administrative distance refers to historical governmental ties, such as those between India and the United Kingdom. This makes sense; they have the same sorts of laws, regulations, institutions, and policies. Membership in the same trading block is also a key similarity. Conversely, the greater the administrative differences between nations, the more difficult the trading relationship—whether at the national or corporate level. It can also refer simply to the level and nature of government involvement in one industry versus another. Farming, for instance, is subsidized in many countries, and this creates similar conditions.

3. **Geography.** This is perhaps the most obvious difference between countries. You can see that the market for a product in Los Angeles is separated from the market for that same product in Singapore by thousands of miles. Generally, as distance goes up, trade goes down, since distance usually increases the cost of transportation. Geographic differences also include time zones, access to ocean ports, shared borders, topography, and climate. You may recall from the opening case that even Google was affected by geographic distance when it felt the speed of the Internet connection to Google.com was slowed down because the Chinese were accessing server farms in other countries, as none were set up in China (prior to the setup of Google.cn).

4. **Economics.** Economic distance refers to differences in demographic and socioeconomic conditions. The most obvious economic difference between countries is size (as compared by gross domestic product, or GDP).

Another is per capita income. This distance is likely to have the greatest effect when (1) the nature of demand varies with income level, (2) economies of scale are limited, (3) cost differences are significant, (4) the distribution or business systems are different, or (5) organizations have to be highly responsive to their customers' concerns. Disassembling a company's economy reveals other differences, such as labor costs, capital costs, human capital (e.g., education or skills), land value, cheap natural resources, transportation networks, communication infrastructure, and access to capital.

Each of these CAGE dimensions shares the common notion of distance. CAGE differences are likely to matter most when the CAGE distance is great. That is, when CAGE differences are small, there will likely be a greater opportunity to see business being conducted across borders. A CAGE analysis also requires examining an organization's particular industry and products in each of these areas. When looking at culture, consider how culturally sensitive the products are. When looking at administration, consider whether other countries coddle certain industries or support "national champions." When looking at geography, consider whether products will survive in a different climate. When looking at economics, consider such issues as the effect of per capita income on demand.

An Amusing Anecdote

Pankaj Ghemawat provides this anecdote in partial support of his multidomestic (or anti-flat-world) view. "It takes an aroused man to make a chicken affectionate" is probably not the best marketing slogan ever devised. But that's the one Perdue Chicken used to market its fryers in Mexico. Mexicans were nonplussed, to say the least, and probably wondered what was going on in founder Frank Perdue's henhouse. How did the slogan get approved? Simple: it's a literal translation of Perdue's more appetizing North American slogan "It takes a tough man to make a tender chicken." As Perdue discovered, at least through his experience with the literal translation of his company motto into Spanish, cultural and economic globalization have yet to arrive. Consider the market for capital. Some say capital "knows no boundaries." Recent data, however, suggests capital knows its geography quite well and is sticking close to home. For every dollar of capital investment globally, only a dime comes from firms investing "outside their home countries." For every $100 US investors put in the stock market, they spend $15 on international stocks. For every one hundred students in Organization for Economic Co-operation (OECD) universities, perhaps five are foreigners. These and other key measures of internationalization show that the world isn't flat. It's 90 percent round, like a rugby ball. [8]

While the world may not be flat, it is probably safe to say that it is flattening. We will use the CAGE framework throughout this book to better understand this evolving dynamic.

KEY TAKEAWAYS

- The globalization debate pits the opinions of Thomas Friedman against those of Pankaj Ghemawat. Their differing views help you better understand the context of international business. Through exposure to Friedman's ideas, you gain a better perspective on the forces, or "flatteners," that are making cross-border business more prominent.

- Ghemawat portrays a world that is "semiglobalized" and "multidomestic," where global strategy begins with noticing national differences.

- Ghemawat's CAGE framework covers four factors—culture, administration, geography, and economics.

EXERCISES

(AACSB: Reflective Thinking, Analytical Skills)

1. What are the basic tenets of the flat-world perspective?
2. Why does Ghemawat disagree with the flat-world perspective?
3. What are the four components of the CAGE analytical framework?

[1] William J. Bernstein, A Splendid Exchange: How Trade Shaped the World (New York: Atlantic Monthly Press, 2008).
[2] Thomas L. Friedman, The World Is Flat (New York: Farrar, Straus and Giroux, 2005).
[3] Thomas L. Friedman, "It's a Flat World, After All," New York Times Magazine, April 3, 2005, accessed June 2, 2010,http://www.nytimes.com/2005/04/03/magazine/03DOMINANCE.html.
[4] Thomas L. Friedman, The World Is Flat (New York: Farrar, Straus and Giroux, 2005), 48–159.
[5] Pankaj Ghemawat, "Distance Still Matters," Harvard Business Review 79, no. 8 (2001): 137–47.
[6] Pankaj Ghemawat, "Distance Still Matters," Harvard Business Review 79, no. 8 (2001): 137–47.
[7] "I Am Canadian," YouTube video, posted by "vinko," May 22, 2006, accessed May 4, 2011, http://www.youtube.com/watch?v=BRI-A3vakVg.
[8] Pankaj Ghemawat, Redefining Global Strategy: Crossing Borders in a World Where Differences Still Matter (Boston: Harvard Business School Press, 2007), 42.

1.5 Ethics and International Business
LEARNING OBJECTIVES

1. Learn about the field of ethics.
2. Gain a general understanding of business ethics.
3. See why business ethics might be more challenging in international settings.

A Framework for Ethical Decision Making

The relationship between ethics and international business is a deep, natural one. Definitions of ethics and ethical behavior seem to have strong historical and cultural roots that vary by country and region. The field of ethics is a branch of philosophy that seeks virtue. Ethics deals with morality about what is considered "right" and "wrong" behavior for people in various situations. While business ethics emerged as a field in the 1970s, *international* business ethics didn't arise until the late 1990s. Initially, it looked back on the international developments of the late 1970s and 1980s, such as the Bhopol disaster in India or the infant milk-formula debate in Africa. [1] Today, those who are interested in international business ethics and ethical behavior examine various kinds of business activities and ask, "Is the business conduct ethically right or wrong?"

While ethical decision making is tricky stuff, particularly regarding international business issues, it helps if you start with a specific decision-making framework, such as the one summarized from the Markkula Center for Applied Ethics at Santa Clara University. [2]

1. **Is it an ethical issue?** Being ethical doesn't always mean following the law. And just because something is possible, doesn't mean it's ethical—hence the global debates about biotechnology advances, such as cloning. Also, ethics and religion don't always concur. This is perhaps the trickiest stage in ethical decision making; sometimes the subtleties of the issue are above and beyond our knowledge and experience. Listen to your instincts—if it feels uncomfortable making the decision on your own, get others involved and use their collective knowledge and experience to make a more considered decision.

2. **Get the facts.** What do you know and, just as important, what don't you know? Who are the people affected by your decision? Have they been consulted? What are your options? Have you reviewed your options with someone you respect?

3. **Evaluate alternative actions.** There are different ethical approaches that may help you make the most

ethical decision. For example, here are five approaches you can consider:

a) **Utilitarian approach.** Which action results in the most good and least harm?

b) **Rights-based approach.** Which action respects the rights of everyone involved?

c) **Fairness or justice approach.** Which action treats people fairly?

d) **Common good approach.** Which action contributes most to the quality of life of the people affected?

e) **Virtue approach.** Which action embodies the character strengths you value?

Test your decision. Could you comfortably explain your decision to your mother? To a man on the street? On television? If not, you may have to rethink your decision before you take action.

Just do it—but what did you learn? Once you've made the decision, implement it. Then set a date to review your decision and make adjustments if necessary. Often decisions are made with the best information on hand at the time, but things change and your decision making needs to be flexible enough to change too. Even a complete about-face may be the most appropriate action later on.

Ethics in Action

You might know that almost 60 percent of the soccer balls in the world are made in the city of Sialkot, Pakistan. Historically, these balls were hand-stitched in peoples' homes, often using child labor. During the 1996 European Championships, the media brought attention to the 7,000 seven- to fourteen-year-old children working full time stitching balls. NGOs (nongovernmental organizations) and industry groups stepped up to take action. [3] UNICEF, the World Federation of the Sporting Goods Industry, the International Labour Organization (ILO), and the Sialkot Chamber of Commerce signed the Atlanta Agreement to eliminate the use of child labor in Pakistan's soccer ball industry. [4] The Atlanta Agreement got ball production out of the home and into stitching centers, which could be monitored more easily. This also led to the centralization of production in approved "stitching centers." On the one hand, the centers made it easier for the Independent Monitoring Association for Child Labor (IMAC)—an NGO created to watch over the Atlanta Agreement—to make sure no child labor was used. On the other hand, the centralization sometimes forced workers to commute farther to get to work. As a result, child labor has to a large extent disappeared from

this sector. [5] Moreover, global fair-trade companies, such as GEPA, have set up village-based stitching centers that solely employ women. [6] Custom and religion prohibit women from working with men in Pakistan, and the women-only soccer ball stitching centers give them an opportunity to have a job and improve their families' incomes.

What Ethics Is Not

Two of the biggest challenges to identifying ethical standards relate to questions about what the standards should be based on and how we apply those standards in specific situations. Experts on ethics agree that the identification of ethical standards can be very difficult, but they *have* reached some agreement on what ethics is *not*. At the same time, these areas of agreement suggest why it may be challenging to obtain consensus across countries and regions as to "what is ethical?" Let's look at this five-point excerpt from the Markkula Center for Applied Ethics at Santa Clara University about what ethics is not:

Ethics is not the same as feelings. Feelings provide important information for our ethical choices. Some people have highly developed habits that make them feel bad when they do something wrong, but many people feel good even though they are doing something wrong. And often our feelings will tell us it is uncomfortable to do the right thing if it is hard.

Ethics is not religion. Many people are not religious, but ethics applies to everyone. Most religions do advocate high ethical standards but sometimes do not address all the types of problems we face.

Ethics is not following the law. A good system of law does incorporate many ethical standards, but law can deviate from what is ethical. Law can become ethically corrupt, as some totalitarian regimes have made it. Law can be a function of power alone and designed to serve the interests of narrow groups. Law may have a difficult time designing or enforcing standards in some important areas, and may be slow to address new problems.

Ethics is not following culturally accepted norms. Some cultures are quite ethical, but others become corrupt—or blind to certain ethical concerns (as the United States was to slavery before the Civil War). "When in Rome, do as the Romans do" is not a satisfactory ethical standard.

Ethics is not science. Social and natural science can provide important data to help us make better ethical choices. But science alone does not tell us what we ought to do. Science may provide an explanation for what humans are like. But ethics provides reasons for how humans ought to act. And just because something is scientifically or technologically possible, it may not be ethical to do it. [7]

KEY TAKEAWAYS

- The subject of ethics is important in almost any context—be it medicine, science, law, or business. You learned a framework for ethical decision making as well as some opinions on what ethics is not.

- Many would argue that international business ethics can have a strong foundation in national culture. Some argue that ethics shouldn't follow culturally accepted norms. However, business managers should have a good understanding of which norms their ethical standards are based on and why and how they believe they should apply in other national contexts.

EXERCISES

(AACSB: Reflective Thinking, Analytical Skills)
1. To what does the term *business ethics* refer?
2. What are the five steps in the ethical decision-making framework?
3. What five areas have experts agreed are not ethics?

[1] Georges Enderle, ed., International Business Ethics: Challenges and Approaches (Notre Dame, IN: University of Notre Dame Press, 1999), 1.
[2] "A Framework for Thinking Ethically," Markkula Center for Applied Ethics, Santa Clara University, last modified May 2009, accessed January 26, 2010,http://www.scu.edu/ethics/practicing/decision/framework.html.
[3] "Child Labour Case Study," The Global Compact, accessed November 12, 2010, http://human-rights.unglobalcompact.org/case_studies/child-labour/child_labour/combating_child_labour_in_football_production.html.
[4] "Atlanta Agreement," Independent Monitoring Association for Child Labor, accessed November 12,
2010, http://www.imacpak.org/atlanta.htm.
[5] "Child Labour Eliminated in Manufacturing Soccer Balls," The Nation, April 19, 2010, accessed November 12,
2010, http://www.nation.com.pk/pakistan-news-newspaper-daily-english-online/Business/18-Apr-2010/Child-labour-eliminated-in-manufacturing-soccer-balls.
[6] GEPA website, accessed January 20, 2010,
http://www.gepa.de/p/index.php/mID/1/lan/en.
[7] "A Framework for Thinking Ethically," Markkula Center for Applied Ethics, Santa Clara University, last modified May 2009, accessed January 26, 2010,http://www.scu.edu/ethics/practicing/decision/framework.html.

1.6 End-of-Chapter Questions and Exercises

These exercises are designed to ensure that the knowledge you gain from this book about international business meets the learning standards set out by the international Association to Advance Collegiate Schools of Business (AACSB International). [1] AACSB is the premier accrediting agency of collegiate business schools and accounting programs worldwide. It expects that you will gain knowledge in the areas of communication, ethical reasoning, analytical skills, use of information technology, multiculturalism and diversity, and reflective thinking.

EXPERIENTIAL EXERCISES

(AACSB: Communication, Use of Information Technology, Analytical Skills)
1. One of your friends plans to return to the family alfalfa farm in central California after college and has an idea to export a compressed form of alfalfa (alfalfa pellets) to be used as high-quality animal feed. Your friend knows that you are studying international business and has asked you for guidance. Prepare a summary for your friend of the issues that need to be considered; you can consult the "A Basic Guide to Exporting" series of webinars found on the globalEDGE website (http://globaledge.msu.edu). What other resources did you find helpful?

2. You like international business so much that you are inspired to start up an international business club at your school. While some of your classmates share this interest, you would like to start the club with strong membership numbers. Your teacher has agreed to give you ten minutes at the start of the next class to introduce your club idea and build support for it. You think that you can also use this presentation to build awareness of international business among students who might really enjoy the class and the topic if they knew more about it. Develop a ten-minute presentation that explains why you are passionate about international business, what international business people do, and what types of organizations are involved in international business.

3. You are browsing YouTube and come across the video "RMIT Business—International Business" (http://www.youtube.com/watch?v=jVmaBDalFsU). You share this video with your international business instructor. She is so impressed by the video that she asks you to develop a two- to three-minute video for your class that can be posted on YouTube as well. Adapt your presentation from Exercise 2 into a YouTube production and share it with your class.

Ethical Dilemmas

(AACSB: Ethical Reasoning, Multiculturalism, Reflective Thinking, Analytical Skills)
1. In Section 1.5 "Ethics and International Business", under the subhead "What Ethics Is Not," you read the statement "Ethics is not following culturally accepted norms." This is a tough statement as many argue that ethics is impacted by cultural values. What are some

examples of culturally accepted norms from one country that challenge the ethical beliefs in another?

2. Giving gifts is an accepted and legal tradition in the Japanese business setting but is discouraged (and in some cases illegal) in the US business setting. Does this difference affect the competitive advantage of Japanese firms doing business in the United States or US firms doing business in Japan?

[1] The Association to Advance Collegiate Schools of Business website, accessed January 26, 2010, http://www.aacsb.edu.

NOTES:

Chapter 2:
International Trade and Foreign Direct Investment

WHAT'S IN IT FOR ME?

1. What is international trade theory?
2. How do political and legal factors impact international trade?
3. What is foreign direct investment?

It's easy to think that trade is just about business interests in each country. But global trade is much more. There's a convergence and, at times, a conflict of the interests of the different stakeholders—from businesses to governments to local citizens. In recent years, advancements in technology, a renewed enthusiasm for entrepreneurship, and a global sentiment that favors free trade have further connected people, businesses, and markets—all flatteners that are helping expand global trade and investment. An essential part of international business is understanding the history of international trade and what motivates countries to encourage or discourage trade within their borders. In this chapter we'll look at the evolution of international trade theory to our modern time. We'll explore the political and legal factors impacting international trade. This chapter will provide an introduction to the concept and role of foreign direct investment, which can take many forms of incentives, regulations, and policies. Companies react to these business incentives and regulations as they evaluate with which countries to do business and in which to invest. Governments often encourage foreign investment in their own country or in another country by providing loans and incentives to businesses in their home country as well as businesses in the recipient country in order to pave the way for investment and trade in the country. The opening case study shows how and why China is investing in the continent of Africa.

OPENING CASE: CHINA IN AFRICA

Foreign companies have been doing business in Africa for centuries. Much of the trade history of past centuries has been colored by European colonial powers promoting and preserving their economic interests throughout the African continent. [1] After World War II and since independence for many African nations, the continent has not fared as well as other former colonial countries in Asia. Africa remains a continent plagued by a continued combination of factors, including competing colonial political and economic

interests; poor and corrupt local leadership; war, famine, and disease; and a chronic shortage of resources, infrastructure, and political, economic, and social will. [2] And yet, through the bleak assessments, progress is emerging, led in large part by the successful emergence of a free and locally powerful South Africa. The continent generates a lot of interest on both the corporate and humanitarian levels, as well as from other countries. In particular in the past decade, Africa has caught the interest of the world's second largest economy, China. [3]

At home, over the past few decades, China has undergone its own miracle, managing to move hundreds of millions of its people out of poverty by combining state intervention with economic incentives to attract private investment. Today, China is involved in economic engagement, bringing its success story to the continent of Africa. As professor and author Deborah Brautigam notes, China's "current experiment in Africa mixes a hard-nosed but clear-eyed self-interest with the lessons of China's own successful development and of decades of its failed aid projects in Africa." [4]

According to CNN, "China has increasingly turned to resource-rich Africa as China's booming economy has demanded more and more oil and raw materials." [5] Trade between the African continent and China reached $106.8 billion in 2008, and over the past decade, Chinese investments and the country's development aid to Africa have been increasing steadily. [6] "Chinese activities in Africa are highly diverse, ranging from government to government relations and large state owned companies (SOE) investing in Africa financed by China's policy banks, to private entrepreneurs entering African countries at their own initiative to pursue commercial activities." [7]

Since 2004, eager for access to resources, oil, diamonds, minerals, and commodities, China has entered into arrangements with resource-rich countries in Africa for a total of nearly $14 billion in resource deals alone. In one example with Angola, China provided loans to the country secured by oil. With this investment, Angola hired Chinese companies to build much-needed roads, railways, hospitals, schools, and water systems. Similarly, China provided nearby Nigeria with oil-backed loans to finance projects that use gas to generate electricity. In the Republic of the Congo, Chinese teams are building a hydropower project funded by a Chinese government loan, which will be repaid in oil. In Ghana, a Chinese government loan will be repaid in cocoa beans. [8]

The Export-Import Bank of China (Ex-Im Bank of China) has funded and has provided these loans at market rates, rather than as foreign aid. While these loans certainly promote development, the risk for the local countries is that the Chinese bids to provide the work aren't competitive. Furthermore, the benefit to local workers may be diminished as Chinese companies bring in some of their own workers, keeping local wages and working standards low.

In 2007, the UNCTAD (United Nations Conference on Trade and Development) Press Office noted the following:

Over the past few years, China has become one of Africa's important partners for trade and economic cooperation. Trade (exports and imports) between Africa and China increased from US$11 billion in 2000 to US$56 billion in 2006….with Chinese companies present in 48 African countries, although Africa still accounts for only 3 percent of China's outward FDI [foreign direct investment]. A few African countries have attracted the bulk of China's FDI in Africa: Sudan is the largest recipient (and the 9th largest recipient of Chinese FDI worldwide), followed by Algeria (18th) and Zambia (19th). [9]

Observers note that African governments can learn from the development history of China and many Asian countries, which now enjoy high economic growth and upgraded industrial activity. These Asian countries made strategic investments in education and infrastructure that were crucial not only for promoting economic development in general but also for attracting and benefiting from efficiency-seeking and export-oriented FDI. [10]

Criticized by some and applauded by others, it's clear that China's investment is encouraging development in Africa. China is accused by some of ignoring human rights crises in the continent and doing business with repressive regimes. China's success in Africa is due in large part to the local political environment in each country, where either one or a small handful of leaders often control the power and decision making. While the countries often open bids to many foreign investors, Chinese firms are able to provide low-cost options thanks in large part to their government's project support. The ability to forge a government-level partnership has enabled Chinese businesses to have long-term investment

perspectives in the region. China even hosted a summit in 2006 for African leaders, pledging to increase trade, investment, and aid over the coming decade. [11] The 2008 global recession has led China to be more selective in its African investments, looking for good deals as well as political stability in target countries. Nevertheless, whether to access the region's rich resources or develop local markets for Chinese goods and services, China intends to be a key foreign investor in Africa for the foreseeable future. [12]

OPENING CASE EXERCISES

(AACSB: Ethical Reasoning, Multiculturalism, Reflective Thinking, Analytical Skills)

1. Describe China's strategy in Africa.
2. If you were the head of a Chinese business that was operating in Sudan, how would you address issues of business ethics and doing business with a repressive regime? Should businesses care about local government ethics and human rights policies?
3. If you were a foreign businessperson working for a global oil company that was eager to get favorable government approval to invest in a local oil refinery in an African country, how would you handle any demands for paybacks (i.e., bribes)?

[1] Martin Meredith, The Fate of Africa (New York: Public Affairs, 2005).
[2] "Why Africa Is Poor: Ghana Beats Up on Its Biggest Foreign Investors," Wall Street Journal, February 18, 2010, accessed February 16, 2011, http://online.wsj.com/article/SB100014240527487048042045750695117466613890.html.
[3] Andrew Rice, "Why Is Africa Still Poor?" The Nation, October 24, 2005, accessed December 20, 2010, http://www.thenation.com/article/why-africa-still-poor?page=0,1.
[4] Deborah Brautigam, "Africa's Eastern Promise: What the West Can Learn from Chinese Investment in Africa," Foreign Affairs, January 5, 2010, accessed December 20, 2010, http://www.foreignaffairs.com/articles/65916/deborah-brautigam/africa%E2%80%99s-eastern-promise.
[5] "China: Trade with Africa on Track to New Record," CNN, October 15, 2010, accessed April 23, 2011, http://articles.cnn.com/2010-10-15/world/china.africa.trade_1_china-and-africa-link-trade-largest-trade-partner?_s=PM:WORLD.
[6] "China-Africa Trade up 45 percent in 2008 to $107 Billion," China Daily, February 11, 2009, accessed April 23, 2011, http://www.chinadaily.com.cn/china/2009-02/11/content_7467460.htm.
[7] Tracy Hon, Johanna Jansson, Garth Shelton, Liu Haifang, Christopher Burke, and Carine Kiala, Evaluating China's FOCAC Commitments to Africa and Mapping the Way Ahead(Stellenbosch, South Africa: Centre for Chinese Studies, University of Stellenbosch, 2010), 1, accessed December 20, 2010, http://www.ccs.org.za/wp-content/uploads/2010/03/ENGLISH-Evaluating-Chinas-FOCAC-commitments-to-Africa-2010.pdf.
[8] Deborah Brautigam, "Africa's Eastern Promise: What the West Can Learn from Chinese Investment in Africa," Foreign Affairs, January 5, 2010, accessed December 20, 2010,

http://www.foreignaffairs.com/articles/65916/deborah-brautigam/africa%E2%80%99s-eastern-promise.
[9] United Nations Conference on Trade and Development, "Asian Foreign Direct Investment in Africa: United Nations Report Points to a New Era of Cooperation among Developing Countries," press release, March 27, 2007, accessed December 20, 2010, http://www.unctad.org/Templates/Webflyer.asp?docID=8172&intItemID=3971&lang=1.
[10] United Nations Conference on Trade and Development, "Foreign Direct Investment in Africa Remains Buoyant, Sustained by Interest in Natural Resources," press release, September 29, 2005, accessed December 20, 2010, http://news.bbc.co.uk/2/hi/africa/7086777.stm.
[11] "Summit Shows China's Africa Clout," BBC News, November 6, 2006, accessed December 20, 2010, http://news.bbc.co.uk/2/hi/business/6120500.stm.
[12] "China in Africa: Developing Ties," BBC News, November 26, 2007, accessed December 20, 2010, http://news.bbc.co.uk/2/hi/africa/7086777.stm.

2.1 What Is International Trade Theory?
LEARNING OBJECTIVES

1. Understand international trade.
2. Compare and contrast different trade theories.
3. Determine which international trade theory is most relevant today and how it continues to evolve.

What Is International Trade?

International trade theories are simply different theories to explain international trade. Trade is the concept of exchanging goods and services between two people or entities. *International trade* is then the concept of this exchange between people or entities in two different countries.

People or entities trade because they believe that they benefit from the exchange. They may need or want the goods or services. While at the surface, this many sound very simple, there is a great deal of theory, policy, and business strategy that constitutes international trade.

In this section, you'll learn about the different trade theories that have evolved over the past century and which are most relevant today. Additionally, you'll explore the factors that impact international trade and how businesses and governments use these factors to their respective benefits to promote their interests.

What Are the Different International Trade Theories?

"Around 5,200 years ago, Uruk, in southern Mesopotamia, was probably the first city the world had ever seen, housing more than 50,000 people within its six miles of wall. Uruk, its agriculture made prosperous by sophisticated irrigation canals, was home to the first class of middlemen, trade

intermediaries…A cooperative trade network…set the pattern that would endure for the next 6,000 years." [1]

In more recent centuries, economists have focused on trying to understand and explain these trade patterns. Chapter 1 "Introduction", Section 1.4 "The Globalization Debate" discussed how Thomas Friedman's flat-world approach segments history into three stages: Globalization 1.0 from 1492 to 1800, 2.0 from 1800 to 2000, and 3.0 from 2000 to the present. In Globalization 1.0, nations dominated global expansion. In Globalization 2.0, multinational companies ascended and pushed global development. Today, technology drives Globalization 3.0.

To better understand how modern global trade has evolved, it's important to understand how countries traded with one another historically. Over time, economists have developed theories to explain the mechanisms of global trade. The main historical theories are called *classical* and are from the perspective of a country, or country-based. By the mid-twentieth century, the theories began to shift to explain trade from a firm, rather than a country, perspective. These theories are referred to as *modern* and are firm-based or company-based. Both of these categories, classical and modern, consist of several international theories.

Classical or Country-Based Trade Theories

Classical Country-Based Theories	Modern Firm-Based Theories
Mercantilism	Country Similarity
Absolute Advantage	Product Life Cycle
Comparative Advantage	Global strategic Rivalry
Heckscher-Ohlin	Porter's National Competitive Advantage

Mercantilism

Developed in the sixteenth century, mercantilism was one of the earliest efforts to develop an economic theory. This theory stated that a country's wealth was determined by the amount of its gold and silver holdings. In its simplest sense, mercantilists believed that a country should increase its holdings of gold and silver by promoting exports and discouraging imports. In other words, if people in other countries buy more from you (exports) than they sell to you (imports), then they have to pay you the difference in gold and silver. The objective of each country was to have a trade surplus, or a situation where the value of exports are greater than the value of imports, and to avoid a trade deficit, or a situation where the value of imports is greater than the value of exports.

A closer look at world history from the 1500s to the late 1800s helps explain why mercantilism flourished. The 1500s marked the rise of new nation-states, whose rulers wanted to strengthen their nations by building larger armies and national institutions. By increasing exports and trade, these rulers were able to amass more gold and wealth for their countries. One way that many of these new nations promoted exports was to impose restrictions on imports. This strategy is called protectionism and is still used today.

Nations expanded their wealth by using their colonies around the world in an effort to control more trade and amass more riches. The British colonial empire was one of the more successful examples; it sought to increase its wealth by using raw materials from places ranging from what are now the Americas and India. France, the Netherlands, Portugal, and Spain were also successful in building large colonial empires that generated extensive wealth for their governing nations.

Although mercantilism is one of the oldest trade theories, it remains part of modern thinking. Countries such as Japan, China, Singapore, Taiwan, and even Germany still favor exports and discourage imports through a form of neo-mercantilism in which the countries promote a combination of protectionist policies and restrictions and domestic-industry subsidies. Nearly every country, at one point or another, has implemented some form of protectionist policy to guard key industries in its economy. While export-oriented companies usually support protectionist policies that favor their industries or firms, other companies and consumers are hurt by protectionism. Taxpayers pay for government subsidies of select exports in the form of higher taxes. Import restrictions lead to higher prices for consumers, who pay more for foreign-made goods or services. Free-trade advocates highlight how free trade benefits all members of the global community, while mercantilism's protectionist policies only benefit select industries, at the expense of both consumers and other companies, within and outside of the industry.

Absolute Advantage
In 1776, Adam Smith questioned the leading mercantile theory of the time in *The Wealth of Nations*. [2] Smith offered a new trade theory called absolute advantage, which focused on the ability of a country to produce a good more efficiently than another nation. Smith reasoned that trade between countries shouldn't be regulated or restricted by government policy or intervention. He stated that trade should flow naturally according to market forces. In a hypothetical two-country world, if Country A could produce a good cheaper or faster (or both) than Country B, then Country A had the advantage and could focus on specializing on producing that good. Similarly, if Country B was better at producing another good, it could focus on specialization as well. By specialization, countries would generate efficiencies, because their labor force would become more skilled by doing the same tasks. Production would also become more efficient, because there would be an incentive to create faster and better production methods to increase the specialization.

Smith's theory reasoned that with increased efficiencies, people in both countries would benefit and trade should be encouraged. His theory stated that a nation's wealth shouldn't be judged by how much gold and silver it had but rather by the living standards of its people.

Comparative Advantage
The challenge to the absolute advantage theory was that some countries may be better at producing both goods and, therefore, have an advantage in *many* areas. In contrast, another country may not have *any* useful absolute advantages. To answer this challenge, David Ricardo, an English economist, introduced the theory of comparative advantage in 1817. Ricardo reasoned that even if Country A had the absolute advantage in the production of *both* products, specialization and trade could still occur between two countries.

Comparative advantage occurs when a country cannot produce a product more efficiently than the other country; however, it *can* produce that product better and more efficiently than it does other goods. The difference between these two theories is subtle. Comparative advantage focuses on the relative productivity differences, whereas absolute advantage looks at the absolute productivity.

Let's look at a simplified hypothetical example to illustrate the subtle difference between these principles. Miranda is a Wall Street lawyer who charges $500 per hour for her legal services. It turns out that Miranda can also type faster than the administrative assistants in her office, who are paid $40 per hour. Even though Miranda clearly has the absolute advantage in both skill sets, should she do both jobs? No. For every hour Miranda decides to type instead of do legal work, she would be giving up $460 in income. Her productivity and income will be highest if she specializes in the higher-paid legal services and hires the most qualified administrative assistant, who can type fast, although a little slower than

Miranda. By having both Miranda and her assistant concentrate on their respective tasks, their overall productivity as a team is higher. This is comparative advantage. A person or a country will specialize in doing what they do *relatively* better. In reality, the world economy is more complex and consists of more than two countries and products. Barriers to trade may exist, and goods must be transported, stored, and distributed. However, this simplistic example demonstrates the basis of the comparative advantage theory.

Heckscher-Ohlin Theory (Factor Proportions Theory)

The theories of Smith and Ricardo didn't help countries determine which products would give a country an advantage. Both theories assumed that free and open markets would lead countries and producers to determine which goods they could produce more efficiently. In the early 1900s, two Swedish economists, Eli Heckscher and Bertil Ohlin, focused their attention on how a country could gain comparative advantage by producing products that utilized factors that were in abundance in the country. Their theory is based on a country's production factors—land, labor, and capital, which provide the funds for investment in plants and equipment. They determined that the cost of any factor or resource was a function of supply and demand. Factors that were in great supply relative to demand would be cheaper; factors in great demand relative to supply would be more expensive. Their theory, also called the factor proportions theory, stated that countries would produce and export goods that required resources or factors that were in great supply and, therefore, cheaper production factors. In contrast, countries would import goods that required resources that were in short supply, but higher demand.

For example, China and India are home to cheap, large pools of labor. Hence these countries have become the optimal locations for labor-intensive industries like textiles and garments.

Leontief Paradox

In the early 1950s, Russian-born American economist Wassily W. Leontief studied the US economy closely and noted that the United States was abundant in capital and, therefore, should export more capital-intensive goods. However, his research using actual data showed the opposite: the United States was importing more capital-intensive goods. According to the factor proportions theory, the United States should have been importing labor-intensive goods, but instead it was actually exporting them. His analysis became known as the Leontief Paradox because it was the reverse of what was expected by the factor proportions theory. In subsequent years, economists have noted historically at that point in time, labor in the United States was both available in steady supply and more productive than in many other countries; hence it made sense to export labor-intensive goods. Over the decades, many economists have used theories and data to explain and minimize the impact of the paradox. However, what remains clear is that international trade is complex and is impacted by numerous and often-changing factors. Trade cannot be explained neatly by one single theory, and more importantly, our understanding of international trade theories continues to evolve.

Modern or Firm-Based Trade Theories

In contrast to classical, country-based trade theories, the category of modern, firm-based theories emerged after World War II and was developed in large part by business school professors, not economists. The firm-based theories evolved with the growth of the multinational company (MNC). The country-based theories couldn't adequately address the expansion of either MNCs or intra-industry trade, which refers to trade between two countries of goods produced in the same industry. For example, Japan exports Toyota vehicles to Germany and imports Mercedes-Benz automobiles from Germany.

Unlike the country-based theories, firm-based theories incorporate other product and service factors, including brand and customer loyalty, technology, and quality, into the understanding of trade flows.

Country Similarity Theory

Swedish economist Steffan Linder developed the country similarity theory in 1961, as he tried to explain the concept of intraindustry trade. Linder's theory proposed that consumers in countries that are in the same or similar stage of development would have similar preferences. In this firm-based theory, Linder suggested that companies first produce for domestic consumption. When they explore exporting, the companies often find that markets that look similar to their domestic one, in terms of customer preferences, offer the most potential for success. Linder's country similarity theory then states that most trade in manufactured goods will be between countries with similar per capita incomes, and intraindustry trade will be common. This theory is often most useful in understanding trade in goods where brand names and product reputations are important factors in the buyers' decision-making and purchasing processes.

Product Life Cycle Theory

Raymond Vernon, a Harvard Business School professor, developed the product life cycle theory in the 1960s. The theory, originating in the field of marketing, stated that a product life cycle has three distinct stages: (1) new product, (2) maturing product, and (3) standardized product. The theory assumed that production of the new product will occur completely in the home country of its innovation. In the 1960s this was a useful theory to explain the manufacturing success of the United States. US manufacturing was the globally dominant producer in many industries after World War II.

It has also been used to describe how the personal computer (PC) went through its product cycle. The PC was a new product in the 1970s and developed into a mature product during the 1980s and 1990s. Today, the PC is in the standardized product stage, and the majority of manufacturing and production process is done in low-cost countries in Asia and Mexico.

The product life cycle theory has been less able to explain current trade patterns where innovation and manufacturing occur around the world. For example, global companies even conduct research and development in developing markets where highly skilled labor and facilities are usually cheaper. Even though research and development is typically associated with the first or new product stage and therefore completed in the home country, these developing or emerging-market countries, such as India and China, offer both highly skilled labor and new research facilities at a substantial cost advantage for global firms.

Global Strategic Rivalry Theory

Global strategic rivalry theory emerged in the 1980s and was based on the work of economists Paul Krugman and Kelvin Lancaster. Their theory focused on MNCs and their efforts to gain a competitive advantage against other global firms in their industry. Firms will encounter global competition in their industries and in order to prosper, they must develop competitive advantages. The critical ways that firms can obtain a sustainable competitive advantage are called the barriers to entry for that industry. The barriers to entry refer to the obstacles a new firm may face when trying to enter into an industry or new market. The barriers to entry that corporations may seek to optimize include:

- research and development,
- the ownership of intellectual property rights,
- economies of scale,
- unique business processes or methods as well as extensive experience in the industry, and

- the control of resources or favorable access to raw materials.

Porter's National Competitive Advantage Theory

In the continuing evolution of international trade theories, Michael Porter of Harvard Business School developed a new model to explain national competitive advantage in 1990. Porter's theory stated that a nation's competitiveness in an industry depends on the capacity of the industry to innovate and upgrade. His theory focused on explaining why some nations are more competitive in certain industries. To explain his theory, Porter identified four determinants that he linked together. The four determinants are (1) local market resources and capabilities, (2) local market demand conditions, (3) local suppliers and complementary industries, and (4) local firm characteristics.

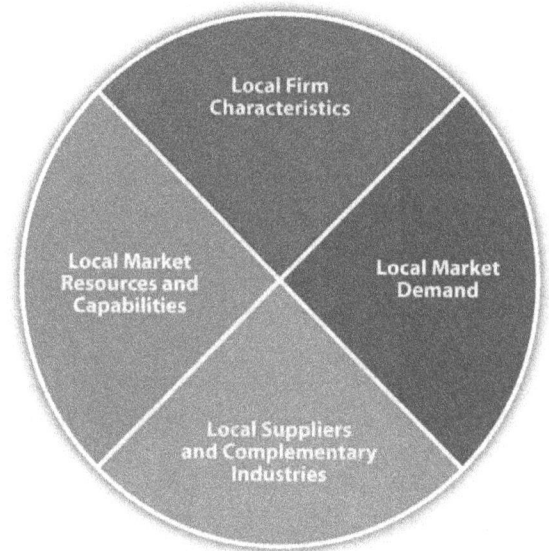

1. **Local market resources and capabilities (factor conditions).** Porter recognized the value of the factor proportions theory, which considers a nation's resources (e.g., natural resources and available labor) as key factors in determining what products a country will import or export. Porter added to these basic factors a new list of advanced factors, which he defined as skilled labor, investments in education, technology, and infrastructure. He perceived these advanced factors as providing a country with a sustainable competitive advantage.

2. **Local market demand conditions.** Porter believed that a sophisticated home market is critical to ensuring ongoing innovation, thereby creating a sustainable competitive advantage. Companies whose domestic markets are sophisticated, trendsetting, and demanding forces continuous innovation and the development of

new products and technologies. Many sources credit the demanding US consumer with forcing US software companies to continuously innovate, thus creating a sustainable competitive advantage in software products and services.

3. **Local suppliers and complementary industries.** To remain competitive, large global firms benefit from having strong, efficient supporting and related industries to provide the inputs required by the industry. Certain industries cluster geographically, which provides efficiencies and productivity.

4. **Local firm characteristics.** Local firm characteristics include firm strategy, industry structure, and industry rivalry. Local strategy affects a firm's competitiveness. A healthy level of rivalry between local firms will spur innovation and competitiveness.

In addition to the four determinants of the diamond, Porter also noted that government and chance play a part in the national competitiveness of industries. Governments can, by their actions and policies, increase the competitiveness of firms and occasionally entire industries.

Porter's theory, along with the other modern, firm-based theories, offers an interesting interpretation of international trade trends. Nevertheless, they remain relatively new and minimally tested theories.

Which Trade Theory Is Dominant Today?

The theories covered in this chapter are simply that—theories. While they have helped economists, governments, and businesses better understand international trade and how to promote, regulate, and manage it, these theories are occasionally contradicted by real-world events. Countries don't have absolute advantages in many areas of production or services and, in fact, the factors of production aren't neatly distributed between countries. Some countries have a disproportionate benefit of some factors. The United States has ample arable land that can be used for a wide range of agricultural products. It also has extensive access to capital. While its labor pool may not be the cheapest, it is among the best educated in the world. These advantages in the factors of production have helped the United States become the largest and richest economy in the world. Nevertheless, the United States also imports a vast amount of goods and services, as US consumers use their wealth to purchase what they need and want—much of which is now manufactured in other countries that have sought to create their own comparative advantages through cheap labor, land, or production costs.

As a result, it's not clear that any one theory is dominant around the world. This section has sought to highlight the basics of international trade theory to enable you to understand the realities that face global businesses. In practice, governments and companies use a combination of these theories to both interpret trends and develop strategy. Just as these theories have evolved over the past five hundred years, they will continue to change and adapt as new factors impact international trade.

KEY TAKEAWAYS

- Trade is the concept of exchanging goods and services between two people or entities. International trade is the concept of this exchange between people or entities in two different countries. While a simplistic definition, the factors that impact trade are complex, and economists throughout the centuries have attempted to interpret trends and factors through the evolution of trade theories.

- There are two main categories of international trade—classical, country-based and modern, firm-based.

- Porter's theory states that a nation's competitiveness in an industry depends on the capacity of the industry to innovate and upgrade. He identified four key determinants: (1) local market resources and capabilities (factor conditions), (2) local market demand conditions, (3) local suppliers and complementary industries, and (4) local firm characteristics.

EXERCISES

(AACSB: Reflective Thinking, Analytical Skills)

1. What is international trade?
2. Summarize the classical, country-based international trade theories. What are the differences between these theories, and how did the theories evolve?
3. What are the modern, firm-based international trade theories?
4. Describe how a business may use the trade theories to develop its business strategies. Use Porter's four determinants in your explanation.

[1] Matt Ridley, "Humans: Why They Triumphed," Wall Street Journal, May 22, 2010, accessed December 20, 2010, http://online.wsj.com/article/SB10001424052748703691804575254533386933138.html.

[2] Adam Smith, An Inquiry into the Nature and Causes of the Wealth of Nations (London: W. Strahan and T. Cadell, 1776). Recent versions have been edited by scholars and economists.

2.2 Political and Legal Factors That Impact International Trade

1. Know the different political systems.
2. Identify the different legal systems.
3. Understand government-business trade relations and how political and legal factors impact international business.

Why should businesses care about the different political and legal systems around the world? To begin with, despite the globalization of business, firms must abide by the local rules and regulations of the countries in which they operate. In the case study in Chapter 1 "Introduction", you discovered how US-based Google had to deal with the Chinese government's restrictions on the freedom of speech in order to do business in China. China's different set of political and legal guidelines made Google choose to discontinue its mainland Chinese version of its site and direct mainland Chinese users to a Hong Kong version.

Until recently, governments were able to directly enforce the rules and regulations based on their political and legal philosophies. The Internet has started to change this, as sellers and buyers have easier access to each other. Nevertheless, countries still have the ability to regulate or strong-arm companies into abiding by their rules and regulations. As a result, global businesses monitor and evaluate the political and legal climate in countries in which they currently operate or hope to operate in the future.

Before we can evaluate the impact on business, let's first look at the different political and legal systems.

What Are the Different Political Systems?

The study of political systems is extensive and complex. A political system is basically the system of politics and government in a country. It governs a complete set of rules, regulations, institutions, and attitudes. A main differentiator of political systems is each system's philosophy on the rights of the individual and the group as well as the role of government. Each political system's philosophy impacts the policies that govern the local economy and business environment.

There are more than thirteen major types of government, each of which consists of multiple variations. Let's focus on the overarching modern political philosophies. At one end of the extremes of political philosophies, or ideologies, is anarchism, which contends that individuals should control

political activities and public government is both unnecessary and unwanted. At the other extreme is totalitarianism, which contends that every aspect of an individual's life should be controlled and dictated by a strong central government. In reality, neither extreme exists in its purest form. Instead, most countries have a combination of both, the balance of which is often a reflection of the country's history, culture, and religion. This combination is called pluralism, which asserts that both public and private groups are important in a well-functioning political system. Although most countries are pluralistic politically, they may lean more to one extreme than the other.

In some countries, the government controls more aspects of daily life than in others. While the common usage treats totalitarian and authoritarian as synonyms, there is a distinct difference. For the purpose of this discussion, the main relevant difference is in ideology. Authoritarian governments centralize all control in the hands of one strong leader or a small group of leaders, who have full authority. These leaders are not democratically elected and are not politically, economically, or socially accountable to the people in the country. Totalitarianism, a more extreme form of authoritarianism, occurs when an authoritarian leadership is motivated by a distinct ideology, such as communism. In totalitarianism, the ideology influences or controls the people, not just a person or party. Authoritarian leaders tend not to have a guiding philosophy and use more fear and corruption to maintain control.

Democracy is the most common form of government around the world today. Democratic governments derive their power from the people of the country, either by direct referendum (called a direct democracy) or by means of elected representatives of the people (a representative democracy). Democracy has a number of variations, both in theory and practice, some of which provide better representation and more freedoms for their citizens than others.

Did You Know?

It may seem evident that businesses would prefer to operate in open, democratic countries; however, it can be difficult to determine which countries fit the democratic criteria. As a result, there are a variety of institutions, including the *Economist*, which analyze and rate countries based on their openness and adherence to democratic principles.

There is no consensus on how to measure democracy, definitions of democracy are contested and there is an ongoing lively debate on the subject. Although the terms "freedom" and "democracy" are often used interchangeably, the two are not synonymous. Democracy can be seen as a set of practices and principles that institutionalize and thus ultimately protect freedom. Even if a consensus on precise definitions has proved elusive, most observers today would agree that, at a minimum, the fundamental features of a democracy include government based on majority rule and the consent of the governed, the existence of free and fair elections, the protection of minorities and respect for basic human rights. Democracy presupposes equality before the law, due process and political pluralism. [1]

To further illustrate the complexity of the definition of a democracy, the *Economist* Intelligence Unit's annual "Index of Democracy" uses a detailed questionnaire and analysis process to provide "a snapshot of the current state of democracy worldwide for 165 independent states and two territories (this covers almost the entire population of the world and the vast majority of the world's independent states (27 micro states are excluded) [as of 2008)]." [2] Several things stand out in the 2008 index.

Although almost half of the world's countries can be considered to be democracies, the number of "full democracies" is relatively low (only 30); 50 are rated as "flawed democracies." Of the remaining 87 states, 51 are authoritarian and 36 are considered to be "hybrid regimes." As could be expected, the developed OECD countries dominate among full democracies, although there are two Latin American, two central European and one African country, which suggest that the level of development is not a binding constraint. Only two Asian countries are represented: Japan and South Korea.

Half of the world's population lives in a democracy of some sort, although only some 14 percent reside in full democracies. Despite the advances in democracy in recent decades, more than one third the world's population still lives under authoritarian rule. [3]

What businesses must focus on is how a country's political system impacts the economy as well as the particular firm and industry. Firms need to assess the balance to determine how local policies, rules, and regulations will affect their business. Depending on how long a company expects to operate in a country and how easy it is for it to enter and exit, a firm may also assess the country's political risk and stability. A company may ask several questions regarding a prospective country's government to assess possible risks:

1. How stable is the government?
2. Is it a democracy or a dictatorship?
3. If a new party comes into power, will the rules of business change dramatically?
4. Is power concentrated in the hands of a few, or is it clearly outlined in a constitution or similar national legal document?
5. How involved is the government in the private sector?
6. Is there a well-established legal environment both to enforce policies and rules as well as to challenge them?
7. How transparent is the government's political, legal, and economic decision-making process?

While any country can, in theory, pose a risk in all of these factors, some countries offer a more stable business environment than others. In fact, political stability is a key part of government efforts to attract foreign investment to their country. Businesses need to assess if a country believes in free markets, government control, or heavy intervention (often to the benefit of a few) in industry. The country's view on capitalism is also a factor for business consideration. In the broadest sense, capitalism is an economic system in which the means of production are owned and controlled privately. In contrast, a planned economy is one in which the government or state directs and controls the economy, including the means and decision making for production. Historically, democratic governments have supported capitalism and authoritarian regimes have tended to utilize a state-controlled approach to managing the economy.

As you might expect, established democracies, such as those found in the United States, Canada, Western Europe, Japan, and Australia, offer a high level of political stability. While many countries in Asia and Latin America also are functioning democracies, their stage of development impacts the stability of their economic and trade policy, which can fluctuate with government changes. Chapter 4 "World Economies" provides more details about developed and developing countries and emerging markets.

Within reason, in democracies, businesses understand that most rules survive changes in government. Any changes are usually a reflection of a changing economic environment, like the world economic crisis of 2008, and not a change in the government players.

This contrasts with more authoritarian governments, where democracy is either not in effect or simply a token process. China is one of the more visible examples, with its strong government and limited individual rights. However, in the past two decades, China has pursued a new balance of how much the state plans and manages the national economy. While the government still remains the dominant force by controlling more than a third of the economy, more private businesses have emerged. China has successfully combined state intervention with private investment to develop a robust, market-driven economy—all within a communist form of government. This system is commonly referred to as "a socialist market economy with Chinese characteristics." The Chinese are eager to portray their version of combining an authoritarian form of government with a market-oriented economy as a better alternative model for fledging economies, such as those in Africa. This new combination has also posed more questions for businesses that are encountering new issues—such as privacy, individual rights, and intellectual rights protections—as they try to do business with China, now the second-largest economy in the world behind the United States. The Chinese model of an authoritarian government and a market-oriented economy has, at times, tilted favor toward companies, usually Chinese, who understand how to navigate the nuances of this new system. Chinese government control on the Internet, for example, has helped propel homegrown, Baidu, a Chinese search engine, which earns more than 73 percent of the Chinese search-engine revenues. Baidu self-censors and, as a result, has seen its revenues soar after Google limited its operations in the country. [4]

It might seem straightforward to assume that businesses prefer to operate only in democratic, capitalist countries where there is little or no government involvement or intervention. However, history demonstrates that, for some industries, global firms have chosen to do business with countries whose governments control that industry. Businesses in industries, such as commodities and oil, have found more authoritarian governments to be predictable partners for long-term access and investment for these commodities. The complexity of trade in these situations increases, as throughout history, governments have come to the aid and protection of their nation's largest business interests in markets around the world. The history of the oil industry shows how various governments have, on occasion, protected their national companies' access to oil through political force. In current times, the Chinese government has been using a combination of government loans and investment in Africa to obtain access for Chinese companies to utilize local resources and commodities. Many business analysts mention these issues in discussions of global business ethics and the role and responsibility of companies in different political environments.

What Are the Different Legal Systems?

Let's focus briefly on how the political and economic ideologies that define countries impact their legal systems. In essence, there are three main kinds of legal systems—common law, civil law, and religious or theocratic law. Most countries actually have a combination of these systems, creating hybrid legal systems.

Civil law is based on a detailed set of laws that constitute a code and focus on how the law is applied to the facts. It's the most widespread legal system in the world.
Common law is based on traditions and precedence. In common law systems, judges interpret the law and judicial rulings can set precedent.

Religious law is also known as theocratic law and is based on religious guidelines. The most commonly known example of religious law is Islamic law, also known as Sharia. Islamic law governs a number of Islamic nations and communities around the world and is the most widely accepted religious law system. Two additional religious law systems are the Jewish Halacha and the Christian Canon system, neither of which is practiced at the national level in a country. The Christian Canon system is observed in the Vatican City.

The most direct impact on business can be observed in Islamic law—which is a moral, rather than a commercial, legal system. Sharia has clear guidelines for aspects of life. For example, in Islamic law, business is directly impacted by the concept of interest. According to Islamic law, banks cannot charge or benefit from interest. This provision has generated an entire set of financial products and strategies to simulate interest—or a gain—for an Islamic bank, while not technically being classified as interest. Some banks will charge a large up-front fee. Many are permitted to engage in sale-buyback or leaseback of an asset. For example, if a company wants to borrow money from an Islamic bank, it would sell its assets or product to the bank for a fixed price. At the same time, an agreement would be signed for the bank to sell back the assets to the company at a later date and at a higher price. The difference between the sale and buyback price functions as the interest. In the Persian Gulf region alone, there are twenty-two Sharia-compliant, Islamic banks, which in 2008 had approximately $300 billion in assets. [5] Clearly, many global businesses and investment banks are finding creative ways to do business with these Islamic banks so that they can comply with Islamic law while earning a profit.

Government—Business Trade Relations: The Impact of Political and Legal Factors on International Trade

How do political and legal realities impact international trade, and what do businesses need to think about as they develop their global strategy? Governments have long intervened in international trade through a variety of mechanisms. First, let's briefly discuss some of the reasons behind these interventions.

Why Do Governments Intervene in Trade?

Governments intervene in trade for a combination of political, economic, social, and cultural reasons.

Politically, a country's government may seek to protect jobs or specific industries. Some industries may be considered essential for national security purposes, such as defense, telecommunications, and infrastructure—for example, a government may be concerned about who owns the ports within its country. National security issues can impact both the import and exports of a country, as some governments may not want advanced technological information to be sold to unfriendly foreign interests. Some governments use trade as a retaliatory measure if another country is politically or economically unfair. On the other hand, governments may influence trade to reward a country for political support on global matters.

Did You Know?

State Capitalism: Governments Seeking to Control Key Industries
Despite the movement toward privatizing industry and free trade, government interests in their most valuable commodity, oil, remains constant. The thirteen largest oil companies (as measured by the reserves they control) in the world are all state-run and all are bigger than ExxonMobil, which is the world's largest private oil company. State-owned companies control more than 75 percent of all crude oil production, in contrast with only 10 percent for private multinational oil firms. [6]

Table 2.1 The Major Global State-Owned Oil Companies

Aramco	Saudi Arabia
Gazprom	Russia
China National Petroleum Corp.	China
National Iranian Oil Co.	Iran
Petróleos de Venezuela	Venezuela
Petrobras	Brazil
Petronas	Malaysia

Source: Energy Intelligence Group, "*Petroleum Intelligence Weekly* Ranks World's Top 50 Oil Companies (2009)," news release, December 1, 2008, accessed December 21, 2010, http://www.energyintel.com/documentdetail.asp?document_id=245527.

In the past thirty years, governments have increasingly privatized a number of industries. However, "in defense, power generation, telecoms, metals, minerals, aviation, and other sectors, a growing number of emerging-market governments, not content with simply regulating markets, are moving to dominate them." [7]

State companies, like their private sector counterparts, get to keep the profits from oil production, creating a significant incentive for governments to either maintain or regain control of this very lucrative industry. Whether the motive is economic (i.e., profit) or political (i.e., state control), "foreign firms and investors find that national and local rules and regulations are increasingly designed to favor domestic firms at their expense. Multinationals now find themselves competing as never before with state-owned companies armed with substantial financial and political support from their governments." [8]

Governments are also motivated by economic factors to intervene in trade. They may want to protect young industries or to preserve access to local consumer markets for domestic firms.

Cultural and social factors might also impact a government's intervention in trade. For example, some countries' governments have tried to limit the influence of American culture on local markets by limiting or denying the entry of American companies operating in the media, food, and music industries.

How Do Governments Intervene in Trade?

While the past century has seen a major shift toward free trade, many governments continue to intervene in trade. Governments have several key policy areas that can be used to create rules and regulations to control and manage trade.

- **Tariffs.** Tariffs are taxes imposed on imports. Two kinds of tariffs exist—specific tariffs, which are levied as a fixed charge, and ad valorem tariffs, which are calculated as a percentage of the value. Many governments still charge ad valorem tariffs as a way to regulate imports and raise revenues for their coffers.
- **Subsidies.** A subsidy is a form of government payment to a producer. Types of subsidies include tax breaks or low-interest loans; both of which are common. Subsidies can also be cash grants and government-equity participation, which are less common because they require a direct use of government resources.

- **Import quotas and VER.** Import quotas and voluntary export restraints (VER) are two strategies to limit the amount of imports into a country. The importing government directs import quotas, while VER are imposed at the discretion of the exporting nation in conjunction with the importing one.
- **Currency controls.** Governments may limit the convertibility of one currency (usually its own) into others, usually in an effort to limit imports. Additionally, some governments will manage the exchange rate at a high level to create an import disincentive.
- **Local content requirements.** Many countries continue to require that a certain percentage of a product or an item be manufactured or "assembled" locally. Some countries specify that a local firm must be used as the domestic partner to conduct business.
- **Antidumping rules.** Dumping occurs when a company sells product below market price often in order to win market share and weaken a competitor.
- **Export financing.** Governments provide financing to domestic companies to promote exports.
- **Free-trade zone.** Many countries designate certain geographic areas as free-trade zones. These areas enjoy reduced tariffs, taxes, customs, procedures, or restrictions in an effort to promote trade with other countries.
- **Administrative policies.** These are the bureaucratic policies and procedures governments may use to deter imports by making entry or operations more difficult and time consuming.

Did You Know?

Government Intervention in China

As shown in the opening case study, China is using its economic might to invest in Africa. China's ability to focus on dominating key industries inspires both fear and awe throughout the world. A closer look at the solar industry in China illustrates the government's ability to create new industries and companies based on its objectives. With its huge population, China is in constant need of energy to meet the needs of its people and businesses.

As a result, the government has placed a priority on energy related technologies, including solar energy. China's expanding solar-energy industry is dependent on polycrystalline silicon, the main raw material for solar panels. Facing a shortage in 2007, growing domestic demand, and high prices from foreign companies that dominated production, China declared the development of domestic polysilicon supplies a priority. Domestic Chinese manufacturers received quick loans with favorable terms as well as speedy approvals. One entrepreneur, Zhu Gongshan, received $1 billion in funding, including a sizeable investment from China's sovereign wealth fund, in record time, enabling his firm GCL-Poly Energy Holding to become one of the world's biggest in less than three years. The company now has a 25 percent market share of polysilicon and almost 50 percent of the global market for solar-power equipment. [9] How did this happen so fast? Many observers note that it was the direct result of Chinese government intervention in what was deemed a key industry.

Central to China's approach are policies that champion state-owned firms and other so-called national champions, seek aggressively to obtain advanced technology, and manage its exchange rate to benefit exporters. It leverages state control of the financial system to channel low-cost capital to domestic industries—and to resource-rich foreign nations (such as those we read in the opening case) whose oil and minerals China needs to maintain rapid growth. [10]

Understanding the balance between China's government structure and its ideology is essential to doing business in this complex country. China is both an emerging market and a rising superpower. Its leaders see the economy as a tool to preserving the state's power, which in turn is essential to maintaining stability and growth and ensuring the long-term viability of the Communist Party. [11]

Contrary to the approach of much of the world, which is moving more control to the private sector, China has steadfastly maintained its state control. For example, the Chinese government owns almost all the major banks, the three largest oil companies, the three telecommunications carriers, and almost all of the media.

China's Communist Party outlines its goals in five-year plans. The most recent one emphasizes the government's goal for China to become a technology powerhouse by 2020 and highlights key areas such as green technology, hence the solar industry expansion. Free trade advocates perceive this government-directed intervention as an unfair tilt against the global private sector. Nevertheless, global companies continue to seek the Chinese market, which offers much-needed growth and opportunity. [12]

KEY TAKEAWAYS

- There are more than thirteen major types of government and each type consists of multiple variations. At one end of the political ideology extremes is anarchism, which contends that individuals should control political activities and public government is both unnecessary and unwanted. The other extreme is totalitarianism, which contends that every aspect of an individual's life should be controlled and dictated by a strong central government. Neither extreme exists in its purest form in the real world. Instead, most countries have a combination of both. This combination is called pluralism, which asserts that both public and private groups are important in a well-functioning political system. Democracy is the most common form of government today. Democratic governments derive their power from the people of the country either by direct referendum, called a direct democracy, or by means of elected representatives of the people, known as a representative democracy.

- Capitalism is an economic system in which the means of production are owned and controlled privately. In contrast a planned economy is one in which the government or state directs and controls the economy.

- There are three main types of legal systems: (1) civil law, (2) common law, and (3) religious law. In practice, countries use a combination of one or more of these systems and often adapt them to suit the local values and culture.

- Government-business trade relations are the relationships between national governments and global businesses. Governments intervene in trade to protect their nation's economy and industry, as well as promote and preserve their social, cultural, political, and economic structures and philosophies. Governments have several key policy areas in which they can create rules and regulations in order to control and manage trade, including tariffs, subsidies; import quotas and VER, currency controls, local content requirements, antidumping rules, export financing, free-trade zones, and administrative policies.

EXERCISES

(AACSB: Reflective Thinking, Analytical Skills)

1. Identify the main political ideologies.
2. What is capitalism? What is a planned economy? Compare and contrast the two forms of economic ideology discussed in this section.
3. What are three policy areas in which governments can create rules and regulations in order to control, manage, and intervene in trade.

[1] "Liberty and Justice for Some," Economist, August 22, 2007, accessed December 21, 2010, http://www.economist.com/node/8908438.

[2] Economist Intelligence Unit, "The Economist Intelligence Unit's Index of Democracy 2008," Economist, October 29, 2008, accessed December 21, 2010, http://graphics.eiu.com/PDF/Democracy%20Index%202008.pdf.

[3] Economist Intelligence Unit, "The Economist Intelligence Unit's Index of Democracy 2008," Economist, October 29, 2008, accessed December 21, 2010, http://graphics.eiu.com/PDF/Democracy%20Index%202008.pdf.

[4] Rolfe Winkler, "Internet Plus China Equals Screaming Baidu," Wall Street Journal, November 9, 2010, accessed December 21, 2010, http://online.wsj.com/article/SB100014240527487035149045756027811 30437538.html.

[5] Tala Malik, "Gulf Islamic Bank Assets to Hit $300bn," Arabian Business, February 20, 2008, accessed December 21, 2010, http://www.arabianbusiness.com/511804-gulf-islamic-banks-assets-to-hit-300bn.

[6] Ian Bremmer, "The Long Shadow of the Visible Hand," Wall Street Journal, May 22, 2010, accessed December 21, 2010,http://online.wsj.com/article/SB10001424052748704852004575258541875590852.html; "Really Big Oil," Economist, August 10, 2006, accessed December 21, 2010,http://www.economist.com/node/7276986.

[7] Ian Bremmer, "The Long Shadow of the Visible Hand," Wall Street Journal, May 22, 2010, accessed December 21, 2010, http://online.wsj.com/article/SB10001424052748704852004575258541875590852.html.

[8] Ian Bremmer, "The Long Shadow of the Visible Hand," Wall Street Journal, May 22, 2010, accessed December 21, 2010, http://online.wsj.com/article/SB10001424052748704852004575258541875590852.html.

[9] Jason Dean, Andrew Browne, and Shai Oster, "China's 'State Capitalism' Sparks Global Backlash," Wall Street Journal, November 16, 2010, accessed December 22, 2010, http://online.wsj.com/article/SB10001424052748703514904575602731006315198.html.

[10] Jason Dean, Andrew Browne, and Shai Oster, "China's 'State Capitalism' Sparks Global Backlash," Wall Street Journal, November 16, 2010, accessed December 22, 2010, http://online.wsj.com/article/SB10001424052748703514904575602731006315198.html.

[11] Jason Dean, Andrew Browne, and Shai Oster, "China's 'State Capitalism' Sparks Global Backlash," Wall Street Journal, November 16, 2010, accessed December 22, 2010, http://online.wsj.com/article/SB10001424052748703514904575602731006315198.html.

[12] Jason Dean, Andrew Browne, and Shai Oster, "China's 'State Capitalism' Sparks Global Backlash," Wall Street Journal, November 16, 2010, accessed December 22, 2010, http://online.wsj.com/article/SB10001424052748703514904575602731006315198.html.

2.3 Foreign Direct Investment
LEARNING OBJECTIVES

1. Understand the types of international investments.
2. Identify the factors that influence foreign direct investment (FDI).
3. Explain why and how governments encourage FDI in their countries.

Understand the Types of International Investments

There are two main categories of international investment—portfolio investment and foreign direct investment. Portfolio investment refers to the investment in a company's stocks, bonds, or assets, but not for the purpose of controlling or directing the firm's operations or management. Typically, investors in this category are looking for a financial rate of return as well as diversifying investment risk through multiple markets.

Foreign direct investment (FDI) refers to an investment in or the acquisition of foreign assets with the intent to control and manage them. Companies can make an FDI in several ways, including purchasing the assets of a foreign company; investing in the company or in new property, plants, or equipment; or participating in a joint venture with a foreign company, which typically involves an investment of capital or know-how. FDI is primarily a long-term strategy. Companies usually expect to benefit through access to local markets and resources, often in exchange for expertise, technical know-how, and capital. A country's FDI can be both inward and outward. As the terms would suggest, inward FDI refers to investments coming into the country and outward FDI are investments made by companies from that country into foreign companies in other countries. The difference between inward and outward is called the net FDI inflow, which can be either positive or negative.

Governments want to be able to control and regulate the flow of FDI so that local political and economic concerns are addressed. Global businesses are most interested in using FDI to benefit their companies. As a result, these two players—governments and companies—can at times be at odds. It's important to understand why companies use FDI as a business strategy and how governments regulate and manage FDI.

Factors That Influence a Company's Decision to Invest

Let's look at why and how companies choose to invest in foreign markets. Simply purchasing goods and services or deciding to invest in a local market depends on a business's needs and overall strategy. Direct investment in a country occurs when a company chooses to set up facilities to produce or market their products; or seeks to partner with, invest in, or purchase a local company for control and access to the local market, production, or resources. Many considerations influence its decisions:

- **Cost.** Is it cheaper to produce in the local market than elsewhere?
- **Logistics.** Is it cheaper to produce locally if the transportation costs are significant?
- **Market.** Has the company identified a significant local market?
- **Natural resources.** Is the company interested in obtaining access to local resources or commodities?
- **Know-how.** Does the company want access to local technology or business process knowledge?
- **Customers and competitors.** Does the company's clients or competitors operate in the country?
- **Policy.** Are there local incentives (cash and noncash) for investing in one country versus another?
- **Ease.** Is it relatively straightforward to invest and/or set up operations in the country, or is there another country in which setup might be easier?
- **Culture.** Is the workforce or labor pool already skilled for the company's needs or will extensive training be required?
- **Impact.** How will this investment impact the company's revenue and profitability?
- **Expatriation of funds.** Can the company easily take profits out of the country, or are there local restrictions?
- **Exit.** Can the company easily and orderly exit from a local investment, or are local laws and regulations cumbersome and expensive?

These are just a few of the many factors that might influence a company's decision. Keep in mind that a company doesn't need to sell in the local market in order to deem it a good option for direct investment. For example, companies set up manufacturing facilities in low-cost countries but export the products to other markets.

There are two forms of FDI—horizontal and vertical. Horizontal FDI occurs when a company is trying to open up a new market—a retailer, for example, that builds a store in a new country to sell to the local market. Vertical FDI is when a company invests internationally to provide input into its core operations—usually in its home country. A firm may invest in production facilities in another country. When a firm brings the goods or components back to its home country (i.e., acting as a supplier), this is referred to as backward vertical FDI. When a firm sells the goods into the local or regional market (i.e., acting as a distributor), this is termed forward vertical FDI. The largest global companies often engage in both backward and forward vertical FDI depending on their industry.

Many firms engage in backward vertical FDI. The auto, oil, and infrastructure (which includes industries related to enhancing the infrastructure of a country—that is, energy, communications, and transportation) industries are good examples of this. Firms from these industries invest in production or plant facilities in a country in order to supply raw materials, parts, or finished products to their home country. In recent years, these same industries have also started to provide forward FDI by supplying raw materials, parts, or finished products to newly emerging local or regional markets.

There are different kinds of FDI, two of which—greenfield and brownfield—are increasingly applicable to global firms. Greenfield FDIs occur when multinational corporations enter into developing countries to build new factories or stores. These new facilities are built from scratch—usually in an area where no previous facilities existed. The name originates from the idea of building a facility on a green field, such as farmland or a forested area. In addition to building new facilities that best meet their needs, the firms also create new long-term jobs in the foreign country by hiring new employees. Countries often offer prospective companies tax breaks, subsidies, and other incentives to set up greenfield investments.

A brownfield FDI is when a company or government entity purchases or leases existing production facilities to launch a new production activity. One application of this strategy is where a commercial site used for an "unclean" business purpose, such as a steel mill or oil refinery, is cleaned up and used for a less polluting purpose, such as commercial office space or a residential area. Brownfield investment is usually less expensive and can be implemented faster; however, a company may have to deal with many challenges, including existing employees, outdated equipment, entrenched processes, and cultural differences.

You should note that the terms *greenfield* and *brownfield* are not exclusive to FDI; you may hear them in various business contexts. In general, greenfield refers to starting from the beginning, and brownfield refers to modifying or upgrading existing plans or projects.

Why and How Governments Encourage FDI

Many governments encourage FDI in their countries as a way to create jobs, expand local technical knowledge, and increase their overall economic standards. [1] Countries like Hong Kong and Singapore long ago realized that both global trade and FDI would help them grow exponentially and improve the standard of living for their citizens. As a result, Hong Kong (before its return to China) was one of the easiest places to set up a new company. Guidelines were clearly available, and businesses could set up a new office within days. Similarly, Singapore, while a bit more discriminatory on the size and type of business, offered foreign companies a clear, streamlined process for setting up a new company.

In contrast, for decades, many other countries in Asia (e.g., India, China, Pakistan, the Philippines, and Indonesia) restricted or controlled FDI in their countries by requiring extensive paperwork and bureaucratic approvals as well as local partners for any new foreign business. These policies created disincentives for many global companies. By the 1990s (and earlier for China), many of the countries in Asia had caught the global trade bug and were actively trying to modify their policies to encourage more FDI. Some were more successful than others, often as a result of internal political issues and pressures rather than from any repercussions of global trade. [2]

How Governments Discourage or Restrict FDI

In most instances, governments seek to limit or control foreign direct investment to protect local industries and key resources (oil, minerals, etc.), preserve the national and local culture, protect segments of their domestic population, maintain political and economic independence, and manage or control economic growth. A government use various policies and rules:

- **Ownership restrictions.** Host governments can specify ownership restrictions if they want to keep the control of local markets or industries in their citizens' hands. Some countries, such as Malaysia, go even further and encourage that ownership be maintained by a person of Malay origin, known locally as *bumiputra*. Although the country's Foreign Investment Committee guidelines are being relaxed, most foreign businesses understand that having a *bumiputra* partner will improve their chances of obtaining favorable contracts in Malaysia.

- **Tax rates and sanctions.** A company's home government usually imposes these restrictions in an effort to persuade companies to invest in the domestic market rather than a foreign one.

How Governments Encourage FDI

Governments seek to promote FDI when they are eager to expand their domestic economy and attract new technologies, business know-how, and capital to their country. In these instances, many governments still try to manage and control the type, quantity, and even the nationality of the FDI to achieve their domestic, economic, political, and social goals.

- **Financial incentives.** Host countries offer businesses a combination of tax incentives and loans to invest. Home-country governments may also offer a combination of insurance, loans, and tax breaks in an effort to promote their companies' overseas investments. The opening case on China in Africa illustrated these types of incentives.

- **Infrastructure.** Host governments improve or enhance local infrastructure—in energy, transportation, and communications—to encourage specific industries to invest. This also serves to improve the local conditions for domestic firms.

- **Administrative processes and regulatory environment.** Host-country governments streamline the process of establishing offices or production in their countries. By reducing bureaucracy and regulatory environments, these countries appear more attractive to foreign firms.

- **Invest in education.** Countries seek to improve their workforce through education and job training. An educated and skilled workforce is an important investment criterion for many global businesses.

- **Political, economic, and legal stability.** Host-country governments seek to reassure businesses that the local operating conditions are stable, transparent (i.e., policies are clearly stated and in the public domain), and unlikely to change.

Ethics in Action
Encouraging Foreign Investment

Governments seek to encourage FDI for a variety of reasons. On occasion, though, the process can cross the lines of ethics and legality. In November 2010, seven global companies paid the US Justice Department "a combined $236 million in fines to settle allegations that they or their contractors bribed foreign officials to smooth the way for importing equipment and materials into several countries." [3] The companies included Shell and contractors Transocean, Noble, Pride International, Global Santa Fe, Tidewater, and Panalpina World Transport. The bribes were paid to officials in oil-rich countries—Nigeria, Brazil, Azerbaijan, Russia, Turkmenistan, Kazakhstan, and Angola. In the United States, global firms—including ones headquartered elsewhere, but trading on any of the US stock exchanges—are prohibited from paying or even offering to pay bribes to foreign government officials or

employees of state-owned businesses with the intent of currying business favors. While the law and the business ethics are clear, in many cases, the penalty fines remain much less onerous than losing critical long-term business revenues. [4]

Did You Know?
Hong Kong: From Junks to Jets? The Rise of a Global Powerhouse

Policies of openness to FDI and international trade have enabled countries around the world to leapfrog economically over their neighbors. The historical rise of Hong Kong is one example. Hong Kong's economic strengths can be traced to a combination of factors, including its business-friendly laws and policies, a local population that is culturally oriented to transacting trade and business, and Hong Kong's geographic proximity to the major economies of China, Japan, and Taiwan.

Hong Kong has always been open to global trade. Many people, from the Chinese to the Japanese to the British, have occupied Hong Kong over the centuries, and all of them have contributed to its development as one of the world's great ports and trading centers.

In 1997, Hong Kong reverted back to Chinese control; however, free enterprise will be governed under the agreement of Basic Law, which established Hong Kong as a separate Special Administrative Region (SAR) of China. Under its Basic Law, in force until 2047, Hong Kong will retain its legal, social, economic, and political systems apart from China's. Thus, Hong Kong is guaranteed the right to its own monetary system and financial autonomy. Hong Kong is allowed to work independently with the international community; to control trade in strategic commodities, drugs, and illegal transshipments; and to protect intellectual property rights. Under the Basic Law, the Hong Kong SAR maintains an independent tax system and the right to free trade.

Hong Kong has an open business structure, which freely encourages foreign direct investment. Any company that wishes to do business here is free to do so as long as it complies with local laws. Hong Kong's legal and institutional framework combined with its good banking and financial facilities and business-friendly tax systems have encouraged foreign direct investment as many multinationals located their regional headquarters in Hong Kong.

As a base for doing business with China, Hong Kong now accounts for half of all direct investments in the mainland

and is China's main conduit for investment and trade. China has also become a major investor in Hong Kong.

Culturally, many foreign firms are attracted to Hong Kong by its skilled workforce and the fact that Hong Kong still conducts business in English, a remnant of its British colonial influence. The imprint of the early British trading firms, known as *hongs*, is particularly strong today in the area of property development. Jardine Matheson and Company, for instance, founded by trader William Jardine, remains one of Hong Kong's preeminent firms. In many of these companies, British management practices remain firmly in place. Every aspect of Hong Kong's business laws—whether pertaining to contracts, taxes, or trusts—bears striking similarities to the laws in Britain. All these factors contribute to a business culture that is familiar to people in many multinationals.

Chinese cultural influences have always affected business and are increasingly so today. Many pundits claim that Hong Kong already resembles China's free-trade zone. And, indeed, the two economies are becoming increasingly intertwined. Much of this economic commingling began in the 1990s, when Hong Kong companies began relocating production centers to the mainland—especially to Guangdong province.

Because of the shift in production to mainland China and other Asian countries, there is not much manufacturing left in Hong Kong. What remains is light in nature and veers toward high-value-added products. In fact, 80 percent of Hong Kong's gross domestic product now comes from its high value-added service sector: finance, business and legal services, brokerage services, the shipping and cargo industries, and the hotel, food, and beverage industry.

Local Hong Kong companies, as well as foreign businesses based there, are uniquely positioned to play important roles as brokers and intermediaries between the mainland and global corporations. Doing business in China is not only complex and daunting but also requires connections, locally known as *guanxi*, to influential people and an understanding of local laws and protocol. Developing these relationships and this knowledge is almost impossible without the assistance of an insider. It is in this role that the Hong Kong business community stands to contribute enormously.

Hong Kong's openness to foreign investment coupled with its proximity to China will ensure its global economic competitiveness for decades to come.

KEY TAKEAWAYS

- There are two main categories of international investment: portfolio investment and foreign direct investment (FDI). Portfolio investment refers to the investment in a company's stocks, bonds, or assets, but not for the purpose of controlling or directing the firm's operations or management. FDI refers to an investment in or the acquisition of foreign assets with the intent to control and manage them.

- Direct investment in a country occurs when a company chooses to set up facilities to produce or market its products or seeks to partner with, invest in, or purchase a local company for control and access to the local market, production, or resources. Many considerations can influence the company's decisions, including cost, logistics, market, natural resources, know-how, customers and competitors, policy, ease of entry and exit, culture, impact on revenue and profitability, and expatriation of funds.

- Governments discourage or restrict FDI through ownership restrictions, tax rates, and sanctions. Governments encourage FDI through financial incentives; well-established infrastructure; desirable administrative processes and regulatory environment; educational investment; and political, economic, and legal stability.

EXERCISES

(AACSB: Reflective Thinking, Analytical Skills)

1. What are three factors that impact a company's decision to invest in a country?
2. What is the difference between vertical and horizontal FDI? Give one example of an industry for each type.
3. How can governments encourage or discourage FDI?

[1] Ian Bremmer, The End of the Free Market: Who Wins the War Between States and Corporations (New York: Portfolio, 2010).
[2] UNCTAD compiles statistics on foreign direct investment (FDI): "Foreign Direct Investment database," UNCTAD United Nations Conference on Trade and Development, accessed February 16, 2011, http://unctadstat.unctad.org/ReportFolders/reportFolders.aspx?sRF_ActivePath=P,5,27&sRF_Expanded=,P,5,27&sCS_ChosenLang=en.
[3] Kara Scannell, "Shell, Six Other Firms Settle Foreign-Bribery Probe," Wall Street Journal, November 5, 2010, accessed December 23, 2010, http://online.wsj.com/article/SB10001424052748704805204575594311301043920.html.
[4] Kara Scannell, "Shell, Six Other Firms Settle Foreign-Bribery Probe," Wall Street Journal, November 5, 2010, accessed December 23, 2010, http://online.wsj.com/article/SB10001424052748704805204575594311301043920.html.

2.4 Tips in Your Entrepreneurial Walkabout Toolkit

Attracting Trade and Investment

Governments around the world seek to attract trade and investment, but some are better at achieving this objective than others. Are you wondering where the best country to start a business might be? The *Wall Street Journal* recently made an effort to answer this question by reviewing data from global surveys. Contrary to what you might think given the global push toward globalization and a flat world, most governments still actively limit and control foreign investment.

Governments in the developing world, for instance, often impose high costs and numerous procedures on people who are trying to get a company off the ground. In Zimbabwe, entrepreneurs will have to fork over about 500 percent of the country's average per-capita income in government fees. Compare that with 0.7 percent in the U.S. In Equatorial Guinea, owners have to slog through 20 procedures to get their venture going, versus just one in Canada and New Zealand. Still, lots of countries are making progress. In a World Bank study of red tape, Samoa was singled out for making the most strides in reforming its practices. It went from one of the toughest places in the world to start a company last year—131st out of 183—to No. 20 this year…China, for instance, ranks as just the 40th best place in the world to start a company. Yet China and its up-and-coming peers score high on forward-looking measures like expectations for job creation—so they're likely to catch up fast with more-advanced economies. [1]

Quick Facts

- *What's the best place in the world to start a business?* Denmark.
- *What country has the biggest share of women who launch new businesses?* Peru.
- *Where does it cost the most to start a company?* You'll have to pony up the most money in the Netherlands.
- *Where does it take an average of 694 days to clear government red tape and get a company off the ground?* Suriname. [2]

[1] Jeff May, "The Best Country to Start a Business…and Other Facts You Probably Didn't Know about Entrepreneurship around the World," Wall Street Journal, November 15, 2010, accessed December 27, 2010,http://online.wsj.com/article/SB1000142405274870385920457552583366862428.html.
[2] Jeff May, "The Best Country to Start a Business…and Other Facts You Probably Didn't Know about Entrepreneurship around the World," Wall Street Journal, November 15, 2010, accessed December 27, 2010,http://online.wsj.com/article/SB1000142405274870385920457552583366862428.html.

2.5 End-of-Chapter Questions and Exercises

These exercises are designed to ensure that the knowledge you gain from this book about international business meets the learning standards set out by the international Association to Advance Collegiate Schools of Business (AACSB International). [1] AACSB is the premier accrediting agency of collegiate business schools and accounting programs worldwide. It expects that you will gain knowledge in the areas of communication, ethical reasoning, analytical skills, use of information technology, multiculturalism and diversity, and reflective thinking.

EXPERIENTIAL EXERCISES

(AACSB: Communication, Use of Information Technology, Analytical Skills)

1. Define the differences between the classical, country-based trade theories and the modern, firm-based trade theories. If you were a manager for a large manufacturing company charged with developing your firm's global strategy, how would you use these theories in your analysis? Which theories seem most appealing to you and which don't seem to apply?

2. Pick a country as a potential new market for your firm's operations. Using what you have learned in this chapter and from online resources (e.g., https://www.cia.gov/library/publications/the-world-factbook/index.html andhttp://globaledge.msu.edu/), [2] assess the local political, economic, and legal factors of the country. Would you recommend to your senior management that your firm establish operations and invest in this country? Which factors do you think are most important in this decision?

Ethical Dilemmas

(AACSB: Ethical Reasoning, Multiculturalism, Reflective Thinking, Analytical Skills)

1. Imagine that you are working for a US business that is evaluating whether it should move its manufacturing to India or China. You have been asked to present the pros and cons of this investment. Based on what you have learned in this chapter, what political, legal, economic, social, and business factors would you need to assess for each country? Use the Internet for country-specific research. [3]

2. Imagine that you work for a large, global company that builds power plants for electricity. This industry has a long-term perspective and requires stable, reliable countries in order to make FDIs. You are assigned to evaluate which of the following would be better for a long-term investment: South Africa, Nigeria, Algeria, or

Kenya. Recall what you've learned in this chapter about political and legal factors and political ideologies—as well as earlier discussions about global business ethics and bribery. Then, using online resources to support your opinion, provide your recommendations to senior management.

[1] Association to Advance Collegiate Schools of Business website, accessed January 26, 2010, http://www.aacsb.edu.
[2] Central Intelligence Agency, World Factbook, Central Intelligence Agency website, accessed February 16, 2011, https://www.cia.gov/library/publications/the-world-factbook/index.html; globalEDGE website, International Business Center, Michigan State University, accessed February 16, 2011, http://globaledge.msu.edu.
[3] globalEDGE website, International Business Center, Michigan State University, accessed February 16, 2011, http://globaledge.msu.edu.

NOTES:

NOTES:

Chapter 3:
Culture and Business

1. What is culture? What kinds of culture are there?
2. What are the key methods used to describe cultures? What are the additional determinants of cultures?
3. How does culture impact local business practices and how does cultural understanding apply to business negotiating?
4. What is global business ethics and how is it impacted by culture?
5. How do ethics impact global businesses?

This chapter will take a closer look at how two key factors, culture and ethics, impact global business. Most people hear about culture and business and immediately think about protocol—a list of dos and don'ts by country. For example, don't show the sole of your foot in Saudi Arabia; know how to bow in Japan. While these practices are certainly useful to know, they are just the tip of the iceberg. We often underestimate how critical local culture, values, and customs can be in the business environment. We assume, usually incorrectly, that business is the same everywhere. Culture does matter, and more and more people are realizing its impact on their business interactions.

Culture, in the broadest sense, refers to how and why we think and function. It encompasses all sorts of things—how we eat, play, dress, work, think, interact, and communicate. Everything we do, in essence, has been shaped by the cultures in which we are raised. Similarly, a person in another country is also shaped by his or her cultural influences. These cultural influences impact how we think and communicate.

This chapter will discuss what culture means and how it impacts business. We'll review a real company, Dunkin' Brands, that has learned to effectively incorporate, interpret, and integrate local customs and habits, the key components of culture, into its products and marketing strategy.

OPENING CASE: DUNKIN' BRANDS—DUNKIN' DONUTS AND BASKIN-ROBBINS: MAKING LOCAL GLOBAL

High-tech and digital news may dominate our attention globally, but no matter where you go, people still need to eat.

Food is a key part of many cultures. It is part of the bonds of our childhood, creating warm memories of comfort food or favorite foods that continue to whet our appetites. So it's no surprise that sugar and sweets are a key part of our food focus, no matter what the culture. Two of the most visible American exports are the twin brands of Dunkin' Donuts and Baskin-Robbins.

Owned today by a consortium of private equity firms known as the Dunkin' Brands, Dunkin' Donuts and Baskin-Robbins have been sold globally for more than thirty-five years. Today, the firm has more than 14,800 points of distribution in forty-four countries with $6.9 billion in global sales.

After an eleven-year hiatus, Dunkin' Donuts returned to Russia in 2010 with the opening of twenty new stores. Under a new partnership, "the planned store openings come 11 years after Dunkin' Donuts pulled out of Russia, following three years of losses exacerbated by a rogue franchisee who sold liquor and meat pies alongside coffee and crullers." [1] Each culture has different engrained habits, particularly in the choices of food and what foods are appropriate for what meals. The more globally aware businesses are mindful of these issues and monitor their overseas operations and partners. One of the key challenges for many companies operating globally with different resellers, franchisees, and wholly owned subsidiaries is the ability to control local operations.

This wasn't the first time that Dunkin' had encountered an overzealous local partner who tried to customize operations to meet local preferences and demands. In Indonesia in the 1990s, the company was surprised to find that local operators were sprinkling a mild, white cheese on a custard-filled donut. The company eventually approved the local customization since it was a huge success. [2]

Dunkin' Donuts and Baskin-Robbins have not always been owned by the same firm. They eventually came under one entity in the late 1980s—an entity that sought to leverage the two brands. One of the overall strategies was to have the morning market covered by Dunkin' Donuts and the afternoon-snack market covered by Baskin-Robbins. It is a strategy that worked well in the United States and was one the company employed as it started operating and expanding in different countries. The company was initially unprepared for the wide range of local cultural preferences and habits that would culturally impact its business. In Russia, Japan, China, and most of Asia, donuts, if they were known at all, were regarded more as a sweet type of bakery treat, like an éclair or cream puff. Locals primarily purchased and consumed them at shopping malls as an "impulse purchase" afternoon-snack item and not as a breakfast food.

In fact, in China, there was no equivalent word for "donut" in Mandarin, and European-style baked pastries were not common outside the Shanghai and Hong Kong markets. To further complicate Dunkin' Donuts's entry into China, which took place initially in Beijing, the company name could not even be phonetically spelled in Chinese characters that made any sense, as Baskin-Robbins had been able to do in Taiwan. After extensive discussion and research, company executives decided that the best name and translation for Dunkin' Donuts in China would read Sweet Sweet Ring in Chinese characters.

Local cultures also impacted flavors and preferences. For Baskin-Robbins, the flavor library is controlled in the United States, but local operators in each country have been the source of new flavor suggestions. In many cases, flavors that were customized for local cultures were added a decade later to the main menus in major markets, including the United States. Mango and green tea were early custom ice cream flavors in the 1990s for the Asian market. In Latin America, dulce de leche became a favorite flavor. Today, these flavors are staples of the North American flavor menu.

One flavor suggestion from Southeast Asia never quite made it onto the menu. The durian fruit is a favorite in parts of Southeast Asia, but it has a strong, pungent odor. Baskin-Robbins management was concerned that the strong odor would overwhelm factory operations. (The odor of the durian fruit is so strong that the fruit is often banned in upscale hotels in several Asian countries.) While the durian never became a flavor, the company did concede to making ice cream flavored after the ube, a sweetened purple yam, for the Philippine market. It was already offered in Japan, and the company extended it to the Philippines. In Japan, sweet corn and red bean ice cream were approved for local sale and became hot sellers, but the two flavors never made it outside the country.

When reviewing local suggestions, management conducts a market analysis to determine if the global market for the flavor is large enough to justify the investment in research and development and eventual production. In addition to the market analysis, the company always has to make sure they have access to sourcing quality flavors and fruit. Mango proved to be a challenge, as finding the correct fruit puree differed by country or culture. Samples from India, Hawaii, Pakistan, Mexico, the Philippines, and Puerto Rico were taste-tested in the mainland United States. It seems that the mango is culturally regarded as a national treasure in every country where it is grown, and every country thinks its mango is the best. Eventually the company settled on one particular flavor of mango.

A challenging balance for Dunkin' Brands is to enable local operators to customize flavors and food product offerings without diminishing the overall brand of the companies. Russians, for example, are largely unfamiliar with donuts, so Dunkin' has created several items that specifically appeal to Russian flavor preferences for scalded cream and raspberry jam. [3]

In some markets, one of the company's brands may establish a market presence first. In Russia, the overall "Dunkin' Brands" already ranks as a dessert purveyor. Its Baskin-Robbins ice-cream chain boasts 143 shops there, making it the No. 2 Western restaurant brand by number of stores behind the hamburger chain McDonald's Corp." [4] The strength of the company's ice cream brand is now enabling Dunkin' Brands to promote the donut chain as well.

OPENING CASE EXERCISES
(AACSB: ETHICAL REASONING, MULTICULTURALISM, REFLECTIVE THINKING, ANALYTICAL SKILLS)

1. If you were a manager for Baskin-Robbins, how would you evaluate a request from a local partner in India to add a sugar-cane-flavored ice cream to its menu? What cultural factors would you look at?

2. Do you think Dunkin' Brands should let local operators make their own decisions regarding flavors for ice creams, donuts, and other items to be sold in-country? How would you recommend that the company's global management assess the cultural differences in each market? Should there be one global policy?

[1] Kevin Helliker, "Dunkin' Donuts Heads Back to Russia," Wall Street Journal, April 27, 2010, accessed February 15, 2011,
http://online.wsj.com/article/SB10001424052748704464704575208320044839374.html.
[2] David Jenkins (former director, International Operations Development, Allied-Domecq QSR International Ltd.), interview with the author, 2010.
[3] Kevin Helliker, "Dunkin' Donuts Heads Back to Russia," Wall Street Journal, April 27, 2010, accessed February 15, 2011,
http://online.wsj.com/article/SB10001424052748704464704575208320044839374.html.

[4] Kevin Helliker, "Dunkin' Donuts Heads Back to Russia," *Wall Street Journal*, April 27, 2010, accessed February 15, 2011, http://online.wsj.com/article/SB10001424052748704464704575208320044839374.html.

3.1 What Is Culture, Anyhow? Values, Customs, and Language

LEARNING OBJECTIVES

1. Understand what is meant by *culture*.
2. Know that there are different kinds of culture.
3. Identify several different kinds of culture.

As the opening case about Dunkin' Brands illustrates, local preferences, habits, values, and culture impact all aspects of doing business in a country. But what exactly do we mean by culture? Culture is different from personality. For our purposes here, let's define *personality* as a person's identity and unique physical, mental, emotional, and social characteristics. [1] No doubt one of the highest hurdles to cross-cultural understanding and effective relationships is our frequent inability to decipher the influence of culture from that of personality. Once we become culturally literate, we can more easily read individual personalities and their effect on our relationships.

So, What Is Culture, Anyway?

Culture in today's context is different from the traditional, more singular definition, used particularly in Western languages, where the word often implies refinement. Culture is the beliefs, values, mind-sets, and practices of a group of people. It includes the behavior pattern and norms of that group—the rules, the assumptions, the perceptions, and the logic and reasoning that are specific to a group. In essence, each of us is raised in a belief system that influences our individual perspectives to such a large degree that we can't always account for, or even comprehend, its influence. We're like other members of our culture—we've come to share a common idea of what's appropriate and inappropriate.

Culture is really the collective programming of our minds from birth. It's this collective programming that distinguishes one group of people from another. Much of the problem in any cross-cultural interaction stems from our expectations. The challenge is that whenever we deal with people from another culture—whether in our own country or globally—we expect people to behave as we do and for the same reasons. Culture awareness most commonly refers to having an understanding of another culture's values and perspective. This does not mean automatic acceptance; it simply means understanding another culture's mind-set and how its history, economy, and society have impacted what people think. Understanding so you can properly interpret someone's

words and actions means you can effectively interact with them.

When talking about culture, it's important to understand that there really are no rights or wrongs. People's value systems and reasoning are based on the teachings and experiences of their culture. Rights and wrongs then really become perceptions. Cross-cultural understanding requires that we reorient our mind-set and, most importantly, our expectations, in order to interpret the gestures, attitudes, and statements of the people we encounter. We reorient our mind-set, but we don't necessarily change it.

There are a number of factors that constitute a culture—manners, mind-set, rituals, laws, ideas, and language, to name a few. To truly understand culture, you need to go beyond the lists of dos and don'ts, although those are important too. You need to understand what makes people tick and how, as a group, they have been influenced over time by historical, political, and social issues. Understanding the "why" behind culture is essential.

When trying to understand how cultures evolve, we look at the factors that help determine cultures and their values. In general, a value is defined as something that we prefer over something else—whether it's a behavior or a tangible item. Values are usually acquired early in life and are often nonrational—although we may believe that ours are actually quite rational. Our values are the key building blocks of our cultural orientation.

Odds are that each of us has been raised with a considerably different set of values from those of our colleagues and counterparts around the world. Exposure to a new culture *may* take all you've ever learned about what's good and bad, just and unjust, and beautiful and ugly and stand it on its head.

Human nature is such that we see the world through our own cultural shades. Tucked in between the lines of our cultural laws is an unconscious bias that inhibits us from viewing other cultures objectively. Our judgments of people from other cultures will always be colored by the frame of reference we've been taught. As we look at our own habits and perceptions, we need to think about the experiences that have blended together to impact our cultural frame of reference.

In coming to terms with cultural differences, we tend to employ generalizations. This isn't necessarily bad. Generalizations can save us from sinking into what may be abstruse, esoteric aspects of a culture. However, recognize that cultures and values are not static entities. They're constantly evolving—merging, interacting, drawing apart, and reforming. Around the world, values and cultures are evolving from generation to generation as people are influenced by things outside their culture. In modern times, media and technology have probably single-handedly impacted cultures the most in the shortest time period—giving people around the world instant glimpses into other cultures, for better or for worse. Recognizing this fluidity will help you avoid getting caught in outdated generalizations. It will also enable you to interpret local cues and customs and to better understand local cultures.

Understanding what we mean by culture and what the components of culture are will help us better interpret the impact on business at both the macro and micro levels. Confucius had this to say about cultural crossings: "Human beings draw close to one another by their common nature, but habits and customs keep them apart."

What Kinds of Culture Are There?

Political, economic, and social philosophies all impact the way people's values are shaped. Our cultural base of reference—formed by our education, religion, or social structure—also impacts business interactions in critical ways. As we study cultures, it is very important to remember that all cultures are constantly evolving. When we say "cultural," we don't always just mean people from different countries. Every group of people has its own unique culture—that is, its own way of thinking, values, beliefs, and mind-sets. For our purposes in this chapter, we'll focus on national and ethnic cultures, although there are subcultures within a country or ethnic group.

Precisely where a culture begins and ends can be murky. Some cultures fall within geographic boundaries; others, of course, overlap. Cultures within one border can turn up within other geographic boundaries looking dramatically different or pretty much the same. For example, Indians in India or Americans in the United States may communicate and interact differently from their countrymen who have been living outside their respective home countries for a few years.

The countries of the Indian subcontinent, for example, have close similarities. And cultures within one political border can turn up within other political boundaries looking pretty much the same, such as the Chinese culture in China and the overseas Chinese culture in countries around the world. We often think that cultures are defined by the country or nation, but that can be misleading because there are different cultural

groups (as depicted in the preceding figure). These groups include nationalities; subcultures (gender, ethnicities, religions, generations, and even socioeconomic class); and organizations, including the workplace.

Nationalities

A national culture is—as it sounds—defined by its geographic and political boundaries and includes even regional cultures within a nation as well as among several neighboring countries. What is important about nations is that boundaries have changed throughout history. These changes in what territory makes up a country and what the country is named impact the culture of each country.

In the past century alone, we have seen many changes as new nations emerged from the gradual dismantling of the British and Dutch empires at the turn of the 1900s. For example, today the physical territories that constitute the countries of India and Indonesia are far different than they were a hundred years ago. While it's easy to forget that the British ran India for two hundred years and that the Dutch ran Indonesia for more than one hundred and fifty years, what is clearer is the impact of the British and the Dutch on the respective bureaucracies and business environments. The British and the Dutch were well known for establishing large government bureaucracies in the countries they controlled. Unlike the British colonial rulers in India, the Dutch did little to develop Indonesia's infrastructure, civil service, or educational system. The British, on the other hand, tended to hire locals for administrative positions, thereby establishing a strong and well-educated Indian bureaucracy. Even though many businesspeople today complain that this Indian bureaucracy is too slow and focused on rules and regulations, the government infrastructure and English-language education system laid out by the British helped position India for its emergence as a strong high-tech economy.

Even within a national culture, there are often distinct regional cultures—the United States is a great example of diverse and distinct cultures all living within the same physical borders. In the United States, there's a national culture embodied in the symbolic concept of "all-American" values and traits, but there are also other cultures based on geographically different regions—the South, Southwest, West Coast, East Coast, Northeast, Mid-Atlantic, and Midwest.

Subcultures

Many groups are defined by ethnicity, gender, generation, religion, or other characteristics with cultures that are unique to them. For example, the ethnic Chinese business community has a distinctive culture even though it may include Chinese businesspeople in several countries. This is particularly evident throughout Asia, as many people often refer to Chinese businesses as making up a single business community. The overseas Chinese business community tends to support one another and forge business bonds whether they are from Indonesia, Malaysia, Singapore, or other ASEAN (Association of Southeast Asian Nations) countries. This group is perceived differently than Chinese from mainland China or Taiwan. Their common experience being a minority ethnic community with strong business interests has led to a shared understanding of how to quietly operate large businesses in countries. Just as in mainland China, *guanxi*, or "connections," are essential to admission into this overseas Chinese business network. But once in the network, the Chinese tend to prefer doing business with one another and offer preferential pricing and other business services.

Organizations

Every organization has its own workplace culture, referred to as the organizational culture. This defines simple aspects such as how people dress (casual or formal), how they perceive and value employees, or how they make decisions (as a group or by the manager alone). When we talk about an entrepreneurial culture in a company, it might imply that the company encourages people to think creatively and respond to new ideas fairly quickly without a long internal approval process. One of the issues managers often have to consider when operating with colleagues, employees, or customers in other countries is how the local country's culture will blend or contrast with the company's culture.

For example, Apple, Google, and Microsoft all have distinct business cultures that are influenced both by their industries and by the types of technology-savvy employees that they hire, as well as by the personalities of their founders. When these firms operate in a country, they have to assess how new employees will fit their respective corporate cultures, which usually emphasize creativity, innovation, teamwork balanced with individual accomplishment, and a keen sense of privacy. Their global employees may appear relaxed in casual work clothes, but underneath there is often a fierce competitiveness. So how do these companies effectively hire in countries like Japan, where teamwork and following rules are more important than seeking new ways of doing things? This is an ongoing challenge that human resources (HR) departments continually seek to address.

KEY TAKEAWAYS

- Culture is the beliefs, values, mind-sets, and practices of a specific group of people. It includes the behavior pattern and norms of a specific group—the rules, the assumptions, the perceptions, and the logic and reasoning that are specific to a group. Culture is really the collective programming of our minds from birth. It's this collective programming that distinguishes one group of people from another. Cultural awareness most commonly refers to having an understanding of another culture's values and perspective.

- When trying to understand how cultures evolve, we look at the factors that help determine cultures and their values. In general, a *value* is defined as something that we prefer over something else—whether it's a behavior or a tangible item. Values are usually acquired early in life and are usually nonrational. Our values are the key building blocks of our cultural orientation.

- When we say cultural, we don't always just mean people from different countries. Cultures exist in all types of groups. There are even subcultures within a country or target ethnic group. Each person belongs to several kinds of cultures: national, subcultural (regional, gender, ethnic, religious, generational, and socioeconomic), and group or workplace (corporate culture).

EXERCISES

(AACSB: Reflective Thinking, Analytical Skills)
1. What is culture?
2. What are the different levels or types of cultures?
3. Identify your national culture and describe the subcultures within it.

[1] Dictionary.com, s.v. "personality," accessed February 22, 2011, http://dictionary.reference.com/browse/personality.

3.2 What Are the Key Methods Used to Describe Cultures?

LEARNING OBJECTIVES

1. Know several methods to describe cultures.
2. Define and apply Hofstede's and Hall's categories for cultural identification.
3. Identify and discuss additional determinants of culture.

The study of cross-cultural analysis incorporates the fields of anthropology, sociology, psychology, and communication. The combination of cross-cultural analysis and business is a new and evolving field; it's not a static understanding but changes as the world changes. Within cross-cultural analysis, two names dominate our understanding of culture—Geert Hofstede and Edward T. Hall. Although new ideas are continually presented, Hofstede remains the leading thinker on how we see cultures.

This section will review both the thinkers and the main components of how they define culture and the impact on communications and business. At first glance, it may seem irrelevant to daily business management to learn about these approaches. In reality, despite the evolution of cultures, these methods provide a comprehensive and enduring understanding of the key factors that shape a culture, which in turn impact every aspect of doing business globally. Additionally, these methods enable us to compare and contrast cultures more objectively. By understanding the key researchers, you'll be able to formulate your own analysis of the different cultures and the impact on international business.

Hofstede and Values

Geert Hofstede, sometimes called the father of modern cross-cultural science and thinking, is a social psychologist who focused on a comparison of nations using a statistical analysis of two unique databases. The first and largest database composed of answers that matched employee samples from forty different countries to the same survey questions focused on attitudes and beliefs. The second consisted of answers to some of the same questions by Hofstede's executive students who came from fifteen countries and from a variety of companies and industries. He developed a framework for understanding the systematic differences between nations in these two databases. This framework focused on value dimensions. Values, in this case, are *broad preferences for one state of affairs over others*, and they are mostly unconscious.

Most of us understand that values are our own culture's or society's ideas about what is good, bad, acceptable, or unacceptable. Hofstede developed a framework for understanding how these values underlie organizational behavior. Through his database research, he identified five key value dimensions that analyze and interpret the behaviors, values, and attitudes of a national culture: [1]

1. Power distance
2. Individualism
3. Masculinity
4. Uncertainty avoidance (UA)
5. Long-term orientation

Power distance refers to how openly a society or culture accepts or does not accept differences between people, as in hierarchies in the workplace, in politics, and so on. For example, *high power distance* cultures openly accept that a boss is "higher" and as such deserves a more formal respect and authority. Examples of these cultures include Japan, Mexico, and the Philippines. In Japan or Mexico, the senior person is almost a father figure and is automatically given respect and usually loyalty without questions.

In Southern Europe, Latin America, and much of Asia, power is an integral part of the social equation. People tend to accept relationships of servitude. An individual's status, age, and seniority command respect—they're what make it all right for the lower-ranked person to take orders. Subordinates expect to be told what to do and won't take initiative or speak their minds unless a manager explicitly asks for their opinion.

At the other end of the spectrum are *low power distance* cultures, in which superiors and subordinates are more likely to see each other as equal in power. Countries found at this end of the spectrum include Austria and Denmark. To be sure, not all cultures view power in the same ways. In Sweden, Norway, and Israel, for example, respect for equality is a warranty of freedom. Subordinates and managers alike often have carte blanche to speak their minds.

Interestingly enough, research indicates that the United States tilts toward low power distance but is more in the middle of the scale than Germany and the United Kingdom.

Let's look at the culture of the United States in relation to these five dimensions. The United States actually ranks somewhat lower in power distance—under forty as noted in Figure 3.1 "The United States' Five Value Dimensions". The United States has a culture of promoting participation at the office while maintaining control in the hands of the manager. People in this type of culture tend to be relatively laid-back about status and social standing—but there's a firm understanding of who has the power. What's surprising for many people is that countries such as the United Kingdom and Australia actually rank lower on the power distance spectrum than the United States.

Individualism, noted as IDV in Figure 3.1 "The United States' Five Value Dimensions", is just what it sounds like. It refers to people's tendency to take care of themselves and their immediate circle of family and friends, perhaps at the expense of the overall society. In individualistic cultures, what counts most is self-realization. Initiating alone, sweating alone, achieving alone—not necessarily collective efforts—are what win applause. In individualistic cultures, competition is the fuel of success.

The United States and Northern European societies are often labeled as individualistic. In the United States, individualism is valued and promoted—from its political structure (individual rights and democracy) to entrepreneurial zeal (capitalism). Other examples of high-individualism cultures include Australia and the United Kingdom.

On the other hand, in collectivist societies, group goals take precedence over individuals' goals. Basically, individual members render loyalty to the group, and the group takes care of its individual members. Rather than giving priority to "me," the "us" identity predominates. Of paramount importance is pursuing the common goals, beliefs, and values of the group as a whole—so much so, in some cases, that it's nearly impossible for outsiders to enter the group. Cultures that prize collectivism and the group over the individual include Singapore, Korea, Mexico, and Arab nations. The protections offered by traditional Japanese companies come to mind as a distinctively group-oriented value.

The next dimension is masculinity, which may sound like an odd way to define a culture. When we talk about masculine or feminine cultures, we're not talking about diversity issues. It's about how a society views traits that are considered masculine or feminine.

This value dimension refers to how a culture ranks on traditionally perceived "masculine" values: assertiveness, materialism, and less concern for others. In masculine-oriented cultures, gender roles are usually crisply defined. Men tend to be more focused on performance, ambition, and material success. They cut tough and independent personas, while women cultivate modesty and quality of life. Cultures in Japan and Latin American are examples of masculine-oriented cultures.

In contrast, feminine cultures are thought to emphasize "feminine" values: concern for all, an emphasis on the quality of life, and an emphasis on relationships. In feminine-oriented cultures, both genders swap roles, with the focus on quality of life, service, and independence. The Scandinavian cultures rank as feminine cultures, as do cultures in Switzerland and New Zealand. The United States is actually more moderate, and its score is ranked in the middle between masculine and feminine classifications. For all these factors, it's important to remember that cultures don't necessarily fall neatly into one camp or the other.

The next dimension is uncertainty avoidance (UA). This refers to how much uncertainty a society or culture is willing to accept. It can also be considered an indication of the risk propensity of people from a specific culture.

People who have high uncertainty avoidance generally prefer to steer clear of conflict and competition. They tend to appreciate very clear instructions. At the office, sharply defined rules and rituals are used to get tasks completed. Stability and what is known are preferred to instability and the unknown. Company cultures in these countries may show a preference for low-risk decisions, and employees in these companies are less willing to exhibit aggressiveness. Japan and France are often considered clear examples of such societies.

In countries with low uncertainty avoidance, people are more willing to take on risks, companies may appear less formal and structured, and "thinking outside the box" is valued. Examples of these cultures are Denmark, Singapore, Australia, and to a slightly lesser extent, the United States. Members of these cultures usually require less formal rules to interact.

The fifth dimension is long-term orientation, which refers to whether a culture has a long-term or short-term orientation. This dimension was added by Hofstede after the original four you just read about. It resulted in the effort to understand the difference in thinking between the East and the West. Certain values are associated with each orientation. The long-term orientation values persistence, perseverance, thriftiness, and having a sense of shame. These are evident in traditional Eastern cultures. Based on these values, it's easy to see why a Japanese CEO is likely to apologize or take the blame for a faulty product or process.

The short-term orientation values tradition only to the extent of fulfilling social obligations or providing gifts or favors. These cultures are more likely to be focused on the immediate or short-term impact of an issue. Not surprisingly, the United Kingdom and the United States rank low on the long-term orientation.

Long- and short-term orientation and the other value dimensions in the business arena are all evolving as many people earn business degrees and gain experience outside their home cultures and countries, thereby diluting the significance of a single cultural perspective. As a result, in practice, these five dimensions do not occur as single values but are really woven together and interdependent, creating very complex cultural interactions. Even though these five values are constantly shifting and not static, they help us begin to understand how and why people from different cultures may think and act as they do. Hofstede's study demonstrates that there are national and regional cultural groupings that affect the behavior of societies and organizations and that these are persistent over time.

Edward T. Hall

Edward T. Hall was a respected anthropologist who applied his field to the understanding of cultures and intercultural communications. Hall is best noted for three principal categories that analyze and interpret how communications and interactions between cultures differ: context, space, and time.

Context: High-Context versus Low-Context Cultures

High and low context refers to how a message is communicated. In high-context cultures, such as those found in Latin America, Asia, and Africa, the physical context of the message carries a great deal of importance. People tend to be more indirect and to expect the person they are communicating with to decode the implicit part of their message. While the person sending the message takes painstaking care in crafting the message, the person receiving the message is expected to read it within context. The message may lack the verbal directness you would expect in a low-context culture. In high-context cultures, body language is as important and sometimes more important than the actual words spoken.

In contrast, in low-context cultures such as the United States and most Northern European countries, people tend to be explicit and direct in their communications. Satisfying individual needs is important. You're probably familiar with some well-known low-context mottos: "Say what you mean" and "Don't beat around the bush." The guiding principle is to minimize the margins of misunderstanding or doubt. Low-context communication aspires to get straight to the point.

Communication between people from high-context and low-context cultures can be confusing. In business interactions, people from low-context cultures tend to listen only to the words spoken; they tend not to be cognizant of body language. As a result, people often miss important clues that could tell them more about the specific issue.

Space

Space refers to the study of physical space and people. Hall called this the study of proxemics, which focuses on space and distance between people as they interact. *Space* refers to everything from how close people stand to one another to how people might mark their territory or boundaries in the

workplace and in other settings. Stand too close to someone from the United States, which prefers a "safe" physical distance, and you are apt to make them uncomfortable. How close is too close depends on where you are from. Whether consciously or unconsciously, we all establish a comfort zone when interacting with others. Standing distances shrink and expand across cultures. Latins, Spaniards, and Filipinos (whose culture has been influenced by three centuries of Spanish colonization) stand rather close even in business encounters. In cultures that have a low need for territory, people not only tend to stand closer together but also are more willing to share their space—whether it be a workplace, an office, a seat on a train, or even ownership of a business project.

Attitudes toward Time: Polychronic versus Monochronic Cultures

Hall identified that time is another important concept greatly influenced by culture. In polychronic cultures—*polychronic* literally means "many times"—people can do several things at the same time. In monochronic cultures, or "one-time" cultures, people tend to do one task at a time.

This isn't to suggest that people in polychronic cultures are better at multitasking. Rather, people in monochronic cultures, such as Northern Europe and North America, tend to schedule one event at a time. For them, an appointment that starts at 8 a.m. is an appointment that starts at 8 a.m.— or 8:05 at the latest. People are expected to arrive on time, whether for a board meeting or a family picnic. Time is a means of imposing order. Often the meeting has a firm end time as well, and even if the agenda is not finished, it's not unusual to end the meeting and finish the agenda at another scheduled meeting.

In polychronic cultures, by contrast, time is nice, but people and relationships matter more. Finishing a task may also matter more. If you've ever been to Latin America, the Mediterranean, or the Middle East, you know all about living with relaxed timetables. People might attend to three things at once and think nothing of it. Or they may cluster informally, rather than arrange themselves in a queue. In polychronic cultures, it's not considered an insult to walk into a meeting or a party well past the appointed hour.

In polychronic cultures, people regard work as part of a larger interaction with a community. If an agenda is not complete, people in polychronic cultures are less likely to simply end the meeting and are more likely to continue to finish the business at hand.

Those who prefer monochronic order may find polychronic order frustrating and hard to manage effectively. Those raised with a polychronic sensibility, on the other hand, might resent the "tyranny of the clock" and prefer to be focused on completing the tasks at hand.

What Else Determines a Culture?

The methods presented in the previous sections note how we look at the structures of cultures, values, and communications. They also provide a framework for a comparative analysis between cultures, which is particularly important for businesses trying to operate effectively in multiple countries and cultural environments.

Additionally, there are other external factors that also constitute a culture—manners, mind-sets, values, rituals, religious beliefs, laws, arts, ideas, customs, beliefs, ceremonies, social institutions, myths and legends, language, individual identity, and behaviors, to name a few. While these factors are less structured and do not provide a comparative framework, they are helpful in completing our understanding of what impacts a culture. When we look at these additional factors, we are seeking to understand how each culture views and incorporates each of them. For example, are there specific ceremonies or customs that impact the culture and for our purposes its business culture? For example, in some Chinese businesses, feng shui—an ancient Chinese physical art and science—is implemented in the hopes of enhancing the physical business environment and success potential of the firm.

Of these additional factors, the single most important one is communication.

Communication

Verbal Language

Language is one of the more conspicuous expressions of culture. As Hall showed, understanding the context of how language is used is essential to accurately interpret the meaning. Aside from the obvious differences, vocabularies are actually often built on the cultural experiences of the users. For example, in the opening case with Dunkin' Donuts, we saw how the local culture complicated the company's ability to list its name in Chinese characters.

Similarly, it's interesting to note that Arabic speakers have only one word for ice, *telg*, which applies to ice, snow, hail, and so on. In contrast, Eskimo languages have different words for each type of snow—even specific descriptive words to indicate the amounts of snow.

Another example of how language impacts business is in written or e-mail communications, where you don't have the benefit of seeing someone's physical gestures or posture. For example, India is officially an English-speaking country, though its citizens speak the Queen's English. Yet many businesspeople experience miscommunications related to misunderstandings in the language, ranging from the comical to the frustrating. Take something as simple as multiplication and division. Indians will commonly say "6 into 12" and arrive at 72, whereas their American counterparts will divide to get an answer of 2. You'd certainly want to be very clear if math were an essential part of your communication, as it would be if you were creating a budget for a project.

Another example of nuances between Indian and American language communications is the use of the word *revert*. The word means "to go back to a previously existing condition." To Indians, though, the common and accepted use of the word is much more simplistic and means "to get back to someone."

To see how language impacts communications, look at a situation in which an American manager, in negotiating the terms of a project, began to get frustrated by the e-mails that said that the Indian company was going to "revert back." He took that to mean that they had not made any progress on some issues, and that the Indians were going back to the original terms. Actually, the Indians simply meant that they were going to get back to him on the outstanding issues—again, a different connotation for the word because of cultural differences.

The all-encompassing "yes" is one of the hardest verbal cues to decipher. What does it really mean? Well, it depends on where you are. In a low-context country—the United States or Scandinavian countries, for example—"yes" is what it is: yes. In a high-context culture—Japan or the Philippines, for example—it can mean "yes," "maybe," "OK," or "I understand you,"—but it may not always signify agreement. The meaning is in the physical context, not the verbal.

Language or words become a code, and you need to understand the word and the context.

Did You Know?

English Required in Japan

It's commonly accepted around the world that English is the primary global business language. In Japan, some companies have incorporated this reality into daily business practice. By 2012, employees at Rakuten, Japan's biggest online retailer by sales, will be "required to speak and correspond with one another in English, and executives have been told they will be fired if they aren't proficient in the language by then. Rakuten, which has made recent acquisitions in the U.S. and Europe, says the English-only policy is crucial to its goal of becoming a global company. It says it needed a common language to communicate with its new operations, and English, as the chief language of international business, was the obvious choice. It expects the change, among other things, to help it hire and retain talented non-Japanese workers." [2]

Rakuten is only one of many large and small Japanese companies pursuing English as part of its ongoing global strategy. English is key to the business culture and language at Sony, Nissan Motor, and Mitsubishi, to name a few Japanese businesses. English remains the leading global business language for most international companies seeking a standard common language with its employees, partners, and customers.

Body Language

How you gesture, twitch, or scrunch up your face represents a veritable legend to your emotions. Being able to suitably read—and broadcast—body language can significantly increase your chances of understanding and being understood. In many high-context cultures, it is essential to understand body language in order to accurately interpret a situation, comment, or gesture.

People may not understand your words, but they will certainly interpret your body language according to *their* accepted norms. Notice the word *their*. It is *their* perceptions that will count when you are trying to do business with them, and it's important to understand that those perceptions will be based on the teachings and experiences of their culture—not yours.

Another example of the "yes, I understand you" confusion in South Asia is the infamous head wobble. Indians will roll their head from side to side to signify an understanding or acknowledgement of a statement—but not necessarily an acceptance. Some have even expressed that they mistakenly thought the head wobble meant "no." If you didn't understand the context, then you are likely to misinterpret the gesture and the possible verbal cues as well.

Did You Know?

OK or Not OK?
Various motions and postures can mean altogether divergent things in different cultures. Hand gestures are a classic example. The American sign for OK means "zero" in Tunisia and southern France, which far from signaling approval, is considered a threat. The same gesture, by the way, delivers an obscenity in Brazil, Germany, Greece, and Russia. If you want to tell your British colleagues that victory on a new deal is close at hand by making the V sign with your fingers, be sure your palm is facing outward; otherwise you'll be telling them where to stick it, and it's unlikely to win you any new friends.

Eye contact is also an important bit of unspoken vocabulary. People in Western cultures are taught to look into the eyes of their listeners. Likewise, it's a way the listener reciprocates interest. In contrast, in the East, looking into someone's eyes may come off as disrespectful, since focusing directly on someone who is senior to you implies disrespect. So when you're interacting with people from other cultures, be careful not to assume that a lack of eye contact means anything negative. There may be a cultural basis to their behavior.

Amusing Anecdote

Kiss, Shake, Hug, or Bow
Additionally, touching is a tacit means of communication. In some cultures, shaking hands when greeting someone is a must. Where folks are big on contact, grown men might embrace each other in a giant bear hug, such as in Mexico or Russia.

Japan, by contrast, has traditionally favored bowing, thus ensuring a hands-off approach. When men and women interact for business, this interaction can be further complicated. If you're female interacting with a male, a kiss on the cheek may work in Latin America, but in an Arab country, you may not even get a handshake. It can be hard not to take it personally, but you shouldn't. These interactions reflect centuries-old traditional cultural norms that will take time to evolve.

Ethnocentrism

A discussion of culture would not be complete without at least mentioning the concept of ethnocentrism. Ethnocentrism is the view that a person's own culture is central and other cultures are measured in relation to it. It's akin to a person thinking that their culture is the "sun" around which all other cultures revolve. In its worst form, it can create a false sense of superiority of one culture over others.

Human nature is such that we see the world through our own cultural shades. Tucked in between the lines of our cultural laws is an unconscious bias that inhibits us from viewing other cultures objectively. Our judgments of people from other cultures will always be colored by the frame of reference in which we have been raised.

The challenge occurs when we feel that our cultural habits, values, and perceptions are superior to other people's values. This can have a dramatic impact on our business relations. Your best defense against ethnocentric behavior is to make a point of seeing things from the perspective of the other person. Use what you have learned in this chapter to extend your understanding of the person's culture. As much as possible, leave your own frame of reference at home. Sort out what makes you and the other person different—*and* what makes you similar.

KEY TAKEAWAYS

- There are two key methods used to describe and analyze cultures. The first was developed by Geert Hofstede and focuses on five key dimensions that interpret behaviors, values, and attitudes: power distance, individualism, masculinity, uncertainty avoidance, and long-term orientation. The second method was developed by Edward T. Hall and focuses on three main categories for how communications and interactions between cultures differ: high-context versus low-context communications, space, and attitudes toward time.

- In addition to the main analytical methods for comparing and contrasting cultures, there are a number of other determinants of culture. These determinants include manners, mind-sets, values, rituals, religious beliefs, laws, arts, ideas, customs, beliefs, ceremonies, social institutions, myths and legends, language, individual identity, and behaviors. Language includes both verbal and physical languages.

EXERCISES

(AACSB: Reflective Thinking, Analytical Skills)

1. Define Hofstede's five value dimensions that analyze and interpret behaviors, values, and attitudes.
2. Identify Hall's three key factors on how communications and interactions between cultures differ.
3. What are the two components of communications?
4. Describe two ways that verbal language may differ between countries.
5. Describe two ways that body language may differ between cultures.
6. What is ethnocentrism?

[1] "Dimensions of National Cultures," Geert Hofstede, accessed February 22, 2011, http://www.geerthofstede.nl/culture/dimensions-of-national-cultures.aspx.
[2] Daisuke Wakabayashi, "English Gets the Last Word in Japan," Wall Street Journal, August 6, 2010, accessed February 22, 2011, http://online.wsj.com/article/SB10001424052748703954804575382011407926080.html.

3.3 Understanding How Culture Impacts Local Business Practices

LEARNING OBJECTIVES

1. Identify the ways that culture can impact how we do business.
2. Understand the aspects of business most impacted by culture.

Professionals err when thinking that, in today's shrinking world, cultural differences are no longer significant. It's a common mistake to assume that people think alike just because they dress alike; it's also a mistake to assume that people think alike just because they are similar in their word choices in a business setting. Even in today's global world, there are wide cultural differences, and these differences influence how people do business. Culture impacts many things in business, including

- The pace of business;
- Business protocol—how to physically and verbally meet and interact;
- Decision making and negotiating;
- Managing employees and projects;
- Propensity for risk taking; and
- Marketing, sales, and distribution.

There are still many people around the world who think that business is just about core business principles and making money. They assume that issues like culture don't really matter. These issues do matter—in many ways. Even though people are focused on the bottom line, people do business with people they like, trust, and understand. Culture determines all of these key issues.

The opening case shows how a simple issue, such as local flavor preferences, can impact a billion-dollar company. The influence of cultural factors on business is extensive. Culture impacts how employees are best managed based on their values and priorities. It also impacts the functional areas of marketing, sales, and distribution.

It can affect a company's analysis and decision on how best to enter a new market. Do they prefer a partner (tending toward uncertainty avoidance) so they do not have to worry about local practices or government relations? Or are they willing to set up a wholly owned unit to recoup the best financial prospects?

When you're dealing with people from another culture, you may find that their business practices, communication, and management styles are different from those to which you are accustomed. Understanding the culture of the people with whom you are dealing is important to successful business interactions and to accomplishing business objectives. For example, you'll need to understand

- How people communicate;
- How culture impacts how people view time and deadlines;
- How they are likely to ask questions or highlight problems;
- How people respond to management and authority;
- How people perceive verbal and physical communications; and
- How people make decisions.

To conduct business with people from other cultures, you must put aside preconceived notions and strive to learn about the culture of your counterpart. Often the greatest challenge is learning not to apply your own value system when judging people from other cultures. It is important to remember that there are no right or wrong ways to deal with other people— just different ways. Concepts like time and ethics are viewed differently from place to place, and the smart business professional will seek to understand the rationale underlying another culture's concepts.

For younger and smaller companies, there's no room for errors or delays—both of which may result from cultural misunderstandings and miscommunications. These miscues can and often do impact the bottom line.

Spotlight on Cultures and Entrepreneurship

With global media reaching the corners of the earth, entrepreneurship has become increasingly popular as more people seek a way to exponentially increase their chances for success. Nevertheless, entrepreneurs can face challenges in starting to do business in nations whose cultures require introductions or place more value on large, prestigious, brand-name firms.

Conversely, entrepreneurs are often well equipped to negotiate global contracts or ventures. They are more likely to be flexible and creative in their approach and have less

rigid constraints than their counterparts from more established companies. Each country has different constraints, including the terms of payment and regulations, and you will need to keep an open mind about how to achieve your objectives.

In reality, understanding cultural differences is important whether you're selling to ethnic markets in your own home country or selling to new markets in different countries. Culture also impacts you if you're sourcing from different countries, because culture impacts communications. Your understanding of culture will affect your ability to enter a local market, develop and maintain business relationships, negotiate successful deals, conduct sales, conduct marketing and advertising campaigns, and engage in manufacturing and distribution. Too often, people send the wrong signals or receive the wrong messages; as a result, people get tangled in the cultural web. In fact, there are numerous instances in which deals would have been successfully completed if finalizing them had been based on business issues alone, but cultural miscommunications interfered. Just as you would conduct a technical or market analysis, you should also conduct a cultural analysis.

It's critical to understand the history and politics of any country or region in which you work or with which you intend to deal. It is important to remember that each person considers his or her "sphere" or "world" the most important and that this attitude forms the basis of his or her individual perspective. We often forget that cultures are shaped by decades and centuries of experience and that ignoring cultural differences puts us at a disadvantage.

Spotlight on Impact of Culture on Business in Latin America

The business culture of Latin America differs throughout the region. A lot has to do with the size of the country, the extent to which it has developed a modern industrial sector, and its openness to outside influences and the global economy.

Some of the major industrial and commercial centers embody a business culture that's highly sophisticated, international in outlook, and on a par with that in Europe or North America. They often have modern offices, businesspeople with strong business acumen, and international experience.

Outside the cities, business culture is likely to be much different as local conditions and local customs may begin to impact any interaction. Farther from the big cities, the infrastructure may become less reliable, forcing people to become highly innovative in navigating the challenges facing them and their businesses.

Generally speaking, several common themes permeate Latin American business culture. Businesses typically are hierarchical in their structure, with decisions made from the top down. Developing trust and gaining respect in the business environment is all about forging and maintaining good relationships. This often includes quite a bit of socializing.

Another important factor influencing the business culture is the concept of time. In Latin America, "El tiempo es como el espacio." In other words, time is space. More often than not, situations take precedence over schedules. Many people unfamiliar with Latin American customs, especially those from highly time-conscious countries like the United States, Canada, and those in Northern Europe, can find the lack of punctuality and more fluid view of time frustrating. It's more useful to see the unhurried approach as an opportunity to develop good relations. This is a generalization, though, and in the megacities of Latin America, such as Mexico City, São Paulo, and Buenos Aires, time definitely equals money.

In most Latin American countries, old-world manners are still the rule, and an air of formality is expected in most business interactions and interpersonal relationships, especially when people are not well acquainted with one another. People in business are expected to dress conservatively and professionally and be polite at all times. Latin Americans are generally very physical and outgoing in their expressions and body language. They frequently stand closer to one another when talking than in many other cultures. They often touch, usually an arm, and even kiss women's cheeks on a first meeting.

In business and in social interactions, Latin America is overwhelmingly Catholic, which has had a deep impact on culture, values, architecture, and art. For many years and in many countries in the region, the Catholic Church had absolute power over all civil institutions, education, and law. However, today, the church and state are now officially separated in most countries, the practice of other religions is freely allowed, and Evangelical churches are growing rapidly. Throughout the region, particularly in Brazil, Indians and some black communities have integrated many of their own traditional rituals and practices with Christianity, primarily Catholicism, to produce hybrid forms of the religion.

Throughout Latin America, the family is still the most important social unit. Family celebrations are important, and there's a clear hierarchy within the family structure, with the head of the household generally being the oldest male—the father or grandfather. *In family-owned businesses, the patriarch, or on occasion matriarch, tends to retain the key decision-making roles.*

Despite the social and economic problems of the region, Latin Americans love life and value the small things that provide color, warmth, friendship, and a sense of community. Whether it's sitting in a café chatting, passing a few hours in the town square, or dining out at a neighborhood restaurant, Latin Americans take time to live.

From Mexico City to Buenos Aires—whether in business or as a part of the vibrant society—the history and culture of Latin America continues to have deep and meaningful impact on people throughout Latin America. [1]

KEY TAKEAWAYS

- Professionals often err when they think that in today's shrinking world, cultural differences no longer pertain. People mistakenly assume that others think alike just because they dress alike and even sound similar in their choice of words in a business setting. Even in today's global world, there are wide cultural differences and these differences influence how people do business. Culture impacts many elements of business, including the following:
  o the pace of business
  o business protocol—how to physically and verbally meet and interact
  o decision making and negotiating
  o managing employees and projects
  o propensity for risk taking
  o marketing, sales, and distribution
- When you're dealing with people from another culture, you may find that their business practices and communication and management styles are different from what you are accustomed to. Understanding the culture of the people you are dealing with is important to successful business interactions as well as to accomplishing business objectives. For example, you'll need to understand the following:
  o how people communicate
  o how culture impacts how people view time and deadlines
  o how people are likely to ask questions or highlight problems
  o how people respond to management and authority
  o how people perceive verbal and physical communications
  o how people make decisions

(AACSB: Reflective Thinking, Analytical Skills)

1. How does culture impact business?
2. What are three steps to keep in mind if you are evaluating a business opportunity in a culture or country that is new to you?
3. If you are working for a small or entrepreneurial company, what are some of the challenges you may face when trying to do business in a new country? What are some advantages?

[1] CultureQuest Doing Business: Latin America (New York: Atma Global, 2011).

3.4 Global Business Ethics

LEARNING OBJECTIVES

1. Define what global business ethics are, and discover how culture impacts business ethics.
2. Learn how ethical issues impact global business.
3. Identify how companies develop, implement, and enforce ethical standards.

Chapter 1 "Introduction" provided a solid introduction to the concept of global ethics and business. The relationship between ethics and international business is extensive and is impacted by local perceptions, values, and beliefs.

Global Business Ethics

The field of ethics is a branch of philosophy that seeks to address questions about morality—that is, about concepts such as good and bad, right and wrong, justice, and virtue. [1] Ethics impacts many fields—not just business—including medicine, government, and science, to name a few. We must first try to understand the "origins of ethics—whether they come from religion, philosophy, the laws of nature, scientific study, study of political theory relating to ethical norms created in society or other fields of knowledge." [2] The description below on the field of ethics shows how people think about ethics in stages, from where ethical principles come from to how people should apply them to specific tasks or issues.

The field of ethics (or moral philosophy) involves systematizing, defending, and recommending concepts of right and wrong behavior. Philosophers today usually divide ethical theories into three general subject areas: metaethics, normative ethics, and applied ethics. *Metaethics* investigates where our ethical principles come from, and what they mean. Are they merely social inventions? Do they involve more than expressions of our individual emotions? Metaethical answers

to these questions focus on the issues of universal truths, the will of God, the role of reason in ethical judgments, and the meaning of ethical terms themselves. *Normative ethics* takes on a more practical task, which is to arrive at moral standards that regulate right and wrong conduct. This may involve articulating the good habits that we should acquire, the duties that we should follow, or the consequences of our behavior on others. Finally, *applied ethics* involves examining specific controversial issues, such as…animal rights, environmental concerns…capital punishment, or nuclear war. [3]

This approach will be used in this chapter to help you understand global business ethics in a modern and current sense. As with this chapter's review of culture, this section on global business ethics is less about providing you with a tangible list of dos and don'ts than it is about helping you understand the thinking and critical issues that global managers must deal with on an operational and strategic basis.

Where Do Our Values Come From?

Just as people look to history to understand political, technical, and social changes, so too do they look for changes in thinking and philosophy. There's a history to how thinking has evolved over time. What may or may not have been acceptable just a hundred years ago may be very different today—from how people present themselves and how they act and interact to customs, values, and beliefs.

Ethics can be defined as a system of moral standards or values. You know from the discussion in Section 3.1 "What Is Culture, Anyhow? Values, Customs, and Language" that cultural programming influences our values. A sense of ethics is determined by a number of social, cultural, and religious factors; this sense influences us beginning early in childhood. People are taught how to behave by their families, exposure to education and thinking, and the society in which they live. Ethical behavior also refers to behavior that is generally accepted within a specific culture. Some behaviors are universally accepted—for example, people shouldn't physically hurt other people. Other actions are less clear, such as discrimination based on age, race, gender, or ethnicity.

Culture impacts how local values influence global business ethics. There are differences in how much importance cultures place on specific ethical behaviors. For example, bribery remains widespread in many countries, and while people may not approve of it, they accept it as a necessity of daily life. Each professional is influenced by the values, social programming, and experiences encountered from childhood on. These collective factors impact how a person perceives an issue and the related correct or incorrect behaviors. Even within a specific culture, individuals have different ideas of what constitutes ethical or unethical behavior. Judgments may differ greatly depending on an individual's social or economic standing, education, and experiences with other cultures and beliefs. Just as in the example of bribery, it should be noted that there is a difference between ethical behavior and normal practice. It may be acceptable to discriminate in certain cultures, even if the people in that society know that it is not right or fair. In global business ethics, people try to understand what the ethical action is and what the normal practice might be. If these are not consistent, the focus is placed on how to encourage ethical actions.

While it's clear that ethics is not religion, values based on religious teachings have influenced our understanding of ethical behavior. Given the influence of Western thought and philosophy over the world in the last few centuries, many would say that global business has been heavily impacted by the mode of thinking that began with the Reformation and post-Enlightenment values, which placed focus on equality and individual rights. In this mode of thinking, it has become accepted that all people in any country and of any background are equal and should have equal opportunity. Companies incorporate this principle in their employment, management, and operational guidelines; yet enforcing it in global operations can be both tricky and inconsistent.

Did You Know?

What Are the Reformation and Enlightenment?

Modern political and economic philosophies trace their roots back to the Reformation and Enlightenment. The Reformation was a period of European history in the sixteenth century when Protestant thinkers, led by Martin Luther, challenged the teachings of the Roman Catholic Church. As a result of the Reformation, the Catholic Church lost its control over all scientific and intellectual thought. While there were a number of debates and discussions over the ensuing decades and century, the Reformation is widely believed to have led to another historical period called the Age of Enlightenment, which refers to a period in Western philosophical, intellectual, scientific, and cultural life in the eighteenth century. The Enlightenment, as it is commonly called, promoted a set of values in which reason, not religion, was advocated as the primary source for legitimacy and authority. As a result, it is also known as the Age of Reason. It's important to understand the impact and influence of these two critical historical periods on our modern sense of global business ethics. The prevailing corporate values—including those of institutional and individual equality; the right of every employee to work hard and reap the rewards,

financial and nonfinancial; corporate social responsibility; and the application of science and reason to all management and operational processes—have their roots in the thoughts and values that arose during these periods.

Impact of Ethics on Global Business

At first, it may seem relatively easy to identify unethical behavior. When the topic of business ethics is raised, most people immediately focus on corruption and bribery. While this is a critical result of unethical behavior, the concept of business ethics and—in the context of this book—global business ethics is much broader. It impacts human resources, social responsibility, and the environment. The areas of business impacted by global perceptions of ethical, moral, and socially responsible behavior include the following:

- Ethics and management
- Ethics and corruption
- Corporate social responsibility

Ethics and Management Practices

Ethics impacts various aspects of management and operations, including human resources, marketing, research and development, and even the corporate mission.

The role of ethics in management practices, particularly those practices involving human resources and employment, differs from culture to culture. Local culture impacts the way people view the employee-employer relationship. In many cultures, there are no clear social rules preventing discrimination against people based on age, race, gender, sexual preference, handicap, and so on. Even when there are formal rules or laws against discrimination, they may not be enforced, as normal practice may allow people and companies to act in accordance with local cultural and social practices.

Culture can impact how people see the role of one another in the workplace. For example, gender issues are at times impacted by local perceptions of women in the workplace. So how do companies handle local customs and values for the treatment of women in the workplace? If you're a senior officer of an American company, do you send a woman to Saudi Arabia or Afghanistan to negotiate with government officials or manage the local office? Does it matter what your industry is or if your firm is the seller or buyer? *In theory*, most global firms have clear guidelines articulating antidiscrimination policies. *In reality*, global businesses routinely self-censor. Companies often determine whether a person—based on their gender, ethnicity, or race—can be effective in a specific culture based on the prevailing values in that culture. The largest and most respected global companies, typically the *Fortune* Global 500, can often make management and employment decisions regardless of local practices. Most people in each country will want to deal with these large and well-respected companies. The person representing the larger company brings the clout of their company to any business interaction. In contrast, lesser-known, midsize, and smaller companies may find that *who* their representative is will be more important. Often lacking business recognition in the marketplace, these smaller and midsize companies have to rely on their corporate representatives to create the professional image and bond with their in-country counterparts.

Cultural norms may make life difficult for the company as well as the employee. In some cultures, companies are seen as "guardians" or paternal figures. Any efforts to lay off or fire employees may be perceived as culturally unethical. In Japan, where lifelong loyalty to the company was expected in return for lifelong employment, the decade-long recession beginning in the 1990s triggered a change in attitude. Japanese companies finally began to alter this ethical perception and lay off workers without being perceived as unethical.

Global corporations are increasingly trying to market their products based not only on the desirability of the goods but also on their social and environmental merits. Companies whose practices are considered unethical may find their global performance impacted when people boycott their products. Most corporations understand this risk. However, ethical questions have grown increasingly complicated, and the "correct" or ethical choice has, in some cases, become difficult to define.

For example, the pharmaceutical industry is involved in a number of issues that have medical ethicists squirming. First, there's the well-publicized issue of cloning. No matter *what* choice the companies make about cloning, they are sure to offend a great many consumers. At the same time, pharmaceutical companies must decide whether to forfeit profits and give away free drugs or cheaper medicines to impoverished African nations. Pharmaceutical companies that *do* donate medicines often promote this practice in their corporate marketing campaigns in hopes that consumers see the companies in a favorable light.

Tobacco companies are similarly embroiled in a long-term ethical debate. Health advocates around the world agree that smoking is bad for a person's long-term health. Yet in many countries, smoking is not only acceptable but can even confer social status. The United States has banned tobacco companies from adopting marketing practices that target young consumers by exploiting tobacco's social cache. However, many other countries don't have such regulations. Should tobacco companies be held responsible for knowingly marketing harmful products to younger audiences in other countries?

Ethics and Corruption

To begin our discussion of corruption, let's first define it in a business context. Corruption is "giving or obtaining advantage through means which are illegitimate, immoral, and/or inconsistent with one's duty or the rights of others. Corruption often results from patronage." [4]

Our modern understanding of business ethics notes that following culturally accepted norms is not always the ethical choice. What may be acceptable at certain points in history, such as racism or sexism, became unacceptable with the further development of society's mind-set. What happens when cultures change but business practices don't? Does that behavior become unethical, and is the person engaged in the behavior unethical? In some cultures, there may be conflicts with global business practices, such as in the area of gift giving, which has evolved into bribery—a form of corruption.

Paying bribes is relatively common in many countries, and bribes often take the form of *grease payments*, which are small inducements intended to expedite decisions and transactions. In India and Mexico, for example, a grease payment may help get your phones installed faster—at home or at work. Transparency International tracks illicit behavior, such as bribery and embezzlement, in the public sector in 180 countries by surveying international business executives. It assigns a CPI (Corruption Perceptions Index) rating to each country. New Zealand, Denmark, Singapore, and Sweden have the lowest levels of corruption, while the highest levels of corruption are seen in most African nations, Russia, Myanmar, and Afghanistan. [5]

Even the most respected of global companies has found itself on the wrong side of the ethics issue and the law. In 2008, after years of investigation, Siemens agreed to pay more than 1.34 billion euros in fines to American and European authorities to settle charges that it routinely used bribes and slush funds to secure huge public-works contracts around the world. "Officials said that Siemens, beginning in the mid-1990s, used bribes and kickbacks to foreign officials to secure government contracts for projects like a national identity card project in Argentina, mass transit work in Venezuela, a nationwide cell phone network in Bangladesh and a United Nations oil-for-food program in Iraq under Saddam Hussein.

'Their actions were not an anomaly,' said Joseph Persichini Jr., the head of the Washington office of the Federal Bureau of Investigation. 'They were standard operating procedures for corporate executives who viewed bribery as a business strategy.'" [6]

Ethics in Action

Each year Transparency International analyzes trends in global corruption. The following is an excerpt from their 2010 Global Corruption Barometer report.

"Corruption has increased over the last three years, say six out of 10 people around the world. One in four people report paying bribes in the last year. These are the findings of the 2010 Global Corruption Barometer.

The 2010 Barometer captures the experiences and views of more than 91,500 people in 86 countries and territories, making it the only world-wide public opinion survey on corruption.

Views on corruption were most negative in Western Europe and North America, where 73 per cent and 67 per cent of people respectively thought corruption had increased over the last three years.

"The fall-out of the financial crises continues to affect people's opinions of corruption, particular in North America and Western Europe. Institutions everywhere must be resolute in their efforts to restore good governance and trust," said Huguette Labelle, Chair of Transparency International.

In the past 12 months one in four people reported paying a bribe to one of nine institutions and services, from health to education to tax authorities. The police are cited as being the most frequent recipient of bribes, according to those surveyed. About 30 per cent of those who had contact with the police reported having paid a bribe.

More than 20 countries have reported significant increases in petty bribery since 2006. The biggest increases were in Chile, Colombia, Kenya, FYR Macedonia, Nigeria, Poland, Russia, Senegal and Thailand. More than one in two people in Sub-Saharan Africa reported paying a bribe—more than anywhere else in the world.

Poorer people are twice as likely to pay bribes for basic services, such as education, than wealthier people. A third of all people under the age of 30 reported paying a bribe in the past 12 months, compared to less than one in five people aged 51 years and over.

Most worrying is the fact that bribes to the police have almost doubled since 2006, and more people report paying bribes to the judiciary and for registry and permit services than five years ago.

Sadly, few people trust their governments or politicians. Eight out of 10 say political parties are corrupt or extremely corrupt, while half the people questioned say their government's action to stop corruption is ineffective.

"The message from the 2010 Barometer is that corruption is insidious. It makes people lose faith. The good news is that people are ready to act," said Labelle. "Public engagement in the fight against corruption will force those in authority to act—and will give people further courage to speak out and stand up for a cleaner, more transparent world." [7]

Gift giving in the global business world is used to establish or pay respects to a relationship. Bribery, on the other hand, is more commonly considered the practice in which an individual would benefit with little or no benefit to the company. It's usually paid in relation to winning a business deal, whereas gift giving is more likely to be ingrained in the culture and not associated with winning a specific piece of business. Bribery, usually in the form of a cash payment, has reached such high proportions in some countries that even locals express disgust with the corruption and its impact on daily life for businesses and consumers.

The practice of using connections to advance business interests exists in just about every country in the world. However, the extent and manner in which it is institutionalized differs from culture to culture.

In Western countries, connections are viewed informally and sometimes even with a negative connotation. In the United States and other similar countries, professionals prefer to imply that they have achieved success on their own merits and without any connections. Gift giving is not routine in the United States except during the winter holidays, and even then gift giving involves a modest expression. Businesses operating in the United States send modest gifts or cards to their customers to thank them for business loyalty in the previous year. Certain industries, such as finance, even set clear legal guidelines restricting the value of gifts, typically a maximum of $100.

In contrast, Asian, Latin American, and Middle Eastern cultures are quick to value connections and relationships and view them quite positively. Connections are considered essential for success. In Asia, gift giving is so ingrained in the culture, particularly in Japan and China, that it is formalized and structured.

For example, gift giving in Japan was for centuries an established practice in society and is still taken seriously. There are specific guidelines for gift giving depending on the identity of the giver or recipient, the length of the business relationship, and the number of gifts exchanged. The Japanese may give gifts out of a sense of obligation and duty as well as to convey feelings such as gratitude and regret. Therefore, much care is given to the appropriateness of the gift as well as to its aesthetic beauty. Gift giving has always been widespread in Japan.

Today there are still business gift-giving occasions in Japan, specifically *oseibo* (year's end) and *ochugen* (midsummer). These are must-give occasions for Japanese businesses. Oseibo gifts are presented in the first half of December as a token of gratitude for earlier favors and loyalty. This is a good opportunity to thank clients for their business. *Ochugen* usually occurs in mid-July in Tokyo and mid-August in some other regions. Originally an occasion to provide consolation to the families of those who had died in the first half of the year, ochugen falls two weeks before *obon*, a holiday honoring the dead.

Businesses operating in Japan at these times routinely exchange oseibo and ochugen gifts. While a professional is not obligated to participate, it clearly earns goodwill. At the most senior levels, it is not uncommon for people to exchange gifts worth $300 or $400. There is an established price level that one should pay for each corporate level.

Despite these guidelines, gift giving in Japan has occasionally crossed over into bribery. This level of corruption became more apparent in the 1980s as transparency in global business gained media attention. Asians tend to take a very different view of accountability than most Westerners. In the 1980s and 1990s, several Japanese CEOs resigned in order to apologize and take responsibility for their companies' practices, even when they did not personally engage in the offending practices. This has become an accepted managerial practice in an effort to preserve the honor of the company. While Japanese CEOs may not step down as quickly as in the past, the notion of honor remains an important business characteristic.

Long an established form of relationship development in all business conducted in Asia, the Arab world, and Africa, gift giving was clearly tipping into outright bribery. In the past two decades, many countries have placed limits on the types and value of gifts while simultaneously banning bribery in any

form. In the United States, companies must adhere to the Foreign Corrupt Practices Act, a federal law that specifically bans any form of bribery. Even foreign companies that are either listed on an American stock exchange or conduct business with the US government come under the purview of this law.

There are still global firms that engage in questionable business gift giving; when caught, they face fines and sanctions. But for the most part, firms continue with business as usual. Changing the cultural practices of gift giving is an evolving process that will take time, government attention, and more transparency in the awarding of global business contracts.

Companies and their employees routinely try to balance ethical behavior with business interests. While corruption is now widely viewed as unethical, firms still lose business to companies that may be less diligent in adhering to this principle. While the media covers stories of firms that have breached this ethical conduct, the misconduct of many more companies goes undetected. Businesses, business schools, and governments are increasingly making efforts to deter firms and professionals from making and taking bribes. There are still countless less visible gestures that some would argue are also unethical. For example, imagine that an employee works at a firm that wants to land a contract in China. A key government official in China finds out that you went to the business school that his daughter really wants to attend. He asks you to help her in the admission process. Do you? Should you? Is this just a nice thing to do, or is it a potential conflict of interest if you think the official will view your company more favorably? This is a gray area of global business ethics. Interestingly, a professional's answer to this situation may depend on his or her culture. Cultures that have clear guidelines for right and wrong behavior may see this situation differently than a culture in which doing favors is part of the normal practice. A company may declare this inappropriate behavior, but employees may still do what they think is best for their jobs. Cultures that have a higher tolerance for ambiguity, as this chapter discusses, may find it easier to navigate the gray areas of ethics—when it is not so clear.

Most people agree that bribery in any form only increases the cost of doing business—a cost that is either absorbed by the company or eventually passed on to the buyer or consumer in some form. While businesses agree that corruption is costly and undesirable, losing profitable business opportunities to firms that are less ethically motivated can be just as devastating to the bottom line. Until governments in every country consistently monitor and enforce anticorruption laws, bribery will remain a real and very challenging issue for global businesses.

Corporate Social Responsibility

Corporate social responsibility (CSR) is defined as "the corporate conscience, citizenship, social performance, or sustainable responsible business, and is a form of corporate self-regulation integrated into a business model. CSR policy functions as a built-in, self-regulating mechanism whereby business monitors and ensures its active compliance with the spirit of the law, ethical standards, and international norms." [8]

CSR emerged more than three decades ago, and it has gained increasing strength over time as companies seek to generate goodwill with their employees, customers, and stakeholders. "Corporate social responsibility encompasses not only what companies do with their profits, but also how they make them. It goes beyond philanthropy and compliance and addresses how companies manage their economic, social, and environmental impacts, as well as their relationships in all key spheres of influence: the workplace, the marketplace, the supply chain, the community, and the public policy realm." [9] Companies may support nonprofit causes and organizations, global initiatives, and prevailing themes. Promoting environmentally friendly and green initiatives is an example of a current prevailing theme.

Coca-Cola is an example of global corporation with a long-term commitment to CSR. In many developing countries, Coca-Cola promotes local economic development through a combination of philanthropy and social and economic development. Whether by using environmentally friendly containers or supporting local education initiatives through its foundation, Coca-Cola is only one of many global companies that seek to increase their commitment to local markets while enhancing their brand, corporate image, and reputation by engaging in socially responsible business practices. [10]

Companies use a wide range of strategies to communicate their socially responsible strategies and programs. Under the auspices of the United Nations, the Global Compact "is a strategic policy initiative for businesses that are committed to aligning their operations and strategies with ten universally accepted principles in the areas of human rights, labour, environment and anti-corruption." [11] The Global Compact will be discussed in more detail in Chapter 5 "Global and Regional Economic Cooperation and Integration".

Enforcement of Ethical Guidelines and Standards

The concept of culture impacting the perception of ethics is one that many businesspeople debate. While culture does impact business ethics, international companies operate in multiple countries and need a standard set of global operating guidelines. Professionals engage in unethical behavior primarily as a result of their own personal ethical values, the corporate culture within a company, or from unrealistic performance expectations.

In the interest of expediency, many governments—the US government included—may not strictly enforce the rules governing corporate ethics. The practice of gift giving is one aspect of business that many governments don't examine too closely. Many companies have routinely used gifts to win favor from their customers, without engaging in direct bribery. American companies frequently invite prospective buyers to visit their US facilities or attend company conferences in exotic locales with all expenses paid. These trips often have perks included. Should such spending be considered sales and marketing expenses, as they are often booked, or are these companies engaging in questionable behavior? It's much harder to answer this question when you consider that most of the company's global competitors are likely to engage in similarly aggressive marketing and sales behavior.

Governments often do not enforce laws until it's politically expedient to do so. Take child labor, for example. Technically, companies operating in India or Pakistan are not permitted to use child labor in factories, mines, and other areas of hazardous employment. However, child labor is widespread in these countries due to deep-rooted social and economic challenges. Local governments are often unable and unwilling to enforce national rules and regulations. Companies and consumers who purchase goods made by children are often unaware that these practices remain unchecked.

The Evolution of Ethics

Ethics evolves over time. It is difficult for both companies and professionals to operate within one set of accepted standards or guidelines only to see them gradually evolve or change. For example, bribery has been an accepted business practice for centuries in Japan and Korea. When these nations adjusted their practices in order to enter the global system, the questionable practices became illegal. Hence a Korean businessman who engaged in bribery ten or twenty years ago may not do so today without finding himself on the other side of the law. Even in the United States, discrimination and business-regulation laws have changed tremendously over the last several decades. And who can know what the future holds? Some of the business practices that are commonly accepted today may be frowned on tomorrow.

It's clear that changing values, as influenced by global media, and changing perceptions and cultures will impact global ethics. The most challenging aspect is that global business does not have a single definition of "fair" or "ethical." While culture influences the definitions of those ideas, many companies are forced to navigate this sensitive area very carefully, as it impacts both their bottom line and their reputations.

KEY TAKEAWAYS

- Culture impacts how local values influence the concept of global business ethics. Each professional is influenced by the values, social programming, and experiences he or she has absorbed since childhood. These collective factors impact how a person perceives an issue and the related correct or incorrect behavior. For some cultures, the evolution of international business and culture sometimes creates a conflict, such as what is seen in gift-giving practices or views on women in the workplace.

- Ethics impacts global business in the areas of management, corruption, and corporate social responsibility.

EXERCISES

(AACSB: Reflective Thinking, Analytical Skills)
1. Define ethics and discuss how it impacts global business.
2. How does culture impact global business ethics?
3. How can global firms develop and enforce ethical guidelines and standards?

[1] Wikipedia s.v. "ethics," last modified February 13, 2011, accessed February 22, 2011, http://en.wikipedia.org/wiki/Ethics.
[2] Wallace R. Baker, "A Reflection on Business Ethics: Implications for the United Nations Global Compact and Social Engagement and for Academic Research," April 2007, accessed February 22, 2011, http://portal.unesco.org/education/en/files/53748/11840802765Baker.pdf/Baker.pdf.
[3] James Fiserv, "Ethics," Internet Encyclopedia of Philosophy, last updated May 10, 2009, accessed February 22, 2011, http://www.iep.utm.edu/ethics.
[4] BusinessDictionary.com, s.v. "corruption," accessed January 9, 2011, http://www.businessdictionary.com/definition/corruption.html.
[5] Transparency International, "Corruption Perceptions Index 2010," accessed February 22, 2011, http://www.transparency.org/policy_research/surveys_indices/cpi/2010/results.
[6] Eric Lichtblau and Carter Dougherty, "Siemens to Pay $1.34 Billion in Fines," New York Times, December 15, 2008, accessed February 22, 2011, http://www.nytimes.com/2008/12/16/business/worldbusiness/16siemens.html.
[7] Transparency International, "Global Corruption Barometer 2010," accessed February 22, 2011, http://www.transparency.org/policy_research/surveys_indices/gcb/2010.
[8] Wikipedia, s.v. "Corporate social responsibility," last modified February 17, 2011, accessed February 22, 2011, http://en.wikipedia.org/wiki/Corporate_social_responsibility.
[9] "Defining Corporate Social Responsibility," Corporate Social Responsibility Initiative, Harvard Kennedy School, last modified 2008, accessed March 26, 2011, http://www.hks.harvard.edu/m-rcbg/CSRI/init_define.html.
[10] "Sustainability," The Coca-Cola Company, accessed March 27, 2011, http://www.thecoca-colacompany.com/citizenship/index.html.
[11] United Nations Global Compact website, accessed January 9, 2011, http://www.unglobalcompact.org.

3.5 Tips in Your Entrepreneurial Walkabout Toolkit

Conducting Business and Negotiating

In this chapter, you have learned about the methods of analyzing cultures, how values may differ, and the resulting impact on global business. Let's take a look at how you as a businessperson might incorporate these ideas into a business strategy. The following are some factors to take into consideration in order to take to equip yourself for success and avoid some cultural pitfalls.

1. **One of the most important cultural factors in many countries is the emphasis on networking or relationships.** Whether in Asia or Latin America or somewhere in between, it's best to have an introduction from a common business partner, vendor, or supplier when meeting a new company or partner. Even in the United States and Europe, where relationships generally have less importance, a well-placed introduction will work wonders. In some countries, it can be almost impossible to get through the right doors without some sort of introduction. Be creative in identifying potential introducers. If you don't know someone who knows the company with which you would like to do business, consider indirect sources. Trade organizations, lawyers, bankers and financiers, common suppliers and buyers, consultants, and advertising agencies are just a few potential introducers. Once a meeting has been set up, foreign companies need to understand the nuances that govern meetings, negotiations, and ongoing business expansion in the local culture.

2. **Even if you have been invited to bid on a contract, you are still trying to sell your company and yourself.** Do not act in a patronizing way or assume you are doing the local company or its government a favor. They must like and trust you if you are to succeed. Think about your own business encounters with people, regardless of nationality, who were condescending and

arrogant. How often have you given business to people who irritated you?

3. **Make sure you understand how your overseas associates think about time and deadlines.** How will that impact your timetable and deliverables?

4. **You need to understand the predominant corporate culture of the country you are dealing with—particularly when dealing with vendors and external partners.** What's the local hierarchy? What are the expected management practices? Are the organizations you're dealing with uniform in culture, or do they represent more than one culture or ethnicity? Culture affects how people develop trust and make decisions as well as the speed of their decision making and their attitudes toward accountability and responsibility.

5. **Understand how you can build trust with potential partners.** How are people from your culture viewed in the target country, and how will it impact your business interactions? How are small or younger companies viewed in the local market? Understand the corporate culture of your potential partner or distributor. More entrepreneurial local companies may have more in common with a younger firm in terms of their approach to doing business.

6. **How do people communicate?** There are also differences in how skills and knowledge are taught or transferred. For example, in the United States, people are expected to ask questions—it's a positive and indicates a seriousness about wanting to learn. In some cultures, asking questions is seen as reflecting a lack of knowledge and could be considered personally embarrassing. It's important to be able to address these issues without appearing condescending. Notice the word *appearing*—the issue is less whether you think you're being condescending and more about whether the professional from the other culture perceives a statement or action as condescending. Again, let's recall that culture is based on perceptions and values.

7. **Focus on communications of all types and learn to find ways around cultural obstacles.** For example, if you're dealing with a culture that shies away from providing bad news or information—don't ask yes-or-no questions. Focus on the process and ask questions about the stage of the business process or deliverable. Many people get frustrated by the lack of information or clear communications. You certainly don't want to be surprised by a delayed shipment to your key customers.

8. **There are no clear playbooks for operating in every culture around the world.** Rather, we have to understand the components that affect culture,

understand how it impacts our business objectives, and then equip ourselves and our teams with the know-how to operate successfully in each new cultural environment. Once you've established a relationship, you may opt to delegate it to someone on your team. Be sure that your person understands the culture of the country, and make sure to stay involved until there is a successful operating history of at least one or more years. Many entrepreneurs stay involved in key relationships on an ongoing basis. Be aware that your global counterparts may require that level of attention.

9. **Make sure in any interaction that you have a decision maker on the other end.** On occasion, junior employees get assigned to work with smaller companies, and you could spend a lot of time with someone who is unable to finalize an agreement. If you have to work through details with a junior employee, try to have that person get a senior employee involved early on so you run fewer chances of losing time and wasting energy.

10. **When negotiating with people from a different culture, try to understand your counterpart's position and objectives.** This does not imply that you should compromise easily or be soft in your style. Rather, understand how to craft your argument in a manner that will be more effective with a person of that culture.

11. **Even in today's wired world, don't assume that everyone in every country is as reliant on the Internet and e-mail as you are.** You may need to use different modes of communication with different countries, companies, and professionals. Faxes are still very common, as many people consider signed authorizations more official than e-mail, although that is changing.

12. **As with any business transaction, use legal documents to document relationships and expectations.** Understand how the culture you are dealing with perceives legal documents, lawyers, and the role of a business's legal department. While most businesspeople around the world are familiar with legal documents, some take the law more seriously than others. Some cultures may be insulted by a lengthy document, while others will consider it a normal part of business.

Many legal professionals recommend that you opt to use the international courts or a third-party arbitration system in case of a dispute. Translate contracts into both languages, and have a second independent translator verify the copies for the accuracy of concepts and key terminology. But be warned: translations may not be exactly the same, as legal terminology is both culture- and country-specific. At the end of the day, even a good contract has many limitations in its use. You have to be willing to enforce infractions. [1]

[1] {Author's Name retracted as requested by the work's original creator or licensee}, Straight Talk about Starting and Growing Your Own Business (New York: McGraw-Hill, 2005).

3.6 End-of-Chapter Questions and Exercises

These exercises are designed to ensure that the knowledge you gain from this book about international business meets the learning standards set out by the international Association to Advance Collegiate Schools of Business (AACSB International). [1] AACSB is the premier accrediting agency of collegiate business schools and accounting programs worldwide. It expects that you will gain knowledge in the areas of communication, ethical reasoning, analytical skills, use of information technology, multiculturalism and diversity, and reflective thinking.

EXPERIENTIAL EXERCISES

(AACSB: Communication, Use of Information Technology, Analytical Skills)

1. As people look at their own habits and perceptions, they need to think about the experiences that have blended together to impact our cultural frame of reference. Many of you in this course come from around the United States, and some of you are from overseas. Furthermore, many of us have immigrant heritages adding to the number of influences that have affected our values. All of this just begins to illustrate how intricate the cultural web can be. Make a list of the most important factors that you think have contributed to how you see your own culture and other cultures.

2. Identify two national cultures among your classmates. Visit http://www.geert-hofstede.com and research Hofstede's five value dimensions for each country. If you were working for a company from one of the two countries selected, how would you advise the senior management on the compatibility of the two cultures? Are the cultures individualistic or collectivist? Do they have a high or low tolerance for risk? Do they have similar or opposite approaches to long-term orientation?

3. Identify someone in your class or a colleague who has recently come from another country. Ask this person what their first impressions were when they came to the new country. Use Hofstede's and Hall's methodologies and determinants to analyze your classmate's or colleague's impressions and experiences. How might you feel if you were to relocate to their country?

4. Pick a country that Dunkin' Brands is not currently operating in. Outline key cultural issues that

management should consider before entering that market. Use the cultural methodologies and determinants that this chapter discusses.

Ethical Dilemmas

(AACSB: Ethical Reasoning, Multiculturalism, Reflective Thinking, Analytical Skills)

1. Section 3.1 "What Is Culture, Anyhow? Values, Customs, and Language" and Section 3.4 "Global Business Ethics" discuss how culture impacts local values and the perception of global business ethics. Each professional is influenced by the values, social programming, and experiences he or she has absorbed since childhood. These collective factors impact how a person perceives an issue and the related correct or incorrect behavior. Culture can also impact how people see the role of one another in workplace. For example, gender issues are at times impacted by local perceptions of women in the workplace. Knowing this, imagine you are a Western businesswoman doing business in Kuwait. Go to Geert Hofstede's site at http://www.geert-hofstede.com, click on Arab World, and review Hofstede's value dimensions and Hall's categories to discuss how local businessmen may perceive your role. Discuss how you would handle an introduction, establish credentials at a first meeting, and conduct ongoing business. Would being a woman be the most difficult impediment to doing business? What other factors might impact your ability to conduct business effectively? How could you prepare yourself to be successful in this market?

2. Both Chapter 1 "Introduction" and this chapter address global business ethics and gift giving in international business. Imagine you are the global business development director for a large American aircraft parts manufacturing firm. You want to make a big sale to an overseas government client. How would you handle a situation where you are doing business with a person from this culture in which gift giving is a routine part of traditional business life? Imagine that your competitors are from other countries, some of which are less concerned about the ethics of gift giving as this book defines it. Discuss if and how you can still win business in such a situation. How would you advise your senior management?

3. You work for a pulp and paper manufacturing company. Using the Corruption Perceptions Index on Transparency International's website (http://www.transparency.org/policy_research/survey s_indices/cpi/2010/results), discuss how you would advise your senior management reviewing the possible setup of operations in either Latin America or Africa.

Which countries would suggest further research and which countries would pose ethical challenges? How important do you think the Corruption Perceptions Index is to your business objectives? Should it be a factor in determining where you set up operations?

[1] Association to Advance Collegiate Schools of Business website, accessed January 26, 2010, http://www.aacsb.edu.

3.7 Additional References

In addition to the textbook, the following are some useful and insightful sources and references:

- Roger E. Axtell, Do's and Taboos Around the World (Hoboken, NJ: John Wiley & Sons, 1993).
- CultureQuest Doing Business In series (New York: Atma Global, 2010).
- {Author's Name retracted as requested by the work's original creator or licensee}, Doing Business in Asia: The Complete Guide (San Francisco: Jossey-Bass, 1998).
- Business Ethics, accessed May 20, 2011, http://business-ethics.com.
- Edward T. Hall, Beyond Culture (New York: Anchor Press/Doubleday, 1976).
- Edward T. Hall and Mildred Reed-Hall, Understanding Cultural Differences (Boston: Intercultural Press, 1990).
- Geert Hofstede, Culture's Consequences (Thousand Oaks, CA: Sage Publications, 1984).
- Samuel P. Huntington, A Clash of Civilizations (New York: Simon & Schuster, 1996).
- Bryan Magee, The Story of Thought: The Essential Guide to the History of Western Philosophy (New York: DK Publishing, 1998).

NOTES:

NOTES:

Chapter 4:
World Economies

WHAT'S IN IT FOR ME?

1. How are economies classified?
2. What is the developed world?
3. What is the developing world?
4. Which are the emerging markets?

From the title of this chapter, you may be wondering—is this chapter going to cover the world? And, in a sense, the answer is yes. When global managers explore how to expand, they start by looking at the world. Knowing the major markets and the stage of development for each allows managers to determine how best to enter and expand. The manager's goal is to hone in on a new country—hopefully, before their competitors and usually before the popular media does. China and India were expanding rapidly for several years before the financial press, such as the Wall Street Journal, elevated them to their current hot status.

It's common to find people interested in doing business with a country simply because they've read that it's the new "hot" economy. They may know little or nothing about the market or country—its history, evolution of thought, people, or how interactions are generally managed in a business or social context. Historically, many companies have only looked at new global markets once potential customers or partners have approached them. However, trade barriers are falling, and new opportunities are fast emerging in markets of the Middle East and Africa—further flattening the world for global firms. Companies are increasingly identifying these and other global markets for their products and services and incorporating them into their long-term growth strategies.

Savvy global managers realize that to be effective in a country, they need to know its recent political, economic, and social history. This helps them evaluate not only the current business opportunity but also the risk of political, economic, and social changes that can impact their business. First, Section 4.1 "Classifying World Economies" outlines how businesses and economists evaluate world economies. Then, the remaining sections review what developed and developing worlds are and how they differ, as well as explain how to evaluate the expanding set of emerging-market countries, which started with the BRIC countries (i.e., Brazil, Russia, India, and China) and has now expanded to include twenty-eight countries. Effective global managers need to be able to identify the markets that offer the best opportunities for their products and services. Additionally, managers need to monitor these emerging markets for new local companies that take advantage of business conditions to become global competitors.

OPENING CASE: CHINA VERSUS INDIA: WHO WILL WIN??

India and China are among the world's fastest-growing economies, contributing nearly 30 percent to global economic growth. Both China and India are not emerging economies—they're actually "re-emerging," having spent centuries at the center of trade throughout history: "These two Asian giants, which until 1800 used to make up half the world economy, are not, like Japan and Germany, mere nation states. In terms of size and population, each is a continent—and for all the glittering growth rates, a poor one." [1]

Both India and China are in fierce competition with each other as well as in their quest to catch up with the major economies in the developed world. Each have particular strengths and competitive advantages that have allowed each of them to weather the recent global financial crisis better than most countries. China's growth has been mainly investment and export driven, focusing on low-cost manufacturing, with domestic consumption as low as 36 percent of gross domestic product (GDP). On the other hand, India's growth has been derived mostly from a strong services sector and buoyant domestic consumption. India is also much less dependent on trade than China, relying on external trade for about 20 percent of its GDP versus 56 percent for China. The Chinese economy has doubled every eight years for the last three decades—the fastest rate for a major economy in recorded history. By 2011, China is the world's second largest economy in the world behind the United States. [2] A recent report by PricewaterhouseCoopers forecasts that China could overtake the US economy as early as 2020. [3]

China is also the first country in the world to have met the poverty-reduction target set in the UN Millennium Development Goals and has had remarkable success in lifting more than 400 million people out of poverty. This contrasts sharply with India, where 456 million people (i.e., 42 percent of the population) still live below the poverty line, as defined by the World Bank at $1.25 a day. [4] Section 4.1 "Classifying World Economies" will review in more detail how we classify countries. China has made greater strides in improving the conditions for its people, as measured by the HDI. All of this contributes to the local business conditions by both developing the skill sets of the workforce as well as expanding the number of middle-class consumers and their disposable incomes.

India has emerged as the fourth-largest market in the world when its GDP is measured on the scale of purchasing power parity. Both economies are increasing their share of world GDP, attracting high levels of foreign investment, and are recovering faster from the global crisis than developed countries. "Each country has achieved this with distinctly different approaches—India with a 'grow first, build later' approach versus a 'top-down, supply driven' strategy in China." [5]

The Chinese economy historically outpaces India's by just about every measure. China's fast-acting government implements new policies with blinding speed, making India's fractured political system appear sluggish and chaotic. Beijing's shiny new airport and wide freeways are models of modern development, contrasting sharply with the sagging infrastructure of New Delhi and Mumbai. And as the global economy emerges from the Great Recession, India once again seems to be playing second fiddle. Pundits around the world laud China's leadership for its well-devised economic policies during the crisis, which were so effective in restarting economic growth that they helped lift the entire Asian region out of the downturn. [6]

As recently as the early 1990s, India was as rich, in terms of national income per head. China then hurtled so far ahead that it seemed India could never catch up. But India's long-term prospects now look stronger. While China is about to see its working-age population shrink, India is enjoying the sort of bulge in manpower which brought sustained booms elsewhere in Asia. It is no longer inconceivable that its growth could outpace China's for a considerable time. It has the advantage of democracy—at least as a pressure valve for discontent. And India's army is, in numbers, second only to China's and America's…And because India does not threaten the West, it has powerful friends both on its own merits and as a counterweight to China. [7]

India's domestic economy provides greater cushion from external shocks than China's. Private domestic consumption accounts for 57 percent of GDP in India compared with only 35 percent in China. India's confident consumer didn't let the economy down. Passenger car sales in India in December jumped 40 percent from a year earlier. [8]

Since 1978, China's economic growth and reform have dramatically improved the lives of hundreds of millions of Chinese, increased social mobility. The Chinese leadership has reduced the role of ideology in economic policy by adopting a more pragmatic perspective on many political and socioeconomic problems. China's ongoing economic transformation has had a profound impact not only on China but on the world. The market-oriented reforms China has implemented over the past two decades have unleashed individual initiative and entrepreneurship. The result has been the largest reduction of poverty and one of the fastest increases in income levels ever seen.

China used to be the third-largest economy in the world but has overtaken Japan to become the second-largest in August 2010. It has sustained average economic growth of over 9.5 percent for the past 26 years. In 2009 its $4.814 trillion economy was about one-third the size of the United States economy. [9] China leapfrogged over Japan and became the world's number two economy in the second quarter of 2010, as receding global growth sapped momentum and stunted a shaky recovery.

India's economic liberalization in 1991 opened gates to businesses worldwide. In the mid- to late 1980s, Rajiv Gandhi's government eased restrictions on capacity expansion, removed price controls, and reduced corporate taxes. While his government viewed liberalizing the economy as a positive step, political pressures slowed the implementation of policies. The early reforms increased the rate of growth but also led to high fiscal deficits and a worsening current account. India's major trading partner then, the Soviet Union, collapsed. In addition, the first Gulf War in 1991 caused oil prices to increase, which in turn led to a major balance-of-payments crisis for India. To be able to cope with these problems, the newly elected Prime Minister Narasimha Rao along with Finance Minister Manmohan Singh initiated a widespread economic liberalization in 1991 that is widely credited with what has led to the Indian economic engine of today. Focusing on the barriers for private sector investment and growth, the reforms enabled faster approvals and began to dismantle the License Raj, a term dating back to India's colonial historical administrative legacy from the British and referring to a complex system of regulations governing Indian businesses. [10]

Since 1990, India has been emerging as one of the wealthiest economies in the developing world. Its economic progress has been accompanied by increases in life expectancy, literacy rates, and food security. Goldman Sachs predicts that India's GDP in current prices will overtake France and Italy by 2020; Germany, the United Kingdom, and Russia by 2025; and Japan by 2035 to become the third-largest economy of the world after the United States and China. India was cruising at 9.4 percent growth rate until the financial crisis of 2008–9, which affected countries the world over. [11]

Both India and China have several strengths and weaknesses that contribute to the competitive battleground between them.

China's Strengths

1. *Strong government control.* China's leadership has a development-oriented ideology, the ability to promote capable individuals, and a system of collaborative policy review. The strong central government control has enabled the country to experience consistent and managed economic success. The government directs economic policy and its implementation and is less susceptible than democratic India to sudden changes resulting from political pressures.
2. *WTO and FDI.* China's entry into the World Trade Organization (WTO) and its foreign direct investment (FDI) in other global markets has been an important factor in the country's successful growth. Global businesses also find the consistency and predictability of the Chinese government a plus when evaluating direct investment.
3. *Cheap, abundant labor.* China's huge population offers large pools of skilled and unskilled workers, with fewer labor regulations than in India.
4. *Infrastructure.* The government has prioritized the development of the country's infrastructure including roads and highways, ports, airports, telecommunications networks, education, public health, law and order, mass transportation, and water and sewer treatment facilities.
5. *Effectiveness of two-pronged financial system.* "The first prong is a well-run directed-credit system that channels funds from bank and postal deposits to policy-determined public uses; the second is a profit-oriented and competitive system, albeit in early and inefficient stages of development. Both prongs continue to undergo rapid

government-sponsored reforms to make them more effective." [12]

India's Strengths

1. *Quality manpower.* India has a technologically competent, English-speaking workforce. As a major exporter of technical workers, India has prioritized the development of its technology and outsourcing sectors. India is the global leader in the business process outsourcing (BPO) and call-center services industries.
2. *Open democracy.* India's democratic traditions are ingrained in its social and cultural fabric. While the political process can at times be tumultuous, it is less likely than China to experience big uncertainties or sudden revolutionary changes as those recently witnessed in the Middle East in late 2010 and early 2011.
3. *Entrepreneurship.* India entrepreneurial culture has led to global leaders, such as the Infosys cofounder, Narayana Murthy. Utilizing the global network of Indians in business and Indian business school graduates, India has an additional advantage over China in terms of entrepreneurship-oriented bodies, such as the TiE network (The Indus Entrepreneurs) or the Wadhwani Foundation, which seek to promote entrepreneurship by, among other things, facilitating investments. [13]
4. *Reverse brain drain.* Historically many emerging and developing markets experienced what is known as brain drain—where its best young people, once educated, moved to developed countries to access better jobs, incomes, and prospects for career advancement. In the past decade, economists have observed that the fast-growing economies of China and India are experiencing the reverse. Young graduates are remaining in India and China to pursue dynamic domestic opportunities. In fact, older professionals are returning from developed countries to seek their fortunes and career advancements in the promising local economies—hence the term reverse brain drain. The average age of the Indian returnees is thirty years old, and these adults are well educated—66 percent hold a master's degree, while 12 percent hold PhDs. The majority of these degrees are in management, technology, and science. Indians returning home are encouraged by the increasing transparency in business and government as well as the political freedoms and the prospects for economic growth. [14]
5. *Indian domestic-market growth.* According to the Trade and Development Report 2010, for sustainable growth, policies "should be based on establishing a balanced mix of domestic and overseas demand." [15] India has a good mix of both international and domestic markets.

Each country has embraced the trend toward urbanization differently. Global businesses are impacted in the way cities are run:

China is in much better shape than India is. While India has barely paid attention to its urban transformation, China has developed a set of internally consistent practices across every element of the urbanization operating model: funding, governance, planning, sectorial policies, and shape. India has underinvested in its cities; China has invested ahead of demand and given its cities the freedom to raise substantial investment resources by monetizing land assets and retaining a 25 percent share of value-added taxes. While India spends $17 per capita in capital investments in urban infrastructure annually, China spends $116. Indian cities have devolved little real power and accountability to its cities; but China's major cities enjoy the same status as provinces and have powerful and empowered political appointees as mayors. While India's urban planning system has failed to address competing demands for space, China has a mature urban planning regime that emphasizes the systematic development of run-down areas consistent with long-range plans for land use, housing, and transportation. [16]

Despite the urbanization challenges, India is likely to benefit in the future from its younger demographics: "By 2025, nearly 28 percent of China's population will be aged 55 or older compared with only 16 percent in India." [17] The trend toward urbanization is evident in both countries. By 2025, 64 percent of China's population will be living in urban areas, and 37 percent of India's people will be living in cities. [18] This historically unique trend offers global businesses exciting markets.

So what markets are likely to benefit the most from these trends? In India, by 2025, the largest markets will be transportation and communication, food, and health care followed by housing and utilities, recreation, and education. Even India's slower-growing spending categories will represent significant opportunities for businesses because these markets will still be growing rapidly in comparison with their counterparts in other parts of the world. In China's cities today, the fastest-growing categories are likely to be transportation and communication, housing and utilities, personal products, health care, and recreation and education. In addition, in both China and India, urban infrastructure markets will be massive. [19]

While both India and China have unique strengths as well as many similarities, it's clear that both countries will continue to grow in the coming decades offering global businesses exciting new domestic markets. [20]

OPENING CASE EXERCISE

(AACSB: Ethical Reasoning, Multiculturalism, Reflective Thinking, Analytical Skills)

1. Pick an industry and company that interests you. As a global manager of the firm you've selected, you're asked to review China and India and determine which market to enter first. How would you evaluate each market and its potential customers? Use your understanding of the stage of development for each country from the case study as well as online resources. Which country would you recommend entering first? Based on your understanding of these markets, would you recommend a strategy for only one country or both?

[1] "Contest of the Century," Economist, August 19, 2010, accessed January 3, 2011, http://www.economist.com/node/16846256.

[2] Gopal Ethiraj, "China Edges Out Japan to Become World's No. 2 Economy," Asian Tribune, August 18, 2010, accessed January 7, 2011, http://www.asiantribune.com/news/2010/08/18/china-edges-out-japan-become-world%E2%80%99s-no-2-economy.

[3] Suzanne Rosselet, "Strengths of China and India to Take Them into League of Developing Countries," Economic Times, May 7, 2010, accessed January 3, 2011,http://economictimes.indiatimes.com/features/corporate-dossier/Strengths-of-China-and-India-to-take-them-into-league-of-developing-countries/articleshow/5900893.cms.

[4] Suzanne Rosselet, "Strengths of China and India to Take Them into League of Developing Countries," Economic Times, May 7, 2010, accessed January 3, 2011,http://economictimes.indiatimes.com/features/corporate-dossier/Strengths-of-China-and-India-to-take-them-into-league-of-developing-countries/articleshow/5900893.cms.

[5] Suzanne Rosselet, "Strengths of China and India to Take Them into League of Developing Countries," Economic Times, May 7, 2010, accessed January 3, 2011,http://economictimes.indiatimes.com/features/corporate-dossier/Strengths-of-China-and-India-to-take-them-into-league-of-developing-countries/articleshow/5900893.cms.

[6] Michael Schuman, "India vs. China: Whose Economy Is Better?," Time, January 28, 2010, accessed January 3, 2011, http://www.time.com/time/world/article/0,8599,1957281,00.html.

[7] "Contest of the Century," Economist, August 19, 2010, accessed January 3, 2011, http://www.economist.com/node/16846256.

[8] Michael Schuman, "India vs. China: Whose Economy Is Better?," Time, January 28, 2010, accessed January 3, 2011, http://www.time.com/time/world/article/0,8599,1957281,00.html.

[9] "Background Note: China," Bureau of East Asian and Pacific Affairs, US Department of State, August 5, 2010, accessed January 3, 2011,http://www.state.gov/r/pa/ei/bgn/18902.htm.

[10] "Economic History of India," History of India, accessed January 7, 2011, http://www.indohistory.com/economic_history_of_india.html.

[11] Mamta Badkar, "Race of the Century: Is India or China the Next Economic Superpower?," Business Insider, February 5, 2011, accessed May 18, 2011, http://www.businessinsider.com/are-you-betting-on-china-or-india-2011-1?op=1.

[12] Albert Keidel, "E-Notes: Assessing China's Economic Rise: Strengths, Weaknesses and Implications," Foreign Policy Research Institute, July

2007, accessed January 3, 2011,
http://www.fpri.org/enotes/200707.keidel.assessingchina.html.
[13] "Entrepreneurship: Riding Growth in India and China," INSEAD,
accessed January 3,
2011, http://knowledge.insead.edu/contents/Turner.cfm.
[14] Vivek Wadhwa, "Beware the Reverse Brain Drain to India and
China," TechCrunch, October 17, 2009, accessed January 7,
2011, http://techcrunch.com/2009/10/17/beware-the-reverse-brain-
drain-to-india-and-china.
[15] Pioneer Edit Desk, "Expand Domestic Market," The Pioneer,
September 20, 2010, accessed January 7,
2011, http://dailypioneer.com/284197/Expand-domestic-market.html.
[16] Richard Dobbs and Shirish Sankhe, "Opinion: China vs.
India," Financial Times, May 18, 2010, reprinted on McKinsey Global
Institute website, accessed January 3,
2011,http://www.mckinsey.com/mgi/mginews/opinion_china_vs_india.a
sp.
[17] Richard Dobbs and Shirish Sankhe, "Opinion: China vs.
India," Financial Times, May 18, 2010, reprinted on McKinsey Global
Institute website, accessed January 3,
2011,http://www.mckinsey.com/mgi/mginews/opinion_china_vs_india.a
sp.
[18] Richard Dobbs and Shirish Sankhe, "Opinion: China vs.
India," Financial Times, May 18, 2010, reprinted on McKinsey Global
Institute website, accessed January 3,
2011,http://www.mckinsey.com/mgi/mginews/opinion_china_vs_india.a
sp.
[19] Richard Dobbs and Shirish Sankhe, "Opinion: China vs.
India," Financial Times, May 18, 2010, reprinted on McKinsey Global
Institute website, accessed January 3,
2011,http://www.mckinsey.com/mgi/mginews/opinion_china_vs_india.a
sp.
[20] See also "India's Surprising Economic Miracle," Economist,
September 30, 2010, accessed January 3,
2011, http://www.economist.com/node/17147648; "A Bumpier but Freer
Road," Economist, September 3, 2010, accessed January 3,
2011,http://www.economist.com/node/17145035; Chris
Monasterski, "Education: India vs. China," Private Sector Development
Blog, World Bank, April 25, 2007, accessed January 7,
2011, http://psdblog.worldbank.org/psdblog/2007/04/education_india.ht
ml; Shreyasi Singh, "India vs. China," The Diplomat, August 27, 2010,
accessed January 7, 2011,http://the-diplomat.com/indian-
decade/2010/08/27/india-vs-china; "The India vs. China Debate: One Up
for India?," Benzinga, January 29, 2010, accessed January 7,
2011,http://www.benzinga.com/global/104829/the-india-vs-china-
debate-one-up-for-india; Steve Hamm, "India's Advantages over
China," Bloomberg Business, March 6, 2007, accessed January 7,
2011,http://www.businessweek.com/globalbiz/blog/globespotting/archiv
es/2007/03/indias_advantag.html.

4.1 Classifying World Economies

LEARNING OBJECTIVES

1. Understand how economies are classified.
2. Evaluate the statistics used in classifications: GNP, GDP, PPP as well as HDI, HPI, GDI, and GEM.

Classification of Economies

Experts debate exactly how to define the level of economic development of a country—which criteria to use and, therefore, which countries are truly developed. This debate crosses political, economic, and social arguments.

When evaluating a country, a manager is assessing the country's income and the purchasing power of its people; the legal, regulatory, and commercial infrastructure, including communication, transportation, and energy; and the overall sophistication of the business environment.

Why does a country's stage of development matter? Well, if you're selling high-end luxury items, for example, you'll want to focus on the per capita income of the local citizens. Can they afford a $1,000 designer handbag, a luxury car, or cutting-edge, high-tech gadgets? If so, how *many* people can afford these expensive items (i.e., how large is the domestic market)? For example, in January 2011, the *Financial Times* quotes Jim O'Neill, a leading business economist, who states, "South Africa currently accounts for 0.6 percent of world GDP. South Africa can be successful, but it won't be big." [1] Section 4.4 "Emerging Markets" discusses the debate around the term *emerging markets* and which countries should be labeled as such. But clearly the size of the local market is an important key factor for businesspeople.

Even in developing countries, there are always wealthy people who want and can afford luxury items. But these consumers are just as likely to head to the developed world to make their purchase and have little concern about any duties or taxes they may have to pay when bringing the items back into their home country. This is one reason why companies pay special attention to understanding their global consumers as well as where and how these consumers purchase goods. Global managers also focus on understanding if a country's target market is growing and by what rate. Countries like China and India caught the attention of global companies, because they had large populations that were eager for foreign goods and services but couldn't afford them. As more people in each country acquired wealth, their buying appetites increased. The challenge is how to identify which consumers in which countries are likely to become new customers. Managers focus on globally standard statistics as one set of criteria to understand the stage of development of any country that they're exploring for business. [2]

Let's look more closely at some of these globally standard statistics and classifications that are commonly used to define the stage of a country's development.

Statistics Used in Classifications

Gross Domestic Product

Gross domestic product (GDP) is the value of all the goods and services produced by a country in a single year. Usually quoted in US dollars, the number is an official accounting of the country's output of goods and services. For example, if a country has a large black, or underground, market for transactions, it will not be included in the official GDP. Emerging-market countries, such as India and Russia, historically have had large black-market transactions for varying reasons, which often meant their GDP was underestimated.

Figure 4.1 shows the total size of the economy, but a company will want to know the income per person, which may be a better indicator of the strength of the local economy and the market opportunity for a new consumer product. GDP is often quoted on a per person basis. Per capita GDP is simply the GDP divided by the population of the country.

The per capita GDP can be misleading because actual costs in each country differ. As a result, more managers rely on the GDP per person adjusted for purchasing power to understand how much income local residents have. This number helps professionals evaluate what consumers in the local market can afford.

Companies selling expensive goods and services may be less interested in economies with low per capita GDP. Figure 4.2 "Per Capita GDP on a Purchasing Power Parity Basis" shows the income (GDP) on a per person basis. For space, the chart has been condensed by removing lower profile countries, but the ranks are valid. Surprisingly, some of the hottest emerging-market countries—China, India, Turkey, Brazil, South Africa, and Mexico—rank very low on the income per person charts. So, why are these markets so exciting? One reason might be that companies selling cheaper, daily-use items, such as soap, shampoos, and low-end cosmetics, have found success entering developing, but promising, markets.

Purchasing Power Parity

To compare production and income across countries, we need to look at more than just GDP. Economists seek to adjust this number to reflect the different costs of living in specific countries. Purchasing power parity (PPP) is, in essence, an economic theory that adjusts the exchange rate between countries to ensure that a good is purchased for the same price in the same currency. For example, a basic cup of coffee should cost the same in London as in New York.

A nation's GDP at purchasing power parity (PPP) exchange rates is the sum value of all goods and services produced in the country valued at prices prevailing in the United States. This is the measure most economists prefer when looking at per-capita welfare and when comparing living conditions or use of resources across countries. The measure is difficult to compute, as a US dollar value has to be assigned to all goods and services in the country regardless of whether these goods and services have a direct equivalent in the United States (for example, the value of an ox-cart or non-US military equipment); as a result, PPP estimates for some countries are based on a small and sometimes different set of goods and services. In addition, many countries do not formally participate in the World Bank's PPP project to calculate these measures, so the resulting GDP estimates for these countries may lack precision. For many developing countries, PPP-based GDP measures are multiples of the official exchange rate (OER) measure. The differences between the OER- and PPP-denominated GDP values for most of the wealthy industrialized countries are generally much smaller. [3]

In some countries, like Germany, the United Kingdom, or Japan, the cost of living is quite high and the per capita GDP (nominal) is higher than the GDP adjusted for purchasing power. Conversely, in countries like Mexico, Brazil, China, and India, the per capita GDP adjusted for purchasing power is higher than the nominal per capita GDP, implying that local consumers in each country can afford more with their incomes.

Human Development Index (HDI)

GDP and purchasing power provide indications of a country's level of economic development by using an income-focused statistic. However, in recent years, economists and business analysts have focused on indicators that measure whether people's needs are satisfied and whether the needs are equally met across the local population. One such indication is the human development index (HDI), which measures people's satisfaction in three key areas—long and healthy life in terms of life expectancy; access to quality education equally; and a decent, livable standard of living in the form of income.

Since 1990, the United Nations Development Program (UNDP) has produced an annual report listing the HDI for countries. The HDI is a summary composite index that measures a country's average achievements in three basic aspects of human development: health, knowledge, and a decent standard of living. Health is measured by *life expectancy* at birth; knowledge is measured by a combination of the adult *literacy* rate and the combined primary, secondary, and tertiary gross enrollment ratio; and standard of living by (*income as measured by*) GDP per capita (PPP US$). [4]

While the HDI is not a complete indicator of a country's level of development, it does help provide a more comprehensive picture than just looking at the GDP. The HDI, for example, does not reflect political participation or gender inequalities. The HDI and the other composite indices can only offer a broad proxy on some of the key the issues of human development, gender disparity, and human poverty. [5] Table 4.1 "Human Development Index (HDI)—2010 Rankings" shows the rankings of the world's countries for the HDI for 2010 rankings. Measures such as the HDI and its components allow global managers to more accurately gauge the local market.

Table 4.1 Human Development Index (HDI)—2010 Rankings

Very High Human Development	High Human Development	Medium Human Development	Low Human Development
1. Norway	43. Bahamas	86. Fiji	128. Kenya
2. Australia	44. Lithuania	87. Turkmenistan	129. Bangladesh
3. New Zealand	45. Chile	88. Dominican Republic	130. Ghana
4. United States	46. Argentina	89. China	131. Cameroon
5. Ireland	47. Kuwait	90. El Salvador	132. Myanmar
6. Liechtenstein	48. Latvia	91. Sri Lanka	133. Yemen
7. Netherlands	49. Montenegro	92. Thailand	134. Benin
8. Canada	50. Romania	93. Gabon	135. Madagascar
9. Sweden	51. Croatia	94. Suriname	136. Mauritania
10. Germany	52. Uruguay	95. Bolivia (Plurinational State of)	137. Papua New Guinea
11. Japan	53. Libyan Arab Jamahiriya	96. Paraguay	138. Nepal
12. Korea (Republic of)	54. Panama	97. The Philippines	139. Togo
13. Switzerland	55. Saudi Arabia	98. Botswana	140. Comoros
14. France	56. Mexico	99. Moldova (Republic of)	141. Lesotho
15. Israel	57. Malaysia	100. Mongolia	142. Nigeria
16. Finland	58. Bulgaria	101. Egypt	143. Uganda
17. Iceland	59. Trinidad and Tobago	102. Uzbekistan	144. Senegal
18. Belgium	60. Serbia	103. Micronesia (Federated States of)	145. Haiti
19. Denmark	61. Belarus	104. Guyana	146. Angola
20. Spain	62. Costa Rica	105. Namibia	147. Djibouti
21. Hong Kong, China (SAR)	63. Peru	106. Honduras	148. Tanzania (United Republic of)
22. Greece	64. Albania	107. Maldives	149. Côte d'Ivoire
23. Italy	65. Russian Federation	108. Indonesia	150. Zambia
24. Luxembourg	66. Kazakhstan	109. Kyrgyzstan	151. Gambia
25. Austria	67. Azerbaijan	110. South Africa	152. Rwanda
26. United Kingdom	68. Bosnia and Herzegovina	111. Syrian Arab Republic	153. Malawi
27. Singapore	69. Ukraine	112. Tajikistan	154. Sudan
28. Czech Republic	70. Iran (Islamic Republic of)	113. Vietnam	155. Afghanistan
29. Slovenia	71. The former Yugoslav Republic of Macedonia	114. Morocco	156. Guinea
30. Andorra	72. Mauritius	115. Nicaragua	157. Ethiopia
31. Slovakia	73. Brazil	116. Guatemala	158. Sierra Leone
32. United Arab Emirates	74. Georgia	117. Equatorial Guinea	159. Central African Republic
33. Malta	75. Venezuela (Bolivarian Republic of)	118. Cape Verde	160. Mali
34. Estonia	76. Armenia	119. India	161. Burkina Faso
35. Cyprus	77. Ecuador	120. Timor-Leste	162. Liberia
36. Hungary	78. Belize	121. Swaziland	163. Chad

Very High Human Development	High Human Development	Medium Human Development	Low Human Development
37. Brunei Darussalam	79. Colombia	122. Lao People's Democratic Republic	164. Guinea-Bissau
38. Qatar	80. Jamaica	123. Solomon Islands	165. Mozambique
39. Bahrain	81. Tunisia	124. Cambodia	166. Burundi
40. Portugal	82. Jordan	125. Pakistan	167. Niger
41. Poland	83. Turkey	126. Congo	168. Congo (Democratic Republic of the)
42. Barbados	84. Algeria 85. Tonga	127. São Tomé and Príncipe	169. Zimbabwe

Source: UNDP, "Human Development Index (HDI)—2010 Rankings," *Human Development Reports*, accessed January 6, 2011, http://hdr.undp.org/en/statistics.

In 1995, the UNDP introduced two new measures of human development that highlight the status of women in each society.

The first, *gender-related development index (GDI)*, measures achievement in the same basic capabilities as the HDI does, but takes note of inequality in achievement between women and men. The methodology used imposes a penalty for inequality, such that the GDI falls when the achievement levels of both women and men in a country go down or when the disparity between their achievements increases. The greater the gender disparity in basic capabilities, the lower a country's GDI compared with its HDI. The GDI is simply the HDI discounted, or adjusted downwards, for gender inequality.

The second measure, *gender empowerment measure (GEM)*, is a measure of agency. It evaluates progress in advancing women's standing in political and economic forums. It examines the extent to which women and men are able to actively participate in economic and political life and take part in decision making. While the GDI focuses on expansion of capabilities, the GEM is concerned with the use of those capabilities to take advantage of the opportunities of life. [6]

In 1997, UNDP added a further measure—the human poverty index (HPI).

If human development is about enlarging choices, poverty means that opportunities and choices most basic to human development are denied. Thus a person is not free to lead a long, healthy, and creative life and is denied access to a decent standard of living, freedom, dignity, self-respect and the respect of others. From a human development perspective, poverty means more than the lack of what is necessary for material well-being.

For policy-makers, the poverty of choices and opportunities is often more relevant than the poverty of income. The poverty of choices focuses on the causes of poverty and leads directly to strategies of empowerment and other actions to enhance opportunities for everyone. Recognizing the poverty of choices and opportunities implies that poverty must be addressed in all its dimensions, not income alone. [7]

Rather than measure poverty by income, the HPI is a composite index that uses indicators of the most basic dimensions of deprivation: a short life (longevity), a lack of basic education (knowledge), and a lack of access to public and private resources (decent standard of living). There are two different HPIs—one for developing countries (HPI-1) and another for a group of select high-income OECD (Organization for Economic and Development) countries (HPI-2), which better reflects the socioeconomic differences between the two groups. HPI-2 also includes a fourth indicator that measures social exclusion as represented by the rate of long-term unemployment. [8]

Why Does All This Matter to Global Business?

So, the richest countries—like Liechtenstein, Qatar, and Luxembourg—may *not* always have big local markets or, in contrast, the poorest countries may *have* the largest local market as determined by the size of the local population. Savvy business managers need to compare and contrast a number of different classifications, statistics, and indicators before they can interpret the strength, depth, and extent of a local market opportunity for their particular industry and company.

The goal of this chapter is to review a sampling of countries in the developed, developing, and emerging markets to understand how economists and businesspeople perceive market opportunities. Of course, one chapter can't do justice to all of these markets, but through select examples, you'll see how countries have evolved in the post–World War II global economic, political, and social environments. Remember that the goal of any successful businessperson is to monitor the changing markets and spot opportunities and trends ahead of his or her peers.

Advice to Students

The major classifications used by analysts are evolving. The primary criteria for determining the stage of development may change within a decade as demonstrated with the addition of the gender and poverty indices. In addition, with every global crisis or event, there's a tendency to add more acronyms and statistics into the mix. Savvy global managers have to sort through these to determine what's relevant to their industry and their business objectives in one or more countries. For example, in the fall of 2010, after two years of global financial crisis, global investors started using a new acronym to describe the changing economic fortunes among countries: HIICs, or heavily indebted industrialized countries. These countries include the United States, the United Kingdom, and Japan. "'Developed markets are basically behaving like emerging markets,' says HSBC's Richard Yetsenga. 'And emerging markets are quickly becoming more developed.'" [9] Investors are pulling money from the developed countries and into the BRIC countries (i.e., Brazil, Russia, India, and China), which are "'where the population growth is, where the raw materials are, and where the economic growth is,' says Michael Penn, global equity strategist at Bank of America Merrill Lynch." [10] *The key here is to understand that classifications—just like countries and international business—are constantly evolving.*

Rather than being overwhelmed by the evolving data, it's critical to understand *why* the changes are occurring, *what* attitudes and perceptions are shifting, and *if* they are supported by real, verifiable data. In the above example of HIICs, investors from the major economies are likely motivated by quick gains on stock prices and the prevailing perception that emerging markets offer companies the best growth prospects. But as a businessperson, the timeline for your company would be in years, not months; so it's important to evaluate information based on your company's goals rather than relying on the media, investment markets, or other singularly focused industry professionals.

To truly monitor the global business arena and select prospective countries, you need to follow the news, trends, and available information for a period of time. Over time, savvy global managers develop a geographic, industrial, or product expertise—or some combination. Those who become experts on a specific country spend a great deal of time in the country, sometimes learn the language, and almost always develop an understanding of the country's political, economic, and social history as well as its culture and evolution. They gain a deeper knowledge of more than just the country's current business environment. In the business world, these folks are affectionately called "old hands"—as

in he is an "old China hand" or an "old Indonesia hand." This is a reflection of how seasoned or experienced a person is with a country.

KEY TAKEAWAYS

- There are some classifications that are commonly used to define a stage of a country's development. The GDP is the value of all the goods and services produced by a country in a single year. The income per person, a better indicator of the strength of the local economy and the market opportunity for a new consumer product, is the nominal per capita GDP—the GDP divided by the population of the country. Finally, to compare production and income across countries, economists adjust this number to reflect the different costs of living in specific countries. PPP adjusts the exchange rate between countries to ensure that a good is purchased for the same price in the same currency.

- The HDI measures people's satisfaction in three key areas: (1) long and healthy life in terms of life expectancy; (2) access to quality education equally; and (3) a decent standard of living in the form of income. Health is measured by *life expectancy* at birth; knowledge is measured by a combination of the adult *literacy* rate and the combined primary, secondary, and tertiary gross enrollment ratio; and standard of living by *(income as measured by)* per capita GDP.

- Standards are constantly evolving to meet changing global scenarios; for instance, in 1997, the UNDP added the HPI to factor in the denial of basic opportunities and choices to those who live in poverty. It's critical to understand *why* the changes are occurring, *what* attitudes and perceptions are shifting, and *if* they are supported by real, verifiable data.

EXERCISES

(AACSB: Reflective Thinking, Analytical Skills)
1. Describe the main criteria used to classify economies.
2. Select two countries on Figure 4.1 identifying GDP per person and research the local economy. Are your findings consistent with what you would expect based on the country rankings? What is the human development ranking for each country? In your opinion, are these rankings consistent with the GDP rankings?

[1] Jennifer Hughes, "'Bric' Creator Adds Newcomers to List," Financial Times, January 16, 2010, accessed January 7, 2011, http://www.ft.com/cms/s/0/f717c8e8-21be-11e0-9e3b-00144feab49a.html#ixzz1MKbbO8ET.

[2] "Global Economies," CultureQuest Global Business Multimedia Series (New York: Atma Global, 2010).

[3] US Central Intelligence Agency, "Country Comparison: GDP (PPP)," World Factbook, accessed January 3, 2011, https://www.cia.gov/library/publications/the-world-factbook/rankorder/2001rank.html.

[4] UNDP, "Frequently Asked Questions (FAQs) about the Human Development Index (HDI): What Is the HDI?" Human Development Reports, accessed May 15, 2011,http://hdr.undp.org/en/statistics/hdi.

[5] UNDP, "Is the HDI Enough to Measure a Country's Level of Development?" Human Development Reports, accessed May 15, 2011, http://hdr.undp.org/en/statistics/hdi.

[6] UNDP, "Measuring Inequality: Gender-related Development Index (GDI) and Gender Empowerment Measure (GEM)," Human Development Reports, accessed January 3, 2011, http://hdr.undp.org/en/statistics/indices/gdi_gem.

[7] UNDP, "The Human Poverty Index (HPI)," Human Development Reports, accessed January 3, 2011, http://hdr.undp.org/en/statistics/indices/hpi.

[8] UNDP, "The Human Poverty Index (HPI)," Human Development Reports, accessed January 3, 2011, http://hdr.undp.org/en/statistics/indices/hpi.

[9] Kelly Evans, "'HIIC' Nations Are Acting Like Backwaters," Wall Street Journal, October 1, 2010, accessed January 3, 2011, http://online.wsj.com/article/SB1000142405274870478940457552440205 9410506.html.

[10] Kelly Evans, "'HIIC' Nations Are Acting Like Backwaters," Wall Street Journal, October 1, 2010, accessed January 3, 2011, http://online.wsj.com/article/SB1000142405274870478940457552440205 9410506.html.

4.2 Understanding the Developed World

LEARNING OBJECTIVES

1. Understand what the developed world is.
2. Identify the major developed economies.

The Developed World

Many people are quick to focus on the developing economies and emerging markets as offering the brightest growth prospects. And indeed, this is often the case. However, you shouldn't overlook the developed economies; they too can offer growth opportunities, depending on the specific product or service. The key is to understand what developed economies are and to determine their suitability for a company's strategy.

In essence, developed economies, also known as advanced economies, are characterized as postindustrial countries—typically with a high per capita income, competitive industries, transparent legal and regulatory environments, and well-developed commercial infrastructure. Developed countries also tend to have high human development index (HDI) rankings—long life expectancies, high-quality health care, equal access to education, and high incomes. In addition, these countries often have democratically elected governments.

In general, the developed world encompasses Canada, the United States, Western Europe, Japan, South Korea, Australia, and New Zealand. While these economies have moved from a manufacturing focus to a service orientation, they still have a solid manufacturing base. However, just because an economy is developed doesn't mean that it's among the largest economies. And, conversely, some of the world's largest economies—while growing rapidly—don't have competitive industries or transparent legal and regulatory environments. The infrastructure in these countries, while improving, isn't yet consistent or substantial enough to handle the full base of business and consumer demand. Countries like Brazil, Russia, India, and China—also known as BRIC—are hot emerging markets but are not yet considered developed by most widely accepted definitions. Section 4.4 "Emerging Markets" covers the BRIC countries and other emerging markets.

The following sections contain a sampling of the largest developed countries that focuses on the business culture, economic environment, and economic structure of each country. [1]

The United States

Geographically, the United States is the fourth-largest country in the world—after Russia, China, and Canada. It sits in the middle of North America, bordered to the north by Canada and to the south by Mexico. With a history steeped in democratic and capitalist institutions, values and entrepreneurship, the United States has been the driver of the global economy since World War II.

The US economy accounts for nearly 25 percent of the global gross domestic product (GDP). Recently, the severe economic crisis and recession have led to double-digit unemployment and record deficits. Nevertheless, the United States remains a global economic engine, with an economy that is about twice as large as that of the next single country, China. With an annual GDP of more than $14 trillion, only the entire European Union can match the US economy in size. An economist's proverb notes that when the US economy sneezes, the rest of the world catches a cold. Despite its massive wealth, 12 percent of the population lives below the poverty line. [2]

Throughout the cycles of growth and contractions, the US economy has a history of bouncing back relatively quickly. In recessions, the government and the business community tend to respond swiftly with measures to reduce costs and encourage growth. Americans often speak in terms of bull and bear markets. A bull market is one in which prices rise for a prolonged period of time, while a bear market is one in which prices steadily drop in a downward cycle.

The strength of the US economy is due in large part to its diversity. Today, the United States has a service-based economy. In 2009, industry accounted for 21.9 percent of the GDP; services (including finance, insurance, and real estate) for 76.9 percent; and agriculture for 1.2 percent. [3] Manufacturing is a smaller component of the economy; however, the United States remains a major global manufacturer. The largest manufacturing sectors are highly diversified and technologically advanced—petroleum, steel, motor vehicles, aerospace, telecommunications, chemicals, electronics, food processing, consumer goods, lumber, and mining.

The sectors that have grown the most in the past decades are financial services, car manufacturing, and, most important, information technology (IT), which has more than doubled its output in the past decade. It now accounts for nearly 10 percent of the country's GDP. As impressive as that figure is, it hardly takes into account the many ways in which IT has transformed the US economy. After all, improvements in information technology and telecommunications have increased the productivity of nearly every sector of the economy.

The United States is so big that its abundant natural resources account for only 4.3 percent of its GDP. Even so, it has the largest agricultural base in the world and is among the world's leading producers of petroleum and timber products. US farms produce about half the world's corn—though most of it is grown to feed beef and dairy cattle. The US imports about 30 percent of its oil, despite its own massive reserves. That's because Americans consume roughly a quarter of the world's total energy and more than half its oil, making them dependent on other oil-producing nations in some fairly troublesome ways.

The US retail and entertainment industries are very valuable to the economy. The country's media products, including movies and music, are the country's most visible exports. When it comes to business, the United States might well be called the "king of the jungle." Emboldened by a strong free-market economy, legions of US companies have achieved unparalleled success. One by-product of this competitive spirit is an abundance of secure, well-managed business partnerships at home and abroad. And although the majority of US companies aren't multinational giants, an emphasis on hard work and a sense of fair play pervade the business culture.

In a culture where entrepreneurialism is practically a national religion, the business landscape is broad and diverse. At one end are enduring multinationals, like Coca-Cola and General Electric, which were founded by visionary entrepreneurs and are now run by boards of directors and appointed managers who answer to shareholders. At the other end of the spectrum are small businesses—millions of them—many owned and operated by a single person.

Today, more companies than ever are "going global," fueled by an increased demand for varied products and services around the world. Expanding into new markets overseas—often through joint ventures and partnerships—is becoming a requirement for success in business.

Another trend that has gained much media attention is outsourcing—subcontracting work, sometimes to foreign companies. It's now quite common for companies of all sizes to pay outside firms to do their payroll, provide telecommunications support, and perform a range of operational services. This has led to a growth in small contractors, often operating out of their homes, who offer a variety of services, including advertising, public relations, and graphic design. [4]

European Union

Today, the European Union (EU) represents the monetary union of twenty-seven European countries. (Chapter 5 "Global and Regional Economic Cooperation and Integration", Section 5.2 "Regional Economic Integration" reviews the history of the EU and the factors impacting its outlook.) One of the primary purposes of the EU was to create a single market for business and workers accompanied by a single currency, the euro. Internally, the EU has made strides toward abolishing trade barriers, has adopted a common currency, and is striving toward convergence of living standards. Internationally, the EU aims to bolster Europe's trade position and its political and economic power. Because of the great differences in per capita income among member states (i.e., from $7,000 to $79,000) and historic national animosities, the EU faces difficulties in devising and enforcing common policies. The EU's strengths also come from the formidable strengths of some of its economic powerhouse members. Germany is the leading economy in the EU.

Spotlight on Germany

Germany has the fifth-largest economy in the world, after the United States, China, Japan, and India. With a heavily export-oriented economy, the country is a leading exporter of machinery, vehicles, chemicals, and household equipment and benefits from a highly skilled labor force. It remains the largest and strongest economy in Europe and the second most-populous country after Russia in Europe.

The country has a socially responsible market economy that encourages competition and free initiative for the individual and for business. The *Grundgesetz* (Basic Law) guarantees private enterprise and private property, but stipulates that these rights must be exercised in the welfare and interest of the public.

Germany's economic development has been shaped, in large part, by its lack of natural resources, making it highly dependent on other countries. This may explain why the country has repeatedly sought to expand its power, particularly on its eastern flank.

Since the end of World War II, successive governments have sought to retain the basic elements of Germany's complex economic system (the *Soziale Marktwirtschaft*). Notably, relationships between employer and employee and between private industry and government have remained stable. Over the years, the country has had few industrial disputes. Furthermore, active participation by all groups in the economic decision making process has ensured a level of cooperation unknown in many other Western countries. Nevertheless, high unemployment and high fiscal deficits are key issues.

Overall, living standards are high, and Germany is a prosperous nation. The majority of Germans live in comfortable housing with modern amenities. The choice of available food is broad and includes cuisine from around the world. Germans enjoy luxury cars, and technology and fashion are big industries. Under federal law, workers are guaranteed minimum income, vacation time, and other benefits. Recently, the government has focused on economic reforms, particularly in the labor market, and tax reduction.

Germany is home to some of the world's most important businesses and industries. Daimler, Volkswagen, and BMW are global forces in the automotive field. Germany remains the fourth-largest auto manufacturer behind China, Japan, and the United States. German BASF, Hoechst, and Bayer are giants in the chemical industry. Siemens, a world leader in electronics, is the country's largest employer, while Bertelsmann is the largest publishing group in the world. In the banking industry, Deutsche Bank is one of the world's largest. In addition to these international giants, Germany has many small- and medium-sized, highly specialized firms.

These businesses make up a disproportionately large part of Germany's exports.

Services drive the economy, representing 72.3 percent (in 2009) of the total GDP. Industry accounts for 26.8 percent of the economy, and agriculture represents 0.9 percent. Despite the strong services sector, manufacturing remains one of the most important components of the Germany economy. Key German manufacturing industries are among the world's largest and most technologically advanced producers of iron, steel, coal, cement, chemicals, machinery, vehicles, machine tools, electronics, food and beverages, shipbuilding, and textiles. Manufacturing provides not only significant sources of revenue but also the know-how that Germany exports around the world. [5]

Japan

Located off the east coast of Asia, the Japanese archipelago consists of four large islands—Honshu, Hokkaido, Kyushu, and Shikoku—and about four thousand small islands, which when combined are equal to the size of California.

The American occupation of Japan following World War II laid the foundation for today's modern economic and political society. The occupation was intended to demilitarize Japan, to fully democratize the government, and to reform Japanese society and the economy. The Americans revised the then-existing constitution along the lines of the British parliamentary model. The Japanese adopted the new constitution in 1946 as an amendment to their original 1889 constitution. On the whole, American reforms rebuilt Japanese industry and were welcomed by the Japanese. The American occupation ended in 1952, when Japan was declared an independent state.

As Japan became an industrial superpower in the 1950s and 1960s, other countries in Asia and the global superpowers began to expect Japan to participate in international aid and defense programs and in regional industrial-development programs. By the late 1960s, Japan had the third-largest economy in the world. However, Japan was no longer free from foreign influences. In one century, the country had gone from being relatively isolated to being dependent on the rest of the world for its resources with an economy reliant on trade.

In the post–World War II period, Japanese politics have not been characterized by sharp divisions between liberal and conservative elements, which in turn have provided enormous support for big business. The Liberal Democratic Party (LDP), created in 1955 as the result of a merger of two of the country's biggest political parties, has been in power for most of the postwar period. The LDP, a major proponent of big business, generally supports the conservative viewpoint. The "Iron Triangle," as it is often called, refers to the tight relationship among Japanese politicians, bureaucrats, and big business leaders.

Until recently, the overwhelming success of the economy overshadowed other policy issues. This is particularly evident with the once powerful Ministry of International Trade and Industry (MITI). For much of Japan's modern history, MITI has been responsible for establishing, coordinating, and regulating specific industry policies and targets, as well as having control over foreign trade interests. In 2001, its role was assumed by the newly created METI, the Ministry of Economy, Trade and Industry.

Japan's post–World War II success has been the result of a well-crafted economic policy that is closely administered by the government in alliance with large businesses. Prior to World War II, giant corporate holding companies called *zaibatsu* worked in cooperation with the government to promote specific industries. At one time, the four largest zaibatsu organizations were Mitsui, Mitsubishi, Sumitomo, and Yasuda. Each of the four had significant holdings in the fields of banking, manufacturing, mining, shipping, and foreign marketing. Policies encouraged lifetime employment, employer paternalism, long-term relationships with suppliers, and minimal competition. Lifetime employment continues today, although it's coming under pressure in the ongoing recession. This policy is often credited as being one of the stabilizing forces enabling Japanese companies to become global powerhouses. [6]

The zaibatsus were dismantled after World War II, but some of them reemerged as modern-day *keiretsu*, and many of their policies continue to have an effect on Japan. Keiretsu refers to the intricate web of financial and nonfinancial relationships between companies that virtually links together in a pattern of formal and informal cross-ownership and mutual obligation. The keiretsu nature of Japanese business has made it difficult for foreign companies to penetrate the commercial sector. In response to recent global economic challenges, the government and private businesses have recognized the need to restructure and deregulate parts of the economy, particularly in the financial sector. However, they have been slow to take action, further aggravating a weakened economy.

Japan has very few mineral and energy resources and relies heavily on imports to bring in almost all of its oil, iron ore,

lead, wool, and cotton. It's the world's largest importer of numerous raw materials including coal, copper, zinc, and lumber. Despite a shortage of arable land, Japan has gone to great lengths to minimize its dependency on imported agricultural products and foodstuffs, such as grains and beef. Agriculture represents 1.6 percent of the economy. The country's chief crops include rice and other grains, vegetables, and fruits. Japanese political and economic protectionist policies have ensured that the Japanese remain fully self-sufficient in rice production, which is their main staple.

As with other developed nations, services lead the economy, representing 76.5 percent of the national GDP. [7] Industry accounts for 21.9 percent of the country's output. Japan benefits from its highly skilled workforce. However, the high cost of labor combined with the cost of importing raw materials has significantly affected the global competitiveness of its industries. Japan excels in high-tech industries, particularly electronics and computers. Other key industries include automobiles, machinery, and chemicals. The service industry is beginning to expand and provide high-quality computer-related services, advertising, financial services, and other advanced business services. [8]

KEY TAKEAWAYS

- The developed economies, also known as advanced economies, are characterized as postindustrial countries—typically with a high per capita income, competitive industries, transparent legal and regulatory environments, and well-developed commercial infrastructure. Developed countries also tend to have high human development index (HDI) rankings (i.e., long life expectancies, high-quality health care, equal access to education, and high incomes). In addition, these countries often have democratically elected governments.
- The major developed economies include Canada, the United States, Western Europe, Japan, South Korea, Australia, and New Zealand.
- The United States is the fourth-largest country in the world—after Russia, China, and Canada. However, the United States is the world's largest single-country economy and accounts for nearly 25 percent of the global gross domestic product (GDP). The strength of the US economy is due in large part to its diversity. Today, the United States has a service-based economy. In 2009, industry accounted for 21.9 percent of the GDP; services (including finance, insurance, and real estate) for 76.9 percent; and agriculture for 1.2 percent.

- Germany, a member of the EU (European Union), has the fifth-largest economy in the world. The country is a leading exporter of machinery, vehicles, chemicals, and household equipment and benefits from a highly skilled labor force. It is the largest and strongest economy in Europe. Services drive the economy, representing 72.3 percent (in 2009) of the total GDP. Industry accounts for 26.8 percent of the economy, and agriculture represents 0.9 percent.

- Japan's post–World War II success has been the result of a well-crafted economic policy closely administered by the government in alliance with large businesses. It also benefits from its highly skilled workforce. Japan has very few mineral and energy resources and relies heavily on imports to bring in almost all of its oil, iron ore, lead, wool, and cotton. It is the world's largest importer of numerous raw materials including coal, copper, zinc, and lumber. As with other developed nations, services lead the economy, representing 76.5 percent of the national GDP, while industry accounts for 21.9 percent of the country's output.

EXERCISES

(AACSB: Reflective Thinking, Analytical Skills)

1. Describe the main characteristics of developed economies.
2. Select one developed country. Utilize a combination of the *World Factbook* at https://www.cia.gov/library/publications/the-world-factbook/geos/xx.html and the HDI at http://hdr.undp.org/en/statistics/, and formulate an opinion of why you think the country is a developed country. Identify the country's per capita GDP and HDI ranking to assess its level of development.

[1] The sections that follow are excerpted in part from two resources owned by author {Author's Name retracted as requested by the work's original creator or licensee}'s firm, Atma Global: CultureQuest Business Multimedia Series and bWise: Business Wisdom Worldwide. The excerpts are reprinted with permission and attributed to the country-specific product when appropriate.

[2] US Central Intelligence Agency, "North America: United States: Economy," World Factbook, accessed January 7, 2011, https://www.cia.gov/library/publications/the-world-factbook/geos/us.html.

[3] US Central Intelligence Agency, "North America: United States: Economy," World Factbook, accessed January 7, 2011, https://www.cia.gov/library/publications/the-world-factbook/geos/us.html.

4.3 Developing World
LEARNING OBJECTIVES

1. Understand what the developing world is.
2. Identify the major developing economies and regions.

The Developing World

The developing world refers to countries that rank lower on the various classifications from. The residents of these economies tend to have lower discretionary income to spend on nonessential goods (i.e., goods beyond food, housing, clothing, and other necessities). Many people, particularly those in developing countries, often find the classifications limiting or judgmental. The intent here is to focus on understanding the information that a global business professional will need to determine whether a country, including a developing country, offers an interesting local market. Some countries may perceive the classification as a slight; others view it as a benefit. For example, in global trade, being a developing country sometimes provides preferences and extra time to meet any requirements dismantling trade barriers.

[In the World Trade Organization (WTO), t] here are no WTO definitions of "developed" and "developing" countries. Members announce for themselves whether they are "developed" or "developing" countries. However, other members can challenge the decision of a member to make use of provisions available to developing countries.

Developing country status in the WTO brings certain rights. There are for example provisions in some WTO Agreements which provide developing countries with longer transition periods before they are required to fully implement the agreement and developing countries can receive technical assistance.

That a WTO member announces itself as a developing country does not automatically mean that it will benefit from the unilateral preference schemes of some of the developed country members such as the Generalized System of Preferences (GSP). In practice, it is the preference giving country which decides the list of developing countries that will benefit from the preferences. [1]

Developing countries sometimes find that their economies improve and gradually they become emerging markets. Many developing economies represent old cultures and rich histories. Focusing only on today's political, economic, and social conditions distorts the picture of what these countries have been and what they might become again. This category hosts the greatest number of countries around the world.

Did You Know?

It's important to understand that the term *developing countries* is different from Third-World countries, which was a traditional classification for countries along political and economic lines. It helps to understand how this terminology has evolved.

When people talk about the poorest countries of the world, they often refer to them with the general term Third World, and they think everybody knows what they are talking about. But when you ask them if there is a Third World, what about a Second or a First World, you almost always get an evasive answer…

The use of the terms First, the Second, and the Third World is a rough, and it's safe to say, outdated model of the geopolitical world from the time of the cold war.

There is no official definition of the first, second, and the third world. Below is OWNO's [One World—Nations Online] explanation of the terms…

After World War II the world split into two large geopolitical blocs and spheres of influence with contrary views on government and the politically correct society:

1. The bloc of democratic-industrial countries within the American influence sphere, the "First World."

2. The Eastern bloc of the communist-socialist states, the "Second World."

3. The remaining three-quarters of the world's population, states not aligned with either bloc were regarded as the "Third World."

4. The term "Fourth World," coined in the early 1970s by Shuswap Chief George Manuel, refers to widely unknown nations (cultural entities) of indigenous peoples, "First Nations" living within or across national state boundaries…

The term "First World" refers to so-called developed, *capitalist*, industrial countries, roughly, a bloc of countries aligned with the United States after World War II, with more or less common political and economic interests: North America, Western Europe, Japan and Australia. [2]

Developing economies typically have poor, inadequate, or unequal access to infrastructure. The low personal incomes result in a high degree of poverty, as measured by the human poverty index (HPI) from. These countries, unlike the developed economies, don't have mature and competitive industries. Rather, the economies usually rely heavily on one or more key industries—often related to commodities, like oil, minerals mining, or agriculture. Many of the developing countries today are in Africa, parts of Asia, the Middle East, parts of Latin America, and parts of Eastern Europe.

Developing countries can seem like an oxymoron in terms of technology. In daily life, high-tech capabilities in manufacturing coexist alongside antiquated methodologies. Technology has caused an evolution of change in just a decade or two. For example, twenty years ago, a passerby looking at the metal shanties on the sides of the streets of Mumbai, India, or Jakarta, Indonesia, would see abject poverty in terms of the living conditions; today, that same passerby peering inside the small huts would see the flicker of a computer screen and almost all the urban dwellers—in and around the shanties—sporting cell phones. Installing traditional telephone infrastructure was more costly and time-consuming for governments, and consumers opted for the faster and relatively cheaper option of cell phones.

Did You Know?

Gillette's Innovative Razor Sales
Companies find innovative ways to sell to developing world markets. Procter & Gamble (P&G)'s latest innovation is a Gillette-brand eleven-cent blade. "Gillette commands about 70 percent of the world's razor and blade sales, but it lags behind rivals in India and other developing markets, mainly because those consumers can't afford to buy its flagship products." [3] The company has designed a basic blade, called the Gillette Guard, that isn't available in the United States or other richer economies. The blade is designed for the developing world, with the goal of bringing "'more consumers into Gillette,' says Alberto Carvalho, P&G's vice president of male grooming in emerging markets…Winning over low-income consumers in developing markets is crucial to the growth strategy,….The need to grow in emerging markets is pushing P&G to change its product development strategy. In the past, P&G would sell basically the same premium Pampers diapers, Crest toothpaste, or Olay moisturizers in developing countries, where only the wealthiest consumers could afford them." [4] The company's approach now is to determine what the consumers can afford in each country and adjust the product features to meet the target price.

Global companies also recognize that in many developing countries, the local government is the buyer—particularly for higher value-added products and services, such as high-tech items, equipment, and infrastructure development. In addition, companies assess the political and economic environment in order to evaluate the risks and opportunities for business in managing key government relationships. In much of Africa and the Middle East, where the economies rely on one or two key industries, the governments remain heavily involved in sourcing and awarding key contracts. The lack of competitive domestic industry and local transparency has also made these economies ripe for graft. [5]

Ethics in Action

Studies have shown that developing countries that are known to be rich in hydrocarbons [mainly oil] are plagued with corruption and environmental pollution. Paradoxically, most extractive resource-rich developing countries are found in the bottom third of the World Bank's composite governance indicator rankings. Again, on the Transparency International Corruption Perception Index (CPI), 2007—most of the countries found at the bottom of the table are rich in mineral resources. This is indicative of high prevalence of corruption in these countries. [6]

Major Developing Economies and Regions

The Middle East

The Middle East presents an interesting challenge and opportunity for global businesses. Thanks in large part to the oil-dependent economies, some of these countries are quite wealthy. In looking at per capita gross domestic product (GDP) adjusted for purchasing power parity (PPP) for select countries, interestingly enough Qatar, Kuwait, United Arab Emirates (UAE), and Bahrain all rank in the top twenty-five. Only Saudi Arabia ranks much lower, due mainly to its larger population; however, it still has a per capita GDP (PPP) twice as high as the global average.

While the income level suggests a strong opportunity for global businesses, the inequality of access to goods and services, along with an inadequate and uncompetitive local economy, present both concerns and opportunities. Many of these countries are making efforts to shift from being an oil-dependent economy to a more service-based economy. Dubai, one of the seven emirates in the UAE, has sought to be the premier financial center for the Middle East. The financial crisis of 2008 has temporarily hampered, but not destroyed, these ambitions.

Spotlight on the UAE

Tucked into the southeastern edge of the Arabian Peninsula, the UAE borders Oman, Qatar, and Saudi Arabia. The UAE is a federation of seven states, called emirates because they are ruled by a local emir. The seven emirates are Abu Dhabi (capital), Dubai, Al-Shāriqah (or Sharjah), Ajmān, Umm al-Qaywayn, Ras'al-Khaymah, and Al-Fujayrah (or Fujairah). Dubai and Abu Dhabi have received the most global attention as commercial, financial, and cultural centers.

Amusing Anecdote

Dubai, the Las Vegas of the Middle East
Dubai is sometimes called the Vegas of the Middle East in reference to its glitzy malls, buildings, and consumerism culture. Luxury brands and excessive wealth dominate the culture as oil wealth is displayed brashly. Among other things, Dubai is home to Mall of the Emirates and its indoor alpine ski resort. [7] Dubai also features aggressive architectural projects, including the spire-topped Burj Khalifa, which is the tallest skyscraper in the world, and the Palm Islands, which are man-made, palm-shaped, phased land-reclamation developments. Visionary proposals include the world's first underwater hotel, the Hydropolis. Dubai's tourism attracts visitors from its more religiously conservative neighbors such as Saudi Arabia as well as from countries in South Asia, primarily for its extensive shopping options. Dubai as well as other parts of the UAE hope to become major global-tourist destinations and have been building hotels, airports, attractions, shops, and infrastructure in order to facilitate this economic diversification goal.

The seven emirates merged in the early 1970s after more than a century of British control of their defense and military affairs. Thanks to its abundant oil reserves, the UAE has grown from an impoverished group of desert states to a wealthy regional commercial and financial center in just thirty years. Its oil reserves are ranked as the world's seventh-largest and the UAE possesses one of the most-developed economies in West Asia. [8] It is the twenty-second-largest economy at market exchange rates and has a high per capita gross domestic product, with a nominal per capita GDP of US$49,995 as per the International Monetary Fund (IMF). [9] It is the second-largest in purchasing power per capita and has a relatively high human development index (HDI) for the Asian continent, ranking thirty-second globally. [10] The UAE is classified as a high-income developing economy by the IMF. [11]

For more than three decades, oil and global finance drove the UAE's economy; however, in 2008–9, the confluence of falling oil prices, collapsing real estate prices, and the international banking crisis hit the UAE especially hard. [12]

Today, the country's main industries are petroleum and petrochemicals (which account for a sizeable 25 percent of total GDP), fishing, aluminum, cement, fertilizers, commercial ship repair, construction materials, some boat building, handicrafts, and textiles. With the UAE's intense investment in infrastructure and greening projects, the coastlines have been enhanced with large parks and gardens. Furthermore, the UAE has transformed offshore islands into agricultural projects that produce food.

A key issue for the UAE is the composition of its residents and workforce. The UAE is perhaps one of the few countries in the world where expatriates outnumber the local citizens, or nationals. In fact, of the total population of almost 5 million people, only 20 percent are citizens, and the workforce is composed of individuals from 202 different countries. As a result, the UAE is an incredible melting pot of cultural, linguistic, and religious groups. Migrant workers come mainly from the Indian subcontinent: India, Pakistan, Bangladesh, and Sri Lanka as well as from Indonesia, Malaysia, the Philippines, and other Arab nations. A much smaller number of skilled managers come from Europe, Australia, and North America. While technically the diverse population results in a higher level of religious diversity than neighboring Arab countries, the UAE is an Islamic country.

The UAE actively encourages foreign companies to open branches in the country, so it is quite common and easy for foreign corporations to do so. Free-trade zones allow for 100 percent foreign ownership and no taxes. Nevertheless, it's common and in some industries required for many companies outside the free-trade zone to have an Emirati sponsor or partner.

While the UAE is generally open for global business, recently Research in Motion (RIM) found itself at odds with the UAE government, which wanted to block Blackberry access in the country. RIM uses a proprietary encryption technology to protect data and sends it to offshore servers in North America. For some countries, such as the UAE, this data encryption is perceived as a national security threat. Some governments want to be able to access the communications of people they consider high security threats. The UAE government and RIM were able to resolve this issue, and Blackberry service was not suspended.

Human rights concerns have forced the UAE government to address the rights of children, women, minorities, and guest workers with legal consistency, a process that is continuing to evolve. Today, the UAE is focused on reducing its dependence on oil and its reliance on foreign workers by diversifying its economy and creating more opportunities for nationals through improved education and increased private sector employment. [13]

Africa

For the past fifty years, Africa has been ignored in large part by most global businesses. Initial efforts that focused on access to minerals, commodities, and markets have given way to extensive local corruption, wars, and high political and economic risk.

When the emerging markets came into focus in the late 1980s, global business turned its attention to Asia. However, that's changing as companies look for the next growth opportunity. "A growing number of companies from the U.S., China, Japan, and Britain are eager to tap the potential growth of a continent with 1 billion people—especially given the weak outlook in many developed nations….Meanwhile, African governments are luring investments from Chinese companies seeking to tap the world's biggest deposits of platinum, chrome, and diamonds." [14]

Within the continent, local companies are starting to and expanding to compete with global companies. These homegrown firms have a sense of African solidarity.

Big obstacles for businesses remain. Weak infrastructure means higher energy costs and trouble moving goods between countries. Cumbersome trade tariffs deter investment in new African markets. And the majority of the people in African countries live well below the poverty line, limiting their spending power.

Yet many African companies are finding ways around these barriers. Nigerian fertilizer company, Notore Chemicals Ltd., for example, has gone straight to governments to pitch the benefits of improved regional trade, and recently established a distribution chain that the company hopes will stretch across the 20 nations of Francophone Africa. [15]

While the focus remains on South Africa, it's only a matter of time until businesses shift their attention to other African nations. Political unrest, poverty, and corruption remain persistent challenges for the entire continent. A key factor in the continent's success will be its ability to achieve political stability and calm the social unrest that has fueled regional civil conflicts.

Google in Africa

Africa has some of the lowest Internet access in the world, and yet Google has been attracted to the continent by its growth potential. Africa with its one billion people is an exciting growth market for many companies.

"The Internet is not an integral part of everyday life for people in Africa," said Joe Mucheru of Google's Kenya office...

[Yet] Google executives say Africa represents one of the fastest growth rates for Internet use in the world. Nigeria already has about 24 million users and South Africa and Kenya aren't far behind, according to World Bank and research sites like Internet World Stats...

Other technology companies have also set their sights on the continent. Microsoft Corp., International Business Machines Corp. [IBM], Cisco Systems Inc., and Hewlett-Packard Co. have sales offices throughout Africa, selling laptops, printers and software to fast-growing companies and an emerging middle class. [16]

Infrastructure, oil, gas and technology firms are not the only businesses looking to Africa; the world of advertising has now set its sights on the continent, following their largest global corporate clients.

Advertising growth in Africa is soaring, driven by telecom companies, financial services firms and makers of consumer products...

"All of our major clients, as they are looking for geographical expansion opportunities, have Africa and the Middle East high up on their priority list, if not at the top," said Martin Sorrell, chief executive of WPP, the world's largest advertising company by revenue...

Nigeria, Angola, Kenya and Ghana have some of the highest growth potential, ad executives say....

And with so many languages and big cultural differences, crafting ads can be labor-intensive, marketing executives say. Ads in Nigeria, for example, need to be in five different languages to reach a large audience.

Africa and the Middle East together represent only about 2.9 percent, or around $14 billion, of the total $482.6 billion global ad market, according to market research firm, eMarketer. [17]

This small percentage indicates the potential for significant advertising growth and a huge opportunity for global advertising and marketing firms.

Spotlight on Nigeria
Located in West Africa, Nigeria shares borders with the Republic of Benin, Chad, Cameroon, and Niger. Its southern

coast lies on the Atlantic Ocean. Nigeria is Africa's most populous country and its second largest economy. Goldman Sachs included Nigeria in its listing of the "Next Eleven" emerging economies after the BRIC countries (Brazil, Russia, India and China). [18]

Since its independence from the United Kingdom in 1960, Nigeria has seen civil war, ethnic tensions and violence, and military rule. Although recent elections have been marred by violence and accusations of voter fraud, Nigeria is technically experiencing its longest period of civilian government since its independence. However, Nigeria remains a fractious nation, divided along ethnic and religious lines.

As noted in the Ethics in Action sidebar in this section, developing country economies that are primarily dependent on oil have widespread government corruption. The Nigerian government continues to face the challenge of reforming a petroleum-based economy, whose revenues have been squandered through corruption and mismanagement, and institutionalizing the early efforts at democracy. "Oil-rich Nigeria, long hobbled by political instability, corruption, inadequate infrastructure, and poor macroeconomic management, has undertaken several reforms over the past decade. Nigeria's former military rulers failed to diversify the economy away from its overdependence on the capital-intensive oil sector, which provides 95 percent of foreign exchange earnings and about 80 percent of budgetary revenues." [19]

The economy of Nigeria is one of the largest in the world, with GDP (PPP) at $341 billion. However on a per capita basis, the country ranks at a dismal 183rd in the world, with a per capita GDP (PPP) at just $2,300. Seventy percent of its population remains below the poverty line, and the country ranks at 142nd on the human development index (HDI) rankings for 2010. Despite the low quality of life rankings for the country, Nigeria's population of more than 152 million make it an interesting long-term prospect for global businesses, particularly as economic conditions enable more Nigerians to achieve middle-income status.[20]

Nigeria's economy is about evenly split between agriculture (which accounts for 32.5 percent), industry at 33.8 percent, and services at 33.7 percent. The country's main industries are crude oil, coal, tin, columbite, rubber products, wood, hides and skins, textiles, cement and other construction materials, food products, footwear, chemicals, fertilizer, printing, ceramics, and steel. [21]

Nigeria received IMF funding in 2000 but pulled out of the program in 2002, when it failed to meet the economic reform requirements, specifically failing to meet spending and exchange rate targets. In recent years, the Nigerian government has begun showing the political will to implement the market-oriented reforms urged by the IMF, such as to modernize the banking system, to curb inflation by blocking excessive wage demands, and to resolve regional disputes over the distribution of earnings from the oil industry. The country's main issues remain government corruption, poverty, inadequate infrastructure, and ethnic violence, mainly over the oil producing Niger Delta region. Nevertheless, with continued economic and political reforms, the expanding economy and large potential domestic market will continue to attract global business attention to Nigeria. [22]

How Do Developing Countries Become Emerging Markets?

It's important to remember that all of the emerging-market countries were once considered developing nations. What resulted in the transition? Are today's developing countries turning into tomorrow's emerging markets? These are the questions that not only global economists and development experts ask, but—more relevantly—global businesses as well.

Typically, the factors that result in the classification of many countries as developing economies are the same ones that— once addressed and corrected—enable these countries to become emerging markets. Countries that seek to implement transparency in the government as well as in the political and economic institutions help inspire business confidence in their countries. Developing the local commercial infrastructure and reducing trade barriers attract foreign businesses. Educating the population equally and creating a healthy domestic workforce that is both skilled and relatively cheap is another incentive for global business investment.

Unlike emerging markets, developing and underdeveloped countries still need special attention from international aid agencies to prevent starvation, mass disease and political instability. Developing countries need to improve their education systems and create a strategy to begin their transition to the global emerging market. Companies from developed and emerging markets should play an important role in this process. Companies from emerging markets are especially crucial, as they have a great deal of experience operating in conditions of non-developed economies. [23]

While developing countries comprise the largest category, it's important to remember that there are wide differences between the nations in this classification. If a company wants to stay ahead of the competition, it must be able to identify those countries ripe for development. Early entrance into these markets helps create first-mover advantage in terms of brand recognition, forging essential relationships with the government and the private sector, and harnessing any early-stage cost advantages. First-mover advantage refers the benefits that a company gains by entering into a market first or introducing a new product or service before its competitors.

Did You Know?

Mongolia Is Becoming Hot!
For most people, the country of Mongolia conjures images of a remote place near China—a movie location. It hasn't been at the forefront of anyone's attention for almost two decades, and yet the "IMF says that Mongolia will be one of the fastest-growing economies over the next decade." [24] This is a remarkable turnaround for a country that lost its Soviet assistance—one-third of its economy—in 1990 with the fall of the Soviet Union. Traditionally an agriculture-based economy, Mongolia is landlocked by its borders with China and Russia and is the approximately the size of Western Europe, with a relatively small population. However, its tremendous untapped mineral resources, which include coal, copper, molybdenum, fluorspar, tin, tungsten, gold, and oil, are attracting foreign investment. The country is a major exporter to China—its large, relatively rich neighbor. The country is exploring new resources as well; according to Prime Minister Sukhbaatar Batbold, "Wind power could be a major opportunity for Mongolia and for export to China." [25]

KEY TAKEAWAYS

- The developing world refers to countries that rank lower on the various classifications from. The residents of these economies tend to have lower discretionary income to spend on nonessential goods.

- The poorest countries of the world are often referred to as the Third World. However, the Third World is not synonymous with the developing world, instead it is part of an outdated model of the geopolitical world from the time of the Cold War. It encompasses three-quarters of the world's population and consists of the states that were not aligned with either the democratic-industrial bloc or the eastern, communist-socialist bloc.

- A developing country, in order to evolve into an emerging market, must (1) seek to implement transparency in its government as well as in its political and economic institutions to help inspire business confidence in its country, (2) develop the local commercial infrastructure and reduce trade barriers to attract foreign businesses, and (3) educate the population equally and create a healthy domestic workforce that's both skilled and relatively cheap.

EXERCISES

(AACSB: Reflective Thinking, Analytical Skills)

1. Describe the main characteristics of developing economies.
2. Select one developing country. Utilize a combination of the *World Factbook* at https://www.cia.gov/library/publications/the-world-factbook/geos/xx.html and the HDI at http://hdr.undp.org/en/statistics/, and formulate an opinion of why you think the country is a developing country. Identify its per capita GDP and HDI ranking to assess its level of development.

[1] "Who Are the Developing Countries in the WTO?" World Trade Organization, accessed January 5, 2011, http://www.wto.org/english/tratop_e/devel_e/d1who_e.htm.

[2] "Worlds within the World?" One World—Nations Online, accessed January 5, 2011, http://www.nationsonline.org/oneworld/third_world_countries.htm.

[3] Ellen Byron, "Gillette's Latest Innovation in Razors: The 11-Cent Blade," Wall Street Journal, October 1, 2010, accessed January 5, 2011, http://online.wsj.com/article/SB10001424052748704789404575524273890970954.html.

[4] Ellen Byron, "Gillette's Latest Innovation in Razors: The 11-Cent Blade," Wall Street Journal, October 1, 2010, accessed January 5, 2011, http://online.wsj.com/article/SB10001424052748704789404575524273890970954.html.

[5] The sections that follow are excerpted in part from two resources owned by author {Author's Name retracted as requested by the work's original creator or licensee}'s firm, Atma Global: CultureQuest Business Multimedia Series and bWise: Business Wisdom Worldwide. The excerpts are reprinted with permission and attributed to the country-specific product when appropriate.

[6] Gilbert Sam, "Ghana's Oil Find: Benefits and Nightmares," Daily Guide, April 30, 2009, reprinted on Modern Ghana website, accessed January 5, 2011, http://www.modernghana.com/news/213863/1/ghanas-oil-find-benefits-and-nightmares.html.

[7] "About Mall of the Emirates," Mall of the Emirates, accessed January 5, 2011, http://www.malloftheemirates.com/MOE/En/MainMenu/AboutMOE/tabid/64/Default.aspx.

[8] US Central Intelligence Agency, "Country Comparison: Oil—Proved Reserves," World Factbook, accessed January 5, 2011, https://www.cia.gov/library/publications/the-world-factbook/rankorder/2178rank.html.

[9] "IMF Data Mapper," International Monetary Fund, accessed January 5, 2011, http://www.imf.org/external/datamapper/index.php.

[10] UNDP, "Human Development Index (HDI)—2010 Rankings," Human Development Report 2010: The Real Wealth of Nations and Pathways to Human Development, November 4, 2010, accessed January 5, 2011, http://hdr.undp.org/en/statistics.

[11] Wikipedia, s.v. "United Arab Emirates," last modified February 15, 2011, accessed February 16, 2011, http://en.wikipedia.org/wiki/United_Arab_Emirates.

[12] US Central Intelligence Agency, "Middle East: United Arab Emirates," World Factbook, accessed January 5, 2011, https://www.cia.gov/library/publications/the-world-factbook/geos/ae.html.

[13] bWise: Business Wisdom Worldwide: U.A.E. (New York: Atma Global, 2011).

[14] Renee Bonorchis, "Africa Is Looking Like a Dealmaker's Paradise," BusinessWeek, September 30, 2010, accessed January 5, 2011, http://www.businessweek.com/magazine/content/10_41/b4198020648051.htm.

[15] Will Connors and Sarah Childress, "Africa's Local Champions Begin to Spread Out," Wall Street Journal, May 26, 2010, accessed January 5, 2011, http://online.wsj.com/article/SB10001424052748704912004575252593400609032.html.

[16] Will Connors, "In Africa, Google Sows the Seeds for Future Growth," Wall Street Journal, May 15, 2010, accessed January 5, 2011, http://online.wsj.com/article/SB100014240527487048662045752238635726307000.html.

[17] Ruth Bender and Suzanne Vranica, "Global Ad Agencies Flocking to Africa," Wall Street Journal, October 22, 2010, accessed January 5, 2011, http://online.wsj.com/article/SB100014240527023047414045755641937839503520.html.

[18] Jim O'Neill and Anna Stupnytska, "Global Economics Paper No. 192: The Long-Term Outlook for the BRICs and N-11 Post Crisis," accessed February 16, 2011, http://www2.goldmansachs.com/ideas/brics/long-term-outlook-doc.pdf.

[19] US Central Intelligence Agency, "Africa: Nigeria," World Factbook, accessed January 5, 2011, https://www.cia.gov/library/publications/the-world-factbook/geos/ni.html.

[20] US Central Intelligence Agency, "Africa: Nigeria," World Factbook, accessed January 5, 2011, https://www.cia.gov/library/publications/the-world-factbook/geos/ni.html; UNDP, "Nigeria," International Human Development Indicators 2010, accessed January 5, 2011, http://hdrstats.undp.org/en/countries/profiles/NGA.html.

[21] US Central Intelligence Agency, "Africa: Nigeria," World Factbook, accessed January 5, 2011, https://www.cia.gov/library/publications/the-world-factbook/geos/ni.html.

[22] US Central Intelligence Agency, "Africa: Nigeria," World Factbook, accessed January 5, 2011, https://www.cia.gov/library/publications/the-world-factbook/geos/ni.html.

[23] Vladimir Kvint, "Define Emerging Markets Now," Forbes, January 28, 2008, accessed January 5, 3011, http://www.forbes.com/2008/01/28/kvint-developing-countries-oped-cx_kv_0129kvint.html.

[24] Charlie Rose, "Charlie Rose Talks to Mongolia's Prime Minister," BusinessWeek, September 30, 2010, accessed January 5, 2011, http://www.businessweek.com/magazine/content/10_41/b4198014855514.htm.

[25] Charlie Rose, "Charlie Rose Talks to Mongolia's Prime Minister," BusinessWeek, September 30, 2010, accessed January 5, 2011, http://www.businessweek.com/magazine/content/10_41/b4198014855514.htm.

4.4 Emerging Markets

LEARNING OBJECTIVES

1. Understand what the emerging markets and BRIC countries are.
2. Identify key emerging markets.

What Exactly Is an Emerging Market?

On September 18, 2008, the *Economist* argued that the term *emerging market* is dated.

Is it time to retire the phrase "emerging markets"? Many of the people interviewed for this special report think so. Surely South Korea, with sophisticated companies such as Samsung, has fully emerged by now. And China already has the world's fourth-largest economy. [*Note:* As of summer 2010, China has the world's second-largest economy.]

The term "emerging markets" dates back to 1981, recalls the man who invented it, Antoine van Agtmael. He was trying to start a "Third-World Equity Fund" to invest in developing-country shares, but his efforts to attract money were constantly rebuffed. "Racking my brain, at last I came up with a term that sounded more positive and invigorating: emerging markets. 'Third world' suggested stagnation; 'emerging markets' suggested progress, uplift and dynamism." [1]

The 2008 article clearly articulates the challenge for global businesses, as well as analysts, who are trying to both define and understand the group of countries typically termed the emerging market. In a 2008 *Forbes* article, Vladimir Kvint, president of the International Academy of Emerging Markets, noted the following:

During the last 20 years, the global business world has gone through drastic, but mostly positive changes. In the 1980s, international business was essentially an exclusive club of the 20 richest countries. This changed as dictatorships and command economies collapsed throughout the world. Countries that once prohibited foreign investment from operating on their soil and were isolated from international cooperation are now part of the global marketplace.

I remember well when, in 1987, the first $80 million of foreign origin was allowed to be invested in the former Soviet Union. So-called "patriots" accused Mikhail Gorbachev of selling their motherland. Twenty years later, in 2007, Russia received about $43 billion of foreign direct investment, and emerging-market countries received about 40 percent of the $1.5 trillion FDI [foreign direct investment] worldwide. [2]

The definition of an emerging market is complex and inconsistent. As discussed in Section 4.1 "Classifying World Economies", there is a plethora of statistics and data available. The application and interpretation of this information varies depending on who is doing the analysis—a private sector business, the World Bank, the International Monetary Fund (IMF), the World Trade Organization (WTO), the United Nations (UN), or any number of global economic, political,

and trade organizations. The varying statistics, in turn, produce a changing number of countries that "qualify" as emerging markets. For many businesspeople, the definition of an emerging market has been simply a country that was once a developing country but has achieved rapid economic growth, modernization, and industrialization. However, this approach can be limiting.

Knowing that there are wide inconsistencies, how do we define emerging markets consistently from the perspective of global businesses? First, understand that there are some common characteristics in terms of local population size, growth opportunities with changes in the local commercial infrastructure, regulatory and trade policies, efficiency improvements, and an overall investment in the education and well-being of the local population, which in turn is expected to increase local incomes and purchasing capabilities.

As a leading economic and strategic thinker in the area of emerging markets, Kvint concludes from his research that there are several major characteristics of emerging markets, which create "a comfortable and attractive environment for global business, foreign investment and international trade. Based on my study, an emerging market country can be defined as a society transitioning from a dictatorship to a free market-oriented economy, with increasing economic freedom, gradual integration within the global marketplace, an expanding middle class, improving standards of living and social stability and tolerance, as well as an increase in cooperation with multilateral institutions." [3]

In April 2010, the chief of HSBC, the largest bank in Europe, forecasted a change for the next ten years in which six new countries (the CIVETS: Colombia, Indonesia, Vietnam, Egypt, Turkey and South Africa) will replace the BRIC countries (Brazil, Russia, India and China) of the last decade:

"Each has a very bright future," HSBC CEO Michael Geoghegan said of the CIVETS, named after the cat-like animals found in some of the countries. "Each has large, young, growing population. Each has a diverse and dynamic economy. And each, in relative terms is politically stable."...

"Within three years, for the first time, the economic firepower of emerging markets will overtake the developed world, measured by purchasing power parity. It's a defining moment."

The size of the emerging market middle class will swell to 1.2 billion people by 2030, from 250 million in 2000, he said.

That bodes well for financial services, as households tend to open bank accounts and ask for other products when income reaches about $10,000, Geoghegan said.

"Many Chinese households are about to hit this level. They number about 33 million now. But they will quadruple to 155 million by 2014. In India, the change will also be dramatic," he said. [4]

In addition, to illustrate how experts debate the next group of emerging-market countries, the Goldman Sachs economist who created the term *BRIC* in 2001 in a report for the investment bank has added a new group, *MITSK*. A January article in the British *Financial Times* newspaper notes, "Jim O'Neill, who coined the term 'Bric', is about to redefine further emerging markets. The chairman of Goldman Sachs Asset Management (until end of 2010) plans to add Mexico, South Korea, Turkey and Indonesia into a new grouping with the Brics—Brazil, Russia, India and China—that he dubs 'growth markets. It's just pathetic to call these four "emerging markets." [5]

The *Financial Times* continues to note how the Brics have frequently been dismissed as a marketing ploy. However, the nine-year-old term has spawned government summits, investment funds, business strategies and a host of countries keen to join. Adding that Mr. O'Neill himself stated that the term "emerging markets" was no longer helpful because it encompassed countries with too great a range of economic prospects. Mexico and South Korea account for 1.6 per cent each of global GDP in nominal terms. Turkey and Indonesia are worth 1.2 and 1.1 per cent respectively. China is the world's second-largest economy, at 9.3 per cent of global GDP (the US is worth 23.6 per cent), while Brazil, India and Russia combined provide a further 8 per cent. O'Neill offers a new approach that will involve looking at fresh ways to measure exposure to equity markets beyond market capitalization—for example, looking at gross domestic product, corporate revenue growth and the volatility of asset returns. [6]

These opinions and analyses by different economists are highlighted in this chapter to illustrate that the category of emerging markets is complex, evolving, and subject to wide interpretation. So how then do savvy global professionals sort through all of this information? Managers focus on the criteria for emerging markets in an effort to take advantage of newly emerging ones. While there are differing opinions on which countries are emerging, it's clear that global businesses are focused on the groups of countries offering strong domestic markets. Many of these emerging-market

countries are also home to companies that are taking advantage of the improved business conditions there. These companies are becoming world-class global competitors in their industries. Regardless of which definition or classification is used, the largest emerging markets remain lucrative and promising. [7]

Key Emerging Markets

Asia

Spotlight on China

Located below Russia on the western seaboard of the Pacific Ocean, China is about as large as the continent of Europe and slightly larger than the United States. It is the third-largest country in the world after Russia and Canada.

For more than fifty years, China has had a centrally planned economy in which the state controlled most of the commercial activity. Under Mao Zedong's over forty-year leadership, the Chinese government kept a firm grip on the country's economic activity. That grip has been loosening since the 1980s as a result of Deng Xiaoping's reforms, which introduced some strong capitalist characteristics into China's centrally planned economy. Since the early 1980s, the Chinese economy has been in transition away from central planning and toward a market-driven economy. In today's model, market forces work in conjunction with state ownership and intervention. This system is commonly referred to as "a socialist market economy with Chinese characteristics." The government now realizes that it can't provide all the resources needed to fuel the economy by itself and that the private sector has a major role to play in providing investment—and jobs. Today, China's economy is caught between two opposing forces—a burgeoning market sector that is outgrowing government control and the inability of that market to function efficiently due to continued influence by the state on production and prices.

In 1979, China instituted economic reforms, established "special economic zones," and opened its economy to foreign investments and companies. This change in attitude brought remarkable changes to the socialist market economy, resulting in improved living standards and new social attitudes. As local provinces have benefited from foreign investment, particularly in the south, central economic control has weakened. Since 1978, industrial output has increased more than six-fold, in large part due to foreign manufacturers and investors who have established operations in China (usually as joint ventures with corporations owned or influenced by the Chinese government but also with some private-sector companies).

In many areas, China remains a predominantly agricultural society. Major crops include rice, barley, millet, tobacco, sweet potatoes, wheat, soybeans, cotton, tea, raw silk, rapeseed, corn, peanuts, watermelon, and sesame seed. Under the 1979 regulations, peasants were permitted to lease land for private farming and were allowed to sell for profit any surplus produce above the quota demanded by the state in the open market. There are still more collectives than family farms, but this is changing. Besides agriculture, the leading industries include textiles, machinery, cement, chemicals, communications and transportation equipment, building materials, and electronic machinery and equipment.

The results of these reforms have been spectacular—China's economy has grown an average of 9 percent per year over the last fifteen years and is now the second largest in the world. If it continues at this rate of expansion, some pundits predict China could eventually replace the United States in first place.

One of the most interesting facets of China's economic transition has been the rise of the middle class. Prior to the 1980s, there was only a small middle class, with most people occupying the lower echelons of the economic ladder. Now it's estimated that some 300 million Chinese have entered the middle-class cohort, fueling a huge increase in consumer spending.

In the 1990s, the seven-day workweek was progressively lowered to five days. With increased time off and longer national holidays, the average Chinese person now has more leisure time—and more time to spend money on consumer goods.

Take a look at some of China's major cities—particularly those along the eastern coast—and you'll see soaring skyscrapers, glitzy boutiques, luxury hotels, and expensive cars. There's a feeling of economic prosperity and high-powered consumerism. Apartment buildings aimed at the prosperous middle-class market are sprouting up all over China's major cities.

Travel just a few hundred miles from the cities, though, and you'll encounter farming scenes reminiscent of the early days of the twentieth century. The economic disparity between the urban rich and the rural poor and all its accompanying problems are likely to continue for the foreseeable future.

With a burgeoning market sector that's outgrowing government control, China is now at the crossroads of reform. Yet despite the high growth rates, enormous challenges remain, including marked regional inequality, an entrenched and at times inflexible bureaucracy, high unemployment, a large floating population, and environmental degradation. Most commentators agree that the country has recognized the complex issues facing its economic future and is now ready to address them.

The growth of China's telecommunications industry is outstripping expectations. The number of mobile-phone subscribers, for example, has grown from 1 million in 1994 to around 700 million in 2009. [8] But the industry's expansion hasn't automatically led to large profits. The growth has been fueled by an increase in competition, putting downward pressure on prices. In fact, a 2009 *China Daily* article claims that China's telecom market the biggest battlefield in the world. [9]

Internet use is also expanding rapidly, although its spread is hindered by the government's attempts to regulate the sector and control access as evidenced in the case between the government and Google in the spring of 2010, as discussed in the case study in Chapter 1 "Introduction". Keeping up with the newest technology in the areas of delivery networks, broadband access, payment procedures, and security has created enormous opportunities. The government has made extensive efforts to invest in infrastructure and emerging technologies.

In 2009, agriculture accounted for an estimated 10.6 percent of China's gross domestic product (GDP), industry represented 46.8 percent, and services totaled 42.6 percent. Apart from agriculture, China's leading industries include "mining and ore processing of iron, steel, aluminum, and other metals, coal; machine building; armaments; textiles and apparel; petroleum; cement; chemicals; fertilizers; consumer products, including footwear, toys, and electronics; food processing; transportation equipment, including automobiles, rail cars and locomotives, ships, and aircraft; telecommunications equipment; commercial space launch vehicles; and satellites." [10] The production of consumer goods is now one of the fastest-growing sectors in the economy. Once a source of cheap consumer electronics for the West, China is now producing those items for its own rapidly expanding internal market.

Chinese economic statistics must still be regarded with a degree of skepticism. Often it's unclear where the numbers have originated or how they have been derived. Still, there's no doubt that phenomenal growth is taking place, and there are pressures for a more transparent economic reporting system.

In the past, China didn't see the environment as an issue in its race to industrialize. Now, there is an increasing sense of environmental awareness. "China is changing from the factory of the world to the clean-tech laboratory of the world. It has the unique ability to pit low-cost capital with large-scale experiments to find models that work." [11]

Government attention and foreign investment have been focused on further developing the country's inadequate infrastructure, including roads, railways, seaports, communications systems, and power generation. Industrial capability, in both light and heavy industries, has also improved. China is a vast country rich in natural resources, including coal, oil, gas, various metals, ores, and minerals.

The largest Chinese companies are those that have capitalized on China's natural strengths and have state backing or are state-run. For example, PetroChina is the country's largest oil and gas producer and distributor. PetroChina is the listed arm of state-owned China National Petroleum Corporation (CNPC). It is one of the world's largest oil producers and is the world's most valuable company by market value as of 2010, exceeding a trillion-dollar market capitalization. China's largest companies have benefited from this combination of government support through access to capital and markets along with private-sector efficiencies.

China joined the WTO in December 2001, and it will likely be drawn even more into the global economy as companies continue to vie for access to its 1.3 billion consumers and cheap and productive labor pool. Most companies expect that dealing with China will now become more straightforward, if not easier. Whatever the future brings, the Chinese economy continues to be a powerhouse of growth and opportunity. [12]

Spotlight on India
India is officially called the Republic of India and is also known as Hindustan or Bharat. As the seventh-largest country in the world, India spans 1.267 million square miles; it's about one-third the size of the United States. India shares borders in the northwest with Pakistan; in the north with China, Bhutan, and Nepal; and in the east with Bangladesh and Myanmar (Burma). The Indian Territory also extends to the Andaman and Nicobar Islands in the Bay of Bengal as well as to Lakshadweep in the Arabian Sea.

Prior to the mid-1980s, the country pursued a policy of socialism with the state planning and controlling many

sectors of the economy. Foreign investment had been discouraged except in the area of technology transfers. Since the early 1990s, India has embarked on an economic liberalization scheme that has proven beneficial to the country.

In 1991, India was on the brink of defaulting on its foreign debt. The government responded with a series of successful measures to initiate widespread economic reforms, including reducing export and import barriers, dismantling some of its swollen bureaucracy, making the currency partially convertible, and eliminating the black market for foreign currency and gold. Efforts were also made to privatize or increase the efficiencies of unprofitable state companies. Finance Minister Manmohan Singh (who later became prime minister) was successful in beginning to dismantle the "License Raj," an intricate system of government economic control through permits and quotas. Various policies initiated by the government provided a larger role for the private sector and encouraged foreign investment. As a result, investment increased, though at much lower levels than in other Asian countries.

Since the 1990s, central government intervention, licensing, and regulation have decreased, as have bureaucratic inefficiencies. India boasts an established free-market system; a sophisticated industrial and manufacturing base; and a huge pool of skilled, low-to-moderate-cost workers, including professional managers. Economic gains, particularly as a result of further integration into the global economy, have provided improved the standard of living for all communities. The country's 2.1 percent annual population growth ensures that its population will surpass China's within the next decade and remains a significant problem for the government, as limited resources threaten the distribution of economic reform benefits.

The country is rich in natural resources, such as rubber, timber, chromium, coal, iron, manganese, copper ore, petroleum, bauxite, titanium, mica salt, limestone, and gypsum. The country is one of the world's leading producers of iron ore, and coal accounts for nearly 40 percent of all mined minerals. India also has reserves of natural gas and oil, but it remains a net importer of crude oil because its domestic generation is insufficient to meet demand. In addition, India has deposits of precious stones, including diamonds, emeralds, gold, and silver. Cut diamonds are one of India's biggest exports.

Agriculture remains an important economic sector, contributing roughly 17 percent of the country's GDP and employing almost 52 percent of the workforce. Major crops include rice, wheat, pulses, sugarcane, cotton, jute, oilseeds, tea, coffee, tobacco, onions, and potatoes. Other important agricultural interests include dairy products, sheep, goats, poultry, and fish.

Until the mid-1960s, India imported much of its food. The Green Revolution focused on improving farming techniques, increasing mechanization, and irrigating as well as introducing high-yielding seeds. All of these have increased agricultural production and made the country self-sufficient in food production. The government also provides incentives to farmers to expand production. Most of India's farms tend to be small and provide subsistence for the families that operate them. They aren't geared for commercial purposes. Northern fertile areas, such as those in the state of Punjab, account for much of the export production.

While India has more cattle than any other country, it isn't farmed for food consumption as Hindus are not supposed to eat beef. The animals are used for a variety of other purposes, including plowing land, producing milk for dairy products, and supplying leather.

The growth of Indian industry, which accounts for about 28.2 percent of its GDP and 14 percent of employment, has resulted in widespread improvements and diversity in the country's manufacturing base. The major manufacturing industries include cotton and jute textiles; iron, steel, and other basic metals; petrochemicals; electrical machinery and appliances; transport equipment; chemicals; cement; fertilizers; software; medicines and pharmaceuticals; and food products. The power, electronics, food processing, software, transportation equipment, and telecommunications industries are developing rapidly. The financial sector, including banking and insurance, is well developed, although efforts to modernize it are underway.

State-run entities continue to control some areas of telecommunications, banking, insurance, public utilities, and defense, as well as the production of minerals, steel, other metals, coal, natural gas, and petroleum. There have been some steps taken to shift more control to the private sector, although on a gradual and closely monitored scale.

Services account for 54.9 percent of the GDP, but employ only 34 percent of the workforce. The most dramatic change in the economy has come from the computer-programming industry, as companies around the world have turned to India for outsourcing. With its skilled, relatively cheap, and English-speaking professional workforce, India has received a much-needed boost in the form of investment and foreign earnings. This is expected to have continued significant impact on the economy, business environment, and the social values and expectations of the Indian population.

India's technology firms have gained global recognition. One of the best known is Infosys. Founded in 1981 by seven Indian entrepreneurs, Infosys today is a NASDAQ-listed global consulting and information technology services company—with $5.4 billion in revenues. Throughout twenty-nine years of growth, Infosys, in addition to other well-managed Indian companies, has been well positioned to take advantage of the Indian government's efforts at economic liberalization that began in the early 1990s. Under this program, the government has systematically reduced trade barriers and embraced globalization. These changes have led to India's emergence as the global destination for software services talent. [13]

Amusing Anecdote

India's Currency Gets a Visible Promotion
A clear sign of a currency's importance is its symbol. All of the major global economies' currencies (e.g., the dollar, pound, euro, and yen) have one. In July 2010, the Indian government announced that there was a new symbol for the rupee. Not yet available on keyboards or any electronic devices, the symbol will replace the often-used Rs. "The symbol is a matter of national pride, underscoring 'the robustness of the Indian economy,' said Ambika Soni, India's Information Minister" to the *New York Times*. [14]

Europe

Spotlight on Russia
Russia is the largest country in the world, stretching across two continents and eleven time zones. Eleven seas and two oceans wash the banks of this 6.6 million square mile territory. The south and southeast of the country are covered with mountains, and the central part is a plain, furrowed with rivers. Around 7,000 lakes spread over the western part of Russia. The border between Europe and Asia runs down the west side of the Ural Mountains, about 807 miles east of Moscow.

Anyone looking to do business in Russia today needs to comprehend the array of changes that have impacted the nation over the past three decades. Rising to power in the 1980s, General Secretary Mikhail Gorbachev was the first leader to end repressive political controls and to suffer nationalist movements in the constituent republics. Gorbachev set the forces in action that would overturn the Communist regime and seal his own expulsion. He relaxed government control on the media and the Russian culture, implementing a policy of *glasnost*, or openness and candor. Gorbachev also sought *perestroika* (i.e., restructuring) of the economy and political system that preserved some of the more positive elements of socialism. Gorbachev gained international fame as the head of the Soviet bloc who helped put an end to the Cold War. To reach a common understanding, Gorbachev met repeatedly with US Presidents Ronald Reagan and George Bush, helping broker arms-reduction agreements.

During Gorbachev's term, Communist regimes began to fall all over Eastern Europe. In an abrupt departure from previous Soviet policy, Gorbachev refused to intervene. The Berlin Wall fell in 1989, and Gorbachev did nothing to stop it. Sensing weakness, republic parliaments all over the Soviet bloc asserted their sovereignty; a few even went so far as to assert complete independence. In 1991, when Gorbachev attempted to negotiate with the republics, alarmed Soviet leaders attempted a coup. The coup failed, but Gorbachev had lost his political cache to rival Boris Yeltsin, who succeeded Gorbachev as the hero of the era. This changed political, economic, and military dynamics around the world.

While the changes Gorbachev implemented did little to develop the Soviet Union's struggling economy, he did overhaul Soviet elections by reintroducing multiparty elections in 1989. This essentially invited political dissidents and reform-minded leaders into the parliament. These individuals soon began to challenge Gorbachev's leadership, pushing him to implement more changes. In 1991, Gorbachev conceded to their demands and installed their leader, Boris Yeltsin, as the president of Russia.

The economic and political challenges the newly independent country faced were considerable. The inefficiency of the Soviet government had left its stamp on every area of the economy. Russia's industries had to update their technology, retrain their workers, and cut back their workforces. Russians were largely unfamiliar with Western ways of doing business and found it difficult to make the changes mandated by capitalism. Unemployment soared, and the plight of most Russians grew increasingly desperate.

In this climate of desperation, Yeltsin's government instituted a so-called shock therapy program intended to galvanize the economy by reducing barriers to free trade. These policies, while well intentioned, produced sweeping inflation that almost completely devalued Russian currency. Western newspapers were plastered with images of Russians waiting in long lines, carrying bags of devalued bills. In an attempt to address the crisis, the government introduced a privatization program, which resulted in rampant cronyism and theft of state property.

While the government encouraged the emergence of small businesses and the already-flourishing black-market trade was finally legitimized, small businesses faced many obstacles inadvertently caused by the government's inefficiency. The tax system was so disorganized that the government couldn't obtain the funds necessary to sustain adequate police or military forces. Health care and other basic welfare systems collapsed, and organized crime forced small businesses to make regular payoffs.

As quality of life took a precipitous drop for the majority of the Russian population, the gap between the rich and poor broadened dramatically. But crime lords weren't the only ones profiting from the gap, the privatization of government assets enabled a few well-placed individuals to turn those assets into their private property. The nouveau riche, as this class of Russians was called, tended to be ostentatious, and the construction of elaborate mansions at a time when ordinary Russians were suffering, outraged the citizens' sense of justice.

Since 1991, Russia has struggled to establish a market economy. The country "has undergone significant changes since the collapse of the Soviet Union, moving from a globally-isolated, centrally-planned economy to a more market-based and globally-integrated economy." [15] Today, Russia has shifted back to a more centralized, semi-authoritarian state. "Economic reforms in the 1990s privatized most industry, with notable exceptions in the energy and defense-related sectors. Nonetheless, the rapid privatization process, including a much criticized 'loans-for-shares' scheme that turned over major state-owned firms to politically-connected 'oligarchs', has left equity ownership highly concentrated." [16] Corruption remains a challenge for businesses operating in Russia. New business legislation, including a commercial code and the establishment of an arbitration court to resolve business disputes, has passed. However, the "protection of property rights is still weak and the private sector remains subject to heavy state interference." [17] However, the system continues to evolve. Additionally, global economic conditions have impacted the value of the ruble and the status of the country's international debts. [18]

Russian industry is primarily split between globally competitive commodity producers—in 2009 Russia was the world's largest exporter of natural gas, the second largest exporter of oil, and the third largest exporter of steel and primary aluminum—and other less competitive heavy industries that remain dependent on the Russian domestic market. This reliance on commodity exports makes Russia vulnerable to boom and bust cycles that follow the highly volatile swings in global commodity prices. The government since 2007 has embarked on an ambitious program to reduce this dependency and build up the country's high-technology sectors but with few results so far. A revival of Russian agriculture in recent years has led to Russia shifting from being a net grain importer to a net grain exporter. Russia has a highly industrialized and agrarian economy. Almost ten million people are engaged in the agriculture industry. Along with its vast spaces, Russia has always been known for its amazing resources. The country produces 30 percent of the world's nonferrous, rare, and noble metals; 17 percent of the world's crude oil; 30 percent of natural gas; and it holds 40 percent of the world's known natural gas deposits. Today, agriculture accounts for 4.7 percent of the economy, industry represents 34.8 percent, and services total 60.5 percent (based on a 2009 estimate). [19]

Did You Know?

Russia, the Summer of 2010 Drought, and Wheat: Understanding the Domino Effect on Countries and Business

Think global business is all about leading-edge, high-tech gadgets, consumer products, or industrial manufacturing items? Think again. Since the early days of ancient trade, commodities, such as wheat, corn, spices, rice, and cotton, have been the primary objects of trade. Even today, wheat and corn, the most basic of foodstuffs across all cultures, can still make governments and economies—developed, developing, and emerging—quiver as a result of natural and unnatural disruptions to their marketplaces. Recently, in the summer of 2010, Russia experienced a crippling drought that led to a four-month ban on all grain exports. "Russia has become an increasingly important force in the global supply of grains and the move reignited fears that nervous governments would begin hoarding their own supplies, potentially causing a shortage….Countries such as Egypt, the world's number one importer of wheat, which had bought Russian wheat, now must consider other options." [20] Russia provided almost 15 percent of the world's wheat supply for global exports from the 2009–10 crop. As a result of the ban, many global packaged-foods companies, including Swiss giants, Migros-Genossenschafts-Bund and Coop Schweiz, and British-based Premier Foods, considered possible price increases as a result of the wheat ban. [21]

Like China, Russia's largest companies are either state-run or have state backing, providing the government with access to resources, capital, and markets. Business analysts and investors are eager for the government to privatize more of the largest firms. "The Economic Development Ministry said in July [of 2010] that the privatization list for 2011–2013 included oil pipeline monopoly Transneft, Russia's largest shipping company Sovcomflot, oil major Rosneft, the country's largest banks Sberbank and VTB, the Federal Grid Company of Unified Energy System, the Russian Agricultural Bank, hydropower holding company RusHydro and other assets." [22]

RUSAL is one of Russia's largest privately held companies. Headquartered in Moscow, RUSAL is the world's largest aluminum company and accounts for almost 11 percent of the world's primary aluminum output and 13 percent of the world's alumina production. The company has aggressively used a strategy of global mergers and acquisition to grow its operations, which now cover nineteen countries and five continents. To raise capital, the company listed on the Hong Kong Stock Exchange in 2010. [23]

Africa

Spotlight on South Africa

South Africa makes up the southern portion of the continent of Africa, from the Atlantic Ocean in the west to the Indian Ocean in the east. With a total land area of 750,000 miles, including the Prince Edward Islands, the country is the twenty-seventh largest in the world, or approximately the same size as France, Spain, and Portugal combined.

Initially a refueling station for Dutch sailors traveling to the East, South Africa gradually developed an agricultural sector, based on fruit, wine, and livestock production, along the coast of the Cape of Good Hope. All of this changed dramatically with the discovery of minerals in the late nineteenth century. Subsequently, the country emerged as the leading manufacturing and industrial economy on the African continent.

Surging prices for gold and the high demand for base metals and other mineral products propelled the country's economy after World War II. South Africa was fortunate to have this strong economic base when international sanctions were applied in the 1970s and 1980s.

Nonetheless, import substitution and sanction busting were necessary for economic survival, and the country as a whole became increasingly isolated. A handful of massive corporations controlled most of the country's wealth and provided the majority of goods and services. The national government controlled those sectors of the economy seen as critical to the national interest of the apartheid state, including transportation, telecommunications, and the media.

South Africa practiced legal racial segregation, under the apartheid system. In the 1970s, worldwide disapproval of apartheid led to economic sanctions against South Africa. An international oil embargo was imposed in 1974, and the country was suspended from participating in the United Nations. "Disinvestment (or divestment) from South Africa was first advocated in the 1960s, in protest of South Africa's system of Apartheid, but was not implemented on a significant scale until the mid-1980s. The disinvestment campaign…is credited as pressuring the South African Government to embark on negotiations ultimately leading to the dismantling of the apartheid system." [24]

During the 1980s, there was global political and economic isolation. Many global investment firms pulled out of South Africa as a result of the public outcry and investor pressures against apartheid. While global firms, such as PepsiCo, Coca-Cola, IBM, ExxonMobil, and others, didn't leave South Africa, they endured public boycotts and protests in their home countries. The moral arguments against apartheid eventually won. After F. W. de Klerk was elected president in 1989, change was immediate. Political prisoners were released, and a national debate was initiated on the future of the country. The ban was lifted on the African National Congress (ANC), and in February 1990, Nelson Mandela was released from prison after twenty-seven years behind bars. He was elected president in 1994, and to further unite the country, de Klerk agreed to serve as deputy president in his administration.

Following the 1994 election, South Africa's period as an international outcast came to a swift end. The country was readmitted into the United Nations, and sanctions were lifted. For the first time South Africans could travel freely, had a free press, and participated in truly democratic institutions. Global businesses could once again do business with South Africa without fear of investor or public backlash.

South Africa has emerged as a free-market economy with an active private sector. The country strives to develop a prosperous and balanced regional economy that can compete in global markets. As an emerging-market country, South Africa relies heavily on industrial imports and capital. Specialty minerals and metals, machinery, transport equipment, and chemicals are important import sectors.

Minerals and energy are central to South Africa's economic activity, and manufacturing, the country's largest industry, is still based to a large extent on mining. South Africa receives more foreign currency for its gold than for any other single item, although it exports other minerals including platinum, diamonds, coal, chrome, manganese, and iron ore. It is the world's largest producer of platinum, gold, and chromium. Agricultural products, such as fruit, wool, hides, corn, wheat, sugarcane, fruits, vegetables, beef, poultry, mutton, dairy products, and grains, account for 3 percent of its GDP.

Today, industry accounts for 31 percent of the country's GDP, focusing on mining and automobile assembly, metalworking, machinery, textiles, iron and steel, chemicals, fertilizer, foodstuffs, and commercial ship repair.

During the years of apartheid, the economy of South Africa stagnated and appeared directionless. That changed after the election of the Government of National Unity in 1994. The post apartheid government has clear priorities, including economic growth, job creation, and inequality reduction.

Under apartheid, large conglomerates achieved near-cartel status and stifled competition. In many instances, this occurred with tacit government approval, and many promising small companies were bought or forced out of the market by financial muscle. The overall effect was a blunting of innovation and growth throughout the country. Since the end of apartheid, the government has made significant strides in promoting small-business development, in part by offering large corporations incentives to donate funds to small companies.

With the growth of their international market, South African businesses are expanding their focus outward. Companies such as Anglo American and South African Breweries (SAB) are listed on the London Stock Exchange, and Sappi (formerly South African Pulp and Paper Industries), a giant paper concern, has invested in the US market.

As part of its effort to improve South Africa's business climate, the government has made a strong commitment to privatization. To date, it has sold parts of South African Airways and Telkom (the former telecommunications monopoly), as well as other companies. The government is also offering incentives to overseas companies to partner with disadvantaged community-owned South African enterprises and requires businesses with government contracts to make contributions to social programs.

Since the end of apartheid, corporate life in South Africa has changed dramatically, and the business scene is now evolving at a fast pace. The government is committed to liberalizing the country's economy in fundamental ways, and corporate culture is changing in response. Programs to encourage economic growth and globalization have attracted new companies from abroad and introduced new approaches to doing business. Companies have also experienced a boost in creative energy. Today, the hallmarks of the South African business culture are change and transformation.

Day to day, doing business in South Africa is relatively easy and becoming easier as regulations are modified to reflect international norms. At the same time, new policies, particularly in matters of employment and labor, are making business life more complex.

While South African society is officially color free, in practical terms there are many areas of business that are still segregated. Overseas companies looking to break into public-sector contract work would be wise to establish joint ventures with companies owned by blacks.

South Africa has one of the highest union-membership rates in the world—a total of 3.2 million workers, or 25 percent of the employed workforce. Although the labor movement has a reputation for militancy, strikes are virtually unheard of since the job market has become so tight, and labor relations have generally improved.

Because of the country's strong union culture, managers tend to be highly sensitive to union concerns in the workplace, and union issues are never far from the surface in decision making. In fact, unions used rolling mass action to disrupt the apartheid economy, and this weapon is still available.

Services now total 65 percent of the economy. South Africa has a well-developed financial services sector, and the South African Futures Exchange ranks among the top-ten international (i.e., non US) stock exchanges. Trade with countries on the African continent has been increasing rapidly. Finished goods and prepared foodstuffs, as well as base metals and chemicals, are in particularly high demand. [25] Overall, the country has the most-sophisticated market economy on the African continent. Between its economic profile and its well-developed physical infrastructure, South Africa has become an attractive place to do business. [26]

"For much of the past decade, Asia has been the go-to continent for companies interested in tapping fast-growing economies. Now, Wal-Mart Stores' agreement on September 27, 2010 to buy South African retailer Massmart Holdings for $4.6 billion may signal a shift toward Africa as another deal-making destination for multinationals." [27] The deal was Walmart's largest in a decade, which indicates just how serious global businesses are taking the emerging opportunity in Africa. Other large representative acquisitions include HSBC's stake in Nedbank Group and Japan's Nippon Telephone & Telegraph (NTT) purchase of Dimension Data. While these acquisitions are South African companies, it's only a matter of time until the rest of Africa triggers global commercial interest as well.

Latin America

Spotlight on Brazil

With nearly 3.4 million square miles in area, Brazil is about the size of the continental United States and the fifth-largest country in the world. It covers nearly half of the South American continent, and, with the exception of Chile and Ecuador, it shares a border with every country in South America.

Brazil remains Latin America's largest market, the world's fifth-most-populous country, and the world's tenth-largest economy in GDP terms. Government policies for disinflation and income support programs for the poorest families have contributed to a significant reduction in poverty rates and income inequality in recent years. However, poverty remains a stubborn challenge for Brazil.

Brazil's economic history has progressed in cycles, each focused on a single export item. Soon after the arrival of the first Europeans, wood was the hot commodity. In the sixteenth and seventeenth centuries, the scramble was for sugar. Eighteenth-century traders lusted for gems, gold, and silver; and finally, in the nineteenth and twentieth centuries, coffee was king. Rubber had its day as well. Also of economic importance during these cycles were cattle and agriculture, though they mainly served the domestic market.

Brazil is best known as a leading world producer of coffee and sugar. These commodities, no doubt, enable the country to trade on the world's stage and remain critical to the Brazilian economy to this day. Brazil is also one of the largest producers and exporters of soybeans, orange juice, cocoa, and tropical fruits. A little known fact, however, is that today, nonagricultural products—namely, auto parts, aircraft, and machinery—bring in more money. Ironically, it's the oft-maligned industrial programs of the 1960s and 1970s that deserve much of the credit for these successes.

Industry came to Brazil in the mid-1800s. The depression of 1929 threw a wrench in development, but the setback was only temporary; during subsequent decades, expansion was steady. Growth was especially healthy between the 1960s and the oil crisis of 1979. It wasn't until the 1980s, when interest rates busted the charts, that the economy began its descent. The flow of foreign and domestic capital slowed to a trickle, devaluations played havoc with the national currency, and foreign companies initiated debilitating cutbacks or left the country altogether. Severely handicapped in its ability to invest, Brazil plunged into a period of runaway inflation and negative growth rates. To this day, the 1980s are referred to as "the lost decade."

In the 1990s, the government honed in on three economic goals: (1) trade reform, (2) stabilizing the economy, and (3) building the country's relationship with the global financial community. In 1994, Minister of Finance Fernando Henrique Cardoso (often called FHC), launched the Real Plan, which inspired the name for Brazil's currency (i.e., the real). The plan, with its emphasis on the need for a strong currency, high interest rates, strict limits on government spending, and an opening up of the economy, touched off a boom in Brazil. Foreign capital began pouring in. Brazil's economic wizards outwitted the forces that wracked Mexico in the mid-1990s as well as Southeast Asia in 1997 and 1998. Their main premise was a strong (i.e., increasingly overvalued) real and spiraling interest rates. However, this premise lost validity in January 1999, when the Central Bank stopped defending the real and let the currency float freely.

Economically, the remainder of the 1990s was a qualified success. In 2001 and 2002, Brazil managed to avoid the fate of its neighbor, Argentina. Nevertheless, the country's finances remained a disaster. Improved prudent economic policy led to early repayment of IMF loans in 2005 and stabilized the economy. Although Brazil has seen significant rates of economic growth in recent years, this growth hasn't benefited all sectors or all groups to the same extent. Simultaneously, the economy is undergoing major structural changes as large-scale privatization of formerly state-owned enterprises continues. [28]

Today, "characterized by large and well-developed agricultural, mining, manufacturing, and service sectors, Brazil's economy outweighs that of all other South American countries, and Brazil is expanding its presence in world markets." [29] Its industry accounts for 25.4 percent of the GDP and focuses on textiles, shoes, chemicals, cement, lumber, iron ore, tin, steel, aircraft, motor vehicles and parts, and other machinery and equipment. Agriculture, including coffee, soybeans, wheat, rice, corn, sugarcane, cocoa, citrus, and beef, accounts for 6.1 percent of the economy, while services total 68.5 percent. [30]

Since 2003, Brazil has steadily improved macroeconomic stability, building up foreign reserves, reducing its debt profile by shifting its debt burden toward real-denominated and domestically held instruments, adhering to an inflation target, and committing to fiscal responsibility. Brazil has also experienced the global "recession, as global demand for Brazil's commodity-based exports dwindled and external credit dried up. However, Brazil was one of the first emerging markets to begin a recovery." [31]

Today, Brazil is home to several global firms. Embraer builds innovative small jets and has become the world's biggest producer of smaller jet aircraft. The Brazilian food processors, Sadia and Perdigao, exemplify the international entrepreneurship of modern Brazil. Each is a $2 billion enterprise and exports about half of its annual production. Brazil's abundant resources for producing pork, poultry, and grains and its ideal growing conditions for animal feed provide these companies with many advantages. Both Sadia and Perdigao also have world-class global distribution and supply-chain management systems for product categories in frozen foods, cereals, and ready-to-eat meals.

KEY TAKEAWAYS

- There are some common characteristics of emerging markets in terms of the size of the local population, the opportunity for growth with changes in the local commercial infrastructure, the regulatory and trade policies, improvements in efficiencies, and an overall investment in the education and well-being of the local population, which in turn is expected to increase local incomes and purchasing capabilities.

- A current definition of an emerging market is a country that can be defined as a society transitioning from a centrally managed economy to a free-market-oriented economy, with increasing economic freedom, gradual integration within the global marketplace, an expanding middle class, and improving standards of living, social stability, and tolerance, as well as an increase in cooperation with multilateral institutions.

EXERCISES

(AACSB: Reflective Thinking, Analytical Skills)
1. Describe the main characteristics of emerging-market economies.
2. Select one emerging-market country. Utilize a combination of the *World Factbook* at https://www.cia.gov/library/publications/the-world-factbook/geos/xx.html and the HDI at http://hdr.undp.org/en/statistics, and formulate an

opinion of why you think the country is an emerging country. Identify its per capita GDP and HDI ranking to assess its level of development.

[1] "Ins and Outs: Acronyms BRIC Out All Over," Economist, September 18, 2008, accessed January 6,

2011, http://www.economist.com/node/12080703.

[2] Vladimir Kvint, "Define Emerging Markets Now," Forbes, January 28, 2008, accessed January 5,

3011, http://www.forbes.com/2008/01/28/kvint-developing-countries-oped-cx_kv_0129kvint.html.

[3] Vladimir Kvint, "Define Emerging Markets Now," Forbes, January 28, 2008, accessed January 5,

3011, http://www.forbes.com/2008/01/28/kvint-developing-countries-oped-cx_kv_0129kvint.html.

[4] Steven Slater, "After BRICs, Look to CIVETS for Growth—HSBC CEO," Reuters, April 27, 2010, accessed January 6, 2011, http://www.reuters.com/article/idUSLDE63Q26Q20100427.

[5] Jennifer Hughes, "'Bric' Creator Adds Newcomers to List," Financial Times, January 16, 2010, accessed January 5,

3011, http://www.ft.com/cms/s/0/f717c8e8-21be-11e0-9e3b-00144feab49a.html#ixzz1MKbbO8ET.

[6] Jennifer Hughes, "'Bric' Creator Adds Newcomers to List," Financial Times, January 16, 2010, accessed January 5,

3011, http://www.ft.com/cms/s/0/f717c8e8-21be-11e0-9e3b-00144feab49a.html#ixzz1MKbbO8ET.

[7] The sections that follow are excerpted in part from two resources owned by author {Author's Name retracted as requested by the work's original creator or licensee}'s firm, Atma Global: CultureQuest Business Multimedia Series and bWise: Business Wisdom Worldwide. The excerpts are reprinted with permission and attributed to the country-specific product when appropriate. The discussion about Asia also draws heavily from the author's book Doing Business in Asia: The Complete Guide, 2nd ed. (New York: Jossey-Bass, 1998).

[8] Wang Xing, "Battle Begins over 3G Market," China Daily, October 19, 2009, accessed May 17,

2011, http://www.chinadaily.com.cn/business/2009-10/19/content_8808873.htm.

[9] Wang Xing, "Battle Begins over 3G Market," China Daily, October 19, 2009, accessed May 17,

2011, http://www.chinadaily.com.cn/business/2009-10/19/content_8808873.htm.

[10] US Central Intelligence Agency, "East & Southeast Asia: China," World Factbook, accessed January 6,

2011, https://www.cia.gov/library/publications/the-world-factbook/geos/ch.html.

[11] Thomas L. Friedman, "World, Not U.S., Takes Lead with Green Technology," Post-Bulletin, September 21, 2010, accessed January 6, 2011, http://www.postbulletin.com/newsmanager/templates/localnews_story.asp?z=12&a=470550.

[12] CultureQuest Business Multimedia Series: China (New York: Atma Global, 2010); bWise: Business Wisdom Worldwide: China (New York: Atma Global, 2011).

[13] CultureQuest Business Multimedia Series: India (New York: Atma Global, 2010); bWise: Business Wisdom Worldwide: India (New York: Atma Global, 2011).

[14] "The Rupee Gets Its Own Mark," New York Times, July 18, 2010, accessed January 6,

2011, http://www.nytimes.com/2010/07/18/weekinreview/18grist.html#

[15] US Central Intelligence Agency, "Central Asia: Russia," World Factbook, accessed January 6,

2011, https://www.cia.gov/library/publications/the-world-factbook/geos/rs.html.

[16] US Central Intelligence Agency, "Central Asia: Russia," World Factbook, accessed January 6,

2011, https://www.cia.gov/library/publications/the-world-factbook/geos/rs.html.

[17] US Central Intelligence Agency, "Central Asia: Russia," World Factbook, accessed January 6,

2011, https://www.cia.gov/library/publications/the-world-factbook/geos/rs.html.

[18] CultureQuest Business Multimedia Series: Russia (New York: Atma Global, 2010); bWise: Business Wisdom Worldwide: Russia (New York: Atma Global, 2011).

[19] US Central Intelligence Agency, "Central Asia: Russia," World Factbook, accessed January 6,

2011, https://www.cia.gov/library/publications/the-world-factbook/geos/rs.html.

[20] Liam Pleven, Gregory Zuckerman, and Scott Kilman, "Russian Export Ban Raises Global Food Fears," Wall Street Journal, August 6, 2010, accessed January 6, 2011,

http://online.wsj.com/article/SB10001424052748703748904575410740617512592.html.

[21] Liam Pleven, Gregory Zuckerman, and Scott Kilman, "Russian Export Ban Raises Global Food Fears," Wall Street Journal, August 6, 2010, accessed January 6, 2011,

http://online.wsj.com/article/SB10001424052748703748904575410740617512592.html.

[22] "Russia Unlikely to Privatize Largest Companies in 2010," RIA Novosti, August 30, 2010, accessed January 6,

2011, http://en.rian.ru/business/20100830/160394304.html.

[23] "Who We Are," RUSAL, accessed May 18,

2011, http://rusal.ru/en/about.aspx.

[24] Wikipedia, s.v. "Disinvestment from South Africa," last modified February 13, 2011, accessed February 16, 2011,

http://en.wikipedia.org/wiki/Disinvestment_from_South_Africa.

[25] bWise: Business Wisdom Worldwide: South Africa (New York: Atma Global, 2011).

[26] CultureQuest Business Multimedia Series: South Africa (New York: Atma Global, 2010).

[27] Renee Bonorchis, "Africa Is Looking Like a Dealmaker's Paradise," BusinessWeek, September 30, 2010, accessed January 5, 2011, http://www.businessweek.com/magazine/content/10_41/b4198020648051.htm.

[28] CultureQuest Business Multimedia Series: Brazil (New York: Atma Global, 2010); bWise: Business Wisdom Worldwide: Brazil (New York: Atma Global, 2011).

[29] US Central Intelligence Agency, "Central America: Brazil," World Factbook, accessed January 7,

2011, https://www.cia.gov/library/publications/the-world-factbook/geos/br.html.

[30] US Central Intelligence Agency, "Central America: Brazil," World Factbook, accessed January 7,

2011, https://www.cia.gov/library/publications/the-world-factbook/geos/br.html.

[31] US Central Intelligence Agency, "Central America: Brazil," World Factbook, accessed January 7,

2011, https://www.cia.gov/library/publications/the-world-factbook/geos/br.html.

4.5 Tips in Your Entrepreneurial Walkabout Toolkit Researching the Local Market

When you begin to consider expanding globally, research the local market thoroughly and learn about the country and its culture. Understand the unique business and regulatory relationships that impact your industry. Early in your research and planning process, take a look to see where your competitors are already selling. You can't enter multiple markets at the same time. You need to prioritize. By studying others' successes and failures, you'll be well positioned to determine which markets make the most sense.

You may, for example, decide that Asia is a good place to do business. Within Asia, you should pick two or three countries and plan to enter a new market only once every two to three years. Regional strategies have the added value of marketing synergies. But as with domestic channels, don't try to take on more than one new market or distribution at a time. Some younger companies tend to choose countries closer to their headquarters and time zones. Conducting business can be harder if you're in opposite time zones, unless everything is done via e-mail. Some companies highlight several countries and then choose their first market based on available sales or distribution options. For example, they may have a salesperson eager to start working in a specific market. Often, local partners and salespeople will approach you even before you have formally decided to enter a new global market. It can seem easy to simply let the person start selling, but first make sure you have a plan in place. It will help set goals, manage everyone's expectations, and determine what a success or failure will look like in terms of revenues, profitability, and time frame.

Large global companies often have a bevy of resources in the form of budgets and consultants to provide information on local markets. Small and midsize companies typically have smaller or no consulting budgets and need to research local markets creatively with existing resources.

A number of resources are available to companies considering new global markets—some more useful than others, depending on the country and on whether the new market is for sourcing or for selling into. The Internet is often the best place to start any research, and e-mail is the best way to contact some of the offices noted below. Many of these organizations operate online exchanges where companies can find partners, customers, and suppliers. The following are key steps to follow when researching a new market:

1. Develop a relationship with your home country's embassy and commercial service office in the target country. Many governments realize that large companies have multiple options and that the companies most likely to need their services and insight are smaller or midsize. Some offices charge modest fees for researching lists of potential partners or distributors. Whether you need this list or not, the added insight from an experienced country expert can be quite useful. These commercial service officers will be able to tell you about the track records of other companies within a specific industry or with specific distributors. Even learning about the lack of other companies entering the market may be helpful, as you may identify the reasons for their lack of success or interest. The US Department of State publishes useful information online at http://www.state.gov/e/eeb/cba/index.htm. The site also provides more general country information.

2. Contact the target country's commercial office within its embassy or consulate in your home country. If the country doesn't have a trade office, contact the respective diplomatic offices. Even tourist offices can provide you with general information. Most country offices are eager to promote their local economies, even on a small scale. If you're considering sourcing from the country, they're usually even more eager to provide you with resources and lists of potential companies as partners or manufacturers.

3. Contact the chamber of commerce for that country in your home country. These are different from the commercial office noted in the first point, as they tend to be funded by private-sector companies. Many smaller or still-emerging countries may not have a chamber of commerce office yet. You may also want to contact your home nation's chamber of commerce in the foreign country of interest. For example, in the United States, there are two types of chambers: American Chambers of Commerce (located in numerous countries) and binational chambers of commerce offices (located in the United States).

The primary difference between the two types of chambers is their location. Both organizations seek to facilitate business interactions between the United States and the respective country, often collaborating on specific projects as well as lobbying governments for protection of US business interests. The American Chambers of Commerce Abroad (AmChams) are affiliated with the US Chamber of Commerce and tend to focus on American business interests in the target country. [1] A list of overseas AmChams can be obtained by contacting the United States Chamber of Commerce in Washington, DC [2]

The binational chambers of commerce located in the United States promote both US business interests and other countries' interests in the United States. It's important to note that these are not the International Chamber of Commerce or its World Chambers Federation division, whose mission is to create a business and legal environment that encourages global trade. Instead the binational chambers of commerce are focused on bilateral issues. For example, the American Indonesian Chamber of Commerce is located in New York.

These binational chambers tend to be run by executive directors who really know the countries well, have excellent networks of US and domestic companies, and can supply needed information or facilitate business introductions. Offices run by people who have been in-country for a lengthy period of time will more likely be knowledgeable and full of useful information. Both AmChams and binational organizations tend to be dominated by large, well-established companies, but they can be very useful in research and information gathering as well as in obtaining introductions to possible partners. Again, the strength of any of these organizations usually rests with the executive director.

Chambers of commerce are also great places to get in touch with others who are experienced in dealing with a country, either as advisors, consultants, or hires. Utilize the expatriate community located within that country, as well as those who have recently returned to your home country, as sources for valuable information about the country and its business climate and practices.

4. Contact the US Department of Commerce's International Trade Administration office in your state and in Washington, DC, or the respective trade office in your home country, and speak with the desk officer for the country of interest. In the United States, general trade information can be obtained at http://www.ita.doc.gov or http://www.usatrade.com. Government trade offices also provide an export program guide that lists resources available at http://www.ita.doc.gov/exportamerica/AskTheTIC/03_02qa.html.

5. Find out if your home state or city has a "sister" state/city relationship with specific countries and if promotional opportunities are available.

6. If possible, conduct a fact-finding trip to your country of interest. Participate in any delegation or trade mission that the US Department of Commerce, your local chamber of commerce office, or other trade organizations sponsor. Always review the agenda and list of meetings carefully. Make sure not only that they fit the needs of your industry and company but also that the people are decision makers and not just political figureheads.

7. Attend trade shows in the country or region of interest. Trade shows have become particularly popular for smaller companies, as many organizers offer smaller booth options with lower fees or allow companies to share both spaces and costs. In many cases, country trade offices also facilitate trade trips to a target country or trade show. The delegation often shares exhibition space to minimize cost. Most of these shows are organized by the specific industries; schedules are available online and through the country's trade or diplomatic offices.

8. Be creative. Find common connections with companies in the country. Also seek connections with individuals who have experience doing business in the country or with the specific company with which you are dealing (e.g., a company or individual that you interact with that also does business in your target country). Talk to natives from the country that live in your home nation. Even if there is no direct business application for the information you glean from such sources, you will be able to gather a great deal of cultural and social information that you may be able to put to good use.

9. Approach vendors and clients. If you are hoping to win local business through government contracts, you may want to approach larger vendors that are more likely to obtain the overseas contracts. Many of them have blanket government contracts and look to subcontract for specific goods and services. Further, they often have a requirement to utilize small businesses, particularly those that are owned by women or minorities.

The entire government-contracting industry is very time-consuming and will require resources up front to cultivate the necessary relationships and process the required paperwork. Unless you're sure that your product or service is required or have established buying relationships, it's not the best first sales prospect given the lengthy sales cycle. Many service companies start to work in new markets through project contracts for specific tasks and time periods. It can take longer to build a sustainable business in a country, but the projects allow you to learn about the country and its business practices as well as identify local partners. Most young companies initially choose to partner with a local service firm rather than try to establish their own office.

Recognize that some embassies, offices, and individual officers are better able to assist you in your efforts. For example, junior-ranking career people who have spent more time in the local country are often more insightful and knowledgeable than senior and politically appointed officers with less in-country experience. Over time and through research and references, you will learn which officers and professionals have the most experience and knowledge. As a safety measure, double-check all information with at least two independent sources. Also, be aware that the embassies in your home country may differ in their degree of responsiveness to foreign interest. Don't automatically assume that the embassies or trade representatives of the larger or more economically advanced countries are more efficient or helpful. [3]

[1] "American Chambers of Commerce Abroad," US Chamber of Commerce, accessed January 7,
2011, http://www.uschamber.com/international/directory.
[2] "International," US Chamber of Commerce, accessed January 7, 2011, http://www.uschamber.com/international.
[3] Excerpted from {Author's Name retracted as requested by the work's original creator or licensee}, Straight Talk about Starting and Growing Your Own Business (New York: McGraw-Hill, 2006).

4.6 End-of-Chapter Questions and Exercises

These exercises are designed to ensure that the knowledge you gain from this book about international business meets the learning standards set out by the international Association to Advance Collegiate Schools of Business (AACSB International). [1] AACSB is the premier accrediting agency of collegiate business schools and accounting programs worldwide. It expects that you will gain knowledge in the areas of communication, ethical reasoning, analytical skills, use of information technology, multiculturalism and diversity, and reflective thinking.

EXPERIENTIAL EXERCISES

(AACSB: Communication, Use of Information Technology, Analytical Skills)

1. Compare and contrast the impact of the regulatory strength of national ministries of trade in Japan or Germany versus India. How did the developed country successfully lead the country to long-term growth? Discuss the role of the bureaucracy in India and if you think it can successfully lead the country to long-term economic growth.

2. Select one developing country that you think may become an emerging market in the next ten years. Discuss which statistics and criteria led to your selection.

Ethical Dilemmas

(AACSB: Ethical Reasoning, Multiculturalism, Reflective Thinking, Analytical Skills)

1. Discuss how global ethics are impacting the development of the local economies of emerging markets. Select two countries and review how the local government is addressing the issues of corruption in business. Have these efforts been successful? Why or why not? How would you handle them if you were doing business in those countries?

2. If you were the manager of new global business development for a consumer products firm, discuss how you would review the prospects for Nigeria. Does Nigeria offer a growing and strong market for consumer products? Is the government stable? Is the economy stable? Are the legal, political, and economic institutions transparent and have the reforms been effective? What concerns would you express to your management?

[1] Association to Advance Collegiate Schools of Business website, accessed January 26, 2010, http://www.aacsb.edu.

NOTES:

Chapter 5:
Global and Regional Economic Cooperation and Integration

WHAT'S IN IT FOR ME?

1. What is international economic cooperation among nations?
2. What is regional economic integration?
3. What is the United Nations (UN), and how do the UN and peace impact global trade?

Following World War II, there's been a shift in thinking toward trade. Nations have moved away from thinking that trade was a zero-sum game of either win or lose to a philosophy of increasing trade for the benefit of all. Additionally, coming out of a second global war that destroyed nations, resources, and the balance of peace, nations were eager for a new model that would not only focus on promoting and expanding free trade but would also contribute to world peace by creating international economic, political, and social cooperative agreements and institutions to support them. While this may sound impossible to achieve, international agreements and institutions have succeeded—at a minimum—in creating an ongoing forum for dialogue on trade and related issues. Reducing the barriers to trade and expanding global and regional cooperation have functioned as flatteners in an increasingly flat world. andreview the specific economic agreements governing global and regional trade—the successes and the challenges. also looks at the United Nations as a key global institution and its impact on free and fair global trade. To start, the opening case study assesses one of the more important trade pacts of the past fifty years, the European Union (EU). What has been the impact of the 2010 debt crisis in Greece on the EU, its members, and its outlook?

DID YOU KNOW?

Before the twentieth century, states (nations) usually increased their power by attacking and absorbing others. In 1500, there were about 500 political units in Europe; by 1900 there were just 25—a consolidation brought by (royal) marriage and dynastic expansion but largely through force. [1]

OPENING CASE: MAKING SENSE OF THE ECONOMIC CHAOS IN THE EUROPEAN UNION

In this chapter, you'll learn more about how governments seek to cooperate with one another by entering into trade agreements in order to facilitate business.

The European Union (EU) is one such example. The EU started after World War II, initially as a series of trade agreements between six European countries geared to avoid yet another war on European soil. Six decades later, with free-flowing trade and people, a single currency, and regional peace, it's easy to see why so many believed that an economic union made the best sense. However, the EU is facing its first major economic crisis, and many pundits are questioning how the EU will handle this major stress test. Will it survive? To better answer this question, let's look at what really happened during the financial crisis in Europe and in particular in Greece.

At its most basic level, countries want to encourage the growth of their domestic businesses by expanding trade with other countries—primarily by promoting exports and encouraging investment in their nations. Borders that have fewer rules and regulations can help businesses expand easier and more cheaply. While this sounds great in theory, economists as well as businesspeople often ignore the realities of the political and sociocultural factors that impact relationships between countries, businesses, and people.

Critics have longed argued that while the EU makes economic sense, it goes against the long-standing political, social, and cultural history, patterns, and differences existing throughout Europe. Not until the 2010 economic crisis in Greece did these differences become so apparent.

What Really Happened in Greece?

What is the European debt crisis? While experts continue to debate the causes of the crisis, it's clear that several European countries had been borrowing beyond their capacity.

Let's look at one such country, Greece, which received a lot of press attention in 2010 and has been considered to have a very severe problem. The financial crisis in the EU, in large part, began in Greece, which had concealed the true levels of its debts. Once the situation in Greece came to light, investors began focusing on the debt levels of other EU countries.

In April 2010, following a series of tax increases and budget cuts, the Greek prime minister officially announced that his country needed an international bailout from the EU and International Monetary Fund (IMF) to deal with its debt crisis.

The crisis began in 2009 when the country faced its first negative economic growth rate since 1993. There was a fast-growing crisis, and the country couldn't make its debt payments. Its debt costs were rising because investors and bankers became wary of lending more money to the country and demanded higher rates. Economic historians have accused the country of covering up just how bad the deficits were with a massive deficit revision of the 2009 budget.

This drastic bailout was necessitated by the country's massive budget deficits, the economy's lack of transparency, and its excess corruption. In Greece, corruption has been so widespread that it's an ingrained part of the culture. Greeks have routinely used the terms fakelaki, which means bribes offered in envelopes, and rousfeti, which means political favors among friends. Compared with its European member countries, Greece has suffered from high levels of political and economic corruption and low global-business competitiveness.

What's the Impact on Europe and the EU?

In the ashes of Europe's debt crisis, some see the seeds of long-term hope. That's because the threat of bankruptcy is forcing governments to implement reforms that economists argue are necessary to help Europe prosper in a globalized world—but were long viewed politically impossible because of entrenched social attitudes. "Together, Europe's banks have funneled $2.5 trillion into the five shakiest euro-zone economies: Greece, Ireland, Belgium, Portugal, and Spain." [2]

So if it's just a handful of European countries, why should the other stronger economies in the EU worry? Well, all of the sixteen member countries that use the euro as their currency now have their economies interlinked in a way that other countries don't. Countries that have joined the euro currency have unique challenges when economic times are tough. A one-size-fits-all monetary policy doesn't give the

member countries the flexibility needed to stimulate their economies. But the impact of one currency for sixteen markets has made countries like Portugal, Spain, and Greece less cost competitive on a global level. In practice, companies in these countries have to pay their wages and costs in euros, which makes their products and services more expensive than goods from cheaper, low-wage countries such as Poland, Turkey, China, and Brazil. Because they share a single common currency, highly indebted EU countries can't just devalue their currency to stimulate exports.

Rigid EU rules don't enable member governments to navigate their country-specific problems, such as deficit spending and public works projects. Of note, a majority of the sixteen countries in the monetary union have completely disregarded the EU's Stability and Growth Pact by running excessive deficits—that is, borrowing or spending more than the country has in its coffers. Reducing deficits and cutting social programs often comes at a high political cost.

As Steven Erlanger noted in the New York Times,

The European Union and the 16 nations that use the euro face two crises. One is the immediate problem of too much debt and government spending. Another is the more fundamental divide, roughly north and south, between the more competitive export countries like Germany and France and the uncompetitive, deficit countries that have adopted the high wages and generous social protections of the north without the same economic ethos of strict work habits, innovation, more flexible labor markets and high productivity.

As Europe grapples with its financial crisis, the more competitive, wealthier countries are reluctantly rescuing more profligate economies, including Greece and Ireland, from fiscal and bank woes, while imposing drastic cuts in spending there. [3]

Early on, EU critics had expressed concern that countries wouldn't want to give up their sovereign right to make economic and political policy. Efforts to create a European constitution and move closer to a political union fell flat in 2005, when Belgium and France rejected the efforts. Critics suggest that a political union is just not culturally feasible. European countries have deep, intertwined histories filled with cultural and ethnic biases, old rivalries, and deep-rooted preferences for their own sovereignty and independence. This first major economic crisis has brought this issue to the forefront.

There were two original arguments against the creation of the EU and euro zone: (1) fiscal independence and sovereignty and (2) centuries-old political, economic, social, and cultural issues, biases, and differences.

Despite these historical challenges, most Europeans felt that the devastation of two world wars were worse. World War I started as a result of the cumulative and somewhat convoluted sequence of political, economic, and military rivalries between European countries and then added in Japan and the United States. World War II started after Germany, intent on expanding its empire throughout Europe, invaded Poland in 1939. All told, these two wars led to almost one hundred million military and civilian deaths, shattered economies, destroyed industries, and severely demoralized and exhausted the global population. European and global leaders were determined that there would never be another world war. This became the early foundations of today's global and regional economic and political alliances, in particular the EU and the United Nations (UN).

Of course, any challenges to the modern-day EU have brought back old rivalries and biases between nations. Strong economies, like Germany, have been criticized for condescending to the challenges in Greece, for example when German commentators used negative Greek stereotypes. Germany was also initially criticized for possibly holding up a bailout of Greece, because it was unpopular with German voters.

European leaders first joined with the IMF in May 2010 and agreed on a $1 trillion rescue fund for financially troubled countries. Then, Greece announced deep budget cuts, Spain cut employer costs, and France raised its retirement age. France also joined Germany and the United Kingdom in imposing harsh budget cuts. Governments now face a crucial test of political will. Can they implement the reforms they've announced? The short-term response to those moves has been a wave of strikes, riots, and—in Spain, Italy, Ireland, and France—demonstrations.

Yet supporters of the EU argue that the mutual common interests of the EU countries will ensure that reforms are implemented. Memories of the fragility of the continent after the wars still lingers. Plus, more realistically, Europeans know that in order to remain globally competitive, they will be stronger as a union than as individual countries—particularly when going up against such formidable economic giants as the United States and China.

What Does This All Mean for Businesses?

The first and most relevant reminder is that global business and trade are intertwined with the political, economic, and social realities of countries. This understanding has led to an expansion of trade agreements and country blocs, all based on the fundamental premise that peace, stability, and trade are interdependent. Both the public and private sectors have embraced this thinking.

Despite the crises in varying European countries, businesses still see opportunity. UK-based Diageo, the giant global beverage company and maker of Ireland's famous Guinness beer, just opened a new distillery in Roseisle, Scotland, located in the northern part of the United Kingdom.

The new distillery is a symbol of optimism for the industry after the uncertainty of the global economic downturn. The scotch industry had been riding high when the financial crisis hit and the subsequent collapse in demand in 2009 ricocheted through important markets like South Korea, where sales contracted by almost 25 percent. Sales in Spain and Singapore were down 5 percent and 9 percent respectively. There was also evidence of drinkers trading down to cheaper spirits—such as hard-up Russians returning to vodka.

David Gates, global category director for whiskies at Diageo, says emerging markets are leading the recovery: "The places we're seeing demand pick up quickest are Asia, Latin America and parts of Eastern Europe. Southern Europe is more concerning because Spain and Greece, which are big scotch markets, remain in very difficult economic situations."…

The renaissance of Scotland's whisky industry has had little to do with Scottish consumption. Drinks groups have concentrated on the emerging middle-class in countries such as Brazil, where sales shot up 44 percent last year.

In Mexico whisky sales were up 25 percent as locals defected from tequila. [4]

While Europe continues to absorb the impact of the 2008 global recession, there is hope for the future.

It is too soon to write off the EU. It remains the world's largest trading block. At its best, the European project is remarkably liberal: built around a single market of 27 rich and poor countries, its internal borders are far more porous to goods, capital and labour than any comparable trading area.…

For free-market liberals, the enlarged union's size and diversity is itself an advantage. By taking in eastern countries with lower labour costs and workers who are far more mobile than their western cousins, the EU in effect brought globalization within its own borders. For economic liberals, that flexibility and dynamism offers Europe's best chance of survival. [5]

UNDERSTANDING THE BASICS OF WHY COUNTRIES BORROW MONEY

Governments operate first from tax revenues before resorting to borrowing. Countries like Saudi Arabia, Brunei, or Qatar that have huge tax revenues from oil don't need to borrow. However, countries that don't have these huge tax revenues might need to borrow money. In addition, if tax revenues go down—for example in a recession or because taxes aren't paid or aren't collected properly—then countries might need to borrow.

Countries usually borrow for four main reasons:

1. *Recession.* During a recession, a country may need to borrow money in order to keep its basic public services operating until the economy improves and businesses and workers can resume paying sufficient tax revenues to make borrowing less of a need.
2. *Investment.* A country may borrow money in order to invest in the public sector and build infrastructure, which may be anything related to keeping a society operating, including roads, airports, telecommunications, schools, and hospitals.
3. *War.* A country may borrow in order to fund wars or military expansion.
4. *Politics.* A country may borrow money in order to reduce tax rates either because of political pressure from its citizens and businesses or to stimulate its economy. Usually countries have a much harder time cutting government spending. People don't want to give up a benefit or service or, in the case of a recession, may need the services, such as food stamps or unemployment benefits, thus making it very difficult to cut government programs.

When countries borrow, they increase their debt. When debt levels become too high, investors get concerned that the country may not be able to repay the money. As a result, investors and bankers (in the form of the credit market) may view the debt as higher risk. Then, investors or bankers ask for a higher interest rate or return as compensation for the higher risk. This, in turn, leads to higher borrowing costs for the country.

The national deficit is the amount of borrowing that a country does from either the private sector or other countries. However, the national deficit is different from the current account deficit, which refers to imports being greater than exports.

Even healthy countries run national deficits. For example, in the case of borrowing to invest long term in domestic facilities and programs, the rationale is that a country is investing in its future by improving infrastructure, much like a business would borrow to build a new factory.

OPENING CASE EXERCISES
(AACSB: Ethical Reasoning, Multiculturalism, Reflective Thinking, Analytical Skills)

1. What are two reasons for the creation of the European Union (EU)?
2. What are four reasons a country might have for borrowing money?

[1] Richard Rosecrance, "Bigger Is Better: The Case for a Transatlantic Economic Union," Foreign Affairs, May/June 2010, accessed January 2, 2011, http://www.foreignaffairs.com/articles/66225/richard-rosecrance/bigger-is-better.
[2] Stefan Theil, "Worse Than Wall Street," Newsweek, July 2, 2010, accessed December 28, 2010, http://www.newsweek.com/2010/07/02/worse-than-wall-street.html.
[3] Steven Erlanger, "Euro Zone Is Imperiled by North-South Divide," New York Times, December 2, 2010, accessed January 2, 2011, http://www.nytimes.com/2010/12/03/world/europe/03divide.html?_r=1&ref=stevenerlanger.
[4] Zoe Wood, "Diageo Opens the First Major New Whisky Distillery for a Generation,"Guardian, October 3, 2010, accessed January 2, 2011, http://www.guardian.co.uk/business/2010/oct/03/diageo-roseisle-distillery-opens.
[5] "Staring into the Abyss," Economist, July 8, 2010, accessed December 28, 2010, http://www.economist.com/node/16536898.

5.1 International Economic Cooperation among Nations
LEARNING OBJECTIVES

1. Understand the global trading system.
2. Explain how and why the GATT was created and what its historical role in international trade is.
3. Know what the WTO is and what its current impact on international trade is.

In the post–World War II environment, countries came to realize that a major component of achieving any level of global peace was global cooperation—politically, economically, and socially. The intent was to level the trade playing field and reduce economic areas of disagreement, since inequality in these areas could lead to more serious conflicts. Among the initiatives, nations agreed to work together to promote free trade, entering into bilateral and multilateral agreements. The General Agreement on Tariffs and Trade (GATT) resulted from these agreements. In this section, you'll review GATT—why it was created and what its historical successes and challenges are. You'll then look at the World Trade Organization (WTO), which replaced GATT in 1995, and study the impact of both these organizations on international trade. While GATT started as a set of rules between countries, the WTO has become an institution overseeing international trade.

General Agreement on Tariffs and Trade (GATT)

The General Agreement on Tariffs and Trade (GATT) is a series of rules governing trade that were first created in 1947 by twenty-three countries. By the time it was replaced with the WTO, there were 125 member nations. GATT has been credited with substantially expanding global trade, primarily through the reduction of tariffs.

The basic underlying principle of GATT was that trade should be free and equal. In other words, countries should open their markets equally to member nations, and there should be neither discrimination nor preferential treatment. One of GATT's key provisions was the most-favored-nation clause (MFN). It required that once a benefit, usually a tariff reduction, was agreed on between two or more countries, it was automatically extended to all other member countries. GATT's initial focus was on tariffs, which are taxes placed on imports or exports.

Did You Know?

MFN Is Everywhere
As a concept, MFN can be seen in many aspects of business; it's an important provision. Companies require MFN of their trading partners for pricing, access, and other provisions. Corporate or government customers require it of the company from which they purchase goods or services. Venture capitalists (VC) require it of the companies in which they invest. For example, a VC wants to make sure that it has negotiated the best price for equity and will ask for this provision in case another financier negotiates a cheaper purchase price for the equity. The idea behind the concept of MFN is that the country, company, or entity that has MFN status shouldn't be disadvantaged in comparison with others in similar roles as a trading partner, buyer, or investor. In practice, the result is that the signing party given MFN status benefits from any better negotiation and receives the cheaper price point or better term. This terminology is also used in sales contracts or other business legal agreements.

Gradually, the GATT member countries turned their attention to other nontariff trade barriers. These included government procurement and bidding, industrial standards, subsidies, duties and customs, taxes, and licensing. GATT countries agreed to limit or remove trade barriers in these areas. The only agreed-on export subsidies were for agricultural products. Countries agreed to permit a wider range of imported products to enter their home markets by simplifying licensing guidelines and developing consistent product standards between imports and domestically produced goods. Duties had to result from uniform and consistent procedures for the same foreign and domestically produced items.

The initial successes in these categories led some countries to get more creative with developing barriers to trade as well as entering into bilateral agreements and providing more creative subsidies for select industries. The challenge for the member countries of GATT was enforcement. Other than complaining and retaliating, there was little else that a country could do to register disapproval of another country's actions and trade barriers.

Gradually, trade became more complex, leading to the Uruguay Round beginning in 1986 and ending in 1994. These trade meetings were called rounds in reference to the series of meetings among global peers held at a "roundtable." Prior to a round, each series of trade discussions began in one country. The round of discussions was then named after that country. It sometimes took several years to conclude the topic discussions for a round. The Uruguay Round took eight years and actually resulted in the end of GATT and the creation of the World Trade Organization (WTO). The current Doha Development Round began in 2001 and is actually considered part of the WTO.

World Trade Organization (WTO)

Brief History and Purpose

The World Trade Organization (WTO) developed as a result of the Uruguay Round of GATT. Formed officially on January 1, 1995, the concept of the WTO had been in development for several years. When the WTO replaced GATT, it absorbed all of GATT's standing agreements. In contrast to GATT, which was a series of agreements, the WTO was designed to be an actual institution charged with the mission of promoting free and fair trade. As explained on its website, the WTO "is the only global international organization dealing with the rules of trade between nations. At its heart are the WTO agreements, negotiated and signed by the bulk of the world's trading nations and ratified in their parliaments. The goal is to help producers of goods and services, exporters, and importers conduct their business." [1]

The global focus on multilateral trade agreements and cooperation has expanded trade exponentially. "The past 50 years have seen an exceptional growth in world trade. Merchandise exports grew on average by 6 percent annually. Total trade in 2000 was 22-times the level of 1950. GATT and the WTO have helped to create a strong and prosperous trading system contributing to unprecedented growth." [2]

The WTO's primary purpose is to serve as a negotiating forum for member nations to dispute, discuss, and debate trade-related matters. More than just a series of trade agreements, as it was under GATT, the WTO undertakes discussions on issues related to globalization and its impact on people and the environment, as well as trade-specific matters. It doesn't necessarily establish formal agreements in all of these areas but does provide a forum to discuss how global trade impacts other aspects of the world.

Headquartered in Geneva, Switzerland, the current round is called the Doha Round and began in 2001. With 153 member nations, the WTO is the largest, global trade organization. Thirty nations have observer status, and many of these are seeking membership. With so many member nations, the concept of MFN has been eased into a new principle of normal trade relations (NTR). Advocates say that no nation really has a favored nation status; rather, all interact with each other as a normal part of global trade.

The biggest change from GATT to the WTO is the provision for the settlement of disputes. If a country finds another country's trade practices unfair or discriminatory, it may bring the charges to the WTO, which will hear from both countries and mediate a solution.

The WTO has also undertaken the effort to focus on services rather than just goods. Resulting from the Uruguay Round, the General Agreement on Trade in Services (GATS) seeks to reduce the barriers to trade in services. Following the GATT commitment to nondiscrimination, GATS requires member nations to treat foreign service companies as they would domestic ones. For example, if a country requires banks to maintain 10 percent of deposits as reserves, then this percentage should be the same for foreign and domestic banks. Services have proven to be more complex to both define and regulate, and the member nations are continuing the discussions.

Similar to GATS is the WTO Agreement on Trade-Related Aspects of Intellectual Property Rights (TRIPS). Intellectual property refers to just about anything that a person or entity creates with the mind. It includes inventions, music, art, and writing, as well as words, phrases, sayings, and graphics—to name a few. The basic premise of intellectual property rights (IPR) law is that the creator of the property has the right to financially benefit from his or her creation. This is particularly important for protecting the development for the creation, known as the research and development (R&D) costs. Companies can also own the intellectual property that their employees generate. This section focuses on the protection that countries agree to give to intellectual property created in another country.

Over the past few decades, companies have become increasingly diligent in protecting their intellectual property and pursuing abusers. Whether it's the knock-off designer handbag from China that lands on the sidewalks of New York or the writer protecting her thoughts in the written words of a book (commonly understood as content), or the global software company combating piracy of its technical know-how, IPR is now formally a part of the WTO agreements and ongoing dialogue.

Current Challenges and Opportunities

Agriculture and textiles are two key sectors in which the WTO faces challenges. Trade in agriculture has been impacted by export-country subsidies, import-country tariffs and restrictions, and nontariff barriers. Whether the United States provides low-cost loans and subsidies to its farmers or Japan restricts the beef imports, agriculture trade barriers are an ongoing challenge for the WTO. Global companies and trade groups that support private-sector firms seek to have their governments raise critical trade issues on their behalf through the WTO.

For example, Japan's ban of beef imports in response to mad cow disease has had a heavy impact on the US beef industry.

At the moment, unfortunately there's some distance between Japan and the U.S.," Japan Agriculture Minister Hirotaka Akamatsu told reporters in 2010 after meeting [US Agriculture Secretary Tom] Vilsack in Tokyo. "For us, food safety based on Japan's scientific standards is the priority. The OIE standards are different from the Japanese scientific ones.

The U.S. beef industry is losing about $1 billion a year in sales because of the restrictions, according to the National Cattlemen's Beef Association, [a trade group supporting the interests of American beef producers]. Japan was the largest foreign buyer of U.S. beef before it banned all imports when the first case of the brain-wasting disease, also known bovine spongiform encephalopathy [i.e., mad cow disease], was discovered in the U.S.

The ban was eased in 2005 to allow meat from cattle aged 20 months or less, which scientists say are less likely to have contracted the fatal illness....

Japan was the third-largest destination for U.S. beef [in 2009], with trade totaling $470 million, up from $383 million in 2008, according to the U.S. Meat Export Federation. That compares with $1.39 billion in 2003.

Mexico and Canada were the biggest buyers of U.S. beef [in 2009]. [3]

The role of the WTO is to facilitate agreements in difficult bilateral and multilateral trade disputes, but this certainly isn't easy. Japan's reluctance for American beef may appear to be the result of mad cow disease, but business observers note Japan's historical cultural preference for Japanese goods, which the country often claims are superior. A similar trade conflict was triggered in the 1980s when Japan discouraged the import of rice from other countries. The prevailing Japanese thought was that its local rice was easier for the Japanese to digest. After extensive discussions in the Uruguay Round, on "December 14, 1993 the Japanese government accepted a limited opening of the rice market under the GATT plan." [4]

Antidumping is another area on which the WTO has focused its attention. Dumping occurs when a company exports to a foreign market at a price that is either lower than the domestic prices in that country or less than the cost of production. Antidumping charges can be harder to settle, as the charge is against a company and not a country. One example is in India, which has, in the past, accused Japan and Thailand of dumping acetone, a chemical used in drugs and explosives, in the Indian market. In an effort to protect domestic manufacturers, India has raised the issue with the WTO. In fact, India was second only to Argentina among the G-20 (or Group of Twenty) nations in initiating antidumping investigations during 2009, according to a recent WTO report. [5]

Future Outlook
While the end of the Doha Round is uncertain, the future for the WTO and any related organizations remains strong. With companies and countries facing a broader array of trade issues than ever before, the WTO plays a critical role in promoting and ensuring free and fair trade. Many observers expect that the WTO will have to emphasize the impact of

the Internet on trade. In most cases, the WTO provides companies and countries with the best options to dispute, discuss, and settle unfair business and trade practices.

KEY TAKEAWAYS

- The General Agreement on Tariffs and Trade (GATT) is a series of rules governing trade that were first created in 1947 by twenty-three countries. It remained in force until 1995, when it was replaced by the WTO.
- The World Trade Organization (WTO) is the only global, international organization dealing with the rules of trade between nations. The WTO agreements that have been negotiated and signed by the organization's 153 member nations and ratified in their parliaments are the heart of the organization. Its goal is to help the producers, exporters, and importers of goods and services conduct business. The current round of the WTO is called the Doha Round.

EXERCISES

(AACSB: Reflective Thinking, Analytical Skills)
1. Define GATT and discuss the importance of the successive rounds. Do you think that GATT was essential to promoting world trade or would we be in the same place today without it? Why or why not?
2. Define WTO. In what ways do you think the WTO is still essential to global trade? Discuss how a private-sector firm would use the WTO to protect its business interests.
3. Read the following excerpt from a 2010 *Wall Street Journal* article about the WTO:

The World Trade Organization formally condemned European subsidies to civil-aircraft maker Airbus, concluding the first half of the most expensive trade dispute in WTO history.

Its main finding was that more than $20 billion in low-interest government loans used to develop six models of passenger jet constituted prohibited export subsidies.
The ruling could force the parent company of Airbus, European Aeronautic Defence & Space Co., to repay some aid money or risk giving the U.S. the right to raise import tariffs in retaliation on goods imported from Europe, such as cars, wines and cheese. [6]

Do you agree with the WTO's assessment? Is it fair for the United States to retaliate against the airplane manufacturer with tariffs on other imported products? How might US consumers react to additional taxes imposed on popular imported products such as cars, wine, and cheese?

[1] "What Is the WTO?" World Trade Organization, accessed December 29, 2010, http://www.wto.org/english/thewto_e/whatis_e/whatis_e.htm.
[2] "The Multilateral Trading System—Past, Present and Future," World Trade Organization, accessed December 29, 2010, http://www.wto.org/english/thewto_e/whatis_e/inbrief_e/inbr01_e.htm.
[3] Jae Hur and Ichiro Suzuki, "Japan, U.S. to Continue Dialogue on Beef Import Curbs (Update 1)," BusinessWeek, April 7, 2010, accessed December 29, 2010, http://www.businessweek.com/news/2010-04-07/japan-u-s-to-continue-dialogue-on-beef-import-curbs-update1-.html.
[4] "Japan Rice Trade," case study on American University website, accessed January 2, 2010, http://www1.american.edu/ted/japrice.htm.
[5] Press Trust of India, "Govt Initiates Anti-Dumping Probe against Acetone Imports," Business Standard, November 3, 2009, accessed December 29, 2010, http://www.business-standard.com/india/news/govt-initiates-anti-dumping-probe-against-acetone-imports/375153/.
[6] John W. Miller and Daniel Michaels, "WTO Condemns Airbus Subsidies," Wall Street Journal, July 1, 2010, accessed December 29, 2010, http://online.wsj.com/article/SB10001424052748703426004575338773153793294.html.

5.2 Regional Economic Integration
LEARNING OBJECTIVES

1. Understand regional economic integration.
2. Identify the major regional economic areas of cooperation.

What Is Regional Economic Integration?
Regional economic integration has enabled countries to focus on issues that are relevant to their stage of development as well as encourage trade between neighbors.

There are four main types of regional economic integration.

1. **Free trade area.** This is the most basic form of economic cooperation. Member countries remove all barriers to trade between themselves but are free to independently determine trade policies with nonmember nations. An example is the North American Free Trade Agreement (NAFTA).
2. **Customs union.** This type provides for economic cooperation as in a free-trade zone. Barriers to trade are removed between member countries. The primary difference from the free trade area is that members agree to treat trade with nonmember countries in a similar manner. The Gulf Cooperation Council (GCC) [1] is an example.
3. **Common market.** This type allows for the creation of economically integrated markets between member countries. Trade barriers are removed, as are any restrictions on the movement of labor and capital between member countries. Like customs unions, there

is a common trade policy for trade with nonmember nations. The primary advantage to workers is that they no longer need a visa or work permit to work in another member country of a common market. An example is the Common Market for Eastern and Southern Africa (COMESA). [2]
4. **Economic union.** This type is created when countries enter into an economic agreement to remove barriers to trade and adopt common economic policies. An example is the European Union (EU). [3]

In the past decade, there has been an increase in these trading blocs with more than one hundred agreements in place and more in discussion. A trade bloc is basically a free-trade zone, or near-free-trade zone, formed by one or more tax, tariff, and trade agreements between two or more countries. Some trading blocs have resulted in agreements that have been more substantive than others in creating economic cooperation. Of course, there are pros and cons for creating regional agreements.

Pros
The pros of creating regional agreements include the following:
- **Trade creation.** These agreements create more opportunities for countries to trade with one another by removing the barriers to trade and investment. Due to a reduction or removal of tariffs, cooperation results in cheaper prices for consumers in the bloc countries. Studies indicate that regional economic integration significantly contributes to the relatively high growth rates in the less-developed countries.
- **Employment opportunities.** By removing restrictions on labor movement, economic integration can help expand job opportunities.
- **Consensus and cooperation.** Member nations may find it easier to agree with smaller numbers of countries. Regional understanding and similarities may also facilitate closer political cooperation.

Cons
The cons involved in creating regional agreements include the following:
- **Trade diversion.** The flip side to trade creation is trade diversion. Member countries may trade more with each other than with nonmember nations. This may mean increased trade with a less efficient or more expensive producer because it is in a member country. In this sense, weaker companies can be protected inadvertently with the bloc agreement acting as a trade barrier. In essence,

regional agreements have formed new trade barriers with countries outside of the trading bloc.

- **Employment shifts and reductions.** Countries may move production to cheaper labor markets in member countries. Similarly, workers may move to gain access to better jobs and wages. Sudden shifts in employment can tax the resources of member countries.

- **Loss of national sovereignty.** With each new round of discussions and agreements within a regional bloc, nations may find that they have to give up more of their political and economic rights. In the opening case study, you learned how the economic crisis in Greece is threatening not only the EU in general but also the rights of Greece and other member nations to determine their own domestic economic policies.

Major Areas of Regional Economic Integration and Cooperation

There are more than one hundred regional trade agreements in place, a number that is continuously evolving as countries reconfigure their economic and political interests and priorities. Additionally, the expansion of the World Trade Organization (WTO) has caused smaller regional agreements to become obsolete. Some of the regional blocs also created side agreements with other regional groups leading to a web of trade agreements and understandings.

North America: NAFTA

Brief History and Purpose

The North American Free Trade Agreement (NAFTA) came into being during a period when free trade and trading blocs were popular and positively perceived. In 1988, the United States and Canada signed the Canada–United States Free Trade Agreement. Shortly after it was approved and implemented, the United States started to negotiate a similar agreement with Mexico. When Canada asked to be party to any negotiations to preserve its rights under the most-favored-nation clause (MFN), the negotiations began for NAFTA, which was finally signed in 1992 and implemented in 1994.

The goal of NAFTA has been to encourage trade between Canada, the United States, and Mexico. By reducing tariffs and trade barriers, the countries hope to create a free-trade zone where companies can benefit from the transfer of goods. In the 1980s, Mexico had tariffs as high as 100 percent on select goods. Over the first decade of the agreement, almost all tariffs between Mexico, Canada, and the United States were phased out.

The rules governing origin of content are key to NAFTA. As a free trade agreement, the member countries can establish their own trading rules for nonmember countries. NAFTA's rules ensure that a foreign exporter won't just ship to the NAFTA country with the lowest tariff for nonmember countries. NAFTA rules require that at least 50 percent of the net cost of most products must come from or be incurred in the NAFTA region. There are higher requirements for footwear and cars. For example, this origin of content rule has ensured that cheap Asian manufacturers wouldn't negotiate lower tariffs with one NAFTA country, such as Mexico, and dump cheap products into Canada and the United States. Mexican *maquiladoras* have fared well in this arrangement by being the final production stop before entering the United States or Canada. *Maquiladoras* are production facilities located in border towns in Mexico that take imported materials and produce the finished good for export, primarily to Canada or the United States.

Current Challenges and Opportunities

Canadian and US consumers have benefited from the lower-cost Mexican agricultural products. Similarly, Canadian and US companies have sought to enter the expanding Mexican domestic market. Many Canadian and US companies have chosen to locate their manufacturing or production facilities in Mexico rather than Asia, which was geographically far from their North American bases.

When it was introduced, NAFTA was highly controversial, particularly in the United States, where many felt it would send US jobs to Mexico. In the long run, NAFTA hasn't been as impactful as its supporters had hoped nor as detrimental to workers and companies as its critics had feared. As part of NAFTA, two side agreements addressing labor and environmental standards were put into place. The expectation was that these side agreements would ensure that Mexico had to move toward improving working conditions.

Mexico has fared the best from NAFTA as trade has increased dramatically. *Maquiladoras* in Mexico have seen a 15 percent annual increase in income. By and large, Canadians have been supportive of NAFTA and exports to the region have increased in the period since implementation. "Trilateral [merchandise] trade has nearly tripled since NAFTA came into force in 1994. It topped $1 trillion in 2008." [4]

Future Outlook

Given the 2008 global economic recession and challenging impact on the EU, it isn't likely that NAFTA will move beyond the free-trade zone status to anything more comprehensive (e.g., the EU's economic union). In the opening case study, you read about the pressures on the EU and the resistance by each of the governments in Europe to make policy adjustments to address the recession. The United States, as the largest country member in NAFTA, won't give up its rights to independently determine its economic and trade policies. Observers note that there may be the opportunity for NAFTA to expand to include other countries in Latin America. [5] Chile was originally supposed to be part of NAFTA in 1994, but President Clinton was hampered by Congress in his ability to formalize that decision. [6] Since then, Canada, Mexico, and the United States have each negotiated bilateral trade agreements with Chile, but there is still occasional mention that Chile may one day join NAFTA. [7]

Did You Know?

Mexico, NAFTA, and the Maquiladoras
The Mexican economy has undergone dramatic changes during the last decade and a half as the country has become integrated into the global marketplace. Once highly protected, Mexico is now open for business. Successive governments have instituted far-reaching economic reforms, which have had a major impact on the way business is conducted. The scale of business has changed as well. Forced to compete with large multinationals and Mexican conglomerates, many traditional family-owned firms have had to close because they were unable to compete in the global marketplace.

NAFTA has added to the already-strong US influence on Mexico's corporate and business practices. In particular, competitiveness and efficiency have become higher priorities, although company owners and managers still like to surround themselves with people they know and to groom their sons and sometimes their daughters to be their successors. US influence is also pervasive in the products and services offered throughout Mexico.

Mexico has always had a strong entrepreneurial business culture, but until NAFTA, it was protected from the pressures of international finance and the global marketplace. Business and particularly interpersonal business relationships were viewed as something that should be pleasurable, like other important aspects of life.

Long-term relationships are still the foundation on which trust is established and business is built. In Mexico, patience and the willingness to wait are still highly valued—and necessary—in business transactions. This is slowly changing, spurred in part by an aggressive cadre of young professionals who pursued graduate education in the United States.

Since the mid-1960s, production facilities known as *maquiladoras* have been a regular feature of Mexican border towns, especially along the Texas and New Mexico borders. US multinational companies, such as John Deere, Zenith, Mattel, and Xerox, run the majority of the more than 3,600 maquiladoras in northern Mexico. Billions of dollars' worth of products—from televisions to clothes to auto parts—are assembled in maquiladoras and then shipped back, tax free, to the United States for sale to US consumers.

Maquiladoras employ more than a million Mexicans, mostly unskilled women in their twenties and early thirties who work long hours. Wages and benefits are generally poor but much better than in the rest of Mexico. The huge growth in trade between the United States and Mexico has greatly expanded the role—and scale—of these assembly operations.

Along with the benefits, challenges have also come with the increased trade. A large number of Mexicans are concerned that wealth is distributed more unevenly than ever. For example, many commentators see the political situation in the state of Chiapas as underscoring the alienation large groups have suffered as a result of the opening of the Mexican economy to global forces. A rural region in southern Mexico, Chiapas is home to extremely poor Mayan, Ch'ol, Zoque, and Lacandón Indians. Although it is the poorest state in Mexico, Chiapas has the richest natural resources, including oil, minerals, and electrical power.

On January 1, 1994, the day NAFTA officially took effect, a group of Indian peasants, commanded by Subcomandante Marcos, rose up in armed rebellion. This was shocking not only to Mexico's leadership but to the international community. The unrest in Chiapas stems from long-standing economic and social injustice in the region and from the Indians' isolation and exploitation by the local oligarchy of landowners and mestizo bosses (*caciques*). While NAFTA clearly advanced the goals of free trade, global businesses are often forced to deal with local economic, political, and social realities within a country.

The Mexican government has indicated that improving the social conditions in the region is a high priority. However, only partial accords have been reached between the government and the peasants. At the same time, the army continues to exert tight control over the state, particularly in and around towns where residents are known to support the rebels.

The low standard of living in Chiapas and of Indians throughout Mexico remains a significant challenge for the Mexican government. In the years following the Chiapas uprising, poverty in southern Mexico has risen to about 40 percent, while in the north, poverty has decreased thanks to closer economic links with the United States. [8]

South America: MERCOSUR

The Common Market of the South, Mercado Común del Sur or MERCOSUR, was originally established in 1988 as a regional trade agreement between Brazil and Argentina and then was expanded in 1991 to include Uruguay and Paraguay. Over the past decade, Bolivia, Chile, Colombia, Ecuador, and Peru have become associate members, and Venezuela is in the process for full membership.

MERCOSUR constituents compose nearly half of the wealth created in all of Latin America as well as 40 percent of the population. Now the world's fourth-largest trading bloc after the EU, NAFTA, and the Association of South East Asian Nations (ASEAN), [9] the group has been strategically oriented to develop the economies of its constituents, helping them become more internationally competitive so that they would not have to rely on the closed market arena. MERCOSUR has brought nations with long-standing rivalries together. Although this is an economic trade initiative, it has also been designed with clear political goals. MERCOSUR is committed to the consolidation of democracy and the maintenance of peace throughout the southern cone. For example, it has taken stride to reach agreements between Brazil and Argentina in the nuclear field. [10]

MERCOSUR has emerged as one of the most dynamic and imaginative initiatives in the region. Surging trade, rising investment, and expanding output are the economic indicators that point to the group's remarkable achievement. More than this, the integration is helping transform national relations among South American nations and with the world as a whole, forging a new sense of shared leadership and shared purpose, which is sending ripples of hope across the continent and beyond.

Other Trade Agreements in the Americas

CARICOM and Andean Community

The Caribbean Community and Common Market (CARICOM), or simply the Caribbean Community, was formed in 1973 by countries in the Caribbean with the intent of creating a single market with the free flow of goods, services, labor, and investment. [11] The Andean Community (called the Andean Pact until 1996) [12] is a free trade agreement signed in 1969 between Bolivia, Chile, Colombia, Ecuador, and Peru. Eventually Chile dropped out, while

Venezuela joined for about twenty years and left in 2006. This trading bloc had limited impact for the first two decades of its existence but has experienced a renewal of interest after MERCOSUR's implementation. In 2007, MERCOSUR members became associate members of the Andean Community, and more cooperative interaction between the trading groups is expected. [13]

CAFTA-DR

The Dominican Republic–Central America–United States Free Trade Agreement (CAFTA-DR) is a free trade agreement signed into existence in 2005. Originally, the agreement (then called the Central America Free Trade Agreement, or CAFTA) encompassed discussions between the US and the Central American countries of Costa Rica, El Salvador, Guatemala, Honduras, and Nicaragua. A year before the official signing, the Dominican Republic joined the negotiations, and the agreement was renamed CAFTA-DR. [14]

The goal of the agreement is the creation of a free trade area similar to NAFTA. For free trade advocates, the CAFTA-DR is also seen as a stepping stone toward the eventual establishment of the Free Trade Area of the Americas (FTAA)—the more ambitious grouping for a free trade agreement that would encompass all the South American and Caribbean nations as well as those of North and Central America (except Cuba). Canada is currently negotiating a similar treaty called the Canada Central American Free Trade Agreement. It's likely that any resulting agreements will have to reconcile differences in rules and regulations with NAFTA as well as any other existing agreements. [15]

Did You Know?

As a result of CAFTA-DR, more than 80 percent of goods exported from the United States into the region are no longer subject to tariffs. [16] Given its physical proximity, Florida is the main investment gateway to the CAFTA-DR countries: about three hundred multinational firms have their Latin American and Caribbean regional headquarters in Florida. In all, more than two thousand companies headquartered outside the United States operate in Florida.

US companies, for example, sell more than $25 billion in products to the Latin American and Caribbean regions annually, ranking it among the top US export markets. With the removal of virtually all tariffs and other barriers to trade, the CAFTA-DR agreement is making commerce with these countries even easier, opening opportunities to a range of industries. At the same time, it's making the CAFTA-DR countries richer and increasing the purchasing power of their citizens.

For international companies looking to access these markets, the United States, recognized worldwide for its stable regulatory and legal framework and for its robust infrastructure, is the most logical place to set up operations. And within the United States, no location is as well positioned as Florida to act as the gateway to the CAFTA-DR markets. For a variety of reasons—from geography and language to well-developed business and family connections—this is a role that Florida has been playing very successfully for a number of years and which, with the implementation of CAFTA-DR, is only gaining in importance. [17]

Europe: EU

Brief History and Purpose

The European Union (EU) is the most integrated form of economic cooperation. As you learned in the opening case study, the EU originally began in 1950 to end the frequent wars between neighboring countries in the Europe. The six founding nations were France, West Germany, Italy, and the Benelux countries (Belgium, Luxembourg, and the Netherlands), all of which signed a treaty to run their coal and steel industries under a common management. The focus was on the development of the coal and steel industries for peaceful purposes.

In 1957, the six nations signed the Treaty of Rome, which established the European Economic Community (EEC) and created a common market between the members. Over the next fifty years, the EEC added nine more members and changed its name twice—to European Community (EC) in the 1970s and the European Union (EU) in 1993. [18]

The entire history of the transformation of the EEC to the EU has been an evolutionary process. However, the Treaty of Maastricht in 1993 stands out as an important moment; it's when the *real* economic union was created. With this treaty, the EU identified three aims. The first was to establish a single, common currency, which went into effect in 1999. The second was to set up monetary and fiscal targets for member countries. Third, the treaty called for a political union, which would include the development of a common foreign and defense policy and common citizenship. The opening case study addressed some of the current challenges the EU is facing as a result of the impact of these aims. Despite the challenges, the EU is likely to endure given its historic legacy. Furthermore, a primary goal for the

development of the EU was that Europeans realized that they needed a larger trading platform to compete against the US and the emerging markets of China and India. Individually, the European countries would never have the economic power they now have collectively as the EU.

Today, the EU has twenty-seven member countries. Croatia, Iceland, Macedonia, and Turkey are the next set of candidates for future membership. In 2009, the twenty-seven EU countries signed the Treaty of Lisbon, which amends the previous treaties. It is designed to make the EU more democratic, efficient, and transparent and to tackle global challenges, such as climate change, security, and sustainable development.

The European Economic Area (EEA) was established on January 1, 1994, following an agreement between the member states of the European Free Trade Association (EFTA) and the EC (later the EU). Specifically, it has allowed Iceland (now an EU candidate), Liechtenstein, and Norway to participate in the EU's single market without a conventional EU membership. Switzerland has also chosen to not join the EU, although it is part of similar bilateral agreements.

CEFTA

Central European Free Trade Agreement (CEFTA) is a trade agreement between non-EU countries in Central and Southeastern Europe, which currently includes Albania, Bosnia and Herzegovina, Croatia, Macedonia, Moldova, Montenegro, Serbia, and the United Nations Interim Administration Mission on behalf of Kosovo (UNMIK)—all of whom joined in 2006. [19]

Originally signed in 1992, CEFTA's founding members were the Visegrad Group, also called the Visegrad Four or V4, which is an alliance of four Central European states—the Czech Republic, Hungary, Poland, and Slovakia. All of the Visegrad Group have relatively developed free-market economies and have formal ties. [20]

Many of the Central European nations have left CEFTA to become members of the EU. In fact, CEFTA has served as a preparation for full EU membership and a large proportion of CEFTA foreign trade is with EU countries. Poland, the Czech Republic, Hungary, Slovakia, and Slovenia joined the EU on May 1, 2004, with Bulgaria and Romania following suit on January 1, 2007. [21]Croatia and Macedonia are in the process of becoming EU members. [22]

Amusing Anecdote

There are twenty-three official and working languages within the EU, and all official documents and legislation are translated into all of these languages. With this in mind, it's easy to see why so many Europeans see the need to speak more than one language fluently!

Official and Working Languages of the EU	
Bulgarian	Italian
Czech	Irish
Danish	Latvian
Dutch	Lithuanian
English	Maltese
Estonian	Polish
Finnish	Portuguese
French	Romanian
German	Slovene
Greek	Spanish
Hungarian	Swedish

EU Governance

The EU is a unique organization in that it is not a single country but a group of countries that have agreed to closely cooperate and coordinate key aspects of their economic policy. Accordingly, the organization has its own governing and decision-making institutions.

- **European Council.** The European Council provides the political leadership for the EU. The European Council meets four times per year, and each member has a representative, usually the head of its government. Collectively it functions as the EU's "Head of State."
- **European Commission.** The European Commission provides the day-to-day leadership and initiates legislation. It's the EU's executive arm.
- **European Parliament.** The European Parliament forms one-half of the EU's legislative body. The parliament consists of 751 members, who are elected by popular vote in their respective countries. The term for each member is five years. The purpose of the parliament is to debate and amend legislation proposed by the European Commission.
- **Council of the European Union.** The Council of the European Union functions as the other half of the EU's legislative body. It's sometimes called the Council or the Council of Ministers and should not be confused with the European Council above. The Council of the European Union consists of a government minister from each member country and its representatives may change depending on the topic being discussed.
- **Court of Justice.** The Court of Justice makes up the judicial branch of the EU. Consisting of three different courts, it reviews, interprets, and applies the treaties and laws of the EU. [23]

Current Challenges and Opportunities

The biggest advantage of EU membership is the monetary union. Today, sixteen member countries use the euro. Since its launch, the euro has become the world's second-largest reserve currency behind the US dollar. It's important to remember several distinctions. First, the EU doesn't consist of the same countries as the continent of Europe. Second, there are more EU member countries than there are countries using the euro. Euro markets, or euro countries, are the countries using the euro.

The European single market is the foremost advantage of being a member of EU. According to Europa, which is the official website of the EU (http://europa.eu), the EU member states have formed a single market with more than five hundred million people, representing 7 percent of the world's population. This single market permits the free flow of goods, service, capital, and people within the EU. [24] Although there is a single tariff on goods entering an EU country, once in the market, no additional tariffs or taxes can be levied on the goods. [25]

Businesses conducting business with one country in the EU now find it easier and cheaper, in many cases, to transact business with the other EU countries. There's no longer a currency–exchange rate risk, and the elimination of the need to convert currencies within euro markets reduces transaction costs. Further, having a single currency makes pricing more transparent and consistent between countries and markets.

Despite the perceived benefits, economic policymakers in the EU admit that the Union's labor markets are suffering from rigidity, regulation, and tax structures that have contributed to high unemployment and low employment responsiveness to economic growth. This is the case, particularly, for relatively low-skilled labor.

Future Outlook

Europe's economy faces a deeper recession and a slower recovery than the United States or other parts of the world.

Because the EU's $18.4 trillion economy makes up 30 percent of the world economy, its poor prospects are likely to rebound on the United States, Asia, and other regions. [26] Fixing the EU's banking system is particularly tricky, because sixteen of the twenty-seven countries share the euro currency and a central bank, but banking regulation mostly remains under the control of the national governments. [27]

The Europe 2020 strategy put forth by the European Commission sets out a vision of the EU's social market economy for the twenty-first century. It shows how the EU can come out stronger from this crisis and how it can be turned into a smart, sustainable, and inclusive economy delivering high levels of employment, productivity, and social cohesion. It calls for stronger economic governance in order to deliver rapid and lasting results. [28]

Asia: ASEAN

The Association of Southeast Asian Nations (ASEAN) was created in 1967 by five founding-member countries: Malaysia, Thailand, Indonesia, Singapore, and the Philippines. Since inception, Myanmar (Burma), Vietnam, Cambodia, Laos, and Brunei have joined the association. [29]

ASEAN's primary focus is on economic, social, cultural, and technical cooperation as well as promoting regional peace and stability. Although less emphasized today, one of the primary early missions of ASEAN was to prevent the domination of Southeast Asia by external powers—specifically China, Japan, India, and the United States.

In 2002, ASEAN and China signed a free trade agreement that went into effect in 2010 as the ASEAN–China Free Trade Area (ACFTA). In 2009, ASEAN and India also signed the ASEAN–India Free Trade Agreement (FTA). In 2009, ASEAN signed a free trade agreement with New Zealand and Australia. It also hopes to create an ASEAN Economic Community by 2015. [30] While the focus and function remains in discussion, the intent is to forge even closer ties among the ten member nations, enabling them to negotiate more effectively with global powers like the EU and the United States. [31]

Asia: APEC

The Asia–Pacific Economic Cooperation (APEC) was founded in 1989 by twelve countries as an informal forum. It now has twenty-one member economies on both sides of the Pacific Ocean. APEC is the only regional trading group that uses the term *member economies*, rather than countries, in deference to China. Taiwan was allowed to join the forum, but only under the name Chinese Taipei. [32]

As a result of the Pacific Ocean connection, this geographic grouping includes the United States, Canada, Mexico, Chile, Peru, Russia, Papua New Guinea, New Zealand, and Australia with their Asia Pacific Rim counterparts. [33] This assortment of economies and cultures has, at times, made for interesting and heated discussions. Focused primarily on economic growth and cooperation, the regional group has met with success in liberalizing and promoting free trade as well as facilitating business, economic, and technical cooperation between member economies. With the Doha Round of the WTO dragging, APEC members have been discussing establishing a free-trade zone. Given its broader membership than ASEAN, APEC has found good success—once its member countries agree. The two organizations often share common goals and seek to coordinate their efforts.

China Seeks to Create a Trading Bloc

On June 29, 2010, China and Taiwan signed the Economic Cooperation Framework Agreement (ECFA), a preferential trade agreement between the two governments that aims to reduce tariffs and commercial barriers between the two sides. It's the most significant agreement since the two countries split at the end of the Chinese Civil War in 1949. [34] It will boost the current $110 billion bilateral trade between both sides. China already absorbed Hong Kong in 1999, after the hundred-year lease to Britain ended. While Hong Kong is now managed by China as a Special Administrative Region (SAR), it continues to enjoy special economic status. China is eager for Hong Kong and Taiwan to serve as gateways to its massive market. Taiwan's motivation for signing the agreement was in large part an effort to get China to stop pressuring other countries from signing trade agreements with it. [35]

"An economically stronger Taiwan would not only gain clout with the mainland but also have more money to entice allies other than the 23 nations around the globe that currently recognize the island as an independent state. Beijing is hoping closer economic ties will draw Taiwan further into its orbit." [36] While opposition in Taiwan sees the agreement as a cover for reunification with China, the agreement does reduce tariffs on both sides, enabling businesses from both countries to engage in more trade.

Middle East and Africa: GCC

The Cooperation Council for the Arab States of the Gulf, also known as the Gulf Cooperation Council (GCC), was created in 1981. The six member states are Bahrain, Kuwait, Saudi Arabia, Oman, Qatar, and the United Arab Emirates (UAE). As a political and economic organization, the group focuses on trade, economic, and social issues. [37] The GCC has become as much a political organization as an economic one. Among its various initiatives, the GCC calls for the coordination of a unified military presence in the form of a Peninsula Shield Force. [38]

In 1989, the GCC and the EU signed a cooperation agreement. "Trade between the EU and the GCC countries totaled €79 billion in 2009 and should increase under the FTA. And while strong economic relations remain the basis for mutual ties, the EU and the GCC also share common interests in areas such as the promotion of alternative energy, thus contributing to the resolution of climate change and other pressing environmental concerns; the promotion of proper reform for the global economic and financial policies; and the enhancement of a comprehensive rules-based international system." [39]

In 2008, the GCC formed a common market, enabling free flow of trade, investment, and workers. [40] In December 2009, Bahrain, Saudi Arabia, Kuwait, and Qatar created a monetary council with the intent of eventually creating a shared currency. [41] Since its creation, the GCC has contributed not only to the expansion of trade but also to the development of its countries and the welfare of its citizens, as well as promoting peace and stability in the region. [42]

Middle East and Africa: AEC

The African Economic Community (AEC) is an organization of the African Union states. Signed in 1991 and implemented in 1994, it provides for a staged integration of the regional economic agreements. Several regional agreements function as pillars of the AEC: [43]

- Community of Sahel-Saharan States (CEN-SAD)
- Common Market for Eastern and Southern Africa (COMESA)
- East African Community (EAC)
- Economic Community of Central African States (ECCAS/CEEAC)
- Economic Community of West African States (ECOWAS)
- Intergovernmental Authority on Development (IGAD)
- Southern African Development Community (SADC)
- Arab Maghreb Union (AMU/UMA)

Economists argue that free trade zones are particularly suited to African countries which were created under colonial occupation when land was divided up, often with little regard for the economic sustainability of the newly created plot. Plus, post-independence conflict in Africa has left much of the continent with a legacy of poor governance and a lack of political integration which free trade zones aim to address….

[In October 2008,] plans were agreed to create a "super" free trade zone encompassing 26 African countries, stretching from Libya in the north to South Africa. The GDP of this group of nations is put at $624bn (£382.9bn). [44]

Ambitiously, in 2017 and after, the AEC intends to foster the creation of a free-trade zone and customs union in its regional blocs. Beyond that, there are hopes for a shared currency and eventual economic and monetary union.

How Do These Trade Agreements and Efforts Impact Business?

Overall, global businesses have benefited from the regional trade agreements by having more consistent criteria for investment and trade as well as reduced barriers to entry. Companies that choose to manufacture in one country find it easier and cheaper to move goods between member countries in that trading bloc without incurring tariffs or additional regulations.

The challenges for businesses include finding themselves outside of a new trading bloc or having the "rules" for their industry change as a result of new trade agreements. Over the past few decades, there has been an increase in bilateral and multilateral trade agreements. It's often called a "spaghetti bowl" of global bilateral and multilateral trade agreements, because the agreements are not linear strands lining up neatly; instead they are a messy mix of crisscrossing strands, like a bowl of spaghetti, that link countries and trading blocs in self-benefiting trading alliances. Businesses have to monitor and navigate these evolving trade agreements to make sure that one or more agreements don't negatively impact their businesses in key countries. This is one reason why global businesses have teams of in-house professionals monitoring the WTO as well as the regional trade alliances.

For example, American companies doing business in one of the ASEAN countries often choose to become members of the US–ASEAN Business Council, so that they can monitor and possibly influence new trade regulations as well as advance their business interests with government entities.

The US–ASEAN Business Council is the premiere advocacy organization for U.S. corporations operating within the dynamic Association of Southeast Asian Nations (ASEAN). ASEAN represents nearly 600 million people and a combined GDP of USD $1.5 trillion across Brunei Darussalam, Cambodia, Indonesia, Laos, Malaysia, Myanmar, the Philippines, Singapore, Thailand and Vietnam. The Council's members include the largest U.S. companies working in ASEAN, and range from newcomers to the region to companies that have been working in Southeast Asia for over 100 years....

The Council leads major business missions to key economies; convenes multiple meetings with ASEAN heads of state and ministers; and is the only U.S. organization to be given the privilege of raising member company concerns in consultations with the ASEAN Finance and Economic Ministers, as well as with the ASEAN Customs Directors-General at their annual meetings. Having long-established personal and professional relationships with key ASEAN decision makers, the Council is able to arrange genuine dialogues, solve problems and facilitate opportunities in all types of market conditions, and provide market entry and exclusive advisory services. [45]

US–ASEAN member companies read like the *Fortune* Global 500 and include AT&T, Coca-Cola, Microsoft, Johnson & Johnson, Chevron, Ford Motor Company, and General Electric. While other countries and the EU have ongoing dialogues with ASEAN, the US–ASEAN Business Council is the most formal approach. For a list of ongoing ASEAN relationships with key trading partners, visit http://www.aseansec.org/9731.htm.

It's easy to see how complicated the relationships can be with just one trading bloc. A global firm with operations in North America, the EU, and Asia could easily find itself at the crosshairs of competing trade interests. Staffed with lawyers in an advocacy department, global firms work to maintain relationships with all of the interested parties. If you are curious about a business career in trade, then you may want to consider combining a business degree with a legal degree for the most impact.

KEY TAKEAWAYS

- Regional economic integration refers to efforts to promote free and fair trade on a regional basis.

There are four main types of economic integration:

a. *Free trade area* is the most basic form of economic cooperation. Member countries remove all barriers to trade between themselves, but are free to independently determine trade policies with nonmember nations.

b. *Customs union* provides for economic cooperation. Barriers to trade are removed between member countries, and members agree to treat trade with nonmember countries in a similar manner.

c. *Common market* allows for the creation of an economically integrated market between member countries. Trade barriers and any restrictions on the movement of labor and capital between member countries are removed. There is a common trade policy for trade with nonmember nations, and workers no longer need a visa or work permit to work in another member country of a common market.

d. *Economic union* is created when countries enter into an economic agreement to remove barriers to trade and adopt common economic policies.

The largest regional trade cooperative agreements are the European Union (EU), the North American Free Trade Agreement (NAFTA), and the Asia–Pacific Economic Cooperation (APEC). The African Economic Community (AEC) has more member countries than the EU, NAFTA, and APEC but represents a substantially smaller portion of global trade than these other cooperatives.

EXERCISES

(AACSB: Reflective Thinking, Analytical Skills)

1. Describe the EU and why it's considered the most integrated economic cooperative agreement.
2. What are two ways that regional economic integration can help global companies?

[1] Cooperation Council for the Arab States of the Gulf website, accessed April 30, 2011, http://www.gcc-sg.org/eng/index.html.
[2] Common Market for Eastern and Southern Africa website, accessed April 30, 2011, http://www.comesa.int.
[3] Europa, the Official Website of the European Union, accessed April 30, 2011, http://europa.eu.
[4] Foreign Affairs and International Trade Canada, "Fast Facts: North American Free Trade Agreement," December 15, 2009, accessed December 30, 2010, http://www.international.gc.ca/trade-agreements-accords-commerciaux/agr-acc/nafta-alena/fast_facts-faits_saillants.aspx?lang=eng.
[5] William M. Pride, Robert James Hughes, and Jack R. Kapoor, Business, 9th ed. (Boston: Houghton Mifflin, 2008), 89, accessed April 30, 2011, http://books.google.com/books?id=z2tEhXnm1rAC&pg=PA88&lpg=PA88&dq=will+chile+join+nafta+2009&source=bl&ots=iohSe7YV0E&sig=BjQr2KOx0lsrAGhv5vMqeb9LhFU&hl=en&ei=hLu8TZ3LPNDAgQeZusjqBQ&sa=X&oi=book_result&ct=result&resnum=6&ved=0CDoQ6AEwBQ#v=onepage&q=will%20chile%20join%20nafta%202009&f=false.
[6] David A. Sanger, "Chile Is Admitted as North American Free Trade Partner," New York Times, December 12, 1994, accessed April 30, 2011, http://www.nytimes.com/1994/12/12/world/chile-is-admitted-as-north-american-free-trade-partner.html.

[7] Anthony DePalma, "Passing the Torch on a Chile Trade Deal," New York Times, January 7, 2001, accessed April 30, 2011, http://www.nytimes.com/2001/01/07/business/economic-view-passing-the-torch-on-a-chile-trade-deal.html.

[8] CultureQuest Doing Business in Mexico (New York: Atma Global, 2011).

[9] Joanna Klonsky and Stephanie Hanson, "Mercosur: South America's Fractious Trade Bloc," Council on Foreign Relations, August 20, 2009, accessed April 30, 2011, http://www.cfr.org/trade/mercosur-south-americas-fractious-trade-bloc/p12762.

[10] Joanna Klonsky and Stephanie Hanson, "Mercosur: South America's Fractious Trade Bloc," Council on Foreign Relations, August 20, 2009, accessed April 30, 2011, http://www.cfr.org/trade/mercosur-south-americas-fractious-trade-bloc/p12762.

[11] Caribbean Community (CARICOM) Secretariat website, accessed April 30, 2011, http://www.caricom.org/index.jsp.

[12] Andean Community of Nations—Andean Pact website, accessed April 30, 2011, http://www.grouplamerica.com/andean_pact.htm.

[13] European Commission, "Andean Community Regional Strategy Paper 2007–2013," December 4, 2007, accessed April 30, 2011, http://www.eeas.europa.eu/andean/rsp/07_13_en.pdf.

[14] "Dominican Republic–Central America–United States Free Trade Agreement (CAFTA-DR)," Export.gov, accessed April 30, 2011, http://www.export.gov/FTA/cafta-dr/index.asp.

[15] "What Is CAFTA?" CAFTA Intelligence Center, accessed April 30, 2011,http://www.caftaintelligencecenter.com/subpages/What_is_CAFTA.asp.

[16] "Dominican Republic–Central America–United States Free Trade Agreement (CAFTA-DR)," Export.gov, accessed April 30, 2011, http://www.export.gov/FTA/cafta-dr/index.asp.

[17] Enterprise Florida, "Your Business: International," The CAFTA Intelligence Center, accessed December 30, 2010, http://www.caftaintelligencecenter.com/subpages/location-International.asp.

[18] "History of the European Union," Europa, accessed April 30, 2011, http://europa.eu/abc/history/index_en.htm.

[19] Andzej Arendarski, Ludovit Cernak, Vladimir Dlouhy, and Bela Kadar, "Central European Free Trade Agreement," December 21, 1992, accessed April 30, 2011, http://www.worldtradelaw.net/fta/agreements/cefta.pdf.

[20] "About the Visegrad Group," International Visegrad Fund, accessed December 30, 2010, http://visegradgroup.eu/main.php?folderID=858.

[21] "About CEFTA," Central European Free Trade Agreement, accessed April 30, 2011, http://cefta.net.

[22] "About CEFTA," Central European Free Trade Agreement, accessed April 30, 2011,http://cefta.net; Andzej Arendarski, Ludovit Cernak, Vladimir Dlouhy, and Bela Kadar, "Central European Free Trade Agreement," December 21, 1992, accessed April 30, 2011,http://www.worldtradelaw.net/fta/agreements/cefta.pdf; Wikipedia, s.v. "Central European Free Trade Agreement," last modified February 12, 2011, accessed February 16, 2011,http://en.wikipedia.org/wiki/Central_European_Free_Trade_Agreement.

[23] "Institutions and Bodies of the European Union," Europa, accessed April 30, 2011, http://europa.eu/about-eu/institutions-bodies/index_en.htm.

[24] "Four Market Freedom Which Benefit Us All," Europa, accessed December 30, 2010, http://europa.eu/pol/singl/index_en.htm.

[25] "Basic Information on the European Union," Europa, accessed April 30, 2011, http://europa.eu/about-eu/basic-information/index_en.htm.

[26] "Staring into the Abyss," Economist, July 8, 2010, accessed December 28, 2010, http://www.economist.com/node/16536898.

[27] Liz Alderman, "Contemplating the Future of the European Union," New York Times, February 13, 2010, accessed April 30, 2011, http://www.nytimes.com/2010/02/14/weekinreview/14alderman.html.

[28] "Future for Europe," Europa, accessed April 30, 2011, http://europa.eu/abc/12lessons/lesson_12/index_en.htm.

[29] {Author's Name retracted as requested by the work's original creator or licensee}, Doing Business in Asia: The Complete Guide, 2nd ed. (San Francisco: Jossey-Bass, 1998).

[30] "ASEAN Countries to Integrate Regional Capital Markets by 2015," Asia Economic Institute, accessed April 30, 2011, http://www.asiaecon.org/special_articles/read_sp/12174.

[31] "About ASEAN," Association of Southeast Asian Nations, accessed April 30, 2011, http://www.aseansec.org/about_ASEAN.html.

[32] {Author's Name retracted as requested by the work's original creator or licensee}, Doing Business in Asia: The Complete Guide, 2nd ed. (San Francisco: Jossey-Bass, 1998).

[33] "About APEC: History," Asia–Pacific Economic Cooperation, accessed April 30, 2011, http://www.apec.org/About-Us/About-APEC/History.aspx.

[34] Keith B. Richburg, "China, Taiwan Sign Trade Pact," Washington Post, June 30, 2010, accessed April 30, 2011, http://www.washingtonpost.com/wp-dyn/content/article/2010/06/29/AR2010062900163.html.

[35] Lucy Hornby, "Taiwan and China Sign Trade Pact," Reuters, June 29, 2010, accessed April 30, 2011, http://www.reuters.com/article/2010/06/29/us-china-taiwan-signing-idUSTRE65S17Z20100629.

[36] Isaac Stone Fish, "Taiwan Inks Risky Deal with China," Newsweek, July 2, 2010, accessed December 31, 2010, http://www.newsweek.com/2010/07/02/taiwan-inks-a-risky-deal-with-china.html.

[37] Cooperation Council for the Arab States of the Gulf website, accessed April 30, 2011, http://www.gcc-sg.org/eng/index.html.

[38] "Stop Meddling in Our Affairs: GCC Countries Tell Iran," The Middle East Times, April 4, 2011, accessed April 30, 2011, http://www.mideast-times.com/left_news.php?newsid=1628.

[39] Gonzalo de Benito, Luigi Narbone, and Christian Koch, "The Bonds between the GCC and EU Grow Deeper," The National, June 12, 2010, accessed May 23, 2011,http://www.grc.ae/index.php?frm_module=contents&frm_action=detail_book&frm_type_id=&op_lang=en&override=Articles+%3E+The+Bonds+between+the+GCC+and+EU+Grow+Deeper&sec=Contents&frm_title=&book_id=69542.

[40] P. K. Abdul Ghafour, "GCC Common Market Becomes a Reality," Arab News, January 2, 2008, accessed April 30, 2011, http://archive.arabnews.com/?page=1&section=0&article=105173&d=1&m=1&y=2008.

[41] Mohsin Khan, "The GCC Monetary Union: Choice of Exchange Rate Regime," Peterson Institute for International Economics, April 2009, accessed April 30, 2011, http://www.iie.com/publications/wp/wp09-1.pdf.

[42] Nadim Kawach, "Unrest Will Not Affect GCC Monetary Union: Bahrain Central Bank Governor Says Union Remains Open for Other Members," Emirates 24/7, March 12, 2011, accessed April 30, 2011, http://www.emirates247.com/2.266/finance/unrest-will-not-affect-gcc-monetary-union-2011-03-12-1.366972.

[43] Wikipedia, s.v. "African Economic Community," accessed April 30, 2011, http://en.wikipedia.org/wiki/African_Economic_Community.

[44] Louise Greenwood, "Q&A: Free Trade Zones in Africa," BBC Africa Business Report, BBC News, August 21, 2009, accessed December 31, 2010, http://news.bbc.co.uk/2/hi/business/8208254.stm.

[45] "About the US–ASEAN Business Council," US–ASEAN Business Council, accessed December 31, 2010, http://www.usasean.org/Aboutus/index.asp.

5.3 The United Nations and the Impact on Trade
LEARNING OBJECTIVE

1. Understand how and why peace impacts business.
2. Describe the role of the United Nations.
3. Identify how global businesses benefit from political and economic stability

The final section in this chapter reviews an institution, the United Nations, whose primary purpose is to promote peace between countries. Peace fosters stability and that stability provides the framework for the expansion of business interests and trade.

Why Does Peace Impact Business?
The opening case study demonstrated how political, economic, and military instability in Europe led to two world wars and eventually the development of the EU. It's clear that conflict between countries significantly reduces international trade and seriously damages national and global economic welfare.

It's worth noting that there is a wide range of businesses that benefit from war—for example, companies in industries that manufacture arms, plastics, clothing (uniforms), and a wide range of supplies and logistics. Companies such as BAE Systems, Lockheed Martin, Finmeccanica, Thales Group, General Dynamics, KBR (Halliburton), Rolls-Royce, Boeing, and Honeywell are just some of the world's largest companies in this sector, and all receive benefits that are woven into economic and trade policy from their respective governments directly as well as through general preferences in trade policies and agreements.

Did You Know?

Industrialized countries negotiate free trade and investment agreements with other countries, but exempt military spending from the liberalizing demands of the agreement. Since only the wealthy countries can afford to devote billions on military spending, they will always be able to give their corporations hidden subsidies through defence contracts, and maintain a technologically advanced industrial capacity.

And so, in every international trade and investment agreement one will find a clause which exempts government programs and policies deemed vital for national security. [1]

Nevertheless, military conflict can be extremely disruptive to economic activity and impede long-term economic performance. As a result, most global businesses find that operating in stable environments leads to the best business operations for a range of reasons:

- **Staffing.** It's easier to recruit skilled labor if the in-country conditions are stable and relatively risk-free. Look at the challenges companies have in recruiting nonmilitary personnel to work in the fledging private sectors of Iraq or Afghanistan. Even development organizations have been challenged to send in skilled talent to develop banking-, finance-, and service-sector initiatives. Historically, regardless of which country or conflict, development staff has only been sent into a country after stability has been secured by military force. Companies have to pay even higher levels of hardship and risk pay and may still not necessarily be able to bring in the best talent.
- **Operations.** In unstable environments, companies fear loss or damage to property and investment. For example, goods in transit can easily be stolen, and factories or warehouses can be damaged.
- **Regulations.** Unclear and constantly changing business rules make it hard for firms to plan for the long term.
- **Currency convertibility and free-flowing capital.** Often countries experiencing conflict often impose capital controls (i.e., restrictions on money going in and out of their countries) as well as find that their currency may be devalued or illiquid. Financial management is a key component of global business management.

While bilateral or multilateral trade doesn't always dissuade countries from pursuing military options, countries that are engaged in trade discussions are more likely to use these forums to discuss other conflict areas. Furthermore, the largest global companies—Siemens, General Electric, Boeing, Airbus, and others—have the economic might to influence governments to promote initiatives to benefit their companies or industries.

Ethics in Action

Business in Conflict Zones: Angola and Conflict Diamonds
Angola, located in southern Africa, is a country that faced internal devastation from an intense civil war raging from its independence in 1975 until 2002. For many businesspeople, Angola may seem a relatively obscure country. However, it is the second-largest petroleum and diamond producer in sub-Saharan Africa. While the oil has brought economic success,

the diamonds, known as conflict or blood diamonds, have garnered global attention. Even Hollywood has called attention to this illicit trade in a 2006 movie entitled *Blood Diamond* as well as numerous other movie plots focusing on conflict diamonds, including one in the James Bond franchise. So what are conflict diamonds? The United Nations (UN) defines them as follows:

Conflict diamonds are diamonds that originate from areas controlled by forces or factions opposed to legitimate and internationally recognized governments, and are used to fund military action in opposition to those governments, or in contravention of the decisions of the Security Council….

Rough diamond caches have often been used by rebel forces to finance arms purchases and other illegal activities. Neighbouring and other countries can be used as trading and transit grounds for illicit diamonds. Once diamonds are brought to market, their origin is difficult to trace and once polished, they can no longer be identified. [2]

First discovered in 1912, diamonds are a key industry for Angola. During its twenty-seven years of conflict, which cost up to 1.5 million lives, rebel groups in Angola traded diamonds to fund armed conflict, hence the term *conflict diamonds*. Some estimate that Angola's main rebel group, National Union for the Total Independence of Angola (UNITA), sold more than $3.72 billion in conflict diamonds to finance its war against the government. [3]

These morally tainted conflict diamonds, along with those from other conflict countries, were bad for the global diamond industry—damaging the reputation and integrity of their key commodity product.

In 1999, the UN applied sanctions to ban the Angolan rebels' trade in conflict diamonds, but a portion of diamonds continued to be traded by the rebels. The UN conducted extensive investigations. "The Security Council's diamond campaign is part of an ongoing UN effort to make sanctions more selective, better targeted and more rigorously enforced instruments for maintaining international peace and security." [4]

Eventually, the UN, various governments, the diamond industry, and nongovernmental organizations, including Global Witness, Amnesty International, and Partnership Africa Canada (PAC), recognized the need for a global system to prevent conflict diamonds from entering the legitimate diamond supply chain and thus helping fund conflicts. The process that was established in 2003 provides for certification process to assure consumers that by

purchasing certified diamonds they weren't financing war and human rights abuses. As a result, seventy-four governments have adopted the Kimberley Process certification system, and more than 99 percent of the world's diamonds are from conflict-free sources. [5]

The Kimberley Process and global attention have addressed a critical global-business ethics issue. By taking collective ethical action, the global diamond industry, including firms such as De Beers, Cartier, and Zale, have not only done the right thing but have also helped preserve and grow their businesses while restoring the reputation of their industry.

For example, South African De Beers is the world's largest diamond mining and trading company. Prior to UN action and the Kimberley Process, De Beers was buying conflict diamonds from guerilla movements in three African countries, thereby financing regional conflicts. One UN investigation in Angola found that rebel forces bartered uncut diamonds for weaponry, thereby allowing the civil war to continue in 1998 despite international economic and diplomatic sanctions. In 1999, under UN pressure, De Beers decided to stop buying any outside diamonds in order to guarantee the conflict-free status of its diamond. [6]

Today, De Beers states that 100 percent of the diamonds it sells are conflict-free and that all De Beers diamonds are purchased in compliance with national law, the Kimberley Process, and its own Best Practice Principles. [7]

Angola is still dealing with the loss and devastation of an almost thirty-year conflict with its quality of life among the worst in the world in terms of life expectancy and infant mortality. Nevertheless, the country has made rapid economic strides since 2002 and is now one of the fastest-growing economies in Africa. Conflict diamonds are no longer traded in Angola. The country is a Kimberley Process participant and currently produces approximately 9 percent of the world's diamonds. [8]

The United Nations
The United Nations (UN) was formed in 1945 at the end of World War II to replace the League of Nations, which had been formed in 1919. Its original goals remain the same today: to maintain international peace and security; to develop friendly relations between nations; and to foster international cooperation in solving economic, social, humanitarian, and cultural issues. There is an underlying premise of human rights and equality. Almost all of the world's countries are members—currently 192 nations—with only a few smaller territories and Taiwan, out of

deference to China, given observer status and not membership. The UN is funded by member countries' assessments and contributions.

The work of the UN reaches every corner of the globe. Throughout the world, the UN and its agencies assist refugees, set up programs to clear landmines, help expand food production, and lead the fight against AIDS. They also help protect the environment, fight diseases, reduce poverty, and strive for better living standards and human rights. Although the UN is often best known for peacekeeping, peace building, conflict prevention, and humanitarian assistance, the organization also works on a broad range of fundamental social, economic, environment, and health issues. In the Ethics in Action sidebar on Angola, you learned how the UN led the way to resolving the problem of conflict diamonds and partnered with the global diamond industry to develop a long-term solution to a thorny ethical trading problem and promote peace and stability in former conflict countries like Angola.

A secretary-general leads the UN and serves for a five-year term. Structurally, the UN consists of six main bodies:

1. **General Assembly.** This is the deliberative body of the UN and consists of all of the member countries that meet in regular sessions throughout the year. All of the members have an equal vote in the General Assembly.
2. **Security Council.** This body is responsible for addressing issues related to peace and security. It has fifteen members, five of which are permanent country representations—the United States, the United Kingdom, Russia, China, and France. The remaining ten are elected by the General Assembly every two years. As you may expect, there's a great deal of political wrangling by countries to be on the Security Council, which is deemed to have significant power. All decisions by the Security Council are supposed to be binding on the rest of the member nations of the UN.
3. **Economic and Social Council (ECOSOC).** This body is responsible for issues related to economics, human rights, and social matters. A number of smaller commissions and specialized agencies carry out this council's work. The ECOSOC works closely with the World Bank and the International Monetary Fund.
4. **Secretariat.** The Secretariat oversees the operations of the UN and is technically headed by the Secretary-General
5. **International Court of Justice.** Located in The Hague, this body hears disputes between nations. The court consists of fifteen judges who are elected by the General Assembly and the Security Council. The court reviews cases concerning war crimes, genocide, ethnic cleansing, and illegal interference by one country in the affairs of another, among others.
6. **UN Trusteeship Council.** While an official part of the UN Charter charged with overseeing all trustee territories under UN custody, this body is currently inactive.

Did You Know?

A strong UN is the world's most effective voice for international cooperation on behalf of peace, development, human rights, and the environment. The UN has also sought to forge partnerships outside of the traditional diplomatic arena. One such partnership that is of growing interest to private sector businesses is the UN Global Compact. This is a strategic policy initiative for businesses that are committed to aligning their operations and strategies with ten universally accepted principles. Why would companies want to align their businesses with these principles? For starters, some businesses see it as a way to be a good global corporate citizen, a label that they can use to attract and retain the best workforce as well as use in marketing efforts to exhibit their global corporate responsibility. The UN is motivated to engage the private sector in helping solve the world's most pressing problems, often with for-profit solutions.

The United Nations Global Compact presents a unique strategic platform for participants to advance their commitments to sustainability and corporate citizenship. Structured as a public-private initiative, the Global Compact offers a policy framework for the development, implementation, and disclosure of sustainability principles and practices related to its four core areas: human rights, labour, the environment and anti-corruption. Indeed, managing the enterprise risks and opportunities related to these areas is today a widely understood aspect of long-term "value creation"—value creation that can simultaneously benefit the private sector and societies at large.

With over 7700 business participants and other stakeholders from more than 130 countries, the Global Compact offers participants a wide spectrum of specialized work streams, management tools and resources, and topical programs and projects—all designed to help advance sustainable business models and markets in order to contribute to the initiative's overarching objective of helping to build a more sustainable and inclusive global economy. [9]

Companies use their participation in the UN Global Compact to illustrate that they are good global corporate citizens, in an effort to satisfy the objectives of consumers, suppliers, and investors as well as government and nongovernment entities—all of whose support a global company needs to achieve its global business objectives.

One example is Coca-Cola and its adherence to maintaining its good global business citizenship also earns it the ability to influence trade and economic policy with governments and organizations that can positively impact its business interests in select markets around the world. For example, Coca-Cola highlights its commitment on its website and in global reports. The company explains on its website, "In March 2006, The Coca-Cola Company became a signatory to the United Nations (UN) Global Compact, affirming our commitment to the advancement of its 10 universal accepted principles…in the areas of human rights, labor, the environment and anti-corruption. Several of our bottling partners are also signatories." [10]

The Ten Principles of the UN Global Compact

Human Rights
- Principle 1: Businesses should support and respect the protection of internationally proclaimed human rights; and
- Principle 2: make sure that they are not complicit in human rights abuses.

Labour
- Principle 3: Businesses should uphold the freedom of association and the effective recognition of the right to collective bargaining;
- Principle 4: the elimination of all forms of forced and compulsory labour;
- Principle 5: the effective abolition of child labour; and
- Principle 6: the elimination of discrimination in respect of employment and occupation.

Environment
- Principle 7: Businesses should support a precautionary approach to environmental challenges;
- Principle 8: undertake initiatives to promote greater environmental responsibility; and
- Principle 9: encourage the development and diffusion of environmentally friendly technologies.

Anti-Corruption
- Principle 10: Businesses should work against corruption in all its forms, including extortion and bribery. [11]

UN as a Business Partner

The UN has a very clear diplomatic role on the global stage. It's also important to remember that it works closely with the private sector, which actually carries out the vast amount of services and projects around the world. Global businesses sell to the UN just as they do to their own governments and public-sector organizations. Each arm of the UN has a procurement office. The UN Procurement Division does business with vendors from all over the world and is actively working to increase its sources of supply from developing countries and countries with economies in transition.

KEY TAKEAWAYS

- While certain industries (e.g., defense companies) benefit from conflict, in general global firms prosper best in peaceful times. The primary impact for businesses is in the areas of staffing, operations, regulations, and currency convertibility and financial management.
- The United Nations (UN) was formed at the end of World War II in 1945. Its original intent remains the same: to maintain international peace and security; to develop friendly relations between nations; and to foster international cooperation in solving economic, social, humanitarian, and cultural issues.
- The six main bodies of the UN are the (1) Secretariat, (2) Security Council, (3) General Assembly, (4) Economic and Social Council, (5) International Court of Justice, and (6) UN Trusteeship Council. The Secretary-General leads the UN.

EXERCISES

(AACSB: Reflective Thinking, Analytical Skills)
1. GE makes both military equipment and consumer products. Research GE and its product range on its website (http://www.ge.com/products_services/directory/by_product.html). Do you think a company like GE prefers conflict zones or peaceful countries? What issues do you think senior management has to consider when reviewing the company's operations in Angola? Use what you learned in the Ethics in Action sidebar on Angola and research the country's civil war. Visit GE's Angola website at http://www.ge.com/ao/ to obtain

more information on the company's in-country operations.

2. The Did You Know? sidebar on the UN Global Compact reviewed how the UN is partnering with global businesses. Visit http://www.unglobalcompact.org. List the ten principles to which businesses must agree. Select one global company and evaluate if you think the ten principles are reasonable and worthwhile for the company to follow.

[1] Stephen Staples, "Confronting the Military-Corporate Complex" (presented at the Hague Appeal for Peace, The Hague, May 12, 1999).
[2] United Nations Department of Public Information in cooperation with the Sanctions Branch, Security Council Affairs Division, Department of Political Affairs, "Conflict Diamonds: Sanctions and War," United Nations, March 21, 2001, accessed December 31,
2010, http://www.un.org/peace/africa/Diamond.html.
[3] Wikipedia, s.v. "Blood diamond," last modified February 9, 2011, accessed February 15,
2011, http://en.wikipedia.org/wiki/Blood_diamond.
[4] Michael Fleshman, "Targeting 'Conflict Diamonds' in Africa," Africa Recovery 14, no. 4 (January 2001): 6, accessed December 31, 2010, http://www.un.org/ecosocdev/geninfo/afrec/subjindx/144diam.htm.
[5] World Diamond Council, "Eliminating Conflict Diamonds," accessed December 31,
2010, http://diamondfacts.org/conflict/eliminating_conflict_diamonds.html#kim.
[6] Dick Durham, "De Beers Sees Threat of Blood Diamonds," January 18, 2001, accessed April 30, 2011,
http://www.cnnstudentnews.cnn.com/2001/WORLD/africa/01/18/diamonds.debeers/index.html.
[7] De Beers Group, "FAQs: What Has De Beers Done about Conflict Diamonds?" 2008, accessed December 31,
2010,http://www.debeersgroup.com/en/Global/FAQs/#Section755.
[8] Wikipedia, s.v. "Angola," last modified February 13, 2011, accessed February 16, 2011, http://en.wikipedia.org/wiki/Angola.
[9] "How to Participate," United Nations Global Compact, accessed January 1, 2011,
http://www.unglobalcompact.org/HowToParticipate/Business_Participation/index.html.
[10] "UN Global Compact," Coca-Cola Company, accessed January 1, 2011, http://www.thecoca-colacompany.com/citizenship/un_global_compact.html.
[11] "The Ten Principles," United Nations Global Compact, accessed April 30, 2011,
http://www.unglobalcompact.org/AboutTheGC/TheTenPrinciples/index.html.

5.4 End-of-Chapter Questions and Exercises

These exercises are designed to ensure that the knowledge you gain from this book about international business meets the learning standards set out by the international Association to Advance Collegiate Schools of Business (AACSB International). [1] AACSB is the premier accrediting agency of collegiate business schools and accounting programs worldwide. It expects that you will gain knowledge in the areas of communication, ethical reasoning, analytical skills,

use of information technology, multiculturalism and diversity, and reflective thinking.

EXPERIENTIAL EXERCISES

(AACSB: Communication, Use of Information Technology, Analytical Skills)

1. Review the WTO and the regional trading agreements. Which do you think is more effective in promoting free trade, the global or regional cooperative agreements? Why?

2. Based on what you have learned in Chapter 3 "Culture and Business", the opening case study on the EU in this chapter, and Section 5.2 "Regional Economic Integration", do you think countries with distinctively different cultural, historical, and economic histories can effectively enter into a trade agreement? Select one regional trading bloc and discuss the economic motivations for that group of countries to form an agreement. Use Hofstedes cultural dimensions at http://www.geert-hofstede.com/geert_hofstede_resources.shtml. Do you think the countries in the trading bloc you selected are likely to have cross-cultural similarities or differences?

Ethical Dilemma

(AACSB: Ethical Reasoning, Multiculturalism, Reflective Thinking, Analytical Skills)

1. Based on what you learned in Chapter 3 "Culture and Business" and this chapter, do you feel that countries enforce trade rules fairly? What factors might affect how one government interprets violations of trade rules? Using a sports analogy, is the WTO a fair referee for trade issues? Is the UN a fair referee for trade and other issues? Why or why not? Research the voting rules for each organization to support for your answer.

2. Based on what you have learned about economic unions and the current issues facing the EU, do you think that NAFTA could become an economic union in the foreseeable future? Why or why not? Use your understanding of economic and monetary unions as well as your understanding of the cultures of the countries in NAFTA. Review the two arguments against the EU as outlined in the opening case. How do you feel that culture, politics, society, and history would impact any possible economic union for NAFTA?

3. The *Wall Street Journal* highlighted the issue of conflict minerals in an article entitled "Retailers Fight to Escape 'Conflict Minerals' Law." Retailers, including Walmart and Target, are protesting part of a new US law that requires companies to verify that products with minerals

from Central Africa are not taxed or controlled by rebel regimes: "Some of the largest U.S. retailers argue they shouldn't have to comply with the rule if they don't exercise direct control over the manufacturing of goods carrying their own brands....Tracing the source of minerals is a tricky task, companies say, because many intermediaries stand between them and the mines." [2] Based on what you learned in this chapter and the sidebar on conflict diamonds in Angola, do you agree or disagree with the statement above and the retailers' position? Why or why not? Should retailers that have their name on a product be responsible for how the product is made?

[1] Association to Advance Collegiate Schools of Business website, accessed January 26, 2010, http://www.aacsb.edu.
[2] Jessica Holzer, "Retailers Fight to Escape Conflict Minerals Law," Wall Street Journal, December 2, 2010, accessed January 2, 2010, http://online.wsj.com/article/SB1000142405274870386500457564899296 4733232.html.

NOTES:

NOTES:

Chapter 6:
International Monetary System

1. What is the international monetary system?
2. What role do the International Monetary Fund (IMF) and the World Bank play?
3. How do the global monetary institutions impact global business?

Global trade depends on the smooth exchange of currencies between countries. Businesses rely on a predictable and stable mechanism. This chapter takes a look at the recent history of global monetary systems and how they have evolved over the past two centuries. While the current monetary system continues to evolve, lessons learned over the past fifty years help determine the best future options. As part of the post–World War II monetary environment, two institutions were created; these institutions have expanded to play an increasingly larger role in world economy. Understanding the role of the IMF and the World Bank provides insight into how governments in developing countries prioritize and fund projects and work with the private sector to implement these initiatives.

OPENING CASE: MCKINSEY & COMPANY: LINKING THE BUSINESS WORLD, GOVERNMENTS, AND GLOBAL INSTITUTIONS

Who Is McKinsey?

McKinsey & Company is a privately held global management-consulting firm that serves as a trusted adviser to the world's leading businesses, governments, and institutions. Recognized as a global leader, it has ranked first as the most prestigious firm in the management consulting industry by Vault.com. [1]

James O. "Mac" McKinsey, an accounting professor at the University of Chicago, founded McKinsey & Company in Chicago in 1926. Over the decades, McKinsey & Company has grown to global prominence by providing expert consulting services and garnering results for companies in a wide range of industries and governments.

Today, McKinsey has a revenue of $6 billion and employs almost 17,000 people worldwide, with more than 9,000 at the director level. "The firm is among the largest hirers of newly minted MBAs in the United States." [2]McKinsey's employees come from around the world, speaking over 120 languages and representing more than one hundred nationalities.

What Does the Firm Do?

As a management consultant firm, McKinsey is approached by its clients to analyze and solve complex problems. Its industry expertise ranges from media and entertainment to the automotive industry, chemicals, and manufacturing. Functional expertise includes all aspects of running a business, including, finance, technology, sales, marketing, risk, and operations. McKinsey has its own Global Institute whose "independent investigations combine McKinsey's microeconomic understanding of companies and industries with the rigor of leading macroeconomic thinking to derive perspectives on the global forces shaping business, government, and society." [3]

The Global Institute is one of McKinsey's paths to assisting governments and global institutions with complex economic and business issues. "Twenty years of McKinsey Global Institute research shows that the mix of sectors within an economy explains very little of the difference in a country's GDP growth rate. In other words, dynamism doesn't turn on whether an economy has a large financial sector, or big manufacturers, or a semiconductor industry, but instead on whether the sectors are competitive or not. Instead of picking winners and funneling subsidies to them, countries must get the basics right. These include a solid rule of law, with patents and protections for intellectual property, enforceable contracts, and courts to resolve disputes; access to finance, particularly for startups; and an efficient physical and communications infrastructure." [4]

Why Does the Firm Matter to International Business?

This chapter discusses the international monetary system, the IMF and the World Bank. In learning about these critical parts of the global business environment, you may find yourself wondering how exactly these institutions and government-led monetary systems interact with the business world. Learning about the business of a management consulting firm like McKinsey helps to illustrate this link.

Over the decades, McKinsey has helped global businesses understand how to enter new markets around the world, how to compete more effectively against their global competitors, and how to harness efficiencies and make improvements in all levels of business. Simultaneously, McKinsey has discreetly been an advisor to governments around the world on diverse issues, including how to amend policy and regulation to encourage more trade and investment in their countries; developing and implementing processes for privatizing industries; and creating more efficiencies in the public sector. At the same time, McKinsey has helped the IMF and the World Bank craft policy to meet their evolving roles in the world economy. Given the often politically charged global environment, it's clear why a company like McKinsey prefers to remain out of the public eye. Much of the work that the firm is engaged in impacts the daily lives of people around the world. Businesses and governments are attracted to McKinsey not only for its sound analysis and advice but also for its discretion and long-term perspective.

McKinsey's consultants form an enviable global network that extends even to former employees. McKinsey operates under a practice of "up or out," meaning that consultants must either advance in their consulting careers within a predefined time frame or leave the firm. It's not uncommon to find that a consultant will leave McKinsey to join their clients in the private sector or work for a government or global institution. This network of "McKinsey-ites," as they are sometimes called, is evident in their influence on policy that could impact their business clients—either on a country basis or industry basis. This network helps attract some of the best business school graduates to the firm.

As noted on its website, people "who join McKinsey find themselves part of a unique culture, shaped by shared values and a desire to help clients make substantial improvements in their performance. When consultants leave, their connection to our firm and their former colleagues remains strong. Our alumni number nearly 23,000 and work in virtually every business sector in almost 120 countries. Through formal events and informal networking, former McKinsey consultants make and sustain professional relationships. This dynamic network is a lasting benefit of a career with McKinsey. Our firm provides support to alumni who want to stay in touch with us and with each other, sponsoring events worldwide." [5]

One of the more interesting aspects of McKinsey's business approach is its nonexclusivity. Consultants develop expertise and can work for direct competitors after short holding periods of one or two years. Other companies in the same industry often see this as an opportunity to learn more about their competitors' strategies—knowing that a competitor has hired McKinsey provides a strong impetus for companies to seek McKinsey's assistance themselves. However, McKinsey does keep its client list confidential, and consultants themselves are not allowed to discuss their work with other teams.

The McKinsey mystique is another interesting aspect of the firm that adds to the secrecy that surrounds it. Despite its size, the firm does not discuss specific client situations and maintains a carefully crafted and low-profile external image, which also protects it from public scrutiny. The McKinsey commitment to discretion has earned it global private and public-sector clients and respect.

Roundly considered to be the most prestigious company of its kind, it has achieved a level of renown so great as to be known even to laymen, despite shrouding details of its work—and its client list—in secrecy. In its practice areas, it addresses strategic, organizational, operational and technological issues, always with a focus—according to the firm—of doing what is right for the client's business, not what is best for McKinsey's bottom line. As for the range of those specialties, the list of industrial sectors the firm serves encompasses everything from commodities and natural resources to the worlds of media, entertainment and high tech. While it doesn't give up the names of its clients (even in case studies it refers to them with pseudonyms such as "BigBank") the firm does claim to serve more than 70 percent of Fortune's Most Admired Companies list, roughly 90 percent of the top-100 corporations worldwide and 80 percent of the 100 largest U.S.-based companies. [6]

While it's hard to know exact details of its pricing, client base, success rate, and profitability, it's clear that the company continues to earn the trust and loyalty of many of the world's companies, governments, and global institutions.

OPENING CASE EXERCISES
(AACSB: Ethical Reasoning, Multiculturalism, Reflective Thinking, Analytical Skills)
1. How does the business of a management consultant illustrate the link between businesses, governments, and global institutions?
2. Discuss how a global consulting firm might assist a government client.
3. Why would a global business in the private sector want to hire McKinsey if McKinsey had already done consulting work for a competitor?

[1] "McKinsey & Company," Vault, accessed February 9, 2011,http://www.vault.com/wps/portal/usa/companies/company-profile?WCM_GLOBAL_CONTEXT=/wps/wcm/connect/Vault_Content_Library/companies+site/companies/parent_mckinsey+_+company/mckinsey+_+company_0/mckinsey+_+company_0&companyId=328.

[2] "America's Largest Private Companies: #54 McKinsey & Co.," Forbes, October 28, 2009, accessed February 9, 2011, http://www.forbes.com/lists/2009/21/private-companies-09_McKinsey-Co_IPPW.html (emphasis added).

[3] "McKinsey Global Institute," McKinsey & Company, accessed February 9, 2011, http://www.mckinsey.com/mgi.

[4] James Manyika, Susan Lund, and Byron Auguste, "From the Ashes," Newsweek, August 16, 2010, accessed February 9, 2011, http://www.newsweek.com/2010/08/16/mckinsey-institute-create-jobs-by-losing-them.html.

[5] "Alumni," McKinsey & Company, accessed February 9, 2011, http://www.mckinsey.com/aboutus/alumni.

[6] "McKinsey & Company," Vault, accessed February 9, 2011,http://www.vault.com/wps/portal/usa/companies/company-profile?WCM_GLOBAL_CONTEXT=/wps/wcm/connect/Vault_Content_Library/companies+site/companies/parent_mckinsey+_+company/mckinsey+_+company_0/mckinsey+_+company_0&companyId=328.

6.1 What Is the International Monetary System?
LEARNING OBJECTIVES

1. Understand the role and purpose of the international monetary system.
2. Describe the purpose of the gold standard and why it collapsed.
3. Describe the Bretton Woods Agreement and why it collapsed.
4. Understand today's current monetary system, which developed after the Bretton Woods Agreement collapse.

Why do economies need money? This chapter defines *money* as a unit of account that is used as a medium of exchange in transactions. Without money, individuals and businesses would have a harder time obtaining (purchasing) or exchanging (selling) what they need, want, or make. Money provides us with a universally accepted medium of exchange. Before the current monetary system can be fully appreciated, it's helpful to look back at history and see how money and systems governing the use of money have evolved.

Thousands of years ago, people had to barter if they wanted to get something. That worked well if the two people each wanted what the other had. Even today, bartering exists.

History shows that ancient Egypt and Mesopotamia—which encompasses the land between the Euphrates and Tigris Rivers and is modern-day Iraq, parts of eastern Syria, southwest Iran, and southeast Turkey—began to use a system based on the highly coveted coins of gold and silver, also known as bullion, which is the purest form of the precious metal. However, bartering remained the most common form of exchange and trade.

Gold and silver coins gradually emerged in the use of trading, although the level of pure gold and silver content impacted the coins value. Only coins that consist of the pure precious metal are bullions; all other coins are referred to simply as *coins*. It is interesting to note that gold and silver lasted many centuries as the basis of economic measure and even into relatively recent history of the gold standard, which we'll cover in the next section. Fast-forward two thousand years and bartering has long been replaced by a currency-based system. Even so, there have been evolutions in the past century alone on how—globally—the monetary system has evolved from using gold and silver to represent national wealth and economic exchange to the current system.

Did You Know?
Throughout history, some types of money have gained widespread circulation outside of the nations that issued them. Whenever a country or empire has regional or global control of trade, its currency becomes the dominant currency for trade and governs the monetary system of that time. In the middle of a period that relies on one major currency, it's easy to forget that, throughout history, there have been other primary currencies—a historical cycle. Generally, the best currency to use is the most liquid one, the one issued by the nation with the biggest economy as well as usually the largest import-export markets. Rarely has a single currency been the exclusive medium of world trade, but a few have come close. Here's a quick look at some of some of the most powerful currencies in history:

- **Persian daric.** The daric was a gold coin used in Persia between 522 BC and 330 BC.
- **Roman currency.** Currencies such as the aureus (gold), the denarius (silver), the sestertius (bronze), the dupondius (bronze), and the as (copper) were used during the Roman Empire from around 250 BC to AD 250.
- **Thaler.** From about 1486 to 1908, the thaler and its variations were used in Europe as the standard against which the various states' currencies could be valued.
- **Spanish American pesos.** Around 1500 to the early nineteenth century, this contemporary of the thaler was widely used in Europe, the Americas, and the Far East; it became the first world currency by the late eighteenth century.
- **British pound.** The pound's origins date as early as around AD 800, but its influence grew in the 1600s as the unofficial gold standard; from 1816 to around 1939

the pound was the global reserve currency until the collapse of the gold standard.

- **US dollar.** The Coinage Act of 1792 established the dollar as the basis for a monetary account, and it went into circulation two years later as a silver coin. Its strength as a global reserve currency expanded in the 1800s and continues today.
- **Euro.** Officially in circulation on January 1, 1999, the euro continues to serve as currency in many European countries today.

Let's take a look at the last century of the international monetary system evolution. International monetary system refers to the system and rules that govern the use and exchange of money around the world and between countries. Each country has its own currency as money and the international monetary system governs the rules for valuing and exchanging these currencies.

Until the nineteenth century, the major global economies were regionally focused in Europe, the Americas, China, and India. These were loosely linked, and there was no formal monetary system governing their interactions. The rest of this section reviews the distinct chronological periods over the past 150 years leading to the development of the modern global financial system. Keep in mind that the system continues to evolve and each crisis impacts it. There is not likely to be a final international monetary system, simply one that reflects the current economic and political realities. This is one main reason why understanding the historical context is so critical. As the debate about the pros and cons of the current monetary system continues, some economists are tempted to advocate a return to systems from the past. Businesses need to be mindful of these arguments and the resulting changes, as they will be impacted by new rules, regulations, and structures.

Pre–World War I

As mentioned earlier in this section, ancient societies started using gold as a means of economic exchange. Gradually more countries adopted gold, usually in the form of coins or bullion, and this international monetary system became known as the gold standard. This system emerged gradually, without the structural process in more recent systems. The gold standard, in essence, created a fixed exchange rate system. An exchange rate is the price of one currency in terms of a second currency. In the gold standard system, each country sets the price of its currency to gold, specifically to one ounce of gold. A fixed exchange

rate stabilizes the value of one currency vis-à-vis another and makes trade and investment easier.

Our modern monetary system has its roots in the early 1800s. The defeat of Napoleon in 1815, when France was beaten at the Battle of Waterloo, made Britain the strongest nation in the world, a position it held for about one hundred years. In Africa, British rule extended at one time from the Cape of Good Hope to Cairo. British dominance and influence also stretched to the Indian subcontinent, the Malaysian peninsula, Australia, New Zealand—which attracted British settlers— and Canada. Under the banner of the British government, British companies advanced globally and were the largest companies in many of the colonies, controlling trade and commerce. Throughout history, strong countries, as measured mainly in terms of military might, were able to advance the interests of companies from their countries—a fact that has continued to modern times, as seen in the global prowess of American companies. Global firms in turn have always paid close attention to the political, military, and economic policies of their and other governments.

In 1821, the United Kingdom, the predominant global economy through the reaches of its colonial empire, adopted the gold standard and committed to fixing the value of the British pound. The major trading countries, including Russia, Austria-Hungary, Germany, France, and the United States, also followed and fixed the price of their currencies to an ounce of gold.

The United Kingdom officially set the price of its currency by agreeing to buy or sell an ounce of gold for the price of 4.247 pounds sterling. At that time, the United States agreed to buy or sell an ounce of gold for $20.67. This enabled the two currencies to be freely exchanged in terms of an ounce of gold. In essence,

£4.247 = 1 ounce of gold = $20.67.

The exchange rate between the US dollar and the British pound was then calculated by

$20.67 / £4.247 = $4.867 to £1.

The Advantages of the Gold Standard

The gold standard dramatically reduced the risk in exchange rates because it established fixed exchange rates between currencies. Any fluctuations were relatively small. This made it easier for global companies to manage costs and pricing. International trade grew throughout the world, although economists are not always in agreement as to whether the gold standard was an essential part of that trend.

The second advantage is that countries were forced to observe strict monetary policies. They could not just print money to combat economic downturns. One of the key features of the gold standard was that a currency had to actually have in reserve enough gold to convert all of its currency being held by anyone into gold. Therefore, the volume of paper currency could not exceed the gold reserves.

The third major advantage was that gold standard would help a country correct its trade imbalance. For example, if a country was importing more than it is exporting, (called a trade deficit), then under the gold standard the country had to pay for the imports with gold. The government of the country would have to reduce the amount of paper currency, because there could not be more currency in circulation than its gold reserves. With less money floating around, people would have less money to spend (thus causing a decrease in demand) and prices would also eventually decrease. As a result, with cheaper goods and services to offer, companies from the country could export more, changing the international trade balance gradually back to being in balance. For these three primary reasons, and as a result of the 2008 global financial crises, some modern economists are calling for the return of the gold standard or a similar system.

Collapse of the Gold Standard

If it was so good, what happened? The gold standard eventually collapsed from the impact of World War I. During the war, nations on both sides had to finance their huge military expenses and did so by printing more paper currency. As the currency in circulation exceeded each country's gold reserves, many countries were forced to abandon the gold standard. In the 1920s, most countries, including the United Kingdom, the United States, Russia, and France, returned to the gold standard at the same price level, despite the political instability, high unemployment, and inflation that were spread throughout Europe.

However, the revival of the gold standard was short-lived due to the Great Depression, which began in the late 1920s. The Great Depression was a worldwide phenomenon. By 1928, Germany, Brazil, and the economies of Southeast Asia were depressed. By early 1929, the economies of Poland, Argentina, and Canada were contracting, and the United States economy followed in the middle of 1929. Some economists have suggested that the larger factor tying these countries together was the international gold standard, which they believe prolonged the Great Depression. [1] The gold standard limited the flexibility of the monetary policy of each country's central banks by limiting their ability to expand the money supply. Under the gold standard, countries could not expand their money supply beyond what was allowed by the gold reserves held in their vaults.

Too much money had been created during World War I to allow a return to the gold standard without either large currency devaluations or price deflations. In addition, the US gold stock had doubled to about 40 percent of the world's monetary gold. There simply was not enough monetary gold in the rest of the world to support the countries' currencies at the existing exchange rates.

By 1931, the United Kingdom had to officially abandon its commitment to maintain the value of the British pound. The currency was allowed to float, which meant that its value would increase or decrease based on demand and supply. The US dollar and the French franc were the next strongest currencies and nations sought to peg the value of their currencies to either the dollar or franc. However, in 1934, the United States devalued its currency from $20.67 per ounce of gold to $35 per ounce. With a cheaper US dollar, US firms were able to export more as the price of their goods and services were cheaper vis-à-vis other nations. Other countries devalued their currencies in retaliation of the lower US dollar. Many of these countries used arbitrary par values rather than a price relative to their gold reserves. Each country hoped to make its exports cheaper to other countries and reduce expensive imports. However, with so many countries simultaneously devaluing their currencies, the impact on prices was canceled out. Many countries also imposed tariffs and other trade restrictions in an effort to protect domestic industries and jobs. By 1939, the gold standard was dead; it was no longer an accurate indicator of a currency's real value.

Post–World War II

The demise of the gold standard and the rise of the Bretton Woods system pegged to the US dollar was also a changing reflection of global history and politics. The British Empire's influence was dwindling. In the early 1800s, with the strength of both their currency and trading might, the United Kingdom had expanded its empire. At the end of World War I, the British Empire spanned more than a quarter of the world; the general sentiment was that "the sun would never set on the British empire." British maps and globes of the time showed the empire's expanse proudly painted in red. However, shortly after World War II, many of the colonies fought for and achieved independence. By then, the United States had clearly replaced the United Kingdom as the dominant global economic center and as the political and military superpower as well.

Did You Know?

Just as the United States became a global military and political superpower, US businesses were also taking center stage. Amoco (today now part of BP), General Motors (GM), Kellogg's, and Ford Motor Company sought to capitalize on US political and military strength to expand in new markets around the world. Many of these companies followed global political events and internally debated the strategic directions of their firms. For example, GM had an internal postwar planning policy group.

Notwithstanding the economic uncertainties that were bound to accompany the war's end, a few of the largest U.S. corporations, often with considerable assets seized or destroyed during the war, began to plan for the postwar period. Among these was General Motors. As early as 1942 the company had set up a postwar planning policy group to estimate the likely shape of the world after the war and to make recommendations on GM's postwar policies abroad.

In 1943 the policy group reported the likelihood that relations between the Western powers and the Soviet Union would deteriorate after the war. It also concluded that, except for Australia, General Motors should not buy plants and factories to make cars in any country that had not had facilities before the conflict. At the same time, though, it stated that after the war the United States would be in a stronger state politically and economically than it had been after World War I and that overseas operations would flourish in much of the world. The bottom line for GM, therefore, was to proceed with caution once the conflict ended but to stick to the policy it had enunciated in the 1920s—seeking out markets wherever they were available and building whatever facilities were needed to improve GM's market share. [2]

Bretton Woods

In the early 1940s, the United States and the United Kingdom began discussions to formulate a new international monetary system. John Maynard Keynes, a highly influential British economic thinker, and Harry Dexter White, a US Treasury official, paved the way to create a new monetary system. In July 1944, representatives from forty-four countries met in Bretton Woods, New Hampshire, to establish a new international monetary system.

"The challenge," wrote Ngaire Woods in his book *The Globalizers: The IMF, the World Bank, and Their Borrowers*, "was to gain agreement among states about how to finance postwar reconstruction, stabilize exchange rates, foster trade, and prevent balance of payments crises from unraveling the system." [3]

Did You Know?

Throughout history, political, military, and economic discussions between nations have always occurred simultaneously in an effort to create synergies between policies and efforts. A key focus of the 1940s efforts for a new global monetary system was to stabilize war-torn Europe. In the decade following the war the administrations of both Harry Truman and Dwight Eisenhower looked to the private sector to assist in the recovery of Western Europe, both through increased trade and direct foreign investments. In fact, the $13 billion Marshall Plan, which became the engine of European recovery between 1948 and 1952, was predicated on a close working relationship between the public and private sectors. Similarly, Eisenhower intended to bring about world economic recovery through liberalized world commerce and private investment abroad rather than through foreign aid. Over the course of his two administrations (1953–1961), the president modified his policy of "trade not aid" to one of "trade and aid" and changed his focus from Western Europe to the Third World, which he felt was most threatened by communist expansion.

In particular he was concerned by what he termed a "Soviet economic offensive" in the Middle East, that is, Soviet loans and economic assistance to such countries as Egypt and Syria. But even then he intended that international commerce and direct foreign investments would play a major role in achieving global economic growth and prosperity. [4]

The resulting Bretton Woods Agreement created a new dollar-based monetary system, which incorporated some of the disciplinary advantages of the gold system while giving countries the flexibility they needed to manage temporary economic setbacks, which had led to the fall of the gold standard. The Bretton Woods Agreement lasted until 1971 and established several key features.

Fixed Exchange Rates

Fixed exchange rates are also sometimes called pegged rates. One of the critical factors that led to the fall of the gold standard was that after the United Kingdom abandoned its commitment to maintaining the value of the British pound, countries sought to peg their currencies to the US dollar. With the strength of the US economy, the gold supply in the United States increased, while many countries had less gold in reserve than they did currency in circulation. The Bretton Woods system worked to fix this by tying the value of the US dollar to gold but also by tying all of the other countries to the US dollar rather than directly to gold. The par value of the US dollar was fixed at $35 to one ounce of gold. All other countries then set the value of their currencies to the US dollar. In reflection of the changing times, the British pound had undergone a substantial loss in value and by that point, its value was $2.40 to £1. Member countries had to maintain the value of their currencies within 1 percent of the fixed exchange rate. Lastly, the agreement established that only governments, rather than anyone who demanded it, could convert their US dollar holdings into gold—a major improvement over the gold standard. In fact, most businesspeople eventually ignored the technicality of pegging the US dollar to gold and simply utilized the actual exchange rates between countries (e.g., the pound to the dollar) as an economic measure for doing business.

National Flexibility

To enable countries to manage temporary but serious downturns, the Bretton Woods Agreement provided for a devaluation of a currency—more than 10 percent if needed. Countries could not use this tool to competitively manipulate imports and exports. Rather, the tool was intended to prevent the large-scale economic downturn that took place in the 1930s.

Creation of the International Monetary Fund and the World Bank

Section 6.2 "What Is the Role of the IMF and the World Bank?" looks at the International Monetary Fund and the World Bank more closely, as they have survived the collapse of the Bretton Woods Agreement. In essence, the IMF's initial primary purpose was to help manage the fixed rate exchange system; it eventually evolved to help governments correct temporary trade imbalances (typically deficits) with loans. The World Bank's purpose was to help with post–World War II European reconstruction. Both institutions continue to serve these roles but have evolved into broader institutions that serve essential global purposes, even though the system that created them is long gone. Section 6.2 "What Is the Role of the IMF and the World Bank?" explores them in greater detail and addresses the history, purpose, evolution, and current opportunities and challenges of both institutions.

Collapse of Bretton Woods

Despite a fixed exchange rate based on the US dollar and more national flexibility, the Bretton Woods Agreement ran into challenges in the early 1970s. The US trade balance had turned to a deficit as Americans were importing more than they were exporting. Throughout the 1950s and 1960s, countries had substantially increased their holdings of US dollars, which was the only currency pegged to gold. By the late 1960s, many of these countries expressed concern that the US did not have enough gold reserves to exchange all of the US dollars in global circulation. This became known as the Triffin Paradox, named after the economist Robert Triffin, who identified this problem. He noted that the more dollars foreign countries held, the less faith they had in the ability of the US government to convert those dollars. Like banks, though, countries do not keep enough gold or cash on hand to honor all of their liabilities. They maintain a percentage, called a reserve. Bank reserve ratios are usually 10 percent or less. (The low reserve ratio has been blamed by many as a cause of the 2008 financial crisis.) Some countries state their reserve ratios openly, and most seek to actively manage their ratios daily with open-market monetary policies—that is, buying and selling government securities and other financial instruments, which indirectly controls the total money supply in circulation, which in turn impacts supply and demand for the currency.

The expense of the Vietnam War and an increase in domestic spending worsened the Triffin Paradox; the US government began to run huge budget deficits, which further weakened global confidence in the US dollar. When nations began demanding gold in exchange for their dollars, there was a huge global sell-off of the US dollar, resulting in the Nixon Shock in 1971.

The Nixon Shock was a series of economic decisions made by the US President Richard Nixon in 1971 that led to the demise of the Bretton Woods system. Without consulting the other member countries, on August 15, 1971, Nixon ended the free convertibility of the US dollar into gold and instituted price and wage freezes among other economic measures.

Later that same year, the member countries reached the Smithsonian Agreement, which devalued the US dollar to $38 per ounce of gold, increased the value of other countries' currencies to the dollar, and increased the band within which a currency was allowed to float from 1 percent to 2.25 percent. This agreement still relied on the US dollar to be the strong reserve currency and the persistent concerns over the high inflation and trade deficits continued to weaken confidence in the system. Countries gradually dropped out of system—notably Germany, the United Kingdom, and Switzerland, all of which began to allow their currencies to float freely against the dollar. The Smithsonian Agreement was an insufficient response to the economic challenges; by 1973, the idea of fixed exchange rates was over.

Before moving on, recall that the major significance of the Bretton Woods Agreement was that it was the first formal institution that governed international monetary systems. By having a formal set of rules, regulations, and guidelines for decision making, the Bretton Woods Agreement established a higher level of economic stability. International businesses benefited from the almost thirty years of stability in exchange rates. Bretton Woods established a standard for future monetary systems to improve on; countries today continue to explore how best to achieve this. Nothing has fully replaced Bretton Woods to this day, despite extensive efforts.

Post–Bretton Woods Systems and Subsequent Exchange Rate Efforts

When Bretton Woods was established, one of the original architects, Keynes, initially proposed creating an international currency called Bancor as the main currency for clearing. However, the Americans had an alternative proposal for the creation of a central currency called unitas. Neither gained momentum; the US dollar was the reserve currency. Reserve currency is a main currency that many countries and institutions hold as part of their foreign exchange reserves. Reserve currencies are often international pricing currencies for world products and services. Examples of current reserve currencies are the US dollar, the euro, the British pound, the Swiss franc, and the Japanese yen.

Many feared that the collapse of the Bretton Woods system would bring the period of rapid growth to an end. In fact, the transition to floating exchange rates was relatively smooth, and it was certainly timely: flexible exchange rates made it easier for economies to adjust to more expensive oil, when the price suddenly started going up in October 1973. Floating rates have facilitated adjustments to external shocks ever since.

The IMF responded to the challenges created by the oil price shocks of the 1970s by adapting its lending instruments. To help oil importers deal with anticipated current account deficits and inflation in the face of higher oil prices, it set up the first of two oil facilities. [5]

After the collapse of Bretton Woods and the Smithsonian Agreement, several new efforts tried to replace the global system. The most noteworthy regional effort resulted in the European Monetary System (EMS) and the creation of a single currency, the euro. While there have been no completely effective efforts to replace Bretton Woods on a global level, there have been efforts that have provided ongoing exchange rate mechanisms.

Jamaica Agreement

In 1976, countries met to formalize a floating exchange rate system as the new international monetary system. The Jamaica Agreement established a managed float system of exchange rates, in which currencies float against one another with governments intervening only to stabilize their currencies at set target exchange rates. This is in contrast to a completely free floating exchange rate system, which has no government intervention; currencies float freely against one another. The Jamaica Agreement also removed gold as the primary reserve asset of the IMF. Additionally, the purpose of the IMF was expanded to include lending money as a last resort to countries with balance-of-payment challenges.

The Gs Begin

In the early 1980s, the value of the US dollar increased, pushing up the prices of US exports and thereby increasing the trade deficit. To address the imbalances, five of the world's largest economies met in September 1985 to determine a solution. The five countries were Britain, France, Germany, Japan, and the United States; this group became known as the Group of Five, shortened to G5. The 1985 agreement, called the Plaza Accord because it was held at the Plaza Hotel in New York City, focused on forcing down the value of the US dollar through collective efforts.

By February 1987, the markets had pushed the dollar value down, and some worried it was now valued too low. The G5 met again, but now as the Group of Seven, adding Italy and Canada—it became known as the G7. The Louvre Accord, so named for being agreed on in Paris, stabilized the dollar. The countries agreed to support the dollar at the current valuation. The G7 continued to meet regularly to address ongoing economic issues.

The G7 was expanded in 1999 to include twenty countries as a response to the financial crises of the late 1990s and the growing recognition that key emerging-market countries were not adequately included in the core of global economic discussions and governance. It was not until a decade later, though, that the G20 effectively replaced the G8, which was made up of the original G7 and Russia. The European Union was represented in G20 but could not host or chair the group.

Keeping all of these different groups straight can be very confusing. The news may report on different groupings as countries are added or removed from time to time. The key point to remember is that anything related to a G is likely to be a forum consisting of finance ministers and governors of central banks who are meeting to discuss matters related to cooperating on an international monetary system and key issues in the global economy.

The G20 is likely to be the stronger forum for the foreseeable future, given the number of countries it includes and the amount of world trade it represents. "Together, member countries represent around 90 per cent of global gross national product, 80 per cent of world trade (including EU intra-trade) as well as two-thirds of the world's population." [6]

G20 Countries	
Argentina	Japan
Australia	Mexico
Brazil	Russia
Canada	Saudia Arabia
China	South Africa
France	South Korea
Germany	Turkey
India	United Kingdom
Indonesia	United States
Italy	European Union

Did You Know?

G-ology

"At present, a number of groups are jostling to be the pre-eminent forum for discussions between world leaders. The G20 ended 2009 by in effect replacing the old G8. But that is not the end of the matter. In 2010 the G20 began to face a new challenger—G2 [the United States and China]. To confuse matters further, lobbies have emerged advocating the formation of a G13 and a G3." [7] The G20 is a powerful, informal group of nineteen countries and the European Union. It also includes a representative from the World Bank and the International Monetary Fund. The list developed from an effort to include major developing countries with countries with developed economies. Its purpose is to address issues of the international financial system.
So just who's in the current G20?

Today's Exchange Rate System

While there is not an official replacement to the Bretton Woods system, there are provisions in place through the ongoing forum discussions of the G20. Today's system remains—in large part—a managed float system, with the US dollar and the euro jostling to be the premier global currency.

For businesses that once quoted primarily in US dollars, pricing is now just as often noted in the euro as well.

Ethics in Action

The *Wall Street Journal*'s July 30, 2010, edition noted how gangsters are helping provide stability in the euro zone. The highest denomination of a euro is a €500 bill, in contrast to the United States, where the largest bill is a $100 bill.

The high-value bills are increasingly "making the euro the currency of choice for underground and black economies, and for all those who value anonymity in their financial transactions and investments," wrote Willem Buiter, the chief economist at Citigroup....

When euro notes and coins went into circulation in January 2002, the value of €500 notes outstanding was €30.8 billion ($40 billion), according to the ECB [European Central Bank].

Today some €285 billion worth of such euro notes are in existence, an annual growth rate of 32 percent. By value, 35 percent of euro notes in circulation are in the highest denomination, the €500 bill that few people ever see.

In 1998, then-U.S. Treasury official Gary Gensler worried publicly about the competition to the $100 bill, the biggest U.S. bank note, posed by the big euro notes and their likely use by criminals. He pointed out that $1 million in $100 bills weighs 22 pounds; in hypothetical $500 bills, it would weigh just 4.4 pounds.

Police forces have found the big euro notes in cereal boxes, tires and in hidden compartments in trucks, says Soren Pedersen, spokesman for Europol, the European police agency based in The Hague. "Needless to say, this cash is often linked to the illegal drugs trade, which explains the similarity in methods of concealment that are used." [8]

While you might think that the ECB should just stop issuing the larger denominations, it turns out that the ECB and the member governments of the euro zone actually benefit from this demand.

The profit a central bank gains from issuing currency—as well as from other privileges of a central bank, such as being able to demand no-cost or low-cost deposits from banks—is known as seigniorage. It normally accrues to national treasuries once the central banks account for their own costs.

The ECB's gains from seigniorage are becoming increasingly important this year....

In recent years, the profits on its issue of new paper currency have been running at €50 billion." [9]

Some smaller nations have chosen to voluntarily set exchange rates against the dollar while other countries have selected the euro. Usually a country makes the decision between the dollar and the euro by reviewing their largest trading partners. By choosing the euro or the dollar, countries seek currency stability and a reduction in inflation, among other various perceived benefits. Many countries in Latin America once dollarized to provide currency stability for their economy. Today, this is changing, as individual economies have strengthened and countries are now seeking to dedollarize.

Spotlight on Dollarizing and Dedollarizing in Latin America

Many countries in Latin America have endured years of political and economic instability, which has exacerbated the massive inequality that has characterized the societies in modern times. Most of the wealth is in the hands of the white elite, who live sophisticated lives in the large cities, eating in fancy restaurants and flying off to Miami for shopping trips. Indeed, major cities often look much like any other modern, industrialized cities, complete with cinemas, fast-food restaurants, Internet cafés, and shopping malls.

But while the rich enjoy an enviable lifestyle, the vast majority of the continent's large indigenous population often lives in extreme poverty. While international aid programs attempt to alleviate the poverty, a lot depends on the country's government. Corrupt governments slow down the pace of progress.

Over the past two decades, governments in Ecuador and Peru—as well as others in Latin America including Bolivia, Paraguay, Panama, El Salvador, and Uruguay—have opted to dollarize to stabilize their countries' economies. Each country replaced its national currency with the US dollar. Each country has struggled economically despite abundant natural resources. Economic cycles in key industries, such as oil and commodities, contributed to high inflation. While the move to dollarize was not always popular domestically initially, its success has been clearly evident. In both Ecuador and Peru, dollarizing has provided a much needed benefit, although one country expects to continue aligning with the US dollar and the other hopes to move away from it.

In Ecuador, for example, a decade after dollarizing, one cannot dismiss the survival of dollarization as coincidence. Dollarization has provided Ecuador with the longest period of a stable, fully convertible currency in a century. Its foremost result has been that inflation has dropped to single digits and remained there for the first time since 1972. The stability that dollarization has provided has also helped the economy grow an average of 4.3 percent a year in real terms, fostering a drop in the poverty rate from 56 percent of the population in 1999 to 35 percent in 2008. As a result, dollarization has been popular, with polls showing that more than three-quarters of Ecuadorians approve of it. [10]

However, this success could not protect the country from the effects of the 2008 global financial crisis and economic downturn, which led to falling remittances and declining oil revenue for Ecuador. The country "lacks a reliable political system, legal system, or investment climate. Dollarization is the only government policy that provides Ecuadorians with a trustworthy basis for earning, saving, investing, and paying." [11]

Peru first opted to dollarize in the early 1970s as a result of the high inflation, which peaked during the hyperinflation of 1988–90. "With high inflation, the U.S. dollar started to be the preferred means of payments and store of value." [12] Dollarization was the only option to stabilize prices. A key cost of dollarizing, however, is losing monetary independence. Another cost is that the business cycle in the country is tied more closely to fluctuations in the US economy and currency. Balancing the benefits and the costs is an ongoing concern for governments.

Despite attempts to dedollarize in the 1980s, it was not until the recent decade that Peru has successfully pursued a market-driven financial dedollarization. Dedollarization occurs when a country reduces its reliance on dollarizing credit and deposit of commercial banks. In Peru, as in some other Latin American countries—such as Bolivia, Uruguay and Paraguay—dedollarization has been "driven by macroeconomic stability, introduction of prudential policies to better reflect currency risk (such as the management of reserve requirements), and the development of the capital market in soles" (the local Peruvian currency). [13]

Dedollarizing is still a relatively recent phenomenon, and economists are still trying to understand the implications and impact on businesses and the local economy in each country. What is clear is that governments view dedollarizing as one more tool toward having greater control over their economies.

KEY TAKEAWAYS

- The international monetary system had many informal and formal stages. For more than one hundred years, the gold standard provided a stable means for countries to exchange their currencies and facilitate trade. With the Great Depression, the gold standard collapsed and gradually gave way to the Bretton Woods system.

- The Bretton Woods system established a new monetary system based on the US dollar. This system incorporated some of the disciplinary advantages of the gold system while giving countries the flexibility they needed to manage temporary economic setbacks, which had led to the fall of the gold standard.

- The Bretton Woods system lasted until 1971 and provided the longest formal mechanism for an exchange-rate system and forums for countries to cooperate on coordinating policy and navigating temporary economic crises.

- While no new formal system has replaced Bretton Woods, some of its key elements have endured, including a modified managed float of foreign exchange, the International Monetary Fund (IMF), and the World Bank—although each has evolved to meet changing world conditions.

EXERCISES

(AACSB: Reflective Thinking, Analytical Skills)

1. What is the international monetary system?
2. What was the gold standard, and why did it collapse?
3. What was Bretton Woods, and why did it collapse?
4. What is the current system of exchange rates?

[1] The Concise Encyclopedia of Economics, s.v. "Great Depression," accessed July 23, 2010, http://www.econlib.org/library/Enc/GreatDepression.html.

[2] Encyclopedia of the New American Nation, s.v. "Multinational Corporations—Postwar Investment: 1945–1955," accessed February 9, 2011, http://www.americanforeignrelations.com/E-N/Multinational-Corporations-Postwar-investment-1945-1955.html#ixzz18TCwg8VJ.

[3] Ngaire Woods, Globalizers: The IMF, the World Bank, and Their Borrowers (Ithaca, NY: Cornell University Press, 2006), 16.

[4] Encyclopedia of the New American Nation, s.v. "Multinational Corporations—Postwar Investment: 1945–1955," accessed February 9, 2011, http://www.americanforeignrelations.com/E-N/Multinational-Corporations-Postwar-investment-1945-1955.html#ixzz18TCwg8VJ.

[5] "The End of the Bretton Woods System (1972–81)," International Monetary Fund, accessed July 26, 2010, http://www.imf.org/external/about/histend.htm.

[6] "About G-20," G-20, accessed July 25, 2010, http://www.g20.org/en.

[7] Gideon Rachman, "A Modern Guide to G-ology," Economist, November 13, 2009, accessed February 9, 2011, http://www.economist.com/node/14742524.

[8] Stephen Fidler, "How Gangsters Are Saving Euro Zone," Wall Street Journal, July 30, 2010, accessed February 9, 2011, http://online.wsj.com/article/SB10001424052748704533220457539754363 4034112.html.

[9] Stephen Fidler, "How Gangsters Are Saving Euro Zone," Wall Street Journal, July 30, 2010, accessed February 9, 2011, http://online.wsj.com/article/SB10001424052748704533220457539754363 4034112.html.

[10] Pedro P. Romero, "Ecuador Dollarization: Anchor in a Storm," Latin Business Chronicle, January 23, 2009, accessed February 9, 2011, http://www.latinbusinesschronicle.com/app/article.aspx?id=3096.

[11] Pedro P. Romero, "Ecuador Dollarization: Anchor in a Storm," Latin Business Chronicle, January 23, 2009, accessed February 9, 2011, http://www.latinbusinesschronicle.com/app/article.aspx?id=3096.

[12] Mercedes García-Escribano, "Peru: Drivers of De-dollarization," International Monetary Fund, July 2010, accessed May 9, 2011, http://www.bcrp.gob.pe/docs/Publicaciones/Documentos-de-Trabajo/2010/Documento-de-Trabajo-11-2010.pdf.

[13] Mercedes García-Escribano, "Peru: Drivers of De-dollarization, International Monetary Fund," July 2010, accessed May 9, 2011, http://www.bcrp.gob.pe/docs/Publicaciones/Documentos-de-Trabajo/2010/Documento-de-Trabajo-11-2010.pdf.

6.2 What Is the Role of the IMF and the World Bank?

LEARNING OBJECTIVES

1. Understand the history and purpose of the IMF.
2. Describe the IMF's current role and major challenges and opportunities.
3. Understand the history and purpose of the World Bank.
4. Describe the World Bank's current role and major challenges and opportunities.

Section 6.1 "What Is the International Monetary System?" discusses how, during the 1930s, the Great Depression resulted in failing economies. The fall of the gold standard led countries to raise trade barriers, devalue their currencies to compete against one another for export markets and curtail usage of foreign exchange by their citizens. All these factors led to declining world trade, high unemployment, and plummeting living standards in many countries. In 1944, the Bretton Woods Agreement established a new international monetary system. The creation of the International Monetary Fund (IMF) and the World Bank were two of its most enduring legacies.

The World Bank and the IMF, often called the Bretton Woods Institutions, are twin intergovernmental pillars supporting the structure of the world's economic and financial order. Both have taken on expanding roles, and there have been renewed calls for additional expansion of their responsibilities, particularly in the continuing absence of a single global monetary agreement. The two institutions may seem to have confusing or overlapping functions. However, while some similarities exist (see the following figure), they are two distinct organizations with different roles.

Similarities Between the IMF and World Bank

✓ Owned and directed by the governments of member nations

✓ Almost every country on earth is a member of both institutions

✓ Both concern themselves with economic issues

✓ Both focus on broadening and strengthening the economies of their member nations

✓ Hold joint annual meetings

✓ Headquartered in Washington DC, USA

✓ Share joint task forces, sessions and research efforts

"Despite these and other similarities, however, the Bank and the IMF remain distinct. The fundamental difference is this: the Bank is primarily a *development* institution; the IMF is a *cooperative* institution that seeks to maintain an orderly system of payments and receipts between nations. Each has a different purpose, a distinct structure, receives its funding from different sources, assists different categories of members, and strives to achieve distinct goals through methods peculiar to itself." [1] This section explores both of these institutions and how they have evolved in the almost seventy years since their creation.

International Monetary Fund

History and Purpose

The architects of the Bretton Woods Agreement, John Maynard Keynes and Harry Dexter White, envisioned an institution that would oversee the international monetary system, exchange rates, and international payments to enable countries and their citizens to buy goods and services from each other. They expected that this new global entity would ensure exchange rate stability and encourage its member countries to eliminate the exchange restrictions that hindered trade. Officially, the IMF came into existence in December 1945 with twenty-nine member countries. (The Soviets, who were at Bretton Woods, refused to join the IMF.)

In 1947, the institution's first formal year of operations, the French became the first nation to borrow from the IMF. Over the next thirty years, more countries joined the IMF, including some African countries in the 1960s. The Soviet bloc nations remained the exception and were not part of the IMF until the fall of the Berlin Wall in 1989. The IMF experienced another large increase in members in the 1990s with the addition of Russia; Russia was also placed on the IMF's executive committee. Today, 187 countries are members of the IMF; twenty-four of those countries or groups of countries are represented on the executive board.

The purposes of the International Monetary Fund are as follows:

1. To promote international monetary cooperation through a permanent institution which provides the machinery for consultation and collaboration on international monetary problems.

2. To facilitate the expansion and balanced growth of international trade, and to contribute thereby to the promotion and maintenance of high levels of employment and real income and to the development of the productive resources of all members as primary objectives of economic policy.

3. To promote exchange stability, to maintain orderly exchange arrangements among members, and to avoid competitive exchange depreciation.

4. To assist in the establishment of a multilateral system of payments in respect of current transactions between members and in the elimination of foreign exchange restrictions which hamper the growth of world trade.

5. To give confidence to members by making the general resources of the Fund temporarily available to them under adequate safeguards, thus providing them with opportunity to correct maladjustments in their balance of payments without resorting to measures destructive of national or international prosperity.

6. In accordance with the above, to shorten the duration and lessen the degree of disequilibrium in the international balances of payments of members. [2]

In addition to financial assistance, the IMF also provides member countries with technical assistance to create and implement effective policies, particularly economic, monetary, and banking policy and regulations.

Special Drawing Rights (SDRs)

A Special Drawing Right (SDR) is basically an international monetary reserve asset. SDRs were created in 1969 by the IMF in response to the Triffin Paradox. The Triffin Paradox stated that the more US dollars were used as a base reserve currency, the less faith that countries had in the ability of the US government to convert those dollars to gold. The world was still using the Bretton Woods system, and the initial expectation was that SDRs would replace the US dollar as the global monetary reserve currency, thus solving the Triffin Paradox. Bretton Woods collapsed a few years later, but the concept of an SDR solidified. Today the value of an SDR consists of the value of four of the IMF's biggest members' currencies—the US dollar, the British pound, the Japanese yen, and the euro—but the currencies do not hold equal weight. SDRs are quoted in terms of US dollars. The basket, or group of currencies, is reviewed every five years by the IMF executive board and is based on the currency's role in international trade and finance. The following chart shows the current valuation in percentages of the four currencies.

Currency	Weighting
US dollar	44 percent
Euro	34 percent
Japanese yen	11 percent
British pound	11 percent

The SDR is not a currency, but some refer to it as a form of IMF currency. It does not constitute a claim on the IMF, which only serves to provide a mechanism for buying, selling, and exchanging SDRs. Countries are allocated SDRs, which are included in the member country's reserves. SDRs can be exchanged between countries along with currencies. The SDR serves as the unit of account of the IMF and some other international organizations, and countries borrow from the IMF in SDRs in times of economic need.

The IMF's Current Role and Major Challenges and Opportunities

Criticism and Challenging Areas for the IMF

The IMF supports many developing nations by helping them overcome monetary challenges and to maintain a stable international financial system. Despite this clearly defined purpose, the execution of its work can be very complicated and can have wide repercussions for the recipient nations. As a result, the IMF has both its critics and its supporters. The challenges for organizations like the IMF and the World Bank center not only on some of their operating deficiencies but also on the global political environment in which they operate. The IMF has been subject to a range of criticisms that are generally focused on the conditions of its loans, its lack of accountability, and its willingness to lend to countries with bad human rights records. [3]

These criticisms include the following:

1. **Conditions for loans.** The IMF makes the loan given to countries conditional on the implementation of certain economic policies, which typically include the following:

   o Reducing government borrowing (higher taxes and lower spending)
   o Higher interest rates to stabilize the currency
   o Allowing failing firms to go bankrupt
   o Structural adjustment (privatization, deregulation, reducing corruption and bureaucracy) [4]

   The austere policies have worked at times but always extract a political toll as the impact on average citizens is usually quite harsh. The opening case in Chapter 2 "International Trade and Foreign Direct Investment" presents the current impact of IMF policies on Greece. Some suggest that the loan conditions are "based on what is termed the 'Washington Consensus,' focusing on liberalization—of trade, investment and the financial sector—, deregulation and privatization of nationalized industries. Often the conditionalities are attached without due regard for the borrower countries' individual circumstances and the prescriptive recommendations by the World Bank and IMF fail to resolve the economic problems within the countries. IMF conditionalities may additionally result in the loss of a state's authority to govern its own economy as national economic policies are predetermined under IMF packages." [5]

2. **Exchange rate reforms.** "When the IMF intervened in Kenya in the 1990s, they made the Central bank remove controls over flows of capital. The consensus was that this decision made it easier for corrupt politicians to transfer money out of the economy (known as the Goldman scandal). Critics argue this is another example of how the IMF failed to understand the dynamics of the country that they were dealing with—insisting on blanket reforms." [6]

3. **Devaluations.** In the initial stages, the IMF has been criticized for allowing inflationary devaluations. [7]

4. **Free-market criticisms of the IMF.** "Believers in free markets argue that it is better to let capital markets operate without attempts at intervention. They argue attempts to influence exchange rates only make things worse—it is better to allow currencies to reach their market level." [8] They also assert that bailing out countries with large debts is morally hazardous; countries that know that there is always a bailout provision will borrow and spend more recklessly.

5. **Lack of transparency and involvement.** The IMF has been criticized for "imposing policy with little or no consultation with affected countries." [9]

6. **Supporting military dictatorships.** The IMF has been criticized over the decades for supporting military dictatorships. [10]

Opportunities and Future Outlook for the IMF
The 2008 global economic crisis is one of the toughest situations that the IMF has had to contend with since the Great Depression.

For most of the first decade of the twenty-first century, global trade and finance fueled a global expansion that enabled many countries to repay any money they had borrowed from the IMF and other official creditors. These countries also used surpluses in trade to accumulate foreign exchange reserves. The global economic crisis that began with the 2007 collapse of mortgage lending in the United States and spread around the world in 2008 was preceded by large imbalances in global capital flows. Global capital flows fluctuated between 2 and 6 percent of world GDP between 1980 and 1995, but since then they have risen to 15 percent of GDP. The most rapid increase has been experienced by advanced economies, but emerging markets and developing countries have also become more financially integrated.

The founders of the Bretton Woods system had taken for granted that private capital flows would never again resume the prominent role they had in the nineteenth and early twentieth centuries, and the IMF had traditionally lent to members facing current account difficulties. The 2008 global crisis uncovered fragility in the advanced financial markets that soon led to the worst global downturn since the Great Depression. Suddenly, the IMF was inundated with requests for standby arrangements and other forms of financial and policy support.

The international community recognized that the IMF's financial resources were as important as ever and were likely to be stretched thin before the crisis was over. With broad support from creditor countries, the IMF's lending capacity tripled to around $750 billion. To use those funds effectively, the IMF overhauled its lending policies. It created a flexible credit line for countries with strong economic fundamentals and a track record of successful policy implementation. Other reforms targeted low-income countries. These factors enabled the IMF to disburse very large sums quickly; the disbursements were based on the needs of borrowing countries and were not as tightly constrained by quotas as in the past. [11]

Many observers credit the IMF's quick responses and leadership role in helping avoid a potentially worse global financial crisis. As noted in the Chapter 5 "Global and Regional Economic Cooperation and Integration" opening case on Greece, the IMF has played a role in helping countries avert widespread financial disasters. The IMF's

requirements are not always popular but are usually effective, which has led to its expanding influence. The IMF has sought to correct some of the criticisms; according to a Foreign Policy in Focus essay designed to stimulate dialogue on the IMF, the fund's strengths and opportunities include the following:

1. **Flexibility and speed.** "In March 2009, the IMF created the Flexible Credit Line (FCL), which is a fast-disbursing loan facility with low conditionality aimed at reassuring investors by injecting liquidity…Traditionally, IMF loan programs require the imposition of austerity measures such as raising interest rates that can reduce foreign investment…In the case of the FCL, countries qualify for it not on the basis of their promises, but on the basis of their history. Just as individual borrowers with good credit histories are eligible for loans at lower interest rates than their risky counterparts, similarly, countries with sound macroeconomic fundamentals are eligible for drawings under the FCL. A similar program has been proposed for low-income countries. Known as the Rapid Credit Facility, it is front-loaded (allowing for a single, up-front payout as with the FCL) and is also intended to have low conditionality." [12]
2. **Cheerleading.** "The Fund is positioning itself to be less of an adversary and more of a cheerleader to member countries. For some countries that need loans more for reassurance than reform, these changes to the Fund toolkit are welcome." [13] This enables more domestic political and economic stability.
3. **Adaptability.** "Instead of providing the same medicine to all countries regardless of their particular problems, the new loan facilities are intended to aid reform-minded governments by providing short-term resources to reassure investors. In this manner, they help politicians in developing countries manage the downside costs of integration." [14]
4. **Transparency.** The IMF has made efforts to improve its own transparency and continues to encourage its member countries to do so. Supporters note that this creates a barrier to any one or more countries that have more geopolitical influence in the organization. In reality, the major economies continue to exert influence on policy and implementation.

To underscore the global expectations for the IMF's role, China, Russia, and other global economies have renewed calls for the G20 to replace the US dollar as the international reserve currency with a new global system controlled by the IMF.

The *Financial Times* reported that Zhou Xiaochuan, the Chinese central bank's governor, said the goal would be to create a reserve currency that is disconnected from individual nations and is able to remain stable in the long run, thus removing the inherent deficiencies caused by using credit-based national currencies. "'This is a clear sign that China, as the largest holder of US dollar financial assets, is concerned about the potential inflationary risk of the US Federal Reserve printing money,' said Qu Hongbin, chief China economist for HSBC." [15]

Although Mr. Zhou did not mention the US dollar, the essay gave a pointed critique of the current dollar-dominated monetary system:

"The outbreak of the [current] crisis and its spillover to the entire world reflected the inherent vulnerabilities and systemic risks in the existing international monetary system," Mr Zhou wrote.

China has little choice but to hold the bulk of its $2,000bn of foreign exchange reserves in US dollars, and this is unlikely to change in the near future.

To replace the current system, Mr. Zhou suggested expanding the role of special drawing rights, which were introduced by the IMF in 1969 to support the Bretton Woods fixed exchange rate regime but became less relevant once that collapsed in the 1970s....

Mr Zhou said the proposal would require "extraordinary political vision and courage" and acknowledged a debt to John Maynard Keynes, who made a similar suggestion in the 1940s. [16]

China is politically and economically motivated to recommend an alternative reserve currency. Politically, the country whose currency is the reserve currency is perceived as the dominant economic power, as Section 6.1 "What Is the International Monetary System?" discusses. Economically, China has come under increasing global pressure to increase the value of its currency, the renminbi, which Section 6.3 "Understanding How International Monetary Policy, the IMF, and the World Bank Impact Business Practices" discusses in greater depth.

The World Bank and the World Bank Group

History and Purpose

The World Bank came into existence in 1944 at the Bretton Woods conference. Its formal name is the International Bank for Reconstruction and Development (IBRD), which clearly states its primary purpose of financing economic development. The World Bank's first loans were extended during the late 1940s to finance the reconstruction of the war-ravaged economies of Western Europe. When these nations recovered some measure of economic self-sufficiency, the World Bank turned its attention to assisting the world's poorer nations. The World Bank has one central purpose: to promote economic and social progress in developing countries by helping raise productivity so that their people may live a better and fuller life:

[In 2009,] the World Bank provided $46.9 billion for 303 projects in developing countries worldwide, with our financial and/or technical expertise aimed at helping those countries reduce poverty.

The Bank is currently involved in more than 1,800 projects in virtually every sector and developing country. The projects are as diverse as providing microcredit in Bosnia and Herzegovina, raising AIDS-prevention awareness in Guinea, supporting education of girls in Bangladesh, improving health care delivery in Mexico, and helping East Timor rebuild upon independence and India rebuild Gujarat after a devastating earthquake. [17]

Today, The World Bank consists of two main bodies, the International Bank for Reconstruction and Development (IBRD) and the International Development Association (IDA), established in 1960. The World Bank is part of the broader World Bank Group, which consists of five interrelated institutions: the IBRD; the IDA; the International Finance Corporation (IFC), which was established in 1956; the Multilateral Investment Guarantee Agency (MIGA), which was established in 1988; and the International Centre for Settlement of Investment Disputes (ICSID), which was established in 1966. These additional members of the World Bank Group have specific purposes as well. The IDA typically provides interest-free loans to countries with sovereign guarantees. The IFC provides loans, equity, risk-management tools, and structured finance. Its goal is to facilitate sustainable development by improving investments in the private sector. The MIGA focuses on improving the foreign direct investment of developing countries. The ICSID provides a means for dispute resolution between governments and private investors with the end goal of enhancing the flow of capital.

The current primary focus of the World Bank centers on six strategic themes:

1. **The poorest countries.** Poverty reduction and sustainable growth in the poorest countries, especially in Africa.

2. **Postconflict and fragile states.** Solutions to the special challenges of postconflict countries and fragile states.

3. **Middle-income countries.** Development solutions with customized services as well as financing for middle-income countries.

4. **Global public goods.** Addressing regional and global issues that cross national borders, such as climate change, infectious diseases, and trade.

5. **The Arab world.** Greater development and opportunity in the Arab world.

6. **Knowledge and learning.** Leveraging the best global knowledge to support development. [18]

The World Bank provides low-interest loans, interest-free credits, and grants to developing countries. There's always a government (or "sovereign") guarantee of repayment subject to general conditions. The World Bank is directed to make loans for projects but never to fund a trade deficit. These loans must have a reasonable likelihood of being repaid. The IDA was created to offer an alternative loan option. IDA loans are free of interest and offered for several decades, with a ten-year grace period before the country receiving the loan needs to begin repayment. These loans are often called soft loans.

Since it issued its first bonds in 1947, the IBRD generates funds for its development work through the international capital markets (which Chapter 7 "Foreign Exchange and the Global Capital Markets" covers). The World Bank issues bonds, typically about $25 billion a year. These bonds are rated AAA (the highest possible rating) because they are backed by member states' shared capital and by borrowers' sovereign guarantees. Because of the AAA credit rating, the World Bank is able to borrow at relatively low interest rates. This provides a cheaper funding source for developing countries, as most developing countries have considerably low credit ratings. The World Bank charges a fee of about 1 percent to cover its administrative overheads.

What Are the World Bank's Current Role and Major Challenges and Opportunities?

Like the IMF, the World Bank has both its critics and its supporters. The criticisms of the World Bank extend from the challenges that it faces in the global operating environment. Some of these challenges have complicated causes; some result from the conflict between nations and the global financial crisis. The following are four examples of the world's difficult needs that the World Bank tries to address:

1. Even in 2010, over 3 billion people lived on less than $2.50 a day.

2. At the start of the twenty-first century, almost a billion people couldn't read a book or sign their names.

3. Less than 1 percent of what the world spends each year on weapons would have put every child into school by the year 2000, but it didn't happen.

4. Fragile states such as Afghanistan, Rwanda, and Sri Lanka face severe development challenges: weak institutional capacity, poor governance, political instability, and often ongoing violence or the legacy of past conflict.[19]

According to the *Encyclopedia of the New American Nation* and the *New York Times*, the World Bank is criticized primarily for the following reasons:

- **Administrative incompetence.** The World Bank and its lending practices are increasingly scrutinized, with critics asserting that "the World Bank has shifted from being a 'lender of last resort' to an international welfare organization," resulting in an institution that is "bloated, incompetent, and even corrupt." Also incriminating is that "the bank's lax lending standards have led to a rapidly deteriorating loan portfolio." [20]

- **Rewarding or supporting inefficient or corrupt countries.** The bank's lending policies often reward macroeconomic inefficiency in the underdeveloped world, allowing inefficient nations to avoid the types of fundamental reforms that would in the long run end poverty in their countries. Many analysts note that the best example is to compare the fantastic growth in East Asia to the deplorable economic conditions of Africa. In 1950 the regions were alike—South Korea had a lower per capita GDP than Nigeria. But by pursuing macroeconomic reforms, high savings, investing in education and basic social services, and opening their economies to the global trading order, the "Pacific Tigers" have been able to lift themselves out of poverty and into wealth with very little help from the World Bank. Many countries in Africa, however, have relied primarily on multilateral assistance from organizations like the World Bank while avoiding fundamental macroeconomic reforms, with deplorable but predictable results.

Conservatives point out that the World Bank has lent more than $350 billion over a half-century, mostly to the underdeveloped world, with little to show for it. One study argued that of the sixty-six countries that received funding from the bank from 1975 to 2000, well over half were no better off than before, and twenty were actually worse off. The study pointed out that Niger received

$637 million between 1965 and 1995, yet its per capita GNP had fallen, in real terms, more than 50 percent during that time. In the same period Singapore, which received one-seventh as much World Bank aid, had seen its per capita GNP increase by more than 6 percent a year. [21]

- **Focusing on large projects rather than local initiatives.** Some critics claim that World Bank loans give preference to "large infrastructure projects like building dams and electric plants over projects that would benefit the poor, such as education and basic health care." The projects often destroy the local environment, including forests, rivers, and fisheries. Some estimates suggest "that more than two and a half million people have been displaced by projects made possible through World Bank loans." Failed projects, argue environmentalists and antiglobalization groups, are particularly illustrative: "The Sardar Sarovar dam on the Narmada River in India was expected to displace almost a quarter of a million people into squalid resettlement sites. The Polonoroeste Frontier Development scheme has led to large-scale deforestation in the Brazilian rain forest. In Thailand, the Pak Mun dam has destroyed the fisheries of the Mun River, impoverishing thousands who had made their living fishing and forever altering the diet of the region." [22] Further, the larger projects become targets for corruption by local government officials because there is so much money involved.

Another example was in 2009, when an internal audit found that the IFC had "ignored its own environmental and social protection standards when it approved nearly $200 million in loan guarantees for palm oil production in Indonesia…Indonesia is home to the world's second-largest reserves of natural forests and peat swamps, which naturally trap carbon dioxide—the main greenhouse gas that causes climate change. But rampant destruction of the forests to make way for palm oil plantations has caused giant releases of CO_2 into the atmosphere, making Indonesia the third-largest emitter of greenhouse gases on the planet…'For each investment, commercial pressures were allowed to prevail,' auditors wrote." [23] However, such issues are not always as clear-cut as they may seem. The IFC responded to the audit by acknowledging "shortcomings in the review process. But the lender also defended investment in palm oil production as a way to alleviate poverty in Indonesia. 'IFC believes that production of palm oil, when carried out in an environmentally and socially sustainable fashion, can provide core support for

a strong rural economy, providing employment and improved quality of life for millions of the rural poor in tropical areas,' it said." [24]

- **Negative influence on theory and practice.** As one of the two Bretton Woods Institutions, the World Bank plays a large role in research, training, and policy formulation. Critics worry that because "the World Bank and the IMF are regarded as experts in the field of financial regulation and economic development, their views and prescriptions may undermine or eliminate alternative perspectives on development." [25]

- **Dominance of G7 countries.** The industrialized countries dominate the World Bank (and IMF) governance structures. Decisions are typically made and policies implemented by these leading countries—the G7—because they are the largest donors, some suggest without sufficient consultation with poor and developing countries. [26]

Opportunities and Future Outlook for the World Bank

As vocal as the World Bank's critics are, so too are its supporters. The World Bank is praised by many for engaging in development projects in remote locations around the globe to improve living standards and reduce poverty. The World Bank's current focus is on helping countries achieve the Millennium Development Goals (MDGs), which are eight international development goals, established in 2000 at the Millennium Summit, that all 192 United Nations member states and twenty-three international organizations have agreed to achieve by the year 2015. They include reducing extreme poverty, reducing child mortality rates, fighting disease epidemics such as AIDS, and developing a global partnership for development. The World Bank is focused on the following four key issues:

1. **Increased transparency.** In response to the criticisms over the decades, the World Bank has made progress. More of the World Bank's decision making and country assessments are available publicly. The World Bank has continued to work with countries to combat corruption both at the country and bank levels.

2. **Expanding social issues in the fight on poverty.** In 2001, the World Bank began to incorporate gender issues into its policy. "Two years later the World Bank announced that it was starting to evaluate all of its projects for their effects on women and girls," noting that "poverty is experienced differently by men and women" and "a full understanding of the gender dimensions of poverty can significantly change the

definition of priority policy and program interventions." [27]

3. **Improvements in countries' competitiveness and increasing exports.** The World Bank's policies and its role as a donor have helped improve the ability of some countries to secure more of the global revenues for basic commodities. In Rwanda, for example, reforms transformed the country's coffee industry and increased exports. Kenya has expanded its exports of cut flowers, and Uganda has improved its fish-processing industry. World Bank efforts have also helped African financial companies develop. [28]

4. **Improving efficiencies in diverse industries and leveraging the private sector.** The World Bank has worked closely with businesses in the private sector to develop local infrastructure, including power, transportation, telecommunications, health care, and education. [29] In Afghanistan, for example, small dams are built and maintained by the locals themselves to support small industries processing local produce.

The World Bank continues to play an integral role in helping countries reduce poverty and improve the well-being of their citizens. World Bank funding provides a resource to countries to utilize the services of global companies to accomplish their objectives.

KEY TAKEAWAYS

- The IMF is playing an expanding role in the global monetary system. The IMF's key roles are the following:
  - To promote international monetary cooperation
  - To facilitate the expansion and balanced growth of international trade
  - To promote exchange stability
  - To assist in the establishment of a multilateral system of payments
  - To give confidence to members by making the IMF's general resources temporarily available to them under adequate safeguards
  - To shorten the duration and lessen the degree of disequilibrium in the international balances of payments of members
- The World Bank consists of two main bodies, the IBRD and the International Development Association (IDA).
- The World Bank Group includes the following interrelated institutions:
  - IBRD, which makes loans to countries with the purpose of building economies and reducing poverty
  - IDA, which typically provides interest-free loans to countries with sovereign guarantees

  - International Finance Corporation (IFC), which provides loans, equity, risk-management tools, and structured finance with the goal of facilitating sustainable development by improving investments in the private sector
  - Multilateral Investment Guarantee Agency (MIGA), which focuses on improving the foreign direct investment of the developing countries
  - International Centre for Settlement of Investment Disputes (ICSID), which provides a means for dispute resolution between governments and private investors, with the end goal of enhancing the flow of capital

EXERCISES

(AACSB: Reflective Thinking, Analytical Skills)
1. What is the IMF, and what role does it play?
2. What are two criticisms of the IMF and two of its opportunities for the future?
3. Discuss whether SDRs or another global currency created by the IMF should replace the US dollar as the international reserve currency.
4. What is the World Bank, and what role does it play?
5. What are two criticisms of the World Bank and two of its opportunities for the future?

[1] David D. Driscoll, "The IMF and the World Bank: How Do They Differ?" International Monetary Fund, last updated August 1996, accessed February 9, 2011,http://www.imf.org/external/pubs/ft/exrp/differ/differ.htm (emphasis added).

[2] "Articles of Agreement: Article I—Purposes," International Monetary Fund, accessed May 23, 2011, http://www.imf.org/external/pubs/ft/aa/aa01.htm.

[3] David N. Balaam and Michael Veseth, Introduction to International Political Economy, 4th ed. (Upper Saddle River, NJ: Pearson Education International/Prentice Hall), 2005.

[4] "Criticism of IMF," Economics Help, accessed June 28, 2010, http://www.economicshelp.org/dictionary/i/imf-criticism.html.

[5] "What Are the Main Concerns and Criticism about the World Bank and IMF?" Bretton Woods Project, January 25, 2007, accessed February 9, 2011,http://www.brettonwoodsproject.org/item.shtml?x=320869.

[6] "Criticism of IMF," Economics Help, accessed June 28, 2010, http://www.economicshelp.org/dictionary/i/imf-criticism.html.

[7] "Criticism of IMF," Economics Help, accessed June 28, 2010, http://www.economicshelp.org/dictionary/i/imf-criticism.html.

[8] "Criticism of IMF," Economics Help, accessed June 28, 2010, http://www.economicshelp.org/dictionary/i/imf-criticism.html.

[9] "Criticism of IMF," Economics Help, accessed June 28, 2010, http://www.economicshelp.org/dictionary/i/imf-criticism.html.

[10] "Criticism of IMF," Economics Help, accessed June 28, 2010, http://www.economicshelp.org/dictionary/i/imf-criticism.html.

[11] "Globalization and the Crisis (2005–Present)," International Monetary Fund, accessed July 26, 2010, http://www.imf.org/external/about/histglob.htm.

[12] Martin S. Edwards, "The IMF's New Toolkit: New Opportunities, Old Challenges," Foreign Policy in Focus, September 17, 2009, accessed June

28, 2010,
http://www.fpif.org/articles/the_imfs_new_toolkit_new_opportunities_old_challenges.

[13] Martin S. Edwards, "The IMF's New Toolkit: New Opportunities, Old Challenges," Foreign Policy in Focus, September 17, 2009, accessed June 28, 2010,
http://www.fpif.org/articles/the_imfs_new_toolkit_new_opportunities_old_challenges.

[14] Martin S. Edwards, "The IMF's New Toolkit: New Opportunities, Old Challenges," Foreign Policy in Focus, September 17, 2009, accessed June 28, 2010,
http://www.fpif.org/articles/the_imfs_new_toolkit_new_opportunities_old_challenges.

[15] Jamil Anderlini, "China Calls for New Reserve Currency," Financial Times, March 24, 2009, accessed February 9, 2011, http://www.ft.com/cms/s/0/7851925a-17a2-11de-8c9d-0000779fd2ac.html#axzz1DTvW5KyI.

[16] Jamil Anderlini, "China Calls for New Reserve Currency," Financial Times, March 24, 2009, accessed February 9, 2011, http://www.ft.com/cms/s/0/7851925a-17a2-11de-8c9d-0000779fd2ac.html#axzz1DTvW5KyI.

[17] "Projects," The World Bank, accessed February 9, 2011, http://go.worldbank.org/M7ARDFNB60.

[18] "To Meet Global Challenges, Six Strategic Themes," The World Bank, accessed February 9, 2011, http://go.worldbank.org/56O9ZVPO70.

[19] Anup Shah, "Causes of Poverty," Global Issues, last modified April 25, 2010, accessed August 1, 2010, http://www.globalissues.org/issue/2/causes-of-poverty.

[20] Encyclopedia of the New American Nation, s.v., "International Monetary Fund and World Bank—World Bank Critics on the Right and Left," accessed June 29, 2010, http://www.americanforeignrelations.com/E-N/International-Monetary-Fund-and-World-Bank-World-bank-critics-on-the-right-and-left.html.

[21] Encyclopedia of the New American Nation, s.v., "International Monetary Fund and World Bank—World Bank Critics on the Right and Left," accessed June 29, 2010, http://www.americanforeignrelations.com/E-N/International-Monetary-Fund-and-World-Bank-World-bank-critics-on-the-right-and-left.html.

[22] Encyclopedia of the New American Nation, s.v., "International Monetary Fund and World Bank—World Bank Critics on the Right and Left," accessed June 29, 2010, http://www.americanforeignrelations.com/E-N/International-Monetary-Fund-and-World-Bank-World-bank-critics-on-the-right-and-left.html.

[23] Lisa Friedman, "How the World Bank Let 'Deal Making' Torch the Rainforests," New York Times, August 19, 2009, accessed February 9, 2011, http://www.nytimes.com/cwire/2009/08/19/19climatewire-how-the-world-bank-let-deal-making-torch-the-33255.html.

[24] Lisa Friedman, "How the World Bank Let 'Deal Making' Torch the Rainforests," New York Times, August 19, 2009, accessed February 9, 2011, http://www.nytimes.com/cwire/2009/08/19/19climatewire-how-the-world-bank-let-deal-making-torch-the-33255.html.

[25] "What Are the Main Concerns and Criticism about the World Bank and IMF?" Bretton Woods Project, January 25, 2007, accessed February 9, 2011, http://www.brettonwoodsproject.org/item.shtml?x=320869.

[26] "What Are the Main Concerns and Criticism about the World Bank and IMF?" Bretton Woods Project, January 25, 2007, accessed February 9, 2011, http://www.brettonwoodsproject.org/item.shtml?x=320869.

[27] Robert J. Brym et al., "In Faint Praise of the World Bank's Gender Development Policy," Canadian Journal of Sociology Online, March–April 2005, accessed May 23, 2011, http://www.cjsonline.ca/articles/brymetal05.html.

[28] Shanta Devarajan, "African Successes—Listing the Success Stories," Africa Can…End Poverty (blog), The World Bank Group, September 17, 2009, accessed May 23, 2011, http://blogs.worldbank.org/africacan/african-successes-listing-the-success-stories.

[29] Shanta Devarajan, "African Successes—Listing the Success Stories," Africa Can…End Poverty (blog), The World Bank Group, September 17, 2009, accessed May 23, 2011, http://blogs.worldbank.org/africacan/african-successes-listing-the-success-stories.

6.3 Understanding How International Monetary Policy, the IMF, and the World Bank Impact Business Practices

LEARNING OBJECTIVES

1. Understand how the current monetary environment, the IMF, and the World Bank impact business.
2. Explore how you can work in the international development arena with a business background.

How Business Is Impacted by the Current Monetary Environment, the IMF, and the World Bank

All businesses seek to operate in a stable and predictable environment. International businesses make efforts to reduce risks and unexpected issues that can impact both operations and profitability. The global monetary system in essence provides a predictable mechanism for companies to exchange currencies. Global firms monitor the policies and discussions of the G20 and other economic organizations so that they can identify new opportunities and use their leverage to protect their markets and businesses.

Did You Know?

There's even an annual forum that the world's largest businesses attend with senior government officials from around the world and leaders of thought on economic, social, and political issues. The five-day meeting is known more commonly as Davos, in reference to the Swiss town in which it is held. Attendees must be invited; the price tag is rather hefty at about $50,000, but the meeting attracts the world's business and political elite. Davos is run by the World Economic Forum (http://www.weforum.org/en/index.htm). The event started in 1971 as the brainchild of Swiss economics professor Klaus Schwab. Originally it served as a small, private, and discreet way of bringing business and political leaders together to establish common ground and objectives. It has since grown exponentially in size and influence and now attracts media and celebrities—but still only by invitation.

The Bretton Woods Institutions have extensive global influence and occasionally use it to nudge countries to reduce trade barriers and adjust the value of their currency. One recent example involves the International Monetary Fund (IMF) and China. A July 2010 report from the IMF stated that China's trade surplus will increase unless the government takes steps to increase more domestic consumption by the Chinese and also by letting the Chinese currency, the renminbi, appreciate or increase in value. [1] China's export machine has been fueled in large part by the low value of the renminbi, as set and maintained by the government. Letting it currently trade with reduced or no government intervention would likely reduce the country's massive exports. "Both the IMF and China's government agree [that China] still depends too much on exports. Supporting domestic consumption instead 'will reduce China's reliance on external demand and better insulate the economy from shocks in overseas markets,' the IMF said. China gave domestic demand an enormous boost with its stimulus program to combat the effects of the financial crisis, resulting in a surge in imports of raw materials and equipment to feed a construction boom." [2]

While the IMF can only issue a report, action is completely at the discretion of the country's government. However, for global businesses, this can be encouraging in several ways. In this case, companies that are eager to enter the Chinese market to sell their goods and services may find it easier or the general climate more welcoming of foreign businesses. Second, if the renminbi increases in value, the Chinese can purchase more goods and services from overseas firms. On the flip side, companies that compete with Chinese firms in other markets may be frustrated by China's cheap costs and undervalued currency. If the Chinese currency increases in value, Chinese exports will become more expensive, allowing other companies to compete more effectively against Chinese firms. These are just a couple of simple scenarios, but they illustrate the range of issues and concerns that China may have with the IMF report and the opportunities that may arise for global businesses. IMF reports are based on years of research, and it's rare that markets, countries, and businesses are not already aware of the issues in any report. However, by actually releasing the report, the IMF is officially prioritizing and legitimizing the concerns. In this case, the initial report from the IMF was ready for release in 2006, but China effectively blocked the release until some changes were made. It was finally released in July 2010. The impact of the report will take several years to unfold. However, already in early 2011, China announced its intentions to let the renminbi begin to trade more freely. "The People's Bank of China...is pushing for a greater role for the renminbi in global trade and investment so that China can reduce its almost total reliance on the US dollar." [3] Recent efforts have included allowing

for individuals and institutions to buy the renminbi outside of China and also to permit select trading of the currency in other countries, such as Russia and Singapore, as well as in its own territory of Hong Kong. The Chinese government hope is that by internationalizing the currency, it will eventually will be perceived as a reserve currency, a key component of its ambitions to be a global power. [4]

Working in the International Development Arena with a Business Background

Why would international businesses care about quasi-government institutions such as the World Bank and IMF? The opening case discusses how a management consulting firm links businesses, governments, and global institutions by advising on policy and strategy. What many people don't realize at first glance is that the global business in the private sector is heavily impacted by the IMF, the World Bank, and other development organizations.

Many of the projects that the World Bank Group funds in specific countries are put up for competitive bidding by the government of the country receiving the funds; the projects are then managed by a government department. However, global companies in the private sector almost always carry out the actual work. Hence there is a vast industry focused on obtaining these often lucrative and secure contracts. The World Bank has worked hard to increase transparency in the bidding process and to closely monitor and audit how its monies are spent.

Let's look at some of the companies and industries that get involved in World Bank projects. Consulting companies, particularly the large global firms—McKinsey, BearingPoint, and PricewaterhouseCoopers (PwC), for example—are high-profile examples of firms that actively solicit projects from the World Bank and other development organizations. Their capabilities range across diverse industries, from finance and regulation to project management and auditing of infrastructure development. Engineering, chemical, and telecommunications firms also have departments that solicit and bid on World Bank projects.

These firms routinely hire people with business degrees. Those with additional qualifications in foreign languages or technical skills have increased chances of being hired. So how do you find out which companies are getting contracts? Try the following method:
- Start by looking at the Devex site. While it's the biggest and best-known website resource for development work, there are others.

- Explore organizational training programs, such as the World Bank's Young Professionals Program, which is designed for highly qualified, experienced, and motivated individuals (under the age of thirty-two) who are skilled in areas relevant to the World Bank's operations, such as economics, finance, education, public health, social sciences, engineering, urban planning, and natural resource management.

- Research the World Bank site and sites of the other institutions in the World Bank Group to identify which firms are winning bids; then apply to those firms. In an effort to combat the ethics issues, each of these organizations now requires complete transparency in contract awards and has sections where you can search. For example, use the following link for the World Bank contractors search: http://web.worldbank.org/wbsite/external/projects/0,,menuPK:51565~pagePK:95864~piPK:95915~theSitePK:40941,00.html.

- Read the *Economist*, the *Wall Street Journal*, and other global business publications to learn more about projects, loans, and activities of the World Bank, private sector firms, and countries. Many of these publications have job ads. Even if it is for more senior positions, you can learn which companies are working in which sectors and countries.

KEY TAKEAWAYS

- Businesses seek to operate in a stable and predictable environment by reducing risks and unexpected issues that can impact both operations and profitability.

- Global firms monitor the policies and discussions of the G20 and other economic organizations so that they can identify new opportunities and use their leverage to protect their markets and businesses.

- Global business in the private sector is heavily impacted by the IMF, the World Bank, and other development organizations.

- Many of the projects that the World Bank Group funds in specific countries are managed by the local governments, but the actual work is typically done by a private sector firm.

EXERCISES

(AACSB: Reflective Thinking, Analytical Skills)
1. Why are the World Bank and the IMF relevant for global businesses?
2. What types of entities carry out the projects funded by the World Bank?

[1] Andrew Batson, "IMF Report Urges China to Consume More," Wall Street Journal, July 30, 2010, accessed February 9, 2011,http://online.wsj.com/article/SB1000142405274870357810457539695358007 8456.html.
[2] Andrew Batson, "IMF Report Urges China to Consume More," Wall Street Journal, July 30, 2010, accessed February 9, 2011,http://online.wsj.com/article/SB1000142405274870357810457539695358007 8456.html.
[3] "Singapore Aims to Be a Renminbi Hub," Financial Times, April 19, 2011, accessed May 7, 2011, http://www.ft.com/cms/s/0/64bac520-6a4f-11e0-a464-00144feab49a.html#ixzz1LgVcCJKM.
[4] Wieland Wagner, "China Plans Path to Economic Hegemony," Spiegel Online International, January 26, 2011, accessed May 7, 2011, http://www.spiegel.de/international/business/0,1518,741303,00.html.

6.4 Tips in Your Entrepreneurial Walkabout Toolkit
Are You Interested in Jobs in the Development Arena?

Check out dedicated websites like Devex (http://www.devex.com/en/). Devex began as a student project at Harvard University's Kennedy School of Government in 2000. Today, Devex is the largest provider of business intelligence and recruitment services to the development community; it serves a majority of the world's leading donor agencies, companies, NGOs, and development professionals. Devex is the main source of business information related to foreign assistance, including tenders, project information, business advice, and news from the World Bank, UNDP, USAID, DFID, ADB, and more.

You can also try DevNet (http://www.devnetjobs.org), which lists available jobs, and Eldis (http://www.eldis.org), which is a resource for development research, jobs, and industry and country information.

6.5 End-of-Chapter Questions and Exercises
These exercises are designed to ensure that the knowledge you gain from this book about international business meets the learning standards set out by the international Association to Advance Collegiate Schools of Business (AACSB International). [1] AACSB is the premier accrediting agency of collegiate business schools and accounting programs worldwide. It expects that you will gain knowledge in the areas of communication, ethical reasoning, analytical skills, use of information technology, multiculturalism and diversity, and reflective thinking.

EXPERIENTIAL EXERCISES

(AACSB: Communication, Use of Information Technology, Analytical Skills)
1. Research the G20 at its website, http://www.g20.org. Identify the current priorities and focus of the organization. Based on what you have learned about the

history of the international monetary system and recent events and changes, do you agree with the current focus? What would you change?

2. Select a large global consumer products or manufacturing company to work for. Review the sidebar on General Motors in Section 6.1 "What Is the International Monetary System?". You are a member of your company's postwar planning policy group. Review the conflict in Iraq. What would you recommend to your senior management about local prospects for your company in the country and region?

3. Identify two countries, one in Africa and one in either Asia or Latin America. Research each country's history with the IMF and the World Bank. Has the country accepted loans from either organization? What were the terms of the loans? Discuss whether the loans achieved the initial purpose and whether the country is better or worse off as a result of working with these institutions. Have the loans helped expand the prospects for businesses, local and multinational?

Ethical Dilemmas

(AACSB: Ethical Reasoning, Multiculturalism, Reflective Thinking, Analytical Skills)

1. This chapter reviews how the World Bank has dealt with charges of corruption and transparency in the past. It also discusses how many global firms seek to do business for World Bank-funded projects. Imagine you are the director of global business development for a large Swedish engineering company that wants to win the contract to build roads in Kenya through a World Bank–funded project. You need to develop a relationship with the Ministry of Transportation in Kenya. Using what you learned in this chapter, discuss how you would handle a situation in which your firm wants to win the contract but has been directly asked for a bribe by a local official in charge of the decision making. Imagine that your competitors are from other countries, some of which are less concerned about the ethics of gift giving as this book has defined it. How can you still win business in such a situation? What would you advise your senior management?

2. Imagine that you are a consultant for McKinsey & Company, and you are assigned to the team advising Walmart on selecting and entering new markets in Africa and Latin America. You were also recently a member of the team that advised the United Nations on a new strategy for the Global Compact, which is covered in Chapter 5 "Global and Regional Economic Cooperation and Integration". How would you link these two consulting projects, and how might it impact the advice you give to Walmart? Would there be any areas of ethical conflict if you shared information on the Global Compact to the benefit of Walmart? Discuss whether any benefits would accrue to the Global Compact.

[1] Association to Advance Collegiate Schools of Business website, accessed January 26, 2010, http://www.aacsb.edu.

NOTES:

Chapter 7:
Foreign Exchange and the Global Capital Markets

WHAT'S IN IT FOR ME?

1. What do we mean by currency and foreign exchange?
2. How do you determine exchange rates?
3. What are the global capital markets?
4. What is the impact of the global capital markets (particularly the venture capital and global capital markets) on international business?

This chapter explores currencies, foreign exchange rates, and how they are determined. It also discusses the global capital markets—the key components and how they impact global business. Foreign exchange is one aspect of the global capital markets. Companies access the global capital markets to utilize both the debt and equity markets; these are important for growth. Being able to access transparent and efficient capital markets around the world is another important component in the flattening world for global firms. Finally, this chapter discusses how the expansion of the global capital markets has benefited entrepreneurship and venture capitalists.

OPENING CASE: WHY A MAIN STREET FIRM, WALMART, IS IMPACTED BY FOREIGN EXCHANGE FLUCTUATIONS

Most people in North America are familiar with the name Walmart. It conjures up an image of a gigantic, box-like store filled with a wide range of essential and nonessential products. What's less known is that Walmart is the world's largest company, in terms of revenues, as ranked by the Fortune 500 in 2010. With $408 billion in sales, it operates in fifteen global markets and has 4,343 stores outside of the United States, which amounts to about 50 percent of its total stores. More than 700,000 people work for Walmartinternationally. With numbers like this, it's easy to see how important the global markets have become for this company. [1]

Walmart's strength comes from the upper hand it has in its negotiations with suppliers around the world. Suppliers are motivated to negotiate with Walmart because of the huge sales volume the stores offer manufacturers. The business rationale for many suppliers is that while they may lose a certain percentage of profitability per product, the overall sales volume of an order from Walmart can make them far more money overall than orders from most other stores. Walmart's purchasing professionals are known for being aggressive negotiators on purchases and for extracting the best terms for the company.

In order to buy goods from around the world, Walmart has to deal extensively in different currencies. Small changes in the daily foreign currency market can significantly impact the costs for Walmart and in turn both its profitability and that of its global suppliers.

A company like Walmart needs foreign exchange and capital for different reasons, including the following common operational uses:

1. To build new stores, expand stores, or refurbish stores in a specific country
2. To purchase products locally by paying in local currencies or the US dollar, whichever is cheaper and works to Walmart's advantage
3. To pay salaries and benefits for its local employees in each country as well as its expatriate and global workforce
4. To take profits out of a country and either reinvest the money in another country or market or save it and make profits from returns on investment

To illustrate this impact of foreign currency, let's look at the currency of China, the renminbi (RMB), and its impact on a global business like Walmart. Many global analysts argue that the Chinese government tries to keep the value of its currency low or cheap to help promote exports. When the local RMB is valued cheaply or low, Chinese importers that buy foreign goods find that the prices are more expensive and higher.

However, Chinese exporters, those businesses that sell goods and services to foreign buyers, find that sales increase because their prices are cheaper or lower for the foreign buyers. Economists say that the Chinese government has intervened to keep the renminbi cheap in order to keep Chinese exports cheap; this has led to a huge trade surplus with the United States and most of the world. Each country tries to promote its exports to generate a trade advantage or surplus in its favor. When China has a trade surplus, it means the other country or countries are running trade deficits, which has "become an irritant to a lot of China's trading partners and those who are competing with China to sell goods around the world." [2]

For Walmart, an American company, a cheap renminbi means that it takes fewer US dollars to buy Chinese products. Walmart can then buy cheap Chinese products, add a small profit margin, and then sell the goods in the United States at a price lower than what its competitors can offer. If the Chinese RMB increased in value, then Walmart would have to spend more US dollars to buy the same products, whether the products are clothing, electronics, or furniture. Any increase in cost for Walmart will mean an increase in cost for their customers in the United States, which could lead to a decrease in sales. So we can see why Walmart would be opposed to an increase in the value of the RMB.

To manage this currency concern, Walmart often requires that the currency exchange rate be fixed in its purchasing contracts with Chinese suppliers. By fixing the currency exchange rate, Walmart locks in its product costs and therefore its profitability. Fixing the exchange rate means setting the price that one currency will convert into another. This is how a company like Walmart can avoid unexpected drops or increases in the value of the RMB and the US dollar.

While global companies have to buy and sell in different currencies around the world, their primary goal is to avoid losses and to fix the price of the currency exchange so that they can manage their profitability with surety. This chapter takes a look at some of the currency tools that companies use to manage this risk.

Global firms like Walmart often set up local operations that help them balance or manage their risk by doing business in local currencies. Walmart now has 304 stores in China. Each store generates sales in renminbi, earning the company local currency that it can use to manage its local operations and to purchase local goods for sale in its other global markets. [3]

OPENING CASE EXERCISES

(AACSB: Ethical Reasoning, Multiculturalism, Reflective Thinking, Analytical Skills)

1. List two reasons a global company needs foreign exchange.
2. Why is Walmart concerned about foreign exchange rates?

[1] "Walmart Stores Inc. Data Sheet—Worldwide Unit Details November 2010," Walmart Corporation, accessed May 25, 2011, http://walmartstores.com/pressroom/news/10497.aspx.
[2] David Barboza, "Currency Fight with China Divides U.S. Business," New York Times, November 16, 2010, accessed May 25, 2011, http://www.nytimes.com/2010/11/17/business/global/17yuan.html?_r=1&pagewanted=2.
[3] David Barboza, "Currency Fight with China Divides U.S. Business," New York Times, November 16, 2010, accessed May 25, 2011, http://www.nytimes.com/2010/11/17/business/global/17yuan.html?_r=1&pagewanted=2.

7.1 What Do We Mean by Currency and Foreign Exchange?

LEARNING OBJECTIVES

1. Understand what is meant by currency and foreign exchange.
2. Explore the purpose of the foreign exchange market.
3. Understand how to determine exchange rates.

What Are Currency and Foreign Exchange?

In order to understand the global financial environment, how capital markets work, and their impact on global business, we need to first understand how currencies and foreign exchange rates work.

Briefly, currency is any form of money in general circulation in a country. What exactly is a foreign exchange? In essence, foreign exchange is money denominated in the currency of another country or—now with the euro—a group of countries. Simply put, an exchange rate is defined as the rate at which the market converts one currency into another.

Any company operating globally must deal in foreign currencies. It has to pay suppliers in other countries with a currency different from its home country's currency. The home country is where a company is headquartered. The firm is likely to be paid or have profits in a different currency and will want to exchange it for its home currency. Even if a company expects to be paid in its own currency, it must assess the risk that the buyer may not be able to pay the full amount due to currency fluctuations.

If you have traveled outside of your home country, you may have experienced the currency market—for example, when you tried to determine your hotel bill or tried to determine if an item was cheaper in one country versus another. In fact, when you land at an airport in another country, you're likely to see boards indicating the foreign exchange rates for major currencies. These rates include two numbers: the bid and the offer. The bid (or buy) is the price at which a bank or financial services firm is willing to buy a specific currency.

The ask (or the offer or sell), refers to the price at which a bank or financial services firm is willing to sell that currency. Typically, the bid or the buy is always cheaper than the sell; banks make a profit on the transaction from that difference. For example, imagine you're on vacation in Thailand and the exchange rate board indicates that the Bangkok Bank is willing to exchange currencies at the following rates (see the following figure). GBP refers to the British pound; JPY refers to the Japanese yen; and HKD refers to the Hong Kong dollar, as shown in the following figure. Because there are several countries that use the dollar as part or whole of their name, this chapter clearly states "US dollar" or uses US$ or USD when referring to American currency.

Foreign Exchange Rates: Bangkok Bank		
Currency/Baht	Banknotes Buy	Banknotes Sell
USD	31.67	32.32
GBP	50.19	51.80
Euro	41.74	43.00
JOY	36.56	39.01
HKD	4.03	4.22

This chart tells us that when you land in Thailand, you can use 1 US dollar to buy 31.67 Thai baht. However, when you leave Thailand and decide that you do not need to take all your baht back to the United States, you then convert baht back to US dollars. We then have to use more baht—32.32 according to the preceding figure—to buy 1 US dollar. The spread between these numbers, 0.65 baht, is the profit that the bank makes for each US dollar bought and sold. The bank charges a fee because it performed a service— facilitating the currency exchange. When you walk through the airport, you'll see more boards for different banks with different buy and sell rates. While the difference may be very small, around 0.1 baht, these numbers add up if you are a global company engaged in large foreign exchange transactions. Accordingly, global firms are likely to shop around for the best rates before they exchange any currencies.

What Is the Purpose of the Foreign Exchange Market?

The foreign exchange market (or FX market) is the mechanism in which currencies can be bought and sold. A key component of this mechanism is pricing or, more specifically, the rate at which a currency is bought or sold. We'll cover the determination of exchange rates more closely in this section, but first let's understand the purpose of the FX market. International businesses have four main uses of the foreign exchange markets.

Currency Conversion

Companies, investors, and governments want to be able to convert one currency into another. A company's primary purposes for wanting or needing to convert currencies is to pay or receive money for goods or services. Imagine you have a business in the United States that imports wines from around the world. You'll need to pay the French winemakers in euros, your Australian wine suppliers in Australian dollars, and your Chilean vineyards in pesos. Obviously, you are not going to access these currencies physically. Rather, you'll instruct your bank to pay each of these suppliers in their local currencies. Your bank will convert the currencies for you and debit your account for the US dollar equivalent based on the exact exchange rate at the time of the exchange.

Currency Hedging

One of the biggest challenges in foreign exchange is the risk of rates increasing or decreasing in greater amounts or directions than anticipated. Currency hedging refers to the technique of protecting against the potential losses that result from adverse changes in exchange rates. Companies use hedging as a way to protect themselves if there is a time lag between when they bill and receive payment from a customer. Conversely, a company may owe payment to an overseas vendor and want to protect against changes in the exchange rate that would increase the amount of the payment. For example, a retail store in Japan imports or buys shoes from Italy. The Japanese firm has ninety days to pay the Italian firm. To protect itself, the Japanese firm enters into a contract with its bank to exchange the payment in ninety days at the agreed-on exchange rate. This way, the Japanese firm is clear about the amount to pay and protects itself from a sudden depreciation of the yen. If the yen depreciates, more yen will be required to purchase the same euros, making the deal more expensive. By hedging, the company locks in the rate.

Currency Arbitrage

Arbitrage is the simultaneous and instantaneous purchase and sale of a currency for a profit. Advances in technology have enabled trading systems to capture slight differences in price and execute a transaction, all within seconds. Previously, arbitrage was conducted by a trader sitting in one city, such as New York, monitoring currency prices on the Bloomberg terminal. Noticing that the value of a euro is cheaper in Hong Kong than in New York, the trader could then buy euros in Hong Kong and sell them in New York for a profit. Today, such transactions are almost all handled by sophisticated computer programs. The programs constantly search different exchanges, identify potential differences, and execute transactions, all within seconds.

Currency Speculation

Speculation refers to the practice of buying and selling a currency with the expectation that the value will change and result in a profit. Such changes could happen instantly or over a period of time.

High-risk, speculative investments by nonfinance companies are less common these days than the current news would indicate. While companies can engage in all four uses discussed in this section, many companies have determined over the years that arbitrage and speculation are too risky and not in alignment with their core strategies. In essence, these companies have determined that a loss due to high-risk or speculative investments would be embarrassing and inappropriate for their companies.

Understand How to Determine Exchange Rates

How to Quote a Currency

There are several ways to quote currency, but let's keep it simple. In general, when we quote currencies, we are indicating how much of one currency it takes to buy another currency. This quote requires two components: the base currency and the quoted currency. The quoted currency is the currency with which another currency is to be purchased. In an exchange rate quote, the quoted currency is typically the numerator. The base currency is the currency that is to be purchased with another currency, and it is noted in the denominator. For example, if we are quoting the number of Hong Kong dollars required to purchase 1 US dollar, then we note HKD 8 / USD 1. (Note that 8 reflects the general exchange rate average in this example.) In this case, the Hong Kong dollar is the quoted currency and is noted in the numerator. The US dollar is the base currency and is noted in the denominator. We read this quote as "8 Hong Kong dollars are required to purchase 1 US dollar." If you get confused while reviewing exchanging rates, remember the currency that you want to buy or sell. If you want to sell 1 US dollar, you can buy 8 Hong Kong dollars, using the example in this paragraph.

Direct Currency Quote and Indirect Currency Quote

Additionally, there are two methods—the American terms and the European terms—for noting the base and quoted currency. These two methods, which are also known as direct and indirect quotes, are opposite based on each reference point. Let's understand what this means exactly.

The American terms, also known as US terms, are from the point of view of someone in the United States. In this approach, foreign exchange rates are expressed in terms of how many US dollars can be exchanged for one unit of another currency (the non-US currency is the *base currency*). For example, a dollar-pound quote in American terms is USD/GP (US$/£) equals 1.56. This is read as "1.56 US dollars are required to buy 1 pound sterling." This is also called a direct quote, which states the domestic currency price of one unit of foreign currency. If you think about this logically, a business that needs to buy a foreign currency needs to know how many US dollars must be sold in order to buy one unit of the foreign currency. In a direct quote, the domestic currency is a variable amount and the foreign currency is fixed at one unit.

Conversely, the European terms are the other approach for quoting rates. In this approach, foreign exchange rates are expressed in terms of how many currency units can be exchanged for a US dollar (the US dollar is the base currency). For example, the pound-dollar quote in European terms is £0.64/US$1 (£/US$1). While this is a direct quote for someone in Europe, it is an indirect quote in the United States. An indirect quote states the price of the domestic currency in foreign currency terms. In an indirect quote, the foreign currency is a variable amount and the domestic currency is fixed at one unit.

A direct and an indirect quote are simply reverse quotes of each other. If you have either one, you can easily calculate the other using this simple formula:

direct quote = 1 / indirect quote.

To illustrate, let's use our dollar-pound example. The direct quote is US$1.56 = 1/£0.64 (the indirect quote). This can be read as

1 divided by 0.64 equals 1.56.

In this example, the direct currency quote is written as US$/£ = 1.56.

While you are performing the calculations, it is important to keep track of which currency is in the numerator and which is in the denominator, or you might end up stating the quote backward. The direct quote is the rate at which you buy a currency. In this example, you need US$1.56 to buy a British pound.

Tip: Many international business professionals become experienced over their careers and are able to correct themselves in the event of a mix-up between currencies. To illustrate using the example mentioned previously, the seasoned global professional knows that the British pound is historically higher in value than the US dollar. This means that it takes more US dollars to buy a pound than the other way around. When we say "higher in value," we mean that the value of the British pound buys you more US dollars. Using this logic, we can then deduce that 1.56 US dollars are required to buy 1 British pound. As an international businessperson, we would know instinctively that it cannot be less—that is, only 0.64 US dollars to buy a British pound. This would imply that the dollar value was higher in value. While major currencies have changed significantly in value vis-à-vis each other, it tends to happen over long periods of time. As a result, this self-test is a good way to use logic to keep track of tricky exchange rates. It works best with major currencies that do not fluctuate greatly vis-à-vis others.

A useful side note: traders always list the base currency as the first currency in a currency pair. Let's assume, for example, that it takes 85 Japanese yen to purchase 1 US dollar. A currency trader would note this as follows: USD 1 / JPY 85. This quote indicates that the base currency is the US dollar and 85 yen are required to purchase a dollar. This is also called a direct quote, although FX traders are more likely to call it an American rate rather than a direct rate. It can be confusing, but try to keep the logic of which currency you are selling and which you are buying clearly in your mind, and say the quote as full sentences in order to keep track of the currencies.

These days, you can easily use the Internet to access up-to-date quotes on all currencies, although the most reliable sites remain the *Wall Street Journal*, the *Financial Times*, or any website of a trustworthy financial institution.

Spot Rates

The exchange rates discussed in this chapter are spot rates—exchange rates that require immediate settlement with delivery of the traded currency. "Immediate" usually means within two business days, but it implies an "on the spot" exchange of the currencies, hence the term *spot rate*. The spot exchange rate is the exchange rate transacted at a particular moment by the buyer and seller of a currency. When we buy and sell our foreign currency at a bank or at American Express, it's quoted at the rate for the day. For currency traders though, the spot can change throughout the trading day even by tiny fractions.

To illustrate, assume that you work for a clothing company in the United States and you want to buy shirts from either Malaysia or Indonesia. The shirts are exactly the same; only the price is different. (For now, ignore shipping and any

taxes.) Assume that you are using the spot rate and are making an immediate payment. There is no risk of the currency increasing or decreasing in value. (We'll cover forward rates in the next section.)

The currency in Malaysia is the Malaysian ringgit, which is abbreviated MYR. The supplier in Kuala Lumpur e-mails you the quote—you can buy each shirt for MYR 35. Let's use a spot exchange rate of MYR 3.13 / USD 1.

The Indonesian currency is the rupiah, which is abbreviated as Rp. The supplier in Jakarta e-mails you a quote indicating that you can buy each shirt for Rp 70,000. Use a spot exchange rate of Rp 8,960 / USD 1.

It would be easy to instinctively assume that the Indonesian firm is more expensive, but look more closely. You can calculate the price of one shirt into US dollars so that a comparison can be made:

For Malaysia: MYR 35 / MYR 3.13 = USD 11.18For Indonesia: Rp 70,000 / Rp 8,960 = USD 7.81

Indonesia is the cheaper supplier for our shirts on the basis of the spot exchange rate.

Cross Rates

There's one more term that applies to the spot market—the cross rate. This is the exchange rate between two currencies, neither of which is the official currency in the country in which the quote is provided. For example, if an exchange rate between the euro and the yen were quoted by an American bank on US soil, the rate would be a cross rate.

The most common cross-currency pairs are EUR/GBP, EUR/CHF, and EUR/JPY. These currency pairs expand the trading possibilities in the foreign exchange market but are less actively traded than pairs that include the US dollar, which are called the "majors" because of their high degree of liquidity. The majors are EUR/USD, GBP/ USD, USD/JPY, USD/CAD (Canadian dollar), USD/CHF (Swiss franc), and USD/AUD (Australian dollar). Despite the changes in the international monetary system and the expansion of the capital markets, the currency market is really a market of dollars and nondollars. The dollar is still the reserve currency for the world's central banks. Table 7.1 "Currency Cross Rates" contains some currency cross rates between the major currencies. We can see, for example, that the rate for the cross-currency pair of EUR/GBP is 1.1956. This is read as "it takes 1.1956 euros to buy one British pound." Another example is the EUR/JPY rate, which is 0.00901. However, a seasoned trader would not say that it takes 0.00901 euros to buy 1 Japanese yen. He or she would instinctively know to quote the currency pair as the JPY/EUR rate or—more specifically—that it takes 111.088 yen to purchase 1 euro.

Forward Rates

The forward exchange rate is the exchange rate at which a buyer and a seller agree to transact a currency at some date in the future. Forward rates are really a reflection of the market's expectation of the future spot rate for a currency. The forward market is the currency market for transactions at forward rates. In the forward markets, foreign exchange is always quoted against the US dollar. This means that pricing is done in terms of how many US dollars are needed to buy one unit of the other currency. Not all currencies are traded in the forward market, as it depends on the demand in the international financial markets. The majors are routinely traded in the forward market.

For example, if a US company opted to buy cell phones from China with payment due in ninety days, it would be able to access the forward market to enter into a forward contract to lock in a future price for its payment. This would enable the US firm to protect itself against a depreciation of the US dollar, which would require more dollars to buy one Chinese yuan. A forward contract is a contract that requires the exchange of an agreed-on amount of a currency on an agreed-on date and a specific exchange rate. Most forward contracts have fixed dates at 30, 90, or 180 days. Custom forward contracts can be purchased from most financial firms. Forward contracts, currency swaps, options, and futures all belong to a group of financial instruments called derivatives. In the term's broadest definition, derivatives are financial instruments whose underlying value comes from (derives from) other financial instruments or commodities—in this case, another currency.

Swaps, Options, and Futures

Swaps, options, and futures are three additional currency instruments used in the forward market.

A currency swap is a simultaneous buy and sell of a currency for two different dates. For example, an American computer firm buys (imports) components from China. The firm needs to pay its supplier in renminbi today. At the same time, the American computer is expecting to receive RMB in ninety days for its netbooks sold in China. The American firm enters into two transactions. First, it exchanges US dollars and buys yuan renminbi today so that it can pay its supplier. Second, it simultaneously enters into a forward contract to sell yuan and buy dollars at the ninety-day forward rate. By entering into both transactions, the firm is able to reduce its foreign exchange rate risk by locking into the price for both.

Currency options are the option or the right—but not the obligation—to exchange a specific amount of currency on a specific future date and at a specific agreed-on rate. Since a currency option is a right but not a requirement, the parties in an option do not have to actually exchange the currencies if they choose not to. This is referred to as not exercising an option.

Currency futures contracts are contracts that require the exchange of a specific amount of currency at a specific future date and at a specific exchange rate. Futures contracts are similar to but not identical to forward contracts.

Exchange-Traded and Standardized Terms

Futures contracts are actively traded on exchanges, and the terms are standardized. As a result, futures contracts have clearinghouses that guarantee the transactions, substantially reducing any risk of default by either party. Forward contracts are private contracts between two parties and are not standardized. As a result, the parties have a higher risk of defaulting on a contract.

Settlement and Delivery

The settlement of a forward contract occurs at the end of the contract. Futures contracts are marked-to-market daily, which means that daily changes are settled day by day until the end of the contract. Furthermore, the settlement of a futures contract can occur over a range of dates. Forward contracts, on the other hand, only have one settlement date at the end of the contract.

Maturity

Futures contracts are frequently employed by speculators, who bet on the direction in which a currency's price will move; as a result, futures contracts are usually closed out prior to maturity and delivery usually never happens. On the other hand, forward contracts are mostly used by companies, institutions, or hedgers that want to eliminate the volatility of a currency's price in the future, and delivery of the currency will usually take place.

Companies routinely use these tools to manage their exposure to currency risk. One of the complicating factors for companies occurs when they operate in countries that limit or control the convertibility of currency. Some countries limit the profits (currency) a company can take out of a country. As a result, many companies resort to countertrade, where companies trade goods and services for other goods and services and actual monies are less involved.

The challenge for companies is to operate in a world system that is not efficient. Currency markets are influenced not only by market factors, inflation, interest rates, and market psychology but also—more importantly—by government policy and intervention. Many companies move their production and operations to overseas locations to manage against unforeseen currency risks and to circumvent trade barriers. It's important for companies to actively monitor the markets in which they operate around the world.

KEY TAKEAWAYS

In this section you learned about the following:
1. An exchange rate is the rate at which the market converts one currency into another. An exchange rate can be quoted as direct or indirect.
2. The spot rate is an exchange rate that requires immediate settlement with delivery of the traded currency. The forward exchange rate is the exchange rate at which a buyer and seller agree to transact a currency at some date in the future. Swaps, options, and futures are additional types of currency instruments used in the forward market.
3. Companies routinely use these tools to manage their exposure to currency risk. Well-functioning currency markets are a component of the global financial markets and an essential mechanism for global firms that need to exchange currencies.

EXERCISES

(AACSB: Reflective Thinking, Analytical Skills)
1. What is currency and foreign exchange? Why are they so important to international business?
2. What is the difference between American and European terms for quoting currencies? Give an example. If you have traveled outside your home country, discuss how you exchanged currency while abroad. What process did you follow?
3. Describe a spot rate and a forward rate.
4. What are the main differences between a forward contract and a futures contract?

7.2 Understanding International Capital Markets
LEARNING OBJECTIVES

1. Understand the purpose of capital markets, domestic and international.
2. Explore the major components of the international capital markets.
3. Understand the role of international banks, investment banks, securities firms, and financial institutions.

What Are International Capital Markets?

A capital market is basically a system in which people, companies, and governments with an excess of funds transfer those funds to people, companies, and governments that have a shortage of funds. This transfer mechanism provides an efficient way for those who wish to borrow or invest money to do so. For example, every time someone takes out a loan to buy a car or a house, they are accessing the capital markets. Capital markets carry out the desirable economic function of directing capital to productive uses.

There are two main ways that someone accesses the capital markets—either as debt or equity. While there are many forms of each, very simply, debt is money that's borrowed and must be repaid, and equity is money that is invested in return for a percentage of ownership but is not guaranteed in terms of repayment.

In essence, governments, businesses, and people that save some portion of their income invest their money in capital markets such as stocks and bonds. The borrowers (governments, businesses, and people who spend more than their income) borrow the savers' investments through the capital markets. When savers make investments, they convert risk-free assets such as cash or savings into risky assets with the hopes of receiving a future benefit. Since all investments are risky, the only reason a saver would put cash at risk is if returns on the investment are greater than returns on holding risk-free assets. Basically, a higher rate of return means a higher risk.

For example, let's imagine a beverage company that makes $1 million in gross sales. If the company spends $900,000, including taxes and all expenses, then it has $100,000 in profits. The company can invest the $100,000 in a mutual fund (which are pools of money managed by an investment company), investing in stocks and bonds all over the world. Making such an investment is riskier than keeping the $100,000 in a savings account. The financial officer hopes that over the long term the investment will yield greater returns than cash holdings or interest on a savings account.

This is an example of a form of direct finance. In other words, the beverage company bought a security issued by another company through the capital markets. In contrast, indirect finance involves a financial intermediary between the borrower and the saver. For example, if the company deposited the money in a savings account, and then the savings bank lends the money to a company (or a person), the bank is an intermediary. Financial intermediaries are very important in the capital marketplace. Banks lend money to many people, and in so doing create economies of scale. This is one of the primary purposes of the capital markets.

Capital markets promote economic efficiency. In the example, the beverage company wants to invest its $100,000 productively. There might be a number of firms around the world eager to borrow funds by issuing a debt security or an equity security so that it can implement a great business idea. Without issuing the security, the borrowing firm has no funds to implement its plans. By shifting the funds from the beverage company to other firms through the capital markets, the funds are employed to their maximum extent. If there were no capital markets, the beverage company might have kept its $100,000 in cash or in a low-yield savings account. The other firms would also have had to put off or cancel their business plans.

International capital markets are the same mechanism but in the global sphere, in which governments, companies, and people borrow and invest across national boundaries. In addition to the benefits and purposes of a domestic capital market, international capital markets provide the following benefits:

1. **Higher returns and cheaper borrowing costs.** These allow companies and governments to tap into foreign markets and access new sources of funds. Many domestic markets are too small or too costly for companies to borrow in. By using the international capital markets, companies, governments, and even individuals can borrow or invest in other countries for either higher rates of return or lower borrowing costs.
2. **Diversifying risk.** The international capital markets allow individuals, companies, and governments to access more opportunities in different countries to borrow or invest, which in turn reduces risk. The theory is that not all markets will experience contractions at the same time.

The structure of the capital markets falls into two components—primary and secondary. The primary market is where new securities (stocks and bonds are the most common) are issued. If a corporation or government agency needs funds, it issues (sells) securities to purchasers in the primary market. Big investment banks assist in this issuing process as intermediaries. Since the primary market is limited to issuing only new securities, it is valuable but less important than the secondary market.

The vast majority of capital transactions take place in the secondary market. The secondary market includes stock exchanges (the New York Stock Exchange, the London Stock Exchange, and the Tokyo Nikkei), bond markets, and futures and options markets, among others. All these secondary markets deal in the trade of securities. The term securities includes a wide range of financial instruments. You're probably most familiar with stocks and bonds. Investors have essentially two broad categories of securities available to them: equity securities, which represent ownership of a part of a company, and debt securities, which represent a loan from the investor to a company or government entity.

Creditors, or debt holders, purchase debt securities and receive future income or assets in return for their investment. The most common example of a debt instrument is the bond. When investors buy bonds, they are lending the issuers of the bonds their money. In return, they will receive interest payments usually at a fixed rate for the life of the bond and receive the principal when the bond expires. All types of organizations can issue bonds.

Stocks are the type of equity security with which most people are familiar. When investors buy stock, they become owners of a share of a company's assets and earnings. If a company is successful, the price that investors are willing to pay for its stock will often rise; shareholders who bought stock at a lower price then stand to make a profit. If a company does not do well, however, its stock may decrease in value and shareholders can lose money. Stock prices are also subject to both general economic and industry-specific market factors.

The key to remember with either debt or equity securities is that the issuing entity, a company or government, only receives the cash in the primary market issuance. Once the security is issued, it is traded; but the company receives no more financial benefit from that security. Companies are motivated to maintain the value of their equity securities or to repay their bonds in a timely manner so that when they want to borrow funds from or sell more shares in the market, they have the credibility to do so.

For companies, the global financial, including the currency, markets (1) provide stability and predictability, (2) help reduce risk, and (3) provide access to more resources. One of the fundamental purposes of the capital markets, both domestic and international, is the concept of liquidity, which basically means being able to convert a noncash asset into cash without losing any of the principal value. In the case of global capital markets, liquidity refers to the ease and speed by which shareholders and bondholders can buy and sell their securities and convert their investment into cash when necessary. Liquidity is also essential for foreign exchange, as companies don't want their profits locked into an illiquid currency.

Major Components of the International Capital Markets

International Equity Markets

Companies sell their stock in the equity markets. International equity markets consists of all the stock traded outside the issuing company's home country. Many large global companies seek to take advantage of the global financial centers and issue stock in major markets to support local and regional operations.

For example, ArcelorMittal is a global steel company headquartered in Luxembourg; it is listed on the stock exchanges of New York, Amsterdam, Paris, Brussels, Luxembourg, Madrid, Barcelona, Bilbao, and Valencia. While the daily value of the global markets changes, in the past decade the international equity markets have expanded considerably, offering global firms increased options for financing their global operations. The key factors for the increased growth in the international equity markets are the following:

- **Growth of developing markets.** As developing countries experience growth, their domestic firms seek to expand into global markets and take advantage of cheaper and more flexible financial markets.
- **Drive to privatize.** In the past two decades, the general trend in developing and emerging markets has been to privatize formerly state-owned enterprises. These entities tend to be large, and when they sell some or all of their shares, it infuses billions of dollars of new equity into local and global markets. Domestic and global investors, eager to participate in the growth of the local economy, buy these shares.
- **Investment banks.** With the increased opportunities in new emerging markets and the need to simply expand their own businesses, investment banks often lead the way in the expansion of global equity markets. These specialized banks seek to be retained by large companies in developing countries or the governments pursuing privatization to issue and sell the stocks to investors with deep pockets outside the local country.

- **Technology advancements.** The expansion of technology into global finance has opened new opportunities to investors and companies around the world. Technology and the Internet have provided more efficient and cheaper means of trading stocks and, in some cases, issuing shares by smaller companies.

International Bond Markets

Bonds are the most common form of debt instrument, which is basically a loan from the holder to the issuer of the bond. The international bond market consists of all the bonds sold by an issuing company, government, or entity outside their home country. Companies that do not want to issue more equity shares and dilute the ownership interests of existing shareholders prefer using bonds or debt to raise capital (i.e., money). Companies might access the international bond markets for a variety of reasons, including funding a new production facility or expanding its operations in one or more countries. There are several types of international bonds, which are detailed in the next sections.

Foreign Bond

A foreign bond is a bond sold by a company, government, or entity in another country and issued in the currency of the country in which it is being sold. There are foreign exchange, economic, and political risks associated with foreign bonds, and many sophisticated buyers and issuers of these bonds use complex hedging strategies to reduce the risks. For example, the bonds issued by global companies in Japan denominated in yen are called *samurai bonds*. As you might expect, there are other names for similar bond structures. Foreign bonds sold in the United States and denominated in US dollars are called *Yankee bonds*. In the United Kingdom, these foreign bonds are called *bulldog bonds*. Foreign bonds issued and traded throughout Asia except Japan, are called *dragon bonds*, which are typically denominated in US dollars. Foreign bonds are typically subject to the same rules and guidelines as domestic bonds in the country in which they are issued. There are also regulatory and reporting requirements, which make them a slightly more expensive bond than the Eurobond. The requirements add small costs that can add up given the size of the bond issues by many companies.

Eurobond

A Eurobond is a bond issued outside the country in whose currency it is denominated. Eurobonds are not regulated by the governments of the countries in which they are sold, and as a result, Eurobonds are the most popular form of international bond. A bond issued by a Japanese company, denominated in US dollars, and sold only in the United Kingdom and France is an example of a Eurobond.

Global Bond

A global bond is a bond that is sold simultaneously in several global financial centers. It is denominated in one currency, usually US dollars or Euros. By offering the bond in several markets at the same time, the company can reduce its issuing costs. This option is usually reserved for higher rated, creditworthy, and typically very large firms.

Did You Know?

As the international bond market has grown, so too have the creative variations of bonds, in some cases to meet the specific needs of a buyer and issuer community. *Sukuk*, an Arabic word, is a type of financing instrument that is in essence an Islamic bond. The religious law of Islam, Sharia, does not permit the charging or paying of interest, so Sukuk securities are structured to comply with the Islamic law. "An IMF study released in 2007 noted that the Issuance of Islamic securities (sukuk) rose fourfold to $27 billion during 2004–06. While 14 types of sukuk are recognized by the Accounting and Auditing Organization of Islamic Finance Institutions, their structure relies on one of the three basic forms of legitimate Islamic finance, murabahah (synthetic loans/purchase orders), musharakah/mudharabah (profit-sharing arrangements), and ijara (sale-leasebacks), or a combination thereof." [1]

The *Economist* notes "that by 2000, there were more than 200 Islamic banks…and today $700 billion of global assets are said to comply with *sharia* law. Even so, traditional finance houses rather than Islamic institutions continue to handle most Gulf oil money and other Muslim wealth."

"More worrying still, the rules for Islamic finance are not uniform around the world. A Kuwaiti Muslim cannot buy a Malaysian *sukuk* (*sharia*-compliant bond) because of differing definitions of what constitutes usury (interest). Indeed, a respected Islamic jurist recently denounced most *sukuk* as godless. Nor are banking licenses granted easily in most Muslim countries. That is why big Islamic banks are so weak. Often they are little more than loose collections of subsidiaries. They also lack home-grown talent: most senior staff are poached from multinationals." But in 2009, one entrepreneur, Adnan Yousif, made headlines as he tried to change that and create the world's biggest Islamic bank. While his efforts are still in progress, it's clear that Islamic banking is a growing and profitable industry niche. [2]

Eurocurrency Markets

The Eurocurrency markets originated in the 1950s when communist governments in Eastern Europe became concerned that any deposits of their dollars in US banks might be confiscated or blocked for political reasons by the US government. These communist governments addressed their concerns by depositing their dollars into European banks, which were willing to maintain dollar accounts for them. This created what is known as the Eurodollar—US dollars deposited in European banks. Over the years, banks in other countries, including Japan and Canada, also began to hold US dollar deposits and now Eurodollars are any dollar deposits in a bank outside the United States. (The prefix *Euro-* is now only a historical reference to its early days.) An extension of the Eurodollar is the Eurocurrency, which is a currency on deposit outside its country of issue. While Eurocurrencies can be in any denominations, almost half of world deposits are in the form of Eurodollars.

The Euroloan market is also a growing part of the Eurocurrency market. The Euroloan market is one of the least costly for large, creditworthy borrowers, including governments and large global firms. Euroloans are quoted on the basis of LIBOR, the London Interbank Offer Rate, which is the interest rate at which banks in London charge each other for short-term Eurocurrency loans.

The primary appeal of the Eurocurrency market is that there are no regulations, which results in lower costs. The participants in the Eurocurrency markets are very large global firms, banks, governments, and extremely wealthy individuals. As a result, the transaction sizes tend to be large, which provides an economy of scale and nets overall lower transaction costs. The Eurocurrency markets are relatively cheap, short-term financing options for Eurocurrency loans; they are also a short-term investing option for entities with excess funds in the form of Eurocurrency deposits.

Offshore Centers

The first tier of centers in the world are the world financial centers, which are in essence central points for business and finance. They are usually home to major corporations and banks or at least regional headquarters for global firms. They all have at least one globally active stock exchange. While their actual order of importance may differ both on the ranking format and the year, the following cities rank as global financial centers: New York, London, Tokyo, Hong Kong, Singapore, Chicago, Zurich, Geneva, and Sydney.

Did You Know?

The *Economist* reported in December 2009 that a "poll of Bloomberg subscribers in October found that Britain had dropped behind Singapore into third place as the city most likely to be the best financial hub two years from now. A survey of executives…by Eversheds, a law firm, found that Shanghai could overtake London within the next ten years." [3] Many of these changes in rank are due to local costs, taxes, and regulations. London has become expensive for financial professionals, and changes in the regulatory and political environment have also lessened the city's immediate popularity. However, London has remained a premier financial center for more than two centuries, and it would be too soon to assume its days as one of the global financial hubs is over.

In addition to the global financial centers are a group of countries and territories that constitute offshore financial centers. An offshore financial center is a country or territory where there are few rules governing the financial sector as a whole and low overall taxes. As a result, many offshore centers are called tax havens. Most of these countries or territories are politically and economically stable, and in most cases, the local government has determined that becoming an offshore financial center is its main industry. As a result, they invest in the technology and infrastructure to remain globally linked and competitive in the global finance marketplace.

Examples of well-known offshore financial centers include Anguilla, the Bahamas, the Cayman Islands, Bermuda, the Netherlands, the Antilles, Bahrain, and Singapore. They tend to be small countries or territories, and while global businesses may not locate any of their operations in these locations, they sometimes incorporate in these offshore centers to escape the higher taxes they would have to pay in their home countries and to take advantage of the efficiencies of these financial centers. Many global firms may house financing subsidiaries in offshore centers for the same benefits. For example, Bacardi, the spirits manufacturer, has $6 billion in revenues, more than 6,000 employees worldwide, and twenty-seven global production facilities. The firm is headquartered in Bermuda, enabling it to take advantage of the lower tax rates and financial efficiencies for managing its global operations.

As a result of the size of financial transactions that flow through these offshore centers, they have been increasingly important in the global capital markets.

Ethics in Action

Offshore financial centers have also come under criticism. Many people criticize these countries because corporations and individuals hide wealth there to avoid paying taxes on it. Many offshore centers are countries that have a zero-tax basis, which has earned them the title of *tax havens*.

The *Economist* notes that offshore financial centers are typically small jurisdictions, such as Macau, Bermuda, Liechtenstein or Guernsey, that make their living mainly by attracting overseas financial capital. What they offer foreign businesses and well-heeled individuals is low or no taxes, political stability, business-friendly regulation and laws, and above all discretion. Big, rich countries see OFCs as the weak link in the global financial chain…

The most obvious use of OFCs is to avoid taxes. Many successful offshore jurisdictions keep on the right side of the law, and many of the world's richest people and its biggest and most reputable companies use them quite legally to minimize their tax liability. But the onshore world takes a hostile view of them. Offshore tax havens have "declared economic war on honest US taxpayers," says Carl Levin, an American senator. He points to a study suggesting that America loses up to $70 billion a year to tax havens…

Business in OFCs is booming, and as a group these jurisdictions no longer sit at the fringes of the global economy. Offshore holdings now run to $5 trillion–7 trillion, five times as much as two decades ago, and make up perhaps 6–8 percent of worldwide wealth under management, according to Jeffrey Owens, head of fiscal affairs at the OECD. Cayman, a trio of islands in the Caribbean, is the world's fifth-largest banking center, with $1.4 trillion in assets. The British Virgin Islands (BVI) are home to almost 700,000 offshore companies.

All this has been very good for the OFCs' economies. Between 1982 and 2003 they grew at an annual average rate per person of 2.8 percent, over twice as fast as the world as a whole (1.2 percent), according to a study by James Hines of the University of Michigan. Individual OFCs have done even better. Bermuda is the richest country in the world, with a GDP per person estimated at almost $70,000, compared with $43,500 for America…On average, the citizens of Cayman, Jersey, Guernsey and the BVI are richer than those in most of Europe, Canada and Japan. This has encouraged other countries with small domestic markets to set up financial centers of their own to pull in offshore money—most spectacularly Dubai but also Kuwait, Saudi Arabia, Shanghai and even Sudan's Khartoum, not so far from war-ravaged Darfur.

Globalization has vastly increased the opportunities for such business. As companies become ever more multinational, they find it easier to shift their activities and profits across borders and into OFCs. As the well-to-do lead increasingly peripatetic lives, with jobs far from home, mansions scattered across continents and investments around the world, they can keep and manage their wealth anywhere. Financial liberalization—the elimination of capital controls and the like—has made all of this easier. So has the internet, which allows money to be shifted around the world quickly, cheaply and anonymously. [4]

For more on these controversial offshore centers, please see the full article at http://www.economist.com/node/8695139.

The Role of International Banks, Investment Banks, Securities Firms, and Global Financial Firms

The role of international banks, investment banks, and securities firms has evolved in the past few decades. Let's take a look at the primary purpose of each of these institutions and how it has changed, as many have merged to become global financial powerhouses.

Traditionally, international banks extended their domestic role to the global arena by servicing the needs of multinational corporations (MNC). These banks not only received deposits and made loans but also provided tools to finance exports and imports and offered sophisticated cash-management tools, including foreign exchange. For example, a company purchasing products from another country may need short-term financing of the purchase; electronic funds transfers (also called wires); and foreign exchange transactions. International banks provide all these services and more.

In broad strokes, there are different types of banks, and they may be divided into several groups on the basis of their activities. Retail banks deal directly with consumers and usually focus on mass-market products such as checking and savings accounts, mortgages and other loans, and credit cards. By contrast, private banks normally provide wealth-management services to families and individuals of high net worth. Business banks provide services to businesses and other organizations that are medium sized, whereas the clients of corporate banks are usually major business entities. Lastly, investment banks provide services related to financial markets, such as mergers and acquisitions. Investment banks also focused primarily on the creation and sale of securities (e.g., debt and equity) to help companies, governments, and

large institutions achieve their financing objectives. Retail, private, business, corporate, and investment banks have traditionally been separate entities. All can operate on the global level. In many cases, these separate institutions have recently merged, or were acquired by another institution, to create global financial powerhouses that now have all types of banks under one giant, global corporate umbrella.

However the merger of all of these types of banking firms has created global economic challenges. In the United States, for example, these two types—retail and investment banks—were barred from being under the same corporate umbrella by the Glass-Steagall Act. Enacted in 1932 during the Great Depression, the Glass-Steagall Act, officially called the Banking Reform Act of 1933, created the Federal Deposit Insurance Corporations (FDIC) and implemented bank reforms, beginning in 1932 and continuing through 1933. These reforms are credited with providing stability and reduced risk in the banking industry for decades. Among other things, it prohibited bank-holding companies from owning other financial companies. This served to ensure that investment banks and banks would remain separate—until 1999, when Glass-Steagall was repealed. Some analysts have criticized the repeal of Glass-Steagall as one cause of the 2007–8 financial crisis.

Because of the size, scope, and reach of US financial firms, this historical reference point is important in understanding the impact of US firms on global businesses. In 1999, once bank-holding companies were able to own other financial services firms, the trend toward creating global financial powerhouses increased, blurring the line between which services were conducted on behalf of clients and which business was being managed for the benefit of the financial company itself. Global businesses were also part of this trend, as they sought the largest and strongest financial players in multiple markets to service their global financial needs. If a company has operations in twenty countries, it prefers two or three large, global banking relationships for a more cost-effective and lower-risk approach. For example, one large bank can provide services more cheaply and better manage the company's currency exposure across multiple markets. One large financial company can offer more sophisticated risk-management options and products. The challenge has become that in some cases, the party on the opposite side of the transaction from the global firm has turned out to be the global financial powerhouse itself, creating a conflict of interest that many feel would not exist if Glass-Steagall had not been repealed. The issue remains a point of ongoing discussion between companies, financial firms, and policymakers around the world. Meanwhile, global businesses have benefited from the expanded services and capabilities of the global financial powerhouses.

For example, US-based Citigroup is the world's largest financial services network, with 16,000 offices in 160 countries and jurisdictions, holding 200 million customer accounts. It's a financial powerhouse with operations in retail, private, business, and investment banking, as well as asset management. Citibank's global reach make it a good banking partner for large global firms that want to be able to manage the financial needs of their employees and the company's operations around the world.

In fact this strength is a core part of its marketing message to global companies and is even posted on its website (http://www.citigroup.com/citi/products/instinvest.htm): "Citi puts the world's largest financial network to work for you and your organization."

Ethics in Action

Outsourcing Day Trading to China
American and Canadian trading firms are hiring Chinese workers to "day trade" from China during the hours the American stock market is open. In essence, day trading or speculative trading occurs when a trader buys and sells stock quickly throughout the day in the hopes of making quick profits. The *New York Times* reported that as many as 10,000 Chinese, mainly young men, are busy working the night shift in Chinese cities from 9:30 p.m. to 4 a.m., which are the hours that the New York Stock Exchange is open in New York.

The motivation is several fold. First, American and Canadian firms are looking to access wealthy Chinese clients who are technically not allowed to use Chinese currency to buy and sell shares on a foreign stock exchange. However, there are no restrictions for trading stocks in accounts owned by a foreign entity, which in this case usually belongs to the trading firms. Chinese traders also get paid less than their American and Canadian counterparts.

There are ethical concerns over this arrangement because it isn't clear whether the use of traders in China violates American and Canadian securities laws. In a *New York Times* article quotes Thomas J. Rice, an expert in securities law at Baker & McKenzie, who states, "This is a jurisdictional mess for the U.S. regulators. Are these Chinese traders essentially acting as brokers? If they are, they would need to be registered in the U.S." While the regulatory issues may not be clear, the trading firms are doing well and growing: "many Chinese day traders see this as an opportunity to quickly gain new riches." Some American and Canadian trading firms see

the opportunity to get "profit from trading operations in China through a combination of cheap overhead, rebates and other financial incentives from the major stock exchanges, and pent-up demand for broader investment options among China's elite." [5]

KEY TAKEAWAYS

- Capital markets provide an efficient mechanism for people, companies, and governments with more funds than they need to transfer those funds to people, companies, or governments who have a shortage of funds.
- The international equity and bond markets have expanded exponentially in recent decades. This expansion has been fueled by the growth of developing markets, the drive to privatize, the emergence of global financial powerhouses including investment banks, and technology advancements.
- The international bond market consists of major categories of bonds—including foreign bonds, Eurobonds, and global bonds—all of which help companies borrow funds to invest and grow their global businesses.

EXERCISES

(AACSB: Reflective Thinking, Analytical Skills)
1. What is a capital market? What is an international capital market?
2. What is the role of bond and equity markets?
3. Select one global financial center and research its history and evolution to present times. Do you feel that the center will remain influential? Why or why not? Which other global financial centers compete with the one you have chosen?

[1] Andy Jobst, Peter Kunzel, Paul Mills, and Amadou Sy, "Islamic Finance Expanding Rapidly," International Monetary Fund, September 19, 2007, accessed February 2, 2011, http://www.imf.org/external/pubs/ft/survey/so/2007/res0919b.htm.
[2] "Godly but Ambitious," Economist, June 18, 2009, accessed February 2, 2011, http://www.economist.com/node/13856281.
[3] "Foul-Weather Friends," Economist, December 17, 2009, accessed February 2, 2011, http://www.economist.com/node/15127550.
[4] Joanne Ramos, "Places in the Sun," Economist, February 22, 2007, accessed March 2, 2011, http://www.economist.com/node/8695139.
[5] David Barboza, "Day Trading, Conducted Overnight, Grows in China," New York Times, December 10, 2010.

7.3 Venture Capital and the Global Capital Markets

LEARNING OBJECTIVES

1. Understand the impact of the global capital markets on international business through the expansion of international venture capital.
2. Understand international venture capital.
3. Understand the perspective of international venture capitalists.

Every start-up firm and young, growing business needs capital—money to invest to grow the business. Some companies access capital from the company founders or the friends and family of the founders. Growing companies that are profitable may be able to turn to banks and traditional lending companies. Another increasingly visible and popular source of capital is venture capital. Venture capital (VC) refers to the investment made in an early- or growth-stage company. Venture capitalist (also known as VC) refers to the investor.

One of the unintended benefits of the expansion of the global capital markets has been the expansion of international VC. Typically, VCs establish a venture fund with monies from institutions and individuals of high net worth. VCs, in turn, use the venture funds to invest in early- and growth-stage companies. VCs are characterized primarily by their investments in smaller, high-growth firms that are considered riskier than traditional investments. These investments are not liquid (i.e., they cannot be quickly bought and sold through the global financial markets). For this riskier and illiquid feature, VCs earn much higher rates of return that are sometimes astronomical if the VC times the exit correctly.

One of the factors that any VC assesses while determining whether or not to invest in a young and growing company is the exit strategy. The exit strategy is the way that a VC or investor can liquidate an investment, usually for a liquid security or cash. It's great if a company does well, but any investor, including VCs, wants to know how and when they're going to get their money out. While an initial public offering (IPO) is certainly a lucrative exit strategy, it's not for every company. Many VCs also like to see a list of possible strategic acquirers.

Did You Know?

Many large global firms also have internal investment groups that make corporate venture investments in early-stage and growing companies. These corporate VC firms may actually be the exit strategy and eventually acquire the young company if it fits their business objectives. This type of corporate VC is often called a strategic investor because they are more likely to place a higher priority on the strategic value of the investment rather than just the pure financial return on investment.

For example, US-based Intel Corporation, one of the world's largest technology companies, has an internal group called Intel Capital. The vision of Intel Capital is "to be the preeminent global investing organization in the world" and its mission "to make and manage financially attractive investments in support of Intel's strategic objectives." [1]

Intel Capital makes investments in companies around the world to encourage the development and deployment of new technologies, enter into or expand in new markets, and generate returns on their investments. "Since 1991, Intel Capital has invested more than USD 9.5 billion in over 1,050 companies in 47 countries. In that timeframe, 175 portfolio companies have gone public on various exchanges around the world and 241 were acquired or participated in a merger. In 2009, Intel Capital invested USD 327 million in 107 investments with approximately 50 percent of funds invested outside the U.S. and Canada." [2]

Table 7.2 "Intel Capital Investments Announced in November 2010" shows a sample of the global investments made by Intel Capital.

As a result, the expanded global markets offer VCs access to (1) new potential investors in their venture funds; (2) a wider selection of firms in which to invest; (3) more exit strategies, including IPOs in other countries outside their home country; and (4) the opportunity for their portfolio companies to merge or be acquired by foreign firms. Tech-savvy American and European VCs have traced the source of the high-tech talent pool and increased their investments in growing companies in many countries, including Israel, China, India, Brazil, and Russia.

Did You Know?

A July 2010 research survey conducted by Deloitte uncovered the following sentiments among VCs from around the world.

'Traditionally strong markets like the U.S. and Europe will continue to be important hubs despite consolidation in the number of venture firms,' said Mark Jensen, partner, Deloitte & Touche LLP and national managing partner for VC services. 'However, the stage has now been set for emerging markets like China, India and Brazil to rise as drivers of innovation as they are increasingly becoming more competitive with the traditional markets.'...

Overall, only 34 percent of all respondents indicated that they expect to increase their investment activity outside their own country....The countries with the most interest in cross border investing include: France (56 percent), Israel (50 percent) and the United Kingdom (49 percent). Countries indicating the least interest in outside investing were Brazil (19 percent), India (15 percent) and China (11 percent).

'The Asian markets, in particular, are abundant in entrepreneurial spirit, energy and a dedication from both the private and public sectors to push the economic growth pendulum as far as possible,' said Trevor Loy, general partner of Flywheel Ventures. 'The continued rapid growth of emerging markets is also creating a new source of customer revenue, investment capital, job creation, and shareholder liquidity for U.S. based technology start-ups, particularly those leveraging America's deep research and development (R&D) resources to address critical infrastructure needs in energy, water, materials and communications.'...

Top challenges varied in countries around the globe with the exit market being cited the most in the United Kingdom (80 percent), Canada (75 percent), India (71 percent) and Israel (70 percent). Eighty-one percent of respondents in Brazil cited unfavorable tax policies as being a hindrance. An unstable regulatory environment was the most common factor cited by respondents in France (72 percent) and China (62 percent).

'The challenges for a U.S. venture firm trying to do business in Europe include the current weakness in the euro-zone economy, language and cultural differences, and the tendency towards inflexible employment regulations,' said Bruce Evans, managing director of Summit Partners. 'On top of this, U.S. firms have to fund their European expansion from their own profits, and the proposed U.S. tax changes to carried interest—and the taxation of equity interests in fund managers more generally—would serve as an impediment to U.S. venture funds' growth aspirations.'

'Yet, opportunities remain as well,' Evans continued. 'The psychological make-up of successful, driven entrepreneurs in Europe mirrors what we have found in the U.S. In addition, the globalization of technology markets means that successful products are as likely to be developed in Europe as elsewhere. Finally, the days of missionary selling of venture capital in Europe are over, and today there is a broad understanding of our type of financing.' [3]

KEY TAKEAWAYS

In this section, you learned

1. VC is the investment made by an investor in an early- or growth-stage company. *Venture capitalist* (also known as VC) refers to the investor. Typically, VCs establish a venture fund with monies from institutions and individuals of high net worth. Venture capitalists, in turn, use the venture fund(s) to invest in early- and growth-stage companies.

2. VC investments are characterized primarily by the fact that they invest in smaller, high-growth firms that are considered higher risk than traditional investments and that the investments are not liquid—that is, they cannot be quickly bought and sold through the global financial markets. For this riskier and illiquid feature, VCs earn much higher rates of return that are sometimes astronomical if the exit is timed correctly.

3. One of the key factors that any VC assesses while determining whether or not to invest in a young and growing company is the exit strategy. The exit strategy is the way a VC or investor can liquidate investments, usually for a liquid security or cash. As a result, the expansion of the global capital markets has benefited VCs who now have more access to the following:

   o New potential investors in their venture funds
   o A wider selection of firms in different countries in which to invest
   o More exit strategies, including IPOs, in other countries outside their home country and the opportunity for their portfolio companies to merge or be acquired by foreign firms

EXERCISES

(AACSB: Reflective Thinking, Analytical Skills)

1. Why do VCs benefit from increased globalization? List three reasons. If you were a research analyst at a US-based VC firm, what would you recommend to your senior partners about the global market opportunity?

2. What is an exit strategy? Why is it so important to a VC?

[1] "Intel Capital," Intel Capital Corporation, accessed March 2, 2011, http://www.intel.com/about/companyinfo/capital/index.htm.
[2] "About Intel Capital," Intel Capital Corporation, accessed March 2, 2011, http://www.intel.com/about/companyinfo/capital/info/earnings.htm.
[3] "U.S. Venture Capital Industry Expected to Shrink While Emerging Markets Grow: Deloitte, NVCA Study," Deloitte Corporation, July 14, 2010, accessed February 2, 2011, http://www.deloitte.com/view/en_US/us/Insights/browse-by-role/media-role/a8e40f2f800d9210VgnVCM200000bb42f00aRCRD.htm.

7.4 Tips in Your Entrepreneurial Walkabout Toolkit Dealing with Venture Capitalists

Young companies around the world now eagerly—and sometimes successfully—reach out to VCs in other countries. If you are a budding entrepreneur thinking about going the VC route to fund your business, it's important to learn more about the industry and community. At the end of the day, money is what matters—it's business for VCs. This is a harsh point of view for entrepreneurs, who are often quite emotional about their product or service. It can be hard to know just how to evaluate VCs. Here are some tips to follow no matter where in the world the entrepreneur or VCs are located. [1]

1. **Understand the nature of a VC.** They are basically fund managers looking for high returns for their investors. Understand the VC's portfolio's mission and goals. Most have multiple funds in their portfolio each with different investment parameters based in part on the various investors. VC is an industry, and the VCs are your "customer." You need to understand how the industry operates, how to get your "product" (i.e., your company) noticed, and how to close the sale (i.e., get your funding). While there are certainly nuances, treat it like a sales process from start to finish. Remember that VCs run a business, one that they are held accountable to by their investors. More often than not, the people you meet at a VC firm are not the actual investors (although the senior principals may have some of their own money in the fund); they just work for the VC firm.

   VCs focus on market trends, whether it's green technology, social networking websites, or the current perceived "hot" industry. While it's still possible to get funding if you are not in a current trend, it's certainly harder. VCs typically look at groups of investments and generally like to have funds with three or four companies out of ten providing exceptional returns. They expect the rest of the businesses in the portfolio to either be weak performers or to fail. Sounds harsh, perhaps, but this is purely statistical to the VC industry. It's important to ask VCs about their expected returns. When VCs market their funds to potential global institutional and wealthy investors, they have to indicate a vision, strategy, and target range for returns to these potential "buyers"—that is, investors. If you're beginning to think that a VC sounds suspiciously like an entrepreneur, you're correct. You need to realize that in the same way you're raising money from a VC, the VC is raising money from someone else.

2. **Control the interview.** Ask the VC about their mission and goals. Additionally, learn about the VC's investment style. Do they prefer to be heavily involved? Or are they hands-off? Is their investment style consistent with both your operating style and stage of business? Experienced and well-connected VCs can be very useful for an early-stage company. If the VC is a strategic investor, understand the motivations for their interest in your product, service, or market.

3. **Act the part.** Be prepared. Conduct yourself professionally at all times. Dress and act like you're going to a job interview—it's quite similar. Don't drop names or promise too much. Don't make claims about your product or service that can't be substantiated.

   Again, your credibility will suffer even if you actually have a solid product or service. Go to any VC meeting with a clear presentation and detailed business plan. If you can't answer a specific question, say so and promise to get back to them within a specified time frame with further information. Even if you don't have an answer, be sure to get back to them later with a follow-up that indicates you are still researching the answer. Don't act like you're entitled to funding for any reason. You may think your idea is great, but VCs see many "great" ideas. Support your request for funding with clear business rationale and facts. Lose any attitude.

4. **Examine the VCs network/expertise.** What is the VC's network? Is the VC or their network in your industry? Does the VC know both clients and partners, and at what decision-making level are these contacts? Is the VC willing to actively assist you with global networking? Look at the companies in the VC's portfolio to see if there's a synergy across the portfolio. It's helpful if the VC is willing to facilitate interaction with key strategic investors in the fund as well as other complementary portfolio companies.

5. **Does the VC have an ability to guide the company to a suitable exit strategy?** An important issue for most investors and VCs is the exit strategy. It's great if a company does well, but the VC wants to know how and when they're going to get their money out. Experienced VCs usually have a time horizon of three to seven years. The entire life of their fund may be only ten to thirteen years, after which time their investors expect to receive their original investments back with all the returns. While an initial public offering (IPO) is certainly a sexy exit strategy, it's not for every company. If you do business with the companies that are likely to buy your firm, then be sure to highlight this early on. Many VCs

also like to see a list of possible strategic acquirers. As noted earlier in this section, access to global markets benefits many global VCs and entrepreneurs, both of whom now have more options to find investors or companies to invest in as well as more exit strategies.

6. **Check-writing ability.** Can the VC make an initial investment? What is their process for obtaining more funding? Venture capitalists fund companies from one of their portfolio funds. If monies in those funds run out, there's limited ability to find more funding. Most experienced VCs save a portion of each fund for follow-on funding for their portfolio companies (which are companies they have already invested in). Remember that VCs have an interest in your company's success, so long as the business parameters warrant it. They are not likely to keep funding a venture with minimal life left in it.

7. **Beware when a VC has no real management experience.** Find a VC with experience in running a company, not just banking. Venture capitalists still tend to come from the worlds of consulting and investment banking. Most have never worked for a company. As a result, their knowledge base of a corporation tends to be academic and theoretical and doesn't stem from any tangible experiences. They tend to be unfamiliar with corporate operating practices as well as general line management. Despite some efforts to hire entrepreneurs on their teams, most VCs still hire people who are just like themselves, a practice that drastically limits the range of experiences and perspectives of their team. Look at the individual backgrounds to assess any diversity of experience and perspective. If you are targeting key markets globally, make sure your VC has direct experience in those markets.

8. **Avoid unreasonable terms and demands.** Manage return expectations; ensure you and the VC are on the same page as far as expectations. Make sure that you and the VC are both motivated by a mutual win. Don't agree to terms that are potentially dangerous to the long-term health of your company. For example, the VC may try to extract personal terms from you, such as a deferred salary or personal guarantees. Even if you are independently wealthy, terms that may make your personal financial survival more difficult only distract you and make you less focused on the business, which should be your and the VC's priority. In such cases, the VC is less interested in your well-being: after all, everyone needs to pay their bills. These terms are never in anyone's best interest, let alone the company, and will undoubtedly come back to haunt both you and the VC.

The entrepreneur should also be careful not to have unreasonably high compensation demands for themselves.

9. **Level of involvement and fit.** How involved do the VCs want to be? Are they helpful or intrusive? Are your professional and cultural styles compatible? If you're from different cultures, be sure that you understand effective ways to communicate and manage differences and expectations. Negotiating a VC's level of involvement can be really challenging, as expectations may change over time. Some VCs who take a hands-off approach in the beginning may increase their involvement at the first hint of difficulties or problems. Overall, most VCs oversee investments in multiple companies, so they don't always want to be heavily involved. Just be sure that the level of involvement meets the needs and expectations of both you and the VC.

10. **Look for mutual respect.** Sure, you need money, but the VC needs to also be aware that they need good companies with solid ideas in order to be successful and profitable.

Is there a mutual acknowledgment of respect and that you both need each other to succeed? Many VCs appear to operate as if this isn't the case. Just as you will likely turn to your VC for creative financing and exit strategies, the VC should respect your industry and management experiences. Success can only be achieved if there's mutual respect and a focus on creating a win for all involved.

11. **Watch for questionable integrity, greed, ego, and power trips.** Be wary of the VC who shows interest in doing your deal and suggests he or she receive a personal fee for doing so or wants to go on your payroll as an "advisor." Kickbacks are not legally standard in the VC world, although they occur in varied forms more often than not. The only persons who may be entitled to fees are those you have retained as investment bankers, advisors, or intermediaries. Additionally, a VC who operates this way is likely to have a pattern of doing so and is not likely to provide the kind of professional support needed during challenging periods. If your VC is from a country outside your base country, be sure to understand your VC's culture and his or her country's rules. It's not worth engaging in unscrupulous business practices. Even if in the short term it helps to fund your company, the long-term repercussions could be disastrous. Find another source. Above all, strive to keep your integrity in all your business dealings.

VCs who are undeservedly full of themselves may be more interested in satisfying their egos than partnering to grow strong companies. Some VCs will show such characteristics by playing mind games at early meetings. Others may try to intimidate you or be unconstructively condescending—for example, creating a hostile environment by aggressively and rudely demanding that you close your PowerPoint presentation and answer obtuse questions. You may find yourself the target of a barrage of foul language. While every industry has its share of egomaniacs, what you really need to focus on is how you can build a level of professional trust that will enable you and the VC to work together during challenging periods. Some VCs can forget that it's a partnership and that the entrepreneur is likely to have an equity interest in the company as well. The VC may seek to treat the entrepreneur as a subordinate or an employee—and not a co-owner as well. Without a sense of cooperative teamwork, you may not have the VC and board support you need at critical junctures. Interestingly enough, the code of conduct that most professionals are expected to follow in the corporate world is not always standard in the VC world. Stay above any questionable behavior and stay professional. Despite the allure of money, you probably wouldn't want to do business with these types of people in any circumstance. [2]

[1] {Author's Name retracted as requested by the work's original creator or licensee}, Starting Your Business (New York: Business Expert Press, 2010).

[2] {Author's Name retracted as requested by the work's original creator or licensee}, Starting Your Business (New York: Business Expert Press, 2010).

7.5 End-of-Chapter Questions and Exercises

These exercises are designed to ensure that the knowledge you gain from this book about international business meets the learning standards set out by the international Association to Advance Collegiate Schools of Business (AACSB International). [1] AACSB is the premier accrediting agency of collegiate business schools and accounting programs worldwide. It expects that you will gain knowledge in the areas of communication, ethical reasoning, analytical skills, use of information technology, multiculturalism and diversity, and reflective thinking.

EXPERIENTIAL EXERCISES

(AACSB: Communication, Use of Information Technology, Analytical Skills)

1. You work for a global auto-parts company. Describe how you would use the spot and forward markets to manage the potential exchange rate risk between the countries from which you import (buy) components and the countries in which you sell auto parts. Select any three currencies to use in your discussion.

   Access the following URL from fxstreet.com:http://www.fxstreet.com/rates-charts/forward-rates. Use it to determine if forward or futures contracts are available in all the currencies you selected.

2. You are working for the CFO of a global food-products company with extensive operations in North America, South America, Europe, Africa, and Asia. The firm is creating a new finance subsidiary to manage a number of financial transactions, including its foreign exchange, financing, and hedging transactions. Your CFO has asked you to prepare an analysis of two offshore financial centers—Bermuda and Luxembourg. Research the pros and cons of each center and make a recommendation to your CFO.

Ethical Dilemmas

(AACSB: Ethical Reasoning, Multiculturalism, Reflective Thinking, Analytical Skills)

1. Imagine that you are the finance manager in control of purchasing for a small manufacturing company. Your supplier in Russia tells you that there are two quotes, one for payments in US dollars by wire transfer or check and one for a US dollar cash-like transaction. The cash transaction is almost 10 percent cheaper, which could earn your firm a nice profit and a potential year-end bonus for you. How do you handle the phone call and the decision? Discuss the ethical and business issues involved. If you decide against the cash-like transaction, do you tell your senior management? What do you recommend to your management about future dealings with this supplier? Russia is one of the most corrupt countries for businesses. What options does your firm have if it needs to source from Russia? Use fxstreet.com (http://www.fxstreet.com/rates-charts/) to research and discuss more.

2. Global companies transact business in multiple countries and currencies. Using information you learned in this chapter, discuss whether companies should set up offshore companies to manage their currency and financial transactions. More specifically, if you worked for Walmart, would you recommend that the firm set up an offshore company? Why or why not?

[1] Association to Advance Collegiate Schools of Business website, accessed January 26, 2010, http://www.aacsb.edu.

NOTES:

Chapter 8:
International Expansion and Global Market Opportunity Assessment

WHAT'S IN IT FOR ME?

1. What are the inputs into global strategic move choices?
2. What are the components of PESTEL analysis and the factors that favor globalization?
3. What are the traditional entry modes for international expansion?
4. How can you use the CAGE model of market assessment?
5. What is the importance of and inputs into scenario analysis?

This chapter pulls together all the information about choosing to expand internationally and possible ways to make that choice. Section 8.1 "Global Strategic Choices" shows that choosing to expand internationally is rarely black and white. A wide variety of internationalization moves are available after choosing to expand. Moreover, some flatteners make global moves easier, while some make them more difficult. Indeed, even importing and outsourcing can be considered stealth, or at least early, steps in internationalization, because they involve doing business across borders. In Section 8.1 "Global Strategic Choices", you will learn the rationale for international expansion and the planning and due diligence it requires.

This chapter also features a richness of analytical frameworks. In Section 8.2 "PESTEL, Globalization, and Importing", you will learn about PESTEL, the framework for analyzing the political, economic, sociocultural, technological, environmental, and legal aspects of different international markets. Section 8.3 "International-Expansion Entry Modes" describes the strategies available to you when entering a new market. Section 8.4 "CAGE Analysis" will demonstrate how globalization and the CAGE (cultural, administrative, geographic, and economic) framework address questions related to the flattening of markets and how the dimensions they help you assess are essentially flatteners. Finally, in Section 8.5 "Scenario Planning and Analysis", you will learn about scenario analysis, which will prepare you to begin an analysis of which international markets might present the greatest opportunities, as well as suggest possible landmines that you could encounter when exploiting them.

OPENING CASE: THE INVISIBLE GLOBAL RETAILER AND ITS REENTRY INTO US MARKETS

Which corporation owns 123 companies, operates in twenty-seven countries, and has been in the mobile-phone business for over a decade? If you don't know, you're not alone. Many people haven't heard of the Otto Group, the German retailing giant that's second only to Amazon in e-commerce and first in the global mail-order business. The reason you've likely never heard of the Otto Group is because the firm stays in the background while giving its brands the spotlight. This strategy has worked over the company's almost eighty-year history, and Otto continues to apply it to new moves, such as its social media site, Two for Fashion. "They are talking about fashion, not about Otto, unless it suits," explained Andreas Frenkler, the company's division manager of new media and e-commerce, about the site's launch in 2008. [1] The site is now one of the top fashion blogs in Germany and is an integral part of the retailer's marketing strategy.

Leading through Passion, Vision, and Strategy

Today, the Otto Group consists of a large number of companies that operate in the major economic zones of the world. The Otto Group's lines of business include financial services, multichannel retail, and other services. The financial services segment covers an international portfolio of commercial services along the value chain of retail companies, such as information-, collection-, and receivable-management services. The multichannel retail segment covers the Otto Group's worldwide range of retail offerings; goods are marketed across three distribution channels—catalogs, e-commerce, and over-the-counter (OTC) retail. The third segment combines the Otto Group's logistics, travel, and other service providers as well as sourcing companies. Logistics service providers and sourcing companies support both the Otto Group's multichannel retail activities and non-Group clients. Travel service providers offer customers travel offerings across all sales channels. Unique to the Otto Group is the combination of travel agencies, direct marketing, and Internet sites. The combined revenue of these three ventures is growing rapidly, even during the global economic downturn. The travel service revenues for 2010 were 10 billion euros, or about $12 billion. [2]

Even though it operates in a variety of market segments, business ideas, and distribution channels—not to mention its regional diversity—the Otto Group sees itself as a community built on shared values. Otto's passion for success is based on four levels of performance, which together represent the true strength of the Otto Group: "Passion for our customers, passion for innovation, passion for sustainability, and passion for integrated networking." Each one of these performance levels is an integral element of the Otto Group's guiding principle and self-image. [3]

Future growth is guided by the Otto Group's Vision 2020 strategy, which is based on achieving a strong presence in all key markets of the three largest regions—Europe, North America, and Asia. In doing so, the Otto Group relies on innovative concepts in the multichannel business, on current trends in e-commerce, on OTC retail, and on developments in mobile commerce. In keeping with that vision, its focus for near-term expansion is on expanding the Group's strong position in Russia and increasing market share in other economic areas, such as the Chinese and Brazilian markets. Investment options in core European markets are continually being reviewed to strengthen the multichannel strategy. As a global operating group, Otto aims to have a presence in all major markets and will continue to expand OTC retailing.

In 2010, for instance, the Otto Group continued to develop its activities in the growth markets of Central and Eastern Europe. Through takeovers and the acquisition of further shares in various distance-selling concepts, including Quelle Russia, the Otto Group has continued to build on its market leadership in Russian mail order. A further major goal for the future is to expand OTC retail within the multichannel retail segment, making it one of the pillars of Otto alongside its e-commerce and catalog businesses. The foundations of value-oriented corporate management are reflected in the uncompromising customer orientation evident in business activities with both end consumers and corporate clients.

The strategy envisages targeted investments that provide the Otto Group with "Best in Class" business models. Otto not only draws on an excellent range of customer services as the basis for its success in its core business of multichannel retailing but also offers an array of retail-related services for its corporate clients. In the future, the company is looking to expand these services, moving beyond its core business. The buying organization of the Otto Group has been repositioned under the name Otto International and is now a firm fixture in the world's key sourcing markets. Otto International's corporate clients stand to benefit directly from the market power of the Otto Group while providing the volumes to make their own contribution to its growth.

The US Market Reentry Initiative

Germany remains the Otto Group's most-important regional sales market, followed by France, the rest of Europe, North America, and Asia. In the United States, Otto set up a greenfield division called Otto International and quietly launched Field & Stream 1871, a brand of outdoor clothing, outerwear, footwear, and accessories, in 2010. The products are available only on the Field & Stream e-commerce site. As always, the Otto name is almost nowhere on the site, being visible only on the site's privacy policy page.

Industry experts thought it surprising that Otto launched the clothing line because it had previously left the US market after its acquisition of Eddie Bauer's parent company, Spiegel, failed in 2009.

Still, the Otto Group has received much acclaim for its innovations in the retail arena. For example, according to a Microsoft case study, Otto was the first company (1) to use telephone ordering, (2) to produce a CD-ROM version of its catalog in the 1990s (to deal with slow dial-up connections), and (3) to build one of the largest collections of online merchandise, at http://www.otto.de. [4] So the Otto Group may have other innovations planned for Field & Stream. But the US fashion market is saturated with competitors. As WWD reported, Otto may do better to focus on growing its own retail brands and utilizing its impressive in-house manufacturing and logistics divisions, which are now Otto's fastest-growing segment. [5] Otto could use these divisions to build other retail operations—while keeping a low profile, of course.

OPENING CASE EXERCISES

(AACSB: Ethical Reasoning, Multiculturalism, Reflective Thinking, Analytical Skills)

1. How do non-German markets figure into the Otto Group's strategy?
2. What do you think the firm has had to do to plan for this level of international expansion?
3. Which country-entry modes does the firm appear to prefer? Does it vary these modes?
4. After the Otto Group failed in its first effort to enter the US market with Spiegel, why would it try again?
5. How does this latest effort to enter the US market differ from its prior attempt?

[1] Lydia Dishman, "How the Biggest Online Retailer You've Never Heard of Will Take the U.S. Market," BNET, April 16, 2010, accessed August 20, 2010, http://www.bnet.com/blog/publishing-style/how-the-biggest-online-retailer-you-8217ve-never-heard-of-will-take-the-us-market/248.

[2] "Otto Group: Private Company Information," BusinessWeek, accessed February 7, 2011, http://investing.businessweek.com/businessweek/research/stocks/private/snapshot.asp?privcapId=61882597.

[3] "Accelerating toward New Goals," Otto Group, accessed August 20, 2010, http://www.ottogroup.com/en/die-otto-group/daten-und-fakten/segmente.php.

[4] "Microsoft Case Studies," Microsoft, accessed August 20, 2010, http://www.microsoft.com/casestudies/Case_Study_Detail.aspx?CaseStudyID=200504; and "Otto Group: OTTO," accessed February 7, 2011, http://www.ottogroup.com/otto.html?&L=0.

[5] Thomas Brenner, "Otto Group: A German Giant Tiptoes Back to the U.S.," WWD, April 14, 2010, accessed February 7, 2011, http://www.wwd.com/wwd-publications/wwd/2010-04-14?id=3036440&date=today&module=tn/today#/article/retail-news/otto-group-a-german-giant-tiptoes-back-to-the-u-s--3036500?navSection=issues_&navId=3036440.

8.1 Global Strategic Choices

LEARNING OBJECTIVES

1. Learn about the *rationale and motivations for* international expansion.
2. Understand the importance of international due diligence.
3. Recognize the role of regional differences, consumer preferences, and industry dynamics.

The *Why*, *Where*, and *How* of International Expansion

The allure of global markets can be mesmerizing. Companies that operate in highly competitive or nearly saturated markets at home, for instance, are drawn to look overseas for expansion. But overseas expansion is not a decision to be made lightly, and managers must ask themselves whether the expansion will create real value for shareholders. Companies can easily underestimate the costs of entering new markets if they are not familiar with the new regions and the business practices common within the new regions. For some companies, a misstep in a foreign market can put their entire operations in jeopardy, as happened to French retailer Carrefour after their failed entry into Chile, which you'll see later in this section. In this section, as summarized in the following figure, you will learn about the rationale for international expansion and then how to analyze and evaluate markets for international expansion.

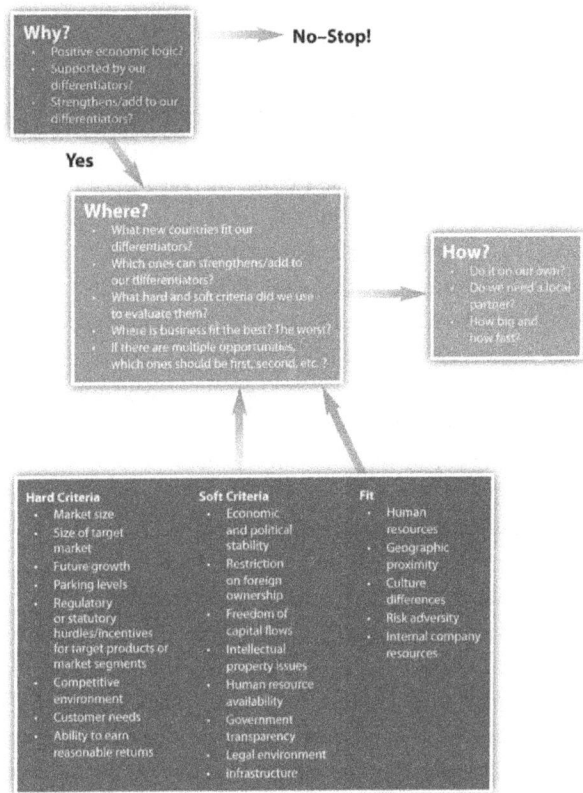

Rationale for International Expansion

Companies embark on an expansion strategy for one or more of the following reasons:

- To improve the cost-effectiveness of their operations
- To expand into new markets for new customers
- To follow global customers

For example, US chemical firm DuPont, Brazilian aerospace conglomerate Embraer, and Finnish mobile-phone maker Nokia are all investing in China to gain new customers. Schneider Logistics, in contrast, initially entered a new market, Germany, not to get new customers but to retain existing customers who needed a third-party logistics firm in Germany. Thus, Schneider followed its customers to Germany. Other companies, like microprocessor maker Intel, are building manufacturing facilities in China to take advantage of the less costly and increasingly sophisticated production capabilities. For example, Intel built a semiconductor manufacturing plant in Dalian, China, for $2.5 billion, whereas a similar state-of-the-art microprocessor plant in the United States can cost $5 billion. [1] Intel has also built plants in Chengdu and Shanghai, China, and in other

Asian countries (Vietnam and Malaysia) to take advantage of lower costs.

Planning for International Expansion

As companies look for growth in new areas of the world, they typically prioritize which countries to enter. Because many markets look appealing due to their market size or low-cost production, it is important for firms to prioritize which countries to enter first and to evaluate each country's relative merits. For example, some markets may be smaller in size, but their strategic complexity is lower, which may make them easier to enter and easier from an operations point of view. Sometimes there are even substantial regional differences within a given country, so careful investigation, research, and planning are important to do before entry.

International Market Due Diligence

International market due diligence involves analyzing foreign markets for their potential size, accessibility, cost of operations, and buyer needs and practices to aid the company in deciding whether to invest in entering that market. Market due diligence relies on using not just published research on the markets but also interviews with potential customers and industry experts. A systematic analysis needs to be done, using tools like PESTEL and CAGE, which will be described in Section 8.2 "PESTEL, Globalization, and Importing" and Section 8.4 "CAGE Analysis", respectively. In this section, we begin with an overview.

Evaluating whether to enter a new market is like peeling an onion—there are many layers. For example, when evaluating whether to enter China, the advantage most people see immediately is its large market size. Further analysis shows that the majority of people in that market can't afford US products, however. But even deeper analysis shows that while many Chinese are poor, the number of people who can afford consumer products is increasing. [2]

Regional Differences

The next part of due diligence is to understand the regional differences within the country and to not view the country as a monolith. For example, although companies are dazzled by China's large market size, deeper analysis shows that 70 percent of the population lives in rural areas. This presents distribution challenges given China's vast distances. In addition, consumers in different regions speak different dialects and have different tastes in food. Finally, the purchasing power of consumers varies in the different cities. City dwellers in Shanghai and Tianjin can afford higher prices than villagers in a western province.

Let's look at a specific example. To achieve the dual goals of reducing operations costs and being closer to a new market of customers, for instance, numerous high-tech companies identify Malaysia as an attractive country to enter. Malaysia is a relatively inexpensive country and the population's English skills are good, which makes it attractive both for finding local labor and for selling products. But even in a small country like Malaysia, there are regional differences. Companies may be tempted to set up operations in the capital city, Kuala Lumpur, but doing a thorough due diligence reveals that the costs in Kuala Lumpur are rising rapidly. If current trends continue, Kuala Lumpur will be as expensive as London in five years. Therefore, firms seeking primarily a lower-cost advantage would do better to locate to another city in Malaysia, such as Penang, which has many of the same advantages as Kuala Lumpur but does not have its rising costs. [3]

Understanding Local Consumers

Entering a market means understanding the local consumers and what they look for when making a purchase decision. In some markets, price is an important issue. In other markets, such as Japan, consumers pay more attention to details—such as the quality of products and the design and presentation of the product or retail surroundings—than they do to price. The Japanese demand for perfect products means that firms entering Japan might have to spend a lot on quality management. Moreover, real-estate costs are high in Japan, as are freight costs such as fuel and highway charges. In addition, space is limited at retail stores and stockyards, which means that stores can't hold much inventory, making replenishment of products a challenge. Therefore, when entering a new market, it's vital for firms to perform full, detailed market research in order to understand the market conditions and take measures to account for them.

How to Learn the Needs of a New Foreign Market

The best way for a company to learn the needs of a new foreign market is to deploy people to immerse themselves in that market. Larger companies, like Intel, employ ethnographers and sociologists to spend months in emerging markets, living in local communities and seeking to understand the latent, unarticulated needs of local consumers. For example, Dr. Genevieve Bell, one of Intel's anthropologists, traveled extensively across China, observing people in their homes to find out how they use technology and what they want from it. Intel then used her insights to shape its pricing strategies and its partnership plans for the Chinese consumer market. [4]

Differentiation and Capability

When entering a new market, companies also need to think critically about how their products and services will be different from what competitors are already offering in the market so that the new offering provides customers value. Companies trying to penetrate a new market must be sure to have some proof that they can deliver to the new market; this proof could be evidence that they have spoken with potential customers and are connected to the market. [5]Related to firm capability, another factor for firms to consider when evaluating which country to enter is that of "corporate fit." Corporate fit is the degree to which the company's existing practices, resources and capabilities fit the new market. For example, a company accustomed to operating within a detailed, unbiased legal environment would not find a good corporate fit in China because of the current vagaries of Chinese contract law. [6] Whereas a low corporate fit doesn't preclude expanding into that country, it does signal that additional resources or caution may be necessary. Two typical dimensions of corporate fit are human resources practices and the firm's risk tolerance.

Did You Know?

Over the years 2005–09, the number of Global 500 companies headquartered in BRIC countries (Brazil, Russia, India, and China) increased significantly. China grew from 8 headquarters to 43, India doubled from 5 to 10, Brazil rose from 5 to 9, and Russia went from 4 to 6. The United States still leads with 181 company headquarters, but it's down from 219 in 2005. [7]

Industry Dynamics

In some cases, the decision to enter a new market will depend on the specific circumstances of the industry in which the company operates. For example, companies that help build infrastructure need to enter countries where the government or large companies have a lot of capital, because infrastructure projects are so expensive. The president of Spanish infrastructure company Fomento de Construcciones y Contratas said, "We focus on those countries where there is more money and there is a gap in the infrastructure," such as China, Singapore, the United States, and Algeria. [8]

Political stability, legal security, and the "rule of law"—the presence of and adherence to laws related to business contracts, for example—are important considerations prior to market entry regardless of which industry a company is in. Fomento de Construcciones y Contratas learned this the hard way and ended up leaving some countries it had entered. The company's president, Baldomero Falcones, explained,

"When you decide whether or not to invest, one factor to take into account is the rule of law. Our ethical code was considered hard to understand in some countries, so we decided to leave during the early stages of the investment." [9]

Ethics in Action

Companies based in China are entering Australia and Africa, primarily to gain access to raw materials. Trade between China and Africa grew an average of 30 percent in the decade up to 2010, reaching $115 billion that year. [10] Chinese companies operate in Zambia (mining coal), the Democratic Republic of the Congo (mining cobalt), and Angola (drilling for oil). To get countries to agree to the deals, China had to agree to build new infrastructure, such as roads, railways, hospitals, and schools. Some economists, such as Dambisa Moyo, who wrote *Dead Aid: Why Aid Is Not Working and How There Is a Better Way for Africa*, believe that the way to help developing countries like those in Africa is not through aid but through trade. Moyo argues that long-term charity is degrading. She advocates business investments and setting up enterprises that employ local workers. Ecobank CEO Arnold Ekpe (whose bank employs 11,000 people in twenty-six African states) says the Chinese look at Africa differently than the West does: "[The Chinese] are not setting out to do good," he says. "They are setting out to do business. It's actually much less demeaning." [11] Deborah Brautigam, associate professor at the American University's International Development Program, agrees. In her book, *The Dragon's Gift: The Real Story of China in Africa*, she says, "The Chinese understand something very fundamental about state building: new states need to build buildings and dignity, not simply strive to end poverty." [12]

Steps and Missteps in International Expansion

Let's look at an example of the steps—as well as the missteps—in international expansion. American retailers entered the Chilean market in the mid- to late 1990s. They chose Chile as the market to enter because of the country's strong economy, the advanced level of the Chilean retail sector, and the free trade agreements signed by Chile. From that standpoint, their due diligence was accurate, but it didn't go far enough, as we'll see.

Retailer JC Penney entered Chile in 1995, opening two stores. French retailer Carrefour also entered Chile, in 1998. Neither company entered through an alliance with a local retailer. Both companies were forced to close their Chilean operations due to the losses they were incurring. Analysis by the Aldolfo Ibáñez University in Chile explained the reasons behind the failures: the managers of these companies were not able to connect with the local market, nor did they understand the variables that affected their businesses in Chile. [13] Specifically, the Chilean retailing market was advanced, but it was also very competitive. The new entrants (JC Penney and Carrefour) didn't realize that the existing major local retailers had their own banks and offered banking services at their retail stores, which was a major reason for their profitability. The outsiders assumed that profitability in this sector was based solely on retail sales. They missed the importance of the bank ties. Another typical mistake that companies make is to assume that a new market has no competition just because the company's traditional competitors aren't in that market.

Now let's continue with the example and watch native Chilean retailers enter a market new to them: Peru.

The Chilean retailers were successful in their own markets but wanted to expand beyond their borders in order to get new customers in new markets. The Chilean retailers chose to enter Peru, which had the same language.

The Peruvian retailing market was not advanced, and it did not offer credit to customers. The Chileans entered the market through partnership with local Peruvian firms, and they introduced the concept of credit cards, which was an innovation in the poorly developed Peruvian market. Entering through a domestic partner helped the Chileans because it eliminated hostility and made the investment process easier. Offering the innovation of credit cards made the Chilean retailers distinctive and offered an advantage over the local offerings. [14]

KEY TAKEAWAYS

- Companies embark on an expansion strategy for one or more of the following reasons: (1) to improve the cost-effectiveness of their operations, (2) to expand into new markets for new customers, and (3) to follow global customers.

- Planning for international expansion involves doing a thorough due diligence on the potential markets into which the country is considering expanding. This includes understanding the regional differences within markets, the needs of local customers, and the firm's own capabilities in relation to the dynamics of the industry.

- Common mistakes that firms make when entering a new market include not doing thorough research prior to entry, not understanding the competition, and not offering a truly targeted value proposition for buyers in the new market.

EXERCISES

(AACSB: Reflective Thinking, Analytical Skills)

1. What are some of the common motivators for companies embarking on international expansion?
2. Why is international market due diligence important?
3. What are some ways in which a company can learn about the needs of local buyers in a new international market?
4. Discuss the meaning of "corporate fit" in relation to international market expansion.
5. Name two common mistakes firms make when expanding internationally

[1] "2011 Global R&D Funding Forecast," R&D Magazine, December 2010, accessed January 2, 2011, http://www.rdmag.com/tags/publications/global-r-and-d-funding-forecast.

[2] Art Kleiner, "Getting China Right," Strategy and Business, March 22, 2010, accessed January 23, 2011, http://www.strategy-business.com/article/00026?pg=al.

[3] Ajay Chamania, Heral Mehta, and Vikas Sehgal, "Five Factors for Finding the Right Site," Strategy and Business, November 23, 2010, accessed May 17, 2011, http://www.strategy-business.com/article/10403?gko=e029a.

[4] Navi Radjou, "R&D 2.0: Fewer Engineers, More Anthropologists," Harvard Business Review (blog), June 10, 2009, accessed January 2, 2011, http://blogs.hbr.org/radjou/2009/06/rd-20-fewer-engineers-more-ant.html.

[5] "How We Do It: Strategic Tests from Four Senior Executives," McKinsey Quarterly, January 2011, accessed January 22, 2011, https://www.mckinseyquarterly.com/PDFDownload.aspx?ar=2712&srid=27.

[6] Carol Wingard, "Ensuring Value Creation through International Expansion," L.E.K. Consulting Executive Insights 5, no. 3, accessed January 15, 2011, http://www.lek.com/sites/default/files/Volume_V_Issue_3.pdf.

[7] Jeanne Meister and Karie Willyerd, The 2020 Workplace (New York: Harper Business, 2010), 22, citing "FT500 2009," Financial Times, accessed November 27, 2009, http://www.ft.com/reports/ft500-2009.

[8] "Practical Advice for Companies Betting on a Strategy of Globalization,"Knowledge@Wharton, January 12, 2011, accessed February 5, 2011, http://knowledge.wharton.upenn.edu/article.cfm?articleid=2541.

[9] "Practical Advice for Companies Betting on a Strategy of Globalization,"Knowledge@Wharton, January 12, 2011, accessed February 5, 2011, http://knowledge.wharton.upenn.edu/article.cfm?articleid=2541.

[10] Paul Redfern, "Africa: Trade between China and Continent at U.S. $115 Billion a Year," Daily Nation, February 11, 2011, accessed February 14, 2011, http://allafrica.com/stories/201102140779.html.

[11] Alex Perry, "Africa, Business Destination," Time, March 12, 2009, accessed February 14, 2011, http://www.time.com/time/specials/packages/article/0,28804,1884779_1884782_1884769,00.html#ixzz1DwbdOXvs.

[12] Steve Bloomfield, "China in Africa: Give and Take," Emerging Markets, May 27, 2010, accessed February 14, 2011, http://www.emergingmarkets.org/Article/2580082/CHINA-IN-AFRICA-Give-and-take.html.

[13] "The Globalization of Chilean Retailing," Knowledge@Wharton, December 12, 2007, accessed January 5, 2011, http://www.wharton.universia.net/index.cfm?fa=viewfeature&id=1450&language=english.

[14] "The Globalization of Chilean Retailing," Knowledge@Wharton, December 12, 2007, accessed January 5, 2011, http://www.wharton.universia.net/index.cfm?fa=viewfeature&id=1 450&language=english.

8.2 PESTEL, Globalization, and Importing

LEARNING OBJECTIVES

1. Know the components of PESTEL analysis.
2. Recognize how PESTEL is related to the dimensions of globalization.
3. Understand why importing might be a stealth form of international entry.

Know the Components of PESTEL Analysis

PESTEL analysis is an important and widely used tool that helps show the big picture of a firm's external environment, particularly as related to foreign markets. PESTEL is an acronym for the political, economic, sociocultural, technological, environmental, and legal contexts in which a firm operates. A PESTEL analysis helps managers gain a better understanding of the opportunities and threats they face; consequently, the analysis aids in building a better vision of the future business landscape and how the firm might compete profitably. This useful tool analyzes for market growth or decline and, therefore, the position, potential, and direction for a business. When a firm is considering entry into new markets, these factors are of considerable importance. Moreover, PESTEL analysis provides insight into the status of key market *flatteners*, both in terms of their present state and future trends.

Firms need to understand the macroenvironment to ensure that their strategy is aligned with the powerful forces of change affecting their business landscape. When firms exploit a change in the environment—rather than simply survive or oppose the change—they are more likely to be successful. A solid understanding of PESTEL also helps managers avoid strategies that may be doomed to fail given the circumstances of the environment. JC Penney's failed entry into Chile is a case in point.

Finally, understanding PESTEL is critical prior to entry into a new country or region. The fact that a strategy is congruent with PESTEL in the home environment gives no assurance that it will also align in other countries. For example, when Lands' End, the online clothier, sought to expand its operations into Germany, it ran into local laws prohibiting it from offering unconditional guarantees on its products. In the United States, Lands' End had built a reputation for quality on its no-questions-asked money-back guarantee. However, this was considered illegal under Germany's regulations governing incentive offers and price discounts. The political skirmish between Lands' End and the German government finally ended when the regulations banning unconditional guarantees were abolished. While the restrictive regulations didn't put Lands' End out of business in Germany, they did inhibit its growth there until the laws were abolished.

There are three steps in the PESTEL analysis. First, consider the relevance of each of the PESTEL factors to your context. Next, identify and categorize the information that applies to these factors. Finally, analyze the data and draw conclusions. Common mistakes in this analysis include stopping at the second step or assuming that the initial analysis and conclusions are correct without testing the assumptions and investigating alternative scenarios.

The framework for PESTEL analysis is presented below. It's composed of six sections—one for each of the PESTEL headings. [1] The framework includes sample questions or prompts, the answers to which can help determine the nature of opportunities and threats in the macroenvironment. These questions are examples of the types of issues that can arise in a PESTEL analysis.

PESTEL Analysis

1. Political
   o How stable is the political environment in the prospective country?
   o What are the local taxation policies? How do these affect your business?
   o Is the government involved in trading agreements, such as the European Union (EU), the North American Free Trade Agreement (NAFTA), or the Association of Southeast Asian Nations (ASEAN)?
   o What are the country's foreign-trade regulations?
   o What are the country's social-welfare policies?
2. Economic
   o What are the current and forecast interest rates?
   o What is the current level of inflation in the prospective country? What is it forecast to be? How does this affect the possible growth of your market?
   o What are local employment levels per capita, and how are they changing?
   o What are the long-term prospects for the country's economy, gross domestic product (GDP) per capita, and other economic factors?
   o What are the current exchange rates between critical markets, and how will they affect production and distribution of your goods?

3. Sociocultural
   o What are the local lifestyle trends?
   o What are the country's current demographics, and how are they changing?
   o What is the level and distribution of education and income?
   o What are the dominant local religions, and what influence do they have on consumer attitudes and opinions?
   o What is the level of consumerism, and what are the popular attitudes toward it?
   o What pending legislation could affect corporate social policies (e.g., domestic-partner benefits or maternity and paternity leave)?
   o What are the attitudes toward work and leisure?
4. Technological
   o To what level do the local government and industry fund research, and are those levels changing?
   o What is the local government's and industry's level of interest and focus on technology?
   o How mature is the technology?
   o What is the status of intellectual property issues in the local environment?
   o Are potentially disruptive technologies in adjacent industries creeping in at the edges of the focal industry?
5. Environmental
   o What are the local environmental issues?
   o Are there any pending ecological or environmental issues relevant to your industry?
   o How do the activities of international activist groups (e.g., Greenpeace, Earth First!, and People for the Ethical Treatment of Animals [PETA]) affect your business?
   o Are there environmental-protection laws?
   o What are the regulations regarding waste disposal and energy consumption?
6. Legal
   o What are the local government's regulations regarding monopolies and private property?
   o Does intellectual property have legal protections?
   o Are there relevant consumer laws?
   o What is the status of employment, health and safety, and product safety laws?

Political Factors

The political environment can have a significant influence on businesses. In addition, political factors affect consumer confidence and consumer and business spending. For instance, how stable is the political environment? This is particularly important for companies entering new markets.

Government policies on regulation and taxation can vary from state to state and across national boundaries. Political considerations also encompass trade treaties, such as NAFTA, ASEAN, and EU. Such treaties tend to favor trade among the member countries but impose penalties or less favorable trade terms on nonmembers.

Economic Factors

Managers also need to consider macroeconomic factors that will have near-term and long-term effects on the success of their strategy. Inflation rates, interest rates, tariffs, the growth of the local and foreign national economies, and exchange rates are critical. Unemployment, availability of critical labor, and the local cost of labor also have a strong bearing on strategy, particularly as related to the location of disparate business functions and facilities.

Sociocultural Factors

The social and cultural influences on business vary from country to country. Depending on the type of business, factors such as the local languages, the dominant religions, the cultural views toward leisure time, and the age and lifespan demographics may be critical. Local sociocultural characteristics also include attitudes toward consumerism, environmentalism, and the roles of men and women in society. For example, Coca-Cola and PepsiCo have grown in international markets due to the increasing level of consumerism outside the United States.

Making assumptions about local norms derived from experiences in your home market is a common cause for early failure when entering new markets. However, even home-market norms can change over time, often caused by shifting demographics due to immigration or aging populations.

Technological Factors

The critical role of technology is discussed in more detail later in this section. For now, suffice it to say that technological factors have a major bearing on the threats and opportunities firms encounter. For example, new technology may make it possible for products and services to be made more cheaply and to a better standard of quality. New technology may also provide the opportunity for more innovative products and services, such as online stock trading and remote working. Such changes have the potential to change the face of the business landscape.

Environmental Factors

The environment has long been a factor in firm strategy, primarily from the standpoint of access to raw materials.

Increasingly, this factor is best viewed as both a direct and indirect cost for the firm.

Environmental factors are also evaluated on the footprint left by a firm on its respective surroundings. For consumer-product companies like PepsiCo, for instance, this can encompass the waste-management and organic-farming practices used in the countries where raw materials are obtained. Similarly, in consumer markets, it may refer to the degree to which packaging is biodegradable or recyclable.

Legal Factors

Finally, legal factors reflect the laws and regulations relevant to the region and the organization. Legal factors can include whether the rule of law is well established, how easily or quickly laws and regulations may change, and what the costs of regulatory compliance are. For example, Coca-Cola's market share in Europe is greater than 50 percent; as a result, regulators have asked that the company give shelf space in its coolers to competitive products in order to provide greater consumer choice. [2]

Many of the PESTEL factors are interrelated. For instance, the legal environment is often related to the political environment, where laws and regulations can only change when they're consistent with the political will.

PESTEL and Globalization

Over the past decade, new markets have been opened to foreign competitors, whole industries have been deregulated, and state-run enterprises have been privatized. So, globalization has become a fact of life in almost every industry. [3] This entails much more than companies simply exporting products to another country. Some industries that aren't normally considered global do, in fact, have strictly domestic players. But these companies often compete alongside firms with operations in multiple countries; in many cases, both sets of firms are doing equally well. In contrast, in a truly global industry, the core product is standardized, the marketing approach is relatively uniform, and competitive strategies are integrated in different international markets. [4] In these industries, competitive advantage clearly belongs to the firms that can compete globally.

A number of factors reveal whether an industry has globalized or is in the process of globalizing. The sidebar below groups globalization factors into four categories: *markets*, *costs*, *governments*, and *competition*. These dimensions correspond well to Thomas Friedman's flatteners

(as described in his book *The World Is Flat*), though they are not exhaustive. [5]

Factors Favoring Industry Globalization

1. Markets
   - Homogeneous customer needs
   - Global customer needs
   - Global channels
   - Transferable marketing approaches
2. Costs
   - Large-scale and large-scope economies
   - Learning and experience
   - Sourcing efficiencies
   - Favorable logistics
   - Arbitrage opportunities
   - High research-and-development (R&D) costs
3. Governments
   - Favorable trade policies
   - Common technological standards
   - Common manufacturing and marketing regulations
4. Competition
   - Interdependent countries
   - Global competitors [6]

Markets

The more similar markets in different regions are, the greater the pressure for an industry to globalize. Coca-Cola and PepsiCo, for example, are fairly uniform around the world because the demand for soft drinks is largely the same in every country. The airframe-manufacturing industry, dominated by Boeing and Airbus, also has a highly uniform market for its products; airlines all over the world have the same needs when it comes to large commercial jets.

Costs

In both of these industries, costs favor globalization. Coca-Cola and PepsiCo realize economies of scope and scale because they make such huge investments in marketing and promotion. Since they're promoting coherent images and brands, they can leverage their marketing dollars around the world. Similarly, Boeing and Airbus can invest millions in new-product R&D only because the global market for their products is so large.

Governments and Competition

Obviously, favorable trade policies encourage the globalization of markets and industries. Governments, however, can also play a critical role in globalization by determining and regulating technological standards. Railroad gauge—the distance between the two steel tracks—would seem to favor a simple technological standard. In Spain, however, the gauge is wider than in France. Why? Because back in the 1850s, when Spain and neighboring France were hostile to one another, the Spanish government decided that making Spanish railways incompatible with French railways would hinder any French invasion.

These are a few key drivers of industry change. However, there are particular implications of technological and business-model breakthroughs for both the pace and extent of industry change. The *rate* of change may vary significantly from one industry to the next; for instance, the computing industry changes much faster than the steel industry. Nevertheless, change in both fields has prompted complete reconfigurations of industry structure and the competitive positions of various players. The idea that all industries change over time and that business environments are in a constant state of flux is relatively intuitive. As a strategic decision maker, you need to ask yourself this question: how accurately does current industry structure (which is relatively easy to identify) predict future industry conditions?

Importing as a Stealth Form of Internationalization

Ironically, the drivers of globalization have also given rise to a greater level of imports. Globalization in this sense is a very strong flattener. Importing involves the sale of products or services in one country that are sourced in another country. In many ways, importing is a stealth form of internationalization. Firms often claim that they have no international operations and yet—directly or indirectly—base their production or services on inputs obtained from outside their home country. Firms that engage in importing must learn about customs requirements, informed compliance with customs regulations, entry of goods, invoices, classification and value, determination and assessment of duty, special requirements, fraud, marketing, trade finance and insurance, and foreign trade zones. Importing can take many forms—from the sourcing of components, machinery, and raw materials to the purchase of finished goods for domestic resale and the outsourcing of production or services to nondomestic providers.

Outsourcing occurs when a company contracts with a third party to do some work on its behalf. The outsourcer may do the work within the same country or may take the work to another country (i.e., offshoring). Offshoring occurs when you take a function out of your country of residence to be performed in another country, generally at a lower cost. International outsourcing, or outsourcing work to a nondomestic third party, has become very visible in business

and corporate strategy in recent years. But it's not a new phenomenon; for decades, Nike has been designing shoes and other apparel that are manufactured abroad. Similarly, Pacific Cycle doesn't make a single Schwinn or Mongoose bicycle in the United States but instead imports them entirely from manufacturers in Taiwan and China. It may seem as if international outsourcing is new because businesses are now more often outsourcing services, components, and raw materials from countries with developing economies (e.g., China, Brazil, and India).

In addition to factors of production, information technologies (IT)—such as telecommunications and the widespread diffusion of the Internet—have provided the impetus for outsourcing services. Business-process outsourcing (BPO) is the delegation of one or more IT-intensive business processes to an external provider that in turn owns, administers, and manages the selected process on the basis of defined and measurable performance criteria. The firms in service and IT-intensive industries—insurance, banking, pharmaceuticals, telecommunications, automotive, and airlines—are among the early adopters of BPO. Of these, insurance and banking are able to generate the bulk of the savings, purely because of the large proportion of processes that they can outsource (i.e., the processing of claims and loans and providing service through call centers). Among those countries housing BPO operations, India experienced the most dramatic growth in services where language skills and education were important. Research firm Gartner anticipates that the BPO market in India will reach $1.8 billion by 2013. [7]

Generally, foreign outsourcing locations tend to be defined by how automated a production process or service can be made and the transportation costs involved. When transportation costs and automation are both high, then the knowledge worker component of the location calculation becomes less important. You can see how you might employ the CAGE framework to evaluate potential outsourcing locations. In some cases, though, firms invest in both plant equipment and the training and development of the local workforce. This becomes important when the broader labor force needs to have a higher level of education to operate complex plant machinery or because a firm's specific technologies also have a cultural component. Brazil is one case in point; Ford, BMW, Daimler, and Cargill have all made significant investments in the educational infrastructure of this significant, emerging economy. [8]

KEY TAKEAWAYS

- A PESTEL analysis examines a target market's political, economic, social, technological, environmental, and legal dimensions in terms of both its current state and possible trends.

- An understanding of the dimensions of PESTEL helps you better grasp the dimensions on which a target market or industry may be more global or local.

- Importing is a stealth form of international entry, because the factors that favor globalization can also lead to a higher level of imports, and inputs can be sourced from anywhere they have either the lowest cost, highest quality, or some combination of these characteristics.

EXERCISES

(AACSB: Reflective Thinking, Analytical Skills)

1. What are the components of PESTEL analysis?
2. What are the four dimensions of pressures favoring globalization?
3. How are the PESTEL and globalization dimensions related to the flatteners (in the context that Thomas Friedman talks about them in his book *The World Is Flat*)?
4. Why might importing be considered a stealth form of internationalization or an internationalization entry mode?
5. What is the difference between outsourcing and offshoring?

[1] {Authors' names retracted as requested by the work's original creator or licensee}, Principles of Management (Nyack, NY:

[2] "EU Curbs Coca-Cola Market Dominance," Food & Beverage Reporter, August 2005, accessed February 18, 2011, http://www.developtechnology.co.za/index.php?option=com_content&task=view&id=18464&Itemid=101.

[3] George S. Yip, "Global Strategy in a World of Nations," Sloan Management Review 31, no. 1 (1989): 29–40.

[4] Michael E. Porter, Competition in Global Industries (Boston: Harvard Business School Press, 1986); George S. Yip, "Global Strategy in a World of Nations," Sloan Management Review 31, no. 1 (1989): 29–40.

[5] Thomas L. Friedman, The World Is Flat (New York: Farrar, Straus and Giroux, 2005).

[6] Adapted from Michael E. Porter, Competition in Global Industries (Boston: Harvard Business School Press, 1986); George S. Yip, "Global Strategy in a World of Nations," Sloan Management Review 31, no. 1 (1989): 29–40.

[7] "Indian BPO Market to Grow 25 percent in 2010," Times of India, March 29, 2010, accessed February 17, 2011, http://timesofindia.indiatimes.com/business/india-business/Indian-BPO-market-to-grow-25-in-2010/articleshow/5739043.cms.

[8] Spencer E. Ante, "IBM Bets on Brazilian Innovation," BusinessWeek, August 17, 2009, accessed February 18, 2011, http://www.businessweek.com/technology/content/aug2009/tc20090817_998497.htm; "Cargill Annual Report 2006," Cargill website,

accessed October 27, 2010,http://www.cargill.com.br/wcm/groups/public/@csf/@brazil/documents/document/br-2006-annual-rpt.pdf; "Ford to Raise Brazil Investments by $281 Million," Reuters, April 8, 2010, accessed February 18, 2011, http://www.reuters.com/article/2010/04/08/ford-brazil-idUSN0821323920100408; "Cargill Investing $210 Million in Brazilian Plant," Forbes, February 2, 2011, accessed February 18, 2011,http://www.forbes.com/feeds/ap/2011/02/02/business-food-retailers-amp-wholesalers-us-cargill-brazil_8289031.htm.

8.3 International-Expansion Entry Modes

LEARNING OBJECTIVES

1. Describe the five common international-expansion entry modes.
2. Know the advantages and disadvantages of each entry mode.
3. Understand the dynamics among the choice of different entry modes.

The Five Common International-Expansion Entry Modes

In this section, we will explore the traditional international-expansion entry modes. Beyond importing, international expansion is achieved through exporting, licensing arrangements, partnering and strategic alliances, acquisitions, and establishing new, wholly owned subsidiaries, also known as greenfield ventures. These modes of entering international markets and their characteristics are shown in Table 8.1 "International-Expansion Entry Modes". [1] Each mode of market entry has advantages and disadvantages. Firms need to evaluate their options to choose the entry mode that best suits their strategy and goals.

Table 8.1 International-Expansion Entry Modes

Type of Entry	Advantages	Disadvantages
Exporting	Fast entry, low risk	Low control, low local knowledge, potential negative environmental impact of transportation
Licensing and Franchising	Fast entry, low cost, low risk	Less control, licensee may become a competitor, legal and regulatory environment (IP and contract law) must be sound
Partnering and Strategic Alliance	Shared costs reduce investment needed, reduced risk, seen as local entity	Higher cost than exporting, licensing, or franchising; integration problems between two corporate cultures

Type of Entry	Advantages	Disadvantages
Acquisition	Fast entry; known, established operations	High cost, integration issues with home office
Greenfield Venture (Launch of a new, wholly owned subsidiary)	Gain local market knowledge; can be seen as insider who employs locals; maximum control	High cost, high risk due to unknowns, slow entry due to setup time

Exporting

Exporting is a typically the easiest way to enter an international market, and therefore most firms begin their international expansion using this model of entry. Exporting is the sale of products and services in foreign countries that are sourced from the home country. The advantage of this mode of entry is that firms avoid the expense of establishing operations in the new country. Firms must, however, have a way to distribute and market their products in the new country, which they typically do through contractual agreements with a local company or distributor. When exporting, the firm must give thought to labeling, packaging, and pricing the offering appropriately for the market. In terms of marketing and promotion, the firm will need to let potential buyers know of its offerings, be it through advertising, trade shows, or a local sales force.

Amusing Anecdotes

One common factor in exporting is the need to translate something about a product or service into the language of the target country. This requirement may be driven by local regulations or by the company's wish to market the product or service in a locally friendly fashion. While this may seem to be a simple task, it's often a source of embarrassment for the company and humor for competitors. David Ricks's book on international business blunders relates the following anecdote for US companies doing business in the neighboring French-speaking Canadian province of Quebec. A company boasted of *lait frais usage*, which translates to "used fresh milk," when it meant to brag of *lait frais employé*, or "fresh milk used." The "terrific" pens sold by another company were instead promoted as *terrifiantes*, or terrifying. In another example, a company intending to say that its appliance could use "any kind of electrical current," actually stated that the appliance "wore out any kind of liquid." And imagine how one company felt when its product to "reduce heartburn" was advertised as one that reduced "the warmth of heart"! [2]

Among the disadvantages of exporting are the costs of transporting goods to the country, which can be high and can have a negative impact on the environment. In addition, some countries impose tariffs on incoming goods, which will impact the firm's profits. In addition, firms that market and distribute products through a contractual agreement have less control over those operations and, naturally, must pay their distribution partner a fee for those services.

Ethics in Action

Companies are starting to consider the environmental impact of where they locate their manufacturing facilities. For example, Olam International, a cashew producer, originally shipped nuts grown in Africa to Asia for processing. Now, however, Olam has opened processing plants in Tanzania, Mozambique, and Nigeria. These locations are close to where the nuts are grown. The result? Olam has lowered its processing and shipping costs by 25 percent while greatly reducing carbon emissions. [3]

Likewise, when Walmart enters a new market, it seeks to source produce for its food sections from local farms that are near its warehouses. Walmart has learned that the savings it gets from lower transportation costs and the benefit of being able to restock in smaller quantities more than offset the lower prices it was getting from industrial farms located farther away. This practice is also a win-win for locals, who have the opportunity to sell to Walmart, which can increase their profits and let them grow and hire more people and pay better wages. This, in turn, helps all the businesses in the local community. [4]

Firms export mostly to countries that are close to their facilities because of the lower transportation costs and the often greater similarity between geographic neighbors. For example, Mexico accounts for 40 percent of the goods exported from Texas. [5] The Internet has also made exporting easier. Even small firms can access critical information about foreign markets, examine a target market, research the competition, and create lists of potential customers. Even applying for export and import licenses is becoming easier as more governments use the Internet to facilitate these processes.

Because the cost of exporting is lower than that of the other entry modes, entrepreneurs and small businesses are most likely to use exporting as a way to get their products into markets around the globe. Even with exporting, firms still face the challenges of currency exchange rates. While larger firms have specialists that manage the exchange rates, small businesses rarely have this expertise. One factor that has helped reduce the number of currencies that firms must deal with was the formation of the European Union (EU) and the move to a single currency, the euro, for the first time. As of 2011, seventeen of the twenty-seven EU members use the euro, giving businesses access to 331 million people with that single currency. [6]

Licensing and Franchising

Licensing and franchising are two specialized modes of entry that are discussed in more detail in Chapter 9 "Exporting, Importing, and Global Sourcing". The intellectual property aspects of licensing new technology or patents is discussed in Chapter 13 "Harnessing the Engine of Global Innovation".

Partnerships and Strategic Alliances

Another way to enter a new market is through a strategic alliance with a local partner. A strategic alliance involves a contractual agreement between two or more enterprises stipulating that the involved parties will cooperate in a certain way for a certain time to achieve a common purpose. To determine if the alliance approach is suitable for the firm, the firm must decide what value the partner could bring to the venture in terms of both tangible and intangible aspects. The advantages of partnering with a local firm are that the local firm likely understands the local culture, market, and ways of doing business better than an outside firm. Partners are especially valuable if they have a recognized, reputable brand name in the country or have existing relationships with customers that the firm might want to access. For example, Cisco formed a strategic alliance with Fujitsu to develop routers for Japan. In the alliance, Cisco decided to co-brand with the Fujitsu name so that it could leverage Fujitsu's reputation in Japan for IT equipment and solutions while still retaining the Cisco name to benefit from Cisco's global reputation for switches and routers. [7]Similarly, Xerox launched signed strategic alliances to grow sales in emerging markets such as Central and Eastern Europe, India, and Brazil. [8]

Strategic alliances are also advantageous for small entrepreneurial firms that may be too small to make the needed investments to enter the new market themselves. In addition, some countries require foreign-owned companies to partner with a local firm if they want to enter the market. For example, in Saudi Arabia, non-Saudi companies looking to do business in the country are required by law to have a Saudi partner. This requirement is common in many Middle Eastern countries. Even without this type of regulation, a local partner often helps foreign firms bridge the differences that otherwise make doing business locally impossible. Walmart, for example, failed several times over nearly a decade to effectively grow its business in Mexico, until it found a strong domestic partner with similar business values.

The disadvantages of partnering, on the other hand, are lack of direct control and the possibility that the partner's goals differ from the firm's goals. David Ricks, who has written a book on blunders in international business, describes the case of a US company eager to enter the Indian market: "It quickly negotiated terms and completed arrangements with its local partners. Certain required documents, however, such as the industrial license, foreign collaboration agreements, capital issues permit, import licenses for machinery and equipment, etc., were slow in being issued. Trying to expedite governmental approval of these items, the US firm agreed to accept a lower royalty fee than originally stipulated. Despite all of this extra effort, the project was not greatly expedited, and the lower royalty fee reduced the firm's profit by approximately half a million dollars over the life of the agreement." [9] Failing to consider the values or reliability of a potential partner can be costly, if not disastrous.

To avoid these missteps, Cisco created one globally integrated team to oversee its alliances in emerging markets. Having a dedicated team allows Cisco to invest in training the managers how to manage the complex relationships involved in alliances. The team follows a consistent model, using and sharing best practices for the benefit of all its alliances. [10]

Did You Know?

Partnerships in emerging markets can be used for social good as well. For example, pharmaceutical company Novartis crafted multiple partnerships with suppliers and manufacturers to develop, test, and produce antimalaria medicine on a nonprofit basis. The partners included several Chinese suppliers and manufacturing partners as well as a farm in Kenya that grows the medication's key raw ingredient. To date, the partnership, called the Novartis Malaria Initiative, has saved an estimated 750,000 lives through the delivery of 300 million doses of the medication. [11]

Acquisitions

An acquisition is a transaction in which a firm gains control of another firm by purchasing its stock, exchanging the stock for its own, or, in the case of a private firm, paying the owners a purchase price. In our increasingly flat world, cross-border acquisitions have risen dramatically. In recent years, cross-border acquisitions have made up over 60 percent of all acquisitions completed worldwide. Acquisitions are appealing because they give the company quick, established access to a new market. However, they are expensive, which in the past had put them out of reach as a strategy for companies in the undeveloped world to pursue. What has changed over the years is the strength of different currencies. The higher interest rates in developing nations has strengthened their currencies relative to the dollar or euro. If the acquiring firm is in a country with a strong currency, the acquisition is comparatively cheaper to make. As Wharton professor Lawrence G. Hrebiniak explains, "Mergers fail because people pay too much of a premium. If your currency is strong, you can get a bargain." [12]

When deciding whether to pursue an acquisition strategy, firms examine the laws in the target country. China has many restrictions on foreign ownership, for example, but even a developed-world country like the United States has laws addressing acquisitions. For example, you must be an American citizen to own a TV station in the United States. Likewise, a foreign firm is not allowed to own more than 25 percent of a US airline. [13]

Acquisition is a good entry strategy to choose when scale is needed, which is particularly the case in certain industries (e.g., wireless telecommunications). Acquisition is also a good strategy when an industry is consolidating. Nonetheless, acquisitions are risky. Many studies have shown that between 40 percent and 60 percent of all acquisitions fail to increase the market value of the acquired company by more than the amount invested. [14]

New, Wholly Owned Subsidiary

The process of establishing of a new, wholly owned subsidiary (also called a greenfield venture) is often complex and potentially costly, but it affords the firm maximum control and has the most potential to provide above-average returns. The costs and risks are high given the costs of establishing a new business operation in a new country. The firm may have to acquire the knowledge and expertise of the existing market by hiring either host-country nationals—possibly from competitive firms—or costly consultants. An advantage is that the firm retains control of all its operations.

Entrepreneurship and Strategy

The Chinese have a "Why not me?" attitude. As Edward Tse, author of *The China Strategy: Harnessing the Power of the World's Fastest-Growing Economy*, explains, this means that "in all corners of China, there will be people asking, 'If Li Ka-shing [the chairman of Cheung Kong Holdings] can be so wealthy, if Bill Gates or Warren Buffett can be so successful, why not me?' This cuts across China's demographic profiles: from people in big cities to people in smaller cities or rural areas, from older to younger people. There is a huge dynamism among them." [15] Tse sees entrepreneurial China as "entrepreneurial people at the grassroots level who are very independent-minded. They're very quick on their feet. They're prone to fearless experimentation: imitating other companies here and there, trying new ideas, and then, if they fail, rapidly adapting and moving on." As a result, he sees China becoming not only a very large consumer market but also a strong innovator. Therefore, he advises US firms to enter China sooner rather than later so that they can take advantage of the opportunities there. Tse says, "Companies are coming to realize that they need to integrate more and more of their value chains into China and India. They need to be close to these markets, because of their size. They need the ability to understand the needs of their customers in emerging markets, and turn them into product and service offerings quickly." [16]

KEY TAKEAWAYS

- The five most common modes of international-market entry are exporting, licensing, partnering, acquisition, and greenfield venturing.
- Each of these entry vehicles has its own particular set of advantages and disadvantages. By choosing to export, a company can avoid the substantial costs of establishing its own operations in the new country, but it must find a way to market and distribute its goods in that country. By choosing to license or franchise its offerings, a firm lowers its financial risks but also gives up control over the manufacturing and marketing of its products in the new country. Partnerships and strategic alliances reduce the amount of investment that a company needs to make because the costs are shared with the partner. Partnerships are also helpful to make the new entrant appear to be more local because it enters the market with a local partner. But the overall costs of partnerships and alliances are higher than exporting, licensing, or franchising, and there is a potential for integration problems between the corporate cultures of the partners. Acquisitions enable fast entry and less risk from the standpoint that the operations are established and known, but they can be expensive and may result in integration issues of the acquired firm to the home office. Greenfield ventures give the firm the best opportunity to retain full control of operations, gain local market knowledge, and be seen as an insider that employs locals. The disadvantages of greenfield ventures are the slow time to enter the market because the firm must set up operations and the high costs of establishing operations from scratch.

- Which entry mode a firm chooses also depends on the firm's size, financial strength, and the economic and regulatory conditions of the target country. A small firm will likely begin with an export strategy. Large firms or firms with deep pockets might begin with an acquisition to gain quick access or to achieve economies of scale. If the target country has sound rule of law and strong adherence to business contracts, licensing, franchising, or partnerships may be middle-of-the-road approaches that are neither riskier nor more expensive than the other options.

EXERCISES

(AACSB: Reflective Thinking, Analytical Skills)
1. What are five common international entry modes?
2. What are the advantages of exporting?
3. What is the difference between a strategic alliance and an acquisition?
4. What would influence a firm's choice of the five entry modes?
5. What is the possible relationship among the different entry modes?

[1] Shaker A. Zahra, R. Duane Ireland, and Michael A. Hitt, "International Expansion by New Venture Firms: International Diversity, Mode of Market Entry, Technological Learning, and Performance," Academy of Management Journal 43, no. 5 (October 2000): 925–50.
[2] David A. Ricks, Blunders in International Business (Hoboken, NJ: Wiley-Blackwell, 1999), 101.
[3] Michael E. Porter and Mark R. Kramer, "The Big Idea: Creating Shared Value," Harvard Business Review, January–February 2011, accessed January 23, 2011, http://hbr.org/2011/01/the-big-idea-creating-shared-value/ar/pr.
[4] Michael E. Porter and Mark R. Kramer, "The Big Idea: Creating Shared Value," Harvard Business Review, January–February 2011, accessed January 23, 2011, http://hbr.org/2011/01/the-big-idea-creating-shared-value/ar/pr.
[5] Andrew J. Cassey, "Analyzing the Export Flow from Texas to Mexico," StaffPAPERS: Federal Reserve Bank of Dallas, No. 11, October 2010, accessed February 14, 2011,http://www.dallasfed.org/research/staff/2010/staff1003.pdf.
[6] "The Euro," European Commission, accessed February 11, 2011, http://ec.europa.eu/euro/index_en.html.
[7] Steve Steinhilber, Strategic Alliances (Cambridge, MA: Harvard Business School Press, 2008), 113.
[8] "ASAP Releases Winners of 2010 Alliance Excellence Awards," Association for Strategic Alliance Professionals, September 2, 2010, accessed February 12, 2011, http://newslife.us/technology/mobile/ASAP-Releases-Winners-of-2010-Alliance-Excellence-Awards.
[9] David A. Ricks, Blunders in International Business (Hoboken, NJ: Wiley-Blackwell, 1999), 101.
[10] Steve Steinhilber, Strategic Alliances (Cambridge, MA: Harvard Business School Press, 2008), 125.
[11] "ASAP Releases Winners of 2010 Alliance Excellence Awards," Association for Strategic Alliance Professionals, September 2, 2010, accessed September 20, 2010,
http://newslife.us/technology/mobile/ASAP-Releases-Winners-of-2010-Alliance-Excellence-Awards.
[12] "Playing on a Global Stage: Asian Firms See a New Strategy in Acquisitions Abroad and at Home," Knowledge@Wharton, April 28, 2010, accessed January 15, 2011, http://knowledge.wharton.upenn.edu/article.cfm?articleid=2473.
[13] "Playing on a Global Stage: Asian Firms See a New Strategy in Acquisitions Abroad and at Home," Knowledge@Wharton, April 28, 2010, accessed January 15, 2011, http://knowledge.wharton.upenn.edu/article.cfm?articleid=2473.
[14] "Playing on a Global Stage: Asian Firms See a New Strategy in Acquisitions Abroad and at Home," Knowledge@Wharton, April 28, 2010, accessed January 15, 2011, http://knowledge.wharton.upenn.edu/article.cfm?articleid=2473.
[15] Art Kleiner, "Getting China Right," Strategy and Business, March 22, 2010, accessed January 23, 2011, http://www.strategy-business.com/article/00026?pg=al.
[16] Art Kleiner, "Getting China Right," Strategy and Business, March 22, 2010, accessed January 23, 2011, http://www.strategy-business.com/article/00026?pg=al.

8.4 CAGE Analysis
LEARNING OBJECTIVES

1. Understand the inputs into CAGE analysis.
2. Know the reasons why CAGE analysis emphasizes distance.
3. See how CAGE analysis can help you identify institutional voids.

The Inputs into CAGE Analysis

Pankaj "Megawatt" Ghemawat is an international strategy guru who developed the CAGE framework to offer businesses a way to evaluate countries in terms of the "distance" between them. [1] In this case, distance is defined broadly to include not only the physical geographic distance between countries but also the cultural, administrative (currencies, trade agreements), and economic differences between them. As summarized in Table 8.2 "The CAGE Framework", the CAGE (cultural, administrative, geographic, and economic) framework offers a broader view of distance and provides another way of thinking about location and the opportunities and concomitant risks associated with global arbitrage. [2]

To apply the CAGE framework, identify locations that offer low raw material costs, access to markets or consumers, or other key decision criteria. You might, for instance, determine that you're interested in markets with strong consumer buying power, so you would use per capita income as your first sorting criterion. As a result, you would likely end up with some type of ranking. Ghemawat provides an example for the fast-food industry, where he shows that on the basis of per capita income, countries like Germany and Japan would be the most attractive markets for the expansion of a North American fast-food company. However, when he adjusts this analysis for distance using the CAGE framework, he shows that Mexico ranks as the second most attractive market for international expansion, far ahead of Germany and Japan. [3] Recall though, that any international expansion strategy still needs to be supported by the specific resources and capabilities possessed by the firm, regardless of the picture presented by the CAGE analysis. To understand the usefulness of the CAGE framework, consider Dell and its efforts to compete effectively in China. The vehicles it used to enter China were just as important in its strategy as its choice of geographic arena. For Dell's corporate clients in China, the CAGE framework would likely have revealed relatively little distance on all four dimensions—even geographic—given the fact that many personal-computer components have been sourced from China. However, for the consumer segment, the distance was rather great, particularly on the dimensions of culture, administration, and economics. For example, Chinese consumers didn't buy over the Internet, which is the primary way Dell sells its products in the United States. One possible outcome could have been for Dell to avoid the Chinese consumer market altogether. However, Dell opted to choose a strategic alliance with distributors whose knowledge base and capabilities allowed Dell to better bridge the CAGE-framework distances. Thus the CAGE framework can be used to address the question of where (which arena) and how (by which entry vehicle) to expand internationally.

CAGE Analysis and Institutional Voids

While you can apply CAGE to consider some first-order distances (e.g., physical distance between a company's home market and the new foreign market) or cultural differences (e.g., the differences between home-market and foreign-market customer preferences), you can also apply it to identify institutional differences. Institutional differences include differences in political systems and in financial markets. The greater the distance, the harder it will be to operate in that country. Emerging markets in particular can have greater differences because these countries lack many of the specialized intermediaries that make institutions like financial markets work. Table 8.3 "Specialized Intermediaries within a Country or Other Geographic Arena" lists examples of specialized intermediaries for different institutions. If an institution lacks these specialized intermediaries, there is an institutional void. An institutional void refers to the absence of key specialized intermediaries found in the markets of finance, managerial talent, and products, which otherwise reduce transaction costs.

Table 8.3 Specialized Intermediaries within a Country or Other Geographic Arena

Institution	Specialized Intermediary
Financial markets	• Venture-capital firms • Private equity providers • Mutual funds • Banks • Auditors • Transparent corporate governance
Markets for managerial talent	• Management institute or business schools • Certification agencies • Headhunting firms • Relocation agencies
Markets for products	• Certification agencies • Consumer reports • Regulatory authorities (e.g., the Food and Drug Administration) • Extrajudicial dispute resolution services
All markets	• Legal and judiciary (for property rights protection and enforcement)

Three Strategies for Handling Institutional Voids

When a firm detects an institutional void, it has three choices for how to proceed in regard to the potential target market: (1) adapt its business model, (2) change the institutional context, or (3) stay away.

For example, when McDonald's tried to enter the Russian market, it found an institutional void: a lack of local suppliers to provide the food products it needs. Rather than abandoning market entry, McDonald's decided to adapt its business model. Instead of outsourcing supply-chain operations like it does in the United States, McDonald's worked with a joint-venture partner to fill the voids. It imported cattle from Holland and russet potatoes from the United States, brought in agricultural specialists from Canada and Europe to improve Russian farmers' management practices, and lent money to farmers so that they could invest in better seeds and equipment. As a result of establishing its own supply-chain and management systems, McDonald's controlled 80 percent of the Russian fast-food market by 2010. The process, however, took fifteen years and $250 million in investments. [4]

An example of the second approach to dealing with an institutional void—changing the institutional context—is that used by the "Big Four" audit firms (i.e., Ernst & Young,

KPMG, Deloitte Touche Tohmatsu, and PricewaterhouseCoopers) when they entered Brazil. At the time, Brazil had a fledgling audit services market. When the four firms set up branches in Brazil, they raised financial reporting and auditing standards across the country, thus bringing a dramatic improvement to the local market. [5]

Finally, the firm can choose the strategy of staying away from a market with institutional voids. For example, The Home Depot's value proposition (i.e., low prices, great service, and good quality) requires institutions like reliable transportation networks (to minimize inventory costs) and the practice of employee stock ownership (which motivates workers to provide great service). The Home Depot has decided to avoid countries with weak logistics systems and poorly developed capital markets because the company would not be able to attain the low cost–great service combination that is its hallmark. [6]

Ethics in Action

Nestlé's Nespresso division is one of the company's fastest-growing divisions. The division makes a single-cup espresso machine along with single-serving capsules of coffees from around the world. Nestlé is headquartered in Switzerland, but the coffee it needs to buy is primarily grown in rural Africa and Latin America. Nespresso set up local facilities in these regions that measure the quality of the coffee. Nespresso also helps local farmers improve the quality of their coffee, and then it pays more for coffee beans that are of higher quality. Nespresso has gone even further by advising farmers on farming practices that improve the yield of beans farmers get per hectare. The results have proven beneficial to all parties: farmers earn more money, Nespresso gets getter quality beans, and the negative environmental impact of the farms has diminished. [7]

KEY TAKEAWAYS

- CAGE analysis asks you to compare a possible target market to a company's home market on the dimensions of culture, administration, geography, and economy.
- CAGE analysis yields insights in the key differences between home and target markets and allows companies to assess the desirability of that market.
- CAGE analysis can help you identify institutional voids, which might otherwise frustrate internationalization efforts. Institutional differences are important to the extent that the absence of specialized intermediaries can raise transaction costs just as their presence can reduce them.

EXERCISES

(AACSB: Reflective Thinking, Analytical Skills)

1. Explain what distance is in relation to the CAGE framework.
2. What are the key elements in CAGE analysis?
3. What is an institutional void?
4. How might CAGE analysis help you identify institutional voids?
5. What are three possible choices firms have when they're considering entering a foreign market with large institutional voids?

[1] Pankaj Ghemawat, "Distance Still Matters," Harvard Business Review 79, no. 8 (September 2001): 1–11.
[2] Pankaj Ghemawat, "The Forgotten Strategy," Harvard Business Review 81, no. 11 (September 2003).
[3] Pankaj Ghemawat, "Distance Still Matters," Harvard Business Review 79, no. 8 (September 2001): 1–11.
[4] "McDonald's in Russia: Accept or Attempt to Change Market Context?," Economic Times of India, April 30, 2010, accessed February 17, 2011, http://economictimes.indiatimes.com/features/corporate-dossier/McDonalds-in-Russia-Accept-or-attempt-to-change-market-context/articleshow/5874306.cms; Tarun Khanna and Krishna G. Palepu, Winning in Emerging Markets: A Road Map for Strategy (Cambridge, MA: Harvard Business School Press, 2010).
[5] Tarun Khanna, Krishna G. Palepu, and Jayant Sinha, "Strategies That Fit Emerging Markets," Harvard Business Review 83, no. 6 (June 2005): 2–16.
[6] Tarun Khanna, Krishna G. Palepu, and Jayant Sinha, "Strategies That Fit Emerging Markets," Harvard Business Review 83, no. 6 (June 2005): 2–16.
[7] Michael E. Porter and Mark R. Kramer, "The Big Idea: Creating Shared Value," Harvard Business Review, January–February 2011, accessed January 23, 2011, http://hbr.org/2011/01/the-big-idea-creating-shared-value/ar/pr.

8.5 Scenario Planning and Analysis

LEARNING OBJECTIVES

1. Understand the history and role of scenario planning and analysis.
2. Know the six steps of scenario planning and analysis.
3. Be able to map scenarios in a two-by-two matrix.

The History and Role of Scenario Planning and Analysis

Strategic leaders use the information revealed by the application of PESTEL analysis, global dimensions, and CAGE analysis to uncover what the traditional SWOT framework calls *opportunities* and *threats*. ASWOT (strengths, weaknesses, opportunities, and threats) assessment is a strategic-management tool that helps you take stock of an organization's internal characteristics, or its strengths and weaknesses, such that any action plan builds on what it does well while overcoming or working around weaknesses; the SWOT assessment also helps a company assess external environmental conditions, or opportunities and threats, that favor or threaten an organization's strategy. In particular, you can use it to evaluate the implications of your industry analysis, both for your focal firm specifically and for the industry in general. However, a SWOT assessment works best with one situation or scenario and provides little direction when you're uncertain about potential changes to critical features of the scenario. Scenario planning can help in these cases.

Scenario Planning

Scenario planning helps leaders develop a detailed, internally consistent picture of a range of plausible outcomes as an industry evolves over time. You can also incorporate the results of scenario planning into your strategy formulation and implementation. Understanding the PESTEL conditions—as well as the level, pace, and drivers of industry globalization and the CAGE framework—will probably equip you with some insight into the outcomes of certain scenarios. The purpose of scenario planning, however, is to provide a bigger picture—one in which you can see specific trends and uncertainties. Developed in the 1950s at the global petroleum giant Shell, the technique is now regarded as a valuable tool for integrating changes and uncertainties in the external context into overall strategy. [1] Since September 11, 2001, the use of scenario planning has increased in businesses. Analysis of Bain & Company's *Management Tools and Trends Survey* shows that in the post-9/11 period, approximately 70 percent of 8,500 global executives reported that their firms used scenarios, in contrast to a usage rate of less than 50 percent in most of the 1990s. [2] In addition, scenarios ranked fifteenth in satisfaction levels among the twenty-five management tools that Bain examined in 1993, while it ranked eighth in 2006. [3]

Unlike forecasts, scenarios are not straight-line, one-factor projections from present to future. Rather, they are complex, dynamic, interactive stories told from a future perspective. To develop useful scenarios, executives need a rich understanding of their industry along with broad knowledge of the diverse PESTEL and global conditions that are most likely to affect them. The six basic steps in scenario planning are detailed below.

Six Basic Steps of Scenario Planning

- **Step 1.** Choose the target issue, scope and time frame that the scenario will explore. The scope will depend on your level of analysis (i.e., industry, subindustry, or strategic group), the stage of planning, and the nature and degree of uncertainty and the rate of change. Generally, four scenarios are developed and summarized in a grid. The four scenarios reflect the extremes of possible worlds. To fully capture critical possibilities and contingencies, it may be desirable to develop a series of scenario sets.

- **Step 2.** Brainstorm a set of key drivers and decision factors that influence the scenario. This could include social unrest, shifts in power, regulatory change, market or competitive change, and technology or infrastructure change. Other significant changes in external contexts, like natural disasters, might also be considered.

- **Step 3.** Define the two dimensions of greatest uncertainty. (For an example, see Table 8.4 "Developing Scenarios for the Global Credit-Union Industry".) These two dimensions form the axes of the scenario framework. These axes should represent two dimensions that provide the greatest uncertainty for the industry. For instance, the example on the global credit-union industry identifies changes in the playing field and technology as the two greatest areas of uncertainty up through the year 2005.

- **Step 4.** Detail the four quadrants of the scenarios with stories. Describe how the four worlds would look in each scenario. It's often useful to develop a catchy name for each world as a way to further develop its distinctive character. One of the worlds will likely represent a slightly future version of the status quo, while the others will be significant departures from it. As shown in the credit-union scenarios, *Chameleon* describes a world in which both the competitive playing field and technology undergo radical change, while *Wallet Wars* is an environment of intense competition but milder technological change. In contrast, in *Technocracy*, the radical changes are in technology, whereas in *Credit Union Power*, credit unions encounter only minor changes on either front. [4]

- **Step 5.** Identify indicators that could signal which scenario is unfolding. These can either be trigger points that signal the change is taking place or milestones that mean the change is more likely. An indicator may be a large industry supplier like Microsoft picking up a particular but little-known technological standard.

- **Step 6.** Assess the strategic implications of each scenario. Microscenarios may be developed to highlight and address business-unit-specific or industry-segment-specific issues. Consider needed variations in strategies, key success factors, and the development of a flexible, robust strategy that might work across several scenarios.

The process of developing scenarios and then conducting business according to the information that the scenarios reveal makes it easier to identify and challenge questionable assumptions. It also exposes areas of vulnerability (e.g., in a country, an industry, or a company), underscores the interplay of environmental factors and the impact of change, allows for robust planning and contingency preparation, and makes it possible to test and compare strategic options. Scenarios also help firms focus their attention on the trends and uncertainties that are likely to have the greatest potential impact on their future.

Once you've determined your target issue, scope, and time frame, you can draw up a list of driving forces that is as complete as possible and is organized into relevant categories (e.g., science-technology, political-economic, regulatory, consumer-social, or industry-market). As you proceed, be sure to identify *key* driving forces—the ones with the greatest potential to affect the industry, subindustry, or strategic group in which you're interested.

Trends and Uncertainties

Among the driving forces for change, be sure to distinguish between *trends* and *uncertainties*. Trends are forces for change whose direction—and sometimes timing—can be predicted. For example, experts can be reasonably confident in projecting the number of consumers in North America, Europe, and Japan who will be over sixty-five years old in the year 2020 because those people are alive now. If your firm targets these consumers, then the impact of this population growth will be significant to you; you may view it as a key trend. For other trends, you may know the direction but not the pace. China and India, for example, are experiencing a trend of economic growth, and many foreign investments depend on the course of infrastructure development and consumer-spending power in this enormous market. Unfortunately, the future pace of these changes is uncertain.

Did You Know?

In his book *Africa Rising*, Vijay Mahajan documents how trends surrounding the 900 million African consumers may offer businesses more opportunities than they're currently taking advantage of:

Many tourists come to Africa every year to see the big game there—the elephants, lions, and rhinos. But I came for a different type of big game. I was seeking out the successful enterprises that are identifying and capitalizing on the market opportunities, and seeking lessons from those that are not so successful, too. In Nairobi, Maserame Mouyeme of The Coca-Cola Company told me how important it is 'to walk the market.' Then, in Harare, I first heard the term 'consumer safari' in a meeting with Unilever executives. This is what

they call their initiatives to spend a day with consumers in their homes to understand how they use products. Years after I started on this journey, I now had a term to describe the quest I was on. I was on a consumer safari. The market landscape that is Africa is every bit as marvelous and surprising as its geographic landscape. It presents as big an opportunity as China and India. [5]

In contrast, uncertainties—forces for change whose direction and pace are largely unknown—are more important for your scenario. European consumers, for example, tend to distrust the biotechnology industry, and given the number of competing forces at work—industries, academia, consumer groups, regulators, and so on—it is difficult to predict whether the consumers will be more or less receptive to biotechnology products in the future. Labeling regulations, for instance, may be either strengthened or relaxed in response to changing consumer opinion.

You might also want to consider the possibility of significant disruptions—that is, steep changes that have an important and unalterable impact on the business environment. A major disaster—such as the September 11 terrorist attacks—can spur regulatory and other legal reforms with major and lasting impact on certain technologies and competitive practices. Table 8.4 "Developing Scenarios for the Global Credit-Union Industry" provides sample scenarios created for the credit-union industry, providing an idea of how you would do this if asked to apply scenario analysis to another industry setting. As you can see, identifying the entry of new competitors and the impact of technology are the two primary sources of uncertainty about the future.

KEY TAKEAWAYS

- Scenario planning was developed in the 1950s by Shell as a tool for integrating changes and uncertainties in the external context into overall strategy. Today it ranks among the top ten management tools in the world in terms of usage. Scenarios are complex, dynamic, interactive stories told from a future perspective. To develop useful scenarios, you need a rich understanding of your industry along with broad knowledge of the diverse PESTEL and global conditions that are most likely to affect them.
- The six steps in formulating a scenario plan are the following: (1) choose the target issue, scope, and time frame that the scenario will explore; (2) brainstorm a set of key drivers and decision factors that influence the scenario; (3) define the two dimensions of greatest uncertainty; (4) detail the four quadrants of the scenarios

with stories about that future; (5) identify indicators that could signal which scenario is unfolding; and (6) assess the strategic implications of each scenario.

- Considering the distillation of issues and drivers, select two dimensions of change that will serve as the two dimensions of your scenario-planning matrix. You must be able to describe the dimensions as high and low at each extreme.

EXERCISES

(AACSB: Reflective Thinking, Analytical Skills)

1. What is scenario planning and analysis?
2. What is the history of scenario planning and analysis?
3. What is the advantage of scenario planning and analysis over SWOT analysis?
4. What are the six steps involved in scenario planning and analysis?
5. What is the difference between uncertainties and trends in scenario planning and analysis?

[1] Paul J. H. Schoemaker, "When and How to Use Scenario Planning: A Heuristic Approach with Illustration," Journal of Forecasting 10, no. 6 (November 1991): 549–64; Paul J. H. Schoemaker and Cornelius A. J. M. van der Heijden, "Integrating Scenarios into Strategic Planning at Royal Dutch/Shell," Planning Review 20, no. 3 (1992): 41–46; Paul J. H. Schoemaker, "Multiple Scenario Development: Its Conceptual and Behavioral Foundation," Strategic Management Journal 14, no. 3 (March 1993): 193–213.
[2] Darrell Rigby and Barbara Bilodeau, "A Growing Focus on Preparedness," Harvard Business Review 85 (July–August 2007).
[3] Darrell Rigby and Barbara Bilodeau, "A Growing Focus on Preparedness," Harvard Business Review 85 (July–August 2007): 21–22.
[4] Adapted from "Scenarios for Credit Unions 2010: An Executive Report," Credit Union Executives Society, 2004, accessed May 10, 2011, http://www.dsicu.com/pdfs/2010_Scenarios.pdf.
[5] Vijay Mahajan, Africa Rising: How 900 Million African Consumers Offer More Than You Think (Upper Saddle River, NJ: Pearson Prentice Hall, 2008), xii.

8.6 End-of-Chapter Questions and Exercises

These exercises are designed to ensure that the knowledge you gain from this book about international business meets the learning standards set out by the international Association to Advance Collegiate Schools of Business (AACSB International). [1] AACSB is the premier accrediting agency of collegiate business schools and accounting programs worldwide. It expects that you will gain knowledge in the areas of communication, ethical reasoning, analytical skills, use of information technology, multiculturalism and diversity, and reflective thinking.

EXPERIENTIAL EXERCISES

(AACSB: Communication, Use of Information Technology, Analytical Skills)

1. Identify a local company whose products or services you really admire. Conduct an assessment of why, where, and how this company might expand internationally. In class, talk through the pros and cons of what you've recommended.
2. Using the same company from the first exercise, undertake PESTEL, globalization, and scenario analyses of the new international target market. What are the implications of your analyses for the recommendations you compiled? What resources did you draw on and what key questions remain unanswered?
3. Kohl's Corporation is a very large and successful US retailer. It has no physical or Internet retail outlets outside the United States. What opportunities might this company have for global expansion? What modes should it explore? Should Kohl's stay "local"?

Ethical Dilemmas

(AACSB: Ethical Reasoning, Multiculturalism, Reflective Thinking, Analytical Skills)

1. Entry into new markets, regardless of entry mode, typically requires extensive relationship building. In some countries, such relationship building includes the exchange of gifts. At the same time, many companies are bound by laws, regulations, or business associations that prohibit bribery. Bribery is an offer or the receipt of any gift, loan, fee, reward, or other advantage to or from any person as an inducement to do something that is dishonest or illegal. [2] Review the most recent International Chamber of Commerce Commission report on corruption, "ICC Rules of Conduct and Recommendations for Combating Extortion and Bribery" (available at http://www.iccwbo.org/policy/anticorruption/id870/index.html). It discusses what the implications of these rules might be for gifts.
2. For each of the entry modes identified in this chapter, develop a list of the key areas of ethical lapses. Draft a policy statement that a firm can use to manage and prevent these lapses.
3. Using the Internet or your library, conduct a search on the topics of "infant formula" or "disposable diapers" and "emerging economies." What are some of the ethical issues that are raised when discussing the export of these products to emerging markets?

[1] Association to Advance Collegiate Schools of Business website, accessed January 26, 2010, http://www.aacsb.edu.

[2] Hossein Askari, Scheherazade Sabina Rehman, and Noora
Arfaa, Corruption and Its Manifestation in the Persian Gulf (Northampton,
MA: Edward Elgar Publishing, 2010), 9.

NOTES:

NOTES:

Chapter 9:
Exporting, Importing, and Global Sourcing

WHAT'S IN IT FOR ME?

1. What are importing and exporting?
2. What is countertrade?
3. What is global sourcing?
4. How do companies manage importing and exporting?
5. What options do companies have to finance their importing and exporting?

A major part of international business is, of course, importing and exporting. An increase in the level of exports and imports is, after all, one of the symptoms of a flattening world. In a flat world, goods and services can flow fluidly from one part of the globe to another. In Section 9.1, "What is Importing and Exporting?" you'll take a quick look back in time to see importing and exporting in their historical context. Then, you'll discover the reasons why companies export, as well as the pitfalls and risks associated with exporting. Next, you'll venture into more specialized modes of entry into an international market, moving progressively from the least expensive to the most expensive options.

Section 9.2 "Countertrade" focuses on what countertrade is and why companies engage in it. You'll learn about countertrade structures, such as barter and counter purchase, and the role they play in the modern economy.

In Section 9.3 "Global Sourcing and Its Role in Business", you'll explore global sourcing and study the best practices to manage sourcing, to judge quality from afar, and to improve sustainability through well-planned sourcing that's beneficial to the environment. You'll understand what outsourcing is, why companies outsource, and what the hidden costs of outsourcing are. Some of these costs are related to the fact that the world is not all that flat! You'll see tips for managing outsourced services and look at the opportunities that outsourcing offers entrepreneurs.

Section 9.4 "Managing Export and Import" reviews the mechanics of import and export—from the main players involved, to the intermediaries, to the important documentation needed for import and export transactions.

Section 9.5 "What Options Do Companies Have for Export and Import Financing?" concludes the chapter with a look at the options companies have for financing their import/export activities.

OPENING CASE: Q-CELLS

Q-Cells exemplifies the successes and challenges of global importing and exporting. Founded in Germany in 1999, the company became the largest manufacturer of solar cells worldwide. [1] By 2010, however, it was experiencing losses due, in part, to mistiming some of the entry strategies that are covered in Section 9.1 "What is Importing and Exporting?"

First, it's important to know that Germany is a high-cost manufacturing country compared to China or Southeast Asia. On the other hand, Germany is known for its engineering prowess. Q-Cells gambled that customers would be willing to pay a premium for German-made solar panels. The trouble was that solar cells aren't that sophisticated or complex to manufacture, and Asian competitors were able to provide reliable products at 30 percent less cost than Q-Cells.

The Cost Advantage

Q-Cells recognized the Asian cost advantage—not only are labor and utility costs lower in Asia, but so are the selling, general, and administrative (SG&A) costs. What's more, governments like China provide significant tax breaks to attract solar companies to their countries. So, Q-Cells opened a manufacturing plant in Malaysia. Once the Malaysian plant is fully ramped up, the costs to manufacture solar cells there will be 30 percent less than at the Q-Cells plant in Germany.

Then, Q-Cells entered into a joint venture with China-based LDK, in which Q-Cells used LDK silicon wafers to make its solar cells. The two companies also used each other's respective expertise to market their products in China and Europe. [2] Although the joint venture gave Q-Cells local knowledge of the Chinese market, it also locked Q-Cells into buying wafers from LDK. These wafers were priced higher than those Q-Cells could source on the spot market. As a result, Q-Cells was paying about 20 cents more for its wafers than competitors were paying. Thus, in the short term, the joint venture hurt Q-Cells. However, the company was able to renegotiate the price it would pay for LDK wafers.

To stay cost competitive, Q-Cells has decided to outsource its solar-panel production to contract manufacturer Flextronics International. Q-Cells' competitors, SunPower Corp. and BP's solar unit, also have outsourced production to contract manufacturers. The outsourcing has not only saved manufacturing costs but also brought the products physically closer to the Asian market where the greatest demand is currently. This has reduced the costs of shipping, breakage, and inventory carrying. [3]

OPENING CASE EXERCISES

(AACSB: Ethical Reasoning, Multiculturalism, Reflective Thinking, Analytical Skills)

1. Do you think Q-Cells could have avoided its current financial troubles? What could they have done differently?
2. Do you see import or export opportunities for entrepreneurs or small businesses in the solar industry? What advice would you give them?

[1] LDK Solar, "Q-Cells and LDK Solar Announce Formation of Joint Venture for Development of PV Systems in Europe and China," news release, April 8, 2009, accessed October 27, 2010, http://www.ldksolar.com/med_press_list.php?news_id=100.
[2] Richard A. Kessler, "Q-Cells, China's LDK Solar Form Joint Venture for Export Push," Recharge, April 8, 2009, accessed September 9, 2010, http://www.rechargenews.com/regions/north_america/article175506.ece?print=true.
[3] Leonora Walet, "Sun Shines Through for Clean Tech Outsourcing," Reuters, May 3, 2010, accessed September 9, 2010, http://www.reuters.com/article/idUSTRE6421KL20100503.

9.1 What is Importing and Exporting?
LEARNING OBJECTIVES

1. Understand what importing and exporting are.
2. Learn why companies export.
3. Explain the main contractual and investment entry modes.

What Do We Mean by Exporting and Importing?

The history of importing and exporting dates back to the Roman Empire, when European and Asian traders imported and exported goods across the vast lands of Eurasia. Trading along the Silk Road flourished during the thirteenth and fourteenth centuries. [1] Caravans laden with imports from China and India came over the desert to Constantinople and Alexandria. From there, Italian ships transported the goods to European ports. [2]

For centuries, importing and exporting has often involved intermediaries, due in part to the long distances traveled and different native languages spoken. The spice trade of the

1400s was no exception. Spices were very much in demand because Europeans had no refrigeration, which meant they had to preserve meat using large amounts of salt or risk eating half-rotten flesh. Spices disguised the otherwise poor flavor of the meat. Europeans also used spices as medicines. The European demand for spices gave rise to the spice trade. [3] The trouble was that spices were difficult to obtain because they grew in jungles half a world away from Europe. The overland journey to the spice-rich lands was arduous and involved many middlemen along the way. Each middleman charged a fee and thus raised the price of the spice at each point. By the end of the journey, the price of the spice was inflated 1,000 percent. [4]

As explained in Chapter 8 "International Expansion and Global Market Opportunity Assessment", exporting is defined as the sale of products and services in foreign countries that are sourced or made in the home country. Importing is the flipside of exporting. Importing refers to buying goods and services from foreign sources and bringing them back into the home country. Importing is also known as global sourcing, which will be examined in depth in Section 9.4 "Managing Export and Import".

An Entrepreneur's Import Success Story

Selena Cuffe started her wine import company, Heritage Link Brands, in 2005. Importing wine isn't new, but Cuffe did it with a twist: she focused on importing wine produced by black South Africans. Cuffe got the idea after attending a wine festival in Soweto, where she saw more than five hundred wines from eighty-six producers showcased. [5] Cuffe did some market research and learned of the $3 billion wine industry in Africa. She also saw a gap in the existing market related to wine produced by indigenous African vintners and decided to fill it. She started her company with $70,000, financed through her savings and credit cards. (In Section 9.5 "What Options Do Companies Have for Export and Import Financing?" you'll learn about other sources of financing available to entrepreneurs and small businesses as well as to larger enterprises.) In the first year, sales were only $100,000 but then jumped to $1 million in the second year, when Cuffe sold to more than one thousand restaurants, retailers, and grocery stores. [6] Even better, American Airlines began carrying Cuffe's imported wines on flights, thus providing a steady flow of business amid the more uncertain restaurant market. [7] Cuffe has attributed her success to passion as well as to patience for meeting the multiple regulations required when running an import business. [8] (You'll learn more about these regulations in Section 9.4 "Managing Export and Import").

Exporting is an effective entry strategy for companies that are just beginning to enter a new foreign market. It's a low-cost, low-risk option compared to the other strategies. These same reasons make exporting a good strategy for small and midsize companies that can't or won't make significant financial investment in the international market.

Companies can sell into a foreign country either through a local distributor or through their own salespeople. Many government export-trade offices can help a company find a local distributor. Increasingly, the Internet has provided a more efficient way for foreign companies to find local distributors and enter into commercial transactions.

Distributors are export intermediaries who represent the company in the foreign market. Often, distributors represent many companies, acting as the "face" of the company in that country, selling products, providing customer service, and receiving payments. In many cases, the distributors take title to the goods and then resell them. Companies use distributors because distributors know the local market and are a cost-effective way to enter that market.

However, using distributors to help with export can have its own challenges. For example, some companies find that if they have a dedicated salesperson who travels frequently to the country, they're likely to get more sales than by relying solely on the distributor. Often, that's because distributors sell multiple products and sometimes even competing ones. Making sure that the distributor favors one firm's product over another product can be hard to monitor. In countries like China, some companies find that—culturally—Chinese consumers may be more likely to buy a product from a foreign company than from a local distributor, particularly in the case of a complicated, high-tech product. Simply put, the Chinese are more likely to trust that the overseas salesperson knows their product better.

Why Do Companies Export?

Companies export because it's the easiest way to participate in global trade, it's a less costly investment than the other entry strategies, and it's much easier to simply stop exporting than it is to extricate oneself from the other entry modes. An export partner in the form of either a distributor or an export management company can facilitate this process. An export management company (EMC) is an independent company that performs the duties that a firm's own export department would execute. The EMC handles the necessary documentation, finds buyers for the export, and takes title of the goods for direct export. In return, the EMC charges a fee or commission for its services. Because an EMC performs all the functions that a firm's export department would, the firm doesn't have to develop these internal capabilities. Most of all, exporting gives a company quick access to new markets.

Benefits of Exporting: Vitrac

Egyptian company Vitrac was founded by Mounir Fakhry Abdel Nour to take advantage of Egypt's surplus fruit products. At its inception, Vitrac sourced local fruit, made it into jam, and exported it worldwide. Vitrac has acquired money, market, and manufacturing advantages from exporting: [9]

- **Market.** The company has access to a new market, which has brought added revenues.
- **Money.** Not only has Vitrac earned more revenue, but it has also gained access to foreign currency, which benefits companies located in certain regions of the world, such as in Vitrac's home country of Egypt.
- **Manufacturing.** The cost to manufacture a given unit decreased because Vitrac has been able to manufacture at higher volumes and buy source materials in higher volumes, thus benefitting from volume discounts.

Risks of Exporting

There are risks in relying on the export option. If you merely export to a country, the distributor or buyer might switch to or at least threaten to switch to a cheaper supplier in order to get a better price. Or someone might start making the product locally and take the market from you. Also, local buyers sometimes believe that a company which only exports to them isn't very committed to providing long-term service and support once a sale is complete. Thus, they may prefer to buy from someone who's producing directly within the country. At this point, many companies begin to reconsider having a local presence, which moves them toward one of the other entry options.

Ethics in Action

Different Countries, Different Food and Drug Rules
Particular products, especially foods and drugs, are often subject to local laws regarding safety, purity, packaging, labeling, and so on. Companies that want to make a product that can be sold in multiple countries will have to comply with the highest common denominator of all the laws of all the target markets. Complying with the highest standard could increase the overall cost of the product. As a result, some companies opt to stay out of markets where compliance with the regulation would be more costly. Is it ethical to be selling a product in one country that another country deems substandard?

Specialized Entry Modes: Contractual

Exporting is an easy way to enter an international market. In addition to exporting, companies can choose to pursue more specialized modes of entry—namely, contractual modes or investment modes. Contractual modes involve the use of contracts rather than investment. Let's look at the two main contractual entry modes, licensing and franchising.

Licensing

Licensing is defined as the granting of permission by the licenser to the licensee to use intellectual property rights, such as trademarks, patents, brand names, or technology, under defined conditions. The possibility of licensing makes for a flatter world, because it creates a legal vehicle for taking a product or service delivered in one country and providing a nearly identical version of that product or service in another country. Under a licensing agreement, the multinational firm grants rights on its intangible property to a foreign company for a specified period of time. The licenser is normally paid a royalty on each unit produced and sold. Although the multinational firm usually has no ownership interests, it often provides ongoing support and advice. Most companies consider this market-entry option of licensing to be a low-risk option because there's typically no up-front investment.

For a multinational firm, the advantage of licensing is that the company's products will be manufactured and made available for sale in the foreign country (or countries) where the product or service is licensed. The multinational firm doesn't have to expend its own resources to manufacture, market, or distribute the goods. This low cost, of course, is coupled with lower potential returns, because the revenues are shared between the parties.

Franchising

Similar to a licensing agreement, under a franchising agreement, the multinational firm grants rights on its intangible property, like technology or a brand name, to a foreign company for a specified period of time and receives a royalty in return. The difference is that the franchiser provides a bundle of services and products to the franchisee. For example, McDonald's expands overseas through franchises. Each franchise pays McDonald's a franchisee fee and a percentage of its sales and is required to purchase certain products from the franchiser. In return, the franchisee gets access to all of McDonald's products, systems, services, and management expertise.

Specialized Entry Modes: Investment

Beyond contractual relationships, firms can also enter a foreign market through one of two investment strategies: a joint venture or a wholly owned subsidiary.

Joint Ventures

An equity joint venture is a contractual, strategic partnership between two or more separate business entities to pursue a business opportunity together. The partners in an equity joint venture each contribute capital and resources in exchange for an equity stake and share in any resulting profits. (In a nonentity joint venture, there is no contribution of capital to form a new entity.)

To see how an equity joint venture works, let's return to the example of Egyptian company, Vitrac. Mounir Fakhry Abdel Nour founded his jam company to take advantage of Egypt's surplus fruit products. Abdel Nour initially approached the French jam company, Vitrac, to enter into a joint venture with his newly founded company, VitracEgypt. Abdel Nour supplied the fruit and the markets, while his French partner supplied the technology and know-how for producing jams.

In addition to exporting to Australia, the United States, and the Middle East, Vitrac began exporting to Japan. Sales results from Japan indicated a high demand for blueberry jam. To meet this demand—in an interesting twist, given Vitrac's origin—Vitrac had to import blueberries from Canada. Vitrac thus was importing blueberries from Canada, manufacturing the jam in Egypt, and exporting it to Japan. [10]

Using French Vitrac's manufacturing know-how, Abdel Nour had found a new supply and the opportunity to enter new markets with it, thus expanding his partner's reach. The partnership fit was good. The two companies' joint venture continued for three years, until the French company sold its shares to Abdel Nour, making Vitrac a 100 percent owned and operated Egyptian company. Abdel Nour's company reached $22 million in sales and was the Egyptian jam-market leader before being bought by a larger Swiss company, Hero. [11]

Risks of Joint Ventures

Equity joint ventures pose both opportunities and challenges for the companies involved. First and foremost is the challenge of finding the right partner—not just in terms of business focus but also in terms of compatible cultural perspectives and management practices.

Second, the local partner may gain the know-how to produce its own competitive product or service to rival the multinational firm. This is what's currently happening in China. To manufacture cars in China, non-Chinese companies must set up joint ventures with Chinese automakers and share technology with them. Once the contract ends, however, the local company may take the knowledge it gained from the joint venture to compete with its former partner. For example, Shanghai Automotive Industry (Group) Corporation, which worked with General Motors (GM) to build Chevrolets, has plans to increase sales of its own vehicles tenfold to 300,000 in five years and to compete directly with its former partner. [12]

Did You Know?

In the past, joint ventures were the only relationship foreign companies could form with Chinese companies. In fact, prior to 1986, foreign companies could not wholly own a local subsidiary. The Chinese government began to allow equity joint ventures in 1979, which marked the beginning of the Open Door Policy, an economic liberalization initiative. The Chinese government strongly encouraged equity joint ventures as a way to gain access to the technology, capital, equipment, and know-how of foreign companies. The risk to the foreign company was that if the venture soured, the Chinese company could end up keeping all of these assets. Often, Chinese companies only contributed things like land or tax concessions that foreign companies couldn't keep if the venture ended. As of 2010, equity joint ventures between a Chinese company and a foreign partner require a minimum equity investment by the foreign partner of at least 33 to 70 percent of the equity, but there's no minimum investment set for the Chinese partner. [13]

Wholly Owned Subsidiaries

Firms may want to have a direct operating presence in the foreign country, completely under their control. To achieve this, the company can establish a new, wholly owned subsidiary (i.e., a greenfield venture) from scratch, or it can purchase an existing company in that country. Some companies purchase their resellers or early partners (as VitracEgypt did when it bought out the shares that its partner, Vitrac, owned in the equity joint venture). Other companies may purchase a local supplier for direct control of the supply. This is known as vertical integration.

Establishing or purchasing a wholly owned subsidiary requires the highest commitment on the part of the international firm, because the firm must assume all of the risk—financial, currency, economic, and political.

Did You Know?

McDonald's has a plant in Italy that supplies all the buns for McDonald's restaurants in Italy, Greece, and Malta. International sales has accounted for as much as 60 percent of McDonald's annual revenue. [14]

Cautions When Purchasing an Existing Foreign Enterprise

As we've seen, some companies opt to purchase an existing company in the foreign country outright as a way to get into a foreign market quickly. When making an acquisition, due diligence is important—not only on the financial side but also on the side of the country's culture and business practices. The annual disposable income in Russia, for example, exceeds that of all the other BRIC countries (i.e., Brazil, India, and China). For many major companies, Russia is too big and too rich to ignore as a market. However, Russia also has a reputation for corruption and red tape that even its highest-ranking officials admit. Presidential economic advisor Arkady Dvorkovich (whose office in the Kremlin was once occupied by Soviet leader Leonid Brezhnev), for example, advises, "Investors should choose wisely" which regions of Russia they locate their business in, warning that some areas are more corrupt than others. [15]Corruption makes the world less flat precisely because it undermines the viability of legal vehicles, such as licensing, which otherwise lead to a flatter world.

The culture of corruption is even embedded into some Russian company structures. In the 1990s, laws inadvertently encouraged Russian firms to establish legal headquarters in offshore tax havens, like Cyprus. A tax haven is a country that has very advantageous (low) corporate income taxes.

Businesses registered in these offshore tax havens to avoid certain Russian taxes. Even though companies could obtain a refund on these taxes from the Russian government, "the procedure is so complicated you never actually get a refund," said Andrey Pozdnyakov, cofounder of Siberian-based Elecard. [16]

This offshore registration, unfortunately, is a danger sign to potential investors like Intel. "We can't invest in companies that have even a slight shadow," said Intel's Moscow-based regional director Dmitry Konash about the complex structure predicament. [17]

Did You Know?

Some foreign companies believe that owning their own operations in China is an easier option than having to deal with a Chinese partner. For example, many foreign companies still fear that their Chinese partners will learn too much from them and become competitors. However, in most cases, the Chinese partner knows the local culture—both that of the customers and workers—and is better equipped to deal with Chinese bureaucracy and regulations. In addition, even wholly owned subsidiaries can't be totally independent of Chinese firms, on whom they might have to rely for raw materials and shipping as well as maintenance of government contracts and distribution channels.

Collaborations offer different kinds of opportunities and challenges than self-handling Chinese operations. For most companies, the local nuances of the Chinese market make some form of collaboration desirable. The companies that opt to self-handle their Chinese operations tend to be very large and/or have a proprietary technology base, such as high tech or aerospace companies—for example, Boeing or Microsoft. Even then, these companies tend to hire senior Chinese managers and consultants to facilitate their market entry and then help manage their expansion. Nevertheless, navigating the local Chinese bureaucracy is tough, even for the most-experienced companies.

Let's take a deeper look at one company's entry path and its wholly owned subsidiary in China. Embraer is the largest aircraft maker in Brazil and one of the largest in the world. Embraer chose to enter China as its first foreign market, using the joint-venture entry mode. In 2003, Embraer and the Aviation Industry Corporation of China jointly started the Harbin Embraer Aircraft Industry. A year later, Harbin Embraer began manufacturing aircraft.

In 2010, Embraer announced the opening of its first subsidiary in China. The subsidiary, called Embraer China Aircraft Technical Services Co. Ltd., will provide logistics and spare-parts sales, as well as consulting services regarding technical issues and flight operations, for Embraer aircraft in China (both for existing aircraft and those on order). Embraer will invest $18 million into the subsidiary with a goal of strengthening its local customer support, given the steady growth of its business in China.

Guan Dongyuan, president of Embraer China and CEO of the subsidiary, said the establishment of Embraer China Aircraft Technical Services demonstrates the company's "long-term commitment and confidence in the growing Chinese aviation market." [18]

Building Long-Term Relationships
Developing a good relationship with regulators in target countries helps with the long-term entry strategy. Building these relationships may include keeping people in the countries long enough to form good ties, since a deal negotiated with one person may fall apart if that person returns too quickly to headquarters.

Did You Know?
One of the most important cultural factors in China is *guanxi* (pronounced *guan shi*), which is loosely defined as a connection based on reciprocity. Even when just meeting a new company or potential partner, it's best to have an introduction from a common business partner, vendor, or supplier—someone the Chinese will respect. China is a relationship-based society. Relationships extend well beyond the personal side and can drive business as well. With guanxi, a person invests with relationships much like one would invest with capital. In a sense, it's akin to the Western phrase "You owe me one."

Guanxi can potentially be beneficial or harmful. At its best, it can help foster strong, harmonious relationships with corporate and government contacts. At its worst, it can encourage bribery and corruption. Whatever the case, companies without guanxi won't accomplish much in the Chinese market. Many companies address this need by entering into the Chinese market in a collaborative arrangement with a local Chinese company. This entry option has also been a useful way to circumvent regulations governing bribery and corruption, but it can raise ethical questions, particularly for American and Western companies that have a different cultural perspective on gift giving and bribery.

Conclusion
In summary, when deciding which mode of entry to choose, companies should ask themselves two key questions:
1. How much of our resources are we willing to commit? The fewer the resources (i.e., money, time, and expertise) the company wants (or can afford) to devote, the better it is for the company to enter the foreign market on a contractual basis—through licensing, franchising, management contracts, or turnkey projects.
2. How much control do we wish to retain? The more control a company wants, the better off it is establishing or buying a wholly owned subsidiary or, at least, entering via a joint venture with carefully delineated responsibilities and accountabilities between the partner companies.

Regardless of which entry strategy a company chooses, several factors are always important.

- **Cultural and linguistic differences.** These affect all relationships and interactions inside the company, with customers, and with the government. Understanding the local business culture is critical to success.
- **Quality and training of local contacts and/or employees.** Evaluating skill sets and then determining if the local staff is qualified is a key factor for success.
- **Political and economic issues.** Policy can change frequently, and companies need to determine what level of investment they're willing to make, what's required to make this investment, and how much of their earnings they can repatriate.
- **Experience of the partner company.** Assessing the experience of the partner company in the market—with the product and in dealing with foreign companies—is essential in selecting the right local partner.

Companies seeking to enter a foreign market need to do the following:

- Research the foreign market thoroughly and learn about the country and its culture.
- Understand the unique business and regulatory relationships that impact their industry.
- Use the Internet to identify and communicate with appropriate foreign trade corporations in the country or with their own government's embassy in that country. Each embassy has its own trade and commercial desk. For example, the US Embassy has a foreign commercial desk with officers who assist US companies on how best to enter the local market. These resources are best for smaller companies. Larger companies, with more money and resources, usually hire top consultants to do this for them. They're also able to have a dedicated team assigned to the foreign country that can travel the country frequently for the later-stage entry strategies that involve investment.

Once a company has decided to enter the foreign market, it needs to spend some time learning about the local business culture and how to operate within it.

KEY TAKEAWAYS

- Exporting is the sale of products and services in foreign countries that are sourced or made in the home country. Importing refers to buying goods and services from foreign sources and bringing them back into the home country.

- Companies export because it's the easiest way to participate in global trade, it's a less costly investment than the other entry strategies, and it's much easier to simply stop exporting than it is to extricate oneself from the other entry modes. The benefits of exporting include access to new markets and revenues as well as lower manufacturing costs due to higher manufacturing volumes.
- Contractual forms of entry (i.e., licensing and franchising) have lower up-front costs than investment modes do. It's also easier for the company to extricate itself from the situation if the results aren't favorable. On the other hand, investment modes (joint ventures and wholly owned subsidiaries) may bring the company higher returns and a deeper knowledge of the country.

EXERCISES

(AACSB: Reflective Thinking, Analytical Skills)

1. What are the risks and benefits associated with exporting?
2. Name two contractual modes of entry into a foreign country. Which do you think is better and why?
3. Why would a company choose to use a contractual mode of entry rather than an investment mode?
4. What are the advantages to a company using a joint venture rather than buying or creating its own wholly owned subsidiary when entering a new international market?

[1] Jack Goldstone, Why Europe? The Rise of the West in World History 1500–1850 (New York: McGraw-Hill, 2008).

[2] J. O. Swahn, The Lore of Spices (Gothenburg, Sweden: Nordbok, 1991), 15–17.

[3] Antony Wild, The East India Company: Trade and Conquest from 1600 (Guilford, CT: Lyons Press, 2000).

[4] Jack Turner, Spice: The History of a Temptation (Westminster, MD: Alfred A. Knopf, 2004), 5.

[5] Selena Cuffe's bio, African-American Chamber of Greater Cincinnati / Greater Kentucky, accessed September 4, 2010, http://african-americanchamber.com/view-user-profile/selena-cuffe.html.

[6] South African Chamber of Commerce in America, "Heritage Link Brands, Connecting U.S. Palates to African Wines," profile, May 4, 2010, accessed September 4, 2010, http://www.sacca.biz/?m=5&idkey=637.

[7] American Airlines, "Serving Up Wines That Invest in Our Communities," American Airlines Corporate Responsibility page, accessed September 4, 2010, http://www.aa.com/i18n/aboutUs/corporateResponsibility/caseLibrary/supporting-our-communities.jsp.

[8] Maritza Manresa, How to Open and Operate a Financially Successful Import Export Business (Ocala, FL: Atlantic Publishing, 2010), 101.

[9] Japan External Trade Organization, "Big in Japan," case study, accessed August 27, 2010, http://www.jetro.go.jp/en/reports/.

[10] Japan External Trade Organization, "Big in Japan," case study, accessed August 27, 2010, http://www.jetro.go.jp/en/reports/.

[11] "Egypt/Switzerland: Hero Acquires Egyptian Jam Market Leader," Just-Food, October 8, 2002, accessed September 5,

2010, http://www.just-food.com/news/hero-acquires-egyptian-jam-market-leader_id69297.aspx.

[12] Ian Rowley, "Chinese Carmakers Are Gaining at Home," BusinessWeek, June 8, 2009, 30–31.

[13] Atma Global Knowledge Media, "Entry Models into the Chinese Market," CultureQuest 2003.

[14] Annual revenue in 2008 was $23.5 billion, of which 60 percent was international. See Suzanne Kapner, "Making Dough," Fortune, August 17, 2009, 14.

[15] Carol Matlack, "The Peril and Promise of Investing in Russia," BusinessWeek, October 5, 2009, 48–51.

[16] Carol Matlack, "The Peril and Promise of Investing in Russia," BusinessWeek, October 5, 2009, 48–51.

[17] Carol Matlack, "The Peril and Promise of Investing in Russia," BusinessWeek, October 5, 2009, 48–51.

[18] United Press International, "Brazil's Embraer Expands Aircraft Business into China," July 7, 2010, accessed August 27, 2010, http://www.upi.com/Business_News/2010/07/07/Brazils-Embraer-expands-aircraft-business-into-China/UPI-10511278532701.

9.2 Countertrade

LEARNING OBJECTIVES

1. Understand what countertrade is.
2. Recognize why companies engage in countertrade.
3. Know two structures of countertrade.

What Is Countertrade?

Some countries limit the profits (currency) a company can take out of a country. As a result, many companies resort to countertrade, where companies trade goods and services for other goods and services; actual monies are involved only to a lesser degree, if at all. You can imagine that limitations on transferring profits would make the world less flat; so too would the absence of countertrade opportunities in situations where currency transfer limitations are in place. Countertrade is also a resourceful way for exporters to sell their products and services to foreign companies or countries that would be unable to pay for them using hard currency alone.

All kinds of companies, from food and beverage company PepsiCo to power and automation technologies giant the ABB Group, engage in countertrade. When PepsiCo wanted to enter the Indian market, the government stipulated that part of PepsiCo's local profits had to be used to purchase tomatoes. This requirement worked for PepsiCo, which also owned Pizza Hut and could export the tomatoes for overseas consumption.

This is one example of countertrade, specifically counter purchase. By establishing this requirement, the Indian government was able to help a local agricultural industry, thereby mitigating criticism of letting a foreign beverage company into the country.

Another example in which companies exchanged goods and services rather than paying hard currency is Bharat Heavy Electricals Limited (BHEL), the largest power generation equipment manufacturer in India. BHEL wanted to secure additional overseas orders. To accomplish this, BHEL looked for countertrade opportunities with other state-owned firms. The company entered into a joint effort with an Indian, state-owned mineral-trading company, MMTC Ltd., to import palm oil worth $1 billion from Malaysia, in return for setting up a hydropower project in that nation. Malaysia is the second-largest producer of palm oil in the world. Because India imports an average of 8 million tons of edible oil every year but consumes 15 million tons, importing edible oil is valuable. [1]

Why Do Companies Engage in Countertrade?

One reason that companies engage in this practice is that some governments mandate countertrade on very large-scale (over $1 million) deals or if the deal is in a certain industry. For example, South Korea mandates countertrade for government telecommunications procurement over $1 million. When governments impose counter purchase obligations, firms have no choice but to engage in countertrade if they wish to sell goods into that country.

Countertrade also can mitigate the risk of price movements or currency-exchange-rate fluctuations. Because both sides of a countertrade deal in real goods, not financial instruments, countertrade can solve the inflation risk involved in foreign currency procurement. In effect, countertrade can be a better mechanism than financial instruments as a way to hedge against inflation or currency fluctuations. [2]

Finally, countertrade offers a way for companies to repatriate profits. As you'll see in Chapter 15 "Understanding the Roles of Finance and Accounting in Global Competitive Advantage", some governments restrict how much currency can flow out of their country. (Governments do this to preserve foreign exchange reserves.) Countertrade offers a way for companies to get profits back to the home country via goods rather than money.

Structures in Countertrade

The very first trading—thousands of years ago—was based on barter. Barter is simply the direct exchange of one good for another, with no money involved. Thus, barter predates even the invention of money.

Does barter still take place today? Yes—and not just among two local businesses exchanging something like a haircut for a therapeutic massage. Thanks to new innovations and the

Internet, barter is taking place across international borders. For example, consider the Bartercard. Established in 1991, Bartercard functions like a credit card, but instead of funding the card through cash in a bank account, a company funds the card with its own goods and services. No cash is needed. Over 75,000 trading members in thirteen countries are using the Bartercard, doing $1.3 billion in cashless transactions annually. [3]

In a counter purchase structure, the seller receives cash contingent on the seller buying local products or services in the amount of (or a percentage of) the cash. Simply put, counter purchase occurs when the seller receives cash but contractually agrees to buy local products or services with that cash.

Disadvantages of Countertrade

Countertrade has a tarnished image due to its associations with command economies during the Cold War, when the goods received were often useless or of poor quality but were forced upon companies by command-economy government regulations. New research is showing that countertrade transactions have legitimate economic rationales, but the risk of receiving inferior goods continues. [4] Most countertrade structures, except for barter, make sense only for very large firms that can take a product like palm oil and—in turn—trade it in a useful way. That's why BHEL partnered with MMTC on the Malaysia countertrade deal—because MMTC specializes in bulk commodities. Similarly, PepsiCo was able to make use of the tomatoes it was required to counter purchase because it also operates a pizza business.

KEY TAKEAWAYS

- Countertrade refers to companies that trade goods and services for other goods and services; actual monies are involved only to a lesser degree, if at all. Although countertrade had a tainted reputation during the Cold War days, it's a useful way for exporters to trade with developing countries that may not be able to pay for the goods in hard currency.

- Companies engage in countertrade for three main reasons: (1) to satisfy a foreign-government mandate, (2) to hedge against price and currency fluctuations, and (3) to repatriate profits from countries that limit the amount of currency that can be taken out of the country.

- Barter is a structure of countertrade that has been around for thousands of years and continues today. Counter purchase is a countertrade structure that involves the seller receiving cash contingent on the seller

buying local products or services in the amount of (or a percentage of) the cash.

EXERCISES

(AACSB: Reflective Thinking, Analytical Skills)
1. What are some of the disadvantages of countertrade?
2. Describe an example of how counter purchasing works.
3. Does barter still make sense in the modern world? Who might engage in barter? What advantages might they gain?

[1] Utpal Bhaskar and Asit Ranjan, "Bhel Looking at Counter-Trade Deals to Secure Overseas Orders," Live Mint, May 11, 2010, accessed November 18, 2010, http://www.livemint.com/2010/05/11224356/Bhel-looking-at-countertrade.html.
[2] Sang-Rim Choi and Adrian E. Tschoegl, "Currency Risks, Government Procurement and Counter-Trade: A Note," Applied Financial Economics 13, no. 12 (December 2003): 885–89.
[3] Bartercard website, accessed November 23, 2010, http://bci.bartercard.com.
[4] Peter W. Liesch and Dawn Birch, "Research on Business-to-Business Barter in Australia," in Getting Better at Sensemaking, ed. Arch G. Woodside, Advances in Business Marketing and Purchasing, vol. 9 (Bingley, UK: Emerald Group Publishing, 2001), 353–84.

9.3 Global Sourcing and Its Role in Business
LEARNING OBJECTIVES

1. Identify what global sourcing is.
2. Learn what comprises the best practices in global sourcing.
3. Recognize the difference between outsourcing and global sourcing.

What Is Global Sourcing?

Global sourcing refers to buying the raw materials, components, or services from companies outside the home country. In a flat world, raw materials are sourced from wherever they can be obtained for the cheapest price (including transportation costs) and the highest comparable quality.

Recall the discussion of the spice trade in Section 9.1 "What is Importing and Exporting?" Europeans sourced spices from China and India. The long overland trade routes required many payments to intermediaries and local rulers, raising prices of spices 1,000 percent by the end of the journey. Such a markup naturally spurred Europeans to look for other trade routes and sources of spices. The desire for spices and gold is what ultimately led Christopher Columbus to secure funding for his voyage across the Atlantic Ocean. Even before that, Portuguese ships were sailing down the coast of Africa. In the 1480s, Portuguese ships were returning to Europe laden with African melegueta pepper. This pepper was inferior to the Far Eastern varieties, but it was much cheaper. By 1500, pepper prices dropped by 25 percent due to the new sources of supply. [1]

Today, the pattern of global sourcing continues as a way to obtain commodities and raw materials. But sourcing now is much more expanded; it includes the sourcing of components, of complete manufactured products, and of services as well.

There are many companies that export to a country while sourcing from that same country. For example, Apple sells iPods and iPads to China, and it also manufactures and sources components in China.

Best Practices in Global Sourcing

Given the challenges of global sourcing, large companies often have a staff devoted to overseeing the company's overseas sourcing process and suppliers, managing the relationships, and handling legal, tax and administrative issues.

Judging Quality from Afar: ISO 9000 Certification

How can companies know that the products or services they're sourcing from a foreign country are of good quality? The mark of good quality around the world is ISO 9000 certification. In 1987, the International Organization of Standardization (ISO) developed uniform standards for quality guidelines. Prior to December 2000, three ISO standards were used: ISO 9001, ISO 9002, and ISO 9003. These standards were collectively referred to as ISO 9000. In 2000, the standards were merged into a revised ISO 9001 standard named ISO 9001:2000. In 2008, a new revision was issued, ISO 9001:2008. The standards are voluntary, but companies can demonstrate their compliance with the standard by passing certification. (Companies that had achieved ISO 9001:2000 certification were required to be recertified to meet ISO 9001:2008 standards.) The certification is a mark that the company's products and services have met quality standards and that the company has quality management processes in place. Companies of any size can get certified. To ensure high-quality products, some companies require that their suppliers be certified before they will source products or services from them. ISO 9001:2008 certification is a "seal of quality" that is trusted around the world.

In addition to quality standards, ISO also developed ISO 14000 standards, which focus on the environment. Specifically, ISO 14000 certification shows that the company works to minimize any harmful effects it may have on the environment.

Over the years, companies have learned to manage for quality and consistency.

- Companies can use unannounced inspections to verify that their suppliers meet quality-assurance standards (although this is costly when suppliers are far away).

- For consistency, to avoid disruption in getting goods, Walmart makes sure that no supplier does more than 25 percent of their business with Walmart.

- Companies can evaluate supplier performance. Cost isn't everything. Many companies use scorecards to evaluate suppliers from whom they source components. Cost is part of the scorecard, of course, but often it represents only part of the evaluation, not all of it. Instead, companies look at issues such as supply continuity, as well as whether the relationship is based on openness and trust.

Trends in Sourcing: Considering Carbon Costs

One of the rising concerns about global sourcing is that of the carbon footprint of goods traveling long distances. A carbon footprint is a measure of the impact that activities like transportation and manufacturing have on the environment, especially on climate change. (The "footprint" is the impact, and "carbon" is shorthand for all the different greenhouse gases that contribute to global warming. [2]) Everyone's daily activities, such as using electricity or driving, have a carbon footprint because of the greenhouse gases produced by burning fossil fuels for electricity, heating, transportation, and so on. The higher the carbon footprint, the worse the activity is for the environment.

In global sourcing, although transporting goods by air and truck has a high carbon footprint due to the fossil fuels burned, ocean transport doesn't. Also, the carbon-footprint measure doesn't just focus on distance; it looks at all the fossil fuels used in the manufacture of an item. For example, when one looks at the total picture of how much energy is required to make a product, the carbon footprint of transportation may be less than the carbon footprint of the manufacturing process. Some regions have natural advantages. For example, it is more environmentally friendly to smelt aluminum in Iceland than locally because of the tremendous amount of electricity required for smelting. Iceland has abundant geothermal energy, which has no carbon footprint compared to generating electricity by burning coal. It's better for the environment to smelt the aluminum in Iceland and then ship it elsewhere.

Similarly, it is more environmentally sound for people in the United Kingdom to buy virgin wood from Sweden than to buy recycled paper made in the United Kingdom. Why? Sweden uses nuclear energy to make paper, which has a much lower carbon footprint than electricity in the United Kingdom, which is generated by burning coal. Even though the paper is recycled, the electricity costs of recycling make it more harmful to the environment.

Perhaps one of the most-effective changes companies can make to help the environment is to work collaboratively with their trading partners. For example, an agreement between potato-chip manufacturers and potato suppliers eliminated wasted resources. Specifically, the physics of frying potato chips requires boiling off the water in the potato, which consumes a large amount of energy. Although boiling off the water would seem to be a requirement in the cooking process, UK-based Carbon Trust discovered a man-made practice that increased these costs. Potato-chip manufacturers buy potatoes by weight. Potato suppliers, to get the most for their potatoes, soak the potatoes in water to boost their weight, thus adding unnecessary water that has to be boiled off. By changing the contracts so that suppliers are paid more for less-soggy potatoes, suppliers had an incentive to use less water, chip makers needed to expend less energy to boil off less water, and the environment benefited from less water and energy waste. These changes had a much more beneficial impact on the environment than would have been gained by a change in transportation. [3]

Outsourcing versus Global Sourcing

In outsourcing, the company delegates an entire process (e.g., accounts payable) to an outsource vendor. The vendor takes control of the operation and runs the operation as it sees fit. The company pays the outsource vendor for the end result; how the vendor achieves those end results is up to the vendor.

Companies outsource for numerous reasons. There are many advantages to outsourcing:

- Reducing costs by moving labor to a lower-cost country
- Speeding up the pace of innovation by hiring engineers in a developing market at much lower cost
- Funding development projects that would otherwise be unaffordable
- Liberating expensive home-country-based engineers and salespeople from routines tasks, so that they can focus on higher value-added work or interacting with customers
- Putting a standard business practice out to bid, in order to lower costs and let the company respond with flexibility. If a new method of performing the function becomes advantageous, the company can change

vendors to take advantage of the new development, without incurring the delays of hiring and training new employees on the process.

Pharmaceutical company Eli Lilly and Company uses outsourcing to bring down the cost of developing a new drug, which stands at $1.1 billion. Lilly hopes to bring down the cost to $800 million through outsourcing. The company is outsourcing the heart of the research effort—drug development—to contract research organizations (CROs). [4] It does 20 percent of its chemistry work in China, for one-quarter the US cost. Lilly hopes to reduce the cost of clinical trials as well, by expanding those efforts to BRIC countries (i.e., Brazil, Russia, India, and China). [5]

The Hidden Costs of Outsourcing

Although outsourcing's costs savings, such as labor costs, are easy to see, some of the hidden costs aren't as visible. For example, high-tech products that spend months traveling by ocean face product obsolescence, deterioration, spoilage, taxes, loss due to damage or theft, and increased administrative and business travel costs. Threats of terrorism, religious strife, changing governments, and failing economies are further issues of concern. Stanley Furniture, a US maker of home furnishings, decided to bring its offshore production back home after product recalls from cribs made in Slovenia, transportation costs, and intellectual property issues outweighed the advantages of cheap goods and labor. [6] All of these hidden costs add up to a world that is less than flat.

Manufacturing outsourcing is also called contract manufacturing. The move to contract manufacturing means that companies like IBM have less control over manufacturing than they did when they owned the factories. Contract-manufacturing companies such as Celestica are making IBM products alongside Hewlett-Packard (HP) and Dell products. Celestica's own financial considerations influence whether it gives preference to IBM, HP, or Dell if there is a rush on manufacturing. The contract manufacturer's best efforts will go to whichever client negotiated the best terms and highest price; this makes companies more vulnerable to variability.

Quanta Computer, based in Taiwan, is the largest notebook-computer contract manufacturer in the world. Quanta makes laptops for Sony, Dell, and HP, among others. In June 2010, Quanta shipped 4.8 million laptops, a laptop-shipment record. [7] For consumer electronics, outsourcing has become the dominant way of doing business.

Managing Outsourced Services

If a company outsources a service, how does it guarantee the quality of that service? One way is through service-level agreements. Service-level agreements (SLAs) contractually specify the service levels that the outsourcer must meet when performing the service. SLAs are one way that companies ensure quality and performance when outsourcing services. SLAs typically include the following components:

- Scope of services
  - o Frequency of service
  - o Quality expected
  - o Timing required
- Cost of service
- Communications
  - o Dispute-resolution procedures
  - o Reporting and governance
  - o Key contacts
- Performance-improvement objectives

Johns Hopkins Enterprise's SLA for Accounts Receivable

Johns Hopkins Enterprise expects the following service levels for accounts receivable:

- Contact the customer after forty-five days if the open invoice is greater than $10,000.
- Contact the customer after sixty days if the open invoice is between $3,000 and $10,000.
- Contact the customer after ninety days if the open invoice is less than $3,000.
- Contact the department within two days if the customer claims the invoice will not be paid due to performance. At this point, it is the department's responsibility to resolve and the invoice will be closed as uncollectible. Once the disagreement with the customer is resolved, a new invoice will be issued.
- All issues that the A/R Service Center can fix will be completed within three business days. Follow-up calls will be made within five business days. [8]

Entrepreneurial Opportunities from Outsourcing

Crimson Consulting Group is a California-based firm that performs global market research on everything from routers to software for clients including Cisco Systems, HP, and Microsoft. Crimson has only fourteen full-time employees, which would be too few to handle these market research inquiries. But Crimson outsources some of the market research to Evalueserve in India and some to independent experts in China, the Czech Republic, and South Africa. "This allows a small firm like us to compete with McKinsey

and Bain on a very global basis with very low costs," said Crimson CEO Glenn Gow. [9]

For example, imagine a company that has an idea for a new medical device, but lacks market research into the opportunity. The company could outsource its market research to a firm like Evalueserve. For a relatively small fee, the outsourced firm could, within a day, assemble a team of Indian patent attorneys, engineers, and business analysts, start mining global databases, and call dozens of US experts and wholesalers to provide an independent market-research report.

KEY TAKEAWAYS

- Global sourcing refers to buying the raw materials, components, complete products, or services from companies located outside the home country.
- Information technology and communications have enabled the outsourcing of business processes, enabling those processes to be performed in different countries around the world.
- Best practices in global sourcing include the following components:
  - o Using ISO 9001:2008 certification to help ensure the quality of products regardless of where they are produced
  - o Considering not just the quality of products but also the environmental practices of the company providing the products, through ISO 14000 certification
  - o Using service-level agreements to ensure the quality of services
- Entrepreneurs benefit from outsourcing because they can acquire services as needed, without having to build those capabilities internally.

EXERCISES

(AACSB: Reflective Thinking, Analytical Skills)
1. Why do companies source globally?
2. What are some ways in which to ensure quality from unknown suppliers?
3. When and how would you use a service-level agreement?
4. Is contract manufacturing the same as outsourcing?
5. Explain the advantages and disadvantages of outsourcing.

[1] Edwin S. Hunt and James M. Murray, A History of Business in Medieval Europe, 1200–1550 (Cambridge, UK: Cambridge University Press, 1999), 229.

[2] Mike Berners-Lee and Duncan Clark, "What Is a Carbon Footprint?" Green Living Blog,Guardian, June 4, 2010, accessed September 12, 2010,http://www.guardian.co.uk/environment/blog/2010/jun/04/carbon-footprint-definition.

[3] MIT Center for Transportation and Logistics and Council of Supply Chain Management Professionals, "Achieving the Energy-Efficient Supply Chain" (symposium, Royal Sonesta Hotel, Cambridge, MA, April 30, 2007).

[4] Jonathan D. Rockoff, "Lilly Taps Contractors to Revive Pipeline," Wall Street Journal, January 5, 2010, accessed September 7, 2010, http://online.wsj.com/article/SB1000142405274870424750457460450392 2019082.html.

[5] Paul McDougall, "Drug Company Eli Lilly Outsources Clinical Data to India, "InformationWeek, November 20, 2006, accessed September 7, 2010,http://www.informationweek.com/news/global-cio/outsourcing/showArticle.jhtml?articleID=194500067; Patricia Van Arnum, "Outsourcing Clinical Trial Development and Materials," Pharmaceutical Technology 6, no. 34 (June 2, 2010): 44–46.

[6] Sarah Kabourek, "Back in the USA," Fortune, September 28, 2009, 30.

[7] Carter Sprunger, "Quanta Computer Breaks Laptop Shipment Record in June," Notebooks, July 9, 2010, accessed October 28, 2010, http://notebooks.com/2010/07/09/quanta-computer-breaks-laptop-shipment-record-in-june.

[8] "Accounts Receivable Shared Service Center Service Level Agreement," Johns Hopkins Enterprise, last updated July 1, 2009, accessed November 23, 2010, http://ssc.jhmi.edu/accountsreceivable/inter_entity.html.

[9] Pete Engardio with Michael Arndt and Dean Foust, "The Future of Outsourcing," BusinessWeek, January 30, 2006, accessed November 18, 2010, http://www.businessweek.com/magazine/content/06_05/b3969401.htm.

9.4 Managing Export and Import

LEARNING OBJECTIVES

1. Learn the main players in export and import.
2. Recognize the role of intermediaries.
3. Identify some of the documents needed for export and import transactions.

Who Are the Main Actors in Export and Import?

The size of exports in the world grew from less than $100 million after World War II to well over $11 trillion today. Export and import is big business, but it isn't just for big businesses. Most of the participants are small and midsize businesses, making this an exciting opportunity for entrepreneurs.

Importing and exporting require much documentation (i.e., filing official forms) to satisfy the regulations of countries. The value of the documentation is that it enables trade between entities who don't know each other. The parties are able to trust each other because the documentation provides a common framework and process to ensure that each party will do what they say in the import/export transaction.

The main parties involved in export and import transactions are the exporter, the importer, and the carrier.

The exporter is the person or entity sending or transporting the goods out of the country. The importer is the person or entity buying or transporting goods from another country into the importer's home country. The carrier is the entity handling the physical transportation of the goods. Well-known carriers across the world are United Parcel Service (UPS), FedEx, and DHL.

Customs administration offices in both the home country and the country to which the item is being exported are involved in the transaction. In the United States, the US Customs Service became the US Bureau of Customs and Border Protection (CBP) after the terrorist attacks on September 11, 2001. The mandate now isn't simply to move goods through customs quickly and efficiently to facilitate international trade; it also ensures that the items coming into the United States are validated and safe as well. Robert Bonner took the position as commissioner of the Customs Service on September 10, 2001. On his second day on the job at 10:05 a.m. EDT, he had to close all the airports, seaports, and border ports of entry. The priority mission of the Customs Service became security—preventing terrorists and terrorist weapons from entering the country. On the third day, however, the trade and business implications of shutting down the borders became visible. Border crossings that used to take ten to twenty minutes were taking ten to twelve hours. Automobile plants in Detroit, using just-in-time delivery of parts for cars, began to shut down on September 14 due to a lack of incoming supplies and parts. Businesses were going to have a difficult time operating if the borders were closed. Thus, the twin goals of the newly created CBP became security as well as trade facilitation. As Bonner explained, "In the past, the United States had no way to detect weapons coming into our borders. We had built a global trading system that was fast and efficient, but that had no security measures." [1]

Mary Murphy-Hoye, a senior principal engineer at Intel, put it simply: "Our things move in big containers, and the US Department of Homeland Security is worried about them. Security means knowing what is it, where is it, where has it been, and has anyone messed with it." [2]

After September 11, the twin goals of safety and facilitation were met through three interrelated initiatives:

1. The twenty-four-hour rule, requiring advanced information prior to loading
2. An automated targeting system to evaluate all inbound freight
3. Sophisticated detection technology for scanning high-risk containers

Cooperation for Security

The World Customs Organization (WCO) created a framework that calls for cooperation between the customs administrations of different countries. Under the WCO Framework of Standards to Secure and Facilitate Global Trade, if a customs administration in one country identifies problems in cargo from another country, that customs administration could ask the exporting country to do an inspection before goods are shipped. Businesses across the world benefit (in terms of speed and cost) if there is one common set of security standards globally, and the WCO is working toward that goal. [3]

Role of Intermediaries

In addition to the main players described above, intermediaries can get involved at the discretion of the importer or exporter. Entrepreneurs and small and midsize businesses, in particular, make use of these intermediaries, rather than expending their resources to build these capabilities in-house.

A freight forwarder typically prepares the documentation, suggests shipping methods, navigates trade regulations, and assists with details like packing and labeling. At the foreign port, the freight forwarder arranges to have the exported goods clear customs and be shipped to the buyer. The process ends with the freight forwarder sending the documentation to the seller, buyer, or intermediary, such as a bank.

An export management company (EMC) is an independent company that performs the duties a firm's export department would execute. The EMC handles the necessary documentation, finds buyers for the export, and takes title of the goods for direct export. In return, the EMC charges a fee or a commission for its services.

Banks perform the vital role of finance transactions. The role of banks will be examined in Chapter 14 "Competing Effectively through Global Marketing, Distribution, and Supply-Chain Management", Section 14.5 "Global Production and Supply-Chain Management".

What's Needed for Import and Export Transactions?

Various forms of documentation are required for import and export transactions.

The bill of lading is the contract between the exporter and the carrier (e.g., UPS or FedEx), authorizing the carrier to transport the goods to the buyer's destination. The bill of lading acts as proof that the shipment was made and that the goods have been received.

A commercial or customs invoice is the bill for the goods shipped from the exporter to the importer or buyer. Exporters send invoices to receive payment, and governments use these invoices to determine the value of the goods for customs-valuation purposes.

Did You Know?

IBM does business with 160 countries. Daily, it sends 2,500 customs declarations and ships 5.5 million pounds of products worth $68 million. [4]

The export declaration is given to customs and port authorities. The declaration provides the contact information for both the exporter and the importer (i.e., buyer) as well as a description of the items being shipped, which the CPB uses to verify and control the export. The government also uses the information to compile statistics about exports from the country.

Humorous Anecdote

Customs regulations in some countries—particularly emerging-market countries—may impede or complicate international trade. A study of the speed and efficiency of items getting through customs in different countries found that it can take anywhere from three to twenty-one days to clear incoming goods. This variation causes problems because companies can't plan on a steady flow of goods across the border. Some countries have customs idiosyncrasies. In Brazil, for example, no goods move within the country on soccer game days and documents that are not signed in blue ink will incur delays for their accompanying goods. [5]

The certificate of origin, as its name implies, declares the country from which the product originates. These certificates are required for import duties. These import duties are lower for countries that are designated as a "most favored nation."

Certificate of Origin as Marketing Tool

Not all governments or industries require certificates of origin to be produced, but some companies are seeing that a certificate of origin can be used for competitive advantage. For example, Eosta, an importer of organic fruit, puts a three-digit number on each piece of fruit. At the website http://www.natureandmore.com, customers can type in that number and get a profile of the farmer who grew the fruit, getting a glimpse into that farmer's operations. For example, Fazenda Tamanduá, a farm in Brazil, grows mangoes using a variety that needs less water to grow and a drip-irrigation system that optimizes water use. This database gives customers a way to learn about growers and provides a way for growers and others to share what they learn. [6] Providing this type of certification to customers differentiates Eosta products and makes them more attractive to sustainability-minded consumers.

Although not required, insurance certificates show the amount of coverage on the goods and identify the merchandise. Some contracts or invoices may require proof of insurance in order to receive payment.

Some governments require the purchase of a license (i.e., permission to export) for goods due to national security or product scarcity. Interestingly, licenses for import and export date back to the 1500s at least, when Japan required a system of licenses to combat the smuggling of goods taking place. [7]

Impact of Trade Agreements

Trade agreements impact the particulars of doing business. For example, the North American Free Trade Agreement (NAFTA) makes Mexico different from other Latin American countries due to the ease of movement of goods between that country and the United States. Changes in agreements can affect the competitiveness of different countries. When China joined the World Trade Organization (WTO), the rapid elimination of tariffs and quotas on textiles harmed US makers.

The letter of credit is a legal document issued by a bank at the importer's (or buyer's) request. The importer promises to pay a specified amount of money when the bank receives documents about the shipment. Simply put, the letter of credit is like a loan against collateral (in this case, the goods being shipped) in which the funds are placed in an escrow account held by the bank. Letters of credit are trusted forms of payment in international trade because the bank promises to make the payment on behalf of the importer (i.e., buyer) and the bank is a trusted entity. Given that the letter of credit is like a loan, getting one issued from the bank requires proof of the importer's (or buyer's) ability to pay the amount of the loan.

Chapter 14 "Competing Effectively through Global Marketing, Distribution, and Supply-Chain Management", Section 14.5 "Global Production and Supply-Chain Management" is devoted to the broad topic of the payment and financing associated with import and export transactions.

KEY TAKEAWAYS

- There are several main parties involved in export and import transactions:
  - The exporter, who is the person or entity sending or transporting the goods out of the country
  - The importer, who is the person or entity buying or transporting goods from another country into the importer's home country
  - The carrier, which is the entity handling the physical transportation of the goods
  - The customs-administration offices from both the home country and the foreign country
- Intermediaries, such as freight forwarders and export management companies (EMC), provide companies with expert services so that the firms don't have to build those capabilities in-house. You could argue that such intermediaries make the world flatter, while the regulations and institutions that they help the firm deal with actually make the world less flat. Freight forwarders specialize in identifying the best shipping methods, understanding trade regulations, and arranging to have exported goods clear customs. EMCs handle the necessary documentation, find buyers for the export, and take title of the goods for direct export.
- Essential documents for importing and exporting include the bill of lading, which is the contract between the exporter and the carrier; the export declaration, which the customs office uses to verify and control the export; and the letter of credit, which is the legal document in which the importer promises to pay a specified amount of money to the exporter when the bank receives proper documentation about the shipment.

EXERCISES

(AACSB: Reflective Thinking, Analytical Skills)

1. Name the four main players in export and import transactions.
2. What role do intermediaries play in export and import transactions?
3. Explain the purpose of a letter of credit.
4. What is the difference between the export declaration and the commercial or customs invoice? How are they related?

[1] Robert Bonner, "Supply Chain Security: Government-Industry Partnership" (presentation at the Resilient and Secure Supply Chain symposium, MIT, Cambridge, MA, September 29, 2005).
[2] Mary Murphy Hoye, "Future Capabilities in the Supply Chain" (presentation at the MIT Center for Transportation and Logistics conference, MIT, Cambridge, MA, May 8, 2007).

[3] World Customs Organization, "WCO Presents Draft Framework of Standards at Consultative Session in Hong Kong, China," news release, March 25, 2005, accessed September 7, 2010, http://www.wcoomd.org/press/default.aspx?lid=1&id=78.

[4] Theo Fletcher, "Global Collaboration for Security" (presentation at the Resilient and Secure Supply Chain symposium, MIT, Cambridge, MA, September 29, 2005).

[5] "Supply Chain Strategies in Emerging Markets" (roundtable discussion at the MIT Center for Transportation and Logistics, MIT, Cambridge, MA, March 7, 2007).

[6] Daniel Goleman, Ecological Intelligence (New York: Crown Business, 2009), 191.

[7] Maritza Manresa, How to Open and Operate a Financially Successful Import Export Business (Ocala, FL: Atlantic Publishing, 2010), 20.

9.5 What Options Do Companies Have for Export and Import Financing?

LEARNING OBJECTIVES

1. Understand how companies receive or pay for goods and services.
2. Learn the basics of export financing.
3. Discover the role of organizations like OPIC, JETRO, and EX-IM Bank.

How Companies Receive or Pay for Goods and Services

You've already learned about two of the three documents required for getting paid in export/import transactions. The *letter of credit* is a contract between banks that stipulates that the bank of the importer will pay the bank of the exporter upon getting the proper documentation about the merchandise. Because importers and exporters rarely know each other, the letter of credit between two banks ensures that each party will do what it says it will do. The *bill of lading*, which is issued by the carrier transporting the merchandise, proves that the exporter has given the carrier the merchandise and that the carrier owns title to the merchandise until paid by the importer. Both the letter of credit and the bill of lading can function as collateral against loans. The final document, the draft (or bill of exchange) is the document by which the exporter tells the importer to pay a specified amount at a specified time. It is a written order for a certain amount of money to be transferred on a certain date from the person who owes the money or agrees to make the payment. The draft is the way in which an exporter initiates the request for payment.

There are two types of drafts. The sight draft is paid on receipt of the draft (when it is "seen") and the time draft is payable at a later time, typically 30, 60, 90, or 120 days in the future as specified by the time draft.

Giving the importer 120 days to pay the draft is very attractive for the importer because it allows time for the importer to sell the goods before having to pay for them. This helps the importer's cash flow. Importers will prefer to give business to an exporter who offers these attractive payment terms, which is why exporters offer them. However, waiting 120 days to get paid could cause cash-flow problems for the exporter. To avoid this problem, the exporter may choose to factor the contract. In factoring, the exporter sells the draft at a discount to an intermediary (often a bank) that will pay the exporter immediately and then collect the full amount from the importer at the specified later date. For example, the factor (bank) pays the exporter 93 percent of the value of the draft now. The factor now owns the draft and collects the full amount owed 120 days later from the importer. The factor earns roughly a 7 percent return in 120 days (but bears the risk that the importer defaults on the payment or takes longer to pay). Factor rates are typically 5 to 8 percent of the total amount of the draft.

Of course, it's possible for the exporter to ask for cash in advance from the importer or buyer, but this is a risky agreement for the buyer to make. As a result, importers prefer to do business with exporters who do not require cash in advance.

An open account, in direct contrast to cash in advance, is an arrangement in which the exporter ships the goods and then bills the importer. This type of agreement is most risky for the exporter, so exporters avoid it when possible or offer it only to their own subsidiaries or to entities with whom they have long-term relationships.

Basics of Export Financing

Financing against collateral is called secured financing, and it's the most common method of raising new money. Banks will advance funds against payment obligations, shipment documents, or storage documents.

There are several common sources of financing:

- A loan from a commercial bank
- A loan from an intermediary, such as an export management company that provides short-term financing
- A loan from a supplier, for which the buyer can make a down payment and ask to make further payments incrementally
- A loan from the corporate parent
- Governmental or other organizational financing

Did You Know?

Banks like HSBC provide trade finance and related services, including a highly automated trade-processing network of

Internet trade services, export document-preparation system, and electronic documentary-credit advising. Some of these banks also provide specialized financing services, such as factoring.

Some companies have mechanisms for providing credit to their business customers. For example, package delivery company United Parcel Service (UPS) also owns warehouses to which its customers can ship their products. Because UPS can see and track the inventory that its business customers send using this service, it can lend those companies money based on their warehouse inventory and goods-in-transit. Simply put, UPS information systems know that a company's goods are on their way or in the warehouse, so UPS can lend money based on that knowledge.

Success Tips for Entrepreneurs
Entrepreneurs and small businesses can look to the US Small Business Administration (SBA) for help with their import or export businesses. Although the SBA itself doesn't loan money, it does guarantee loans and offers good loan programs for small businesses. Let's look at two programs in particular. The SBA's Export Express loan program is the most flexible program available to small businesses. The funds that small businesses obtain through this program can be used to pay for any activity that will increase exports, be it helping the exporter fund the purchase of the export items, take part in trade shows, obtain letters of credit, or translate marketing materials that it will use to sell the goods in overseas markets. Small businesses can get loans or lines of credit of up to $250,000. Obtaining a loan requires going to a bank or other lender and asking if they are an SBA Export Express lender. If so, the small business can apply for the loan with that lender and then send the application to the SBA for final approval. The SBA will review the application to make sure that the funds will be used to enter new export markets (or to expand the company's current market) and that the company has been in business for at least one year. [1]

A second loan program, the SBA's Export Working Capital Program (EWCP), provides loans for businesses that can generate export sales but don't have the working capital to purchase inventory or to stay in business during the long payment cycles. The maximum loan amount or line of credit for the EWCP is $2 million. More information on these loan programs is available at the SBA's international trade website: http://www.sba.gov/international.

Another useful tip for entrepreneurs is to use the Automated Export System (AES) to file the necessary documentation required for exporting. The AES is available to companies of all sizes but is of particular value to entrepreneurs and small businesses that might otherwise have to fill out all this documentation themselves. By filing the documents electronically, entrepreneurs get immediate feedback if there are any errors in their paperwork and can make the corrections right away. This can save days of costly delays. The AES lets entrepreneurs and businesses submit all the export information required by all the agencies involved in the export process. The process begins by filing the export document. If all the necessary information has been provided, the entrepreneur or business gets a confirmation message with approval. If there have been errors, the error message explains the omission or erroneous information so that it can be corrected. For more information, see http://www.aesdirect.gov.

Finally, entrepreneurs can accept payments in many ways, including checks, credit cards, or services like PayPal.

The Role of Organizations in Providing Financing
Countries often have government-supported organizations that help businesses with import and export activities to and from their country. These services are, for the most part, free and include providing information, contacts, and even financing options.

The Japan External Trade Organization (JETRO) was originally established in the 1950s to help the war-torn Japanese economy by promoting export of Japanese products to other countries. By the 1980s, Japan had massive export surpluses and began to feel the need to promote imports. So JETRO's mission reversed; its focus became to assist foreign companies to export their products into Japan. JETRO now offers such free services as

- market-entry information,
- business partner matching,
- expert business consulting (through bilingual business consultants who're experts in various industries), and
- access to a global network of executives and advisors.

On the financing side, JETRO offers subsidies to potential companies, free offices for up to four months while the foreign firm researches the Japanese market, and exhibition space when the company is ready to display their products to prospective Japanese importers. [2]

The current goal of JETRO is to help Japan attract foreign direct investment (FDI) as part of its economic restructuring plan. FDI refers to an investment in or the acquisition of foreign assets with the intent to control and manage them. Companies can make an FDI in several ways, including purchasing the assets of a foreign company; investing in the company or in new property, plant or equipment; or participating in a joint venture with a foreign company, which typically involves an investment of capital or know-how.

The Overseas Private Investment Corporation (OPIC) was established as an agency of the US government in 1971. OPIC helps US businesses invest overseas, particularly in developing countries. As its website states, "OPIC Financing provides medium- to long-term funding through direct loans and loan guaranties to eligible investment projects in developing countries." [3] It also provides exporters' insurance. The most useful tool of OPIC is that it can "provide financing in countries where conventional financial institutions often are reluctant or unable to lend on such a basis." [4]

The Export-Import Bank of the United States (Ex-Im Bank) helps exporters who have found a buyer, yet the buyer is unable to get financing for the purchase in their own country. Ex-Im Bank can provide credit support (i.e., loans, guarantees, and insurance for small businesses) that covers up to 85 percent of the transaction's export value.

Unlike JETRO, OPIC, and Ex-Im Bank, the Private Export Funding Corporation (PEFCO) is a private-sector organization. PEFCO was formed in 1970 "to assist in financing U.S. exports by supplementing the financing available from commercial banks and other lenders." [5] PEFCO provides medium- to long-term loans if they are secured against nonpayment under an appropriate guarantee or insurance policy issued by Ex-Im Bank or for certain small-business export loans under a guarantee issued by the SBA.

Did You Know?
The Development Bank of Japan (DBJ) has loan programs for foreign-affiliated companies investing in Japan. According to Masaaki Kaji of DBJ, the loans are offered at low fixed interest rates for five- to fifteen-year terms. [6] During the twenty-year history of the program, the three hundred companies that have received financial aid have generated $850 billion dollars in income for the Japanese economy. DBJ also works with regional Japanese banks to provide merger and acquisition advice to small and midsize companies. One of DBJ's most famous projects provided financing and strategic advice for the joint venture established between Starbucks and Sazaby Japan. [7]

- The main financial documents import/export companies use in order to get paid are the letter of credit (which states that the bank will pay the exporter upon getting the proper documentation about the merchandise), the bill of lading (which proves that the exporter has given the carrier the merchandise and that the carrier owns title to the merchandise until paid by the importer), and the draft, or bill of exchange (which tells the importer to pay a specified amount at a specified time).
- Companies can obtain funding via loans from several sources: a commercial bank, an intermediary, a supplier, their corporate parent, or a governmental or other organization.
- The role of organizations like OPIC, JETRO, and Ex-Im Bank is to provide financing, market information, and trade assistance. These organizations are often country specific (e.g., JETRO, which focuses on Japan) or specific to a category of countries (e.g., OPIC, which factors loans to developing countries).

EXERCISES

(AACSB: Reflective Thinking, Analytical Skills)
1. If you were an exporter, would you ever give your buyer three months to pay an invoice? Why or why not?
2. Describe how the SBA can help entrepreneurs and small businesses in their export ventures.
3. Explain the difference between a letter of credit and a draft.

[1] US Small Business Administration, "Finance Start-Up," accessed September 5, 2010, http://www.sba.gov/smallbusinessplanner/start/financestartup/SERV_EXPORT.html.
[2] "Open a Japan Office / Invest in Japan," Japan External Trade Organization, accessed November 22, 2010, http://www.jetro.org/index.php?option=com_content&task=view&id=652.
[3] "Financing," Overseas Private Investment Corporation, accessed November 22, 2010, http://www.opic.gov/financing.
[4] "Financing," Overseas Private Investment Corporation, accessed November 22, 2010, http://www.opic.gov/financing.

9.6 Tips in Your Walkabout Toolkit

Negotiating for Success across Cultures
Your understanding of culture will affect your ability to enter a local market, develop and maintain business relationships, negotiate successful deals, conduct sales, conduct marketing and advertising campaigns, and engage in manufacturing and distribution. Too often, people send the wrong signals or

receive the wrong messages and, as a result, become tangled in the cultural web. In fact, there are numerous instances where deals would have been successfully completed, if finalizing them had been based on business issues alone. Just as you would conduct a technical or market analysis, you should also conduct a cultural analysis.

It's critical to understand the history and politics of any country or region in which you work or with whom you intend to deal. It's important to remember that each person considers his or her "sphere" or "world" the most important; this forms the basis of his or her individual perspective. We often forget that cultures are shaped by decades and centuries of experience and that ignoring cultural differences puts us at a disadvantage.

In general, when considering doing business in a new country, there are a number of factors to consider. Make sure to learn about the country's history, culture, and people, as well as determine its more general suitability for your product or service.

When you're dealing and negotiating with people from another culture, you may find that their business practices, communication, and management styles are different from what you are accustomed to. Understanding the culture of the people with whom you are dealing is key to successful business interactions as well as to accomplishing business objectives. For example, you'll need to understand the following:

- How people communicate
- How culture impacts how people view time and deadlines
- How they are likely to ask questions or highlight problems
- How people respond to management and authority
- How people perceive verbal and physical communications
- How people make decisions

The following are some tips on how to negotiate for success and avoid certain cultural pitfalls.

1. One of the most important cultural factors in many countries is the importance of networking or relationships. Whether in Asia or Latin America or somewhere in between, it's best to have an introduction from a common business partner, vendor, or supplier when meeting a new company or partner. Even in the United States or Europe, where we like to think that relationships have less importance, a well-placed introduction will work wonders. Be creative in identifying potential introducers. If you don't know someone who knows the company with which you would like to do business, consider indirect sources. Trade organizations, lawyers, bankers and financiers, common suppliers and buyers, consultants, and advertising agencies are just a few potential introducers. Once a meeting has been set up, foreign companies need to understand the local cultural nuances that govern meetings, negotiations, and ongoing business expansion.

2. Even if you've been invited to bid on a contract, you're still trying to sell your company and yourself. Don't be patronizing or assume you're doing the local company or its government a favor. They must like and trust you if you are to succeed. Think about your own business encounters with people, regardless of nationality, who were condescending and arrogant. How often have you given business to people who irritated you?

3. Make sure you understand how your overseas associates think about time and deadlines. How will that impact your timetable and deliverables?

4. You need to understand the predominant corporate culture of the country with which you're dealing—particularly when dealing with vendors and partners. What's the local hierarchy? What are the expected management practices? Are the organizations you're dealing with uniform in culture or do they represent more than one culture or ethnicity? Culture affects how people develop trust and make decisions as well as the speed of their decision making and their attitudes toward accountability and responsibility.

5. Understand how you can build trust with potential partners. How are people from your culture viewed in the target country, and how will this view impact your business interactions? How are small or younger companies viewed in the local market? Understand the corporate culture of your potential partner or distributor. More entrepreneurial local companies may have more in common with a younger firm in terms of their approach to doing business.

6. Understand the different ways that people communicate. There are differences in how skills or knowledge is taught or transferred. In the United States, we're expected to ask questions—it's a positive and indicates a seriousness about wanting to learn. In some cultures, asking questions is seen as reflecting a lack of knowledge and could be considered personally embarrassing. It's important to be able to address these issues without appearing condescending. Notice the word is appearing—the issue is less whether you think you're

being condescending and more about whether the professional of the differing culture perceives a statement or action as condescending. Again, culture is based on perceptions and values.

7. Focus on communications of all types and learn to find ways around cultural obstacles. For example, if you're dealing with a culture that shies away from providing bad news or information, don't ask yes-or-no questions. Focus on the process and ask questions about the stage or deliverable. Many people get frustrated by a lack of information or clear communications. You certainly don't want to be surprised by a delayed shipment to your key customers.

8. There are no clear playbooks for operating in every culture around the world. Rather, we have to understand the components that affect culture, understand how it impacts our business objectives, and then equip ourselves and our teams with the know-how to operate successfully in each new cultural environment. Once you've established a relationship, you may opt to delegate it to someone on your team. Be sure that person understands the culture of the country, and stay involved until there is a successful operating history of at least one or more years. Many entrepreneurs stay involved in key relationships on an ongoing basis. Be aware that your global counterparts may require that level of attention.

9. Make sure in any interaction that you have a decision maker on the other end. On occasion, junior people get assigned to work with smaller companies, and you could spend a lot of time with someone who is unable to finalize an agreement. If you have to work through details with a junior person, try to get a senior person involved early on as well This will save you time and energy.

10. When negotiating with people from a different culture, try to understand your counterpart's position and objectives. This doesn't imply that you should compromise easily or be "soft" in your style. Rather, understand how to craft your argument in a manner that will be more effective with a person of that culture.

Entrepreneurs are often well equipped to negotiate global contracts or ventures. They are more likely to be flexible and creative in their approach and have less-rigid constraints than their counterparts from more-established companies. Each country has different constraints, including the terms of payment and regulations, and you'll need to keep an open mind about how to achieve your objectives.

11. Even in today's wired world, don't assume that everyone in every country is equally reliant on the Internet and e-mail. You may need to use different modes of communication with different countries, companies, and professionals. Faxes are still very common, as many people consider signed authorizations more official than e-mail (although that's changing).

12. As with any business transaction, use legal documents to substantiate relationships and expectations. Many legal professionals recommend that you opt to use the international courts or a third-party arbitration system in case of a dispute. Translate contracts into both languages, and have a second independent translator verify the copies for the accuracy of concepts and key terminology. But be warned—no translation can ever be exactly accurate, as legal terminology is both culture- and country-specific. At the end of the day, even a good contract has many limitations in its use. You have to be willing to enforce the penalties for infractions.

The key words to remember for entering any new market successfully are *patience*, *patience*, and *patience*. Flexibility and creativity are also important. You should focus on the end result and find unique ways to get there.

9.7 End-of-Chapter Questions and Exercises
These exercises are designed to ensure that the knowledge you gain from this book about international business meets the learning standards set out by the international Association to Advance Collegiate Schools of Business (AACSB International). [1] AACSB is the premier accrediting agency of collegiate business schools and accounting programs worldwide. It expects that you will gain knowledge in the areas of communication, ethical reasoning, analytical skills, use of information technology, multiculturalism and diversity, and reflective thinking.

EXPERIENTIAL EXERCISES

(AACSB: Communication, Use of Information Technology, Analytical Skills)

1. Imagine that you are working for a company that has been exporting to Europe for five years. The company now sees an opportunity to expand into Asia. Which modes of entry would you suggest that your company pursue for Asia? Would you recommend the same strategy for entering Japan as you would for China? Why or why not?

2. Under what conditions would a company engage in countertrade? Would anyone other than a company

from a developing country suggest a countertrade deal? Why or why not?

3. Imagine that you work for a custom-bicycle company that has thus far only manufactured in the United States. You're under pressure to reduce costs. What options would you explore? Would you consider sourcing some of the components from countries with lower material costs? Would you consider outsourcing some of the manufacturing? Would you set up a subsidiary in a country with lower labor and material costs to handle the manufacturing? Explain the advantages or disadvantages of these options.

4. Compare and contrast the roles of the SBA, Ex-Im Bank, OPIC, and JETRO. When would a company seek out these organizations? Could a bank or EMC take on the role that these other organizations provide? Are these organizations better for small businesses or larger corporations?

5. Imagine that you are an exporter. You've found a buyer who's interested in importing your goods. However, the buyer doesn't have the cash to buy the products in the 100-lot quantities you require. What would you do? Are there ways to help the buyer get financing? Are there financing mechanisms that you yourself can pursue to ease the burden on the buyer?

Ethical Dilemmas

(AACSB: Ethical Reasoning, Multiculturalism, Reflective Thinking, Analytical Skills)

1. In some countries, bribes are a common business practice. One country's definition of corrupt or unethical behavior may be another country's definition of polite relationship development. Under US law, it's permissible for a salesperson to take a potential customer to a baseball game or the golf course but not to give them a gift or cash payment. Imagine that you are a rising young executive sent to oversee imports in your company's Russian subsidiary. Your predecessor shows you the ropes and tells you that bribes are needed for routine tasks like getting imported supplies cleared through customs. "We use customs brokers, and they build bribes into the invoice," he casually explains. Refusing to give payoffs slows down the business greatly. You know that offering bribes is illegal under US law. But in this case, the bribe wouldn't be coming from your company; it would come from the customs broker. You also know that US law doesn't address small payoffs and that even though Russia enacted new anticorruption laws in 2008, the law criminalizes only completed acts of bribery, not the act of demanding or offering bribes. The legislation also doesn't address corruption in the judicial

system that would prosecute such offenses. So, the changes of getting caught or prosecuted are low. Would you continue the practice of giving bribes? Would you risk a business slowdown under your new management if you don't give bribes? Would you alert your boss at headquarters of this practice?

2. The standards of the legal minimum age for employment vary in different countries due to their different circumstances. Nike got skewered in the US press and public opinion when a photograph showed a twelve-year-old Pakistani boy sewing a Nike soccer ball. But a Massachusetts Institute of Technology (MIT) alumnus from Pakistan who interviewed boys making soccer balls for Nike in Pakistan discovered this: "In Pakistan, the reality is that the 14-year-old's father may be a drug addict or dead, and his mother may have 10 other children to raise. As a 14-year-old, he represents the family's best earning potential." [2] To deny the fourteen-year-old boy the ability to earn wages to provide for the family is age discrimination. Indeed, the company could be sued. The notion that a fourteen-year-old is "too young" to work and that working is "not in the best interests of the child" must be tempered by knowledge of the local conditions and the true alternatives facing fourteen-year-olds in developing countries. Sewing soccer balls at fourteen may be damaging to the eyes, but what if the alternative is selling one's body?

An MIT alumnus from Brazil expressed similar views: "In Brazil, a 14-year-old is not the same as a 14-year-old in the U.S. In the U.S., 14-year-olds have the alternative of going to school. After school, maybe they play sports or take music lessons. In Brazil, it's better to be working a part-time job at 14 than to be on the streets and be offered drugs. Limiting the worker age to 16 makes sense for the U.S., but not for Brazil." [3]

How would you handle a situation like this? If it were legal for one of your suppliers to hire children as young as twelve years old, would you let them? Would you ask them to adhere to the US minimum-age standard of sixteen? Is it even your business to tell another company what to do? How might your decision impact your reputation in the United States? How might your actions impact the people in the country where your supplier is located? Can you think of ways to make the hiring of younger workers more palatable to US stakeholders?

[1] Association to Advance Collegiate Schools of Business website, accessed January 26, 2010, http://www.aacsb.edu.

[2] Thomas A. Kochan and Richard Schmalensee, Management: Inventing and Delivering its Future (Cambridge, MA: MIT Press, 2003), 72–73.
[3] Thomas A. Kochan and Richard Schmalensee, Management: Inventing and Delivering its Future (Cambridge, MA: MIT Press, 2003), 72–73.

NOTES:

Chapter 10:
Strategy and International Business

WHAT'S IN IT FOR ME?

1. What are the basics of business and corporate strategy?
2. What is the range of generic strategies?
3. How do generic strategies become international strategies?
4. What are the five facets of good strategies?
5. What is the significance of the P-O-L-C (planning-organizing-leading-controlling) framework?

This chapter takes you deeper into the subjects of strategy and management in international business and within the context of a flattening world. As a business student, you will likely take a full course in strategic management, so you should view this chapter as simply an introduction to the field. You will learn about strategy—specifically, the strategy formulation framework known as the strategy diamond. This will help you better understand how international markets—whether for customers or factors of production—can be an integral part of a firm's strategy. Because you know that the world is not flat, in the sense that Thomas Friedman describes, it is important that an international strategy be adjusted to adapt, overcome, or exploit differences across countries and regions. Finally, provides an introduction to managing international businesses through a brief overview of the P-O-L-C (planning-organizing-leading-controlling) framework.

OPENING CASE: MAKING A SPLASH WITH SPLASH CORPORATION

The tale of husband and wife Rolando and Rosalinda Hortaleza is well known in the Philippines. As the story goes, the couple launched a backyard business in 1985 to supplement their entry-level salaries as doctors at a government hospital. From this humble beginning, the Splash Group of Companies was born.

Beyond the Backyard

Like many entrepreneurs, the Hortalezas sought a big success. In 1987, they spotted an opportunity in hair spray, because "big hair" was the fad in the Philippines at that time. So the couple created a company that offered a high-quality, low-price alternative to imported hair spray. [1] The gambit proved successful, and the Hortalezas earned their first million Philippine pesos in sales that year. Over the years, the company name changed several times, reflecting its growth and evolving strategy. What began as Hortaleza Cosmetics in 1986 became Splash Cosmetics in 1987, Splash Manufacturing Corporation in 1991, and finally Splash Corporation in 2001. [2] Today, Splash Corporation sells more skin-care products than international giants like Johnson and Unilever and local brands. With sales of 90 billion pesos (nearly $2 billion), Splash Corporation is the number one maker of skin-care products in the Philippines and is sixth in the international market, being the only Filipino-owned company to hold a position among global companies and brands. [3] In twenty years, the small business that the Hortalezas started has posted 5 billion Philippine pesos in sales, putting it among the country's 300 largest corporations.

Splash Corporation exports and markets Splash products to almost twenty countries around the world. In Indonesia, unlike the rest of the company's market destinations, Splash entered into a joint venture with an Indonesian company, Parit Padang. By itself, Parit Padang is one of the largest pharmaceutical and health-care distribution companies in Indonesia. The joint venture, called Splash Indonesia PT, began operating in 2000, importing Splash soap and skin-care products every month from Manila. The venture now produces some of its products locally in Indonesia, employing a staff of 40 there in its factory. Splash Indonesia PT has even developed a new product for the local market, the SkinWhite Whitening Bath Soap. This product blends innovative ingredients and technology from the Philippines with a fine Indonesian noodle soap, creating a whitening body soap of a seemingly better quality than other local soaps.

Splash recently launched the Splash Nutraceutical Corporation. The term nutraceutical was coined in the 1990s by Dr. Stephen DeFelice, founder of the US-based Foundation for Innovation in Medicine. DeFelice defined the word as any substance that is a food or part of a food and provides medical or health benefits, including the prevention and treatment of disease. In essence, nutraceuticals are "a food (or part of a food) that provides medical or health benefits, including the prevention and/or treatment of a disease."[4]

The nutraceuticals market is growing rapidly worldwide, especially in such developed countries where disposable incomes are higher and the challenges of diet-disease links, aging populations, and rising health care costs are more pronounced. Nutraceuticals currently address health concerns like cardiovascular disease, osteoporosis, high blood pressure, diabetes, and gastrointestinal disorders. Worldwide sales of nutraceutical products have grown exponentially and are currently estimated at $80 billion.

The establishment of Splash Nutraceuticals completes the company's mission of becoming a total-wellness company. Fondly called "Doc" by Splash employees (while his wife is the "Doctora"), Dr. Rolando Hortaleza considers nutraceuticals a natural extension of the company's personal care line of products. He defines the term wellness as "beauty inside and out—if you feel good about yourself, you then become more productive." He estimates the market potential of nutraceuticals to be in the billions of pesos.

The Values, Mission, and Vision behind Splash

Corporate Cause: We shall uplift the pride and economic well-being of the societies we serve.

Mission: Splash is a world-class company that is committed to making accessible, innovative, high-quality and value personal care products for everyone.

Vision: We are a marketing company in the beauty, personal and health care industries where we shall be known for strong brand management of pioneering, high-quality and innovative products derived from extensive research to improve the well-being of our consumers. We shall do this through:

Leading edge trade and consumer marketing systems.

Pursuit of excellence in all other business systems.

We shall be generous in sharing the rewards with our employees, business partners, stockholders and our community for the realization of our corporate cause. [5]

OPENING CASE EXERCISES

(AACSB: Ethical Reasoning, Multiculturalism, Reflective Thinking, Analytical Skills)

1. Describe Splash Corporation's corporate strategy and business strategy.
2. Use the strategy diamond tool (see) to summarize Splash Corporation's strategy.

[1] Tyrone Solee, "Hortaleza Success Story," Millionaire Acts (blog), February 15, 2009, accessed June 3, 2010, http://www.millionaireacts.com/808/hortaleza-success-story.html.
[2] "Splash Corporation, Making Waves in the Global Beauty and Personal Care Industry," Splash Corporation, accessed November 10, 2010, http://www.splash.com.ph/NewsAndEvents.aspx?ID=8.
[3] Tyrone Solee, "Hortaleza Success Story," Millionaire Acts (blog), February 15, 2009, accessed December 27, 2010, http://www.millionaireacts.com/808/hortaleza-success-story.html.
[4] Vicki Brower, "Nutraceuticals: Poised for a Healthy Slice of the Healthcare Market?" Nature Biotechnology 16, no. 8 (1998): 728–731, quoted in Ekta K. Kalra, "Nutraceutical—Definition and Introduction," AAPS PharmSci 5, no. 2 (2003), accessed November 9, 2010,http://www.aapsj.org/view.asp?art=ps050325#ref1.
[5] "Corporate Cause/Vision/Mission," Splash Corporation, accessed November 9, 2010, http://www.splash.com.ph/our_company.aspx?id=2.

10.1 Business and Corporate Strategy
LEARNING OBJECTIVES

1. Understand the difference between strategy formulation and strategy implementation.
2. Comprehend the relationships among business, corporate, and international strategy.
3. Know the inputs into a SWOT analysis.

What Is Strategy?
A strategy is the central, integrated, externally oriented concept of how a firm will achieve its objectives. Strategy formulation (or simply *strategizing*) is the process of deciding what to do; strategy implementation is the process of performing all the activities necessary to do what has been planned. Neither can succeed without the other; the two processes are interdependent from the standpoint that implementation should provide information that is used to periodically modify the strategy. However, it's important to distinguish between

the two because, typically, different people are involved in each process. In general, the leaders of the organization formulate strategy, while everyone is responsible for strategy implementation.

Figure 10.1 Corporate and Business Strategy summarizes the distinction between business and corporate strategy. The general distinction is that business strategy addresses *how we should compete*, while corporate strategy is concerned with *in which businesses we should compete*. Specifically, business strategy refers to the ways in which a firm plans to achieve its objectives within a particular business. In other words, one of Splash Corporation's business strategies would address its objectives within the nutraceuticals business. This strategy may focus on such things as how it competes against multinationals, including Unilever and Procter & Gamble. Similarly, Walmart managers are engaged in business strategy when they decide how to compete with Sears for consumer dollars.

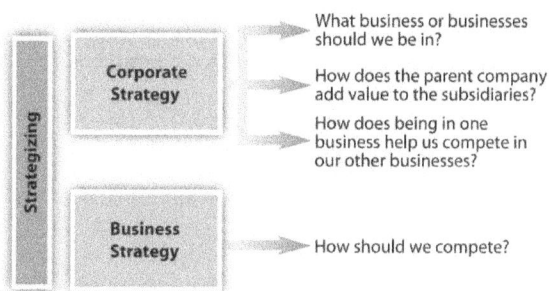

Corporate strategy addresses issues related to three fundamental questions:

1. **In what businesses will we compete?** The Hortalezas, for instance, say that they are in the wellness business; but from the opening case, you can see that they're talking about specific niche markets related to wellness.

2. **How can we, as a corporate parent, add value to our various lines of business (often called subsidiaries)?** For example, Splash's senior management might be able to orchestrate synergies and learning by using new products coming out of the Splash Research Institute. It can also glean market intelligence through health and beauty care retail outlets. Market intelligence can give Splash information on which brands are selling well, and some of those brands might be good targets for Splash to acquire, such as it did with the Hygienix brand line. Hygienix is a brand line of antibacterial skin-care products. Corporate strategy deals with

finding ways to create value by having two or more owned businesses cooperate and share resources.

3. **How can diversifying our business or entering a new industry, help us compete in our other industries?** The Hortalezas' experience with the HBC retailers can provide valuable insights into which new products to develop through the Splash Research Institute; in addition, Splash can sell more of its own products through HBC outlets.

International strategy is specialized in the sense that corporate strategy guides the choice of which markets, including different countries, a firm competes in. Even when a firm doesn't sell products or services outside its home country, its international strategy can include importing, international outsourcing, or offshoring. Importing involves the sale of products or services in one country that are sourced in another country. Penzeys Spices, for instance, sells herbs and spices that it buys from all over the world, yet it has retail outlets in only twenty-three states. However, such activity is not limited to small companies like Penzeys. Kohl's Corporation, one of the largest discount retailers in the country, has stores exclusively in the United States but most of its products are sourced overseas. In outsourcing, the company delegates an entire process (e.g., accounts payable) to the outsource vendor. The vendor takes control of the operation and runs the operation as it sees fit. The company pays the outsource vendor for the end result; how the vendor achieves those end results is up to the vendor. The outsourcer may do the work within the same country or may take it to another country (also known as offshoring). In offshoring, the company takes a function out of its home country and places the function in another country, generally at a lower cost. International outsourcing refers to work that is contracted to a nondomestic third party.

The Strategizing Process

From where does strategy originate? Strategy formulation typically comes from the top managers or owners of an organization, while the responsibility for strategy implementation resides with all organizational members. This entire set of activities is called the strategizing process.

As you can see with the opening case on Splash Corporation, the strategizing process starts with an organization's mission and vision. A mission statement is the organization's statement of purpose and describes who the company is and what it does. Customers, employees, and investors are the stakeholders most often emphasized, but others like government or communities (i.e., in the form of social or environmental impact) can also be impacted. [1] Mission statements are often longer than vision statements. Sometimes mission statements include a summation of the firm's values. Organizational values are those shared principles, standards, and goals.

A vision statement, in contrast, is a future-oriented declaration of the organization's purpose. In many ways, the mission statement lays out the organization's "purpose for being," and the vision statement then says, "on the basis of that purpose, this is what we want to become." The strategy should flow directly from the vision, since the strategy is intended to achieve the vision and satisfy the organization's mission. Along with some form of internal and organizational analysis using SWOT (or the firm's strengths, weaknesses, opportunities, and threats), a strategy is formulated into a strategic plan. This plan should allow for the achievement of the mission and vision. Taking SWOT analysis into consideration, the firm's management then determines how the strategy will be implemented in regard to organization, leadership, and controls. Strategic planning, together with organizing, leading, and controlling, is sometimes referred to by the acronym P-O-L-C. This is the framework managers use to understand and communicate the relationship between strategy formulation and strategy implementation.

Did You Know?

Research suggests that companies from different countries approach strategy from different perspectives of social responsibility. Central to the distinctiveness of the Indian business model is the sense of mission, a social goal for the business that goes beyond making money and helps employees see a purpose in their work. Every company we [the researchers] saw articulated a clear social mission for their business. ITC, a leading conglomerate, echoed the views of the companies we interviewed with this statement, describing the company's purpose: "Envisioning a larger societal purpose has always been a hallmark of ITC. The company sees no conflict between the twin goals of shareholder value enhancement and societal value creation." Contrast this Indian model, where a company's business goal is seen as bettering society, with

the US model, where we try to motivate employees around the corporate goal of making shareholders rich. The US approach is at a sizable disadvantage, because it is difficult for most people to see making money for shareholders as a goal that is personally meaningful. While it is possible to tie pay to shareholder value, it is extremely expensive to pay the average employee enough in share-based incentives to get him or her to focus on shareholder value. [2]

The Fundamentals of SWOT Analysis

SWOT analysis was developed by Ken Andrews in the early 1970s. [3] It is the assessment of a company's strengths and weaknesses—the S and W—which occur as part of organizational analysis; this organizational analysis of S and W is an audit of a company's internal workings. Conversely, examining the opportunities and threats is a part of environmental analysis—the company must look outside the organization to determine the opportunities and threats, over which it has less control.

When conducting a SWOT analysis, a firm asks four basic questions about itself and its environment:

1. What can we do?
2. What do we want to do?
3. What might we do?
4. What do others expect us to do?

Strengths and Weaknesses

A good starting point for strategizing is an assessment of what an organization does well and what it does less well. [4] The general idea is that good strategies take advantage of *strengths* and minimize the disadvantages posed by any *weaknesses*. Michael Jordan, for instance, is an excellent all-around athlete; he excels in baseball and golf, but his athletic skills show best in basketball. As with Jordan's athleticism, when you can identify certain strengths that set an organization apart from actual and potential competitors, that strength is considered a source of competitive advantage. The hardest but most important thing for an organization to do is to develop its competitive advantage into a sustainable competitive advantage—that is, using the organization's strengths in a way that can't be easily duplicated by other firms or made less valuable by changes in the external environment.

Opportunities and Threats

After considering what you just learned about competitive advantage and sustainable competitive advantage, it's easy to see why the external environment is a critical input into strategy. *Opportunities* assess the external attractive factors that represent the reason for a business to exist and prosper. What opportunities exist in the market or the environment from which the organization can benefit? *Threats* include factors beyond your control that could place the strategy or even the business itself at risk. Threats are also external—managers typically have no control over them, but it can be beneficial to have contingency plans in place to address them.

In summary, SWOT analysis helps you identify strategic alternatives that address the following questions:

- **Strengths and opportunities (SO).** How can you use your strengths to take advantage of the opportunities?

- **Strengths and threats (ST).** How can you take advantage of your strengths to avoid real and potential threats?

- **Weaknesses and opportunities (WO).** How can you use your opportunities to overcome the weaknesses you are experiencing?

- **Weaknesses and threats (WT).** How can you minimize your weaknesses and avoid threats? [5]

KEY TAKEAWAYS

- Strategy formulation is coming up with the plan, and strategy implementation is making the plan happen.

- There are different forms of strategy. Business strategy refers to how a firm competes, while corporate strategy answers questions concerning the businesses with which the organization should compete. International strategy is a key feature of many corporate strategies. In some cases, international strategy takes the form of outsourcing or offshoring.

- An overview of the strategizing process involves a SWOT (strengths, weaknesses, opportunities, threats) analysis and the development of the organization's mission and vision.

EXERCISES

(AACSB: Reflective Thinking, Analytical Skills)

1. What is the difference between strategy formulation and strategy implementation?
2. What are the different levels of strategy?

3. To what level of strategy do outsourcing, offshoring, and international strategy belong?

[1] {Authors' names retracted as requested by the work's original creator or licensee}, Principles of Management (Nyack, NY)
[2] Peter Cappelli, Harbir Singh, Jitendra Singh, and Michael Useem, "The India Way: Lessons for the U.S.," Academy of Management Perspectives 24, no. 2 (2010): 6–24.
[3] Kenneth R. Andrews, The Concept of Corporate Strategy (Homewood, IL: Richard D. Irwin, 1971).
[4] {Authors' names retracted as requested by the work's original creator or licensee}, Principles of Management (Nyack, NY)
[5] Heinz Weihrich, "The TOWS Matrix—A Tool for Situational Analysis," Long Range Planning 15, no. 2 (April 1982): 52–64.

10.2 Generic Strategies
LEARNING OBJECTIVES

1. Know the three business-level strategies.
2. Understand the difference between the three dimensions of corporate strategy.
3. Comprehend the importance of economies of scale and economies of scope in corporate strategy.

Types of Business-Level Strategies

Business-level strategies are intended to create differences between a firm's position and those of its rivals. To position itself against its rivals, a firm must decide whether to *perform activities differently* or *perform different activities.* [1] A firm's business-level strategy is a deliberate choice in regard to how it will perform the value chain's primary and support activities in ways that create unique value.

Collectively, these primary and support activities make up a firm's value chain, as summarized in Figure 10.3 "The Value Chain". For example, successful Internet shoe purveyor Zappos has key value-chain activities of purchasing, logistics, inventory, and customer service. Successful use of a chosen strategy results only when the firm integrates its primary and support activities to provide the unique value it intends to deliver. The Zappos strategy is to emphasize customer service, so it invests more in the people and systems related to customer service than do its competitors.

Value is delivered to customers when the firm is able to use competitive advantages resulting from the integration of activities. Superior fit of an organization's functional activities, such as production, marketing, accounting, and so on, forms an activity system—with Zappos, it exhibits superior fit among the value-chain activities of purchasing, logistics, and customer service.

In turn, an effective activity system helps the firm establish and exploit its strategic position. As a result of Zappos's activity system, the company is the leading Internet shoe retailer in North America and has been acquired by Amazon to further build Amazon's clothing and accessories business position.

Favorable positioning is important to develop and sustain competitive advantages. [2] Improperly positioned firms encounter competitive difficulties and can fail to sustain competitive advantages. For example, Sears made ineffective responses to competitors such as Walmart, leaving it in a weak competitive position for years. These ineffective responses resulted from the company's inability to implement appropriate strategies to take advantage of external opportunities and internal competencies and to respond to external threats. Two researchers have described this situation: "Once a towering force in retailing, Sears spent 10 sad years vacillating between an emphasis on hard goods and soft goods, venturing in and out of ill-chosen businesses, failing to differentiate itself in any of them, and never building a compelling economic logic." [3] Firms choose from among three generic business-level strategies to establish and defend their desired strategic position against rivals: (1) *cost leadership*, (2) *differentiation*, and (3) *integrated cost leadership and differentiation*. Each business-level strategy helps the firm establish and exploit a competitive advantage within a particular scope.

When deciding on a strategy to pursue, firms have a choice of two potential types of competitive advantage: (1) lower cost than competitors or (2) better quality (through a differentiated product or service) for which the form can charge a premium price. Competitive advantage is therefore achieved within some scope. Scope includes the geographic markets the company serves as well as the product and customer segments in which it competes. Companies seek to gain competitive advantage by implementing a cost leadership strategy or a differential strategy.

As you read about each of these business-level strategies, it's important to remember that none is better than the others. Rather, how effective each strategy depends on each firm's specific circumstances—namely, the conditions of the firm's external environment as well as the firm's internal strengths, capabilities, resources, and core competencies.

Cost-Leadership Strategy

Choosing to pursue a cost-leadership strategy means that the firm seeks to make its products or provide its services at the lowest cost possible relative to its competitors while maintaining a quality that is acceptable to consumers. Firms achieve cost leadership by building large-scale operations that help them reduce the cost of each unit by eliminating extra features in their products or services, by reducing their marketing costs, by finding low-cost sources or materials or labor, and so forth. Walmart is one of the most cited examples of a global firm pursuing an effective cost-leadership strategy.

One of the primary sets of activities that firms perform is the set of activities around supply-chain management and logistics. Supply-chain management encompasses both inbound and outbound logistics. Inbound logistics include identifying, purchasing, and handling all the raw materials or inputs that go into making a company's products. For example, one of Stonyfield Farm's inputs is organic milk that goes into its organic yogurts. Walmart buys finished products as its inputs, but it must warehouse these inputs and allocate them to its specific retail stores. In outbound logistics, companies transport products to their customer. When pursuing a low-cost strategy, companies can examine logistics activities—sourcing, procurement, materials handling, warehousing, inventory control, transportation—for ways to reduce costs. These activities are particularly fruitful for lowering costs because they often account for a large portion of the firm's expenditures. For example, Marks & Spencer, a British retailer, overhauled its supply chain and stopped its previous practice of buying supplies in one hemisphere and shipping them to another. This will save the company over $250 million dollars over five years—and will greatly reduce carbon emissions. [4]

Differentiation Strategy

Differentiation stems from creating unique value to the customer through advanced technology, high-quality ingredients or components, product features, superior delivery time, and the like. [5] Companies can differentiate their products by emphasizing products' unique features, by coming out with frequent and useful innovations or product upgrades, and by providing impeccable customer service. For example, the construction equipment manufacturer Caterpillar has excelled for years on the durability of its tractors; its worldwide parts availability, which results in quick repairs; and its dealer network.

When pursuing the differentiation strategy, firms examine all activities to identify ways to create higher value for the customer, such as by making the product easier to use, by offering training on the product, or by bundling the product with a service. For example, the Henry Ford West Bloomfield Hospital in West Bloomfield, Michigan, has distinguished itself from other hospitals by being more like a hotel than a hospital. The hospital has only private rooms, all overlooking a pond and landscaped gardens. The hospital is situated on 160 acres of woodlands and wetlands and has twenty-four-hour room service, Wi-Fi, and a café offering healthful foods. "From the get-go, I said that the food in the hospital would be the finest in the country," says Gerard van Grinsven, president and CEO of the hospital. [6] The setting and food are so exquisite that not only has the café become a destination café, but some couples have even held their weddings there. [7]

Integrated Cost-Leadership/Differentiation Strategy

An integrated costleadership and differentiation strateg y is a combination of the cost leadership and the differentiation strategies. Firms that can achieve this combination often perform better than companies that pursue either strategy separately. [8] To succeed with this strategy, firms invest in the activities that create the unique value but look for ways to reduce cost in nonvalue activities.

Types of Corporate Strategy

Remember, business strategy is related to questions about how a firm competes; corporate strategy is related to questions about what businesses to compete in and how these choices work together as a system. Nonprofits and governments have similar decision-making situations, although the element of competition isn't always present. A firm that is making choices about the scope of its operations has several options. Figure 10.4 summarizes how all organizations can expand (or contract) along any of three areas: (1) *vertical*, (2) *horizontal*, and (3) *geographic*.

Vertical Scope

Vertical scope refers to all the activities, from the gathering of raw materials to the sale of the finished product, that a business goes through to make a product. Sometimes a firm expands vertically out of economic necessity. Perhaps it must protect its supply of a critical input, or perhaps firms in the industry that supply certain

inputs are reluctant to invest sufficiently to satisfy the unique or heavy needs of a single buyer. Beyond such reasons as these—which are defensive—firms expand vertically to take advantage of growth or profit opportunities. Vertical expansion in scope is often a logical growth option because a company is familiar with the arena.

Sometimes a firm can create value by moving into suppliers' or buyers' value chains. In some cases, a firm can bundle complementary products. If, for instance, you were to buy a new home, you'd go through a series of steps in making your purchase decision. Now, most homebuilders concentrate on a fairly narrow aspect of the homebuilding value chain. Some, however, have found it profitable to expand vertically into the home-financing business by offering mortgage brokerage services. Pulte Homes Inc., one of the largest homebuilders in the United States, set up a wholly owned subsidiary, Pulte Mortgage LLC, to help buyers get financing for new homes. This service simplifies the home-buying process for many of Pulte's customers and allows Pulte to reap profits in the home-financing industry. Automakers and car dealers have expanded into financing for similar reasons.

Horizontal Scope

Whereas as vertical scope reflects a firm's level of investment in upstream or downstream activities, horizontal scope refers to the number of similar businesses or business activities at the same level of the value chain. A firm increases its horizontal scope in one of two ways:

1. By moving from an industry market segment into another, related segment
2. By moving from one industry into another (the strategy typically called *diversification*)

Examples of horizontal scope include when an oil company adds refineries; an automaker starts a new line of vehicles; or a media company owns radio and television stations, newspapers, books, and magazines. The degree to which horizontal expansion is desirable depends on the degree to which the new industry is related to a firm's home industry. Industries can be related in a number of different ways. They may, for example, rely on similar types of human capital, engage in similar value-chain activities, or share customers with similar needs. Obviously, the more factors present, the greater the degree of relatedness. When, for instance,

Coca-Cola and PepsiCo expanded into the bottled water business, they were able to take advantage of the skill sets that they'd already developed in bottling and distribution. Moreover, because bottled water and soft drinks are substitutes for one another, both appeal to customers with similar demands.

On the other hand, when PepsiCo expanded into snack foods, it was clearly moving into a business with a lesser degree of relatedness. For one thing, although the distribution channels for both businesses are similar (both sell products through grocery stores, convenience stores, delis, and so forth), the technology for producing the products is fundamentally different. In addition, although the two industries sell complementary products—they're often sold at the same time to the same customers—they aren't substitutes.

Economies of Scale, Economies of Scope, Synergies, and Market Power

Why is increased horizontal scope attractive? Primarily because it offers opportunities in four areas:

1. To exploit economies of scale, such as by selling more of the same product in the same geographic market
2. To exploit possible economies of scope by sharing resources common to different products
3. To enhance revenue through synergies—achieved by selling more, but different, products to the same customers
4. To increase market power—achieved by being relatively bigger than suppliers

Economies of scale, in microeconomics, are the cost advantages that a business obtains through expanding in size, which is one reason why companies grow large in certain industries. Economies of scale are also used to justify free-trade policies, because some economies of scale may require a larger market than is possible within a particular country. For example, it wouldn't be efficient for a small country like Switzerland to have its own automaker, if that automaker could only sell to its local market. That automaker may be profitable, however, if it exports cars to international markets in addition to selling to selling them in the domestic market.

Economies of scope are similar in concept to economies of scale. Whereas economies of scale derive primarily from efficiencies gained from marketing or the supply side, such as increasing the scale of production of a single product type, economies of scope refer to efficiencies gained from demand-side changes, such as increasing the scope of marketing and distribution.

Economies of scope gained from marketing and distribution are one reason why some companies market products as a bundle or under a brand family. Because segments in closely related industries often use similar assets and resources, a firm can frequently achieve cost savings by sharing them among businesses in different segments. The fast-food industry, for instance, has many segments—burgers, fried chicken, tacos, pizza, and so forth. Yum! Brands, which operates KFC, Pizza Hut, Taco Bell, A&W Restaurants, and Long John Silver's, has embarked on what the company calls a "multibrand" store strategy. Rather than house all of its fast food in separate outlets, Yum! achieves economies of scope across its portfolio by bundling two outlets in a single facility. The strategy works in part because customer purchase decisions in horizontally related industries are often made simultaneously. In other words, two people walking into a bundled fast-food outlet may desire different things to eat, but both want fast food, and both are going to eat at the same time. In addition, the inherent product and demand differences across breakfast, lunch, dinner, and snacks allows for multiple food franchises to share a resource that would otherwise be largely unused during off-peak hours.

Geographic Scope

A firm increases geographic scope by moving into new geographic areas without entirely altering its business model. In its early growth period, for instance, a company may simply move into new locations in the same country. For example, the US fast-food chain Sonic will only open new outlets in states that are adjacent to states where it already has stores.

More often, however, increased *geographic scope* has come to mean *internationalization*—entering new markets in other parts of the world. For this reason, international strategy is discussed in depth in the next section. For a domestic firm whose operations are confined to its home country, the whole globe is a potential area of expansion. Remember, however, that just as different industries can exhibit different degrees of relatedness, so, too, can different geographic markets—even those within the same industry. We can assess relatedness among different national markets by examining a number of factors, including laws, customs, cultures, consumer preferences, distances from home markets, common borders, language, socioeconomic development, and many others.

Economies of Scale, Economies of Scope, or Reduction in Costs

Geographic expansion can be motivated by economies of scale or economies of scope. Research and development (R&D), for example, represents a significant, relatively fixed cost for firms in many industries. When firms move into new regions of a country or global arenas, they often find that they can amortize their R&D costs over a larger market. For instance, the marginal cost for a pharmaceutical firm to enter a new geographic market is lower than the marginal costs of R&D and running clinical trials, which are required when a company wants to bring a new drug into the US market. Once the costs of development and entry are covered, entering new geographic markets brings in new revenues. Because the fixed costs have been amortized over the new, larger market, the average cost for all the firm's customers goes down. It should come as no surprise, then, that industries with relatively high R&D expenditures, such as pharmaceuticals and computer-related products, are among the most thoroughly globalized industries. Finally, changes in geographic scope can lower costs when operations are moved to lower cost supply markets.

KEY TAKEAWAYS

- There are three different business-level strategies: (1) cost leadership, (2) differentiation, and (3) integrated cost leadership and differentiation.

- All three of these business-level strategies involve choices related to differentiation and cost leadership. Corporate strategy can unfold in terms of vertical integration (or disintegration), horizontal integration (or disintegration), or geographic diversification.

- Choices made with respect to these three aspects of diversification have financial implications in the form of economies of scale or scope. Geographic expansion into new countries can affect profitability through economies of scale, economies of scope, or reduction in costs resulting from less costly inputs.

EXERCISES

(AACSB: Reflective Thinking, Analytical Skills)

1. On what two dimensions are all business strategies based?
2. What are the three dimensions of corporate strategy and how are they different?
3. What are the three ways in which geographic diversification can positively affect financial performance?

[1] Michael E. Porter, "What Is Strategy?" Harvard Business Review 74, no. 6 (November–December 1996): 61–78.
[2] Edward H. Bowman and Constance E. Helfat, "Does Corporate Strategy Matter?" Strategic Management Journal 22, no. 1 (January 2001): 1–4; Bill McEvily and Akbar Zaheer, "Bridging Ties: A Source of Firm Heterogeneity in Competitive Capabilities," Strategic Management Journal 20, no. 12 (December 1999): 1133–56.
[3] Donald C. Hambrick and James W. Fredrickson, "Are You Sure You Have a Strategy?" Academy of Management Executive 19, no. 4 (2005): 52.
[4] Michael E. Porter and Mark R. Kramer, "The Big Idea: Creating Shared Value," Harvard Business Review, January 2011, accessed January 14, 2011, http://hbr.org/2011/01/the-big-idea-creating-shared-value/ar/pr.
[5] Michael E. Porter, Competitive Advantage (New York: Free Press, 1985), 150.
[6] Gerard van Grinsven, "Healthy Living, the Ritz Way" (booklet, BIF-6 Collaborative Innovation Summit, Providence, RI, September 15–16, 2010), 60–61.
[7] Gerard van Grinsven, "Healthy Living, the Ritz Way" (presentation, BIF-6 Collaborative Innovation Summit, Providence, RI, September 15–16, 2010).
[8] Gregory G. Dess, Anil Gupta, Jean-François Hennart, and Charles W. L. Hill, "Conducting and Integrating Strategy Research at the International, Corporate, and Business Levels: Issues and Directions," Journal of Management 21, no. 3 (Fall 1995): 377.

10.3 International Strategy

LEARNING OBJECTIVES

1. Know the trade-offs being made in terms of local responsiveness and global efficiency in regard to international strategies.
2. Distinguish among multidomestic, global, and transnational strategies.
3. Understand how the local environment can impact a firm's international strategy.

At the corporate level, firms choose to use one of three international strategies: multidomestic, global, or transnational (transnational is a combination of multidomestic and global). These three strategies reflect trade-offs between local responsiveness and global efficiency For firms to gain a competitive advantage, they have to devise strategies that take best advantage of the firm's core competencies and that are difficult for competitors to copy.

Multidomestic Strategy

Multidomestic strategy maximizes local responsiveness by giving decentralizing decision-making authority to local business units in each country so that they can create products and services optimized to their local markets. A multidomestic strategy would be appropriate, for instance, where Thomas Friedman's flat-world thesis is not applicable. A multidomestic strategy focuses on competition within each country and maximizes local responsiveness. It assumes that the markets differ and, therefore, are segmented by country boundaries. In other words, consumer needs and desires, industry conditions (e.g., the number and type of competitors), political and legal structures, and social norms vary by country. Using a multidomestic strategy, the firm can customize its products to meet the specific preferences and needs of local customers. As a result, the firm can compete more effectively in each local market and increase its local market share.

The disadvantage of a multidomestic strategy, however, is that the firm faces more uncertainty because of the tailored strategies in different countries. In addition, because the firm is pursuing different strategies in different locations, it cannot take advantage of economies of scale that could help decrease costs for the firm overall. The multidomestic strategy has been more commonly used by European multinational firms because of the variety of cultures and markets found in Europe.

As mentioned earlier, Yum! Brands has a strong incentive to compete internationally with its restaurant concepts (i.e., KFC, Pizza Hut, Taco Bell, A&W Restaurants, and Long John Silver's). Yum! pursues a multidomestic strategy by trying to localize as much as possible. The firm doesn't open restaurants using only the US model. Wherever the company has locations, it consistently adapts to local tastes and negotiates well when cultural and political climates change: "In Japan, for instance, KFC sells tempura crispy strips. In northern England, KFC stresses gravy and potatoes, while in Thailand, it offers fresh rice with soy or sweet chili sauce. In Holland, the company makes a potato-and-onion croquette. In France, it sells pastries alongside chicken. And in China, the chicken gets spicier the farther inland you travel. More and more, if it's only an American brand without a regional appeal, it's going to be difficult to market."[1] Recognizing this constraint, Yum! introduces its products in those foreign markets that are the shortest "taste" distance from its traditional home markets. [2] So, it sticks to high-population areas in which American culture has some appeal as well.

Global Strategy

In contrast to a multidomestic strategy, a global strategy is centralized and controlled by the home office and seeks to maximize global efficiency Under this strategy, products are much more likely to be standardized rather than tailored to local markets. One way to think about global strategies is that if the world is flat, you can sell the same products and services in the same way in every country on the planet. The strategic business units operating in each country are assumed to be interdependent, and the home office attempts to achieve integration across these businesses. Therefore, a global strategy emphasizes economies of scale and offers greater opportunities to utilize innovations developed at the corporate level or in one country in other markets.

Although pursuing a global strategy decreases risk for the firm, the firm may not be able to gain as high a market share in local markets because the global strategy isn't as responsive to local markets. Another disadvantage of the global strategy is that it is difficult to manage because of the need to coordinate strategies and operating decisions across country borders. Consequently, achieving efficient operations with a global strategy requires the sharing of resources as well as coordination and cooperation across country boundaries, which in turn require centralization and headquartered control. Whether the world is flat or flattening can often depend on the industry. In most cases, the world isn't flat, but in a few industries the market characteristics are fairly common. The cement and concrete industry is an example of an industry where the flatteners have taken effect. CEMEX, a Mexico-based cement and building materials company founded in 1906, pursued an international business strategy that led to its growth and position as one of the top building materials companies in the world today. [3] CEMEX acquired companies to grow rapidly, took advantage of economies of scale, and used the Internet to lower its cost structure. Perhaps most crucial to its international expansion success was foreseeing the shifts in distribution technologies that would bring previously disparate regional markets closer together. [4]

In 2009, CEMEX CEO Lorenzo H. Zambrano wrote a message to stakeholders regarding sustainable development:

In 2009, as we coped with the worst crisis to hit the global economy, our industry, and our company in 75 years, we took important and decisive steps to strengthen not only our business model, but also our commitment to sustainable development. As a result, we are a stronger company, well positioned to take advantage of the recovery of the global economy. That is testimony to the quality of our employees, to our company's core values of collaboration, integrity, and leadership, and to the disciplined execution of sound strategies.

We made several difficult decisions during the year to adjust to a rapidly evolving and extraordinarily challenging market environment. For example, we sold assets, most notably our Australian operations, and reorganized our business to improve efficiency and productivity. Together, these measures brought about an unfortunate, but necessary, reduction in our workforce. However, these steps enabled us to weather the crisis and will position our company for long-term success.

Even as the economic crisis unfolded, we deepened our commitment to our stakeholders. We continued our efforts to ensure the safety of our employees, and many of our country operations recorded solid improvements in their safety performance. However, despite our ongoing efforts, I am deeply saddened to report that 33 people—including employees, contractors, and third parties—died in incidents related to our operations during 2009. This is tragic and unacceptable. We are working harder than ever to identify and address the root causes of all fatalities and serious injuries in order to prevent their recurrence. For example, we are expanding and strengthening our efforts in key areas such as safety training for drivers and contractors. Above all, we remain committed to our global long-term goal of zero incidents.

On the environmental front, we continued to reduce our carbon footprint by improving the energy efficiency of our operations and expanding our use of alternative fuels. As a result, in 2009 we increased our use of alternative fuels to 16.4 percent, exceeding our target for 2015 ahead of time. In addition, Eurus, the wind farm project developed by ACCIONA Energía, became fully operational during the year and can supply 25 percent of our plants' electricity needs in Mexico.

Finally, we engaged the communities in which we operate through open and ongoing dialogue, social initiatives, and volunteer efforts. We continued to find ways to promote access to housing and community infrastructure. For example, we launched our most successful low-income housing solution, Patrimonio Hoy, in the Dominican Republic.

As a global company, we are deeply aware of our responsibility to address complex sustainability challenges. We are committed to further reducing our impact on the environment and recognize that we have many opportunities to improve. We reconfirm our commitment to address climate change and to the development of a low-carbon economy.

We actively engage with our global panel of sustainability experts, who provide important and valuable advice. On a personal note, I thank them for their feedback and for continuously challenging us to make further progress.

We present our 2009 sustainable development report within the framework of our overall sustainability website to better communicate our sustainability performance. We have provided an executive summary that highlights our performance on our key sustainability issues. We hope that you find the report engaging, transparent, and comprehensive, and we welcome your feedback.

Sincerely, Lorenzo H. Zambrano

CEMEX Chairman of the Board and Chief Executive Officer [5]

Transnational Strategy

Transnational strategy seeks to combine the best of multidomestic strategy and a global strategy to get both global efficiency and local responsiveness. For many industries, given the differences across markets and the similarities being fostered by the flatteners, this form of strategy is highly desirable and appropriate. The difficulty is that combining the multidomestic and global strategies is hard to do because it requires fulfilling the dual goals of flexibility and coordination. Firms must balance opposing local and global goals. On the positive side, firms that effectively implement a transnational strategy often outperform competitors who use either the multidomestic or global corporate-level strategies. [6]

The Ford Motor Company and BMW are examples of firms pursuing a transnational strategy. Ford, for example, is focusing on the "world car," building one core car that will be sold globally. This strategy lowers Ford's development costs, because rather than developing different cars for different countries or regions, Ford will sell the same car to all markets. The world car strategy, however, poses a major hurdle: how to design a car that appeals to consumers in many different countries. To tackle the issue, Ford took a page from BMW, which uses the concept of "fashion forward" when designing its 3 Series cars for multiple markets. The secret, according to Verena Kloos, president of BMW's DesignworksUSA studio in California, is to "show consumers what the next big thing is, not reflect what they think now." As James D. Farley, Ford's global marketing chief, sees it, the global appeal of the 3 Series rests on trust and aspiration. People worldwide see the same design, which builds trust through ubiquity and familiarity and leads them to aspire to own the car themselves. [7]

International Strategy and the Local Environment

Sometimes, firms expanding into new geographic markets find that they must adapt certain components of their strategies to accommodate local environments. In the United States, for instance, Dell is famous for the business model that allows it to skip middlemen and go directly to suppliers and customers. In its early years, Dell experimented with a brick-and-mortar retail strategy but quickly retrenched. As it expanded into international markets, however, Dell has found that it has to suspend its direct model, at least temporarily. Why? Basically because it needs local intermediaries to help develop both a base of business and acceptable levels of customer awareness and sophistication. Such has been the case first in India and then in China, which constitute huge markets for Dell.

While Dell provides a good example of adaptation, most global firms tend to approach corporate strategy from the perspective of their domestic market constraint, which can be problematic. Microsoft is a case in point. The United States and the European Union (EU) have very different traditions and models of competition, which in turn means that strategies must vary across these important markets. Had you not been aware of

these differences, you might think that Microsoft followed an ideal resource-based corporate strategy in its diversification into Europe. It bundled its Windows operating system with the Internet Explorer browser and other software to increase the company's perceived value and, therefore, customers' willingness to pay. It also used its extensive experience with home-computer software, operating systems, and applications to better penetrate the server market for software and operating systems, where customers are primarily businesses. Finally, Microsoft tried to lock out competitors by including its Windows Media Player as a standard feature in both its server and home PC operating systems.

The EU, however, has made these Microsoft tactics illegal: the bundling strategy "deters innovation and reduces consumer choice in any technologies which Microsoft could conceivably take an interest in and tie with Windows in the future." [8] The EU signaled its disapproval by imposing a fine of over $600 million and giving Microsoft ninety days to release versions of its Windows operating systems for home PCs and servers without the Windows Media Player and to begin providing rivals access to the details of the code underlying its proprietary server systems, used primarily in business settings. This is not the first time such differences in regulatory environments have been ignored or underestimated by global firms. Just a few years earlier, the European Commission's ruling dealt a fatal blow to the all-but-done merger between Honeywell and General Electric (GE), citing that the merger would reduce competition in the aerospace industry. [9]

KEY TAKEAWAYS

- Multidomestic strategy maximizes local responsiveness by giving decentralizing decision-making authority to local business units in each country so that they can create products and services optimized to their local markets. This strategy allows firms to compete more effectively in the local market and increase their share in that market. The disadvantage of a multidomestic strategy, however, is that the firm faces more uncertainty because of the tailored strategies in different countries. In addition, because the firm is pursuing different strategies in different locations, it cannot take advantage of economies of scale that could help decrease costs for the firm overall.

- A global strategy is centralized and controlled by the home office and seeks to maximize global efficiency. Under this strategy, products are much more likely to be standardized rather than tailored to local markets. Although pursuing a global strategy decreases risk for the firm, the firm may not be able to gain as high a market share in local markets because the global strategy isn't as responsive to local markets.

- A transnational strategy offers the advantages of both the multidomestic strategy (efficiency) and global strategy (responsiveness to local conditions) but has the disadvantage that it is difficult to simultaneously execute the dual goals of flexibility and coordination.

EXERCISES

(AACSB: Reflective Thinking, Analytical Skills)

1. When should a firm choose the global strategy rather than a multidomestic strategy?
2. How might a given country's regulatory environment impact a firm's international strategy?
3. How do the international strategies affect the trade-offs managers must make between local responsiveness and global efficiency?

[1] Brian O'Keefe, "What Do KFC and Pizza Hut Conjure Up Abroad?" Fortune, November 26, 2001, 102–10.

[2] Pankaj Ghemawat, "Distance Still Matters," Harvard Business Review 79, no. 8 (2001): 147.

[3] "Strategically Positioned," CEMEX, accessed January 1, 2011, http://www.cemex.com/tc/tc_gl.asp.

[4] Daniel F. Spulber, Global Competitive Strategy (Cambridge, UK: Cambridge University Press, 2007), 217–18.

[5] Lorenzo H. Zambrano, "Addressing Complex Sustainability Challenges," CEMEX, accessed June 7, 2010, http://www.cemex.com/su/Su_oc_me.aspx.

[6] John Child and Yanni Yan, "National and Transnational Effects in International Business: Indications from Sino-Foreign Joint Ventures," Management International Review 41, no. 1 (January 2001): 53–75.

[7] David Kiley, "Can Ford's 'World Car' Bet Pay Off?" BusinessWeek, accessed June 7, 2010, http://www.businessweek.com/magazine/content/09_24/b41 35058974279.htm?campaign_id=rss_innovate.

[8] "EU Lowers Boom on Microsoft," Wired, March 24, 2004, accessed November 10, 2010, http://www.wired.com/techbiz/media/news/2004/03/62789.

[9] Yusaf Akbar, "Grabbing Victory from the Jaws of Defeat: Can the GE-Honeywell Merger Force International Competition Policy Cooperation?" World Competition 25, no. 4 (2002): 26–31.

10.4 The Five Elements of Strategy
LEARNING OBJECTIVES

1. Know the five elements of strategy through the strategy diamond.
2. Understand the interrelationship among the elements in the strategy diamond.
3. Recognize how the strategy diamond helps you develop and articulate international strategy.

Good strategy formulation means refining the elements of the strategy. First of all, don't confuse part of a strategy for a strategy itself. Being a low-cost provider or first mover in a market may be part of a strategy or the underlying logic of a particular strategy, but it's not a complete strategy. It's also important not to confuse your mission or vision with a strategy, even though the former are essential to the development and execution of good strategies.

As noted earlier, a strategy is an integrated and externally oriented concept of how a firm will achieve its objectives—how it will compete against its rivals. A strategy consists of an integrated set of choices. These choices relate to five elements managers must consider when making decisions: (1) *arenas*, (2) *differentiators*, (3) *vehicles*, (4) *staging and pacing*, and (5) *economic logic*. This group of elements, which are central to the strategic management process, makes up the strategy diamond. Most strategic plans focus on one or two such elements, often leaving large gaps in the overall strategy. Only when you have answers to questions about each of these five elements can you determine whether your strategy is an integrated whole; you'll also have a better idea of the areas in which your strategy needs to be revised or overhauled. As the strategy diamond figure shows, a good strategy considers the five key elements in order to arrive at specific answers to five questions:

1. **Arenas.** Where will we be active?
2. **Differentiators.** How will we get there?
3. **Vehicles.** How will we win in the marketplace?
4. **Staging.** What will be our speed and sequence of moves?
5. **Economic logic.** How will we obtain our returns?

Let's take a closer look at each of these elements.

Arenas

Arenas are areas in which a firm will be active. Decisions about a firm's arenas may encompass its products, services, distribution channels, market segments, geographic areas, technologies, and even stages of the value-creation process. Unlike vision statements, which tend to be fairly general, the identification of arenas must be very specific. It clearly tells managers what the firm should and should not do. In addition, because firms can contract with outside parties for everything from employees to manufacturing services, the choice of arenas can be fairly narrowly defined for some firms.

For example, as the largest US bicycle distributor, Pacific Cycle owns the Schwinn, Mongoose, and GT brands and sells its bikes through big-box retail outlets and independent dealers, as well as through independent agents in foreign markets. In addition to these arena choices, Pacific Cycle has entirely outsourced the production of its products to Asian manufacturers. This is important in the sense that the strategy diamond also helps the firm be precise in regard to which activities it will engage itself and which ones it will outsource and where. As you know, Asia happens to be a low-cost source of high-quality manufactured goods. In outsourcing shoes and apparel lines, Nike follows a similar strategy in terms of arenas. One key difference, however, is that Nike, through its Nike Town retail outlets, has also chosen a direct retail presence in addition to its use of traditional retail-distribution channels.

The arenas facet of the strategy diamond helps you answer questions about business strategy—that is, it helps you determine which particular industry or geographic segments are the firm's prime competitive arenas. The arenas facet also allows you to summarize corporate strategy—that is, it allows you to summarize which group of industry and geographic segments the firm competes in.

Differentiators

Differentiators are features and attributes of a company's product or service that help it beat its competitors in the marketplace. Firms can be successful in the marketplace along a number of common dimensions, including image, customization, technical superiority, price, quality, and reliability. Japanese automakers Toyota and Honda have done very well by providing effective combinations of differentiators. They sell both inexpensive cars and high-end cars with high-quality features, and many consumers find the value that they provide hard to match. However, even though the best strategies often combine differentiators, history has shown that firms often perform poorly when they try to be all things to all consumers. It's difficult to imagine, for instance, a single product that boasts both state-of-the-art technology and the lowest price on the market. Part of the problem is perceptual—consumers often associate low quality with low prices. Part of it is practical—leading-edge technologies cost money to develop and command higher prices because of their uniqueness or quality.

There are two critical factors in selecting differentiators:
1. Decisions must be made early. Key differentiators rarely materialize without significant up-front decisions, and without valuable differentiators firms tend to lose marketplace battles.
2. Identifying and executing successful differentiators mean making tough choices—trade-offs. Managers who can't make tough decisions about trade-offs often end up trying to satisfy too broad a spectrum of customer needs; as a result, they execute poorly on most dimensions.

Audi is an example of a company that has aligned these two factors successfully. Several years ago, Audi management realized that its cars were perceived as low-quality but high-priced German automobiles—obviously a poor competitive position. The firm decided that it had to move one way or another—up market or down market. It had to do one of two things: (1) lower its costs so that its pricing was consistent with customers' perceptions of product quality or (2) improve quality sufficiently to justify premium pricing. Given limited resources, the firm couldn't go in both directions; that is, it couldn't produce cars in both the low-price and high-quality strata. Audi made a decision to invest heavily in quality programs and in refining its marketing efforts. Ten years later, the quality of Audi cars has increased significantly, and customer perception has moved them much closer to the level of BMW and Mercedes-Benz. Audi has reaped the benefits of premium pricing and improved profitability, but the decisions behind the strategic up-market move entailed significant trade-offs. Differentiators are what drive potential customers to choose one firm's offerings over those of competitors. The earlier and more consistent the firm is at driving these differentiators, the greater the likelihood that customers will recognize them.

Vehicles

Vehicles are the means for participating in targeted arenas. For instance, a firm that wants to go international can do so in different ways. In a recent drive to enter certain international markets (e.g., Argentina), Walmart has opened new stores and grown organically—meaning that it developed all the stores internally as opposed to acquiring stores already based in the countries it wanted to enter. Elsewhere (namely, in England and Germany), Walmart has purchased existing retailers and is in the process of transferring its unique way of doing business to the acquired companies. Likewise, a firm that requires a new technology could develop it through investments in research and development (R&D). Or it could opt to form an alliance with a competitor or a supplier that already possesses the technology, accelerating the integration of the missing piece into its set of resources and capabilities. Finally, it could simply buy another firm that owns the technology. In this case, the possible vehicles for entering a new arena include acquisitions, alliances, and organic investment and growth.

Staging and Pacing

Staging and pacing refer to the timing and speed, or pace, of strategic moves. Staging choices typically reflect available resources, including cash, human capital, and knowledge. At what point, for example, should Walmart have added international markets to its strategy? Perhaps if the company had pursued global opportunities earlier, it would have been able to develop a better sense of foreign market conditions and even spread the cost of entry over a longer period of time. However, by delaying its international moves, the company was able to focus on dominating the US market, which is—after all—the largest retail market in the world. Despite mixed results overseas, Walmart is the undisputed leader in global retailing and has recently increased its emphasis on international markets as the basis for future growth.

Staging decisions should be driven by several factors—resources, urgency, credibility, and the need for early wins. Because few firms have the resources to do everything they'd like to do immediately, they usually have to match opportunities with available resources. In addition, not all opportunities to enter new arenas are permanent; some have only brief windows. In such cases, early wins and the credibility of certain key stakeholders may be necessary to implement a strategy.

Economic Logic

Economic logic refers to how the firm will earn a profit—that is, how the firm will generate positive returns over and above its cost of capital. Economic logic is the "fulcrum" for profit creation. Earning normal profits, of course, requires a firm to meet all fixed, variable, and financing costs. Achieving desired returns over the firm's cost of capital is a tall order for any organization. In analyzing a firm's economic logic, think of both costs and revenues. Sometimes economic logic resides primarily on the cost side of the equation. Irish airline Ryanair, for example, can fly passengers for significantly lower costs per passenger mile than any major competitor. At other times, economic logic may rest on the firm's ability to increase the customer's willingness to pay premium prices for products (in other words, prices that significantly exceed the costs of providing enhanced products).

When the five elements of strategy are aligned and mutually reinforcing, the firm is generally in a position to perform well. High performance levels, however, ultimately mean that a strategy is also being executed well. This leads to strategy implementation.

The Five Elements and International Strategy

As you learn to apply the strategy diamond to issues about international business, you will probably work through three related questions:

1. Do we need to expand outside our home country?
2. If so, where should we expand?
3. Finally, how should we do that?

Answering the first question requires an understanding of the international strategy's economic logic and how the strategy is supported by the current differentiators. Answering the second question includes identifying specific regions and countries and the criteria that might be used to prioritize potential markets. Finally, the answer to the third question involves whether the organization should enter the new international market on its own, with a partner, or through acquisition.

Considering the responses to these questions, you'll then have a new strategy diamond that addresses the following:

*   **Arenas.** The specific geographic markets and the channels and value-chain activities in those markets.

- **Differentiators.** How being international differentiates the organization from competitors, makes products or services more attractive to future customers, and strengthens the effectiveness of the differentiators in the chosen arenas.
- **Vehicles.** The preference to use organic investment and growth, alliances, or acquisitions as expansion vehicles.
- **Staging and pacing.** When you start expanding, how quickly you expand and the sequence of your expansion efforts.
- **Economic logic.** How your international strategy contributes to the overall economic logic of your business and corporate strategies.

KEY TAKEAWAYS

- The strategy diamond lets you summarize the characteristics of a firm's business and corporate strategy in terms of five facets—arenas, differentiators, vehicles, staging and pacing, and economic logic.
- All five facets are interrelated. When the five elements of strategy are aligned and mutually reinforcing, the firm is generally in a position to perform well.
- The strategy diamond helps you develop international strategy, using three related questions:
  a. Do we need to expand outside our home country?
  b. If so, where should we expand?
  c. How should we expand?

EXERCISES

(AACSB: Reflective Thinking, Analytical Skills)
1. What are the five facets of the strategy diamond?
2. How does the strategy diamond capture a firm's business strategy?
3. How does the strategy diamond capture a firm's corporate strategy?
4. What are some of the strategy-diamond issues a good international strategy must address?

10.5 Managing the International Business with the P-O-L-C Framework

LEARNING OBJECTIVES

1. Know the dimensions of the P-O-L-C framework.
2. Recognize the general inputs into each P-O-L-C dimension.

A manager's primary challenge is to solve problems creatively. In order to help managers respond to the challenge of creative problem solving, principles of management have long been categorized into the four major functions of planning, organizing, leading, and controlling, or the P-O-L-C framework. [1]These four functions are actually highly integrated when carried out in the day-to-day realities of running an organization. So, don't get caught up in trying to closely analyze and understand a complete, clear rationale for the categorization of the skills and practices that comprise the P-O-L-C framework.

It's important to note that this framework is not without criticism. Specifically, these criticisms stem from this observation: while P-O-L-C functions might be ideal, they don't accurately depict the day-to-day actions of actual managers. [2]The typical day in the life of a manager at any level can be fragmented and hectic, with the constant threat of having priorities dictated by the law of the trivial many and important few (i.e., the 80-20 rule). However, the general conclusion seems to be that the P-O-L-C framework of management still provides a very useful way of classifying the activities managers engage in as they attempt to achieve organizational goals. [3]

Planning

You have already been exposed to the essentials of planning in your introduction to strategy and strategic management. "Planning is the function of management that involves setting objectives and determining a course of action for achieving these objectives." [4] In this section, planning reflects the notion of strategizing. To plan well, managers must be aware of the external conditions facing their organizations (recall the O and T in the discussion of SWOT in Section 10.1 "Business and Corporate Strategy"). Managers must also be good decision makers to set a course for achieving organizational objectives. In international business, planning is particularly complex given all the countries and variables involved.

There are five steps in the planning process. First, the process begins with SWOT analysis, which means that planners must be aware of the critical factors facing their organization in terms of economic conditions, their competitors, and their customers.

Second, planners establish organizational objectives. Organizational objectives are statements of what needs to be achieved and when. Third, planners identify multiple ways of achieving those objectives, with an eye toward choosing the best path to reach each objective. Fourth, planners must formulate the necessary steps and ensure effective implementation of plans. Finally, planners must constantly monitor the progress of their plans and evaluate the success of those plans, making adjustments as necessary. Let's look at the three primary types of plans and planning—strategic, tactical, and operational.

Strategic Planning

Strategic planning is the most long-range planning, typically looking three years or more into the future. During strategic planning, an organization's top management analyzes competitive opportunities and threats as well as the strengths and weaknesses of the organization, getting input from across the organization. Then the managers set a plan for how best to position the organization to compete effectively in the environment. Strategic planning is generally conducted across the enterprise and includes setting objectives that reflect the organization's mission.

Tactical Planning

Tactical planning, in contrast to strategic planning, has a shorter time horizon, typically one to three years, and specifies fairly concrete ways to implement the strategic plan. Tactical planning is often done by middle-level managers.

Operational Planning

Operational planning takes the organization-wide or subunit goals and specifies concrete action steps to achieve the strategic and tactical plans. Operational planning is short-range planning (less than a year).

Organizing

Organizing is a management function that develops an organizational structure and coordinates human resources within that structure to achieve organizational objectives. Typically, organizational structure is represented by an organizational chart that graphs the lines of who reports to whom and shows a hierarchical chain of command. In recent years, however, social network analysis has become increasingly popular as a means of identifying who in the organization people consider to be "expert" and turn to when they need help. [5]The advantage of mapping this type of informal network is that it shows who is a valuable, well-connected expert, even if that person is not a de facto "boss." Decisions made about the structure of an organization are generally referred to as organizational design decisions.

Organizing takes place at both the level of the organization and at the level of the job. Organizing at the level of the enterprise or organization involves deciding how best to divide or cluster jobs into departments to effectively allocate and coordinate effort. There are many different ways to departmentalize, such as organizing by a job function, by products, by geographical regions, or by type of customer. Larger organizations often use several methods of departmentalization. When the business crosses borders, the organization must choose a structure that complements its strategy. This often relates to whether there is a separate international division or if each country operates autonomously (and to what degree).

Organizing at the job level means designing individual jobs within the organization. Decisions must be made about the duties and responsibilities associated with each job, as well as the manner in which the duties should be carried out. Decisions made about the nature of jobs within the organization are generally called job design decisions.

Job design involves organizing jobs so that each position makes productive use of an individual's talents. In the past, job design meant narrowing a job's tasks so that the individual could be more proficient at those tasks. But further research showed that too narrow a job function leads to boredom and concomitant job dissatisfaction.

As a result, organizations now try to balance specialization (and the efficiency it brings) with variety and opportunity for autonomy. Human resource specialists use principles such as empowerment, job enrichment, and teamwork when designing jobs. For instance, HUI Manufacturing, a custom sheet-metal fabricator, has done away with traditional departments in order to focus outward on customers rather than internally on departments. As a result, HUI listens and responds to customers. Using small-team "huddles" and company-wide meetings, HUI employees work together to understand their customers and how HUI might service them best. [6] While some employees remain specialists, employees are paid more to develop multiple skill sets—thus a metalworker may also be proficient in design and accounting. As a result, HUI's workforce is highly diverse in terms of individual capabilities.

Leading

Leading involves influencing and inspiring others to take action. Managers who lead well inspire their employees to be enthusiastic about working to achieve organizational goals and objectives.

Managers can become effective leaders by understanding their employees' individual values, personalities, and attitudes. For example, studies of motivation and motivational theory help managers understand how workers can be energized to put forth productive effort. Studies of communication, likewise, provide direction as to how managers can effectively and persuasively communicate. Finally, studies of leadership and leadership style provide information on topics such as how a manager can be a good leader and what leadership styles are most appropriate and effective in certain situations. When an organization's operations cross borders, managers have to make additional choices related to the employment of local workers versus relocating workers from the home country, as well as the degree and frequency with which employees rotate through positions and countries.

Controlling

The controlling function requires monitoring performance so that it meets the performance standards established by the organization. Controlling consists of three steps—setting performance standards based on the company's objectives, measuring and comparing actual performance against standards, and taking corrective action when necessary. For example, a performance standard can be that a technical support staffer will resolve three customer problems per hour. If staffers are consistently only able to resolve three problems per hour, it may mean that the standard was set too high. Setting performance standards is a delicate balance: managers want the task to be attainable but not too easy. If the standard is set at five problem resolutions

per hour and half of the staffers achieve that goal, then they can be recognized for their achievement, while the staffers unable to meet that performance level can be coached, or other measures can be taken to minimize the low performance.

Performance standards can be measured in various ways, such as through financial statements, sales reports, production results, customer satisfaction, and formal performance appraisals. Managers at all levels engage in the function of controlling to some degree.

Don't let the term *control* confuse you into thinking that it means manipulation. Rather, the controlling function is intended to ensure that work is proceeding according to plan. Indeed, effective control requires having plans and objectives and establishing which position will be responsible for correcting deviations that occur.

Effective controls provide valuable feedback mechanisms. For international companies, such feedback includes the methods for transferring knowledge and advantages out of home or foreign countries into the business operations of other countries. Such learning, while a key advantage of global firms, is easier said than done. Even the best firms have found cross-border learning difficult. For example, when Toyota vehicles in the United Kingdom experienced problems with their braking and acceleration systems, these design issues were not communicated to the company's US operations until the same difficulties had reached crisis proportions in the United States.

In summary, the P-O-L-C functions of planning, organizing, leading, and controlling are widely considered to be the best means of describing the manager's job. Managers perform these essential functions despite tremendous changes in their environment and the tools they use to perform their roles.

KEY TAKEAWAYS

- The principles of management can be distilled down to four critical functions. These functions are planning, organizing, leading, and controlling.
- Strategy is a starting point in the P-O-L-C framework, but it also incorporates many additional activities that allow the strategy to be executed well. This framework provides useful guidance into what

the ideal job of a manager should look like in both domestic and international business contexts.

EXERCISES

(AACSB: Reflective Thinking, Analytical Skills)

1. What are the management functions in the P-O-L-C framework?
2. Are there any criticisms of this framework?
3. What function does planning serve?
4. What function does organizing serve?
5. What function does leading serve?
6. What function does controlling serve?

[1] {Authors' names retracted as requested by the work's original creator or licensee}, Principles of Management (Nyack, NY)

[2] Henry Mintzberg, The Nature of Managerial Work (New York: Harper & Row, 1973).

[3] David Lamond, "A Matter of Style: Reconciling Henri and Henry," Management Decision 42, no. 2 (2004): 330–56.

[4] Reference for Business, "Management Functions," Encyclopedia of Business, 2nd ed., accessed August 2, 2008, http://www.referenceforbusiness.com/management/Log-Mar/Management-Functions.html.

[5] Olivier Serrat, "Social Network Analysis," Knowledge Solutions 28 (February 2009), accessed January 3, 2011, http://www.adb.org/Documents/Information/Knowledge-Solutions/Social-Network-Analysis.pdf.

[6] "Your Teams: Overview," HUI Manufacturing, accessed November 9, 2010, http://www.huimfg.com/abouthui-yourteams.aspx.

10.6 End-of-Chapter Questions and Exercises

These exercises are designed to ensure that the knowledge you gain from this book about international business meets the learning standards set out by the international Association to Advance Collegiate Schools of Business (AACSB International). [1] AACSB is the premier accrediting agency of collegiate business schools and accounting programs worldwide. It expects that you will gain knowledge in the areas of communication, ethical reasoning, analytical skills, use of information technology, multiculturalism and diversity, and reflective thinking.

EXPERIENTIAL EXERCISES

(AACSB: Communication, Use of Information Technology, Analytical Skills)

1. One of the reasons that firms expand across borders is to expand the impact and value created by their strong brands. Pick a local company and develop a vision for how it can expand its brand globally. What seem to be the opportunities and barriers to doing this? Review the short YouTube video on global branding by Sanjay Sood, a UCLA professor, and see how you might qualify your recommendations. The video is at http://www.youtube.com/watch?v=X26WHNRhqPk.

2. Visit the corporate websites of Splash Corporation, CEMEX, Procter & Gamble, and 3M. How does it appear that these firms have organized their global business operations? What are their similarities and differences, and what might explain those similarities and differences? How might you characterize their business, corporate, and international strategies?

3. Outsourcing and offshoring are important parts of international strategy, yet they also have a clear ethical dimension. View the trailer for Outsourced: The Movie at http://www.youtube.com/watch?v=LImhTTFu4b8 and the opening sample video clips (starting with "Todd's First Training") at http://www.outsourcedthemovie.com/Clips/ms_educlips.html. What stereotypes do the videos highlight? What does it appear Todd is learning from this experience?

Ethical Dilemmas

(AACSB: Ethical Reasoning, Multiculturalism, Reflective Thinking, Analytical Skills)

1. What are the ethical implications of outsourcing or offshoring business activities?

2. You have been hired by Procter & Gamble (P&G) to work in their cosmetics product development group. P&G is aiming to grow its business by identifying new products where demand is growing quickly in emerging markets. Through a Filipino classmate from your college days, you learn about the skin-lightening product market and how rapidly it is growing in emerging markets. What are some of the ethical considerations you might want to take into account as you evaluate this market and make recommendations to your colleagues at P&G?

3. You are a quality-control manager for Toyota Motor Corporation in the United Kingdom. Over the past six months, you have forwarded information to Toyota's headquarters in Japan about possible brake problems but have seen no action taken. In your heart you believe that the company is just being careful to confirm what the problems actually are and is not intentionally covering up the problem. This morning you read a

piece in *USA Today* about Toyota vehicles in the United States experiencing similar problems. What action do you take?

[1] Association to Advance Collegiate Schools of Business website, accessed January 26, 2010, http://www.aacsb.edu.

NOTES:

Chapter 11:
Global Entrepreneurship and Intrapreneurship

WHAT'S IN IT FOR ME?

1. Who is an entrepreneur, and what is entrepreneurship?
2. What do entrepreneurs do?
3. What is entrepreneurship across borders?
4. How does entrepreneurship lead to global start-ups?
5. What is intrapreneurship?

This chapter will explore the subjects of entrepreneurship and intrapreneurship in international business. It is through both the differences across countries and the flatteners that are reducing such differences that entrepreneurial and intrapreneurial opportunities are created or identified. For instance, countries have different average income levels, but regardless of income level the people in those countries have medical care needs. An entrepreneurial or intrapreneurial move in this setting would be the introduction of a low-cost medical treatment for an ailment common to both high- and low-income countries. As a business student, you may be able to take electives in entrepreneurship, so view this information as sensitizing you to the field, rather than making you an expert. You will gain more knowledge of both entrepreneurial process and its related field, intrapreneurship. Whereas entrepreneurship is concerned with starting new businesses, intrapreneurship is concerned with starting something new, like a new product or service, in an existing, established business. Intrapreneurs may take on more risk than a traditional line-management employee; but it's risk within parameters or within course boundaries—to use sports as an analogy. Entrepreneurship, on the other hand, is more like helicopter skiing—there's no safety net and no safe path or course boundaries. Intrapreneurs who fail are very likely to still have a job, perhaps moving into a new role in their company. Entrepreneurs, most of whom aren't funded, don't have a guaranteed monthly paycheck; failure means complete failure. Throughout this chapter, you'll also learn how entrepreneurship and intrapreneurship are important in global markets.

OPENING CASE: ESYS TECHNOLOGIES

Why Go Global? Because It's What Entrepreneurs Do!

Entrepreneurs are go-getters who seize opportunities and work tirelessly to overcome obstacles. Entrepreneurs who expand internationally face even more risks and challenges, but many of them thrive on those very challenges because those challenges bring previously unseen new opportunities. Our opening vignette, which is about eSys Technologies LLC, provides one case in point. eSys founder Vikas Goel used the global playing field to his advantage to build his company in creative ways.

Vikas, in Sanskrit, Means Growth

Vikas Goel grew eSys at an astonishingly fast rate from very humble beginnings. Goel launched his company in 2000, during the time when companies were cratering due to the dot-com economic crash of tech companies. Few would have bet that Goel's eSys, which aimed to distribute hard disk drives (HDDs), stood a chance in the down environment. But Goel saw things differently.

"An exceptional entrepreneur is able to identify a threat which nobody wants to touch and convert it into an opportunity," said Goel. [1] Goel succeeded in the early years by bootstrapping his success. Operating in Singapore, he went to the Bank of India to ask for a loan, making a presentation directly to the CEO of the bank. Goel's passion and plan garnered him a loan of US $3.5 million, which he immediately put to work. Goel's first job after graduating with his MBA had been with American Components, for whom he distributed (very successfully) Seagate HDDs in India.

Rekindling former ties, Goel offered to distribute Seagate HDDs through eSys. Seagate agreed and, having developed trust and confidence in Goel, gave him rights to distribute Seagate HDDs in other countries as well.

Seagate's competitors, seeing the success Seagate was having through eSys, signed on with eSys as well. By 2004, eSys was distributing Seagate, Maxtor, and Western Digital HDDs to the tune of 20 million disk drive unit sales, making eSys arguably the largest HDD distributor in the world. [2]

A big contributor to Goel's success is his local sales-force approach. Despite operating in twenty-five countries, each eSys sales team is an in-country local team that understands local culture.

Building on the success of his distribution business, Goel next decided to expand into manufacturing. In particular, Goel's vision was to manufacture and sell a PC under the eSys brand that would retail for $250, making it affordable to a broader range of consumers. The price point of $250 was aggressive—none of eSys's competitors could profitably sell a PC for that low a price. To succeed in his goal, Goel would have to be very creative in taking out all unnecessary costs. Goel was able to achieve the $250 PC goal by cleverly taking advantage of country-specific differences. For example, eSys set up manufacturing plants next to its regional logistics hubs. The move seems counter-intuitive. Most firms would set up manufacturing in China to get the lowest cost, but Goel thought through the distribution and tax implications that his costs would be even lower. Labor may be cheap in China, but physically moving inventory from remote places takes time. In addition, China levies a 17 percent value-added tax. Singapore, in contrast, has no such tax and is a logistics hub with fast, easy shipment to all of Asia and beyond. Accordingly, Goel set up manufacturing plants in the hub locations (Singapore, Dubai, Los Angeles, and New Delhi), taking advantage of low inventory costs and building state-of-the-art software-controlled facilities to reduce labor cost.

Goel also made innovative use of financing. For example, he bought insurance on the credit he borrowed, making his lenders the beneficiaries of that insurance. Going the extra step made his lenders and vendors even more comfortable extending credit to eSys, which saved Goel the equivalent of about 2 percent annual interest. [3]

And the Winner Is?

Goel's smart moves won him Ernst & Young's Singapore Entrepreneur of the Year award in 2005 and put him in contention for Ernst & Young's World Entrepreneur of the Year award in 2006. In the end, the E&Y judges didn't choose Goel as the World Entrepreneur of the Year. That honor went to Bill Lynch of South Africa, who, after arriving from Ireland in 1971 with a village-school education, few prospects, and 2,000 British pounds, turned a money-losing car dealership into a $6 billion transport and mobility empire. Thirty years later, Lynch's business was enormous and thriving. Whether Goel's venture could last that long remained to be seen. Some of the E&Y judges questioned the staying power of any company operating with a pretax margin of less than 1 percent. But longevity aside, Goel had already demonstrated that it was possible to improve efficiency and cut costs in just about every area of a business by taking advantage of the technological tools of the new world economy and operating on a truly global scale.

From day one, eSys was the prototypical born-global firm—one that has been defined as "a business organization that, from inception, seeks to derive significant competitive advantage from the use of resources and the sale of outputs in multiple countries." [4]

Even though Goel did not win World Entrepreneur of the Year, Jack Stack, legendary CEO in his own right and a judge at the E&Y World Entrepreneur competition, was truly impressed when he met Goel, calling eSys "the first truly global start-up I'd ever seen. By that I mean it was the first company I knew of to operate worldwide almost from day one, taking advantage of the cost savings available in different countries." [5]

Stack praised Goel for the following:

- Locating eSys distribution hubs in country locations to reduce inventory costs
- Buying insurance from Switzerland and Germany to get the best rates
- Setting up back-office and IT operations in India for lowest wages coupled with high skills
- Handling finances out of Singapore, which has the lowest effective tax rate in the world [6]

In 2007, Goel sold a majority interest in eSys to India's Chennai-based Teledata Informatics Ltd. for $105 million. [7] Teledata and eSys also announced their likely investment of $20 million in Chandigarh, India, to open a total-business-offshoring/outsourcing (TBO) unit, with at least 1,000 employees. Teledata's CEO explained the rationale behind the acquisition: "Every year we buy 3,000–4,000 personal computers for several e-governance projects. This year, we plan to buy 15,000 PCs. The eSys acquisition will now make these projects cost effective." [8] With the acquisition, Goel assumed the title of CEO of Teledata Technologies and will hold 49 percent ownership in that company. eSys already has a PC-manufacturing unit in Delhi and is in the process of setting up another unit in Himachal Pradesh, India, to produce 1 million units per year. Consistent with his track record of cutting costs, Goel noted, "We might shut down the Delhi plant and shift the entire manufacturing capabilities to the new centre." [9] When asked what work means to him, Goel's answer was simple but powerful, "It's about making your business your passion, rather than making your passion your business." [10]

OPENING CASE EXERCISES

(AACSB: Ethical Reasoning, Multiculturalism, Reflective Thinking, Analytical Skills)

1. What kind of people would do well working for eSys? Do you think, for instance, that you would need a good understanding of international business to do well in eSys?

2. Goel's business model might make some people and certain stakeholder groups uncomfortable. What if every company were able to set up operations globally so as to minimize expenses, including taxes? Where would governments get the money for essential functions? What would happen to standards of living around the world? The eSys model is clearly great for eSys, but what if everybody adopted it? Is this a practice the business world should encourage?

3. How should government policymakers work with companies like eSys? Should this type of cross-border arbitrage be entirely unregulated? (For instance, there is no law in the United States regulating whether a US company locates its tax headquarters in the United States or a more tax-favorable country like Bermuda.) Can we rely on each nation to set up its own laws and regulations, or is this an example of why we need supranational governments like the Organization for Economic Co-operation (OECD), the European Union, and trading blocs?

[1] eSys Information Technologies, "Ernst & Young Entrepreneur of the Year 2005 Award Goes to Mr. Vikas Goel of eSys Technologies," news release, March 10, 2006, accessed June 16, 2010, http://www.esys.in/NewsDisplay.php?ID=141.

[2] Vikas Goel, "Vikas Goel and eSys," July 7, 2010, accessed December 23, 2010, http://www.vikas-goel-esys.com/index.php/vikasgoel/vikas-goel-and-esys.html.

[3] Jack Stack and Bo Burlingham, "My Awakening," Inc., April 1, 2007, accessed December 23, 2010, http://www.inc.com/magazine/20070401/features-my-awakening.html.

[4] Benjamin M. Oviatt and Patricia Phillips McDougall, "Toward a Theory of International New Ventures," Journal of International Business Studies, First Quarter 1994, 49, accessed December 24, 2010, http://aib.msu.edu/awards/25_1_94_45.pdf.

[5] Jack Stack and Bo Burlingham, "My Awakening," Inc., April 1, 2007, accessed December 23, 2010, http://www.inc.com/magazine/20070401/features-my-awakening.html.

[6] Jack Stack and Bo Burlingham, "My Awakening," Inc., April 1, 2007, accessed December 23, 2010, http://www.inc.com/magazine/20070401/features-my-awakening.html.

[7] Gabriel Chen, "eSys Lays Off Staff ahead of Teledata Merger," Strait Times, February 22, 2007, accessed December 23, 2010, http://www.sg-electronics.com/Singlenews.aspx?DirID=77&rec_code=60181.

[8] "Teledata Buys Singapore Firm for $105mn," Business Standard, February 19, 2007, accessed June 16, 2010, http://www.business-standard.com/india/news/teledata-buys-singapore-firm-for-105mn/275156/.

[9] "Teledata Buys Singapore Firm for $105mn," Business Standard, February 19, 2007, accessed June 16, 2010, http://www.business-standard.com/india/news/teledata-buys-singapore-firm-for-105mn/275156/.

[10] eSys Information Technologies, "Ernst & Young Entrepreneur of the Year 2005 Award Goes to Mr. Vikas Goel of eSys Technologies," news release, March 10, 2006, accessed June 16, 2010, http://www.esys.in/NewsDisplay.php?ID=141.

11.1 Entrepreneurship
LEARNING OBJECTIVES

1. Identify what entrepreneurship is.
2. Understand who an entrepreneur is.
3. Recognize some of the myths of entrepreneurship.

Entrepreneurship and Entrepreneurs

Entrepreneur is a French word that means "to undertake." In the business world, this term applies to someone who wants to start a business or enterprise. As you may recall, entrepreneurship is defined as "the recognition of opportunities (needs, wants, problems, and challenges) and the use or creation of resources to implement innovative ideas for new, thoughtfully planned ventures." [1] An entrepreneur is a person who engages in entrepreneurship. Entrepreneurs are typically go-getters with high levels of skill and energy. *Webster's* defines an entrepreneur as "the organizer of an economic venture; *especially* one who organizes, owns, manages, and assumes the risks of a business." [2]Entrepreneurship, like strategic management, will help you think about the opportunities available when you connect new ideas with new markets.

Entrepreneurs are distinct from small-business owners in that entrepreneurs often rely on innovation—new products, methods, or markets—to grow their business quickly and broadly. Entrepreneurs rely on innovation and speed to a much greater extent than small-business owners. Small-business owners typically enter established markets, providing a more traditional product or service to a local market. For example, a local dry cleaner may be a small business, whereas a company that develops a revolutionary new way to do dry cleaning and seeks to expand that new method nationally and internationally would be considered entrepreneurial.

Prior to the end of the last century, most people equated the word *entrepreneurship* with risk takers and nonconformists who were usually unable to work in a corporate environment. It was that small segment of the population that was willing to take what most perceive as very high risks. In truth, that is far from the reality. Entrepreneurs are certainly an adventurous group, but most wouldn't describe themselves as aggressive risk takers. More often, they are passionate about an idea and carefully plan how to put it into effect. Most entrepreneurs are more comfortable with managed risk than with dangerous get-rich-quick schemes.

Did You Know?

How do entrepreneurs identify opportunities for new business ventures? First, they actively search for opportunities. That is, they don't just passively wait for an idea to hit them, and they don't just look at traditional sources of information, like news and trade publications. Instead, they search out more unusual sources, such as specialized publications or conversations with personal contacts, to get hints of new opportunities. Second, entrepreneurs are particularly alert to opportunities. Specifically, they look for "changed conditions or overlooked possibilities." [3] Third, research confirms that prior knowledge—information gathered from prior experience—helps entrepreneurs identify potentially profitable opportunities. [4] For example, having prior industry or market experience with customers' needs or struggles to solve particular problems greatly aids entrepreneurs in being able to create innovative new solutions to those problems. The latest research in human cognition shows that these three factors—active search, alertness, and prior experience—combine to help entrepreneurs see patterns among seemingly unrelated events or trends in the external world. As Robert Baron says, these factors help entrepreneurs "connect the dots" between changes in technology, demographics, markets, government policies, and other factors. [5]

Entrepreneurship became a high-profile subject in the 1990s with the dot-com era, which created a whole new breed of "wannabe" entrepreneurs. Entrepreneurship was in vogue, and everyone wanted to be an entrepreneur. That period shaped the expectations and perceptions of an entire generation of potential entrepreneurs. It also made the world of venture capital more commonplace and accessible. Eventually—as with most business cycles—the Internet bubble burst, and the shift reversed. People sought the surety of corporate life once again. Nevertheless, the allure of entrepreneurship has continued to tempt many people.

So You Want to Be an Entrepreneur?

Many people are surprised to learn that successful entrepreneurs do not always have a perfect business plan and marketing and sales strategy in place before launching their businesses. In fact, many often deviate so significantly from the original plan that the business is unrecognizable. Instead, the mark of a successful entrepreneur is the ability to adeptly navigate the daily, weekly, and monthly bumps, twists, and turns in the life of a young or small company. We live in a world of instant gratification. People want immediate success along with everything else. However, there are no prepackaged, absolutely certain paths to successful entrepreneurship. Successful entrepreneurs start a business for what they can get out of it this year, not three to five years down the road—because they're not likely to make it to that future point if they can't take care of today. Pay yourself a salary and strive for profitability. [6]

Truths and Myths about Entrepreneurs

Entrepreneurs work hard and are driven by an intense commitment and determined perseverance; they see the cup half full, rather than half empty; they strive for integrity; they burn with the competitive desire to excel and win; they are dissatisfied with the status quo and seek opportunities to improve almost any situation they encounter; they use failure as a tool for learning and eschew perfection in favor of effectiveness; and they believe they can personally make an enormous difference in the final outcome of their ventures and their lives. [7]

The myths, however, are many. The following five entrepreneurship myths are among the most prevalent:

1. **Entrepreneurs are born, not made.** The most prevalent myth about entrepreneurs is that they are born with the skills that will make them successful and that anyone who's not born with those skills will not succeed. In reality, entrepreneurism is a skill that, like any other skill, can be learned.

2. **Entrepreneurs make more money.** Surprisingly, the typical entrepreneur earns less than he or she would earn if working as an employee. Only the top 10 percent of entrepreneurs earn more than employees. [8]

3. **Being original is essential.** Another entrepreneurial myth is that entrepreneurs who get to the market first gain the most. Research by Joe Tabet, presented at INSEAD's Global Entrepreneurship Forum, has shown that the so-called first mover advantage is a myth: Google, eBay, and Swatch are examples of successful businesses that entered markets later. The key, Tabet says, is to find your niche and serve your customers well. [9]

4. **It takes a lot of money to start a business.** Research by Scott Shane of Case Western Reserve University has shown that the average new business needs only $25,000

in financing and that most of that money can be raised through debt. [10]

5. **Entrepreneurs must be risk takers.** According to this myth, entrepreneurs are good at starting businesses but can't manage them once they grow. Research by Babson College professor Joel Shulman shows that the stocks of publicly traded companies run by entrepreneurs significantly outperform those run by nonentrepreneurs and continue to do so even after adjusting by market cap size, sector, geography, or time period. [11]

Should You Become an Entrepreneur?

Whatever your reasons for becoming an entrepreneur, understand and be clear about your personal motivations. This will help you make decisions and choices along the way. The short survey that follows this section might provide you with helpful insights, though keep in mind that—as the survey says—"no reliable predictive model or entrepreneurial character has successfully been developed."

Beyond such self-assessment and reflection, as you go through the personal decision-making process, try to talk to as many people as you possibly can. Seek out others who have tried entrepreneurship—both those who have been successful and those who have not. Talk to people in your industry, including colleagues, friends, and potential advisors. You'd be surprised how open people can be about their experiences—good and bad. Read lots of books and get a variety of opinions. You're not trying to get people's "permission" to be an entrepreneur, nor are you looking to give yourself permission to try. What you should strive for is to understand the factors critical to success and see if you're comfortable with them. There are no right or wrong answers. Only another entrepreneur can tell you what it's like to lie awake at night stressing about whether you'll make payroll that month. But at the same time, it's that entrepreneur who can tell you what strategy worked to make payroll that month. It's not the issues that define you as an entrepreneur but how you respond to those issues.

As you consider entrepreneurship, you need to assess whether it will provide you with the ability to support and sustain yourself and your family, both in the beginning and later on, when you eventually achieve your personal financial goals. Are you comfortable with the time it may take to grow and sustain your business? Many people start companies expecting to grow them aggressively (in financial terms), only to find that they are actually quite content with a profitable lifestyle business that allows them the ability to pursue other personal goals. Think about what kind of growth you're comfortable with. Do you want a lifestyle business or an

aggressive-growth business? Both are commendable choices, but only you can make that decision.

If you decide to become an entrepreneur, take a look at your professional and personal support systems—particularly the latter. Are they supporting you or thinking you're off your rocker? Even if you are comfortable with the risks, uncertainties, and challenges, a spouse or other key family member may not be. Negative whisperings can rock the very confidence that's required for entrepreneurship. Be wary not only of your own demons but also those of others around you.

Attitude is a key factor. For example, if deep down you're happiest as a sole proprietor but are talking about growing a company because it sounds so much better, then guess what? You're likely to stay a sole proprietor and defeat yourself subconsciously. You will not grow your company, and you'll also be unhappy and unfulfilled, even if your company is successful by financial and market definition. Get in touch with what you really want and how you define success. Be comfortable and confident with your own answers. Confidence is a key component—it will bring customers, investors, and supporters to you.

You also need to assess how you handle stress. How determined are you to succeed? Starting a business isn't always easy. You may have more naysayers than coaches around you. Many businesses fold in the second year despite the fact that the next year might have been the turning point. Most entrepreneurs will tell you that they hit a key milestone of sustainability around the third year of their business. If you can make it to that point, you can keep going, barring any unforeseen problems inside or outside the company. For example, you could be doing great, and then in the fifth year, your largest customer stumbles badly, creating a ripple effect in your company. If you've been astute enough to diversify, it should be no problem—if not, you'll drown, too. Diversification in terms of your customer base is essential.

If you're choosing entrepreneurship as a response to a personal or professional transition, think through your motivations thoroughly. If you're starting a company because you were laid off from your last job, do you see it as a life-changing opportunity, or are you treading water until a suitable full-time position becomes available? If a personal situation or crisis is motivating you to consider entrepreneurship as a way to balance your obligations, you may want to focus on being a sole proprietor for a while, as growing a company of any size is a very time- and energy-consuming endeavor. [12]

Entrepreneurship and the Changing Nature of "Corporate" Life

As corporate life continues to offer less and less security, more people are considering entrepreneurship. Some leave, taking their former corporate employer as their first customer. For others, it's an opportunity to enter an entirely new industry. For most of us, we're hoping to capitalize on our experience and know-how or on a new idea or market to fill a gap in our own industry.

Many entrepreneurs have actually discovered their vision and opportunity through a former employer. If you've spent your professional life in the corporate world, then you can recognize that the early years of an entrepreneurial venture demand very hands-on involvement. It's not a joke when we say that you should be ready to take out the garbage. Most entrepreneurs have in the early days.

When you make the leap from corporate life to entrepreneurship, it involves major changes. The biggest difference is that entrepreneurs don't have a buffer between a mistake and total failure. When a large company makes a bad bet on a product or market, the damage gets absorbed, perhaps with a hit to earnings or the stock price. In the early stages of company growth, a bad bet can destroy everything. There are no shock absorbers.

Many large companies attempt to create the spirit of entrepreneurship inside their organizations. These internal groups, or *intrapreneurs*, may spur more innovation, but this *intrapreneurship* is a far cry from the realities of entrepreneurship. These groups have far more resources than most new ventures. They are protected from feeling the immediate impact of failures and mistakes, and there's no immediate risk of losing a paycheck. [13]

Surveying Your Entrepreneurial Character Traits

The survey below was developed by analyzing the character traits of entrepreneurs. It measures entrepreneurial readiness—whether one considers himself or herself an entrepreneur.

Rate each of the eleven characteristics using the following scale:

+2 = I'm very strong in this characteristic.

+1 = I possess this characteristic.
0 = I don't know.
−1 = I have very little of this characteristic.
−2 = I don't possess this characteristic.

TRAIT	CIRCLE ONE CHOICE IN EACH TRAIT					
Creativity	+2	+1	0	−1	−2	
Calculated Risk Taker	+2	+1	0	−1	−2	
Self-confident	+2	+1	0	−1	−2	
Dynamic	+2	+1	0	−1	−2	
Like to Lead Others	+2	+1	0	−1	−2	
Market Savvy	+2	+1	0	−1	−2	
Resourceful	+2	+1	0	−1	−2	
Perseverant/Determined	+2	+1	0	−1	−2	
Optimistic	+2	+1	0	−1	−2	
Knowledgeable	+2	+1	0	−1	−2	
Energetic	+2	+1	0	−1	−2	
						TOTAL SCORE_____ −

Despite all the academic research around the world covering entrepreneurship, no reliable predictive model exists to identify who could be a successful entrepreneur. Having the traits in the chart doesn't guarantee success, but the higher your total score, the more characteristics you possess that are similar to successful entrepreneurs. [14]

KEY TAKEAWAYS

- Entrepreneurship is defined as the recognition of opportunities (i.e., needs, wants, problems, and challenges) and the use or creation of resources to implement innovative ideas for new, thoughtfully planned ventures.
- The entrepreneur is a person who engages in entrepreneurship. Entrepreneurs are sometimes seen as

people of very high aptitude who pioneer change. *Webster's* defines an entrepreneur as "one who organizes, manages, and assumes the risks of a business or enterprise." [15]

- There are many myths about entrepreneurs—often emphasizing their luck and ability to take risks. The reality is that entrepreneurship is a skill that can be learned (not a trait that you're born with), and that you don't need a lot of money to start a business.

EXERCISES

(AACSB: Reflective Thinking, Analytical Skills)

1. What is entrepreneurship?
2. Who is an entrepreneur?
3. What are some key characteristics of entrepreneurs?
4. What are some common myths about entrepreneurs?
5. What questions would you want to explore to help you better understand whether or not you want to be an entrepreneur?

[1] {Authors' names retracted as requested by the work's original creator or licensee}, Principles of Management (Nyack, NY)

[2] Webster's Third New International Dictionary, Unabridged, s.v. "entrepreneur," accessed November 7, 2010, http://unabridged.merriam-webster.com/cgi-bin/unabridged?va=entrepreneur&x=0&y=0.

[3] Robert A. Baron, "Opportunity Recognition as Pattern Recognition: How Entrepreneurs 'Connect the Dots' to Identify New Business Opportunities," Academy of Management Perspectives, February 2006, 105.

[4] Scott Shane, "Prior Knowledge and the Discovery of Entrepreneurial Opportunities," Organization Science 11, no. 4: 448–69.

[5] Robert A. Baron, "Opportunity Recognition as Pattern Recognition: How Entrepreneurs 'Connect the Dots' to Identify New Business Opportunities," Academy of Management Perspectives, February 2006, 104.

[6] {Author's Name retracted as requested by the work's original creator or licensee}, Starting Your Business (New York: Business Expert Press, 2010), 4–5.

[7] Jeffry A. Timmons, New Venture Creation: Entrepreneurship for the 21st Century, 5th ed. (New York: McGraw-Hill, 1999), 44.

[8] Scott Shane, "Top Ten Myths of Entrepreneurship," How to Change the World (blog), January 10, 2008, accessed January 2, 2011, http://blog.guykawasaki.com/2008/01/top-ten-myths-o.html#tp.

[9] "Debunking Myths about Entrepreneurs," Knowledge (blog), INSEAD, June 10, 2009, accessed January 2, 2011, http://knowledge.insead.edu/Debunkingmythsaboutentrepreneurs090615.cfm.

[10] Scott Shane, "Top Ten Myths of Entrepreneurship," How to Change the World (blog), January 10, 2008, accessed January 2, 2011, http://blog.guykawasaki.com/2008/01/top-ten-myths-o.html#tp.

[11] Jeff Cornwall, "Another Entrepreneurial Myth Busted," The Entrepreneurial Mind (blog), December 17, 2009, accessed January 1, 2011, http://www.drjeffcornwall.com/entrepreneurial-myths.

[12] {Author's Name retracted as requested by the work's original creator or licensee}, Starting Your Business (New York: Business Expert Press, 2010), 17–19.

[13] {Author's Name retracted as requested by the work's original creator or licensee}, Starting Your Business (New York: Business Expert Press, 2010), 19–20.

[14] Adapted from Center for Ethics in Free Enterprise, 21st Century Entrepreneurship, Entrepreneurship Course Workbook (Jacksonville: University of North Florida Press, 1997–99), chap. 1.

[15] Webster's Third New International Dictionary, Unabridged, s.v. "entrepreneur," accessed November 7, 2010, http://unabridged.merriam-webster.com/cgi-bin/unabridged?va=entrepreneur&x=0&y=0.

11.2 What Do Entrepreneurs Do?

LEARNING OBJECTIVES

1. Understand the different contexts in which entrepreneurship takes place.
2. Know the three facets of the entrepreneurial process.
3. Be able to apply the levers of opportunity identification.

What Do Entrepreneurs Do?

Entrepreneurs build for-profit and nonprofit ventures. The most well-known type of entrepreneurial venture is the for-profit, or commercial, venture, which sells products or services for a profit. Entrepreneurs can also launch a nonprofit venture whose purpose is to fulfill a social mission rather than to make money. For example, nonprofits often work to improve societal issues such as health care, the environment, and underserved populations. Entrepreneurs who launch these kinds of nonprofit ventures are often referred to as social entrepreneurs. Social entrepreneurs look for and implement innovative solutions to societal problems. Social entrepreneurs apply the same tools and skill sets as other entrepreneurs—seizing opportunities, organizing and managing tasks and people, improving how something is done—but their focus is to solve a social problem or create a benefit to humanity.

Entrepreneurial ventures can grow large or stay small, and they can operate at any level: local, national, or international.

Ethics in Action

Camila Batmanghelidjh

Being an entrepreneur doesn't mean that the only option open to you is building a successful commercial business. Social entrepreneurs focus on improving people's lives by giving them new opportunities or resources. In that sense, Camila Batmanghelidjh is a social entrepreneur.

Batmanghelidjh was honored with the United Kingdom's Social Entrepreneur of the Year award from Ernst & Young (E&Y). She explained what drove her to found one of the United Kingdom's most remarkable social enterprises:

I founded the Kids Company in 1996 to create a place for children who struggle against relentless deprivation and trauma. Some of these children are homeless; some have parents with drug or alcohol addictions. Some have reached the point of desperation. In some cases, their emotional exhaustion leads to passively suicidal behavior, not caring if they live, die or kill.

All manner of horrors will have been witnessed by these children. One had swallowed her mother's methadone as a toddler. Three years later, her mother took her to a dealer's house to collect her fix when a man burst in with a gun and threw the dealer out of a multi-storey window. The older sister of this child, barely an adolescent, was already bringing home money from prostitution.

We now look after around 5,000 children a year. We have in-school therapeutic services [and] after-school homework clubs and offer sheets and blankets for homeless children. We take them to the doctor and to sexual health clinics and support the children if they get into legal trouble. Above all, we encourage their personal and spiritual development using the arts. This is a vocational organization. We will always strive for excellence. Our workers don't just turn up to a job; they turn up to fulfill a vision. [1]

What Is the Entrepreneurial Process?

There are three essential parts of the entrepreneurial process: (1) opportunity identification, (2) plan and prepare the venture, and (3) resource the venture and take action. Sometimes the process unfolds as depicted in Figure 11.1 "The Entrepreneurial Process", though there are many examples where a formal plan is never put forth, or where a plan and resources lead to the identification of a completely different opportunity. 3M's Post-it self-adhesive notes or W. L. Gore's Glide dental floss are examples of the latter scenario. [2]However, for simplicity, you'll look at the process in the common 1-2-3 order of identifying the opportunity, planning the venture, and funding and staffing it.

Taking the Opportunity

Perhaps the biggest difference between strategy in existing firms and new ventures is the starting point. Most researchers agree that the starting point for new ventures is opportunity, while the strategy for existing firms usually begins with some assessment of the firm's underlying resources and capabilities. [3]

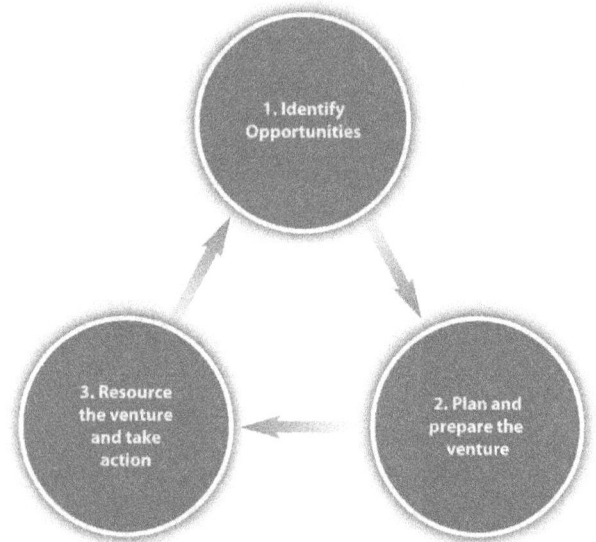

Figure 11.1 The Entrepreneurial Process

How Do People Find Opportunities?

You might be surprised to learn that you already possess at least two tools that might help you unearth a valuable business opportunity. One way to think about opportunities is through a tool shown in Figure 11.2 "Levers That Lead to Opportunity Identification". The first four levers—eliminate, reduce, create, and raise—are summarized in the Blue Ocean Strategy framework made popular by strategy researchers W. Chan Kim and Renée Mauborgne. [4] The fifth characteristic was developed through the work of the authors of the best-selling textbook *Strategic Management: A Dynamic Perspective*. [5] The general idea behind the first four changes is that an entrepreneurial opportunity will offer something new but not necessarily because it is simply adding more features or costs. For instance, Amazon became successful because it provided a greater selection of books than any other store on the planet (increase), allowed greater convenience when shopping for books (reduced time needed), developed a logistics and software infrastructure to manage the process (create/add), and threatened to make brick-and-mortar stores obsolete (eliminate).

New markets can be created when innovations are based on these four characteristics alone. However, experience has shown that the more customers need to change their behaviors, the more slowly they will adopt an innovation. For this reason, the fifth characteristic—what stays the same—becomes a differentiating factor between innovations that take hold and those that don't or do so more slowly. For instance, e-books have taken a long time to gain adoption, even though there are an increasing number of ways for them to be purchased and read. In contrast, Amazon's strategy of selling printed books through an online store has worked largely because the book—the basic product—remained unchanged and thus required less change on the part of the consumer.

Research suggests that new venture opportunities tend to fall into one of three categories—new-market disruptions, low-end disruptions, or hybrid.

Low-End Disruption

A disruptive technology is a technology that can make prior technologies obsolete. For instance, the automobile was a disruptive technology for the horse-and-buggy; CD players and MP3 players were disruptive technologies for the phonograph, or record player; and the computer was a disruptive technology for the typewriter. Some disruptive technologies appear at the low end of an industry offering and are referred to as low-end disruptions. Current players tend to ignore such new entrants because they target the least valuable of their customers. These low-end disruptions rarely offer features that satisfy the best customers in the industry. In fact, the new low-end disruptive technologies usually perform worse than the existing technology at first. [6] For example, early automobiles were less reliable than the horse-and-buggy until improvements made them vastly better. New entrants often use low-end entry to gain a foothold to move into the attractive market once their products or services improve. Indeed, by the time they do improve, these low-end disruptions often satisfy the needs of the center of the market better than incumbents' products do, because the new entrants have been making incremental improvements to satisfy their best clients' demands. Southwest Airlines began as a very successful low-end disrupter, satisfying only the most basic travel needs and eliminating many services that had been taken for granted by established airlines. Over time, Southwest's offerings improved, and its on-time arrival percentage and customer service became the best in the industry. As a result, Southwest Airlines now appeals to more than just low-end customers.

New-Market Disruption

A new-market disruption targets noncustomers rather than low-end customers. Thus, the technology creates a new market in a niche that larger players ignored because it was too small or was considered unprofitable with existing technology.

Hybrid-Disruption Strategies

As you might expect, most newcomers adopt some combination of new-market and low-end disruption strategies; these are hybrid-disruption strategies. Today, it may look as if Amazon has pursued a single-minded, low-end disruption strategy, but along the way, it has also created some new markets, mainly by bringing more buyers into the market for books. Many Amazon customers buy in the quantities they do because of the information that the site makes available. The strategies of such companies as JetBlue, Charles Schwab, and the University of Phoenix are also hybrids of new-market and low-cost disruption strategies. [7] JetBlue's focused, low-cost strategy, for instance, has been able to achieve the lowest cost position in the industry by eliminating many services (a business model it borrowed from Southwest). However, it has also targeted overpriced but underserved markets, thereby stimulating net new demand. Thus, JetBlue has both taken a portion of the existing market and created a new market by attracting consumers who couldn't ordinarily afford air travel. Schwab is another example; it pioneered discount brokerage as a new market but has since captured many clients from full-service brokers, such as Merrill Lynch. The University of Phoenix is taking a strategic path in higher education much like the one blazed by Schwab in the investment market.

All three of these disruption strategies provide you with a solid basis for identifying market opportunities.

Under all these strategies, an entrepreneur identifies an opportunity and then seeks to cobble together the resources and opportunities to exploit it. Individuals in close contact with scientific breakthroughs can also identify opportunities. In fact, scientific, technological, or process discoveries often inspire people to seek market opportunities. This is one reason why universities are increasing investments to support research faculty in the protection of intellectual property and identification of commercial opportunities. The University of Wisconsin–Madison, for instance, maintains its Office of Corporate Relations, which, among other services, assists individual researchers in the creation of new ventures. After all, faculty and staff members who create early-stage technology are often in the best position to develop it. Not only do they possess unsurpassed technical knowledge about their discoveries, but they're also in a position to appreciate the promise that they hold.

The Business Plan

In order to secure start-up financing and launch the new product, many entrepreneurs draw up a formal business plan that brings all the elements of the new venture together for a specific purpose—namely, to ensure key stakeholders that the firm has a well-considered strategy and managerial expertise. A business plan is a formal statement of business goals, the reasons why they are attainable, and the plan for reaching those goals. It may also contain background information about the organization or team attempting to reach the goals. Even if such a plan isn't necessary for communicating with external stakeholders, preparing one is still a good idea. At the very least, it will help you reexamine the five elements of your strategy and prompt you to look for ways to bring them together in order to create a viable and profitable firm. In addition, a business plan provides a vehicle for sharing your goals and objectives—and your plans for implementing them—with members of your entrepreneurial team. Focusing on the staging component of the five elements of strategy, for example, is a good way to set milestones and timelines and otherwise manage the scale and pace of your company's growth. Finally, when it does come time to seek external funding to support the firm's growth, the plan provides a solid basis for engaging professionals who can both help you get financing and advise you on strengthening customer relationships and finding strategic suppliers.

Familiarity with the five elements of strategy, implementation levers, and frameworks for analyzing external organizational context can prepare you to draw up a business plan. Although there are variations on form, the content of most plans covers the same topics. You can find a multitude of examples on the web in addition to software packages for creating a detailed and professional-looking document. [8] For more information, see the sidebar below for a summary of what is normally contained in a comprehensive business plan.

Contents of a Typical Business Plan

1. **Executive summary.** This summary is one to three pages in length and highlights all the key points of the plan in a way that captures the reader's interest. This section stresses the business concept and not the numbers. It's the unique value proposition and business model that really matters.
2. **Company description.** This short section describes the company's business, form of organization, location, structure, and strategy. It provides a summary of the company's capabilities and its goals and plans for the next five years.
3. **Products and services.** This overview explains what products or services the company will sell; it also discusses why customers will want the products or services, what problems the offerings will solve and what benefits they will deliver, and how much customers are likely to pay for them (i.e., the willingness-to-pay criteria).
4. **Market analysis.** This section identifies the need or demand for the product, who the target customers will be, and why the customers will buy the product. The

section also includes a discussion of the company's competitors or potential competitors, and why the product or service will have a competitive advantage over similar offerings from competitors. It also addresses the barriers to entry in this market that may prevent the entry of new competitors, such as high capital costs, difficulty in reaching customers or persuading them to switch loyalties, hard-to-get employee skills, and so forth.

5. **Proprietary position.** If the new venture will rely on patents or licenses to patents, this section discusses how these patents will contribute to the company's competitive position and assesses whether other patents (i.e., competitors or otherwise) might limit the company's ability to market its products. If similar products don't already exist, it discusses the alternative means by which customers are likely to meet the needs the product addresses.
6. **Marketing and sales plan.** This part shows how the company plans to attract and maintain customers and discusses product pricing promotion and positioning strategy.
7. **Management team.** The plan also describes the members of the management team, emphasizing its track record at accomplishing tasks similar to those the company will face. Investors view the management team as the most important asset that will lead to company growth and help respond to unexpected changes.
8. **Operations plan.** Next, the plan describes how the business will operate on a day-to-day basis, explaining how the key assets (labor, processes, and tools) will be used to produce and deliver the products and services. This section includes a description of where the company will be located and where it will do business.
9. **Finances.** This section identifies the capital that will be required to build the business and how it will be used. It includes projections of revenues and expenses that show investors how they will get their money back and what return they can expect on their investment.

Finally, a word of warning: All too often, would-be entrepreneurs tend to equate a good business plan with the probability of success in running a business. Needless to say, however, a well-crafted plan doesn't ensure a successful business. At this point in the process, your probability of success depends more heavily on the strength of the three elements with which you started the process—a good opportunity (including the right timing), the right entrepreneurial team, and the necessary resources and capabilities. A business plan is no substitute for strategy and strong execution. That's why consultants often suggest that entrepreneurs think of the business plan not only as a helpful and necessary starting point but also as a continuous work in progress. [9]

Resourcing the New Venture Plan with People, Money, and Action People

There is no litmus test for determining the characteristics of successful entrepreneurs or those people who make the best members of an entrepreneurial team. However, without them, a new venture will never get off the ground. Sometimes, as you might imagine, key people are among the intangible resources and capabilities that distinguish the potential new venture as an opportunity, rather than just another good idea. As a practical matter, it's the entrepreneur who drives the entrepreneurial process and ensures that all three elements—opportunity, resources and capabilities, and people—are in place and balanced. Because individuals have limits, team members are often selected because they bring skills that complement those of the lead entrepreneur and ensure that the firm has the necessary human capital to achieve its objectives.

Money

Beyond the opportunity and the people, most entrepreneurs would identify money and access to money as one of the scarcest resources. The financing activity of the new venture can take many forms with sources ranging from credit cards to venture capitalists to banks. You might expect most successful ventures to have access to adequate capital, but you'd be surprised. In fact, many successful entrepreneurs (and their investors) suspect that too much money too early does more damage than good. [10] How can excess cash possibly be a problem? Remember, first of all, that financing rarely comes without strings attached. Entrepreneurs who depend on significant cash flow from loans or investor capital often find that their flexibility is considerably reduced. Second, ample funding can obscure potential problems until the consequences are irreversible.

Perhaps most importantly, deep financial pockets shelter the new firm from the need to innovate in all aspects of its business. For example, the best new opportunities are often created by firms that have both new ideas and new, sometimes less costly ways to put those ideas work. Dell's sustained dominance in the personal computer (PC) market, for instance, can be credited to the combination of a new direct-sales model (a new-market opportunity using catalogs and then the Internet) and the direct manufacturing model (a cheaper way of putting together the equipment sold through

direct means) that it fostered. Similarly, Amazon's prowess is equally a function of its introduction of an online book business (again, a new opportunity) and the patented online logistical expertise that the company developed to put the idea into practice (i.e., a cheaper way to merchandise).

The book you are reading (in your hands or on a screen—or "reading" through your headphones) is the most recent product of this marriage of opportunity and a new way of doing things.

Bootstrapping means exploiting a new business opportunity with limited funds. A lot of new ventures are bootstrapped; a recent study of the five hundred fastest-growing small companies in the United States found median start-up capital to be around $20,000 in real terms. [11] Ironically, the fastest-growing firms typically require the most money because they have to support increases in inventories, accounts receivable, staffing, and production and service facilities. The most common form of bootstrapping is simply to use a personal credit card and then pay off the incurred debt. Despite the risk that taking on personal debt has, founders may opt for this method because it gives them more freedom to grow the company their own way and not have to share any equity. Many successful companies, including Dell, were founded this way.

There are different types of bootstrapping, including the following: [12]

- Owner financing
- Sweat equity
- Minimization of the accounts receivable
- Joint utilization
- Delaying payment
- Minimizing inventory
- Subsidy finance
- Personal debt

Despite bootstrapping's advantages, it may not be enough by itself. Entrepreneurs will bring in outside investors if they need a larger sum of capital than they can obtain through personal credit cards or second mortgages. In addition, outside investors can bring useful contacts, experience and accountability to the new venture. Outsiders can range from individuals like angel investors to professionals like venture capitalists, insurance companies, and public and private pension funds.

Action

One thing that does separate successful ventures (and entrepreneurs) from unsuccessful ones is a bias for action, or a "propensity to act or decide without customary analysis or sufficient information" (i.e., a just-do-it-and-contemplate-later mentality). Tom Peters and Robert Waterman, authors of *In Search of Excellence*, identified this as a distinguishing feature of agile, entrepreneurial firms. [13] This perspective is clearly articulated in the following quote from the Babson Entrepreneurship Club:

There is no substitute for action. Until you form the company and attempt to land your first partners and customers, all you really have is a paper-napkin idea. I hate to break it to you, but this country's chock full of paper napkins. It's short on people who will believe in themselves and give it a try. You'll be surprised how much and how quickly you learn once the company's up and running. For a measly few hours of your time, you'll springboard into the category of "business owner" and become part of the select few. [14]

It's important to note that this bias for action relates to activities guided by the business plan or core idea. The plan helps the entrepreneur make choices that make things happen, revise assumptions, and make midcourse corrections in light of new information. Without action, however, there will be no new sources of information to inform these latter parts of the entrepreneurial process.

KEY TAKEAWAYS

- Entrepreneurs operate in both for-profit and nonprofit organizations.

- Entrepreneurship takes place through some combination of opportunity identification, the venture's preparation and plan, and the resources that convert the venture plan into action. Action is a vital component; there is no substitute for action. Until the entrepreneur forms the company and attempts to land the first partners and customers, all the entrepreneur really has is an idea.

- The levers of opportunity identification include the following:
  - New-market-creation strategies that are designed to eliminate, reduce, create, or raise some previously assumed dimension of product/market supply and demand
  - New-market-disruption strategies that are designed to allow a firm that has created a new market to grow into a dominant player in a new but huge industry
  - Low-end-disruption strategies that identify a business that will let you shift customers from a high-cost-to-serve to a low-cost-to-serve business model

EXERCISES

(AACSB: Reflective Thinking, Analytical Skills)

1. In what contexts does entrepreneurship take place?
2. Why would entrepreneurship be important in the context of government or nonprofits?
3. What is social entrepreneurship?
4. What are the three facets of the entrepreneurial process?
5. How might a firm disrupt an existing market?

[1] "It's Not Just Business, It's Life and Death," Ernst & Young, accessed December 24, 2010, http://www.ey.com/GL/en/About-us/Entrepreneurship/Entrepreneur-Of-The-Year/Entrepreneur-Of-The-Year---SEOY---Camila-Batmanghelidjh.

[2] "Inventor of the Week: Robert Gore," MIT School of Engineering, September 2006, accessed May 5, 2011, http://web.mit.edu/invent/iow/gore.html.

[3] Jonathan T. Eckhardt and Scott A. Shane, "Opportunities and Entrepreneurship," Journal of Management 29, no. 3 (June 2003): 333–49; Jonathan T. Eckhardt and Scott A. Shane, "The Individual-Opportunity Nexus: A New Perspective on Entrepreneurship," in Handbook of Entrepreneurship Research: An Interdisciplinary Survey and Introduction, ed. Zoltan J. Acs and David B. Audretsch (Boston: Kluwer, 2003), 161–91.

[4] W. Chan Kim and Renée Mauborgne, "Blue Ocean Strategy: From Theory to Practice," California Management Review 47, no. 3 (Spring 2005): 105–21.

[5] {Author's name retracted as requested by the work's original creator or licensee} and William G. Sanders, Strategic Management: A Dynamic Perspective, Concepts and Cases (Upper Saddle River, NJ: Prentice Hall, 2009).

[6] Clayton Christensen, The Innovator's Dilemma (New York: Harper Business, 2000), xv.

[7] These examples are drawn from an extensive and detailed list provided by Clayton M. Christensen and Michael E. Raynor, The Innovator's Solution: Creating and Sustaining Successful Growth (Boston: Harvard Business School Press, 2003).

[8] See, for example, Business Plans website, accessed November 1, 2010,http://www.bplans.com; U.S. Small Business Administration website, accessed November 1, 2010, http://www.sba.gov/category/navigation-structure/starting-managing-business/starting-business/writing-business-plan; More Business website, accessed November 1, 2010, http://www.morebusiness.com; Center for Business Planning website, accessed November 1, 2010, http://www.businessplans.org.

[9] Jeffry A. Timmons, New Venture Creation: Entrepreneurship for the 21st Century, 5th ed. (New York: McGraw-Hill, 1999).

[10] Jeffry A. Timmons, New Venture Creation: Entrepreneurship for the 21st Century, 5th ed. (New York: McGraw-Hill, 1999); Amar V. Bhide, "Bootstrap Finance: The Art of Start-Ups," Harvard Business Review, 70, no. 66 (November–December 1992): 109–17.

[11] Amar V. Bhide, "Bootstrap Finance: The Art of Start-Ups," Harvard Business Review, 70, no. 66 (November–December 1992): 109–17.

[12] Jay Ebbens and Alec Johnson, "Bootstrapping in Small Firms: An Empirical Analysis of Change over Time," Journal of Business Venturing 21, no. 6 (November 2006): 851–65.

[13] Thomas J. Peters and Robert Waterman Jr., In Search of Excellence (New York: Grand Central Publishing, 1988), 119.

[14] Babson Entrepreneurship Club, "LLC Workshop FAQ," accessed July 1, 2010, http://life.babson.edu/organization/bec.

11.3 Business Entrepreneurship across Borders
LEARNING OBJECTIVES

1. Understand why entrepreneurship can vary across borders.
2. Recognize how entrepreneurship differs from country to country.
3. Access and utilize the *Doing Business* and Global Entrepreneurship Monitor resources.

How the Ease of Doing Business Affects Entrepreneurship across Countries

There are a number of factors that explain why the level of business entrepreneurship varies so much across countries. In 1776, Adam Smith argued in *The Wealth of Nations* that the free-enterprise economic system, regardless of whether it's in the United States, Russia, or anywhere else in the world, encourages entrepreneurship because it permits individuals freedom to create and produce. [1] Such a system makes it easier for entrepreneurs to acquire opportunity. Smith was focused mostly on for-profit businesses. However, constraints on the ownership of property might not necessarily constrain other types of entrepreneurship, such as social entrepreneurship.

Business entrepreneurship and social entrepreneurship are clearly related. Researchers have observed that in countries where it's relatively easy to start a business—that is, to engage in business entrepreneurship—then it's also comparatively easier to be a social entrepreneur as well. One useful information resource in this regard is the World Bank's annual rankings of "doing business"—that is, the *Doing Business* report provides a quantitative measure of all the regulations associated with starting a business, such as hiring employees, paying taxes, enforcing contracts, getting construction permits, obtaining credit, registering property and trading across borders. [2]

Doing Business is based on the concept that economic activity requires good rules. For businesses to operate effectively, they need to know that contracts are binding, that their property and intellectual property rights are protected, and that there is a fair system for handling disputes. The rules need to be clear yet simple to follow so that things like permits can be obtained efficiently.

The World Bank's *Doing Business* Project looks at laws and regulations, but it also examines time and motion indicators. Time and motion indicators measure how long it takes to complete a regulatory goal (e.g., getting a permit to operate a business).

Thanks to ten years of *Doing Business* data, scholars have found that lower costs of entry encourage entrepreneurship, enhance firm productivity, and reduce corruption. [3] Simpler start-up regulations also translate into greater employment opportunities. [4]

Beyond describing local business practices, one of the key objectives of the *Doing Business* Project is to make it easier for entrepreneurship to flourish around the world. Considerable progress has been made each year in this regard, with 2010 being noted as a record year in regard to business-regulation reform. The countries with at least one positive reform are shown in the following figure.

Among the most populated countries, the World Bank suggests it's easiest to do business in the United States, the United Kingdom, Canada, Australia, and Thailand; the most difficult large countries are Côte d'Ivoire, Angola, Cameroon, Venezuela, and the Republic of the Congo. Among the less populated countries, the easiest-to-do-business rankings go to Iceland, Mauritius, Bahrain, Estonia, and Lithuania; the most difficult are Mauritania, Equatorial Guinea, São Tomé and Príncipe, and Guinea-Bissau. You can experiment with sorting the rankings yourself by region, income, and population at http://www.doingbusiness.org/economyrankings.

Differing Attitudes about Entrepreneurship around the World

Entrepreneurship takes place depending on the economic and political climate, as summarized in the World Bank's *Doing Business* surveys. However, culture also plays an important role—as well as the apparent interest among a nation's people in becoming entrepreneurs. This interest is, of course, partly related to the ease of doing business, but the cultural facet is somewhat deeper.

Turkey, for instance, seems a ripe location for entrepreneurship because the country has relatively stable political and economic conditions. Turkey also has a variety of industries that are performing well in the strong domestic market. Third, Turkey has enough consumers who are early adopters, meaning that they will buy technologies ahead of the curve. Again, this attitude would seem to support entrepreneurism. Yet, as Jonathan Ortmans reports in his *Policy Forum Blog*, currently only 6 percent workers are entrepreneurs—a surprisingly low rate given the country's favorable conditions and high level of development. [5]The answer to the mystery can be found in the World Bank's most recent report, which shows Turkey to be among the most difficult countries in which to do business. The Kauffman Foundation, on the basis of its own assessment, likewise identified many hurdles to entrepreneurship in Turkey, such as limited access to capital and a large, ponderous bureaucracy that has a tangle of regulations that are often inconsistently applied and interpreted. Despite all the regulations, intellectual property rights are poorly enforced and big established businesses strong-arm smaller suppliers. [6]

However, the Kauffman study also suggests that perhaps the most difficult problem is Turkey's culture regarding entrepreneurship and entrepreneurs. Although entrepreneurs "by necessity" are generally respected for their work ethic, entrepreneurs "by choice" (i.e., entrepreneurs who could be pursuing other employment) are often discouraged by their families and urged not to become entrepreneurs. The entrepreneurs who succeed are considered "lucky" rather than having earned their position through hard work and skill. In addition, the business and social culture does not have a concept of "win-win," which results in larger businesses simply muscling in on smaller ones rather than encouraging their growth or rewarding them through acquisition that would provide entrepreneurs with a profitable exit. The Kauffman report concludes that Turkey is in as much need of cultural capital as financial capital.

Did You Know?
The late entrepreneur and philanthropist Ewing Marion Kauffman established the Ewing Marion Kauffman Foundation in the mid-1960s. Based in Kansas City, Missouri, the Kauffman Foundation is among the thirty largest foundations in the United States, with an asset base of approximately $2 billion. [7] Here's how Kauffman Foundation CEO Carl Schram describes the vision of the foundation and its activities:

Our vision is to foster "a society of economically independent individuals who are engaged citizens, contributing to the improvement of their communities." In service of this vision and in keeping with our founder's wishes, we focus our grant making and operations on two areas: advancing entrepreneurship and improving the education of children and youth. We carry out our mission through four programmatic areas: Entrepreneurship, Advancing Innovation, Education, and Research and Policy.

Though all major foundation donors were entrepreneurs, Ewing Kauffman was the first such donor to direct his foundation to support entrepreneurship, recognizing that his path to success could and should be achieved by many more people. Today, the Kauffman Foundation is the largest American foundation to focus on entrepreneurship and has more than fifteen years of in-depth experience in the field. Leaders from around the world look to us for entrepreneurship expertise and guidance to help grow their economies and expand human welfare. Our Entrepreneurship team works to catalyze an entrepreneurial society in which job creation, innovation, and the economy flourish. We work with leading educators, researchers, and other partners to further understanding of the powerful economic impact of entrepreneurship, to train the nation's next generation of entrepreneurial leaders, to develop and disseminate proven programs that enhance entrepreneurial skills and abilities, and to improve the environment in which entrepreneurs start and grow businesses. In late 2008, the Foundation embarked on a long-term, multimillion-dollar initiative known as Kauffman Laboratories for Enterprise Creation, which, through a set of innovative programs, is seeking to accelerate the number and success of high-growth, scale firms.

In the area of Advancing Innovation, our research suggests that many innovations residing in universities are slow getting to market, and that many will never reach the market. As we look to improve this complex task, we work to research the reasons why the system is not more productive, explore ways to partner with universities, philanthropists, and industry to ensure greater output, and ultimately foster higher levels of innovative entrepreneurship through the commercialization of university-based technologies.

We believe, as did Mr. Kauffman, that investments in education should lead students on a path to self-sufficiency, preparing them to hold good-paying jobs, raise their families, and become productive citizens. Toward that end, the Foundation's Education team focuses on providing high-quality educational opportunities that prepare urban students for success in college and life beyond; and, advancing student achievement in science, technology, engineering and math.

The Kauffman Foundation has an extensive Research and Policy program that is ultimately aimed at helping us develop effective programs and inform policy that will best advance entrepreneurship and education. To do so, our researchers must determine what we know, commit to finding the answers to what we don't, and then apply that knowledge to how we operate as a Foundation. Kauffman partners with top-tier scholars and is the nation's largest private funder of economic research focused on growth. Our research is contributing to a broader and more in-depth understanding of what drives innovation and economic growth in an entrepreneurial world. [8]

(Click the following link to view Schram's discussion with Charlie Rose about entrepreneurship and education: http://www.charlierose.com/view/interview/11026.)

Is there a way for you to gain insights into a country's entrepreneurial culture and therefore better explain why entrepreneurship varies so much? While there's no perfect answer to this—just as it's impossible to provide you with a survey telling you whether you will be a success or a failure as an entrepreneur—you may find it of interest to compare the motivations for engaging in entrepreneurship across countries. The Global Entrepreneurship Monitor (GEM) is a research program begun in 1999 by London Business School and Babson College. GEM does an annual standardized assessment of the national level of entrepreneurial activity in fifty-six countries. The GEM reports are available at http://www.gemconsortium.org.

GEM shows that there are systematic differences between countries in regard to national characteristics that influence entrepreneurial activity. GEM also shows that entrepreneurial countries experience higher economic growth. On the basis of another set of surveys and the corresponding index prepared annually by the World Economic Forum (WEF), [9] countries are broken out in groups, including factor-driven economies (e.g., Angola, Bolivia, Bosnia and Herzegovina, Colombia, Ecuador, Egypt, India, and Iran), efficiency-driven economies (e.g., Argentina, Brazil, Chile, Croatia, Dominican Republic, Hungary, Jamaica, Latvia, Macedonia, Mexico, Peru, Romania, Russia, Serbia, South Africa, Turkey, and Uruguay), and innovation-driven economies (e.g., Belgium, Denmark, Finland, France, Germany, Greece, Iceland, Ireland, Israel, Italy, Japan, the Netherlands, Norway, Slovenia, South Korea, Spain, the United Kingdom, and the United States). Somewhat like the *Doing Business* survey, the WEF ranks national competitiveness in the form of a Global Competitiveness Index (GCI). The GCI defines competitiveness as "the set of institutions, policies, and factors that determine the level of productivity of a country." The GCI ranks nations on a weighted index of twelve assessed pillars: (1) institutions, (2) infrastructure, (3) macroeconomic stability, (4) health and primary education, (5) higher education and training, (6) goods-market efficiency, (7) labor-market efficiency, (8) financial-market sophistication, (9) technological readiness, (10) market size, (11) business sophistication, and (12) innovation. [10] Current

and past reports are available at http://www.weforum.org/reports.

Entrepreneurship in Factor-Driven Economies

Economic development consists of changes in the quantity and character of economic value added. These changes result in greater productivity and rising per capita incomes, and they often coincide with migration of labor across different economic sectors in the society, for example from primary and extractive sectors to the manufacturing sector and eventually, services. Countries with low levels of economic development typically have a large agricultural sector, which provides subsistence for the majority of the population who mostly still live in the countryside. This situation changes as industrial activity starts to develop often around the extraction of natural resources. As extractive industry starts to develop, this triggers economic growth, prompting surplus population from agriculture to migrate toward extractive and emergent scale-intensive sectors, which are often located in specific regions. The resulting oversupply of labor feeds subsistence entrepreneurship in regional agglomerations, as surplus workers seek to create self-employment opportunities to make a living.

Entrepreneurship in Efficiency-Driven Economies

As the industrial sector develops further, institutions start to emerge to support further industrialization and the buildup of scale in the pursuit of higher productivity through economies of scale. Typically, national economic policies in scale-intensive economies shape their emerging economic and financial institutions to favor large national businesses. As increasing economic productivity contributes to financial capital formation, niches may open in individual supply chains that service these national incumbents. This, combined with the opening up of independent supplies of financial capital from the emerging banking sector, would spur opportunities for the development of small-scale and medium-size manufacturing sectors. Thus, in a scale-intensive economy, one would expect necessity-driven industrial activity to gradually fall and give way to an emerging small-scale manufacturing sector.

Entrepreneurship in Innovation-Driven Economies

As an economy matures, and its wealth increases, one may expect the emphasis in industrial activity to gradually shift toward an expanding service sector that caters to the needs of an increasingly affluent population and supplies the services normally expected of a high-income society. The industrial sector evolves and experiences improvements in variety and sophistication, such a development would typically be associated with increasing research and development and knowledge intensity, as knowledge-generating institutions in the economy gain momentum . This development opens the way for the development of innovative, opportunity-seeking entrepreneurship activity that is not afraid to challenge established incumbents in the economy. Often small and innovative entrepreneurial firms enjoy an innovation productivity advantage over large incumbents, enabling them to operate as 'agents of creative destructions.' To the extent that the economic and financial institutions created during the scale-intensive phase of the economy are able to accommodate and support opportunity-seeking entrepreneurial activity, innovative entrepreneurial firms may emerge as significant drivers of economic growth and wealth creation.

Factor-driven economies are economies that are dependent on natural resources and unskilled labor. For example, Chad is the lowest-ranked country in the GCI, and its economy is dependent on oil reserves. Because its economy is so tied to a commodity, Chad is very sensitive to world economic cycles, commodity prices, and fluctuations in exchange rates. The pillars associated with factor-driven economies are institutions, infrastructure, macroeconomic stability, and health and primary education.

Efficiency-driven economies, in contrast, are found in countries that have well-established higher education and training, efficient goods and labor markets, sophisticated financial markets, a large domestic or foreign market, and the capacity to harness existing technologies, which is also known as technological readiness. The economies compete on production and product quality, as Brazil does. Brazil has a per capita gross domestic product (GDP) of about $7,000.

Innovation-driven economies, finally, are economies that compete on business sophistication and innovation. [11] The

United States, with a per capita GDP of about $46,000, ranks first overall in the GCI due to its mature financial markets, business laws, large domestic size, and flourishing innovation.

Using the criteria for factor-driven, efficiency-driven, and innovation-driven economies and the most recent surveys results, the following figure summarizes the range of activity across a select group of countries.

KEY TAKEAWAYS

- Entrepreneurship differs in various countries; for instance, it is easier to do business in some countries than others, and this would likely have an impact on the level of entrepreneurship in each country. The *Doing Business* and Global Entrepreneurship Monitor resources offer insights into everything from a quantitative measure of regulations for starting a business to an assessment of the national level of entrepreneurial activity.

- Citizens of different countries vary in terms of their attitudes toward entrepreneurs and entrepreneurship. For example, a country where people viewed entrepreneurs as positive role models and entrepreneurship as a viable career alternative might also encourage others to become entrepreneurs.

- A country's stage of development also influences its nature of entrepreneurial activity.

EXERCISES

(AACSB: Reflective Thinking, Analytical Skills)

1. Why might the level of entrepreneurship vary across countries?
2. Would all the factors that promote or constrain business entrepreneurship also affect the level of social entrepreneurship?
3. Do you think some industries would be more affected or less affected by the criteria in the *Doing Business* rankings?
4. Among those factors affecting the level of entrepreneurial activity, which might be the easiest to change and which might be the most difficult? Which might take the most time to change?
5. How might a country's level of economic development affect the nature of entrepreneurial activity?

[1] Adam Smith, An Inquiry into the Nature and Causes of the Wealth of Nations (London: W. Strahan and T. Cadell, 1776). Recent versions have been edited by scholars and economists.
[2] Doing Business website, accessed July 2, 2010, http://www.doingbusiness.org.

[3] For example, Levon Barseghyan, "Entry Costs and Cross-Country Productivity and Output," Journal of Economic Growth 12, no. 2 (2008): 145–67; and Leora F. Klapper, Anat Lewin, and Juan Manuel Quesada Delgado, "The Impact of the Business Environment on the Business Creation Process," World Bank Policy Research Working Paper No. 4937, May 1, 2009.
[4] For example, Roberto Chang, Linda Kaltani, and Norman V. Loayza, "Openness Can Be Good for Growth: The Role of Policy Complementarities," Journal of Development Economics90, no. 1 (September 2009): 33–49; Elhanan Helpman, Marc Melitz, and Yona Rubinstein, "Estimating Trade Flows: Trading Partners and Trading Volumes," The Quarterly Journal of Economics, 123, no. 2 (May 2008): 441–87.
[5] Jonathan Ortmans, "Entrepreneurship in Turkey," Policy Forum Blog, April 5, 2010, accessed July 2, 2010, http://www.entrepreneurship.org/en/Blogs/Policy-Forum-Blog/2010/April/Entrepreneurship-in-Turkey.aspx.
[6] Jonathan Ortmans, "Entrepreneurship in Turkey," Policy Forum Blog, April 5, 2010, accessed July 2, 2010, http://www.entrepreneurship.org/en/Blogs/Policy-Forum-Blog/2010/April/Entrepreneurship-in-Turkey.aspx.
[7] "Foundation Overview," Ewing Marion Kauffman Foundation, accessed July 2, 2010, http://www.kauffman.org/about-foundation/foundation-overview.aspx.
[8] "Foundation Overview," Ewing Marion Kauffman Foundation, accessed July 2, 2010, http://www.kauffman.org/about-foundation/foundation-overview.aspx.
[9] World Economic Forum website, accessed July 2, 2010, http://www.weforum.org/en/index.htm.
[10] "The Global Competitiveness Report 2008-2009: US, 2008," World Economic Forum, accessed January 18, 2011, https://members.weforum.org/pdf/gcr08/United%20States.pdf.
[11] Casey Coleman, "Assessing National Innovation and Competitiveness Benchmarks," U.S. General Services Administration, March 7, 2009, accessed June 10, 2010,http://innovation.gsa.gov/blogs/OCIO.nsf/dx/Assessing-National-Innovation-and-Competitiveness-Benchmarks.

11.4 From Entrepreneurship to Born-Global Firms
LEARNING OBJECTIVES

1. Understand the nature of born-global firms (or global start-ups).
2. See why global start-ups are challenging to manage and yet increasing in prevalence.
3. Know the two phases of global start-up assessment.

Global Start-ups and Born-Global Firms

More and more firms—even very small ones—have operations that bridge national borders soon after their founding. Thanks to the Internet and related information technologies (IT) that enable many of them, this new breed of firms began emerging in the 1990s and is dubbed "born-global" because their operations often span the globe early in their existence. A born-global firm, also commonly called a global start-up, is "a business organization that, from inception, seeks to derive significant competitive advantage from the use of resources and the sale of outputs in multiple countries." [1] A common characteristic of such firms is that their offerings complement the products or capabilities of other global players, take advantage of global IT infrastructure, or otherwise tap into a demand for a product or service that at its core is somewhat uniform across national geographic markets. While many firms may fall into this category by virtue of their products, the operations and customers of born-global firms do actually span the globe—exploiting a combination of exporting and foreign direct investment.

Did You Know?

The born global firm is defined as a business organization that, from inception, seeks to derive significant competitive advantage from the use of resources and the sale of outputs in multiple countries. In due course, these distinctive firms are gradually becoming the norm among companies that do international business. The distinguishing feature of born global firms is that their origins are international, as demonstrated by management's global focus and the commitment of certain types of resources to international activities. Here we emphasize not the size, but rather the age by which the firm ventures into foreign markets. In contrast to the traditional pattern of businesses that operate in the home country for many years and gradually evolve into international trade, born globals begin with a "borderless" view of the world and develop the strategies needed to expand abroad at or soon after the firm's founding. The focus is on the phenomenon of early internationalization and the approaches that companies leverage for achieving superior performance in international business from the inception of the firm. [2]

Logitech, the computer peripherals company, is perhaps one of the best early examples of a successful born-global firm. [3] Focusing first on the PC mouse, the company was founded by two Italians and a Swiss. The company's operations and research and development were initially split between California and Switzerland, and then it expanded rapidly with production in Ireland and Taiwan. With its stylish and ergonomic products, Logitech captured 30 percent of the global computer mouse business by 1989, garnering the start-up a healthy $140 million in revenues.

Today, Logitech is an industry leader in the design and manufacture of computer peripheral devices; has manufacturing facilities in Asia and offices in major cities in North America, Europe, and the Asia-Pacific region; and directly employs more than 6,000 people worldwide. [4]

Skype Limited is a more recent born-global firm. You may already have its software on your laptop or desktop computer

to take advantage of this free Internet phone technology, called voice-over Internet protocol, or VoIP. [5] At any point in time, there are millions of users logged in on Skype; the program and service has made such a strong impression that the term "Skype me" has replaced "call me" in some circles. Niklas Zennstrom and Janus Friis, the same two entrepreneurs who invented KaZaA (one of the most popular Internet file-sharing software programs in the world) also developed Skype. Initially founded in Sweden as Tele2, Skype is now headquartered in Luxembourg and has offices in Europe, the United States, and Asia. Skype and has received significant funding from some of the largest venture-capital firms in the world. [6] Both Logitech and Skype share certain characteristics—ripe conditions for global start-ups, what it takes to build them, and what it takes to make them succeed.

Two Phases of Global Start-up Assessment

Global start-ups need to pass through two phases. If you can answer yes to all or most of the questions from Phase 1, then you need to be sure that you can quickly build the resources and capabilities identified in Phase 2. Research has shown that firms unable to connect the dots in Phase 2 are forced to cease operations after a short, but lively, period of time. [7]

- Phase 1: Should my firm be a global start-up?
    1. Do I want to build the brand around the world right from the start?
    2. Do I need human resources from other countries for my company to succeed?
    3. Do I need financial capital from other countries for my company to succeed?
    4. Will my target customers prefer the services of my company to the services of my competitors if I am global?
    5. Can I put an international system in place more quickly than domestic competitors?
    6. Do I need global scale and scope to justify the financial and human capital investment in the venture?
    7. Will a purely domestic focus now make it harder for me to go global in the future?
- Phase 2: Now that you have committed to going global, here is what you need:
    1. A strong management team with international experience
    2. A broad and deep international network among suppliers, customers, and complements
    3. Preemptive marketing or technology that provides you with a first-mover advantage with customers and

can lock out competitors from key suppliers and complements

4. Strong intangible assets (e.g., both Logitech and Skype have style, hipness, and mindshare via their brands)

5. The ability to keep customers locked in by linking new products and services to the core business while constantly innovating in the core product or service itself

6. Close worldwide coordination and communication among business units, suppliers, complements, and customers

So why is the introduction of global start-ups important at this point in your international business education? One reason is the increasing prevalence of global start-ups, driven in part by globalizing consumer preferences, mobile consumers, large global firms, and the pervasiveness of the Internet and its effects. The other is that global start-ups are very relevant to the subject of intrapreneurship, which you will learn about in Section 11.5 "From Entrepreneurship to Intrapreneurship".

KEY TAKEAWAYS

- Global start-ups, also called born-global firms, are an increasingly important phenomenon in the world of entrepreneurship. A global start-up is a business organization that, from inception, seeks to derive significant competitive advantage from the use of resources and the sale of outputs in multiple countries.

- A common characteristic of such firms is that their offerings complement the products or capabilities of other global players, take advantage of global IT infrastructure, or otherwise tap into a demand for a product or service that at its core is somewhat uniform across national geographic markets.

- There are two phases of global start-up assessment: (1) deciding if a firm should become a global start-up and (2) deciding what the firm needs to do to make that happen.

EXERCISES

(AACSB: Reflective Thinking, Analytical Skills)

1. What are the characteristics of a global start-up?
2. What might explain the increasing number of global start-ups?
3. Why might a global start-up be harder to manage than a purely domestic company?

4. What key pieces of information would you need to assess whether you should launch a global start-up?
5. Once you have decided to launch a global start-up, what key resources and capabilities must you begin putting into place?

[1] Benjamin M. Oviatt and Patricia Phillips McDougall, "Toward a Theory of International New Ventures," Journal of International Business Studies, First Quarter 1994, 47, accessed December 24, 2010, http://aib.msu.edu/awards/25_1_94_45.pdf.

[2] S. Tamer Cavusgil and Gary Knight, Born Global Firms: A New International Enterprise (New York: Business Expert Press, 2009), 1.

[3] Benjamin M. Oviatt and Patricia Phillips McDougall, "Global Start-Ups: Entrepreneurs on a Worldwide Stage," Academy of Management Executive 9, no. 2 (1995): 30–44.

[4] Logitech website, accessed November 1, 2010, http://www.logitech.com.

[5] Skype website, accessed November 1, 2010, http://www.skype.com.

[6] "Where Is Skype?" Skype, accessed December 27, 2010, http://about.skype.com/where-is-skype.

[7] Benjamin M. Oviatt and Patricia Phillips McDougall, "Global Start-Ups: Entrepreneurs on a Worldwide Stage," Academy of Management Executive 9, no. 2 (1995): 30–44.

11.5 From Entrepreneurship to Intrapreneurship
LEARNING OBJECTIVES

1. Understand the background of intrapreneurship.
2. Recognize the difference and relationship between entrepreneurship and intrapreneurship.
3. Know the inputs and challenges to the intrapreneurial organization.

Intrapreneurship and Its Roots

The power and spirit of entrepreneurs and entrepreneurship are also felt in the context of established businesses. In 1992, for instance, *The American Heritage Dictionary* brought intrapreneurship and intrapreneur into the mainstream by adding intrapreneur to its dictionary, defining it as "a person within a large corporation who takes direct responsibility for turning an idea into a profitable finished product through assertive risk taking and innovation."[1]

Intrapreneurship in Action

Google lets its technical employees spend up to 20 percent of their time on projects of their own choosing. This freedom is a "license to pursue your dreams," as Google's Marissa Mayer, one-time VP of search products, called it in *Fast Company* magazine. [2] In 2006, Mayer said that half of the new products and features launched by Google in the last six months of 2005 came from work done under the "20 percent rule." [3]

In the early 1980s, Gifford and Elizabeth Pinchot were developing the concept of the intracorporate entrepreneur and coined the word *intrapreneur*. Under their model, a person wishing to develop an intrapreneurial project would initially have to risk something of value to themselves—a portion of their salary, for instance. The intrapreneur could then sell the completed project for both cash bonuses and intracapital, which could be used to develop future projects. On the basis of the success of some of the early trials of their methods in Sweden, the Pinchots began a school for intrapreneurs. In 1985, they published their first book, *Intrapreneuring*, combining the findings from their research and practical applications. [4]

In their book *Re-Inventing the Corporation*, John Naisbitt and Patricia Aburdene cited intrapreneurship as a way for established businesses to find new markets and new products. [5] Steve Jobs also described the development of the Macintosh computer as an intrapreneurial venture within Apple. In 1990, the concept was established enough that Rosabeth Moss Kanter of the Harvard Business School discussed the need for intrapreneurial development as a key factor in ensuring the survival of the company in her book *When Giants Learn to Dance*. [6]

Differences between Entrepreneurs and Intrapreneurs

The primary difference between the two types of innovators is their context—the intrapreneur acts within the confines of an existing organization. Most organizations would dictate that the intrapreneur should ask for permission before attempting to create a desired future—in practice, the intrapreneur is more inclined to act first and then ask for forgiveness later, rather than ask for permission before acting. The intrapreneur is also typically the intraorganizational revolutionary—challenging the status quo and fighting to change the system from within. This ordinarily creates a certain amount of organizational friction. A healthy dose of mutual respect is required in order to ensure that such friction can be positively channeled. In summary, then, an intrapreneur is someone who operates like an entrepreneur but has the backing of an organization.

Intrapreneurship in Action

Sharon Nunes is a vice president at IBM Technologies. Here, in an excerpt from a 2009 WITI newsletter, she relates her own experience as an intrapreneur at IBM:

The fact that I'm leading IBM's Big Green Innovations group—focused on water management, alternative energy, and carbon management—isn't a coincidence. It's because I wanted to work on something I care deeply about, and I worked hard to raise awareness inside the company that this wasn't just a good idea—it was imperative.

Our Big Green Innovations initiative was started as part of a $100 million investment in ten new businesses based on ideas generated during Innovation Jam in 2006. IBM used Jams to enable broad collaboration, gain new perspectives on problems and challenges, and find important patterns and themes—all with the goal of accelerating decision making and action. Jams are grounded in "crowdsourcing," also known as "wisdom of the crowds." This particular "crowd"—hundreds of thousands of IBMers, their families, and IBM customers—called resoundingly for an effort like Big Green Innovations. And so, it happened. [7]

Gifford Pinchot's book *Intrapreneuring: Why You Don't Have to Leave the Corporation to Become an Entrepreneur* provides Ten Commandments for intrapreneurs:

1. Do any job needed to make your project work, regardless of your job description.
2. Share credit wisely.
3. Remember, it is easier to ask for forgiveness than permission.
4. Come to work each day willing to be fired.
5. Ask for advice before asking for resources.
6. Follow your intuition about people; build a team of the best.
7. Build a quiet coalition for your idea; early publicity triggers the corporate immune system.
8. Never bet on a race unless you are running in it.
9. Be true to your goals, but realistic about ways to achieve them.
10. Honor your sponsors. [8]

The Intrapreneurial Organization

An intrapreneurial organization is one that seeks to systematically promote the spirit of intrapreneurship in targeted parts of the organization. The stellar innovation track records of firms like Merck & Co., 3M, Motorola, Newell Rubbermaid, Johnson & Johnson, Corning Incorporated, General Electric, Hewlett-Packard, Walmart, and many others demonstrate that bigness isn't in itself antithetical to intrapreneurship. At the same time, these are but a few of the thousands of large firms around the world. Understanding the obstacles to entrepreneurship in large, established firms will put you on firmer ground when it comes time to translate what you know about entrepreneurship in general to the process of corporate intrapreneurship.

As you may have guessed by now, intrapreneurs have helped increase the speed and cost-effectiveness of technology transfer from research and development to the marketplace. The following are some methods that have been used by businesses to foster intrapreneurship:

- Intrapreneurial employees are able to participate in the rewards of what they create, such as being granted something like ownership rights in the internal enterprises they create.

- The firm treats intrapreneurial teams as a profit center, rather than as a cost center (i.e., teams are expected to make money). Some companies give their intrapreneurial teams their own internal bank accounts.

- Team members can choose the projects on which they work or the alliances they join.

- Employees have access to training to help them learn new skills.

- Internal enterprises are recognized within the organization and have official standing.

- The organization defines and supports a system of contractual agreements between internal enterprises.

- The intrapreneurship plan includes a method for settling disputes that may arise around the internal enterprise and employees.

Companies that want to gain the benefits of intrapreneurism create systems for identifying employees with intrapreneurial traits and help develop those employees through training and reward them through incentives. The intrapreneurial organization can take on one or a combination of two forms: coexistence or structural separation.

The Coexistence Approach

A firm may seek to develop a new business around some valuable process or technological breakthrough. With the coexistence approach, the new venture activities are conducted within an existing business or business unit. Typically, an executive or group of executives will champion the innovation, and the process will proceed when the business concept has been tentatively validated and many of the major uncertainties resolved or reduced. [9] Attention then shifts from opportunity validation to the process of bringing the new business to life. Efforts are directed at assembling resources and capabilities, meeting production and sales goals, and solidifying organization. Interestingly, researchers note that creating a business climate supportive of entrepreneurial activity is the most difficult task faced by a large company in trying to integrate an innovative new business. [10]

As a general rule, new-venture activities like those described are less predictable and are therefore riskier than those in which a firm traditionally engages. In particular, they face four obstacles:

1. Although false starts and failures can sometimes be important learning mechanisms, most large firms naturally try to mitigate them by improving efficiency.

2. Moreover, new ventures often meet resistance because they challenge long-established assumptions, work practices, and employee skills. After all, *new* by definition means *different*.

3. New ventures can threaten existing businesses beyond simply being different. For instance, a retail store that sets up an Internet sales site has the challenge of growing both its online store and its brick-and-mortar store, even though the Internet may inevitably be cannibalizing the brick-and-mortar store's sales.

4. Ironically—and most importantly—large organizations often lavish *too many resources*, including cash, on new ventures. How can this practice be a problem? To be successful at a new corporate venture, large firms must learn to be simultaneously patient and tolerant of risk on the one hand and stingy on the other. The need for stinginess comes from the observation by strategy researchers that corporate new ventures tend to thrive when their managers must face new markets on the same realistic terms that start-ups outside the corporate bureaucracy typically do.

The Structural-Separation Approach

The second form of organizational intrapreneurship, in which the firm sets up an internal new-venture division, is actually a structural solution to these same problems. In many ways, this division acts like a venture-capitalist or business incubator, working to provide expertise and resources and to impart structure and process in developing the new opportunity. In this case, too, the opportunity may revolve around some proprietary process, product, or technological breakthrough. This approach is designed to achieve one of two possible objectives:

1. To create a high-growth new venture that the firm can sell off through an IPO at a significant profit

2. To create and retain internally a new business that will fuel growth and, perhaps, foster corporate renewal

The advantage of the structural approach is the system for investing in a team that's assigned specifically to the creation of new ventures. If the system is managed properly, these divisions can function like the best venture-capitalist operations—that is, they can be cost conscious while still encouraging risk taking, experimentation, and novel, market-oriented solutions. Even this approach, however, falls far short of creating a win-win situation. A new-venture division—and for that matter, new venturing in any form—is a form of diversification, with the firm betting that it has the resources and capabilities to do something new.

The structural approach first became popular in the late 1960s, when 25 percent of the *Fortune* 500 maintained internal venture divisions. [11] The next wave came in the late 1970s and early 1980s, as large players such as Gillette, IBM, Levi Strauss & Co., and Xerox launched internal new-venture groups. [12] Next came the Internet boom, when many firms set up divisions to run e-commerce operations that mirrored their traditional brick-and-mortar operations. Remember, however, that the hallmark of new-division performance isn't internal rate of return. It's the amount that a dedicated venture capitalist would earn on the same amount of money invested over the same period of time. By this standard, the performance of most internal venturing divisions falls short. [13] Why? Although a firm may have proprietary access to a valuable technology, it probably doesn't possess the necessary venture-capitalist managerial skills and experience. In addition, when it's in the hands of a new-venture division, the new business is isolated from the rest of the organization. As a result, the parent firm is insulated from the new business and, therefore, less likely to learn from its successes and failures. By the same token, the new venture has limited access to other proprietary resources and capabilities possessed by the parent firm.

Is corporate new venturing, then, doomed to failure? Of course not. Firms must, however, be careful to balance the requirements of entrepreneurial ventures—such as a supportive entrepreneurial climate—with the benefits of sustained linkage to the parent firm. Entrepreneurship professor David Garvin of Harvard Business School has recently reviewed the history of corporate new venturing. He suggests that corporate new ventures are more likely to succeed when they

- are developed and validated in firms with supportive, entrepreneurial climates;
- have senior executive sponsorship;
- involve related, rather than radically different, products and services;
- appeal to an emerging subset or current set of customers;
- employ market-experienced personnel;
- test concepts and business models directly with potential users;
- experiment, probe, and prototype repeatedly during early development;

- balance demands for early profitability with realistic timelines;
- introduce required systems and processes in time, but not earlier than the new venture's evolution required; and
- combine disciplined oversight and stinginess with entrepreneurial autonomy. [14]

Garvin's guidelines for successful corporate venturing suggest that there are other inherent tensions in the decision-making process as well. Even when a firm succeeds in creating a climate that's supportive of intrapreneurship, the evolving characteristics of the new venture may result in a unit that's more distinctive from the core businesses than it is complementary to them. In that case, it might be wise for the parent firm to allow the new business to function independently—physically and legally. In part, the increase in new-venture public offerings or carve-outs, where the parent company takes the new business public through an initial public offering, or IPO, can be attributed to the willingness of firms to take this advice.

KEY TAKEAWAYS

- Intrapreneurship is the form of entrepreneurship practiced within existing organizations.
- The intrapreneur is typically the intraorganizational revolutionary—challenging the status quo and fighting to change the system from within. The entrepreneur is the challenger from outside the firm.
- An organization can develop a culture of intrapreneurialism such that it can operate nimbly in an entrepreneurial fashion as the environment changes or that it can act as an industry disruptor. There are two approaches to intrapreneurship—the coexistence approach and the structural-separation approach.

EXERCISES

(AACSB: Reflective Thinking, Analytical Skills)

1. How is intrapreneurship similar to and different from entrepreneurship?
2. How might intrapreneurs differ from entrepreneurs?
3. What challenges might an intrapreneur face?
4. Why might organizations have an interest in becoming intrapreneurial?
5. What challenges do organizations face in becoming more intrapreneurial?

[1] The American Heritage Dictionary (Orlando, FL: Houghton Mifflin, 1992), s.v. "intrapreneur."

[2] Chuck Slater, "Marissa Mayer's 9 Principles of Innovation," Fast Company, February 19, 2008, accessed March 16, 2011, http://www.fastcompany.com/article/marissa-mayer039s-9-principles-innovation.

[3] Jeff Jarvis, What Would Google Do? (New York: Harper Business, 2009), 111.

[4] Gifford Pinchot and Elizabeth Pinchot, Intrapreneuring (New York, NY: Harper & Row Publishers, 1985).

[5] John Naisbitt and Patricia Aburdene, Re-Inventing the Corporation (New York: Warner Bros Publications, 1985).

[6] Rosabeth Moss Kanter, When Giants Learn to Dance (New York: Free Press, 1990).

[7] Sharon Nunes, "Passing the Technical Torch: 'Intrepreneurs' are the New Entrepreneurs," WITI, September 23, 2009, accessed September 17, 2010, http://www.witi.com/wire/articles/view.php?id=117.

[8] Gifford Pinchot and Elizabeth Pinchot, Intrapreneuring (New York, NY: Harper & Row Publishers, 1985), 22.

[9] Diana L. Day, "Raising Radicals: Different Processes for Championing Innovative Corporate Ventures," Organization Science 5, no. 2 (May 1994): 148–72.

[10] David A. Garvin, "A Note on Corporate Venturing and New Business Creation," Harvard Business School Note 302-091, March 2002, 1–20.

[11] Norman D. Fast, The Rise and Fall of Corporate New Venture Divisions (Ann Arbor: UMI Research Press, 1978).

[12] R. E. Gee, "Finding and Commercializing New Business," Research-Technology Management 37, no. 1 (1994): 50.

[13] Henry Chesbrough, "Designing Corporate Ventures in the Shadow of Private Venture Capital," California Management Review 42, no. 3 (Spring 2000): 31–49.

[14] David A. Garvin, "A Note on Corporate Venturing and New Business Creation," Harvard Business School Note 302-091, March 2002, 1–20.

11.6 End-of-Chapter Questions and Exercises

These exercises are designed to ensure that the knowledge you gain from this book about international business meets the learning standards set out by the international Association to Advance Collegiate Schools of Business (AACSB International). [1] AACSB is the premier accrediting agency of collegiate business schools and accounting programs worldwide. It expects that you will gain knowledge in the areas of communication, ethical reasoning, analytical skills, use of information technology, multiculturalism and diversity, and reflective thinking.

EXPERIENTIAL EXERCISES

(AACSB: Communication, Use of Information Technology, Analytical Skills)

1. Complete the survey of entrepreneurial characteristics. Ask your instructor to summarize the class scores and share the means and standard deviations for each scale item and the overall scale. Discuss what you think these results tell you about yourself and your differences and similarities with the rest of the class.

2. Like most popular soft drinks, Red Bull is largely sugar water. At the same time, Red Bull is a great example of an innovative, high-growth company that discovered a little-known, poor-selling product in Thailand and revitalized it, growing into a multibillion-dollar, highly profitable firm as a result. Visit the Red Bull website at http://www.redbull.com. Have you ever run across a product in one country that could be used in another country to grow a company like Red Bull? What are other examples of this type of opportunity?

3. You learned about global start-ups in this chapter, starting with the introductory case on eSys. This chapter identifies other examples of global start-ups as well. Conduct a web search using the search term "global start-ups." What types of firms seem to most commonly fit this label? Which countries seem the most active in this domain?

4. Break up your class into two groups—one made up of students who want to start their own business and the second made up of students who want to work for an established firm. Have each group talk about why they have this preference, and summarize the top ten issues using bullet points. Next, compare the two lists and work to come up with an explanation for why it is difficult for established organizations to be both efficient and entrepreneurial. What recommendations would you have to an established business that wants to attract and hire the budding entrepreneurs in your class?

Ethical Dilemmas

(AACSB: Ethical Reasoning, Multiculturalism, Reflective Thinking, Analytical Skills)

1. Adam Smith, in his 1776 book The Wealth of Nations, essentially argued that free enterprise, regardless of whether it is in the United States, Russia, or anywhere else in the world, encourages entrepreneurship because it permits an individual's freedom to create and produce. Such a system makes it easier for entrepreneurs to acquire opportunity. Is this the same thing as saying that to be an entrepreneur is to be ethical? Why or why not?

2. You are thinking about starting a new business that makes and sells a product similar to Red Bull. However, on a recent trip to Scandinavia you learned that Red Bull has actually been banned in some countries; it is illegal in Denmark, France, and Norway. Why is this magical drink that "gives you wings" banned in several countries? What are the ethical issues surrounding making and selling products that are legal in some countries but illegal in others?

3. Many multinationals are being intrapreneurial in developing new products for the world's poor, particularly in developing and emerging markets. These companies are targeting customers who live on dollar-a-day food budgets. For instance, in Indonesia, the global

food company Danone is targeting ten-cent drinkable yogurts at the poor, and in Mexico, it offers fifteen-cent cups of water. Unilever, likewise, sells Cubitos in developing markets. Cubitos are small cubes of flavoring that cost as little as two cents apiece What ethical issues are these firms grappling with in growing into these markets where poverty is so dire?

[1] Association to Advance Collegiate Schools of Business website, accessed January 26, 2010, http://www.aacsb.edu.

NOTES:

NOTES:

Chapter 12:
Winning through Effective, Global Talent Management

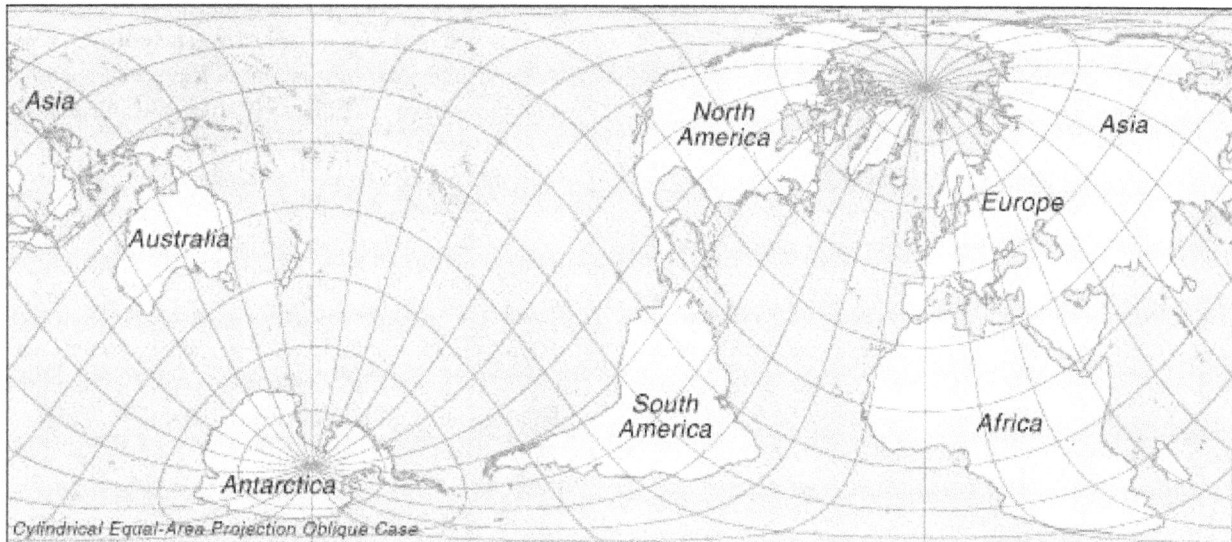

WHAT'S IN IT FOR ME?

1. What is the scope and changing role of global, strategic human resources management (SHRM) in international business?
2. How can you visualize the battlefield in the global war for talent?
3. How can you engage in effective selection and placement strategies?
4. What are the roles of pay structure and pay for performance in effective talent management?
5. How can you use the Workforce Scorecard to gauge and proactively manage human capital, including your own?

You've probably heard the saying "people make the place." Moreover, firms with operations across borders have this added advantage: access to the best and brightest people from around the world, because talent isn't constrained by national borders. Indeed, one of the key forces in flattening the world is new technologies; other trends too are empowering people from every corner of the earth. At the same time, companies large and small are able to find and leverage human capital from the farthest reaches of the planet. This ability to arbitrage and attract human capital worldwide is a key driver in the war for talent, which is a term signifying the strategic importance of attracting top employees to work for your company. In today's fast-changing environment, companies need employees who understand the organization's strategy and are empowered to execute it. To achieve this, organizations need to follow a strategic human resources management (SHRM) approach. SHRM ensures that people are a key factor in a firm's competitive advantage. Organizations need human resources to be a partner in identifying, recruiting, and hiring the types of employees who will be most qualified to help the company achieve its goals. SHRM requires attracting the right employees to the company, identifying metrics to help employees stay on target to meet the company's goals, and rewarding them appropriately for their efforts so that they stay engaged and motivated. Having all these components in place results in a high-performance work system, improves organizational performance, and unleashes employee talent.

OPENING CASE: EMPLOYEE RECRUITMENT, SELECTION, AND DEVELOPMENT STRATEGIES AT ENTERPRISE HOLDINGS

You may know this company through one of its businesses, Enterprise Rent-A-Car, and its "We'll pick you up" jingle. The Enterprise car-rental business is part of a much larger family business—Enterprise Holdings. Through its regional subsidiaries, Enterprise Holdings operates more than 1 million cars and trucks, the largest fleet of passenger vehicles in the world today. [1] It's one of the largest and most comprehensive providers in the car-rental industry, serving approximately 7,600 neighborhood and airport locations in the United States, Canada, Mexico, the Caribbean, Latin America, the United Kingdom, Ireland, Germany, and Asia. In addition, Enterprise Holdings is part of a global strategic alliance with Europcar, creating the world's largest car-rental network. In this case study, you'll see how Enterprise—with more than 68,000 employees and $12 billion revenue—ensures it has the right people with the right skills in the right locations worldwide.

Core Values from the Start

Enterprise was founded in 1957 by Jack Taylor, who returned from World War II to start a car-leasing company in St. Louis. He launched with a total of seven cars and one employee, but he had a vision to grow and a strong motto: "Take care of your customers and your employees first, and the profits will follow." [2] This vision of exceptional customer service means that Enterprise has to identify, attract, and hire employees who would be good at delivering on its customer service mission. To accomplish this, Enterprise looks for potential new hires who have the following set of skills and competencies that support the company's objectives:

1. Customer service focus
2. Sales and listening skills
3. Positive work ethic (a drive to achieve results)
4. Leadership aptitude
5. Communication skills
6. Flexibility

The company has identified the competencies and behaviors that such skills provide and has clearly articulated the benefits that these skills provide to Enterprise. For instance, flexibility is defined as dealing well with challenges, demonstrating resilience, and being able to prioritize. Enterprise believes that it—the company—is better able to cope with changing circumstances when an employee exhibits flexibility.

Enterprise describes the competencies it seeks on its website so that job seekers can determine for themselves whether they will measure up and fit in with the Enterprise culture.

Attracting and Recruiting Employees

Enterprise has a team of 200 recruiters whose job is to identify potential new candidates at over one hundred college campuses each year. [3] Given its growth and international expansion, Enterprise hires 8,000 college graduates a year to fill its future management needs. [4] The recruiting function at Enterprise is decentralized: each recruiter is responsible for recruiting within his or her local market. The rationale for this structure is this: local hires reflect the local community for each branch office. "We try to mirror our communities," says

Pam Webster, assistant vice president for recruiting at Enterprise. [5]

Enterprise also uses an internship program as a way to identify potential future employees. The program is open to college juniors and seniors; interested interns then spend a summer working at Enterprise after graduating. Recruiters stay in touch with interns during the school year through e-mails and lunches. Some even send a care package to interns during final exam time.

In the United Kingdom, Enterprise began using Campus Brand Managers on university campuses to find potential interns and job applicants. These Campus Brand Managers are interns or students who already work for Enterprise and who act as liaisons for potential applicants. [6]

Enterprise also has an employee-referral program through which current employees get a financial reward if they recommend a new employee to Enterprise and that candidate is hired into a full-time position. The referral program has been the company's primary source of minority and female hires, and approximately 40 percent of new hires join Enterprise that way. [7]

Finally, Enterprise recruits online; about 50 percent of Enterprise's UK and Ireland workforce is recruited via the web.

Developing Employees

To develop new recruits who would like to enter the ranks of management, Enterprise offers its Graduate Management Trainee program, which is a program that teaches management skills such as leadership and big-picture thinking; finance and business management skills such as cost control and attention to profits; sales and marketing skills to generate more sales; fleet-control skills such as handling repairs and getting the right number and type of cars; and of course customer service skills. In as little as eight to twelve months, trainees can become assistant managers. Once they become assistant managers, they start to earn performance pay in addition to their salaries. [8] The performance pay is based on branch profits, which means employees can directly benefit from the improvements they make to branch operations.

Enterprise's training program supports the company's promote-from-within philosophy. "We have always hired college grads into our management training program, and from there we promote entirely from within," says Marie

Artim, assistant vice president of recruiting. "It's where I started, it's where our CEO started, and it's where almost all our senior leadership started." [9] Enterprise Holdings' president and chief operating officer (COO), Pamela Nicholson, started as a management trainee in 1981, working behind the rental counter, as did current chairman and CEO Andy Taylor. [10]Nicholson moved steadily through the ranks of the company and in 1999 was promoted to senior vice president of the company's North American operations, then to COO in 2003, and to president in 2008. [11]

Global Entrepreneurship

In addition to customer service, entrepreneurship is another key corporate value at Enterprise. The tradition began with founder Jack Taylor and continued through innovations introduced by Enterprise's branch managers. For example, in 1974 a rental manager in Orlando decided to offer his customers a new service: a free ride to the Enterprise rental office. Other branches emulated this free pick-up service, which demonstrated that employees with a great idea can see it implemented across the company.

Other entrepreneurial ideas include WeCar, which is Enterprise's new car-sharing program for corporations and campuses. [12] For example, Google is using the WeCar program and lets its employees choose among Priuses and Ford Escape Hybrids that Enterprise provides. [13]

Expanding internationally is likewise done through entrepreneurial employees. Enterprise opened its first German office in Ottobrunn in 1997. Enterprise's German pioneer, Jack Cope, said, "It's a lot of fun taking something from nothing and making it big, and I'm on my way to making that happen. A few years ago, Enterprise was unknown here in Germany. Today, thanks to the efforts of our motivated German workforce, the Enterprise mission, philosophy and culture are catching on." [14]

The company entices international entrepreneurs through messages like the following one on its website:

Just imagine the possibilities that come with joining a huge, internationally successful company with a personal, entrepreneurial approach which allows individuals to stand out. Our secret lies in the fact that we're divided up into thousands of smaller, local businesses. So when you take one of our graduate trainee jobs, you'll be learning how to run the business yourself. And how many organizations with a $12 billion turnover can say that? [15]

OPENING CASE EXERCISES

(AACSB: Ethical Reasoning, Multiculturalism, Reflective Thinking, Analytical Skills)

1. How does Enterprise use SHRM to support its customer service objectives?
2. What strategies does Enterprise use to attract new employees?
3. Do you think entrepreneurial employees would be motivated to work at Enterprise? Why or why not?

[1] "Enterprise Holdings Announces Fiscal 2010 Highlights," MarketWire, September 30, 2010, accessed November 24, 2010, http://www.marketwire.com/press-release/Enterprise-Holdings-Announces-Fiscal-2010-Highlights-1328012.htm.

[2] "Heritage," Enterprise Holdings, accessed January 28, 2011, http://www.enterpriseholdings.com/about-us.

[3] "Recruitment and Selection at Enterprise Rent-A-Car," The Times 100, 2009, accessed May 10, 2011, http://www.thetimes100.co.uk/downloads/enterprise/enterprise_14_full.pdf.

[4] Seth Cline, "The Companies Hiring the Most New College Grads," Forbes, June 21, 2010, accessed January 27, 2011, http://www.forbes.com/2010/06/21/companies-hiring-college-graduates-leadership-careers-jobs.html?_boxes=leadershipchannellatest.

[5] Fay Hansen, "Enterprise's Recruiting Model Transforms Interns into Managers, "Workforce Management Online, May 2009, accessed January 30, 2011, http://www.workforce.com/section/recruiting-staffing/feature/enterprises-recruiting-model-transforms-interns-into/index.html.

[6] "Recruitment and Selection at Enterprise Rent-A-Car," The Times 100, 2009, accessed May 10, 2011, http://www.thetimes100.co.uk/downloads/enterprise/enterprise_14_full.pdf.

[7] Fay Hansen, "Enterprise's Recruiting Model Transforms Interns into Managers,"Workforce Management Online, May 2009, accessed January 30, 2011, http://www.workforce.com/section/recruiting-staffing/feature/enterprises-recruiting-model-transforms-interns-into/index.html.

[8] David Lagess, "A 'Stealth Company' No Longer," U.S. News & World Report, October 17, 2008, accessed January 27, 2011, http://money.usnews.com/money/business-economy/small-business/articles/2008/10/17/a-stealth-company-no-longer?PageNr=2.

[9] Seth Cline, "The Companies Hiring the Most New College Grads," Forbes, June 21, 2010, accessed January 27, 2011, http://www.forbes.com/2010/06/21/companies-hiring-college-graduates-leadership-careers-jobs.html?_boxes=leadershipchannellatest.

[10] Anne Fisher, "Get a Great Job after Graduation," Fortune, May 28, 2009, accessed January 27, 2011, http://money.cnn.com/2009/05/28/news/economy/new.grad.jobs.fortune/index.htm?postversion=2009052904.

[11] "An Interview with Pamela M. Nicholson, President and Chief Operating Officer, Enterprise Holdings," Leaders 34, no. 1 (January–March 2011), accessed January 27, 2011, http://www.leadersmag.com/issues/2011.1_Jan/Missouri/LEADERS-Pamela-Nicholson-Enterprise-Holdings.html.

[12] David Lagess, "A 'Stealth Company' No Longer," U.S. News & World Report, October 17, 2008, accessed January 27, 2011, http://money.usnews.com/money/business-economy/small-business/articles/2008/10/17/a-stealth-company-no-longer?PageNr=2.

[13] Elizabeth Olson, "Car Sharing Reinvents the Company Wheels," New York Times, May 6, 2009, accessed January 27, 2011, http://www.nytimes.com/2009/05/07/business/businessspecial/07CAR.html?_r=1&ref=businessspecial.

[14] "For Management Trainees, Ours Really Is a World of Opportunity," About Enterprise, Enterprise Rent-A-Car, accessed January 27, 2011, https://www.enterprisealive.com/about-enterprise/global-locations.

[15] "With a Company as Successful as Ours, It's Easy to Start Getting Ahead of Yourself," About Enterprise, Enterprise Rent-A-Car, accessed January 27, 2011, http://www.enterprisealive.com/about-enterprise/our-industry.

12.1 The Changing Role of Strategic Human Resources Management in International Business

LEARNING OBJECTIVES

1. Understand how human resources management is becoming a strategic partner.
2. Recognize the importance of an organization's human capital.
3. Learn the key elements of SHRM.

HR as a Strategic Partner

The role of human resources management (HRM) is changing in business, particularly in international business. Previously considered a support function, HRM is now becoming a strategic partner in helping a global company achieve its goals. The strategic approach to HRM—strategic human resources management (SHRM)—means going beyond administrative tasks such as payroll processing. Instead, as shown in the opening case on Enterprise, managers need to think more broadly and deeply about how employees will contribute to the company's success.

SHRM is not just a function of the human resources (HR) department—all managers and executives need to be involved because the role of people is so vital to a company's competitive advantage. [1] In addition, organizations that value their employees are more profitable than those that don't. [2] Research shows that successful organizations have several things in common: providing employment security, engaging in selective hiring, using self-managed teams, being decentralized, paying well, training employees, reducing status differences, and sharing information. [3] When organizations enable, develop, and motivate human capital, they improve accounting profits as well as shareholder value in the process. [4] The most successful organizations manage HR as a strategic asset and measure HR performance in terms of its strategic impact. When each piece is in the right place, it creates a high-performance work system (HPWS)—a set of management practices that attempt to create an environment within an organization in which the employee has greater involvement and responsibility.

The following are some questions that HRM should be prepared to answer in this new world: [5]

- **Competence.** To what extent does our company have the required knowledge, skills, and abilities to implement its strategy?
- **Consequence.** To what extent does our company have the right measures, rewards, and incentives in place to align people's efforts with the company strategy?
- **Governance.** To what extent does our company have the right structures, communications systems, and policies to create a high-performing organization?
- **Learning and Leadership.** To what extent can our company respond to uncertainty and learn and adapt to change quickly?

Crucial Role of SHRM in Global Firms

Developing an effective international workforce is much more difficult for a competitor to emulate than buying technology or securing capital. [6] Besides, how well companies manage their HR around the world can mean the difference between success and failure. In a nutshell, firms that effectively manage their international HR typically outperform competitors in terms of identifying new international business opportunities, adapting to changing conditions worldwide, sharing innovation knowledge throughout the firm, effectively coordinating subsidiary operations, conducting successful cross-border acquisitions, and maintaining a high-performing, committed overseas workforce. [7]

Did You Know?

Robert Half International (RHI), a professional consulting firm, has staffing operations in more than 400 locations worldwide. [8] During the recession of 2009, RHI began hiring older, more experienced workers to add to its roster of temporary workers. Typically, temporary workers are low-level employees, but during the recession, many workers with fifteen or twenty years of experience lost their jobs or retired from full-time jobs. RHI hired older highly skilled workers, such as accounting and finance experts, to work on temporary projects—helping a company restructure or emerge from bankruptcy, for instance. The situation is a win-win: companies get access to experts they may not otherwise be able to afford, while retired workers earn extra money or income after a layoff. Zurich-based Adecco, a competitor to

RHI, likewise hired older workers. "More companies are looking for flexible, highly skilled temporary employees because it's much easier to end an assignment than terminate employment," said Doug Arms, chief talent officer at Ajilon Professional Staffing, a unit of Adecco. [9]

In many multinationals, an important challenge is balancing the need to coordinate units scattered around the world with the need for individual units to have the control necessary to deal effectively with local issues. [10] Achieving this balance becomes more difficult as the level of diversity that firms are exposed to increases. For example, consider a situation where the parent firm's national culture differs dramatically from the cultures in its overseas subsidiaries. In this case, it may be harder for the parent firm to share information, technology, and innovations between the home office and foreign outposts. It may also be more difficult to promote needed organizational changes and manage any conflicts that arise between employees in different countries.

Fortunately, international human resources management (IHRM) strategies can overcome such problems. For instance, IHRM professionals can help ensure that top executives understand the different cultures within the company workforce and around the world. They can also offer advice on how to coordinate functions across boundaries and develop outstanding cross-cultural skills in employees (e.g., through various training programs and career paths that involve significant overseas exposure). [11]

Of course, these are general suggestions and a range of HR practices might be used to implement them. Companies should develop an international HR philosophy that describes corporate values about HR—this in turn, will shape the broad outline of what constitutes acceptable IHRM practices for employees all over the world. From there, individual units can fine-tune and select specific practices that best fit their local conditions. But this is easier said than done, especially for firms operating in dozens of countries. Multinationals typically find it extremely difficult, for example, to design a compensation system that is sensitive to cultural differences yet still meets general guidelines of being seen as fair by employees everywhere. Indeed, culture may impact local HRM practices in a variety of ways—from how benefit packages are constructed to the hiring, termination, and promotion practices used, just to name a few. [12]

Nevertheless, selecting the right IHRM strategy can pay off, particularly in difficult foreign markets. Consider multinationals wanting to quickly enter countries with transitional economies—those that are moving from being state-dominated to being market-based (e.g., China and Russia). Choosing to enter those markets by buying local firms, building new plants, or establishing joint ventures may create significant HR challenges that will undercut performance if not handled well. Consequently, global firms need to adopt an appropriate IHRM strategy to meet transition economy challenges.

The Importance of Human Capital

Employees provide an organization's human capital. Your human capital is the set of skills that you have acquired on the job—through training and experience—which increase your value in the marketplace. The Society of Human Resource Management's *Research Quarterly* defined an organization's human capital as "the collective sum of the attributes, life experience, knowledge, inventiveness, energy, and enthusiasm that its people choose to invest in their work." [13]

Focus on Outcomes

Unfortunately, many HR managers are more effective in the technical or operational aspects of HR than they are in the strategic, even though the strategic facet has a much larger effect on the company's success. [14] In the past, HR professionals focused on compliance to rules, such as those set by the federal government, and tracked simple metrics—for instance, the number of employees hired or the number of hours of training delivered. The new principles of management, however, require a focus on outcomes and results, not just numbers and compliance. Just as lawyers count how many cases they've won—not just how many words they used—so too must HR professionals track how employees are using the skills they've learned to attain goals, not just how many hours they've spent in training. [15]

John Murabito, executive vice president and head of Human Resources and Services at CIGNA, says that HR executives need to understand the company's goals and strategy and then provide employees with the skills needed. Too often, HRM executives get wrapped up in their own initiatives without understanding how their role contributes to the business. That's dangerous, because when it comes to the HR department, "anything that is administrative or transactional is going to get outsourced," Murabito says. [16] Indeed, the number of HRM outsourcing contracts over $25 million has been increasing, with nearly 3,000 active company contracts recently under way. [17] For example, Bank of America outsourced its HRM administration to NorthgateArinso. NorthgateArinso now provides timekeeping, payroll processing, and payroll services for 10,000 Bank of America employees outside the United States. [18]To avoid being outsourced, HRM needs to stay relevant and accept accountability for its business results. In short, the people strategy needs to fully align with the company's business strategy, keeping the focus on outcomes.

Key Elements of HRM

Beyond the basic need for compliance with HRM rules and regulations, the four key elements of HR are summarized in Figure 12.1 "Key HRM Elements". In high-performing companies such as Enterprise Holdings, each element of the HRM system is designed to reflect best practices and to maximize employee performance. The different parts of the HRM system are strongly aligned with company goals.

Figure 12.1 Key HRM Elements

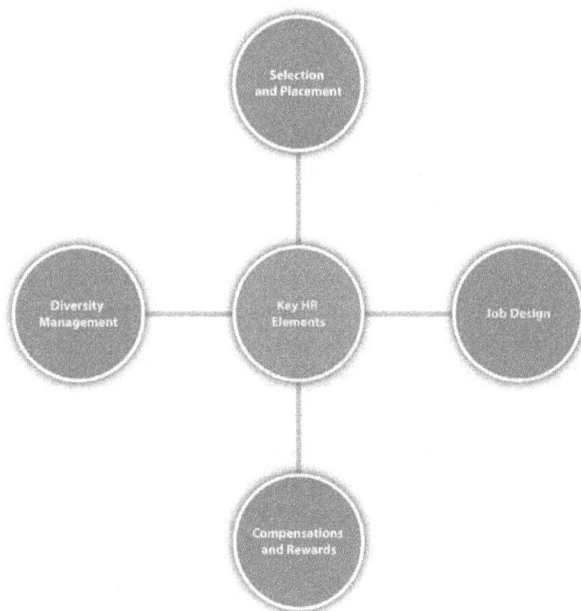

Selection and Placement

It's good for firms to acquaint prospective new hires with the nature of the jobs they'll be expected to fulfill early in the hiring process. This includes explaining the technical competencies needed (e.g., collecting statistical data) and defining behavioral competencies. Behavioral competencies may have a customer focus, such as the ability to show empathy and support of customers' feelings and points of view, or a work-management focus, such as the ability to complete tasks efficiently or to know when to seek guidance.

In addition, an SHRM best practice is to make the organization's culture clear by discussing the values that underpin the organization. For example, firms can describe the "heroes" of the organization—those employees who

embody the values of the organization. For example, a service company's heroes may be the people who go the extra mile to get customers to smile. In a software company, the heroes may be the people who toil through the night to develop new code. By sharing such stories of company heroes with potential hires, the firm helps reinforce the values and behaviors that make the company unique. This, in turn, will help the job candidates determine whether they'll fit well into that organization's culture.

Job Design

Job design refers to the process of combining tasks to form a whole job. The goal is to design jobs that involve doing a whole piece of work and that are challenging but ultimately doable for the employee. Job design also takes into account issues of health and safety of the worker. When planning jobs or assigning people to jobs, HR managers also consider training (ensuring that employees to have the knowledge and skills to perform all parts of their job) and giving them the authority and accountability to do so. [19]

One company that does training right is Motorola. As a global company, Motorola operates in many countries, including China. Operating in China presents particular challenges in terms of finding and hiring skilled employees. In a recent survey conducted by the American Chamber of Commerce in Shanghai, 37 percent of US-owned enterprises operating in China said that recruiting skilled employees was their biggest operational problem. [20] Indeed, polled companies cited HRM as a problem more often than they cited regulatory concerns, bureaucracy, or infringement on intellectual property rights. This is because Chinese universities don't turn out candidates with the skills that multinational companies need. As a result, Motorola has created its own training and development programs to bridge the gap. For example, Motorola's China Accelerated Management Program is designed for local managers. Motorola's Management Foundation program helps train managers in areas such as communication and problem solving. Finally, Motorola offers a high-tech MBA program in partnership with Arizona State University and Tsinghua University, so that top employees can earn an MBA in-house. [21] Such programs are tailor-made to the minimally skilled—but highly motivated—Chinese employees.

Compensation and Rewards

The SHRM function also includes evaluating and paying people on the basis of their performance—not simply for showing up to the job. Firms must offer rewards for skill development and organizational performance, emphasizing teamwork, collaboration, and responsibility for performance.

Good compensation systems include incentives, gainsharing, profit sharing, and skill-based pay that rewards employees who learn new skills and put those skills to work for the organization. Employees who are trained in problem solving and a broad range of skills are more likely to grow on the job and feel more satisfaction. Their training enables them to make more valuable contributions to the company, which, in turn, gains them higher rewards and greater commitment to the company. [22] Likewise, the company benefits from employees' increased flexibility, productivity, and commitment.

When employees have access to information and the authority to act on that information, they're more involved in their jobs, more likely to make the right decision, and more inclined to take the necessary actions to further the organization's goals. Similarly, rewards need to be linked to performance so that employees are naturally inclined to pursue outcomes that will earn rewards and further the organization's success at the same time. [23]

Diversity Management

Another key to successful SHRM in today's business environment is embracing diversity. In past decades, "diversity" meant avoiding discrimination against women and minorities in hiring. Today, diversity goes far beyond this limited definition; diversity management involves actively appreciating and using the differing perspectives and ideas that individuals bring to the workplace. Diversity is an invaluable contributor to innovation and problem-solving success. As James Surowiecki shows in *The Wisdom of Crowds*, the more diverse the group in terms of expertise, gender, age, and background, the more ability the group has to avoid the problems of groupthink. [24] Diversity helps company teams to come up with more creative and effective solutions. Teams whose members have complementary skills are often more successful because members can see one another's blind spots. Diverse people will probably make different kinds of errors, which also means that they'll be more likely to catch and correct each other's mistakes.

KEY TAKEAWAYS

- HRM is becoming increasingly important in organizations because today's knowledge economy requires employees to contribute ideas and be engaged in executing the company's strategy.
- HRM is becoming a strategic partner by identifying the skills that employees need and then providing employees with the training and structures needed to develop and deploy those competencies.

- All the elements of HRM—selection, placement, job design, and compensation—need to be aligned with the company's strategy so that the right employees are hired for the right jobs and rewarded properly for their contributions to furthering the company's goals.

EXERCISES

(AACSB: Reflective Thinking, Analytical Skills)

1. What are the advantages of the new SHRM approach?
2. Name three elements of HRM.
3. What must HRM do to be a true strategic partner of the company?
4. What benefits does a diverse workforce provide the company?
5. If you were an HR manager, what steps would you take to minimize the outsourcing of jobs in your department?

[1] Brian E. Becker and Mark A. Huselid, "Strategic Human Resources Management: Where Do We Go from Here?" Journal of Management 32, no. 6 (2006): 898–925.

[2] Mark A. Huselid, "The Impact of Human Resource Management Practices on Turnover, Productivity, and Corporate Financial Performance," Academy of Management Journal 38, no. 3 (1995): 635–72; Jeffrey Pfeffer, The Human Equation: Building Profits by Putting People First (Boston: Harvard Business School Press, 1998); Jeffrey Pfeffer and John F. Veiga, "Putting People First for Organizational Success," Academy of Management Executive 13, no. 2 (1999): 37–48; Theresa M. Welbourne and Alice O. Andrews, "Predicting Performance of Initial Public Offering Firms: Should HRM be in the Equation?," Academy of Management Journal 39, no. 4 (1996): 910–11.

[3] Jeffrey Pfeffer and John F. Veiga, "Putting People First for Organizational Success," Academy of Management Executive 13, no. 2 (1999): 37–48.

[4] Brian E. Becker, Mark A. Huselid, and David Ulrich, "Six Key Principles for Measuring Human Capital Performance in Your Organization" (working paper, School of Management and Labor Relations, Department of Human Resources Management, Rutgers, State University of New Jersey, 2002).

[5] David Ulrich, Delivering Results (Boston: Harvard Business School Press, 1998).

[6] Dennis R. Briscoe, Randall S. Schuler, and Lisbeth Claus, International Human Resource Management, 3rd ed. (New York: Routledge, 2009).

[7] Mary Yoko Brannen and Mark F. Peterson, "Merging without Alienating: Interventions Promoting Cross-cultural Organizational Integration and Their Limitations," Journal of International Business Studies 40 (2009): 468–89; Yaping Gong, "Toward a Dynamic Process Model of Staffing Composition and Subsidiary Outcomes in Multinational Enterprises," Journal of Management 29, no. 2 (2003): 259–80; Dana Minbaeva, Torben Pedersen, Ingmar Björkman, Carl F. Fey, and Hyeon Jeong Park, "MNC Knowledge Transfer, Subsidiary Absorptive Capacity, and HRM," Journal of International Business Studies 34, no. 6 (2003): 586–99; Gary Oddou, Joyce S. Osland, and Roger N. Blakeney, "Repatriating Knowledge: Variables Influencing the 'Transfer' Process," Journal of International Business Studies 40, no. 2 (2009): 181–99.

[8] "About Us," Robert Half International, accessed January 28, 2011, http://www.rhi.com/AboutUs.

[9] Aili McConnon, "Temp Giant Robert Half Welcomes Boomers," BusinessWeek, May 21, 2009, accessed January 28, 2011,

http://www.businessweek.com/magazine/content/09_22/b413305460132 0.htm.

[10] Randall S. Schuler, Pawan S. Budhwar, and Gary W. Florkowski, "International Human Resource Management," in Handbook for International Management Research, ed. Betty-Jane Punnett and Oded Shenkar (Ann Arbor: University of Michigan Press, 2004), 356–414.

[11] Dennis R. Briscoe, Randall S. Schuler, and Lisbeth Claus, International Human Resource Management, 3rd ed. (New York: Routledge, 2009); Carl F. Fey and Ingmar Björkman, "The Effect of Human Resource Management Practices on MNC Subsidiary Performance in Russia," Journal of International Business Studies 32, no. 1 (2001): 59–75; Patrick M. Wright, Gary C. McMahan, and Abagail McWilliams, "Human Resources and Sustained Competitive Advantage: A Resource-Based Perspective," International Journal of Human Resource Management 5, no. 2 (1994): 301–26.

[12] Dennis R. Briscoe, Randall S. Schuler, and Lisbeth Claus, International Human Resource Management, 3rd ed. (New York: Routledge, 2009).

[13] Leslie A. Weatherly, "Human Capital—the Elusive Asset; Measuring and Managing Human Capital: A Strategic Imperative for HR," 2003 SHRM Research Quarterly, March 2003, accessed November 2, 2010, http://www.ispi.org/pdf/suggestedReading/6_Weatherly_HumanCapital. pdf.

[14] Mark A. Huselid, Susan E. Jackson, and Randall S. Schuler, "Technical and Strategic Human Resource Management Effectiveness as Determinants of Firm Performance," Academy of Management Journal 40, no. 1 (1997): 171–88.

[15] David Ulrich, Delivering Results (Boston: Harvard Business School Press, 1998).

[16] Jessica Marquez, "On the Front Line: A Quintet of 2006's Highest-Paid HR Leaders Discuss How They Are Confronting Myriad Talent Management Challenges as Well as Obstacles to Being Viewed by Their Organizations as Strategic Business Partners," Workforce Management 86, no. 5 (1997): 22.

[17] "TPI Counts 2700+ Outsourcing Contracts," SharedXpertise Forums, December 2007, accessed January 30, 2009, http://www.sharedxpertise.com/content/4301/tpi-counts-2700-outsourcing-contracts.

[18] "Annual Report 2006," Arinso International, accessed March 10, 2011, http://bib.kuleuven.be/ebib/data/jaarverslagen/Arinso_2006eng.pdf.

[19] Edward E. Lawler III, The Ultimate Advantage (San Francisco: Jossey-Bass, 1992).

[20] Kevin Lane and Florian Pollner, "How to Address China's Growing Talent Shortage," McKinsey Quarterly, no. 3 (2008), accessed March 10, 2011, http://www.mckinseyquarterly.com/How_to_address_Chinas_growing_ta lent_shortage_2156.

[21] Kevin Lane and Florian Pollner, "How to Address China's Growing Talent Shortage," McKinsey Quarterly, no. 3 (2008), accessed March 10, 2011, http://www.mckinseyquarterly.com/How_to_address_Chinas_growing_ta lent_shortage_2156.

[22] William F. Barnes, "The Challenge of Implementing and Sustaining High Performance Work Systems in the United States: An Evolutionary Analysis of I/N Tek and Kote" (PhD diss., University of Notre Dame, 2001).

[23] {Authors' names retracted as requested by the work's original creator or licensee}, Principles of Management (Nyack, NY)

[24] James Surowiecki, The Wisdom of Crowds (New York: Anchor Books, 2005).

12.2 The Global War for Talent
LEARNING OBJECTIVES

1. Define talent management.
2. Discover how to attract the right workers to your organization.
3. Understand the benefits of good talent management.

What Talent Management Means

You have likely heard the phrase "the war for talent," which reflects competition among organizations to attract and retain the most able employees. For years, agencies that track demographic trends have been warning that the US workforce will shrink in the second and third decades of the twenty-first century as the baby boom generation (those born between 1945 and 1961) reaches retirement age. According to one source, there will be 11.5 million more jobs than workers in the United States by 2010. [1] Even though many boomers say they want (or have) to continue working past the traditional age of retirement, those who do retire or who leave decades-long careers to pursue "something I've always wanted to do" will force employers to scramble to replace well-trained, experienced workers. As workers compete for the most desirable jobs, employers will have to compete even more fiercely to find the right talent.

Peter Cappelli of the Wharton School defines talent management as anticipating the need for human capital and setting a plan to meet it. Talent management goes hand in hand with succession planning, which refers to the process of recruiting and developing employees to ensure that the key roles in the company are filled. [2] Most companies, unfortunately, don't plan ahead for the talent they need, which means that they face shortages of critical skills at some times and surpluses at other times. Other companies use outdated methods of succession planning that don't accurately forecast the skills they'll need in the future.

Interestingly, however, techniques that were developed to achieve productivity breakthroughs in manufacturing can be applied to talent management. For example, it's expensive to develop all talent internally; training people takes a long time and requires accurate predictions about which skills will be needed. Such predictions are increasingly difficult to make in our uncertain world. Therefore, rather than developing everyone internally, companies can hire from the outside when they need to tap specific skills. In manufacturing, this principle is known as "make or buy." In human resources management (HRM), the solution is to make *and* buy—that is, to train some people and to hire others from the external marketplace. In this case, "making" an employee means hiring a person who doesn't yet have all the needed skills to fulfill the role but who can be trained to develop them. The key to a successful "make" decision is to distinguish between the high-potential employees who don't yet have the skills but who can learn them, from the mediocre employees who merely lack the skills. The "buy" decision means hiring an employee who has all the necessary skills and experience to fulfill the role from day one. The buy decision is useful when it's too difficult to predict exactly which skills will be needed in the future. [3]

Ethics in Action

One month after launching in Kenya, start-up txteagle became one of the country's largest employers with a workforce of 10,000 Kenyans. [4] Nathan Eagle founded txteagle in 2008. Txteagle deconstructs work into microtasks that can be performed on any simple mobile phone through texting. For example, one task is to type in local road signs (the data will be used to create a satellite navigation system). [5] Txteagle is similar to Amazon's Mechanical Turk (mTurk), which also asks workers to complete microtasks such as clicking on photos that contain a particular object. The difference is that workers for txteagle only need a simple mobile phone—no computer or Internet access is necessary. Txteagle distributes the microtasks to thousands of workers (currently primarily in Africa) who complete them and get paid via the mobile phone either in airtime minutes or in cash through the M-Pesa service. [6] "Txteagle is a commercial corporation that enables people to earn small amounts of money on their mobile phones by completing simple tasks for our corporate clients," says Eagle. [7]

Txteagle now has partnerships with 220 mobile operators in more than eighty countries. [8] This expands txteagle 's reach to 2.1 billion cell phone users in sub-Saharan Africa, Brazil, and India, who can all participate as workers. [9] Currently, the firm earns revenues in forty-nine countries. Companies like txteagle and mTurk give citizens in poor countries an opportunity to get work. But some Westerners criticize mTurk because employers can reject a person's work without explanation. The pay scale is also very low—about twenty-four cents an hour, which makes some critics call mTurk a "digital sweatshop." [10] For workers in developing nations, however, where wages are low and unemployment rates are high, such wages may be better than the alternative of no work.

Another principle from manufacturing that works well in talent management is to run smaller batch sizes. [11] That is, rather than sending employees to three-year-long training programs, send them to shorter programs more frequently. With this approach, managers don't have to make the training decision so far in advance. They can wait to decide exactly which skills employees will learn closer to the time the skill is needed, thereby ensuring that employees are trained on the skills they'll actually use.

Attracting the Right Workers to the Organization

Winning the war for talent means more than simply attracting workers to your company. It means attracting the *right* workers—the ones who will be enthusiastic about their work. Enthusiasm for the job requires more than having a good attitude about receiving good pay and benefits—it means that an employee's goals and aspirations also match those of the company. Therefore, it's important to identify employees' preferences and mutually assess how well they align with the company's strategy. To do this, the organization must first be clear about the type of employee it wants. Companies already do this with customers—marketing executives identify specific segments of the universe of buyers to target for selling products. Red Bull, for example, targets college-age consumers, whereas Slim Fast goes for adults of all ages who are overweight. Both companies are selling beverages but to completely different consumer segments. Similarly, companies need to develop a profile of the type of workers they want to attract. Do you want entrepreneurial types who seek autonomy and continual learning, or do you want team players who enjoy collaboration, stability, and structure? Neither employee type is inherently "better," but an employee who craves autonomy may feel constrained within the very same environment in which a team player would thrive.

As stated earlier, it's important to "mutually assess" how well employees' preferences align with the company's strategy. Half of "mutual" refers to the company, but the other half refers to the job candidate. Potential employees need to know whether they'll fit into the company well. One way to help prospective hires make this determination is to describe to them the "signature experience" that sets your company apart. As Tamara Erickson and Lynda Gratton define it, your company's signature experience is the distinctive practice that shows what it's really like to work at your company. [12]

Here are the signature experiences of two companies—Whole Foods Market and Goldman Sachs. At Whole Foods, team-based hiring is a signature experience—employees in each department vote on whether a new employee will be retained after a four-week trial period. This demonstrates to potential hires that Whole Foods is all about collaboration. In contrast, Goldman Sachs's signature experience is multiple one-on-one interviews. The story often told to prospective hires is of the MBA student who went through sixty interviews before being hired. This story signals to new hires that they need to be comfortable meeting endless numbers of new people and building networks across the company. Those who enjoy meeting and being interviewed by so many diverse people are exactly the ones who will fit into Goldman's culture.

The added benefit of hiring workers who match your organizational culture and are engaged in their work is that they will be less likely to leave your company just to get a higher salary.

Keeping Star Employees

The war for talent stems from the approaching shortage of workers. As mentioned earlier in this chapter, the millions of baby boomers reaching retirement age are leaving a gap in the US workforce. What's more, workers are job-hopping more frequently than in the past. According to the US Bureau of Labor Statistics, the average job tenure has dropped from fifteen years in 1980 to four years in 2007. As a manager, therefore, you need to give your employees reasons to stay with your company. One way to do this is to spend time talking with employees about their career goals. Listen to their likes and dislikes so that you can help them fully utilize the skills they like using or develop the new ones they wish to acquire. [13]

Don't be afraid to "grow" your employees. Some managers want to keep their employees in their department. They fear that helping employees grow on the job will mean that employees will outgrow their jobs and leave. [14] However, keeping your employees down is a sure way to lose them. What's more, if you help your employees advance, it'll be easier for you to move up, because your employees will be better able to take on the role you leave behind.

In some cases, your employees may not be sure what career path they want. As a manager, you can help them identify their goals by asking questions such as the following:

- What assignments have you found most engaging?
- Which of your accomplishments in the last six months made you proudest?
- What makes for a great day at work? [15]

What Employees Want

Employees want to grow and develop, stretching their capabilities. They want projects that engage their heads as well as their hearts, and they want to connect with the people and things that will help them achieve their professional goals.

[16] Here are two ways to provide this to your employees: First, connect people with mentors and help them build their networks. Research suggests that successful managers dedicate 70 percent more time to networking activities and 10 percent more time to communication than their less successful counterparts. [17] What makes networks special? Through networks, people energize one another as well as learn, create, and find new opportunities for growth. Second, help connect people with a sense of purpose. Focusing on the need for purpose is especially important for younger workers, who rank meaningful work and challenging experiences at the top of their job-search lists. [18]

Benefits of Good Talent Management

Global consulting firm McKinsey & Company conducted a study to identify a possible link between a company's financial performance and its success in managing talent. The survey results, reported in May 2008, show that there was indeed a relationship between a firm's financial performance and its global talent-management practices. Three talent-management practices, in particular, correlated highly with exceptional financial performance:

- Creating globally consistent talent-evaluation processes
- Achieving cultural diversity in a global setting
- Developing and managing global leaders [19]

The McKinsey survey found that companies achieving scores in the top third of any of these areas had a 70 percent chance of achieving financial performance in the top third of all companies. [20]

Let's take a closer look at what each of these three best practices entail. First, having consistent talent evaluation means that employees around the world are evaluated on the same standards. This is important because it means that if an employee from one country transfers to another, his or her manager can be assured that the employee has been held to the same level of skills and standards. Second, having cultural diversity means having employees who learn something about the culture of different countries, not just acquire language skills. This helps bring about open-mindedness across cultures. Finally, developing global leaders means rotating employees through different cultures, giving them international experience. Companies that do this best also have policies of giving managers incentives to share their employees with other units.

KEY TAKEAWAYS

- The coming shortage of workers makes it imperative for managers to find, hire, retain, and develop their employees.

- Managers first need to define the skills that the company will need for the future. Then they can "make or buy"— that is, train or hire—employees with the needed skills.

- Retaining these employees requires engaging them on the job. Good talent-management practices translate into improved financial performance for the company as a whole.

EXERCISES

(AACSB: Reflective Thinking, Analytical Skills)

1. How might a manager go about identifying the skills that the company will need in the future?

2. Describe the "make or buy" option and how it can be applied to human resources management.

3. How would you go about attracting and recruiting talented workers to your organization? Suggest ideas you would use to retain stars and keep them happy in their jobs.

4. What skills might an organization like a bank need from its employees?

[1] "Extreme Talent Shortage Makes Competition Fierce for Key Jobs and Highlights Needs for Leadership Development," Business Wire, November 26, 2007, 27.

[2] Peter Cappelli, "Talent Management for the Twenty-First Century," Harvard Business Review 86, no. 3 (March 2008): 74–81.

[3] Patricia M. Buhler, "Managing in the New Millennium; Succession Planning: Not Just for the C Suite," Supervision 69, no. 3 (2008): 19–23.

[4] Kate Greene, "Crowd-Sourcing the World," MIT Tech Review, January 21, 2009, accessed January 23, 2011, http://www.technologyreview.com/business/21983.

[5] Robert Bain, "The Power of Text in the Developing World," Research, January 20, 2011, accessed May 17, 2011, http://www.research-live.com/features/the-power-of-text-in-the-developing-world/4004395.article.

[6] Andrea Meyer, "Workforce Innovation: How Txteagle Distributes Microtasks Worldwide," Working Knowledge (blog), January 23, 2011, accessed January 23, 2011,http://workingknowledge.com/blog/?p=1444; Jessica Vaughn, "Q&A: Nathan Eagle, Founder of txteagle," JWT Intelligence, March 3, 2010, accessed January 23, 2011,http://www.jwtintelligence.com/2010/03/qa-nathan-eagle-founder-of-txteagle.

[7] Jessica Vaughn, "Q&A: Nathan Eagle, Founder of txteagle," JWT Intelligence, March 3, 2010, accessed January 23, 2011, http://www.jwtintelligence.com/2010/03/qa-nathan-eagle-founder-of-txteagle.

[8] "Mobile Work," Economist, October 28, 2010, accessed January 23, 2011, http://www.economist.com/node/17366137.

[9] Txteagle website, accessed January 23, 2011, http://txteagle.com.

[10] Bryan Walsh, "Pennies for Your Thoughts," Time, January 31, 2011, accessed January 31, 2011, http://www.time.com/time/magazine/article/0,9171,2043450,00.html.

[11] {Authors' names retracted as requested by the work's original creator or licensee}, Principles of Management (Nyack, NY)

[12] Tamara J. Erickson and Lynda Gratton, "What It Means to Work Here," Harvard Business Review 85, no. 3 (2007): 23–29.

[13] Beverly Kaye, Love 'Em or Lose 'Em (San Francisco: Barrett-Koehler, 2008).

[14] Anne Field and Ken Gordon, "Do Your Stars See a Reason to Stay?" Harvard Management Update 13, no. 6 (2008), http://hbr.org/product/do-your-stars-see-a-reason-to-stay/an/U0806A-PDF-ENG.

[15] Timothy Butler, Getting Unstuck (Boston: Harvard Business School Press, 2007).

[16] Deloitte Research, It's 2008: Do You Know Where Your Talent Is? Why Acquisition and Retention Strategies Don't Work (Geneva, Switzerland: Deloitte Research Report, 2007), accessed May 10, 2011, http://www.deloitte.com/assets/Dcom-Venezuela/Local%20Assets/Documents/VE_Consulting_HC_connect_ta lentmgmt_Feb07.pdf.

[17] Fred Luthans, Richard M. Yodgetts, and Stuart A. Rosenkrantz, Real Managers (Cambridge, MA: Ballinger, 1988).

[18] Peter Sheahan, Generation Y: Thriving (and Surviving) with Generation Y at Work (Victoria, Australia: Hardie Grant Books, 2006).

[19] "McKinsey Global-Talent-Management Survey of Over 450 Executives," December 2007, as cited in Matthew Guthridge and Asmus B. Komm, "Why Multinationals Struggle to Manage Talent," McKinsey Quarterly, May 2008, 19–25, accessed January 30, 2009,http://www.mckinseyquarterly.com/article_print.aspx?L2=18&L3=3 1&ar=2140.

[20] Matthew Guthridge and Asmus B. Komm, "Why Multinationals Struggle to Manage Talent," McKinsey Quarterly, May 2008, 19–25.

12.3 Effective Selection and Placement Strategies

LEARNING OBJECTIVES

1. Identify why a good job description benefits both the employer and the applicant.

2. Learn how company culture can be used in selecting new employees.

3. Know the advantages and disadvantages of personnel testing.

4. Recognize some of the considerations in international staffing and placement.

Job-Description Best Practices

Selecting the right employees and placing them in the right positions within the company is a key human resources management (HRM) function and is vital to a company's success. Companies should devote as much care and attention to this "soft" issue as they do to financial planning, because errors will have a financial impact and adverse effects on a company's strategy.

Let's use a hypothetical example of Walt, a manager in a midsize company who considers himself fortunate that the organizational chart allows him to have a full-time administrative assistant (AA) who reports to him. In the two years Walt has been in his job, however, five people have held this AA job. The most recent AA, who resigned after four weeks, told Walt that she hadn't known what the job would involve. "I don't do numbers; I'm not an accountant," she said. "If you want someone to add up figures and do calculations all day, you should say so in the job description. Besides, I didn't realize how long and stressful my commute would be—the traffic between here and my house is murder!"

Taken aback, Walt contacted the company's HRM department to clarify the job description for the AA position. What he learned was that the description made available to applicants was, indeed, inadequate in a number of ways, which resulted in frequent turnover that was draining Walt's company of resources that could be used for much more constructive purposes.

An accurate and complete job description is a powerful strategic human resources management (SHRM) tool that costs little to produce and can save a bundle in reduced turnover. While the realistic description may discourage some applicants (e.g., those who lack an affinity for calculations might not bother to apply for Walt's AA position), those who follow through with the application process are much more likely to be satisfied with the job once hired. In addition to summarizing what the worker will actually be doing all day, here are some other suggestions for writing an effective job description: [1]

- List the job requirements in bullet form, so that job seekers can scan the posting quickly.
- Use common industry terms, which speak to knowledgeable job seekers.
- Avoid organization-specific terms and acronyms, which would confuse job seekers.
- Use meaningful job titles (not the internal job codes of the organization).
- Use key words taken from the list of common search terms (to maximize the chance that a job posting appears on a job seeker's search).
- Include information about the organization, such as a short summary and links to more detailed information.
- Highlight special intangibles and unusual benefits of the job and workplace (e.g., flextime or travel).
- Specify the job's location (and nearest large city) and provide links to local community pages (to entice job seekers with quality-of-life information).

Tailoring Recruitment to Match Company Culture

Managers who hire well don't just hire for skills or academic background; they ask about the potential employee's philosophy on life or how the candidate likes to spend free time. These questions help the manager assess whether the cultural fit is right. A company in which all work is done in teams needs team players, not just "A" students. Ask questions such as "Do you have a personal mission statement? If not, what would it be if you wrote one today?" to identify a potential hire's preferences. [2]

At Google, for example, job candidates are asked questions such as "If you could change the world using Google's resources, what would you build?" [3] Google wants employees who will think and act on a grand scale—employees who will take on the challenges of their jobs, whatever their jobs may be. Take Josef DeSimone, Google's executive chef. DeSimone, who's worked everywhere from family-style restaurants to Michelin-caliber ones, was amazed to learn that Google had seventeen cafes for its employees. "Nobody changes the menu daily on this scale," he says. "It's unheard of." When he was hired, DeSimone realized, "Wow, you hire a guy who's an expert in food and let him run with it! You don't get in his way or micromanage?" [4] Google applies this approach to all positions; they let employees run with the challenge.

Traditionally, companies have built a competitive advantage by focusing on what they have—structural advantages such as economies of scale, a well-established brand, or dominance in certain market segments. Companies such as Southwest Airlines, by contrast, see its people as their advantage: "Our fares can be matched; our airplanes and routes can be copied. But we pride ourselves on our customer service," said Sherry Phelps, director of corporate employment. That's why Southwest looks for candidates who generate enthusiasm; they lean toward extroverted personalities. Southwest hires for attitude. Flight attendants have been known to sing the safety instructions, and pilots tell jokes over the public address system.

Southwest Airlines makes clear right from the start the kind of people it wants to hire. For example, one recruitment ad depicted Southwest cofounder Herb Kelleher dressed as Elvis and read "Work in a Place Where Elvis Has Been Spotted…The qualifications? It helps to be outgoing. Maybe even a bit off-center. And be prepared to stay awhile. After all, we have the lowest employee turnover rate in the industry." People may scoff or question why Southwest indulges in such showy activities or wonder how an airline can treat its jobs so lightly. Phelps answers, "We do take our work seriously. It's ourselves that we don't." People who don't have a humane, can-do attitude are fired. Southwest has a probationary period during which it determines the compatibility of new hires with the culture. People may be excellent performers, but if they don't match the culture, they're let go. As Kelleher once said, "People will write me and complain, 'Hey, I got terminated or put on probation for purely subjective reasons.' And I'll say, 'Right! Those are the important reasons.'" [5]

In many states, employees are covered under what is known as the at-will employment doctrine. The at-will employment doctrine defines an employment relationship in which either party can break the relationship with no liability, provided there was no express contract for a definite term governing the employment relationship and that the employer doesn't belong to a collective bargaining unit (i.e., a union). [6] However, there are legal restrictions on how purely subjective the reasons for firing can be. For instance, if the organization has written hiring and firing procedures and doesn't follow them in selective cases, then those cases might give rise to claims of wrongful termination. Similarly, in situations where termination is clearly systematic—for example, based on age, race, religion, and so on—wrongful termination can be claimed.

Organized Labor and International Business
Many labor markets around the world have organized labor and labor unions, just as the United States does. Historically, most labor relations departments were decentralized, operating on the individual subsidiary level. With the rise of globalization, however, labor unions are seeing new threats, such as multinational enterprises (MNEs) threatening to move production to another country if the local union is demanding too much.

Because the actions of labor unions can constrain a firm's ability to pursue an effective global strategy, the firm's SHRM function must develop policies and practices that maintain harmony and reduce potential conflict between labor and management. Similarly, MNEs evaluate the labor climate when considering entering a new international location. MNEs typically look for labor markets that do not have a history of strife. MNEs may also try to negotiate better terms with a local union in exchange for locating a new facility in the country. To counter this, organized labor has attempted to organize globally, but this has proven to be difficult due to legal and cultural differences among countries. [7]

Tools and Methods: Interviewing and Testing
To make good selection and placement decisions, a company needs information about the job candidate. Testing and

interviewing are two time-tested methods used to get that information.

A detailed interview begins by asking the candidate to describe his work history and then getting as much background on his most recent position (or the position most similar to the open position). Ask about the candidate's responsibilities and major accomplishments. Then, ask in-depth questions about specific job situations. Called situational interviews, these types of interviews can focus on past experience or future situations. For example, experienced-based questions draw on the employees past performance. One such question may be "What is a major initiative you developed and the steps you took to get it adopted? Describe a problem you had with someone and how you handled it." In contrast, future-oriented situation interview questions ask candidates to describe how they would handle a future hypothetical situation. An example of this kind of question is "Suppose you came up with a faster way to do a task, but your team was reluctant to make the change. What would you do in that situation?"

In addition to what is asked, it's also important that interviewers understand what they should *not* ask, largely because certain questions lead to answers that may be used to discriminate. There are five particularly sensitive areas. First, the only times you can ask about age are when it is a requirement of a job duty or you need to determine whether a work permit is required. Second, it is rarely appropriate or legal to ask questions regarding race, color, national origin, or gender. Third, although candidates may volunteer religious or sexual orientation information in an interview, you still need to be careful not to discriminate. Ask questions that are relevant to work experience or qualifications. Fourth, firms cannot discriminate for health or disabilities; you may not ask about smoking habits, health-related issues, or disabilities in an interview. Finally, you may not ask questions about marital status, children, personal life, pregnancy, or arrest record. These kinds of questions could be tempting to ask if you're interviewing for a position requiring travel; however, you can only explain the travel requirements and confirm that these requirements are acceptable.

In addition to interviews, many employers use testing to select and place job applicants. Any tests given to candidates must be job related and follow guidelines set forth by the US Equal Employment Opportunity Commission to be legal. [8] For the tests to be effective, they should be developed by reputable psychologists and administered by professionally qualified personnel who have had training in occupational testing in an industrial setting. The rationale behind testing is to give the employer more information before making the selection and placement decision—information vital to assessing how well a candidate is suited to a particular job. Most preemployment assessment tests measure thinking styles, behavioral traits, and occupational interests. The results are available almost immediately after a candidate completes the roughly hour-long questionnaire. Thinking-styles tests can tell the potential employer how fast someone can learn new things or how well she can verbally communicate. Behavioral-traits assessments measure energy level, assertiveness, sociability, manageability, and attitude. For example, a high sociability score would be a desirable trait for salespeople. [9]

International Staffing and Placement

In our increasingly global economy, managers need to decide between using expatriates or hiring locals when staffing international locations. An expatriate, or expat, is a person who is living in a country other than his or her home (native) country. Most expatriates only stay temporarily in the foreign country, planning to return to their home country. Some expatriates, however, never return to their country of citizenship. On the surface, this seems a simple choice between the firm-specific expertise of the expatriate and the cultural knowledge of the local hire. In reality, companies often fail to consider the high probability and high cost of expatriates failing to adapt and perform in their international assignments.

There are four predictors of a manager's ability to succeed as an expatriate:

1. **Self-orientation.** The expatriate has attributes that strengthen his or her self-esteem, self-confidence, and mental well-being. [10]
2. **Others orientation.** The expatriate has attributes that enhance his or her ability to interact effectively with host-country nationals (e.g., sociability and openness). [11]
3. **Perceptual ability.** The expatriate has the ability to understand why people of other countries behave the way they do. [12]
4. **Cultural toughness.** The expatriate has the ability to adjust to a particular posting given the culture of the assignment's country. [13]

Individuals who are high on all four dimensions are generally better able to cope and thrive with an expat experience. Research also shows that a global mind-set (i.e., having cognitive complexity—the ability to differentiate, articulate, and integrate—and a cosmopolitan outlook) greatly increases the chances that a global manager will be successful in international assignments. [14] Ironically, however, studies show that most firms select expatriate managers on the basis of technical expertise and do not factor in a global mind-set. Firms that use expatriates to staff international operations must be aware of and prepare for the possibility of expatriate failure, which means that the expatriate returns to the home country before completing the international assignment.

Researchers estimate the expatriate failure rate to be 40 percent to 55 percent. [15] For example, cultural issues can easily create misunderstandings between expatriate managers and employees, suppliers, customers, and local government officials. Given the high cost of expatriate failure, international-assignment decisions are often made too lightly in many companies. There are several factors that contribute to expatriate failure in US-headquartered multinational firms:

- The expatriate's spouse is unable to adapt to a foreign culture, or there are other family-related reasons.
- The expatriate is unable to adjust to the new culture or lacks personal or emotional maturity to function well in the new country.
- The expatriate is unable to handle the larger overseas responsibilities.

The challenge is to overcome the natural tendency to hire a well-known, corporate insider over an unknown local at the international site. Here are some indications to consider in determining whether an expatriate or a local hire would be best.

Managers may want to choose an expatriate when the following factors are true:

- Company-specific technology or knowledge is important.
- Confidentiality in the staff position is an issue.
- There is a need for speed (i.e., assigning an expatriate is usually faster than hiring a local).
- Work rules regarding local workers are restrictive.
- The corporate strategy is focused on global integration.

Managers may want to staff the position with a local hire when the following factors are true:

- The need to interact with local customers, suppliers, employees, or officials is paramount.
- The corporate strategy is focused on multidomestic or market-oriented operations.
- Cost is an issue (i.e., expatriates often bring high relocation/travel costs).
- Immigration rules regarding foreign workers are restrictive.

- There are large cultural distances between the host country and candidate expatriates. [16]

KEY TAKEAWAYS

- Effective selection and placement means finding and hiring the right employees for your organization and then putting them into the jobs for which they are best suited. Providing an accurate and complete job description is a key step in the selection process.

- An important determination is whether the candidate's personality is a good fit for the company's culture. Interviewing is a common selection method. Situational interviews ask candidates to describe how they handled specific situations in the past (experience-based situational interviews) and how they would handle hypothetical questions in the future (future-oriented situational interviews). Other selection tools include cognitive tests, personality inventories, and behavioral-traits assessments. Specific personalities may be best suited for positions that require sales, teamwork, or entrepreneurship, respectively.

- In our increasingly global economy, managers need to decide between using expatriates and hiring locals when staffing international locations.

EXERCISES

(AACSB: Reflective Thinking, Analytical Skills)

1. What kind of information would you include in a job description?
2. Do you think it is important to hire employees who fit into the company culture? Why or why not?
3. List questions that you would ask in a future-oriented situational interview.
4. What requirements must personnel tests meet?
5. If you were hiring to fill a position overseas, how would you go about selecting the best candidate?

[1] {Authors' names retracted as requested by the work's original creator or licensee}, Principles of Management (Nyack, NY)

[2] Jeffrey Pfeffer, The Human Equation: Building Profits by Putting People First (Boston: Harvard Business School Press, 1998).

[3] Chuck Slater, "The Faces and Voices of Google," Fast Company, March 2008, 37–45.

[4] Chuck Slater, "Josef DeSimone—Executive Chef," Fast Company, February 2008, 46–48.

[5] Anne Bruce, "Southwest: Back to the FUNdamentals," HR Focus 74, no. 3 (March 1997): 11; Kevin Freiberg and Jackie Freiberg, Nuts! Southwest Airlines' Crazy Recipe for Business and Personal Success (Austin, TX: Bard, 2003); Roger Hallowell, "Southwest Airlines: A Case Study Linking Employee Needs Satisfaction and Organizational Capabilities to Competitive Advantage," Human Resource Management 35, no. 4 (Winter 1996): 513–29; James L. Heskett and Roger Hallowell, "Southwest Airlines: 1993 (A)," Harvard Business School Case 694-023,

1993; "Southwest Airlines' Herb Kelleher: Unorthodoxy at Work," Management Review, January 1995, 2–9; Polly LaBarre, "Lighten Up! Blurring the Line Between Fun and Work Not Only Humanizes Organizations but Strengthens the Bottom Line," Industry Week 245, no. 3 (February 5, 1996): 53–67; Kenneth Labich, "Is Herb Kelleher America's Best CEO?," Fortune, May 2, 1994, 44–45; Donald J. McNerney, "Employee Motivation: Creating a Motivated Workforce," HR Focus 73, no. 8 (August 1996): 1; Richard Tomkins, "HR: The Seriously Funny Airline," Financial Times, November 11, 1996, 14.

[6] Mark A. Rothstein, Andria S. Knapp, and Lance Liebman, Cases and Materials on Employment Law (New York: Foundation Press, 1987), 738.

[7] James Heskett, "What's the Future of Globally Organized Labor?" HBS Working Knowledge (blog), October 3, 2005, accessed January 31, 2011, http://hbswk.hbs.edu/item/5029.html.

[8] {Authors' names retracted as requested by the work's original creator or licensee}, Principles of Management (Nyack, NY)

[9] Terri Mrosko, "The Personnel Puzzle: Preemployment Testing Can Help Your Bottom Line," Inside Business 8, no. 8 (August 2006): 60–73.

[10] Mark Mendenhall and Gary Oddou, "The Dimensions of Expatriate Acculturation," Academy of Management Review 10 (1985): 39–47.

[11] Paula M. Caligiuri, "Selecting Expatriates for Personality Characteristics: A Moderating Effect of Personality on the Relationship between Host National Contact and Cross-cultural Adjustment," Management International Review 40, no. 1 (2000): 65, accessed January 29, 2011, http://chrs.rutgers.edu/pub_documents/Paula_21.pdf.

[12] Mark Mendenhall and Gary Oddou, "The Dimensions of Expatriate acculturation," Academy of Management Review 10 (1985): 39–47.

[13] J. Stewart Black, Mark Mendenhall, and Gary Oddou, "Toward a Comprehensive Model of International Adjustment: An Integration of Multiple Theoretical Perspectives," Academy of Management Review 16, no. 2 (1991): 291–317.

[14] Joana S. Story, "Testing the Impact of Global Mindset on Positive Organizational Outcomes: A Multi-Level Analysis" (PhD diss., University of Nebraska at Lincoln, April 2010), accessed January 29, 2011, http://digitalcommons.unl.edu/aglecdiss/4; Mansour Javidan, "Bringing the Global Mindset to Leadership," Harvard Business Review (blog), May 19, 2010, accessed January 29, 2011, http://blogs.hbr.org/imagining-the-future-of-leadership/2010/05/bringing-the-global-mindset-to.html.

[15] J. Stewart Black, H. B. Gregersen, Mark Mendenhall, and L. K. Stroh, Globalizing People through International Assignments (Reading, MA: Addison-Wesley, 1999).

[16] Rebecca E. Weems, "Ethnocentric Staffing and International Assignments: A Transaction Cost Theory Approach" (presentation, Academy of Management Conference, San Diego, CA, August 9–12, 1998).

12.4 The Roles of Pay Structure and Pay for Performance

LEARNING OBJECTIVES

1. Explain the factors to be considered when setting pay levels.
2. Understand the value of pay for performance plans.
3. Discuss the challenges of individual versus team-based pay.

Compensation Design Issues for Global Firms

Pay can be thought of in terms of the "total reward" that includes an individual's base salary, variable pay, share ownership, and other benefits. A bonus, for example, is a form of variable pay. A bonus is a one-time cash payment, often awarded for exceptional performance. Providing employees with an annual statement of all the benefits they receive can help them understand the full value of what they are getting. [1]

There are five areas that global firms must manage when designing their compensation strategy. The first involves setting up a worldwide compensation system. What this means is that the firm is coordinating each country's compensation in such a way that the overall collection of countries operates as a system. Management, for instance, will have decided which features of the system to standardize and which ones to adapt to local customs, cultures, and practices. The second part of the strategy involves decisions about how to compensate third-country nationals. A third-country national (TCN) is an individual who is a citizen of neither the United States nor the host country and who is hired by the US government or a government-sanctioned contractor to perform work in the host country. TCNs most often perform work on government contracts in the role of a private military contractor. The term can also be applied to foreign workers employed in private industry in the Arab Gulf region (e.g., Kuwait, Qatar, and Saudi Arabia), in which it's common to outsource work to noncitizens.

The last three areas of compensation strategy relate to questions about international benefits and related taxes, pension plans, and stock-ownership plans. With expatriates, for instance, pay is but a small percentage of total compensation. A typical expatriate package will include the following: [2]

- A cost-of-living allowance to protect the employee's purchasing power (the goal is equalization, not a bonus)
- A mobility premium of 5 percent to 15 percent of gross salary
- A hardship allowance of up to 30 percent for employees moving to difficult areas
- Reasonable costs for moving furniture
- Schooling costs for children between four and eighteen years of age
- Family support to cover language and cultural training and help for the spouse to find work
- A one-off payment, usually of one month's salary, to cover miscellaneous expenses

Did You Know?

As firms enter emerging markets to take advantage of the tremendous growth opportunities there, they are finding that they need to develop in-country talent rather than just send expatriates. The knowledge that in-country managers have of the local culture and the sheer numbers of employees that will be needed to staff local operations drive managers to hire locally. Senior HR professionals need to ask themselves the following questions:

- How many of our current executives live in the countries where we do business?
- Is the number of native executives proportional to the revenue of those countries?
- How many of our senior executive team are from countries where we are experiencing growth?

It takes time to build talent in emerging markets, where the talent pool may be less experienced, so HR managers need to plan ahead.

Pay System Elements

As summarized in Table 12.1 "Elements of a Pay System", pay can take the form of direct or indirect compensation. Nonmonetary pay can include any benefit an employee receives from an employer or job that doesn't involve tangible value. This includes career and social rewards—job security, flexible hours, opportunities for growth, praise and recognition, task enjoyment, and friendships. Direct pay is an employee's base wage. It can be an annual salary, hourly wage, or any performance-based pay that an employee receives, such as profit-sharing bonuses.

Indirect compensation is far more varied, including everything from social security and health insurance to retirement programs, paid leave, child care, and housing. US law requires some indirect-compensation elements (e.g., social security, unemployment, and disability payments). Other indirect elements are up to the employer and can serve as excellent ways to provide benefits to both the employees and the employer. For example, a working parent may take a lower-paying job with flexible hours that will allow him to be home when the children get home from school. A recent graduate may be looking for stable work and an affordable place to live. Both of these individuals have different needs and, therefore, would appreciate different compensation elements.

Setting Pay Levels

When setting pay levels for positions, managers should make sure that the pay level is fair relative to what other employees in the position are being paid. Part of the pay level is determined by similar pay levels at other companies. If your company pays substantially less than others, it's going to be the last choice of employment—unless it offers something overwhelmingly positive to offset the low pay, such as flexible hours or a fun, congenial work atmosphere. Besides these external factors, companies conduct a job evaluation to determine the internal value of the job—the more vital the job to the company's success, the higher the pay level. Jobs are often ranked alphabetically—"A" positions are those on which the company's value depends; "B" positions are somewhat less important in that they don't deliver as much upside to the company; and "C" positions are those of least importance—in some cases, these are outsourced.

The most vital jobs to one company's success may not be the same in other companies. For example, information technology companies may put top priority on their software developers and programmers, whereas retailers such as Nordstrom would consider the frontline employees who provide personalized service as the "A" positions. For an airline, pilots would be a "B" job because, although they need to be well trained, investing further in their training is unlikely to increase the airline's profits. "C" positions for a retailer might include back-office bill processing, while an information technology company might classify customer service as a "C" job.

When setting reward systems, it's important to pay for what the company actually hopes to achieve. Steve Kerr, a senior advisor and former chief learning officer at Goldman Sachs, talks about the common mistakes that companies make with their reward systems, such as saying they value teamwork but only rewarding individual effort. Similarly, companies say they want innovative thinking or risk taking, but they reward people who "make the numbers." [3] If companies truly want to achieve what they hope for, they need payment systems aligned with their goals. For example, if retention of star employees is important to your company, reward managers who retain top talent. At PepsiCo, for instance, a third of a manager's bonus is tied directly to how well the manager did at developing and retaining employees. Tying compensation to retention makes managers accountable. [4]

As you can imagine, one of the reasons that firms seek workers in other countries is to take advantage of the low relative cost of labor. As shown in the following figure, the most recent US Bureau of Labor Statistics data show that the United States is among the costliest countries for manufacturing employees, exceeded only by Canada and countries in the Euro Area (Austria, Belgium, Finland, France, Germany, Greece, Ireland, Italy, Luxembourg, the Netherlands, Portugal, Slovakia, and Spain).

It's important to point out, however, that simply because a company locates an operation in a lower-pay market doesn't necessarily mean that the cost of the operation will be less. For instance, in a 2009 interview Emmanuel Hemmerle, a principal with executive search firm Heidrick & Struggles, noted,

There's a wrong assumption with regard to China. Headquarters in Japan, in Europe, in the US tend to believe that China, because it's low cost, should be cheaper in terms of executives' packages. Nothing is more wrong. In fact, if you want to woo top talent, you're going to have to pay the right amounts. Often you end up with packages for similar skill sets, similar responsibility, scope, size, everything…that is higher in China than what would be the case with similar counterparts in Europe and the US. And we spend a lot of time coaching companies, especially those that are headquartered overseas, that they need to invest in talent [in much the same way as they would] invest to create a new research center, to create new production facilities in China. They need to invest in the talent. If you want top talent, you're going to have to pay for it. We're starting to see some interesting trends. We can start seeing a number of top talents who meet the international best standards, who could compete with their peers in the US or in Europe—and I'm talking about in terms of performance, in terms of skill sets. And probably, we're going to start seeing more and more of that…I believe that it makes less and less sense to have Westerners, or [expatriates], let's say, who are compensated twice or three times as much as the local mainland Chinese, while performance is equivalent or sometimes even lower. That will create issues, very serious issues, in your organization. I'm always concerned and worried when a company tells me that they want to localize because they want to drive down costs. There's a host of reasons that are better reasons than just cost. [5]

As the Heidrick & Struggles example suggests, it's often a dilemma whether a multinational company should localize or globalize its compensation for the local managers. If they pay them on the basis of global standards, a higher cost will emerge. If not, it will be difficult to retain them. Pay inequity will often lead to a sense of unfairness. You can imagine a local manager asking herself, "Why should I get two or three times less pay even when I deliver a better performance than the expatriates?"

Pay for Performance
As its name implies, pay for performance ties pay directly to an individual's performance in meeting specific business goals or objectives. Managers (often together with the employees themselves) design performance targets to which the employees will be held accountable. The targets have

accompanying metrics that enable employees and managers to track performance. The metrics can be financial indicators, or they can be indirect indicators such as customer satisfaction or speed of development. Pay-for-performance schemes often combine a fixed base salary with a variable pay component (e.g., bonuses or stock options) that varies with the individual's performance.

Innovative Employee-Recognition Programs

In addition to regular pay structures and systems, companies often create special programs that reward exceptional employee performance. For example, the financial software company Intuit instituted a program called Spotlight. The purpose of Spotlight is to "spotlight performance, innovation and service dedication." [6] Unlike regular salaries or year-end bonuses, Spotlight awards can be given on the spot for specific behavior that meets the reward criteria, such as filing a patent, inventing a new product, or meeting a milestone for years of service. Rewards can be cash awards of $500 to $3,000 and can be made by managers without high-level approval. In addition to cash and noncash awards, two Intuit awards feature a trip with $500 in spending money. [7]

Pay Structures for Groups and Teams

So far, we have discussed pay in terms of individual compensation, but many employers also use compensation systems that reward all the organization's employees as a group or various groups and teams within the organization. Let's examine some of these less-traditional pay structures.

Gainsharing

Sometimes called profit sharing, gainsharing is a form of pay for performance. In gainsharing, the organization shares the financial gains with employees. Employees receive a portion of the profit achieved from their efforts. How much they receive is determined by their performance against the plan. Here's how gainsharing works: First, the organization must measure the historical (baseline) performance. Then, if employees help improve the organization's performance on those measures, they share in the financial rewards achieved. This sharing is typically determined by a formula.

The effectiveness of a gainsharing plan depends on employees seeing a relationship between what they do and how well the organization performs. The larger the organization, the harder it is for employees to see the effects of their work. Therefore, gainsharing plans are more effective in companies with fewer than 1,000 people. [8] Gainsharing success also requires the company to have good performance metrics in place so that employees can track their process.

The gainsharing plan can only be successful if employees believe and see that if they perform better, they will be paid more. The pay should be given as soon as possible after the performance so that the tie between the two is established.

When designing systems to measure performance, realize that performance appraisals need to focus on quantifiable measures. Designing these measures with input from the employees helps make the measures clear and understandable to employees and increases their gainsharing buy-in.

Team-Based Pay

Many managers seek to build teams but face the question of how to motivate all the members to achieve the team's goals. As a result, team-based pay is becoming increasingly accepted. In 1992, only 3 percent of companies had team-based pay. [9] By 1999, 80 percent of companies had team-based pay. [10] With increasing acceptance and adoption comes different choices and options of how to structure team-based pay. One way is to first identify the type of team you have— parallel, work, project, or partnership—and then choose the pay option that's most appropriate.

Parallel teams are teams that exist alongside (parallel to) an individual's daily team. For example, a person may be working in the accounting department but may also be asked to join a team on productivity. Parallel teams usually meet on a part-time rather than a full-time basis and are often interdepartmental and formed to deal with a specific issue. The reward for performance on this team would typically be a merit increase or a recognition award (cash or noncash) for performance on the team.

A *project team* is another temporary team, but it meets full-time for the life of the project. For example, a team may be formed to develop a new product and then disband when the new product is completed. The pay schemes appropriate for this team include profit sharing, recognition rewards, and stock options. Team members may be asked to evaluate each other's performance.

A *partnership team* is formed around a joint venture or strategic alliance. Profit sharing in the venture is the most common pay structure.

Finally, with the *work team*, all individuals work together daily to accomplish their jobs. Skill-based pay and gainsharing are the payment schemes of choice, with team members evaluating one another's performance.

Pay Systems that Reward Both Team and Individual Performance

There are two main theories of how to reward employees. Nancy Katz characterized the theories as two opposing camps. The first camp advocates rewarding individual performance, through plans such as commissions-sales schemes and merit-based pay. The claim is that this will increase employees' energy, drive, willingness to take risks, and task identification. The disadvantages of rewarding individual performance are that employees will cooperate less, that high performers may be resented by others in the corporation, and that low performers may try to undermine top performers. [11]

The second camp believes that organizations should reward team performance, without regard for individual accomplishment. This reward system is thought to bring the advantages of increased helping and cooperation, sharing of information and resources, and mutual respect among employees. The disadvantages of team-based reward schemes are that they create a lack of drive, that low performers become free riders, and that high performers may withdraw or become "tough cops." Free riders are individuals who benefit from a the actions of others without contributing or paying their fair share of the costs. The term can apply to individuals who do not do their fair share of work on teams, and it can also apply to firms that benefit from a shared resource but do not pay or contribute to its creation or maintenance.

Katz sought to identify reward schemes that achieve the best of both worlds. These hybrid pay systems would reward individual and team performance and promote excellence at both levels. Katz suggested two possible hybrid reward systems. The first system features a base rate of pay for individual performance that increases when the group reaches a target level of performance. In this reward system, individuals have a clear pay-for-performance incentive, and their rate of pay increases when the group as a whole does well. In the second hybrid, the pay-for-performance rate also increases when a target is reached. Under this reward system, however, every team member must reach a target level of performance before the higher pay rate kicks in. In contrast with the first hybrid, this reward system clearly incentivizes the better performers to aid poorer performers. Only when the poorest performer reaches the target does the higher pay rate kick in.

KEY TAKEAWAYS

- Compensation plans reward employees for contributing to company goals. Pay levels should reflect the value of each type of job to the company's overall success. For some companies, technical jobs are the most vital, whereas for others frontline customer-service positions determine the success of the company against its competitors.
- Companies should identify the types of teams they have—parallel, work, project, or partnership—and then choose the pay options that are most appropriate.
- Pay-for-performance plans tie an individual's pay directly to their ability to meet performance targets. These plans can reward individual performance or team performance—or a combination of the two.

EXERCISES

(AACSB: Reflective Thinking, Analytical Skills)
1. What factors would you consider when setting a pay level for a particular job?
2. What might be the "A" level positions in a bank?
3. If you were running a business, would you implement a pay-for-performance scheme? Why or why not?
4. Describe the difference between a base salary, a bonus, and a gainsharing plan.
5. Discuss the advantages and disadvantages of rewarding individual versus team performance.

[1] Inez Anderson, "Human Resources: War or Revolution?" Mondaq Business Briefing, August 1, 2007.
[2] Carly Chynoweth, "King of the Expat Package," Times (London), March 14, 2010, accessed July 26, 2010, http://business.timesonline.co.uk/tol/business/career_and_jobs/senior_executive/article7060648.ece.
[3] Steven Kerr, "On the Folly of Rewarding for A, While Hoping for B," Academy of Management Executive 9, no. 1 (1995): 25–37.
[4] Anne Field and Ken Gordon, "Do Your Stars See a Reason to Stay?" Harvard Management Update 13, no. 6 (2008): 5–6.
[5] Clay Chandler, "Winning the Talent War in China," McKinsey Quarterly, November 2009, accessed July 26, 2010, https://www.mckinseyquarterly.com/Organization/Talent/Winning_the_talent_war_in_China_2472.
[6] David Hoyt, "'Spotlight' Global Strategic Recognition Program," Stanford Graduate School of Business Case Study, accessed January 30, 2009, http://globoblog.globoforce.com/our-customers/case-studies/intuit.html?KeepThis=true.
[7] Eric Mosley, "Intuit Spotlights Strategic Importance of Global Employee Recognition," Global Trends in Human Resource Management (blog), August 15, 2008, accessed January 30, 2009, http://howtomanagehumanresources.blogspot.com/2008/08/intuit-spotlights-strategic-importance.html.
[8] Edward E. Lawler III, The Ultimate Advantage (San Francisco: Jossey-Bass, 1992).
[9] Thomas Flannery, People, Performance, and Pay (New York: Free Press, 1996), 117.

[10] Charlotte Garvey, "Steer Teams with the Right Pay," HR Magazine, May 2002, accessed January 30, 2011, http://findarticles.com/p/articles/mi_m3495/is_5_47/ai_86053654/?tag=untagged.

[11] Nancy. R. Katz, "Promoting a Healthy Balance Between Individual Achievement and Team Success: The Impact of Hybrid Reward Systems" (presentation, "Do Rewards Make a Difference?" session, Academy of Management Conference, San Diego, CA, August 9–12, 1998).

12.5 Tying It All Together—Using the HRM Balanced Scorecard to Gauge and Manage Human Capital, Including Your Own

LEARNING OBJECTIVES

1. Describe the Balanced Scorecard method and how it can be applied to HRM.
2. Discuss what is meant by "human capital."
3. Understand why metrics are important to improving company performance.
4. Consider how your human capital might be mapped on an HRM Balanced Scorecard.

Applying the Balanced Scorecard Method to HRM

You may already be familiar with the Balanced Scorecard, a tool that helps managers measure what matters to a company. Developed by Robert Kaplan and David Norton, the Balanced Scorecard helps managers define the performance categories that relate to the company's strategy. The managers then translate those categories into metrics and track performance on those metrics. Besides traditional financial and quality measures, companies use employee-performance measures to track their employees' knowledge, skills, and contributions to the company. [1]

The employee-performance aspects of the Balanced Scorecard analyze employee capabilities, satisfaction, retention, and productivity. Companies also track whether employees are motivated (e.g., by tracking the number of suggestions made and implemented by employees) and whether employee performance goals are aligned with company goals.

Applying the Balanced Scorecard Method to HRM

Because the Balanced Scorecard focuses on the strategy and metrics of the business, Mark Huselid and his colleagues took this concept a step further and developed the Workforce Scorecard to provide a framework specific to HRM. According to Huselid, the Workforce Scorecard identifies and measures the behaviors, skills, mind-sets, and results required for the workforce to contribute to the company's success. Specifically, as summarized in the following figure, the Workforce Scorecard has four key sequential elements: [2]

1. **Workforce mind-set and culture.** Does the workforce understand the strategy and embrace it? Does the workforce have the culture needed to support strategy execution?
2. **Workforce competencies.** Does the workforce, especially in the strategically important or "A" positions, have the skills it needs to execute the strategy? (Remember that "A" positions are those job categories most vital to the company's success.)
3. **Leadership and workforce behaviors.** Are the leadership team and workforce consistently behaving in ways that will lead to the attainment of the company's key strategic objectives?
4. **Workforce success.** Has the workforce achieved the key strategic objectives for the business? (If the organization can answer yes to the first three elements, then the answer should be yes here as well.) [3]

Human Capital

Implementing the Workforce Scorecard requires a change in perspective, from seeing people as a cost to seeing people as the company's most important asset to be managed—human capital. As discussed in Section 12.1 "The Changing Role of Strategic Human Resources Management in International Business", human capital is the collective sum of the attributes, life experiences, knowledge, inventiveness, energy, and enthusiasm that a company's employees choose to invest in their work. Such an asset is difficult to measure because it's intangible, and factors like "inventiveness" are subjective and open to interpretation. The challenge for managers, then, is to develop measurement systems that are more rigorous and provide a frame of reference. The metrics can range from activity-based (transactional) metrics to strategic ones. Transactional metrics are the easiest to measure and include counting the number of new people hired, fired, transferred, and promoted. The measures associated with these include the cost of each new hire, the length of time and cost associated with transferring an employee, and so forth. Typical ratios associated with transactional metrics include the training cost factor (i.e., the total training cost divided by the number of employees trained) and training cost percentage (i.e., the total training cost divided by the operating expense). [4] But these transactional measures don't get at the strategic issues—namely, whether the right employees are being trained and whether they're remembering and using what they learned. Measuring training effectiveness requires not only devising metrics but also changing the nature of the training.

Ethics in Action

How to Initiate an Ethics Program

The Balanced Scorecard doesn't explicitly have a facet on global ethics, but that doesn't mean you can't add one. Fostering business-ethics awareness in today's multicultural workplace and global marketplace is only the beginning. The following initiatives can be implemented to your corporate ethics program:

- Uncover or discover what the burning ethical issues are in your organization worldwide. This may involve conducting a broad survey to a cross section of all employees, covering all areas and departments of the organization worldwide.

- Make ethics explicit by developing a clear code of conduct that is based on values and that deals directly and cross-culturally with issues. Once articulated, the challenge is to communicate and inculcate this explicit code throughout the organization.

- Provide opportunities to learn about ethical dilemmas and how to resolve them. Practice doing so in nonthreatening, experiential ways, such as through simulation training or case studies. This might involve creating an ethics program built around the organization's explicit code of conduct.

- Network with others in your industry and with ethics personnel from other organizations and industries. This is an effective way to learn the best practices in the field and to benchmark your organization.

- Review the "ethical state of health" on a continual basis by repeatedly revisiting your research, communication and training programs, code of conduct, and so forth. Times change, and strategies shift. Thus there is always a need to revisit the subject. Don't expect the core values to change. However, one word in a definition may need to be edited or replaced, or a new value may emerge that is critical to the future character and success of your business.

The BMO Bank of Montreal has taken this step. "What we're trying to do at the Bank of Montreal is to build learning into what it is that people are doing," said Jim Rush of the Bank of Montreal's Institute for Learning. "The difficulty with training as we once conceived it is that you're taken off your job, you're taken out of context, you're taken away from those things that you're currently working on, and you go through some kind of training. And then you've got to come back and begin to apply that. Well, you walk back to that environment and it hasn't changed. It's not supportive or conducive to you behaving in a different kind of way, so you

revert back to the way you were, very naturally." To overcome this, the bank conducts training such that teams bring in specific tasks on which they're working, so that they learn by doing. This removes the gap between learning in one context and applying it in another. The bank then looks at performance indices directly related to the bottom line. "If we take an entire business unit through a program designed to help them learn how to increase the market share of a particular product, we can look at market share and see if it improved after the training," Rush said. [5]

Motorola has adopted a similar approach, using action learning in its Senior Executive Program. Action learning teams are assigned a specific project by Motorola's CEO and are responsible for implementing the solutions they design. This approach not only educates the team members but also lets them implement the ideas, so they're in a position to influence the organization. In this way, the training seamlessly supports Motorola's goals.

As you can see in these examples, organizations need employees to apply their knowledge to activities that add value to the company. In planning and applying human capital measures, managers should use both retrospective (lagging) and prospective (leading) indicators. Lagging indicators are those that tell the company what it has accomplished (e.g., the Bank of Montreal's documenting the effect that training had on a business unit's performance). Leading indicators are forecasts that help an organization see where it is headed. Leading indicators include employee learning and growth indices. [6]

Ethics in Action

As Mark Vickers of the Human Resource Institute points out, global corporations often have to operate in nations where bribery, sexual harassment, racial discrimination, and a variety of other issues are not uniformly viewed as illegal or even unethical. [7] As a result, companies must grapple with maintaining an enterprise-wide standard of ethics in countries where these practices are not the norm and may even be counter to local traditions. For many companies, China may be the test bed for dealing with these issues. A recent study reported that in China "there is a need to harness the (largely neglected) ethical dimension to transform business practice along international standards...At a minimum, fraud and corruption must be suppressed in an atmosphere where contract and property rights are clearly defined and honored." [8] As countries work together to develop multinational trade and labor agreements, a common set of ethical norms will develop over time, but the process will not happen overnight. In the meantime, companies will need to think internally about how to handle ethical issues in a way that makes sense at home and abroad. [9]

The Payoff

Given the complexity of trying to measure intangibles with metrics and a scorecard, some managers may be inclined to ask, "Why bother doing all this?" Research by John Lingle and William Schiemann provides a clear answer. Companies that make a concerted effort to measure intangibles such as employee performance, innovation, and change in addition to measuring financial benchmarks perform better. Lingle and Schiemann examined how executives measured six strategic performance areas: (1) financial performance, (2) operating efficiency, (3) customer satisfaction, (4) employee performance, (5) innovation and change, and (6) community/environment issues. To evaluate how carefully the measures were tracked, the researchers asked the executives, "How highly do you value the information in each strategic performance area?" and "Would you bet your job on the quality of the information on each of these areas?" The researchers found that the companies that paid the closest attention to the metrics and had the most credible information were the ones that had been identified as industry leaders over the previous three years (e.g., 74 percent of measurement-managed companies but only 44 percent of others) and reported financial performance in the top third of their industry (e.g., 83 percent compared with 52 percent). [10]

The Workforce Scorecard is vital because most organizations have much better control and accountability over their raw materials than they do over their workforce. For example, a retailer can quickly identify the source of a bad product, but the same retailer can't identify a poor manager whose negative attitude is poisoning morale and strategic execution. [11]

KEY TAKEAWAYS

- The Balanced Scorecard, when applied to HRM, helps managers align all HRM activities with the company's strategic goals. Assigning metrics to the HRM activities lets managers track progress on goals and ensure that they're working toward strategic objectives. It adds rigor and lets managers quickly identify gaps.
- Companies that measure intangibles such as employee performance, innovation, and change perform better financially than companies that don't use such metrics.
- Rather than investing equally in training for all jobs, a company should invest disproportionately more in

developing the people in the key strategic ("A") jobs on which the company's success is most dependent.

EXERCISES

(AACSB: Reflective Thinking, Analytical Skills)
1. Define the Balanced Scorecard method.
2. List the elements of a Workforce Scorecard.
3. Discuss how human capital can be managed like a strategic asset.
4. Why is it important to align HRM metrics with company strategy?
5. What kind of metrics would be most useful for HRM to track?

[1] Robert S. Kaplan and David P. Norton, The Balanced Scorecard (Boston: Harvard Business School Press, 1996).
[2] Mark A. Huselid, Brian E. Becker, and Richard W. Beatty, The Workforce Scorecard: Managing Human Capital to Execute Strategy (Boston: Harvard Business School Press, 2005).
[3] Mark A. Huselid, Brian E. Becker, and Richard W. Beatty, "'A Players' or 'A Positions'? The Strategic Logic of Workforce Management," Harvard Business Review 83, no. 12 (December 2005), http://chrs.rutgers.edu/pub_documents/Huselid-Beatty-Becker%20HBR%20Paper.pdf.
[4] Leslie A. Weatherly, "The Value of People: The Challenges and Opportunities of Human Capital Measurement and Reporting," SHRM Research Quarterly 3 (2003): 14–25, accessed February 6, 2011, http://www.shrm.org/Research/Articles/Articles/Documents/0303measurement.pdf.
[5] Jim Rush, interview by Andrea Meyer, Fast Company, July 1995.
[6] Leslie A. Weatherly, "The Value of People: The Challenges and Opportunities of Human Capital Measurement and Reporting," SHRM Research Quarterly 3 (2003): 14–25, accessed February 6, 2011, http://www.shrm.org/Research/Articles/Articles/Documents/0303measurement.pdf.
[7] Mark R. Vickers, "Business Ethics and the HR Role: Past, Present, and Future," Human Resource Planning 28, no. 1 (2005), accessed January 28, 2011, http://www.entrepreneur.com/tradejournals/article/131500182_1.html.
[8] Philip. C. Wright, Szeto Wing-Fu, and S. K. Lee, "Ethical Perceptions in China: The Reality of Business Ethics in an International Context," Management Decision 41, no. 2 (2003): 182.
[9] Philip C. Wright, Szeto Wing-Fu, and S. K. Lee, "Ethical Perceptions in China: The Reality of Business Ethics in an International Context," Management Decision 41, no. 2 (2003): 180–89.
[10] Leslie A. Weatherly "The Value of People: The Challenges and Opportunities of Human Capital Measurement and Reporting," HR Magazine, January 30, 2011, http://findarticles.com/p/articles/mi_m3495/is_9_48/ai_108315188.
[11] Brian E. Becker and Mark A. Huselid, "Strategic Human Resources Management: Where Do We Go from Here?" Journal of Management 32, no. 6 (2006): 898–925.

12.6 Tips in Your Walkabout Toolkit Applying the Balanced Scorecard Method to Your Human Capital

Let's translate the Workforce Scorecard to your own Balanced Scorecard of human capital. As a reminder, the idea behind the HRM scorecard is that if developmental attention is given to each area, then the organization will be more likely to be successful. In this case, however, you use the scorecard to better understand why you may or may not be effective in your current work setting. When you create the Workforce Scorecard for your company, it should comprise four sets of answers and activities. [1]

1. **What are your mind-set and values?** Do you understand the organization's strategy and embrace it, and do you know what to do in order to implement the strategy? If you answered no to either of these questions, then you should consider investing some time in learning about your firm's strategy. For the second half of this question, you may need additional coursework or mentoring to understand what it takes to move the firm's strategy forward.

2. **What are your work-related competencies?** Do you have the skills and abilities to get your job done? If you have aspirations to key positions in the organization, do you have the skills and abilities for those higher roles?

3. **What are the leadership and workforce behaviors?** If you aren't currently in a leadership position, do you know how consistently your leaders are behaving in regard to the achievement of strategic objectives? If you are one of the leaders, are you behaving strategically?

4. **How are you contributing to the organization's success?** Can you tie your mind-set, values, competencies, and behaviors to the organization's performance and success?

This simple scorecard assessment will help you understand why your human capital is helping the organization or needs additional development itself. With such an assessment in hand, you can act to help the firm succeed and identify priority areas for personal growth, learning, and development.

[1] {Authors' names retracted as requested by the work's original creator or licensee}, Principles of Management (Nyack, NY).

12.7 End-of-Chapter Questions and Exercises

These exercises are designed to ensure that the knowledge you gain from this book about international business meets the learning standards set out by the international Association to Advance Collegiate Schools of Business (AACSB International). [1] AACSB is the premier accrediting agency of collegiate business schools and accounting programs worldwide. It expects that you will gain knowledge in the areas of communication, ethical reasoning, analytical skills, use of information technology, multiculturalism and diversity, and reflective thinking.

EXPERIENTIAL EXERCISES

(AACSB: Communication, Use of Information Technology, Analytical Skills)

1. One of the reasons that firms seek to employ people in other countries is the relative cost of labor. Visit the US Bureau of Labor Statistics website and scan the available comparison data for international compensation (http://www.bls.gov/fls/flshcaeindnaics.htm). Which countries have the lowest wages? Which have the highest? Why wouldn't companies always locate their operations where labor costs are the lowest?

2. You are an SHRM consultant called in by an American firm that wants to staff its new international operations with expatriates. They have asked you to compile a checklist of the key concerns the company should address and steps it should go through before embarking on this endeavor. Engage Michigan State University's globalEDGE site (http://globaledge.msu.edu/) and similar resources to prepare your report.

3. Drawing on information in this chapter and in resources such as globalEDGE, design a preparation plan that might improve the chances for success in foreign assignments. Does your plan include selection criteria as well? Why or why not? If so, what might these selection criteria be?

4. Pick a foreign country where you'd like to sign up for a job assignment. How well do you know the business practices in that country? To see how well you understand the ways of doing business in other countries, go to Kwintessential—Language and Cultural Specialists' web page at http://www.kwintessential.co.uk/cultural-services/aims-and-objectives.html. Click on Tools and Resources. From here, you can choose several online quizzes to test your knowledge of business etiquette in a number of countries.

Ethical Dilemmas

(AACSB: Ethical Reasoning, Multiculturalism, Reflective Thinking, Analytical Skills)

1. Your company is just beginning to branch out of the United States, and your CEO suggests that it might be good for the company to put its ethical standards related to SHRM into writing for the entire company. Regarding selection and placement, job design, compensation and rewards, and diversity management, what standards would you propose? How would you go about determining if these standards fit every country in which your company wishes to do business?

2. Your company's home country believes in gender equality. What happens when locals from another

country follow that country's customs by treating a female expatriate employee as a second-class citizen? What obligations does your company have to her? How should she respond?

3. Your company appears to be taking unfair advantage of the working conditions in an overseas subsidiary in which you work. At the same time, however, your company is providing much-sought-after employment in this developing region. Your conscience is bothered.

What should you do? What rights and obligations does your company have in such a situation?

[1] Association to Advance Collegiate Schools of Business website, accessed January 26, 2010, http://www.aacsb.edu.

NOTES:

Chapter 13:
Harnessing the Engine of Global Innovation

WHAT'S IN IT FOR ME?

1. What is the role of research and development (R&D) in innovation?
2. How are intellectual property rights treated around the globe?
3. Where in the world should R&D be located?
4. How are businesses accelerating their innovation efforts?
5. What is innovation for the bottom of the pyramid?

This chapter introduces you to the R&D function and innovation in international business. First, you'll look at R&D and its importance to corporations (Section 13.1 "An Introduction to Research and Development (R&D)") and then move on to consider intellectual property rights around the world (Section 13.2 "Intellectual Property Rights around the Globe"). Section 13.3 "How to Organize and Where to Locate Research and Development Activities" examines how to organize the international R&D function and where to locate R&D activities. Communications and other technologies are flattening the world in regard to innovation, enabling innovation activities to be located anywhere, while the absence of legal property-rights protections in some areas work against this flattener. Section 13.4 "Increasing Speed and Effectiveness of International Innovation" discusses the activities associated with managing innovation and running international R&D to increase the speed and effectivness with which a firm can innovate. You'll learn how the developments enabled by the Internet, such as open innovation, are bringing new innovation opportunities while at the same time making innovation imperative. Section 13.5 "Innovation for the Bottom of the Pyramid" describes innovating for the needs of all the world's consumers, not just the wealthiest ones. Innovation in emerging markets is also depicted in the opening case study on Unilever.

OPENING CASE: A TALE OF EMERGING MARKET-BASED INNOVATION

For most companies, the traditional route to global business is through the export of the products they have developed and manufactured for their home markets. But most of the products sold in developed countries are much too expensive for emerging markets, where most of the people make less

than $1,500 per year. [1] Simply exporting products designed for the United States, Western Europe, or Japan doesn't work well. Nor does simply lowering the price of products, because lower prices mean both lower margins and increased risks of cannibalizing the profits of higher-priced brands.

Moreover, emerging markets, such as Brazil, Russia, India, and China (also collectively known as the BRIC countries), don't have the same needs or capabilities as those found in developed economies. For instance, disposable income levels are relatively low, the availability of basic utilities like water or electricity can be varied, and transportation and transportation infrastructure can be nonexistent. While these emerging economies are attractive by virtue of their massive size, their different needs and capabilities pose unique challenges that are often overcome only through corporate innovation. Let's look at a case in point—Unilever in Brazil.

Among consumer packaged-goods (CPG) companies, Unilever and Procter & Gamble (P&G) often trade punches for customers in the world's emerging markets. Take their efforts in trying to market powdered laundry detergent (sometimes referred to as "washing powders") to the tens of millions of poorer consumers in Brazil. A decade ago, Unilever and P&G held significantly different market shares than they do today. Unilever held an 81 percent market share in the powered detergent sector while P&G was a late entrant in the market and was a distant second behind Unilever. P&G, however, was known for its strong R&D unit and extensive marketing experience worldwide; thus it posed a potential threat to Unilever. [2]

Laercio Cardoso, head of Unilever's Home Care division in Brazil, knew he had to take action to respond to P&G's imminent threat. The solution, as he saw it, was to develop a product targeting the lower end of the market. But Cardoso faced opposition from his own colleagues at Unilever, because they ascribed Unilever's prior success to its premium-quality products. They also argued that any successful move into the low-end market would have to draw demand from Brazil's low-income consumers living in its vast favelas (slums). Over the years, both in Brazil and elsewhere, Unilever had learned that the attitudes and behaviors of this segment of consumers were very different from what Unilever was used to in the more high-end markets.

For example, Unilever knew that low-end consumers in Brazil didn't own washing machines. Instead, mothers washed the family's clothing by hand in the river. Regardless of whether the family lived in a city or rural area, the river was the place where mothers gathered to wash the clothes. What's more, the women shopped at local mom-and-pop stores, not big central shopping centers. To succeed in this new market, therefore, Unilever would have to design a soap that was effective for washing clothes by hand and that could be easily transported to the local mom-and-pop shops.

Drawing on its experience in India, Unilever launched Ala, a brand of detergent created specifically to meet the needs of low-income consumers.[3] The product is designed to work well for laundry washed by hand in river water. It's affordable and effective—and it is sold in small sizes to make it easy to transport and stock in a local store. The technique of small-portion packaging is called "sachet marketing," originating from powered soaps and shampoos sold in sachets in India for two to four cents each.

OPENING CASE EXERCISES

(AACSB: Ethical Reasoning, Multiculturalism, Reflective Thinking, Analytical Skills)

1. View the YouTube video on Unilever's Ala in Brazil (http://www.youtube.com/watch?v=WhmYtfL6s_8). Given that Unilever is viewed as being highly innovative in Brazil, does the video confirm this reputation? Why or why not?
2. Do you think that small, entrepreneurial ventures could be as effectively innovative as an enormous firm like P&G in emerging markets?
3. Visit Trendwatching.com's web page on "Sachet Marketing" athttp://trendwatching.com/trends/sachet_marketing. htm. Why might the concept of a sachet be relevant in international business beyond soap or laundry detergent?

[1] "Sachet Marketing," Trend Watching, accessed May 16, 2010, http://trendwatching.com/trends/sachet_marketing.htm.
[2] Pierre Chandon, "Unilever in Brazil: Marketing Strategies for Low-Income Countries," November 28, 2006, accessed December 19, 2010, http://estrategiasynegocios.wordpress.com/2006/11/28/case-study-unilever-in-brazil-marketing-strategies-for-low-income-countries.
[3] "Sachet Marketing," Trend Watching, accessed May 16, 2010, http://trendwatching.com/trends/SACHET_MARKETING.htm.

13.1 An Introduction to Research and Development (R&D)

LEARNING OBJECTIVES

1. Know what constitutes research and development (R&D).
2. Understand the importance of R&D to corporations.
3. Recognize the role government plays in R&D.

Research and development (R&D) refers to two intertwined processes of research (to identify new knowledge and ideas) and development (turning the ideas into tangible products or processes). Companies undertake R&D in order to develop new products, services, or procedures that will help them grow and expand their operations. Corporate R&D began in the United States with Thomas Edison and the Edison General Electric Company he founded in 1890 (which is today's GE). Edison is credited with 1,093 patents, but it's actually his invention of the corporate R&D lab that made all those other inventions possible. [1]Edison was the first to bring management discipline to R&D, which enabled a much more powerful method of invention by systematically harnessing the talent of many individuals. Edison's 1,093 patents had less to do with individual genius and more to do with management genius: creating and managing an R&D lab that could efficiently and effectively crank out new inventions. For fifty years following the early twentieth century, GE was awarded more patents than any other firm in America. [2]

Edison is known as an inventor, but he was also a great innovator. Here's the difference: an invention brings an idea into tangible reality by embodying it as a product or system. An innovation converts a new idea into revenues and profits. Inventors can get patents on original ideas, but those inventions may not make money. For an invention to become an innovation, people must be willing to buy it in high enough numbers that the firm benefits from making it. [3]

Edison wanted his lab to be a commercial success. "Anything that won't sell, I don't want to invent. Its sale is proof of utility and utility is success," [4] Edison said. Edison's lab in Menlo Park, New Jersey, was an applied research lab, which is a lab that develops and commercializes its research findings. As defined by the National Science Foundation, applied research is "systematic study to gain knowledge or understanding necessary to determine the means by which a recognized and specific need may be met." [5] In contrast, basic research advances the knowledge of science without an explicit, anticipated commercial outcome.

History and Importance

From Edison's lab onward, companies learned that a systematic approach to research could provide big competitive advantages. Companies could not only invent new products, but they could also turn those inventions into innovations that launched whole new industries. For example, the radio, wireless communications, and television industry grew out of early-twentieth-century research by General Electric and American Telephone and Telegraph (AT&T, which founded Bell Labs).

The heyday of American R&D labs came in the 1950s and early 1960s, with corporate institutions like Bell Labs, RCA labs, IBM's research centers, and government institutions such as NASA and DARPA. These labs funded both basic and applied research, giving birth to the transistor, long-distance TV transmission, photovoltaic solar cells, the UNIX operating system, and cellular telephony, each of which led to the creation of not just hundreds of products but whole industries and millions of jobs. [6] DARPA's creation of the Internet (known at its inception as ARPAnet) and Xerox PARC's Ethernet and graphical-user interface (GUI) laid the foundations for the PC revolution. [7]

Companies invest in R&D to gain a pipeline of new products. For a high-tech company like Apple, it means coming up with new types of products (e.g., the iPad) as well as newer and better versions of its existing computers and iPhones. For a pharmaceutical company, it means coming out with new drugs to treat diseases. Different parts of the world have different diseases or different forms of known diseases. For example, diabetes in China has a different molecular structure than diabetes elsewhere in the world, and pharmaceutical company Eli Lilly's new R&D center in Shanghai will focus on this disease variant. [8] Even companies that sell only services benefit from innovation and developing new services. For example, MasterCard Global Service started providing customers with emergency cash advances, directions to nearby ATMs, and emergency card replacements. [9]

Innovation also includes new product and service combinations. For example, heavy-equipment manufacturer John Deere created a product and service combination by equipping a GPS into one of its tractors. The GPS keeps the tractor on a parallel path, even under hands-free operation, and keeps the tractor with only a two-centimeter overlap of those parallel lines. This innovation helps a farmer increase the yield of the field and complete passes over the field in the tractor more quickly. The innovation also helps reduce fuel, seed, and chemical costs because there is little overlap and waste of the successive parallel passes. [10]

Did You Know?

Appliance maker Whirlpool has made innovation a strategic priority in order to stay competitive. Whirlpool has an innovation pipeline that currently numbers close to 1,000 new products. On average, Whirlpool introduces one hundred new products to the market each year. "Every month we report pipeline size measured by estimated sales, and our goal this year is $4 billion," said Moises Norena, director of global innovation at Whirlpool. With Whirlpool's 2008 revenue totaling $18.9 billion, that means roughly 20 percent of sales would be from new products. [11]

Not only do companies benefit from investing in R&D, but the nation's economy benefits as well, as Massachusetts Institute of Technology (MIT) professor Robert Solow discovered. Solow showed mathematically that, in the long run, growth in gross national product per worker is due more to technological progress than to mere capital investment. Solow won a Nobel Prize for his research, and investment in corporate R&D labs grew.

Although R&D has its roots in national interests, it has become globalized. Most US and European *Fortune* 1000 companies have R&D centers in Asia. [12] You'll see the reasons for the globalization of R&D in Section 13.3 "How to Organize and Where to Locate Research and Development Activities".

The Role of Government

Governments have played a large role in the inception of R&D, mainly to fund research for military applications for war efforts. Today, governments still play a big role in innovation because of their ability to fund R&D. A government can fund R&D directly, by offering grants to universities and research centers or by offering contracts to corporations for performing research in a specific area.

Governments can also provide tax incentives for companies that invest in R&D. Countries vary in the tax incentives that they give to corporations that invest in R&D. By giving corporations a tax credit when they invest in R&D, governments encourage corporations to invest in R&D in their countries. For example, Australia gave a 125 percent tax deduction for R&D expenses. The Australian government's website noted, "It's little surprise then, that many companies from around the world are choosing to locate their R&D facilities in Australia." The government also pointed out that "50 percent of the most innovative companies in Australia are foreign-based." [13]

Finally, governments can promote innovation through investments in infrastructure that will support new technology and by committing to buy the new technology. China is doing this in a big way, and it is thus influencing the course of many companies around the world. Since 2000, China has had a policy in place "to encourage tech transfer from abroad and to force foreign companies to transfer their R&D operations to China in exchange for access to China's large volume markets," reported *R&D Magazine* in its 2010 review of global R&D. [14] For example, any automobile manufacturer that wants to sell cars in China must enter into a partnership with a Chinese company. As a result, General Motors (GM), Daimler, Hyundai, Volkswagen (VW), and Toyota have all formed joint ventures with Chinese companies. General Motors and Volkswagen, for example, have both formed joint ventures with the Chinese company Shanghai Automotive Industry Corporation (SAIC), even though SAIC also sells cars under its own brand. [15] The Chinese government made another strategic decision influencing innovation in the automobile industry. Because no Chinese company is a leader in internal combustion engines, the government decided to leapfrog the technology and focus on becoming a leader in electric cars. [16] "Beijing has pledged that it will do whatever it takes to help the Chinese car industry take the lead in electric vehicles," notes industry watcher Brian Dumaine. [17] That includes allocating $8 billion in R&D funds as well as another $10 billion in infrastructure (e.g., installing charging stations). [18] The government will also subsidize the purchase of electric cars by consumers and has committed to buying electric cars for government fleets, thus guaranteeing that there will be buyers for the new electric vehicles that companies invent and develop.

Another role of government is to set high targets that require innovation. In the 1960s, the US Apollo space program launched by President John F. Kennedy inspired US corporations to work toward putting a man on the moon. The government's investments in the Apollo program sped up the development of computer and communications technology and also led to innovations in fuel cells, water purification, freeze-drying food, and digital image processing now used in medical products for CAT scans and MRIs. [19] Today, government policies coming from the European Union mandate ambitious environmental targets, such as carbon-neutral fuels and energy, which are driving global R&D to achieve environmental goals the way the Apollo program drove R&D in the 1960s. [20]

After the 1990s, US investment in R&D declined, especially in basic research. Governments in other countries, however, continue to invest. New government-corporate partnerships are developing around the world. IBM, which for years closely guarded its R&D labs (even IBM employees were required to have special badges to enter the R&D area), is now setting up "collaboratories" around the world. These collaboratories are partnerships between IBM researchers and outside experts from government, universities, and even other companies. "The world is our lab now," says John E. Kelly III, director of IBM Research. [21] IBM has deals for six future collaboratories in China, Ireland, Taiwan, Switzerland, India, and Saudi Arabia.

The reason for the collaboratory strategy is to share R&D costs—IBM's partners must share 50 percent of the funding costs, which means that together the partners can participate in a large-scale effort that they'd be hard pressed to fund on their own. An example is IBM's research partnership with the state-funded Swiss university ETH Zurich. The two are building a $70 million semiconductor lab for nanotech research with the goal of identifying a replacement for the current semiconductor-switch technology. [22] Such a breakthrough could harken the creation of a whole new industry.

Did You Know?
Of all the countries in the world, the United States remains the largest investor in R&D. One-third of all spending on R&D comes from the United States. Just one government agency—the Department of Defense—provides more funding than all the nations of the world except China and Japan. Nonetheless, other countries are increasing the amounts of money they spend on R&D. Their governments are funding R&D at higher levels and are giving more attractive tax incentives to firms that spend on R&D.

Governments can also play a big role in the protection of intellectual property rights, as you'll see in Section 13.2 "Intellectual Property Rights around the Globe".

KEY TAKEAWAYS

- R&D refers to two intertwined processes of research (to identify new facts and ideas) and development (turning the ideas into tangible products and services.) Companies undertake R&D to get a pipeline of new products. Breakthrough innovations can create whole new industries, which can provide thousands of jobs.

- Invention is the creation of a new idea embodied in a product or process, while innovation takes that new idea and commercializes it in a way that enables a company to generate revenue from it.

- Government support of R&D plays a significant role in innovation. It has been generally accepted that it's desirable to encourage R&D for reasons of economic growth as well as national security. This has resulted in massive support from public funds for many sorts of laboratories. Governments influence R&D not only by providing direct funding but also by providing tax incentives to companies that invest in R&D. Governments also stimulate innovation through supporting institutions such as education and providing reliable infrastructure.

EXERCISES

(AACSB: Reflective Thinking, Analytical Skills)

1. What benefits does a company get by investing in R&D?
2. Why do organizations make a distinction between basic research and applied research?
3. Describe three ways in which government can influence R&D.

[1] Andrea Meyer, "High-Value Innovation: Innovating the Management of Innovation," Working Knowledge (blog), August 20, 2009, accessed February 22, 2011, http://workingknowledge.com/blog/?p=594.

[2] Gary Hamel, "The Why, What and How of Management Innovation," Harvard Business Review, February 2006, accessed February 24, 2011, http://hbr.org/2006/02/the-why-what-and-how-of-management-innovation/ar/1.

[3] A. G. Lafley and Ram Charan, The Game-Changer (New York: Crown Publishing Group, 2008), 21.

[4] A. G. Lafley and Ram Charan, The Game-Changer (New York: Crown Publishing Group, 2008), 25.

[5] National Science Foundation, "Definitions of Research and Development," Office of Management and Budget Circular A-11, accessed March 5, 2011, http://www.nsf.gov/statistics/randdef/fedgov.cfm.

[6] Adrian Slywotzky, "How Science Can Create Millions of New Jobs," BusinessWeek, September 7, 2009, accessed May 11, 2011, http://www.businessweek.com/magazine/content/09_36/b4145036678131.htm.

[7] Adrian Slywotzky, "How Science Can Create Millions of New Jobs," BusinessWeek, September 7, 2009, accessed May 11, 2011, http://www.businessweek.com/magazine/content/09_36/b4145036678131.htm.

[8] "2011 Global R&D Funding Forecast," R&D Magazine, December 2010, accessed February 27, 2011, http://www.battelle.org/aboutus/rd/2011.pdf.

[9] Lance Bettencourt, Service Innovation (New York: McGraw-Hill, 2010), 99.

[10] Lance Bettencourt, Service Innovation (New York: McGraw-Hill, 2010), 110.

[11] Jessie Scanlon, "How Whirlpool Puts New Ideas through the Wringer," BusinessWeek, August 3, 2009, accessed January 17, 2011, http://www.businessweek.com/innovate/content/aug2009/id20090083_452757.htm.

[12] "2011 Global R&D Funding Forecast," R&D Magazine, December 2010, accessed February 27, 2011, http://www.battelle.org/aboutus/rd/2011.pdf.

[13] Committee on Prospering in the Global Economy of the 21st Century (U.S.), Committee on Science, Engineering, and Public Policy (U.S.), Rising Above the Gathering Storm (Washington, DC: National Academies Press, 2007), 195.

[14] "2011 Global R&D Funding Forecast," R&D Magazine, December 2010, accessed February 27, 2011, http://www.battelle.org/aboutus/rd/2011.pdf.

[15] Brian Dumaine, "China Charges into Electric Cars," Fortune, November 1, 2010, 140.

[16] Bill Russo, Tao Ke, Edward Tse, and Bill Peng, China's Next Revolution: Transforming The Global Auto Industry, Booz & Company report, 2010, accessed February 27, 2011, http://www.booz.com/media/file/China's_Next_Revolution_en.pdf.

[17] Brian Dumaine, "China Charges into Electric Cars," Fortune, November 1, 2010, 140.

[18] Gordon Orr, "Unleashing Innovation in China," McKinsey Quarterly, January 2011, accessed January 2, 2011, https://www.mckinseyquarterly.com/Strategy/Innovation/Unleashing_innovation_in_China_2725.

[19] Adrian Slywotzky, "How Science Can Create Millions of New Jobs," BusinessWeek, September 7, 2009, accessed May 11, 2011, http://www.businessweek.com/magazine/content/09_36/b4145036678131.htm.

[20] Martin Grueber and Tim Studt, "A Battelle Perspective on Investing in International R&D," R&D Magazine, December 22, 2009, http://www.rdmag.com/Featured-Articles/2009/12/Global-Funding-Forecast-A-Battelle-Perspective-International-R-D.

[21] Steve Hamm, "How Big Blue Is Forging Cutting-edge Partnerships around the World," BusinessWeek, August 27, 2009, accessed January 2, 2010, http://www.businessweek.com/print/magazine/content/09_36/b4145040683083.htm.

[22] Steve Hamm, "How Big Blue Is Forging Cutting-Edge Partnerships around the world," BusinessWeek, August 27, 2009, accessed January 2, 2010, http://www.businessweek.com/print/magazine/content/09_36/b4145040683083.htm.

13.2 Intellectual Property Rights around the Globe
LEARNING OBJECTIVES

1. Understand what intellectual property (IP) is and why it's important for companies to protect their IP.
2. Be able to describe different types of intellectual property.
3. Know that intellectual property protection varies by country.

Intellectual Property Rights

For companies to gain financial benefits from investing in research and coming up with new inventions, there must be legal protection for those inventions. The system of law related to R&D and innovation is referred to as intellectual property rights. Different countries vary in the extent to which they protect intellectual property and enforce intellectual property regulations. The presence of strong, enforceable, consistent property rights serves to make the world flatter. However, as long as significant differences in property rights exist around the globe, the world will be far from flat with respect to innovation.

Intellectual property (IP) refers to creations of the mind—inventions, literary and artistic works, and symbols, names, and images used in commerce.[1] The term *property* connotes ownership that's exclusive, but the owners have the right to license or sell their IP. Under intellectual property law, owners are granted certain exclusive rights—intellectual property rights (IPR)—to the discoveries, inventions, words, phrases, symbols, and designs they create.

Let's look at the ways companies protect their IP and profit from it. The simplest way for a company to protect its intellectual property is to never reveal it—to create what is called a trade secret. This is how Coca-Cola protects the formula for its hugely popular soda. If the secret were discovered or revealed through nefarious intent, then trade secret law would allow punishment of the perpetrator, including criminal prosecution. But if a company somehow developed the same formula on its own, Coca-Cola could do nothing to stop them. Therefore, companies opt for other IP protection—namely, patents and copyrights.

The most common way to protect an industrial discovery or invention is to patent it. A patent is an inventor's exclusive right granted by the government for an invention, whether a product or a process, that is industrially applicable (i.e., useful) or new (i.e., novel) or exhibits a sufficient "inventive step" (i.e., be nonobvious) To get a patent, the company must reveal the details of the invention. The rationale for revealing the invention details is so that others can build on the invention and thus promote further innovation. By revealing the invention, companies obtain legal protection and the right to exclusive sales of the invention (or the right to license or sell its use to others). The patent gives the patent owner a monopoly on the invention for a specific number of years.

Patents can be granted within a single country or internationally. Christian Hahner, head of Intellectual Property & Technology Management at Daimler, said, "Attaining international patent protection is an expensive undertaking. If we believe it's important for our business to actively defend our patent in court in order to prevent unauthorized copies or imitations, then we have to nationalize the patent, which makes it valid in other countries." [2] A patent prohibits other people from selling the identical product built in the same way as the accepted patent. Patents give the owner the right to defend the invention in court, but they don't automatically mean that the owner will win the court case.

"When I make an innovation public in Germany by initially registering a patent, I'm actually defining the state of the art. It then becomes impossible for anyone else in the world to patent that innovation," Hahner said. "The publication of the patent also creates conditions that enable the worldwide utilization of innovations with great value to society—like those related to vehicle safety, for example." [3] That is, by disclosing the invention publicly, the inventor gets legal protection from outright copying of the invention, but society also benefits because others learn about the invention and can try to devise a different, original way to achieve the same outcome. Because of this fear of copying, some companies, such as Microsoft, choose not to patent some of their products. For example, Microsoft does not have a patent on its Windows software because doing so would force it to reveal its source code, which Microsoft does not want to do.

Did You Know?
A car might have one hundred patents associated with it in various parts and components. In contrast, in the pharmaceutical industry, one patent may be all that's needed to cover one product: a patented drug is the product in itself. What's more, much of the innovation in new cars today resides in software. For example, the Chevrolet Volt has more software than a state-of-the-art fighter aircraft. Almost 40 percent of the car's value comes from software, computer controls, and sensors. [4]

A trademark is a distinctive sign that identifies certain goods or services as those produced or provided by a specific person or enterprise. A trademark uniquely identifies the source of the product. Companies trademark brand names and then advertise to build familiarity with that name. [5] Consumers come to trust the name and look for other products by that maker.

For a brief review of the main types of intellectual property rights, see Table 13.1 "Intellectual Property Types", which is reprinted with permission from *Exchanging Value—Negotiating Technology Licensing Agreements—A Training Manual*, which was published jointly by the World Intellectual Property Organization (WIPO) and the International Trade Centre (ITC) (http://www.wipo.int/sme/en/documents/pdf/technology_licensing.pdf).

Licensing IP Rights
The word *license*, according to the World Intellectual Property Organization (WIPO), means permission granted by the owner of the intellectual property to another to use it

according to agreed terms and conditions, for a defined purpose, in a defined territory, and for an agreed period of time. [6] In licensing IP rights, the IP owner gives permission to use the IP but retains ownership of the IP.

Some companies obtain patents mainly to license or sell them to others, thus making money from their inventions without having to manufacture or service anything themselves. In turn, other companies actively seek patents that they can purchase because they want to speed up their own R&D efforts. For example, even Daimler, which registered 2,000 patents in 2009, pays 2,600 outside inventors to use their innovations in Daimler products. [7] Filing patents is relatively inexpensive; even entrepreneurs can afford the filing fee. But defending a patent can be expensive. Given how overworked the patent examiners are, they often err on the side of granting a patent, which means that there are often overlapping patents. "We wind up in these fights over patents where we can't tell what they mean, and the courts can't tell what they mean, and even the patentees can't tell you what they mean," said David Kappos, a lawyer who managed IBM's patent portfolio. [8]

Spotlight on International Strategy and Entrepreneurship

CH2M Hill is a $6 billion environmental services company that partnered with ADA Technologies, to develop patents for an inexpensive and effective way to control mercury emissions from coal-fired power plants. Neither company, however, makes products, so they contributed their IP to a new product-based start-up funded by outside investors. CH2M Hill and the start-up will then jointly market the new mercury-control technology. [9]

IP Protection Varies by Country

The US government's Office of the United States Trade Representative (USTR) monitors intellectual property rights around the world and fights IP theft because IP theft impacts the 18 million Americans whose livelihood depends on IP protection. [10] The USTR evaluates countries and rates them according to how those countries enforce IP rights. The Special 301 Report is an annual review of the global state of IPR protection and enforcement issued by the USTR. The worst offenders are put on a "Priority Watch List." The countries on the 2010 Priority Watch list are China, Russia, Algeria, Argentina, Canada, Chile, India, Indonesia, Pakistan, Thailand, and Venezuela. China, which has been on the Watch List before, continues to be on the list not only because of IP theft and counterfeiting but also because of government practices that severely restrict the market for foreign goods while giving favored treatment to "indigenous

innovation." [11] Countries can get off the Watch List by taking measures to reduce IP theft. The Czech Republic, Hungary, and Poland were all removed from the Watch List because they took significant steps to clamp down on piracy and counterfeiting.

WIPO

The World Intellectual Property Organization (WIPO) is a specialized agency of the United Nations that works to harmonize the intellectual property laws of countries around the world. Although the roots of the WIPO go back to 1883, WIPO became an agency of the United Nations in 1974, with a mandate to administer intellectual property matters recognized by the member states of the UN. In 1996, WIPO expanded its role and further demonstrated the importance of intellectual property rights in the management of globalized trade by entering into a cooperation agreement with the World Trade Organization (WTO). Today, WIPO seeks to

- harmonize national intellectual property legislation and procedures,
- provide services for international applications for industrial property rights,
- exchange intellectual property information,
- provide legal and technical assistance to developing and other countries,
- facilitate the resolution of private intellectual property disputes, and
- marshal information technology as a tool for storing, accessing, and using valuable intellectual property information. [12]

KEY TAKEAWAYS

- Intellectual property (IP) refers to creations of the mind, such as inventions, literary and artistic works, and symbols, names, and images used in commerce.
- Under IP law, owners are granted certain exclusive rights (intellectual property rights) to a variety of intangible assets.
- Through IP protection, owners are given the opportunity to license or sell their innovations to others, which can be an important way of creating value with these assets.
- The World Intellectual Property Organization (WIPO) is the global nongovernmental organization tasked with coordinating and marshaling efforts to harmonize intellectual property rights among countries and regions.

EXERCISES

(AACSB: Reflective Thinking, Analytical Skills)

1. What are IPRs, and why are they important?
2. What are the four main types of IP?
3. How does licensing relate to IPR?
4. Would you do business in a country with poor IP protection? Why or why not?
5. What advantages does a company gain by filing a patent? Why might a company decide not to file a patent on an intellectual asset?

[1] "What Is Intellectual Property?" World Intellectual Property Organization, 2003, accessed March 4, 2011,http://www.wipo.int/freepublications/en/intproperty/450/wipo_pub_450.pdf.

[2] Peter Thomas, "Patents Are the Future of Innovation Management," Technicity, 2010, accessed February 10, 2011, http://www.daimler-technicity.de/en/christianhahner.

[3] Peter Thomas, "Patents Are the Future of Innovation Management." Technicity, 2010, accessed February 10, 2011, http://www.daimler-technicity.de/en/christianhahner.

[4] Jason Paur, "Chevy Volt: King of (Software) Cars," Wired, November 5, 2010, accessed February 27, 2011, http://www.wired.com/autopia/2010/11/chevy-volt-king-of-software-cars.

[5] Steve Steinhilber, Strategic Alliances (Cambridge, MA: Harvard Business School Press, 2008), 98.

[6] Geoffrey Loades, "Exchanging Value: Negotiating Technology Licensing Agreements," World Intellectual Property Organization, 2005, 14.

[7] Peter Thomas, "Patents Are the Future of Innovation Management," Technicity, 2010, accessed February 10, 2011, http://www.daimler-technicity.de/en/christianhahner.

[8] Jeff Howe, Crowdsourcing (New York: Three Rivers Press, 2008), 65.

[9] Henry W. Chesbrough and Andrew R. Garman, "Use Open Innovation to Cope in a Downturn," Harvard Business Review, 2009, http://hbr.harvardbusiness.org/2009/06/web-exclusive-use-open-innovation-to-cope-in-a-downturn/ar/pr.

[10] United States Trade Representative, "USTR Releases 2010 Special 301 Report on Intellectual Property Rights," press release, April 2010, accessed February 27, 2011,http://www.ustr.gov/about-us/press-office/press-releases/2010/april/ustr-releases-2010-special-301-report-intellectual-p.

[11] United States Trade Representative, "USTR Releases 2010 Special 301 Report on Intellectual Property Rights," press release, April 2010, accessed February 27, 2011,http://www.ustr.gov/about-us/press-office/press-releases/2010/april/ustr-releases-2010-special-301-report-intellectual-p.

[12] "WIPO Treaties—General Information," World Intellectual Property Organization, accessed November 22, 2010, http://www.wipo.int/treaties/en/general.

13.3 How to Organize and Where to Locate Research and Development Activities

LEARNING OBJECTIVES

1. Understand two main ways in which to organize research and development (R&D) activities in a global organization.
2. Be able to describe two factors to consider when deciding where in the world to locate R&D activities.
3. Know what an innovation hub is and how governments can influence innovation.

How to Organize R&D Activities

The flattening world is putting more pressure on corporate research and development (R&D) to come up with new products and services in less time and at lower cost. As a result, new models for how a company should organize its R&D activities have emerged. The traditional model of having one central R&D center located in the United States is being replaced by having a network of smaller R&D centers located in various parts of the world. The reasons for this dispersion of R&D activities are to tap talent around the world, to lower costs, and to be better able to develop new products and services tailored to new country markets.

When designing the R&D network, companies need to make sure that all centers use the same communication and information systems platform so that team members can communicate regardless of where they are. Some companies also offer financial and promotion incentives to encourage employees to work in different locations. [1]

The director of HP Labs, Prith Banerjee, explains the benefit and rationale for locating R&D activities in new-market countries in order to innovate more effectively for those markets. Today, HP Labs is located in seven different regions around the world, including India, China, Russia, and Israel. One reason for being in India, besides lower labor costs, is to tap the talent in India and their knowledge of local needs.

The mission of HP Labs India, Banerjee says, is innovation for the next billion customers: "I strongly believe that it is not very easy for researchers sitting in Palo Alto to imagine the problems for the billion people in India, the vegetable vendors in India. What kind of cell phones, what kind of PDA devices would they need to solve their day-to-day problems? Sitting here in Palo Alto, you imagine that the whole world is developed, and it's not. So the researchers in India are actually working on precisely those problems." [2]

One of the challenges of a distributed global network of R&D centers is managing employees located in different countries. Booz & Company surveyed R&D leaders in 186 companies in nineteen nations to ask them their most pressing R&D challenges. The three top challenges executives listed were (1) how to assess the value of a new idea, (2) how to encourage collaboration across geographical locations and functions, and (3) managing the complexity of global R&D projects. [3] One way that large multinationals manage the challenge of globally distributed innovation activities is through specially trained innovation teams. For example, Whirlpool has devised a way to help encourage and share innovation across a globally distributed enterprise. Specifically, Whirlpool designates "i-mentors" and trains them in innovation and deploys them throughout the organization to identify promising new product ideas. [4]Similarly, General Mills has two "innovation squads" to harvest ideas from outside and inside the company, respectively. The cross-functional squads consist of six to eight company veterans with between fifteen and twenty-five years of experience. These people hunt for good business ideas and present them to division heads. The squads also give their top-ten ideas to the company chairman once a quarter. For example, one squad found a patent that had been donated to a university. The patent pertained to a new method for encapsulating calcium. The squad converted it into a very successful new product line of orange juice with added calcium that doesn't taste chalky. [5]

Did You Know?

Between 1975 and 2005, the percentage of R&D sites located outside the markets of their corporate headquarters has risen from 45 percent to 66 percent. [6]

Deciding Where to Locate R&D Activities

As we saw in the above example, HP is locating R&D labs in the countries for which it wants to develop new products. Another strategy is to locate the R&D center in a location known to be an innovation hub.

The concept of an innovation hub is based on Harvard Business School Professor Michael Porter's concept of clusters, which he defined in his book *The Competitive Advantage of Nations*. A cluster is defined as "a geographic concentration of business initiatives, suppliers and associated institutions in a particular field." [7] This particular model of location advantage is summarized in Figure 13.1 "Determinants of Location Advantages". For example, Silicon Valley in California is a cluster for technology companies that have located (or were founded) there. The partnerships and cross-pollination of ideas among the companies created new high-tech businesses whose success in turn brought venture capitalists (VCs) there. VCs looked for new ideas to fund, which led to more high-tech start-ups, thus stimulating even further innovation and new business creation.

Strategy consulting firm McKinsey & Company partnered with the World Economic Forum to evaluate what makes a given region an innovation hub. McKinsey analyzed 700

variables, including business environment, government and regulation, human capital, infrastructure, and local demand. [8] An innovation hub includes universities, government research institutes or labs, and corporate R&D centers. The purpose of the collocation is to create a dense social network. Geographic proximity promotes repeated interactions among people and thus builds trust among the people; companies compete intensely with each other but at the same time they learn from each other about changing markets and technologies. [9]

Innovation hubs usually have a specific industry focus, which can be anything from footwear to technology to life sciences. Let's take a look at examples that make this concept clearer. Zhongguancun is a technology district in northwestern Beijing known as "the Silicon Valley of China." [10] Within a one-mile area are China's top two universities, Tsinghua University and Peking University. Also in the area is Tsinghua Science Park and Shanghai Science and Technology Center. American high-tech company EMC located an R&D facility in this area to be in close proximity to the university talent and encourage some of them to work for EMC. EMC located another R&D center in Bangalore, India, in the Marathahalli-area innovation hub that's home to the R&D centers of IBM, Oracle, HP, Cisco, and Google; it is also home to the India Institute of Management, a university ranked among the top business schools in the world. Cisco's R&D center in Bangalore has 1,400 employees, and Cisco invested $750 million in R&D in India. [11] Illustrating Banerjee's point, however, is that despite all the high-tech companies in the Bangalore area, employees still have to stop their cars for cattle crossing the highway. [12]

The single common factor that drives innovation across all sectors is the availability of a well-qualified talent pool. Talent attracts talent, creating a reinforcing success cycle. People go to work where the work is exciting. If one location has a concentration of R&D labs, universities, and government research facilities, high-caliber people will be attracted to that location.

Hubs are known for the cross-pollination of ideas that takes place when employees of one firm talk with employees of another simply because of their proximity and frequenting the same local restaurants, events, or transportation stops. A specific phenomenon that occurs with this proximity is knowledge spillover. That is, knowledge can "spill over" as locals talk with one another; through those conversations, employees are more likely to understand each other's innovations and build on them. For example, Adam Jaffe and his colleagues analyzed the prior patents that a firm cited when applying for a new patent. [13] Jaffe and his colleagues found that, after controlling for other factors, the cited patents were five to ten times more likely to come from other firms in the same metropolitan area. People were casually sharing and building on each other's ideas. Jaffe's finding also explains why it's harder to take advantage of foreign countries' knowledge if one is not located there: "culture geography and secrecy make knowledge harder to diffuse across international borders." [14]

Below is a graphic from the Global Innovation Index. The graphic shows the main enablers that encourage innovation to take place in a given country. These enablers are Human Capacity, General and ICT (information and communication technology) Infrastructure, Market Sophistication, and Business Sophistication. On the right-hand side are the outputs of innovation—namely, scientific papers, patents, and new products and creative works. Companies evaluate the following things when choosing among countries in which to locate R&D facilities:

- A nation's institutions (the political and regulatory environment)
- A nation's investment in education
- A nation's ICT infrastructure
- The sophistication of the market (access to investors and credit)
- Business sophistication (the innovation ecosystem and openness to competition)

KEY TAKEAWAYS

- In the past, companies centralized R&D activities into one R&D center located in the same country as the company's headquarters. Now, that model is being replaced by a network of R&D clusters located in innovation hubs in the countries where a company hopes to grow its business.

- Innovation hubs are geographic locations that have universities, research labs, and corporate R&D centers clustered together. Proximity attracts the best workers and stimulates innovation through the cross-pollination of ideas. Employees are exposed to new ideas, and knowledge "spills over" during the everyday interactions of employees, university professors, and students.

- Countries and regions vary systematically in their levels of innovation, but governments can encourage innovation by supporting the pillars that enable innovation—namely, Institutions, Human Capacity, General and ICT (information and communication technology) Infrastructure, Market Sophistication, and

Business Sophistication. The Global Innovation Index shows the level of innovation of any country.

EXERCISES

(AACSB: Reflective Thinking, Analytical Skills)

1. Why might the level of innovation vary across countries and regions?
2. What factors would you examine when deciding where to locate an R&D center?
3. Discuss the advantages and disadvantages of organizing corporate R&D into a network of globally distributed R&D centers.
4. How might governments or companies go about encouraging the creation of innovation hubs in a specific region?
5. Do you think that communication technologies enabled by the Internet will influence knowledge spillover? Why or why not?

[1] Thomas Goldbrunner, Yves Doz, and Keeley Wilson, "The Well-Designed Global R&D Network," Strategy and Business, May 30, 2006, accessed January 2, 2011, http://www.strategy-business.com/article/06217?gko=0a6cc.

[2] "Wedding Innovation with Business Value: An Interview with the Director of HP Labs Prith Banerjee," McKinsey Quarterly, February 1, 2010, accessed January 2, 2011, https://www.mckinseyquarterly.com/Strategy/Innovation/Wedding_innovation_with_business_value_An_interview_with_the_director_of_HP_Labs_2522.

[3] Thomas Goldbrunner, Yves Doz, and Keeley Wilson, "The Well-Designed Global R&D Network," Strategy and Business, May 30, 2006, accessed January 10, 2011, http://www.strategy-business.com/article/06217?gko=0a6cc.

[4] Jessie Scanlon, "How Whirlpool Puts New Ideas through the Wringer," Businessweek, August 3, 2009, accessed January 17, 2011, http://www.businessweek.com/innovate/content/aug2009/id2009083_452757.htm.

[5] Peter Erickson, "Innovating on Innovation" (keynote presentation at the Front End of Innovation Conference, Boston, MA, May 2009); MIT Center for Transportation and Logistics, "Future Capabilities in the Supply Chain" (presentation in Cambridge, MA, May 8, 2007).

[6] Thomas Goldbrunner, Yves Doz, and Keeley Wilson, "The Well-Designed Global R&D Network," Strategy and Business, May 30, 2006, accessed January 2, 2011, http://www.strategy-business.com/article/06217?gko=0a6cc.

[7] Juan A. Bertolin, "Convoy Model: The Dynamic Perspective of Porter's Cluster Model," Innovation Management, December 8, 2010, accessed March 10, 2011, http://www.innovationmanagement.se/2010/12/08/convoy-model-the-dynamic-perspective-of-porters-cluster-model.

[8] André Andonian, Christoph Loos, and Luiz Pires, "Building an Innovation Nation," McKinsey & Company: What Matters, March 4, 2009, accessed February 24, 2011, http://whatmatters.mckinseydigital.com/innovation/building-an-innovation-nation.

[9] AnnaLee Saxenian, Regional Advantage (Cambridge, MA: Harvard University Press, 1994), 2–3, 161.

[10] Steve Todd, Innovate with Global Influence (Bangor, ME: Booklocker.com, 2010), 9.

[11] "The New Geography of Global Innovation," Innovation Management, September 20, 2010, accessed February 26, 2011, http://www.innovationmanagement.se/wp-content/uploads/2010/10/The-new-geography-of-global-innovation.pdf.

[12] Steve Todd, Innovate with Global Influence (Bangor, ME: Booklocker.com, 2010), 13.

[13] Adam Jaffe, Manuel Trajtenberg, and Rebecca Henderson, "Geographic Localization of Knowledge Spillovers as Evidenced by Patent Citations," Quarterly Journal of Economics 108, no. 3: 577–98.

[14] Erik Brynjolfsson and Adam Saunders, Wired for Innovation (Cambridge, MA: MIT Press, 2010), 99.

13.4 Increasing Speed and Effectiveness of International Innovation

LEARNING OBJECTIVES

1. Know the difference between product innovation and process innovation.
2. Describe the ways in which open innovation and innovation contests improve innovation outcomes.
3. Understand how businesses encourage intrapreneurs to contribute to the company's innovation efforts.

Process Innovations

We typically think of new products and services as the innovation output of investments in research and development (R&D). However, a significant amount of innovation yields no new products or services, not because of R&D failure, but because the innovations are not related to a company's core processes. A process innovation is an innovation in the way a company does any process, such as taking a customer order. A process is defined as "a specific ordering of work activities across time and place, with a beginning and end, and clearly identified inputs and outputs." [1] Processes can be simple activities (e.g., filling out a travel expense report), longer processes (e.g., issuing an insurance policy), or a broad set of activities (e.g., inventory management and distributions). The broader the process, the more impact innovating that process will have. For example, UPS made a process change when designing the routes its drivers follow when making deliveries. The company's routes give preference to making right turns rather than left turns whenever possible. The reason is that right turns are easier, faster, and safer—and they save fuel compared to left turns. This "right turn" process innovation doesn't involve the customer, but it helps UPS operate more efficiently.

Open Innovation

Among the latest developments in corporate innovation is the concept of open innovation. Open innovation is the intentional leveraging of the research, ideas, or technologies of outsiders—that is, people or companies that are not part of the corporate entity—rather than relying solely on innovations that are generated from inside the company. Open innovation takes innovation beyond a company's R&D lab and lets customers and partners participate in the creation of new product and services.

Procter & Gamble (P&G) embarked on open innovation in 2001 with its Connect + Develop program. For example, the innovation of printing text or images on Pringles chips came about through P&G partnering with a professor in Italy who ran a small bakery and had invented a technology that used ink-jet techniques to print pictures on pastries. [2] P&G adopted the technology to work with potato chips and launched Pringles Prints (chips with images and text printed on them) at a fraction of the cost and time it would have taken to research and develop the technology internally. Since adopting open innovation 2001, P&G's innovation success rate has doubled, while its costs have decreased. [3]

Another example of open innovation is from Kraft Foods. When Irene Rosenfeld took over as CEO of Kraft Foods, she saw an anemic innovation pipeline. The company had 2,000 corporate R&D staff—scientists, engineers and chemists—but new products weren't flowing rapidly enough. [4] To solve the problem, she encouraged Kraft managers to reach out beyond corporate R&D and enlist the help of employees across the whole company, as well as suppliers and partners, to spur innovation. For example, Kraft runs an online "Innovate with Kraft" program whereby anyone can submit product ideas. The idea for Kraft's Bagel-fuls (frozen bagels prefilled with Philadelphia Cream Cheese), for instance, came unsolicited from a bagel supplier. The idea was a win-win for both companies: it solved some technical challenges that Kraft had faced in delivering a bagel-and-cheese combo, and it boosted the revenue of the bagel supplier.

Innovation Contests

One method by which a company can manage and run open innovation is to use a contest or "challenge" method. In the contest method, the company poses a challenge, such as a way "to drop large amounts Humanitarian food and water packages from an aircraft into populated areas such that there is no danger of falling objects (i.e., nonfood items) causing harm to those on the ground" and offers a financial reward to the person, company, or team that solves the problem first. [5]

Companies can run their own open innovation contests, or they can use a third-party provider like InnoCentive (which originated inside Eli Lilly and Company and was spun off as a separate company in 2005). InnoCentive runs contests via the web and has a community of more than 180,000 engineers, scientists, inventors, business professionals, and research organizations in 175 countries who regularly participate in its contests. Financial prizes as high as $1 million are awarded for the best solutions.

The advantages of the open innovation contest approach include the following:

1. Reduced cost of R&D because, rather than funding R&D projects that may fail, the contest approach pays the financial reward only after the solution is found. If no viable solution is found, the company does not pay the financial reward.

2. Faster product development time because multiple teams work on the project at the same time, with an incentive to be the first to develop a viable solution and thus win the prize.

3. Access to experts from around the world. The experts do not have to be employed by the firm but can still contribute an idea or solution. This gives a firm access to experts and talent which it couldn't afford to employ full time.

4. Bigger breakthroughs because experts in a different field can make an unusual connection. For example, InnoCentive's challenge to find a biomarker for ALS disease received a solution proposed by a dermatologist—someone completely outside the ALS research field but who had an idea for a low-cost testing method.

The contest method has had such success that now the US government also uses this approach to reward innovative solutions. See http://challenge.gov for the list of challenges that the government is running.

Role of Intrapreneurship in Corporate Innovation

Large multinationals that have R&D centers also look for other ways to encourage innovation and new ideas. One effective way to stimulate innovation is to devise ways for intrapreneurs to contribute their ideas. Let's look at how one multinational, Shell, does this. Despite spending over $1 billion annually on R&D, Shell also runs a small program called GameChanger to foster radically innovative ideas. Started in 2006, GameChanger is a program to which any Shell employee anywhere in the world can contribute an idea for a product, project, or service. The program is open to nonemployees as well, making it an example of open innovation. Interestingly, about 70 percent of the proposed projects include at least one person who is not a Shell employee. (The nonemployee is typically someone associated with a university.) [6] Under the GameChanger program, a team of experts evaluates all the submitted ideas. Ideas that look promising are awarded funding of $15,000 to $25,000 so that the person who submitted the idea can expand on the proposal, possibly developing a prototype and attracting collaborators. [7] Ideas that pass the next screening by a broader group of experts get funded to the tune of $500,000 to $1 million for a year. After that, the idea may be further developed by a Shell business, spun off as a separate company, or sold to another company. [8]

Did You Know?

Did you know that the best people to run a new idea may be those who have the most passion for it? That's what retailer Best Buy's CMO believes. He encourages the intrapreneurial spirit by letting employees self-select the projects they want to work on and letting those with the most passion for the idea run it: "The Loop [a market prediction tool developed internally at Best Buy] is run by retail operations. They have the passion for it so they run it. Typically at Best Buy one of the ideas is if you've got passion then you may be best suited to take it on regardless of what organization you're in because you have point of view." [9]

User-Led Innovation

The precursor to open innovation was the concept of user-led innovation, first identified by MIT professor Eric von Hippel. Von Hippel noticed that many breakthrough innovations don't come out of a company's lab but rather from the lead users of the company's products. In some cases, the lead users even precede a company. For example, von Hippel says that skateboards were the invention of people who took their roller skates and hammered a piece of board between them. [10] Companies later saw the popularity of the invention and took over the refinement and manufacture of skateboards. Similarly, von Hippel says, M-Pesa did not invent mobile banking. Rather, it saw people in Africa buying minutes for their cell phones and then transferring those minutes to relatives in lieu of money. M-Pesa made the process systematic so that money could be transferred between people who didn't already have a relationship with each other—namely, for business. [11]

Social Networks

One of the features common to both open innovation and user-led innovation is the important and integral role played by social networks. A social network is a social structure made of nodes (which are generally individuals or organizations) that are connected by ties. In other words, it's a set of relationships among people. Your social network is the structure of personal and professional relationships you have with others. Social capital, in turn, is the resources—such as ideas, information, money, and trust—that you're able to access and influence through your social network. While social networks and social capital can be associated with many things, they're particularly important sources of innovation.

In a typical company, innovation relies on a handpicked team leading an innovation project. The trouble is that these teams often have no good way of tapping the expertise of the whole company. They tend to call on the small circle of colleagues they know or on the acknowledged experts in an established field. But such teams often have a hard time identifying people they don't already know but who might have knowledge relevant to the problem at hand. As a result, potential good ideas are lost or hidden—they remain inside the heads of unknown employees. That's where social software tools come in handy. With social software tools, a company can start a discussion on a topic and employees who know about the topic self-identify by posting ideas, refining the ideas of others, and voting on ideas. That is, employees don't need to be "found" by the innovation team. They can post ideas and thus self-identify and demonstrate their knowledge. For example, a company could start a discussion like "Can we develop a new water-filtration product?" People from market research might identify the top-selling filtration products. Someone from human resources who recently bought a water-filtration system for her family might contribute her own insights gathered from what blogs and outside websites were saying about all the competing products (e.g., "Brand B is bad because it's difficult to install"). Other employees might point out the engineering deficits of a proposed technology, such as that a potential filter material is too expensive for consumer water filters. Another person might have good suggestions for how to solve the cost problem (e.g., to coat the expensive filter ingredient on a cheaper material). The point is that with the help of social networking tools, these contributions can come from any employee, not just the handpicked team members and their inner circle. [12]

Software tools that promote social networking are even more important when companies expand internationally, because it will be hard for innovation teams to personally know all the employees who could contribute innovative ideas. With enterprise-wide social networking tools, these employees can self-identify.

KEY TAKEAWAYS

- A process innovation is a new way of doing things—the implementation of a new or significantly improved activity or set of activities. This includes significant changes in techniques, equipment, or software.

- Open innovation allows people outside a company—including university researchers, experts, suppliers, and partners—to contribute ideas and solutions for new products or services. One open innovation method is the holding of contests to solicit solutions and pay rewards for those solutions.

- Open innovation approaches save companies money: companies pay only for results, not for attempts that fail. Open innovation also saves time because concurrent teams work on solving the problem.

- Companies encourage intrapreneurs to propose new ideas and solutions, rewarding them with seed money to develop and grow their ideas.

- User-led innovation, identified by Eric von Hippel, shows how breakthrough innovations can originate from outside the research and development (R&D) lab, coming from users who are passionate about an idea.

- Social networks and social media technology enable innovative ideas to be shared and discussed by employees at all levels.

EXERCISES

(AACSB: Reflective Thinking, Analytical Skills)

1. How are process innovations similar to but different from product innovations?
2. What are the advantages and disadvantages of open innovation?
3. How are open innovation and user-led innovation distinct from ways R&D and innovation were managed in the past?
4. How might a company encourage intrapreneurs to contribute innovative ideas?
5. What benefits do companies gain by using open innovation contests?

[1] Thomas Davenport, Process Innovation (Cambridge, MA: Harvard Business School Press, 1993), 5.

[2] Stefan Lindegaard, The Open Innovation Revolution (New York: John Wiley & Sons, 2010), 9.

[3] Larry Huston and Nabil Sakkab, "Connect and Develop," Harvard Business Review 84, no. 3 (March 2006), accessed January 2, 2011, http://hbr.org/2006/03/connect-and-develop/ar/1.

[4] Andrea Meyer, "Kraft: The '$40 Billion Start-Up' Spurs Innovation," Working Knowledge (blog), October 7, 2009, accessed February 27, 2011, http://workingknowledge.com/blog/?p=878.

[5] "Humanitarian Air Drop Challenge," InnoCentive, March 2, 2011, accessed March 4, 2011, https://gw.innocentive.com/ar/challenge/overview/9932741.

[6] "Boston Consulting Group, Simulation Advantage," Boston Consulting Group, accessed February 26, 2011, http://www.bcg.com/documents/file57197.pdf.

[7] Russell Conser, "Shell GameChanger: Space to Free the Mind," Innosight 6, no. 4 (July–August 2008), accessed January 2, 2011, http://www.innosight.com/innovation_resources/article.html?id=628.

[8] Wendel Broere, "Sparking the Spirit of Innovation," July 13, 2007, accessed January 17, 2011, http://www.shell.com/home/content/innovation/innovative_thinking/game_changer/sparking_innovation/.

[9] Francois Gossieaux and Ed Moran, The Hyper-Social Organization (New York: McGraw-Hill, 2010), 178.

[10] Haydn Shaughnessy, "Eric Von Hippel on Innovation," Innovation Management, February 21, 2011, accessed February 25, 2011,http://www.innovationmanagement.se/2011/02/21/eric-von-hippel-on-innovation/?utm_source=Subscribers+InnovationManagement.se&utm_campaign=2780c497a9-Five+Steps+to+Profitable+Innovation&utm_medium=email.

[11] Haydn Shaughnessy, "Eric Von Hippel on Innovation," Innovation Management, February 21, 2011, accessed February 25, 2011,http://www.innovationmanagement.se/2011/02/21/eric-von-hippel-on-innovation/?utm_source=Subscribers+InnovationManagement.se&utm_campaign=2780c497a9-Five+Steps+to+Profitable+Innovation&utm_medium=email.

[12] Andrea Meyer, "Using Social Media to Improve Corporate Innovation," Working Knowledge (blog), accessed March 4, 2011, http://workingknowledge.com/blog/?p=578.

13.5 Innovation for the Bottom of the Pyramid

LEARNING OBJECTIVES

1. Understand the nature and size of BOP markets.
2. Know examples of firms pursuing BOP strategies.
3. Be conversant with the twelve principles of BOP innovation.

Contemporary View of BOP

In 1998, Professors C. K. Prahalad and Stuart L. Hart defined the bottom of the pyramid (BOP) as the billions of people living on less than $2 per day. Both men expanded this definition of BOP in their subsequent writing (e.g., Prahalad's *The Fortune at the Bottom of the Pyramid* in 2004 and Hart's *Capitalism at the Crossroads* in 2005). [1] The BOP is estimated to comprise between four billion and five billion people.

Too Good to Be True?

Professor Aneel Karnani at the University of Michigan argues that the BOP proposition is indeed too good to be true. "It is seductively appealing, but it is riddled with fallacies. There is neither glory nor fortune at the bottom of the pyramid—it is all a mirage." [2] He argues that the BOP proposition is logically flawed and is not supported by empirical evidence. He proposes an alternative approach for the private sector to alleviate poverty by viewing the poor as producers, not consumers. This shift in view, Karnani argues, is the way to alleviate poverty by raising the incomes of the poor.

In Prahalad and Hart's view, companies that understand the potential for commercial consumption at the BOP can open a new, potentially lucrative market that benefits the business as well as BOP consumers. By innovating to meet the needs of BOP customers, a company treats them with dignity and respect that previously was afforded only to the wealthy, Prahalad and Hart say.

Twelve Principles of BOP Innovation

Addressing the bottom of the pyramid requires a fresh managerial mind-set, summarized below in Prahalad's "12 Principles of BOP Innovation"—which are innovations themselves. [3] In developed markets, Prahalad suggests that one may take the availability of electricity, telephones, credit, refrigeration, and other such amenities for granted. At the BOP, the infrastructure is much spottier and more hostile. Consumers may have to cope with frequent electric-power blackouts and brownouts. Credit may be extremely costly. Refrigeration may be unavailable. Products marketed to the bottom of the pyramid must be able to withstand such an environment.

Below are Prahalad's "12 Principles of BOP Innovation," along with examples of each.

1. **Focus on value and on delivering performance for the price.** The BOP consumer isn't interested merely in cheap prices but in getting the greatest possible performance for the price paid. It's extraordinary how low a price can be and still be highly profitable, if the seller is organized to deliver value. For example, doctors at India's Aravind Eye Care System, the world's largest eye-care business, perform hundreds of thousands of cataract surgeries each year. The prices range from $50 to $300 per surgery, including the hospital stay. Aravind is quite profitable, although 60 percent of its patients pay nothing.

2. **Innovate.** Old technologies can't solve the problems of BOP consumers, and products aimed at the BOP market can't simply be watered-down versions of developed-world products. Instead, products must be rethought to bring radically lower cost while at the same time having features that meet the BOP's highest needs. For example, Hindustan Unilever Limited (HUL), a Unilever subsidiary, developed a new molecular encapsulation

technology to prevent iodized salt from losing its iodine before consumption. To test the efficacy of the technology, the researchers used radioactive tracing techniques pioneered by the Indian Atomic Energy Commission.

3. **Make the solution scalable.** When delivering high performance at affordable prices, profits must be generated through volume sales. The product itself must be low cost, but with four billion to five billion BOP customers across the world, scaling the operation is what will make the venture sustainable. Solutions should be scalable across borders.

4. **Aim to conserve resources.** BOP consumers cannot afford to waste resources. Per capita water consumption in the United States is almost 2,000 cubic meters per year, compared to less than 500 in China and less than 700 in India. The developed world's high standard of living is a water- and waste-intensive lifestyle. Innovations should emphasize conserving resources, recycling materials, and eliminating waste. Creating products for five billion people means designing the products in ways that can be environmentally sustainable. China's focus on electric cars rather than gasoline-powered cars reflects the reality that it's unlikely China could obtain the oil it would need for that many cars and that its extremely polluted cities could handle the additional exhaust fumes.

5. **Identify functionality.** BOP customers likely require different functionality than high-end consumers. For example, prosthetic legs developed for India's BOP consumers needed to meet some special requirements: consumers needed to be able to squat, sit cross-legged, and walk on rough ground. Dr. Pramod Karan Sethi and Ram Chandra developed the Jaipur Foot prosthetic for this purpose. The charity Bhagwan Mahaveer Viklang Sahayata Samiti, which is based in Jaipur, India, made them available for less than $30. [4]

6. **Think in terms of process innovations.** One way to bring costs down dramatically is to standardize processes. That's how Aravind is able to bring down the costs of cataract surgery so dramatically. Aravind made the process highly standardized and trained young village women to prepare patients and handle postoperative care. Thus doctors focus exclusively on surgery and perform only cataract surgery—nothing else. This focused process lets one doctor and two technicians perform fifty surgeries per day.

7. **Reduce the skills required to do the job.** Design products and services suitable to people without skills. Voxiva, a Peruvian start-up, developed a system enabling health-care workers to diagnose illnesses such as smallpox by comparing a patient's lesions to a picture of a similar lesion. With this simplified diagnostic process, health-care workers don't require great skills to know when to call a doctor.

8. **Educate consumers in the use of products.** This may require collaborating with nongovernmental organizations (NGOs), governments, and others. HUL launched a program in some of India's village schools to promote the washing of hands with soap as a way to prevent the childhood diarrhea that kills two million children per year. HUL educated the children, who in turn educated their parents.

9. **Design products and services to operate in very tough infrastructure environments.** For example, when Indian conglomerate ITC built a network connecting Indian villages, it had to provide personal computers that could handle wide voltage fluctuations. ITC included surge suppressors and solar panels to give the system adequate, reliable electricity.

10. **Make the interface simple and the learning curve short.** In Mexico, the chain retailer Elektra uses automated teller machines (ATMs) with a fingerprint identification system so BOP consumers don't have to remember lengthy identification codes.

11. **Innovate in distribution.** Avon has built a Brazilian direct-sales business that delivers revenues of $1.7 billion annually.

12. **Challenge assumptions.** The Jaipur Foot and Aravind Eye Care System hospitals defy conventional wisdom about how (and at what price) it's possible to deliver health care to the poor.

Ethics in Action

NextBillion.net began as an initiative of the World Resources Institute's Markets and Enterprise Program. The name refers to the next billion people to rise from the bottom of the pyramid into the middle class and connotes the next billion in profits that companies can make serving this market. The purpose of the site is to provide a source for news, analysis, research and discussion on development through enterprise and BOP ideas. In addition, the NextBillion.net website has a career center that posts jobs (consulting projects as well as full-time jobs and academic appointments). As the site states, its mission is to "highlight the development and implementation of business strategies that open opportunities and improve the lives of the world's approximately 4 billion low-income producers and consumers." [5]

KEY TAKEAWAYS

- The BOP (or bottom-of-the-pyramid) market refers to the four billion to five billion people living on less than $2 per day.

- When businesses get involved in BOP economies, they can stimulate the creation of new services and products. Though there is some debate as to whether the goal should be to innovate and sell to the BOP or to engage the BOP markets as the source of innovation, all parties agree that engagement with BOP economies is desired and productive.

EXERCISES

(AACSB: Reflective Thinking, Analytical Skills)

1. Why are businesses interested in BOP markets?
2. What are some examples of products developed to profitably serve BOP markets?
3. What are some of the challenges of serving BOP markets?
4. In what ways might BOP markets be a source of innovation?
5. What are some examples of innovations derived from the BOP?

[1] C. K. Prahalad, The Fortune at the Bottom of the Pyramid (Upper Saddle River, NJ: Wharton School Publishing, 2004); Stuart L. Hart, Capitalism at the Crossroads (Upper Saddle River, NJ: Wharton School Publishing, 2005).
[2] Aneel Karnani, "Fortune at the Bottom of the Pyramid: A Mirage," Ross School of Business Working Paper Series, Working Paper No. 1035, July 2006, accessed February 12, 2011, http://deepblue.lib.umich.edu/bitstream/2027.42/41223/5/1035-Karnani_OLD.pdf.
[3] C. K. Prahalad, The Fortune at the Bottom of the Pyramid (Upper Saddle River, NJ: Wharton School Publishing, 2004), 25–27.
[4] Tim McGirk, "The $28 Foot," Time, accessed May 11, 2011, http://www.time.com/time/reports/heroes/foot.html.
[5] "About NextBillion," NextBillion, accessed May 11, 2011, http://www.nextbillion.net/about.

13.6 End-of-Chapter Questions and Exercises

These exercises are designed to ensure that the knowledge you gain from this book about international business meets the learning standards set out by the international Association to Advance Collegiate Schools of Business (AACSB International). [1] AACSB is the premier accrediting agency of collegiate business schools and accounting programs worldwide. It expects that you will gain knowledge in the areas of communication, ethical reasoning, analytical skills, use of information technology, multiculturalism and diversity, and reflective thinking.

EXPERIENTIAL EXERCISES

(AACSB: Communication, Use of Information Technology, Analytical Skills)

1. Visit the websites of several corporations (e.g., General Electric, Procter & Gamble, and Unilever) that you believe may be trying to innovate with R&D operations in one of the BRIC emerging markets. Do you see any common patterns in how they discuss this strategy? Do they make any statements about intellectual property rights?

2. Each year Cornell University's Center for Sustainable Global Enterprise sponsors a BOP-themed essay competition. (Visit the competition's website at http://www.johnson.cornell.edu/Center-for-Sustainable-Global-Enterprise.aspx.) The goal is to "highlight the challenges of implementing business in underserved markets and identify innovative business initiatives or solutions to those challenges." [2] The awards range from $500 to $4,000, and winners are recognized on NextBillion.net. Review the winning essays and, individually or with a team, identify the basis for your own essay. Draft a short summary (approximately five hundred words) of it and share it with the class.

3. Search YouTube for "bottom of the pyramid." You'll find several videos by C. K. Prahalad (e.g., http://www.youtube.com/watch?v=79JOHMrs8m4y and the Maastricht series starting with http://www.youtube.com/watch?v=VJUjzT--HUk). Beyond these videos, what other resources did you find? Poverty is likely to exist in most communities and not just developing economies. What opportunities in the BOP market exist in your community?

Ethical Dilemmas

(AACSB: Ethical Reasoning, Multiculturalism, Reflective Thinking, Analytical Skills)

1. In 1998, Nike launched the World Shoe Project, which is a line of footwear targeted and designed exclusively for emerging markets in Asia, Africa, and Latin America. By January 2001, Tom Hartge and his team at Nike had sold only 404,520 pairs of World Shoes in China. One year later, even though the Nike CEO at the time, Phil Knight, remained a supporter, the World Shoe Project was "alive in spirit only." [3] Part of the explanation for this state of affairs was that Nike expected the same profit margins on products regardless of markets. Should successful companies like Nike be expected to earn lower profits in emerging markets as a way to "give back" to society?

2. What are some of the ethical concerns that come to mind for companies seeking to sell to the BOP? Review the Wikipedia entry on the Nestlé boycott (http://en.wikipedia.org/wiki/Nestlé_boycott) to see if you've identified and addressed all the ethical concerns raised in that case in your answer.

[1] Association to Advance Collegiate Schools of Business website, accessed January 26, 2010, http://www.aacsb.edu.

[2] "BOP Competition," Cornell University Johnson Graduate School of Management, accessed February 12, 2011, http://www.johnson.cornell.edu/Center-for-Sustainable-Global-Enterprise.aspx.

[3] Heather McDonald and Ted London, "Expanding the Playing Field: Case B: Nike's World Shoe Project," World Resources Institute Case Study, 2002.

NOTES:

NOTES:

Chapter 14:
Competing Effectively through Global Marketing, Distribution, and Supply-Chain Management

Best Global Brands
2009 Rankings

2009 Rank	2008 Rank	Brand	Country of Origin	Sector	2009 Brand Value ($m)	Change in Brand Value
1	1	Coca-Cola	United States	Beverages	68,434	3%
2	2	IBM	United States	Computer Services	60,211	2%
3	3	Microsoft	United States	Computer Software	56,647	−4%
4	4	GE	United States	Diversified	47,777	−10%
5	5	NOKIA	Finland	Consumer Electronics	34,864	−3%
6	8	[McDonald's]	United States	Restaurants	32,275	4%
7	10	Google	United States	Internet Services	31,980	25%

WHAT'S IN IT FOR ME?

1. What are the fundamentals of global marketing?
2. What are the trade-offs between standardized and customized products and promotions?
3. What are the fundamentals of distribution?
4. How does international distribution differ from purely domestic distribution?
5. What are the international aspects of supply-chain management?

In this chapter, you'll learn the "hows" of global marketing, distribution, and supply-chain management. Specifically, you'll see how companies decide which products to market internationally, how to source and distribute those products, and how to manage operations for smooth operation throughout the company's supply chain.

The chapter opens with a case study on Yum! Brands' entry into China with KFC restaurants. After initial missteps, Yum! Brands and KFC have had great success and are now pondering ways to sustain that success. In Section 14.1

"Fundamentals of Global Marketing", you'll learn the fundamentals of marketing in an international context. If the world were truly flat, then it would be easy to sell a product or service that is popular in one setting in another country setting with little additional work. However, because the world is not truly flat in terms of culture, administration, geography, and economics (i.e., CAGE), firms must make choices as to how they adapt to or avoid international markets. You'll see how companies like Starbucks adapt and innovate in different markets, how integrated-circuit maker Intel deals with the difficulties of counterfeit markets, and how entertainment giant Bertelsmann makes decisions in emerging markets. You'll also get a glimpse of how consumers in BRIC countries (i.e., Brazil, Russia, India, and China) differ and the special challenges of marketing products to countries where incomes are low.

You'll be following along as companies like Nokia make decisions about whether to adapt products to specific markets. You'll see the innovations that Procter & Gamble and General Electric create as they develop products for BRIC countries and how these innovations earn them additional benefits back home in developed markets. You'll learn how to avoid the pitfalls that trapped Ford Motor Company, and you'll see the entrepreneurial approaches to distribution management that Unilever created. Section 14.4 "Global Sourcing and Distribution" will highlight the difference between outsourcing and offshoring and the advantages and disadvantages they bring. Finally, Section 14.5 "Global Production and Supply-Chain Management" will demonstrate the value of an integrated approach to supply-chain management.

OPENING CASE: COLONEL SANDERS IS NO CHICKEN!

Kentucky Fried Chicken (KFC) was the first American fast-food restaurant to enter China, opening its first outline there in 1987 in Beijing. [1] KFC's US archrival, McDonald's, didn't open a restaurant in China until 1990. [2]Despite initial marketing mistakes—like its "finger lickin' good" slogan being mistranslated into Chinese characters that meant "eat your fingers off"—the company grew and thrived. [3] Today, KFC has 2,872 restaurants in China, which generate over $2 billion in sales for its parent company, Yum! Brands. [4]

The main factor contributing to KFC's success in China is its localization strategy. Let's see how KFC did it.

When KFC first entered the Chinese market, Chinese law stipulated that foreign companies could only operate in China if they had a local partner. KFC selected partners who had connections to government, so that it could benefit from their resources and contacts. [5] KFC learned a lot from its local partners, and once joint ventures were no longer required, KFC chose a leadership team that knew Chinese culture intimately. Rather than sending expatriates to China to lead the expansion, for example, KFC selected people who had "an understanding of China and the Chinese cultural context 'so deep that it is intuitive,' to understand the Chinese people's 'mixed feelings, of love and hate about the West, to understand Chinese history, language, the influence of Confucianism, Buddhism and Taoism, this is especially important if you are in the consumer goods industry,'" said Warren Liu, former vice president of development at KFC China and author of the book KFC in China: Secret Recipe for Success. [6] This leadership team recommended that KFC follow a strategy of localization: offering local Chinese food options on the menu to appeal to local tastes. For example, instead of serving coleslaw, KFC offers bamboo shoots and lotus roots. Likewise, it sells a sandwich in the style that Peking duck is served, simply substituting fried chicken for the duck. [7] The extent of KFC's product localization is extensive, from preserved Sichuan pickle and shredded pork soup to a Chinese-style porridge called congee for breakfast. [8]

KFC's promotional marketing is similarly steep in Chinese culture. As Yu Cui and Zhang Ting explain, "China is a society with relatively high collectivism, where people have a high sense of identity to the traditional culture and traditional food. Since the family members in China often share the similar value and most Chinese people consider that it is necessary to keep on the wonderful family traditions, such as respecting, loving and supporting the elderly, helping others, friendship between individuals and so on. Thus, many advertisements of KFC in recent years try to reveal the background of common Chinese families." [9]

KFC emphasizes speed and convenience rather than chicken. "Choosing to eat at fast food restaurants like KFC doesn't necessarily indicate a desire for Western flavors," said Sun Min, a local government official who eats at KFC because speed and convenience are his top priorities when choosing a place to eat. [10]

Selecting the right place or location for its outlets is also important for convenience, and KFC is opening stores at a pace of nearly one a day in China, to be close to wherever its customers are. [11] KFC also developed its distribution system quickly, right from the start, and its parent, Yum! Brands, owns those distribution centers. Owning its own distribution centers lets Yum! Brands grow it restaurants efficiently as it expands into 402 cities in China. [12]

For the future, David Novak, CEO of Yum! Brands (which owns Pizza Hut and Taco Bell in addition to KFC), said he envisions eventually having more than twenty thousand restaurants in China. "We're in the first inning of a nine-inning ball game in China," Novak told investors in a conference call in February 2010. [13]

OPENING CASE EXERCISES
(AACSB: Ethical Reasoning, Multiculturalism, Reflective Thinking, Analytical Skills)
1. Do you think that Yum's other restaurants—Pizza Hut and Taco Bell—would be successful in China? Why or why not? What would help them be more successful?
2. What advice would you give KFC about how to continue its growth in China?
3. How might KFC's presence in China help the restaurant in other markets?

[1] The Gale Group Inc., "KFC Corporation," International Directory of Company Histories, accessed December 19, 2010, http://www.answers.com/topic/kfc-corporation.

[2] Jennifer Lawinski, "KFC, Taco Bell a Hit for YUM! in China," Slashfood, July 15, 2010, accessed December 14, 2010, http://www.slashfood.com/2010/07/15/kfc-taco-bell-a-hit-for-yum-in-china/#ixzz16JzYnIBS.

[3] Carlye Adler, "Colonel Sanders' March on China," Time, November 17, 2003, accessed December 14, 2010, http://www.time.com/time/magazine/article/0,9171,543845,00.html.

[4] "Restaurant Counts: 2009 Q4 Restaurant Units Activity Summary," Yum! Brands, accessed December 14, 2010, http://www.yum.com/investors/restcounts.asp.

[5] Karen Cho, "KFC China's Recipe for Success," INSEAD, July 1, 2009, accessed December 14, 2010, http://knowledge.insead.edu/KFCinChina090323.cfm?vid=195.

[6] John Sexton, "KFC—'A Foreign Brand with Chinese Characteristics,'" China.org.cn, September 22, 2008, accessed December 14, 2010, http://www.china.org.cn/business/2008-09/22/content_16515747.htm.

[7] "Kentucky Fried China," MSNBC, January17, 2005, accessed December 14, 2010, http://www.msnbc.msn.com/id/6833233/ns/business-world_business.

[8] Aaron Hotfelder, "Why Does China Love KFC More Than McDonald's?" Gadling (blog), June 5, 2010, accessed December 14, 2010, http://www.gadling.com/2010/06/05/why-does-china-love-kfc-more-than-mcdonalds.

[9] Yu Cui and Zhang Ting, "American Fast Food in Chinese Market: A Cross-Cultural Perspective—The Case of KFC and McDonald's" (master's diss. in international marketing, University of Halmstad, Halmstad, Sweden, 2009), 41, accessed December 14, 2010, http://hh.diva-portal.org/smash/get/diva2:286121/FULLTEXT01.

[10] "Western Fast Food Giants Meet the Challenges of Local Culinary Preferences," Alibaba, June 9, 2009, accessed December 15, 2010, http://resources.alibaba.com/topic/531563/KFC_s_localization_strategy_in_China_.htm.

[11] Ben Rooney, "China: The New Fast Food Nation," CNN Money, July 14, 2010, accessed December 15, 2010, http://money.cnn.com/2010/07/13/news/companies/Yum_Brands/index.htm.

[12] "Yum! Execs Discuss China Strategy, Franchising and the Recent Minimum Wage Uproar," Seeking Alpha, May 6, 2007, accessed December 14, 2010, http://seekingalpha.com/article/34612-yum-execs-discuss-china-strategy-franchising-and-the-recent-minimum-wage-uproar.

[13] Samuel Shen, "Kentucky Fried Chicken Banks on China," New York Times, May 5, 2008, accessed December 14, 2010, http://www.nytimes.com/2008/05/05/business/worldbusiness/05iht-kfc.1.12567957.html?_r=1.

14.1 Fundamentals of Global Marketing

LEARNING OBJECTIVES

1. Understand the four Ps of marketing and how they differ in international marketing.
2. Know how to segment international markets.
3. Be able to explain how gray and counterfeit markets can be harmful to companies.

The Four Ps

As we saw in the opening case, KFC has had great success in China after a first failed attempt. Why did KFC try again after its first failure? For the same reason that most companies market their products globally. Specifically, companies expand internationally to reach more customers, gain higher profit opportunities, balance sales across countries in case one country experiences problems, and compete with other brands that are expanding internationally and with global firms in their home markets.

Reaching new consumers is often the main reason for international expansion. The rising standards of living in the developing world, especially BRIC countries (i.e., Brazil, Russia, India, and China) mean billions of new consumers. [1] In fact, 80 percent of the world's population lives in emerging-market countries. Companies based in the mature economies of the West are attracted by the potential for double-digit growth in emerging markets.

What is the best way to reach those international customers? You begin with the core of marketing knowledge—the four Ps—product, price, promotion, and place. While you likely learned this framework in your marketing class, it's important to recognize how this essential tool will help you think about marketing in the context of international business. In a flat world, the answers to questions about the four Ps are all the same; however, because the world isn't really that flat, country differences will have important implications for how product, price, promotion, and place play out when an organization takes its offerings across borders.

The first P—product—refers to any physical good or intangible service that's offered for sale. For example, the product could be physical, like a laser printer, or it could be a service, like printing or photocopying services. The product could also be access to information, such as stock-market reports. Given the differences between countries (e.g., language, culture, laws, and technology standards), a company's products may need to be adapted to different countries. Some products, like Coca-Cola or Starbucks coffee, need little, if any, modification. But even these companies create product variations to suit local tastes. For example, Starbucks introduced a green tea Frappuccino in China. The new flavor was very successful there. We'll learn more about product standardization and customization in the next section.

Did You Know?

Innovation at Starbucks

Annie Young-Scrivner, Starbucks's chief marketing officer, described her company's plans for innovation and international expansion. "We continue to have very solid plans for China," Young-Scrivner said. "As we expand outside of the U.S. and get more depth in [international] markets, we're finding lots of best practices and innovation that we can bring back. There are so many examples of creativity, like flat white [a milk and espresso beverage] in the U.K., black sesame [and] green tea Frappuccino in China. Green tea Frappuccino came from an international market and we launched it here. The local relevance became a tipping point for innovation in other markets for the brand." [2]

The second P—price—is the amount of money that the consumer pays for the product. Pricing can take different forms. For example, pricing can be by item (e.g., a can of corn), by volume (e.g., gasoline), by subscription (e.g., monthly cable service), by usage (e.g., cell-phone minutes), or by performance (e.g., paying more for overnight delivery versus two-day delivery).

Let's spend a little more time on price, because pricing has even more nuances when applied to international products. For example, emerging-market countries often have a less-developed financial system and limited credit available to local consumers and businesses. Some of the biggest challenges in selling to emerging markets involve making the product affordable. In Brazil, 26 percent of the population lives below the poverty line. However, companies have devised ways to help even the poorest consumers afford products. Let's see how Casas Bahia has succeeded in selling to the bottom-of-the-pyramid (BOP) consumers in Brazil.

Did You Know?

Casas Bahia—Selling to BOP Consumers
Some consumers in developing countries are very poor. Often called the *bottom of the pyramid (BOP)* on income scales, they are the four billion people who live on less than $2 a day. Would you market products to these people? Surprisingly, the answer may be yes in many instances. According to C. K. Prahalad, BOP consumers are a viable market segment to target. [3]The key is having the right market mix of product, price, promotion, and place. Let's see how it works.

Casas Bahia is a retailer in Brazil that sells appliances and furniture. It successfully sells to the BOP. In fact, 45 percent of its appliance and furniture products are sold to BOP consumers. First, consider *product*. You might think that a refrigerator is a luxury item for these consumers. In a tropical country like Brazil, however, a refrigerator becomes more of a necessity. Second, *price*: obviously, keeping costs low is key. Casas Bahia does this by buying products in huge volumes to

get huge discounts. It has built large warehouses capable of storing much more inventory than a typical retailer would, in order to handle the large volumes. But low prices alone are not enough, as Walmart learned in its failed expansion into Brazil. Indeed, 70 percent of Casas Bahia customers have no formal or consistent income. How are these customers able to pay for their purchases? Casas Bahia helps them by giving them a passbook—similar to a credit card but with important differences. First, Casas Bahia hires credit analysts and trains them extensively, so that they can accurately assess how much a customer can afford to pay. These credit analysts help steer a customer away from products that may be too expensive for them and instead suggest a more modest model. Second, unlike credit-card statements that come in the mail and are easy to ignore, customers must make passbook payments directly inside the Casas Bahia store. This direct approach builds a personal relationship between the customer and the friendly store employees. Rates of default on passbooks are much lower than they are on credit cards. To recap, many of Casas Bahia's *products* are seen as more of a necessity than a luxury. Low *prices* coupled with credit assessment and friendly employees encourage monthly payments. Selling in retail stores (*place*) reduces the need for external *promotions*, because customers return monthly to make payments, which gives Casas Bahia an opportunity to sell them additional products.

The third P—promotion—refers to all the activities that inform and encourage consumers to buy a given product. [4] Promotions include advertising (whether print, broadcast radio, television, online, billboard, poster, or mobile), coupons, rebates, and personal sales. Like products, promotions are often customized to a country to appeal to local sensibilities. One obvious mistake to avoid is a language translation that misses the nuances of native speakers. For example, a straight translation of Clairol's "Mist Stick" curling iron into German misses the nuance that "mist" in German is slang for manure. Likewise, Coors' "turn it loose" slogan, when translated into Spanish, is interpreted by some locals as "suffer from diarrhea." [5] Less obvious, but important to know, are the different countries' regulations affecting advertising. For example, as discussed in Chapter 8 "International Expansion and Global Market Opportunity Assessment", Section 8.2 "PESTEL, Globalization, and Importing", regulations in Germany prohibited discounts, free gifts, or money-back guarantees with purchase. When US clothier Lands' End expanded into Germany, it was taken to court for its guarantee that "If you're not satisfied with any item, simply return it to us at any time for an exchange or refund of its purchase price." Only recently have these

German laws been repealed to bring them in line with European Union laws. [6]

The final P—place—refers to the location at which a company offers its products for sale. The place could be a small kiosk in a village, a store in town, or an online website. Place poses a particular challenge when selling internationally. Many of the things we take for granted in the United States—national retailers, grocery stores, and extensive railways and roadways to reach them—aren't prevalent everywhere. Section 14.4 "Global Sourcing and Distribution" discusses how to overcome these challenges.

Products reach consumers through a channel of distribution, which is a series of firms or individuals who facilitate the movement of the product from the producer to the final consumer. The shortest channel, called the direct channel, consists of just the producer and the consumer. In this case, the consumer buys directly from the producer, such as when you buy an apple from a local farmer. An indirect channel, in contrast, contains one or more intermediaries between the consumer and the producer. These intermediaries include distributors, wholesalers, agents, brokers, and retailers. In international business, the number of intermediaries can expand due to the regulations affecting import and export across national boundaries. Agents, brokers, international freight forwarders, and trading companies may get involved. Then, once a company's product is in the foreign country, that country may have its own wholesalers who get involved. The firm must pay all these intermediaries for their services, which increases the cost of the product. Firms must raise prices or accept lower margins when confronting these added channel costs.

Even when sales are direct, as with Internet sales, place differences can affect marketing. For example, as mentioned previously, laws in Germany prohibit retailer Lands' End from advertising its unconditional money-back guarantee because returns are allowed only up to fourteen days. [7]

Ethics in Action

The Case of International Marketing
Major international marketing ethical problems derived from applied research are presented with their short definitions as follows:

- Traditional Small Scale Bribery—involves the payment of small sums of money, typically to a foreign official in exchange for him/her violating some official duty or responsibility or to speed routine government actions (grease payments, kickbacks).

- Large Scale Bribery—a relatively large payment intended to allow a violation of the law or designed to influence policy directly or indirectly (e.g., political contribution).
- Gifts/Favors/Entertainment—includes a range of items such as: lavish physical gifts, call girls, opportunities for personal travel at the company's expense, gifts received after the completion of transaction and other extravagant expensive entertainment.
- Pricing—includes unfair differential pricing, questionable invoicing—where the buyer requests a written invoice showing a price other than the actual price paid, pricing to force out local competition, dumping products at prices well below that in the home country, pricing practices that are illegal in the home country but legal in host country (e.g., price fixing agreements).
- Products/Technology—includes products and technology that are banned for use in the home country but permitted in the host country and/or appear unsuitable or inappropriate for use by the people of the host country.
- Tax Evasion Practices—used specifically to evade tax such as transfer pricing (i.e., where prices paid between affiliates and/or parent company adjusted to affect profit allocation) including the use of tax havens, where any profit made is in low tax jurisdiction, adjusted interest payments on intra-firm loans, questionable management and service fees charged between affiliates and /or the parent company.
- Illegal/Immoral Activities in the Host Country—practices such as: polluting the environment, maintaining unsafe working conditions; product/technology copying where protection of patents, trademarks or copyrights has not been enforced and short-weighting overseas shipments so as to charge a country a phantom weight.
- Questionable Commissions to Channel Members—unreasonably large commissions of fees paid to channel members, such as sales agents, middlemen, consultants, dealers and importers. [8]
- Cultural Differences—between cultures involving potential misunderstandings related to the traditional requirements of the exchange process (e.g., transactions) may be regarded by one culture as bribes but be acceptable business practices in another culture. These practices include: gifts, monetary payments, favors, entertainment and political contributions.
- Involvement in Political Affairs—related to the combination of marketing activities and politics

including the following: the exertion of political influence by multinationals, engaging in marketing activities when either home or host countries are at war and illegal technology transfers.

The Marketing Mix

The four Ps together form the marketing mix. Because the four Ps affect each other, marketers look at the mix of product, price, promotion, and place. They fine-tune and adjust each element to meet the needs of the market and to create the best outcome for the company. Promotion has an impact on the other Ps because a product's price, for example, may be lowered during a promotional event. Likewise, holding a special promotional event like a two-for-one deal on a product impacts place, because the company must ensure that it supplies stores with enough product to meet the anticipated demand. Finally, the promotion might affect the product's packaging, such as bundling a shampoo and conditioner together.

A company's marketing mix will often be different for different countries based on

- a country's culture and local preferences,
- a country's economic level,
- what a country's consumers can afford, and
- a country's distribution channels and media.

Market Segmentation

Market segmentation is the process of dividing a larger market into smaller markets that share a common characteristic. The characteristics might be demographics, such as segments divided by age groups (e.g., eighteen to twenty-four year-olds), genders, or household incomes. Segmentation can also be done on the basis of geographic location or by lifestyle (e.g., new moms of different ages might have more in common with each other than they have with identically aged nonmothers.) The purpose of segmentation is to give the company a concrete vision of its customers, so that it can better understand how to market to that customer. Segmentation helps companies target their marketing efforts more effectively.

For example, geographic segmentation is important for language differences. Sometimes, the segmentation must be done even more granularly than at the country level. Some parts of Mexico, for instance, don't use Spanish as the primary language. Because of this, Walmart Mexico's stores in Juchitán conduct business in the local Zapotec tongue. Its female employees wear traditional skirts, and the morning company cheer is in Zapotec. [9]

Each country may have its own cultural groups that divide the country or transcend national boundaries. For example, the northern coast of Colombia is culturally more similar to the Caribbean than it is to the interior of its own country because the Andes Mountains split the country into two regions: east and west. Historically, these regions had been cut off from each other.

Understanding Your Target Customers

Foreign markets are not just copies of US markets; they require products suitable to the local population. Although European and developed country markets are more similar to the United States, emerging markets like the BRIC countries have important differences. Products must meet local needs in terms of cost, quality, performance, and features and, in order to be successful, a company must be aware of the interplay between these factors. Let's look at consumers in emerging countries to get a feel for these differences.

Rising Middle Class

The number of middle-class people in emerging countries has been growing, partly because of Western companies hiring low-cost labor (directly or through outsourcing agreements) in these regions. Providing jobs in these countries has improved household incomes. These fast-rising incomes, especially in urban areas, create vast new pools of disposable income. Eight of the ten largest cities in the world are in emerging markets. Their populations are young, and they're just beginning to adopt the full range of consumer goods found in the developed world.

In some cases, these middle-class consumers will buy more expensive branded goods, if the brands resonate with the interests of the local crowd. Consider the relative sales ratio of $60 Nike basketball shoes versus $120 Yao Ming–branded Nike basketball shoes. In the United States, sales might be 20 percent for the higher priced shoe. In mainland China, it might be 5 percent for the Yao Ming shoe due to cost; but in more prosperous Hong Kong, the sales might be 50 percent for the shoes. [10] Middle-class populations are reading about Western goods and want branded items, but pricing can be an issue depending on the local level of affluence.

Millionaires Are Everywhere

Just because the average income is much lower in emerging markets doesn't mean that no one can afford high-end luxury goods. Some automobile manufacturers, for example, track the number of millionaires in the country as an indicator of the very affluent segment. By recent estimates, China has approximately 477,000 millionaires, [11] Brazil has approximately 143,000, [12] Russia has approximately 136,000, [13] and India has approximately 126,000. [14] These very high net-worth individuals explicitly want the same products that are sold in the West, not down-market versions. Specific cities in emerging-market countries may have a concentration of affluent consumers. In Monterrey, Mexico, for example, the costs of consumer goods are comparable to those of New York City.

Emerging Markets for Business Customers

Business-to-business (B2B) opportunities also abound, as emerging-market businesses grow to serve export or internal markets. Just as with consumers, businesses in emerging markets are different from developed markets. For example, companies in emerging markets may be smaller and less sophisticated and may have lower budgets than their Western counterparts. They may lack the level of automation and information technology that prevails in the developed world. This is especially true in the retail industry. Many developing countries have a predominance of small mom-and-pop stores.

Global Market Research

Global market research includes understanding the market's culture and social trends, because these factors impact which products consumers will like and which advertising appeals will resonate with them.

Some of the same techniques of market research used in the United States can be applied internationally. For example, Procter & Gamble (P&G) uses a variety of focus-group testing and in-home research to understand why people buy the products they buy. P&G researchers watch how consumers use products and ask about what features they might want in the future. The company has learned from past experience that just because a product sells well in one market doesn't imply that it will sell well in another market. For example, although Bounty paper towels sell well in the United States, the European launch of Bounty paper towels did well in only two of twelve markets. Why? P&G quickly learned that Germans found the entire concept of paper towels to be too wasteful and, therefore, didn't buy them.

Dealing with Gray and Counterfeit Markets

The gray market exists because of price discrepancies between different markets. For example, consumer packaged-goods companies may price their products higher in Austria than in the neighboring Czech Republic due to the Austrian citizens' higher income levels. As a result, Austrians might order their goods from Czech retailers and simply drive over the border to pick up the products. The goods in the Czech stores are legitimate and authentic, but the existence of this gray-market activity hurts the producer and their channel partners (e.g., distributors and retailers) in the higher-priced country.

In contrast to gray markets, which are legitimate but—legally—in a gray area, counterfeit markets purposely deceive the buyer. For example, counterfeiters slightly alter the Sony logo to Bony in a way that makes it hard to distinguish without careful inspection.

Counterfeit markets hurt companies that have invested in building intellectual assets such as unique product designs, technological developments, costly media content, and carefully crafted brands. Together, these intellectual assets represent an investment of millions or billions of dollars. If a company's product, technology, or brand is counterfeited, both the company's reputation and financial security suffers. All of its channel partners (i.e., distributors, retailers, and licensing partners) are affected as well. For example, an executive traveling in Hong Kong saw unique styles of Nike shoes. When he asked about them, he was told the shoes were only available in size nine. This fact led him to realize that the shoes were probably prototype samples from a local factory that had been smuggled out of the factory to be sold. Some industries have tried to limit the scope of the counterfeiting and copying of DVDs through regionalized encoding, but even this is too easy to circumvent. That's why musical and entertainment giant Bertelsmann avoids expansion into emerging-market countries that have lax enforcement of intellectual property rights.

Counterfeiters may also tamper with branded products. For example, Intel processor chips vary in price based on their processing speed: the higher the speed, the higher the price of the chip. Counterfeiters buy (or steal) low-end chips, repaint a few numbers on them, and then sell them as high-end chips. The high-end chips sell for $100 or $200 more than the low-end chips. Customers looking for a bargain may unwittingly buy these chips. For Intel, these remarked chips not only cannibalize sales of the higher-margin, high-performance chips, but they also create higher warranty costs because customers turn to Intel when these chips fail. The counterfeiting can also damage the brand's reputation. To defeat counterfeiters, Intel implemented a long list of product-security measures. It replaced removable painted numbers with more-permanent, laser-etched numbers; developed retail packages with holograms and other hard-to-copy markings; and created software to detect any mismatch between the chip's internal rating and operating speed.

Strategically, Intel executives debated whether to even use the Intel name on products at the low end of the spectrum that were sold in emerging markets. Not using the Intel name would prevent the low-priced goods from re-entering Western markets. The downside of that strategy, however, is less brand recognition in the developing country.

KEY TAKEAWAYS

- The fundamentals of global marketing begin with the core of marketing knowledge, the four Ps. The four Ps refer to product, price, promotion, and place. When put together, the four Ps form the marketing mix.

- One or more of the four Ps can differ from country to country. For example, the product can differ from country to country if a company chooses to adapt its product to local tastes or to create a new product specifically for local tastes. Thus, Starbucks introduced a green tea Frappuccino in China.

- The second P, price, refers to the amount of money that the consumer pays for the product. Price represents a special challenge when companies sell to emerging markets because consumers' income levels in these countries are much lower than in developed countries. In addition, the channel of distribution often gets longer when companies sell to international markets. Rather than a direct channel in which a company sells directly to a consumer, intermediaries (i.e., distributors, wholesalers, agents, brokers retailers, international freight forwarders, and trading companies) between the consumer and the producer often characterize the international-market distribution chain. Companies must pay each of these intermediaries, which increases the cost of the product.

- The third P, promotion, refers to the activities that inform and encourage consumers to buy a given product. Companies often customize these promotions to use images and wording that resonate with local markets.

- The final P, place, refers to where a company offers its products for sale. Many emerging countries may lack national retail chains, which means that companies may need to sell their products through a much more fragmented system of small storefronts or kiosks.

- Market segmentation refers to the process of dividing a larger market into smaller markets that share a common characteristic, such as age or lifestyle. It's important to note that not all citizens of a given country can be marketed to uniformly, because besides demographic differences there may be regional differences within each country as well.

- Price discrepancies between markets can cause the development of gray markets. These price discrepancies are hard to avoid because income levels differ in different countries. Companies want to charge prices that locals in different countries can afford. The result, however, is that consumers in wealthier countries may buy the product in a less-affluent country for a cheaper price. Counterfeit markets deceive customers into buying what they think is a branded product at a bargain price.

EXERCISES

(AACSB: Reflective Thinking, Analytical Skills)
1. Why might a company's marketing mix be different for different countries?
2. What problems can gray or counterfeit markets cause for companies?
3. What are some characteristics of emerging-market customers?
4. Explain some ways to segment international markets.
5. Name the four Ps and how they might differ in international marketing.

[1] MIT Center for Transportation and Logistics, "Crossroads of Supply Chain and Strategy Symposium 2008" (symposium, MIT, Cambridge, MA, March 27, 2008).

[2] Emily Bryson York, "The Global CMO Interview: Annie Young-Scrivner, Starbucks: 'Local Relevance Became a Tipping Point for Innovation in Other Markets,'" Advertising Age, June 14, 2010, accessed November 4, 2010, http://adage.com/cmostrategy/article?article_id=144390.

[3] C. K. Prahalad, The Fortune at the Bottom of the Pyramid (Upper Saddle River, NJ: Wharton School Publishing, 2004).

[4] {Authors' names retracted as requested by the work's original creator or licensee}, Launch! Advertising and Promotion in Real Time (Nyack, NY).

[5] Richard P. Carpenter, "What They Meant to Say Was…," Boston Globe, August 2, 1998, M5.

[6] Jan Peter Heidenreich, "The New German Act against Unfair Competition," German Law Archive, accessed August 9, 2010, http://www.iuscomp.org/gla/literature/heidenreich.htm#D3c.

[7] Charles W. Lamb, Joseph F. Hair Jr., and Carl McDaniel, Essentials of Marketing (Mason, OH: South-Western Cengage Learning, 2009), 131.

[8] Recep Yücel, Halil Elibol, and Osman Dagdelen, "Globalization and International Marketing Ethics Problems," International Research Journal of Finance and Economics, no. 26 (2009): 100–101, accessed October 22, 2010, http://www.eurojournals.com/irjfe_26_08.pdf.

[9] "Supply Chain Strategies in Emerging Markets" (roundtable discussion at the MIT Center for Transportation and Logistics, MIT, Cambridge, MA, March 7, 2007).

[10] "Supply Chain Strategies in Emerging Markets" (roundtable discussion at the MIT Center for Transportation and Logistics, MIT, Cambridge, MA, March 7, 2007).

[11] "Number of Millionaires Grows in China," Digital Journal, June 24, 2010, accessed November 25, 2010, http://www.digitaljournal.com/article/293790.

[12] "World Now Has 10 Million Millionaires," MSN Money, June 25, 2008, accessed November 25, 2010,

http://articles.moneycentral.msn.com/Investing/Extra/WorldNowHasTe
nMillionMillionaires.aspx.

[13] "World Now Has 10 Million Millionaires," MSN Money, June 25, 2008, accessed November 25, 2010, http://articles.moneycentral.msn.com/Investing/Extra/WorldNowHasTe
nMillionMillionaires.aspx.

[14] "Asian Millionaires Overtake Europeans in World Wealth Game," Hindustan Times, June 23, 2010, accessed November 25, 2010, http://www.hindustantimes.com/Asian-millionaires-overtake-Europeans-in-world-wealth-game/Article1-562154.aspx.

14.2 Critical Decision Points in Global Marketing
LEARNING OBJECTIVES

1. Understand the advantages and disadvantages of global branding.
2. Know the trade-offs of centralized versus decentralized marketing decision making.
3. Identify the special challenges of branding decisions in emerging markets.

Global Branding

A global brand is the brand name of a product that has worldwide recognition. Indeed, the world does become flatter to the extent a brand is recognized, accepted, and trusted across borders. Some of the most-recognized brands in the world include Coca-Cola, IBM, Microsoft, GE, Nokia, McDonald's, Google, Toyota, Intel, and Disney. [1]

Companies invest a lot in building their brand recognition and reputation because a brand name signals trust. "Trust is what drives profit margin and share price," says Larry Light, CEO of Arcature brand consultancy and a veteran of McDonald's and BBDO Worldwide and Bates Worldwide advertising agencies. "It is what consumers are looking for and what they share with one another." [2]

The advantages of creating a global brand are economies of scale in production and packaging, which lower marketing costs while leveraging power and scope. The disadvantages, however, are that consumer needs differ across countries, as do legal and competitive environments. So while global branding, and consumer acceptance of such, is a flattener, significant country differences remain even when a firm has a strong global brand. Companies may decide to follow a global-brand strategy but also make adjustments to their communications strategy and marketing mix locally based on local needs.

The decision companies face is whether they should market one single brand around the world or multiple brands. Coca-Cola uses the Coke name on its cola products around the world but markets its water under the Dasani brand. Nestlé uses a local branding strategy for its 7,000 brands but also promotes the Nestlé corporate brand globally.

Acer's Multiple-Brand Strategy

PC maker Acer sells its personal computers under four different brands. Using a multibrand strategy is a good choice when a country has a strong, positive association with a particular brand. For example, when Taiwan-based Acer bought US PC-maker Gateway, Acer kept the Gateway brand to use in the United States for midtier PCs. In Europe, however, Acer uses the Packard Bell brand. Acer also has two other brands, which are segmented by price. Acer's eMachines brand is for the lower-end consumer who is most focused on price, whereas the Acer brand is reserved for the highest-quality products aimed at technophiles. This multibrand strategy also helps Acer's distribution. As Acer's chief marketing officer, Gianpiero Morbello, says, "It's difficult to get a retailer to place 50 percent of his space with one brand. It's easier to split that same space with three brands." [3]

Global Brand Web Strategy

Companies that are promoting their global brands successfully on the web include Google, Philips, Skype, Ericsson, Hewlett-Packard, and Cisco Systems. These companies are mindful of the cultural and language differences across countries. They have created websites in local languages and are using images and content specific to each country. At the same time, however, each country website has the same look and feel of the main corporate website to preserve the overall brand. [4]

Planning a Brand Strategy for Emerging Markets

Entering an emerging market with a developed-country brand poses an extra challenge. As noted in Section 14.1 "Fundamentals of Global Marketing", income levels in emerging markets are lower, so companies tend to price their products as inexpensively as possible. This low-cost strategy may have consequences for the company's brand, however. For example, if a company introduces its brand as a "premium" product despite having a lower price, how will it introduce and differentiate its true "premium" brand later as consumers' incomes rise?

Branding Issues: How Low Can You Go?

Many emerging markets call for lower-cost goods. But how low can a company go on quality and performance without damaging the company's brand? The challenge is to balance maintaining a global reputation for quality while serving local markets at lower cost points.

One way to resolve the challenge is to offer the product at quality levels that are the best in that country even though they would be somewhat below developed-country standards. This is the tactic Walmart has successfully used in Mexico. Walmart's flooring, lighting, and air conditioning make its Mexican stores better than any other local stores even if they might seem Spartan to US consumers.

Centralized versus Decentralized Marketing Decisions

Who has the authority to make marketing decisions? In a centralized-marketing organizational structure, the home-country headquarters retains decision-making power. In a decentralized-marketing organizational structure,   the regions are able to make decisions without headquarters' approval. The advantage of the centralized structure is speed, consistency, and economies of scale that can save costs (such as through global-marketing campaigns). The disadvantages are that the marketing isn't tied to local knowledge and doesn't reflect local tastes, so sales aren't optimized to appeal to regional differences.

KEY TAKEAWAYS

- One of the key decisions that must be made when marketing internationally is how to set up the structure of the marketing organization in the company—centralized or decentralized. In a centralized structure, the home-country headquarters makes the decisions, which can save costs and bring consistency to marketing campaigns. In a decentralized organizational structure, the regions are able to make decisions autonomously, which enables regions to tailor their marketing to local sensibilities.

- Another decision concerns whether to pursue a single global-brand strategy or a multiple-brand strategy. A global brand is the brand name of a product that has worldwide recognition, such as Coca-Cola or IBM. Global brands bring economies of scale and marketing power. Multiple brands, however, may resonate more with specific markets, especially if a company merges with or acquires a local brand that is well respected in that region. The purpose of brands is to signal trust. In some cases, consumers may trust a familiar local brand more than a foreign global brand.

- Finally, companies need to plan a brand strategy for emerging markets, where products have to be sold at lower price points, which could hurt a premium brand reputation.

EXERCISES

(AACSB: Reflective Thinking, Analytical Skills)

1. What are the benefits of a centralized-marketing organization?
2. When might a company prefer to make decentralized-marketing decisions?
3. List the advantages of a global-brand strategy.
4. Discuss the advantages of a multibrand strategy.
5. How can a company use the web to promote a global brand while at the same time localizing it?

[1] "Best Global Brands Report 2010," Interbrand, accessed October 22, 2010, http://issuu.com/interbrand/docs/bgb_report_us_version?mode=a_p.
[2] David Kiley and Burt Helm, "The Great Trust Offensive," BusinessWeek, September 17, 2009, accessed November 4, 2010, http://www.businessweek.com/magazine/content/09_39/b414803849293 3.htm.
[3] Bruce Einhorn and Tim Culpan, "With Dell in the Dust, Acer Chases HP," BusinessWeek, March 8, 2010, 58–59.
[4] Chanin Ballance, "Speaking Their Language: How to Localize Your Message for Global Customers," Marketing Profs, March 24, 2009, accessed November 4, 2010, http://www.marketingprofs.com/9/speaking-their-language-localize-message-global-customers-ballance.asp.

14.3 Standardized or Customized Products

LEARNING OBJECTIVES

1. Understand the trade-offs between standardized versus customized products.
2. Know the influence of the country-of-origin effect.
3. Comprehend the benefits of reverse innovation.

Straight Product Extension

Companies deciding to market their products in different countries typically have a choice of three common strategies to pursue. The first is the straight product extension. This means taking the company's current products and selling them in other countries without making changes to the product. The advantages of this strategy are that the company doesn't need to invest in new research, development, or manufacturing. Changes may be made in packaging and labeling, but these are driven by local regulatory requirements. The disadvantages, however, are that its products may not be well suited to local needs and that the products may be more costly due to higher manufacturing and labor costs in the United States.

Product Adaptation

The second strategy is product adaptation and refers to modifying the company's existing product in a way that makes it fit better with local needs. For example, when

Procter & Gamble (P&G) introduced Tide laundry detergent in emerging markets like India, it changed the formulation to remove softeners. The reformulated Tide cost less than the original Tide. This change was important because price was an important factor in India where income levels were lower. Indian consumers were more able to afford the reformulated Tide.

Another way to localize a product is through packaging. Locally appropriate packaging doesn't just mean using the country's language. It also means creating packaging sizes that suit the country. For example, a company wanting to make its products more economical to less-wealthy countries may be tempted to sell larger, economy-sized packaging. But emerging-market consumers often prefer smaller package sizes, even if that increases the cost-per-use. They tend to buy sachets of shampoo rather than economy-size bottles. These smaller sizes are also easier to transport to local villages or to store in smaller-sized homes.

Mobile-phone maker Nokia went a step further in localizing its phones to different markets. The company uses local designers to create mobile-phone handset models that are specifically appropriate for each country. For example, the handsets designed in India are dust resistant and have a built-in flashlight. The models designed in China have a touchscreen, stylus, and Chinese character recognition.

Local designers are more likely to understand the needs of the local population than headquarters-located designers do.

The examples of Tide and Nokia show how companies can create a version of their existing product tailored to specific countries.

Product Invention: P&G Diapers

The third strategy, product invention, is creating an entirely new product for the target market. In this strategy, companies go back to the drawing board and rethink how best to design a product for that country.

The first step in inventing a product for a new country market is to understand the key product characteristics needed to succeed in that market. For example, when P&G wanted to sell diapers in BRIC countries (i.e., Brazil, Russia, India, and China), it started from square one. Rather than merely modifying the existing design, P&G engaged local knowledge and reconsidered all the key features of the design in the context of the needs of the emerging markets.

A major issue was price. To make the diaper affordable, P&G settled on an aggressive price target—each diaper should cost

as much as one egg. But the company also wanted a diaper that could uphold the P&G brand name. At first, the designers thought that the lower-cost product needed to do everything that the current developed-world product did. But further discussions refined and narrowed the definition so that P&G could meet the cost target without damaging the brand.

P&G designers debated features such as absorbency, color, fit, and packaging to find a design that was acceptable on cost targets, acceptable to emerging-market consumers, and acceptable as a P&G-branded product. The designers considered materials and how they could avoid using high-paid, specialized suppliers. Some characteristics, such as packaging, could be adjusted to meet local cost standards. In other cases, a characteristic was nonnegotiable—such as corporate social-responsibility issues. For example, P&G wanted to ensure that none of the suppliers to its diaper business used child labor. In the end, P&G succeeded by understanding both the critical elements of the brand and the emerging-market customers' expectations.

Nuances of Product Extension, Adaptation, and Invention

The product-adaptation strategy is easier for firms to execute than product invention. Nonetheless, even product adaptation requires understanding the local market well. Consider Ford Motor Company's missteps in adapting its midpriced car model to the Indian market. Ford realized that it needed to lower the cost of its car to make it more affordable to Indian consumers. Ford brought a team of designers together in Detroit and tasked them with figuring out how to reduce the cost of the car. The designers looked at removing nonessential elements. The first feature to go was air conditioning. Next, the team decided to remove power windows in the back, keeping them only in the front. These and other such tweaks brought the total cost of the car down from $20,000 to $15,000. Reducing the cost by 25 percent is notable, but unfortunately the design team lacked vital local knowledge about India. First, even though the price of the car was lower, the $15,000 price point in India is still way above what the middle class can afford. The Indians who can afford a $15,000 car are the very rich. Second, the very rich in India who can afford to pay $15,000 for a car can also afford (and will have) a chauffeur. Remember the clever idea of removing the air conditioning and the power windows in the back? The consequence is that the chauffeur is the only one who gets a breeze. Given the sweltering summer temperatures and traffic congestion in Indian cities, you can guess that the Ford car didn't sell well. [1]

Country-of-Origin Effect

The country-of-origin effect refers to consumers using the country where the product was made as a barometer for evaluating the product. Their perceptions of the country influence whether they will perceive the product favorably or unfavorably. That perception influences consumers' purchasing decisions. For example, France is known for its wines and luxury goods. Wines from Chile may be just as good and more affordably priced, but consumers may perceive French wines to be better due to the country-of-origin effect. In the 1960s, "Made in Japan" was a signal of low quality, but over time Japan has changed that perception through a dedicated focus on high quality. Specifically, Japan adopted Total Quality Management (TQM) which is a set of management practices initially introduced to Japan by W. Edwards Deming. The focus of TQM is increasing quality and reducing errors in production or service delivery. TQM consists of systematic processes, planning, measurement, continuous improvement, and customer satisfaction. These days, "made in Japan" is viewed positively, but "made in China" faces more of a stigma. Likewise, consumers in Colombia don't want products that are made in Colombia. A similar problem happens with Mercedes-Benz—Mercedes-Benz cars assembled in Egypt have much lower resale value than those assembled in Germany. In these cases, local assembly in Egypt might be taken as a sign of inferior quality.

Reverse Innovation: How Designing for Emerging Economies Brings Benefits Back Home

Increasingly, marketing and innovation are directly linked. Reverse innovation means designing a product for a developing country and bringing that innovation back to the home country. Creating new products and services for developing countries requires radical innovation and opens new opportunities in developed-world markets as well. For example, GE Healthcare sells sophisticated medical-imaging devices around the world. Historically, GE has sold these high-end machines in emerging economies like India. But only 10 percent of Indian hospitals can afford a $10,000 electrocardiogram (ECG) machine. Reaching the other 90 percent of the market takes more than simply cutting a few costs. It requires radical innovation and an in-depth understanding of local conditions.

One important local fact to know is that most Indians live in rural areas. That means they don't have a local hospital to visit. Therefore, medical equipment needs to go to them, and no rural health care clinic is going to lug a $10,000 ECG machine into the field even if it *could* afford the device. Achieving the goal of a lightweight, reliable, simple-to-use ECG device took radical rethinking. GE built such a device

that could fit in a shoulder bag or backpack. The device has a built-in replaceable printer and costs only $500. In addition, because the device would be used in rural locations with scant access to electricity, GE designed a battery that could do 500 ECGs on one charge. To make it easy to use, GE designed the device to have only three buttons. Finally, just because the device is inexpensive doesn't mean it's dumb. GE installed professional-level analysis software to aid rural doctors.

With its new portable ECG device, GE has unlocked a whole new market in developing countries. Beyond that, GE has also opened up new opportunities back home—and that's the reverse innovation side of the story. How? The portable ECG machine with a $500 price tag is ideal for use in ambulances, saving lives of accident victims in developed countries as well. Cheap, portable, and easy-to-use devices are desirable in any country. [2], [3]

KEY TAKEAWAYS

- There are three strategies for introducing a company's product to a new international market: (1) straight product extension, (2) product adaptation, and (3) product invention.

- A straight product extension involves taking the company's current product and selling it in other countries without making changes to the product. The advantages of this strategy are that the company doesn't need to invest in new research and development or manufacturing. The disadvantages, however, are that its products may not be well suited to local needs and that the products may be more costly due to higher US manufacturing and labor costs.

- Product adaptation refers to modifying the company's existing product in a way that makes it fit better with local needs, as Nokia did by making its mobile phones for India dust-resistant.

- Product invention means creating an entirely new product for the target market, as P&G did by designing a diaper for emerging markets that cost the same as a single egg. Such a price would make the diaper affordable in emerging-market countries.

- When adapting or inventing a product for a new market, it's important to have local knowledge, as the missteps of Ford's car for India have shown. In addition, the country-of-origin effect influences consumers' purchasing decisions. If consumers perceive one country more favorably than another, they're more apt to buy products from that country.

- Inventing a new product for an international country can bring benefits back to the home market. GE Healthcare completely reinvented a $10,000 medical-imaging device to create a $500 portable, imaging device for the Indian market. In the process, GE realized it had created a new product for its home market as well.

EXERCISES

(AACSB: Reflective Thinking, Analytical Skills)

1. Describe three strategies for introducing a product to a new international market.
2. Why might a company want to adapt its product to a local country rather than doing a straight product extension?
3. What are the challenges of the product-invention strategy?
4. Could the country-of-origin effect be used to a company's advantage?
5. Explain reverse innovation and the potential advantages it brings.

[1] Vijay Govindarajan, "Ten Rules for Strategic Innovators" (presentation, World Innovation Forum, New York, NY, May 5–6, 2009).
[2] Vijay Govindarajan, "Reverse Innovation: A New Strategy for Creating the Future" (webinar, HSM Global, March 18, 2010), accessed November 23, 2010, http://us.hsmglobal.com/contenidos/hsm-webinars-vijay.html.
[3] "An ECG for Less Than Rs 10? New, Made-in-India, GE Device, Does IT," India Tech Online, November 25, 2009, accessed August 1, 2010, http://www.indiatechonline.com/ge-mac-i-ecg-168.php.

14.4 Global Sourcing and Distribution
LEARNING OBJECTIVES

1. Understand the advantages of global sourcing.
2. Know the pros and cons of sole-sourcing and multisourcing.
3. Describe the distribution-management choices companies have when entering new international markets.

Global sourcing refers to buying the raw materials or components that go into a company's products from around the world, not just from the headquarters' country. For example, Starbucks buys its coffee from locations like Colombia and Guatemala. The advantages of global sourcing are quality and lower cost. Global sourcing is possible to the extent that the world is flat—for example, buying the highest-quality cocoa beans for making chocolate or buying aluminum from Iceland, where it's cheaper because it's made using free geothermal energy.

When making global-sourcing decisions, firms face a choice of whether to sole-source (i.e., use one supplier exclusively) or to multisource (i.e., use multiple suppliers). The advantage of sole-sourcing is that the company will often get a lower price by giving all of its volume to one supplier. If the company gives the supplier a lot of business, the company may have more influence over the supplier for preferential treatment. For example, during a time of shortage or strained capacity, the supplier may give higher quantities to that company rather than to a competitor as a way of rewarding the company's loyalty.

On the other hand, using multiple suppliers gives a company more flexibility. For instance, if there's a natural disaster or other disruption at one of their suppliers, the company can turn to its other suppliers to meet its needs. For example, when Hurricane Mitch hit Honduras with 180-mile-per-hour winds, 70 to 80 percent of Honduras's infrastructure was damaged and 80 percent of its banana crop was lost. Both Dole Food Company and Chiquita bought bananas from Honduras, but Dole relied more heavily on bananas from Honduras than from other countries. As a result, Dole lost 25 percent of its global banana supply, but Chiquita lost only 15 percent. [1] In the aftermath, Chiquita's revenues increased, while Dole's decreased.

Sole-Sourcing Advantages
- Price discounts based on higher volume
- Rewards for loyalty during tough times
- Exclusivity brings differentiation
- Greater influence with a supplier

Sole-Sourcing Disadvantages
- Higher risk of disruption
- Supplier has more negotiating power on price

Multisourcing Advantages
- More flexibility in times of disruption
- Negotiating lower rates by pitting one supplier against another

Multisourcing Disadvantages
- Quality across suppliers may be less uniform
- Less influence with each supplier
- Higher coordination and management costs
  Whichever sourcing strategy a company chooses, it can reduce risk by visiting its suppliers regularly to ensure the quality of products and processes, the financial health of each supplier, and the supplier's adherence to laws, safety regulations, and ethics.

Ethics in Action

The Case of Global Sourcing

While there is little systematic research on questions related to ethics and global sourcing, one recent survey in the context of clothing manufacturers identified the following most encountered issues: [2]

- **Child labor.** Forty-three percent of the respondents had encountered factories where child labor was being used. India, China, Thailand, and Bangladesh were cited as the worst offenders in this regard, partly because of the absence or unreliability of birth certificates, but also because of the difficulty that Westerners have in assessing the age of workers in these countries. Buyers relied on the management of the factory to check on documents supplied by the employee.

- **Dangerous working conditions and health and safety issues.** Forty-three percent of the respondents had encountered dangerous working conditions in factories. These included unsafe machinery (e.g., machine guards having been removed to speed up production), workers failing to use safety equipment such as cutting gloves, and the use and storage of hazardous chemicals (e.g., those used for dyeing and printing). Fire regulations were also sometimes inadequate, both in factories and in the dormitory accommodation often provided for workers who live away from their home regions. Sometimes fire exits were locked, and fire extinguishers were missing.

- **Bribery and corruption.** Thirty-one percent of respondents said that they had experienced bribery and corruption. One blatantly fraudulent practice mentioned was for suppliers to mislead the buyer over the true source of production. Many suppliers claim that goods are made in one factory, then transfer the production elsewhere, making it difficult for the retailer to audit.

- **Exploitation of the workforce.** Twenty-five percent of respondents mention some aspect of exploitation of the workforce, encompassing the issues of child labor and health and safety. However, it can also cover low wages being paid to workers and excessive overtime being expected by employers. Respondents specifically mentioned that they had encountered worker exploitation. Many spoke of long working hours in factories, especially at peak periods, with employees often working over seventy hours per week.

Distribution Management

Selling internationally means considering how your company will distribute its goods in the market. Developed countries have good infrastructure—passable roads that can accommodate trucks, retailers who display and sell products, and reliable communications infrastructure and media choices. Emerging markets, on the other hand, often have very fragmented distribution networks, limited logistics, and much smaller retailer outlets. Hole-in-the-wall shops, door-to-door peddlers, and street vendors play a much larger role in emerging-market countries. In the emerging countries of Africa, for example, books might be sold from the back of a moped.

In addition, the standards of living in emerging countries vary widely. Most of the middle class lives in cities, but the percentage of the population that lives in rural areas varies by country. In India, 70 percent of the population lives in rural areas, whereas in Latin America only 30 percent does.

Rural logistics are especially problematic. Narrow dirt roads, weight-limited bridges, and mud during the rainy season hamper the movement of goods. An executive at computer storage device manufacturer EMC noted that sometimes the company's refrigerator-sized, data-storage systems have had to be transported on horse-drawn wagons.

How Nokia Tackles Distribution Challenges

Nokia is a $59 billion company with over 123,000 employees. [3] It sells 150 different devices, of which 50 to 60 are newly introduced each year. Each device can be customized on many variants, including language and content. This variation adds greatly to the devices' complexity; three hundred to four hundred components need to arrive on time at factories in order for the devices to be built. Approximately one billion people use Nokia devices worldwide. Countries like China, India, and Nigeria, which ten years ago had almost zero penetration of mobile phones, now have twenty million to forty million users each. Emerging markets now account for over half of Nokia's annual sales.

Nokia has the challenge of selling a growing variety of mobile devices in hundreds of thousands of tiny retail outlets in the developing world. To tackle reaching its rural customers in developing countries, Nokia has 350,000 points of presence in rural areas, from small kiosks and corner shops to organized retail outlets. Nokia has 100,000 such point-of-sale (POS) outlets in India, 80,000 in China, and 120,000 in the Middle East and Africa.

To train salespeople in developing countries, Nokia created an internal university to educate the people who sell its phones in these POS locations—an average of five people per location. Nokia Academy teaches local salespeople about the features of the phones and how to sell them. As Nokia expands further into these emerging markets, it will penetrate deeper into the rural areas and will distribute through local providers.

Nokia's challenge is to maintain its strong brand name—the fifth most recognized brand in the world—across these POS locations. Meeting this challenge has taken years. One way that Nokia maintains control of its brand across these locations is by having managers visit the outlets on a regular basis and using their mobile phones to photograph the shelf layout at each location. This lets Nokia control quality and improve merchandizing techniques at all locations.

Distribution-Management Choices: Partner, Acquire, or Build from Scratch

There are typically three distribution strategies for entering a new market. First, companies can do a joint-venture or partnership with a local company. This is the strategy Walmart used when entering Mexico. A second strategy is to acquire a local company to have immediate access to large-scale distribution. The Home Depot pursued this strategy in China when it acquired a partner with whom it had been working for quite some time. Third, a company can to build its own distribution from scratch. Retailer Carrefour chose this route in China years ago, because it knew China would offer a big opportunity, and Carrefour wanted to develop its own local capabilities. Which strategy the company chooses depends on its timetable for volume in the market, local foreign-ownership laws, and the availability of suitable partners or acquisition targets.

Spotlight on International Strategy and Entrepreneurship

Unilever Solves Distribution Issues in India
Hindustan Unilever Limited (HUL), Unilever's Indian subsidiary, wanted to reach the 70 percent of Indians who live in rural villages. This underserved market is very hard to reach. Not only is marketing to remote villages difficult, but the physical transport of products is no easier. Most of the villages lack paved roads, making traditional truck-based distribution arduous. The only way to reach many of these remote villages is by single-track dirt trails.

In response to these conditions, HUL has created Project Shakti (the word means "strength") and developed a network of 14,000 women and women-owned cooperatives to serve 50,000 villages. The women handle the logistics and door-to-door retailing of a range of personal-care products. To address the needs of the market and this novel distribution

system, HUL has packaged its products in much smaller sizes. The effort has created $250 million in new revenues for HUL, of which 10 percent is used for financing the women entrepreneurs. By using this approach, HUL doesn't have to deal with the problem of moving products in rural India. The women or their employees come to the company's urban distribution centers to get the products.

KEY TAKEAWAYS

- Global sourcing refers to buying the raw materials or components that go into a company's products from around the world, not just from the headquarters' country. The advantages of global sourcing include access to higher quality or lower prices.

- When making sourcing decisions, companies must decide whether to sole-source (i.e., to use one supplier exclusively) or to use two or more suppliers. Sole-sourcing can bring advantages of price discounts based on volume and may give the company greater influence over a supplier or preferential treatment during times of constrained capacity Sole-sourcing can also bring advantages of differentiation or high quality. The disadvantages of sole-sourcing, however, are that the company faces a higher risk of disruption if something happens to that supplier. Also, the supplier may hold more negotiating power on price.

- A company typically has three distribution strategies for entering a new market—to engage in a joint venture, to acquire a local company, or to build its own distribution network from scratch. Establishing a partnership or joint venture is the least costly approach, followed by acquisition. Building a distribution network from scratch is the most costly and time consuming, but it may give the company the most local experience and capabilities for the long term.

- Distribution channels in emerging markets are less developed, which means that companies may need to seek novel solutions to distributing their products, such as Hindustan Unilever Limited creating its own distribution network of 14,000 female independent distributors and cooperatives or Nokia creating Nokia Academy to train salespeople.

EXERCISES

(AACSB: Reflective Thinking, Analytical Skills)
1. Describe three distribution strategies that companies can use when entering a new market.

2. What challenges do companies face when distributing products internationally?
3. What are the distribution challenges in emerging-market countries?
4. When making a sourcing decision, would you choose to sole-source or multisource? Why?
5. What are the advantages of global sourcing?

[1] Yossi Sheffi, The Resilient Enterprise (Cambridge, MA: MIT Press, 2005), 216–17.
[2] Mike Pretious and Mary Love, "Sourcing Ethics and the Global Market: The Case of the UK Retail Clothing Sector," International Journal of Retail & Distribution Management 34, no. 12 (2006): 892–903.
[3] "Nokia Corporation Company Profile," Hoovers, accessed August 6, 2010, http://www.hoovers.com/company/Nokia_Corporation/crxtif-1-1njdap.html.

14.5 Global Production and Supply-Chain Management

LEARNING OBJECTIVES

1. Understand the differences between outsourcing and offshoring.
2. Explain three strategies for locating production operations.
3. Know the value of supply-chain management.

Strategic Choices: Export, Local Assembly, and Local Production

When deciding where and how to produce products for international markets, companies typically have a choice of three strategies. The strategies vary in terms of levels of risk, cost, exposure to exchange-rate fluctuations, and leveraging of local capabilities. Companies need to tailor their strategy to fit their product and the country.

Manufacture in the United States and Then Export

The lowest-investment production strategy is to make the product at the company's existing manufacturing locations and then export them to the new market. Companies use this solution in situations where the total opportunity in the new market doesn't justify opening a plant. For example, EMC supplies its Asia-Pacific customers from plants in the United States and Ireland. This strategy does have several downsides. Specifically, the company faces higher shipping costs, importation delays, local import duties, risks due to exchange-rate fluctuations, and isolation from local knowledge.

Global Components with Local Assembly

The next level of strategy uses of out-of-country suppliers but local assembly. Dell Latin America uses this approach. It buys high-tech computer components globally but performs customized assembly in Brazil. Being closer to the market improves Dell's sales, service, and customer knowledge.

Another example is Iams. Iams makes its proprietary pet food in the United States and ships it to other countries for packaging. This strategy lets Iams do some local customization and offer better customer response, while gaining tax or tariff incentives from local assembly.

Along with these advantages come increased supplier-coordination issues and concerns about supplier quality. In some cases, local assembly can harm the product, which leads back to the country-of-origin effect discussed in Section 14.3 "Standardized or Customized Products". For example, some markets like Colombia don't want to buy Colombian-made goods. In those cases, local assembly can harm product sales.

Local Production

Finally, a company can go completely local, sourcing materials in the foreign country and manufacturing the product there. Nokia used this strategy in India. This strategy takes the greatest advantage of lower-cost labor, regional suppliers, and local knowledge. However, it involves high investment and depends heavily on the quality of local resources. It also exposes the company to political risks. However, going 100 percent local may work well in BRIC countries (i.e., Brazil, Russia, India, and China) for labor-intensive, low-value products. These types of products can tolerate the potentially lower levels of quality associated with local suppliers.

Companies that decide to build a local plant have to decide in which country to locate the plant. The criteria to consider are

- political stability,
- statutory/legal environments,
- infrastructure quality,
- foreign-investment incentives,
- local telecommunications and utility infrastructure,
- workforce quality,
- security and privacy,
- compensation costs,
- tax and regulatory costs, and
- communication costs.

Government Incentives

Countries sometimes offer special incentives to attract companies to their area. Malaysia, for example, set up the Multimedia Super Corridor that offers tax breaks, desirable facilities, and excellent infrastructure to foreign companies.

Similarly, China has special economic zones (SEZs) that promote international high-quality standards in the Hainan Province, Shenzhen, Shantou, and elsewhere. While one component is a government initiative to set up SEZs or corridors that boast excellent communications infrastructure, other factors, such as uninterrupted power supply and connections to transportation infrastructure, play an important role as well. Even though the economic or political picture of a country may appear appealing, companies also need to understand public policy and the regulatory environment of the specific state or municipality in which they plan to set up operations, because laws on a local level may be different and may create roadblocks for new company operations.

Infrastructure Issues

Emerging-market countries are investing in new infrastructure to varying degrees. China is working hard to grow rail, road, and port infrastructure. In other countries, investment may be lagging. And in some cases, companies have been caught in the middle of governmental problems arising from dealing with officials who turn out to be corrupt. Locating a plant in China means having to ship products from China. If a company's primary market is in the United States, China is halfway around the world. The company may save on labor, but there are other added costs—extra shipping costs as well as hidden costs of uncertainty. [1] If the company's products are en route and experience delays, for example, customers might experience a stock-out. A stock-out means that there is no more stock of the company's product. The product is unavailable to customers who want to buy it. To avoid stock-out situations, a company may decide to hold inventory close to its customers.

Called safety stock, this inventory helps ensure that the company won't run out of products if there's a delay or crisis in a distant manufacturing region. The downsides of safety stock, however, include the increased costs of carrying that inventory, such as the investment in the products, taxes and insurance, and storage space. In addition, companies risk obsolescence of the products before they're sold.

It's important to note that China is far away only if the company's primary markets are outside Asia. The distance that truly matters is the distance to the company's markets. Companies that sell their products around the world may want to have production facilities around the world as well, so that their products are closer to customers—wherever those customers may be.

Did You Know?

Intel's Approach to Managing Risk in Global Production

If a company builds plants in different locations, the company may face the issue of differing quality among its plants. Intel, the world leader in the manufacturing, marketing, and sales of integrated circuits for computing and communications industries worldwide has faced this problem. Quality is a major issue when making these tiny, complex integrated-circuit chips. Intel's Atom chips, for example, are the size of a grain of rice. To ensure high quality at all of its plants worldwide, Intel devised a strategy called Copy Exact! [2] That is, Intel builds all of its semiconductor-fabrication plants (also known as "fabs") to the same exact specifications, creating interchangeable processes and interchangeable fabs throughout the company. Intel began the Copy Exact! strategy in the mid-1980s as a way to cope with the complexity of semiconductor manufacturing. Manufacturing integrated computer chips is highly delicate. The smallest variation in temperature, pressure, chemistry, or handling can mean the difference between producing a wafer that made up of hundreds of $1,000 chips and producing a wafer that is a useless silicon disk. Once Intel has a new semiconductor-manufacturing process debugged at one facility, it copies that process—down to the lengths of the hoses on the vacuum pumps—to other Intel facilities. Intel has realized that this Copy Exact! strategy also provides flexibility in manufacturing. For example, Intel can transfer capacity back and forth between facilities to eliminate manufacturing bottlenecks. When the severe acute respiratory syndrome (SARS) flu epidemic hit Asia, for example, Intel simply transferred partially completed wafers from one plant to another for finishing.

The Copy Exact! strategy extends beyond semiconductor fabrication to include the assembly and test factories and the contractors that support building electronic boards, such as personal computer motherboards. "If something happens to that facility, we roll over to a subcontractor at another site that can pick up the same assembly test and make sure that we get the same product coming out and the same amounts for our shipping plans," said Intel's Steve Lund. [3] Copy Exact! even extends to Intel's information technology infrastructure. Identical software and hardware architecture support a range of activities, such as ordering and production planning, at eighteen manufacturing, testing, and assembly sites across three continents.

Outsourcing and Offshoring

Offshoring means setting up operations in a low-cost country for the purpose of hiring local workers at lower labor rates. Offshoring differs from outsourcing in that the firm retains control of the operations and directly hires the employees. In outsourcing, by contrast, the company delegates an entire process (such as accounts payable) to the outsource vendor. The vendor takes control of the operations and runs the operations as they see fit. The company pays the outsource vendor for the end result; how the vendor achieves those end results is up to the vendor. Companies that choose to offshore face the same location-criteria factors as companies that make production-operation decisions.

The advantages of outsourcing include the following:
- Efficient processes (the outsourcer typically specializes in a particular process or set of processes, giving them high levels of expertise with that process)
- Access to specialized equipment that may be too expensive for a company to invest in unless that process is their chief business

India has long been a favorite location for outsourcing services, such as call centers and software testing, because of its English-speaking, highly educated workforce. The labor-rate ratio has been five to one, meaning that a company based in the United Kingdom, for example, could hire five Indian college graduates for the price of hiring one UK college graduate. Given the high demand for their labor, however, Indian employees' wages have begun to rise. Offshoring companies are now faced with a new challenge. The firms hire and train Indian employees only to see them leave in a year for a higher salary elsewhere. [4] This wage inflation and high turnover in India has led some companies, like ABN AMRO Bank, to consider whether they should move offshoring operations to China, where wages are still low. The downside is that graduates in China aren't as knowledgeable about the financial industry, and language problems may be greater.

Diageo, the world's largest purveyor of spirits, used the following criteria when choosing an offshoring-services location. [5] Diageo analyzed nineteen locations in fourteen countries, ultimately choosing Budapest, Hungary, as the location of its offshore shared-services operations. The primary criteria Diageo used were
- a low-cost base, both in terms of start-up and ongoing running costs;
- a favorable general business environment;
- the availability of suitable staff—particularly with regard to language skills;

- a high level of local and international accessibility with good transport links;
- the attractiveness for international staff; and
- a robust regulatory framework. [6]

Companies save on labor costs when offshoring, but the "hidden costs" can be significant. These hidden costs include the costs of additional facilities, telecommunications, and technological infrastructure. Delays or problems with internal project coordination and the need for redundancy can add even more costs.

Did You Know?

Standard Chartered Bank Mitigated Risk by Duplicating Operations in Chennai and Kuala Lumpur
As you can imagine, banks are very concerned about security because of the highly confidential customer information they possess. Some banks try to mitigate the risks by setting up mirror sites. Standard Chartered Bank, for instance, chose Chennai in South India as the hub for its Scope International operations, but some of the tasks are also done in Kuala Lumpur in Malaysia: "Because we run the operations of 52 countries, we have to satisfy information security and business continuity issues in all locations," says Sreeram Iyer, Group Head, Global Shared Services Centers, Standard Chartered Scope International at the time of the decision. "Kuala Lumpur backs up the Chennai center and vice versa." [7]

Supply-Chain Management
Supply-chain management encompasses the planning and management of all activities involved in sourcing and procurement, conversion, and logistics. Importantly, it also includes coordination and collaboration with channel partners, which can be suppliers, intermediaries, third-party service providers, and customers. In essence, supply-chain management integrates supply-and-demand management within and across companies. [8]

Activities in the supply chain include:
- demand management (e.g., forecasting, pricing, and customer segmentation),
- procurement (e.g., purchasing, supplier selection, and supplier-base rationalization),
- inventory management (e.g., raw materials and finished goods),
- warehousing and material handling,

- production planning and control (e.g., aggregate planning, workforce scheduling, and factory operations),
- packaging (i.e., industrial and consumer),
- transportation management,
- order management,
- distribution network design (e.g., facility location and distribution strategy), and
- product-return management.

Cross-organizational teams across the supply chain can bring great perspective to the overall team process. Representatives from design, business, purchasing, manufacturing, equipment purchasing, planning, customer, logistics, information technology, and finance all bring their specialized knowledge to the benefit of the supply chain as a whole. [9]

Spotlight on International Strategy and Entrepreneurship

Entrepreneurial Innovation at P&G

In 2002, Procter & Gamble (P&G) created a test factory, called the Garage, in Vietnam to experiment with low-cost diaper manufacturing for emerging markets. This factory was different from P&G's US-based factories because it didn't use high-tech, automation-intensive manufacturing processes. Rather, P&G wanted a low-cost, low-tech solution. The factory helped P&G devise a new, low-cost approach to manufacturing in emerging-market countries. The strategy required finding local suppliers, some of whom wouldn't have been acceptable for other P&G products but were suitable for this one. P&G formed a network of 150 low-cost machine builders who could supply manufacturing equipment to P&G's Vietnam factory. This manufacturing equipment was appropriate for emerging-market sites and emerging-market prices. The equipment was not on par to P&G's US-based manufacturing equipment, but P&G could use it in other countries and in other product lines. For example, P&G took the lessons and machine-building know-how it had learned from making low-cost diapers in Asia and applied it to reducing the costs of making feminine pads in Mexico. In transferring this know-how from one country to the next, P&G reduced the costs of its feminine pads in Mexico by 20 percent.

P&G has gone a step further and brought its results back home to the United States in two ways. First, thanks to the North American Free Trade Agreement (NAFTA), P&G can import its low-cost feminine pads from Mexico back into the United States. Second, P&G now sees an opportunity to give a second life to obsolete plants in the United States. The experience P&G has gained in emerging markets has taught the company that not every product in every market needs the latest and greatest approaches to manufacturing in order to be successful. P&G's experience with its Vietnamese factory has given it a scalable approach, which has enabled P&G to make diapers and other similar personal-care products in many different emerging-market countries using widely available, low-cost manufacturing equipment.

KEY TAKEAWAYS

- There are several strategic choices available to companies when they decide how to produce their products for international markets. First, companies can manufacture their products in their home countries and export them. This strategy involves the least amount of change but has the downsides of higher supply-chain costs, potential delays, exchange-rate risks, and isolation from local knowledge.
- Second, a company can build components in one country and do local assembly in another. This strategy offers advantages of tax or tariff incentives but increases coordination costs and may bring unfavorable country-of-origin effects.
- Finally, a company can opt for local production. This decision requires a careful evaluation of the risks and rewards of production operations in that country, including assessing political risks, the skills of the local workforce, and the quality of the infrastructure.
- Some companies also choose to outsource or offshore their processes, either giving control to the outsource vendor for the process and paying for the results (i.e., outsourcing) or retaining control of the process while taking advantage of lower labor rates (i.e., offshoring).
- Supply-chain management is the coordination of a host of activities that can give a company a distinct competitive advantage. Cross-organizational teams are the best way to take advantage of the perspectives of each supply-chain function for the benefit of all.

EXERCISES

(AACSB: Reflective Thinking, Analytical Skills)
1. What processes does supply-chain management encompass?
2. If you were going to build a plant overseas, what factors would you take into account when making your location decisions?

3. What strategic choices do international companies have about where to locate production operations?
4. Describe strategies for mitigating some of the risks of overseas production.
5. What are some advantages and disadvantages of outsourcing?

[1] April Terreri, "Supply Chain Trends to Watch," World Trade, July 2010, 16–21.
[2] Yossi Sheffi, The Resilient Enterprise (Cambridge, MA: MIT Press, 2005), 184.
[3] Yossi Sheffi, The Resilient Enterprise (Cambridge, MA: MIT Press, 2005), 184.
[4] Hub Potential Analysis Report 2007: Frost & Sullivan's 2007 Global Shared Services and Outsourcing (SSO) Study (San Antonio, TX: Frost & Sullivan, 2007), accessed May 19, 2011, http://www.frost.com/prod/servlet/cpo/106999825.
[5] Burt Helm, "Diageo Targets the Home Bartender," BusinessWeek, July 6, 2009, 48.
[6] Linda Pavey, "OTC Focus & Solutions," June 6, 2005, accessed August 6, 2010, http://www.ideaslab.info.
[7] Ranganath Iyengar, "Banks: Captive to Third Party Move?" Global Services, October 30, 2006, accessed November 25, 2010,http://www.globalservicesmedia.com/redesign/BPO/Market-Dynamics/Banks:-Captive-to-Third-Party-Move/23/28/0/general200705211425.
[8] "CSCMP Supply Chain Management Definitions," Council of Supply Chain Management Professionals, accessed August 7, 2010, http://cscmp.org/aboutcscmp/definitions.asp.
[9] C. J. Wehlage, "Supply Chain Transformation Leadership: Intel's Low-Cost Supply Chain Model," AMR Research, February 2, 2009, accessed August 4, 2010, http://www.amrresearch.com/content/View.aspx?compURI=tcm:7-39341.

14.6 End-of-Chapter Questions and Exercises

These exercises are designed to ensure that the knowledge you gain from this book about international business meets the learning standards set out by the international Association to Advance Collegiate Schools of Business (AACSB International). [1] AACSB is the premier accrediting agency of collegiate business schools and accounting programs worldwide. It expects that you will gain knowledge in the areas of communication, ethical reasoning, analytical skills, use of information technology, multiculturalism and diversity, and reflective thinking.

EXPERIENTIAL EXERCISES

(AACSB: Communication, Use of Information Technology, Analytical Skills)
1. Your company has a strong brand name in the United States, and you're ready to enter Europe. You decide to acquire a local company in Germany. Taking what you have learned in this chapter about branding, would you use the existing German brand in Germany? Would you use it in all of Europe? Or would you use your strong US brand globally? Would you use both brands in the same markets? Discuss the advantages and disadvantages of the various strategies, taking into account the trust factor of brands, the influence of local differences, and the country-of-origin effect.
2. Pick an item from a store, such as a shirt, and use the Internet to analyze where the shirt might have come from. Which countries could have supplied the raw material? Where might the article have been designed? Where might it have been manufactured? Would these two locations likely be near or far from each other? Why or why not? How would you make these sourcing and production decisions if you were running the company?
3. Your company manufactures hand tools for the do-it-yourself market in the United States, selling to retail stores like The Home Depot and smaller local hardware stores like McGuckin Hardware in Boulder, Colorado. Company executives have decided that the company needs to grow by expanding internationally. They come to you and your team for advice. How would you decide which country to expand into first? Would you recommend customizing the product for this market? Why or why not?

Ethical Dilemmas
(AACSB: Ethical Reasoning, Multiculturalism, Reflective Thinking, Analytical Skills)
1. You have selected a supplier in China who will manufacture one of the components that go into your consumer-electronics device. You learn that this supplier has switched to a manufacturing technique that is leaking potentially hazardous materials into the groundwater. What would you do? Would you tell them to go back to their original method? (Would you pay them more if they said the original method was more expensive to implement?) Would you withdraw your business and try to find another supplier, knowing this will cause delays and possible stock-outs of your products? Would you help the company clean up and solve the hazardous materials leak? Would you report the supplier to the government and let the government handle it (even if the government is prone to turning a blind eye on environmental issues)?
2. You are an organic products company that sells organic milk and dairy products to the United States and Europe. Until now, you've sourced your milk from local organic dairy farmers in the United States to sell to the US market and from farmers in Europe to sell to the European market. Now, you're seeing greater demand for organic milk supply as more and more competitors enter your industry. Prices for organic milk are rising.

What do you do? Would you raise prices and thus pass the additional costs onto your customers? Would you source organic milk from Australia or New Zealand, where organic milk supplies are less expensive? Would you be concerned about the higher carbon footprint that you would be creating by shipping from Australia or New Zealand to the United States and Europe?

[1] Association to Advance Collegiate Schools of Business website, accessed January 26, 2010, http://www.aacsb.edu.

NOTES:

NOTES:

Chapter 15:
Understanding the Roles of Finance and Accounting in Global Competitive Advantage

WHAT'S IN IT FOR ME?

1. What are the role of accounting in business and the impact of international standards?
2. What are the nature of currency risk and the methods of currency translation?
3. What are the sources of financing available to firms?
4. What are capital budgeting and the factors that influence international investment decisions?
5. What are global money management methods that reduce corporate transaction costs and taxes?

In this chapter, you'll learn the principles and techniques of global finance and accounting. In the opening case study, you'll see the increased role that governments are playing in the business finance arena. In a flat world, access to capital (i.e., part of the finance function) is uniform across countries, as are accounting standards. However, access to capital varies significantly across countries and between small and large firms. Accounting standards also vary, though these differences are decreasing.

In Section 15.1 "International Accounting Standards", you'll get a glimpse into why countries developed different accounting rules in the past and how new international accounting standards have emerged to create smoother capital markets functioning in our increasingly global world.

In Section 15.2 "Accounting in International Business", you'll learn the importance of consolidated financial statements, and the challenges they present in currency translation. You'll also explore two techniques of currency translation and two ways to mitigate the risks of currency exposure.

In Section 15.3 "Fundamentals of Finance", you'll learn the sources of financing available to international firms and see how firms like L'Occitane, IBM, Hewlett-Packard, Kimberly-Clark, SAP, and McDonald's are making financing and investment decisions.

In Section 15.4 "Financial Management in International Business", you'll see the factors underlying political risk and economic volatility and learn three ways that multinational firms are structuring their financial organizations to deal with those risks. You'll also find out how religion can impact the financial laws of some countries.

Finally, in Section 15.5 "Global Money Management: Moving Money across Borders", you'll delve into global money management and how firms like Colgate move money across borders to minimize costs and taxes, while gaining maximum returns on their capital.

OPENING CASE: BUCYRUS AND EX-IM BANK

Among the many changes taking place in the international business landscape, numerous leading management consultants predict that government will play an increasingly active role. Governments will no longer simply be an external regulator but will be a direct participant in particular strategic choices and actions. The new normal, in terms of government involvement in business, is one in which government's hand in strategy and strategy execution will be highly visible and significant. Part of this governmental activism is a result of the growing scale and reach of global firms. For instance, even before the global financial meltdown in 2009, McKinsey & Company consultancy noted the following:

As businesses expand their global reach, and as the economic demands on the environment intensify, the level of societal suspicion about big business is likely to increase. The tenets of current global business ideology—for example, shareholder value, free trade, intellectual-property rights, and profit repatriation—are not understood, let alone accepted, in many parts of the world. Scandals and environmental mishaps seem as inevitable as the likelihood that these incidents will be subsequently blown out of proportion, thereby fueling resentment and creating a political and regulatory backlash. This trend is not just of the past 5 years but of the past 250 years. The increasing pace and extent of global business, and the emergence of truly giant global corporations, will exacerbate the pressures over the next 10 years. [1]

Unfortunately for big (and small) business, the apparent systematic risk, managerial excesses, and imprudence that led to the global financial meltdown in 2008 and 2009 have only exacerbated the interest of government in business matters. Let's look at the example of Bucyrus International for how to survive and thrive in this new normal of governmental activism. [2]

Meet Bucyrus

Bucyrus caters to those who mine their own business. [3] To be precise, the company designs and manufactures surface and subsurface mining equipment and aftermarket replacement parts, as well as servicing its equipment. Its mining products are used for unearthing coal, gold, iron ore, oil sands, and other raw materials. The company sells products to customers worldwide, from large companies to small ones to quasi-governmental agencies operating largely in South America, Australia, Canada, China, India, South Africa, and the United States. Even though Bucyrus is a US-based company, international sales account for more than 70 percent of its revenues.

Bucyrus in Emerging Markets

Like many successful multinationals, much of Bucyrus's new work takes place in emerging markets where the growth and need is greatest. For instance, Bucyrus struck a deal in which its mining shovels would be used to dig coal to fire a giant, new power plant being built by Reliance Industries in India. Reliance, with nearly 25,000 employees, is India's largest private-sector conglomerate, with business interests in energy, retailing, chemicals, textiles, and communications. [4]

Although Bucyrus and Reliance had agreed on the deal, the involvement of the Export-Import Bank of the United States (Ex-Im Bank) as a loan guarantor complicated things. Ex-Im Bank is the principal government agency responsible for aiding the export of American goods and services—thereby creating and sustaining US jobs—through a variety of loan, guarantee, and insurance programs. Although supporting US exports is its primary mission, the bank was sued by Friends of the Earth, Greenpeace and four American cities that brought a global warming lawsuit against the bank as well as the Overseas Private Investment Corporation (OPIC), contending that the agencies provided financial assistance to projects without first evaluating the projects' global warming impacts. [5] The lawsuit took seven years to resolve, but in the end the courts ruled that Ex-Im Bank and OPIC must consider the environmental effect of the projects they fund. [6]

In reviewing Bucyrus's loan-guarantee application, Ex-Im Bank expressed concerns about the project's environmental impact. [7] In the end, the bank rejected the application. It stated that the coal-fired power plant that would be fed by the mine conflicted with the Obama administration's environmental goals. [8] The guarantees would have backed loans that Reliance would have used to purchase mining equipment from Bucyrus. If the bank's rejection of the financing stood, Reliance could turn to another country, most likely China, for financing and equipment. [9] The bank's ruling was not appealable, but within hours of hearing about it, Bucyrus CEO Tim Sullivan launched an intense campaign aimed at getting Ex-Im Bank to reverse course before the Indian project's equipment orders went to Chinese companies. Sullivan argued that the rejection could result in a loss of $600 million in equipment sales for Bucyrus and up to 1,000 US jobs could be at stake. [10]

Preparation + Reaching Out to Stakeholders...and a Little Luck

Sullivan fumed at the bank's rejection of his loan application. He had recently gone out on a limb and made the bold move of convincing his board of directors to spend $250 million to expand and refurbish Bucyrus's South Milwaukee operations, while the company's competitors were moving work to China. [11] Instead of accepting defeat with the bank's decision, he went on the attack. Sullivan notified elected officials, many of whom were engaged in reelection campaigns. Given the prevailing tough US economic atmosphere, the officials would likely back an initiative that would retain or increase US jobs. Sullivan also called business and labor union leaders and enlisted support from Bucyrus's hundreds of suppliers. The president of the United Steelworkers of America, Leo Gerard, appealed to the public to participate in a letter-writing campaign to protest Ex-Im Bank's refusal to finance mining equipment that would be made by union members. "At a time when we are losing good-paying jobs, and at a time when President Obama wants to double US exports, how can the Export-Import Bank deny a loan that would create and protect jobs at Bucyrus International? It was a dumb decision," Gerard told the Journal Sentinel. [12]

As Sullivan rallied potential supporters, luck played its role: President Barack Obama was planning for a town hall meeting in Racine, Wisconsin, just a few miles from Bucyrus's headquarters. Even better, the town hall meeting topic was the economy. A local business association took out full-page advertisements in the local newspapers asking the president to help reverse the bank's decision and save US jobs. Sullivan was astute in pushing the right political hot buttons, but getting Obama's attention would have been much harder had he not been coming to Racine.

All-Night Negotiations and a Surprise Reversal of the Ex-Im Bank Decision

It is important to remember that Bucyrus is not a coal miner but instead a supplier to that industry, so Ex-Im Bank's complaint was really with Bucyrus's customer, Reliance. After all-night negotiations, still prior to President Obama's visit to Wisconsin, Reliance and Ex-Im Bank remained in disagreement. The bank's primary mission is to support US exports, [13] but it still wanted Reliance to commit to buying US equipment for renewable energy projects as a condition of its approving the loan guarantees. [14]Reliance, however, stated that making such a promise would violate World Trade Organization rules. The impasse was finally settled when Reliance agreed to pursue renewable energy projects in addition to the coal-fired power plant. [15] In an Export-Import Bank news release, Ex-Im Bank chairman and president Fred P. Hochberg said, "We are pleased that Reliance is making this commitment to renewable energy, which allows us to sustain U.S. jobs and promote both conventional and renewable energy exports." [16] Renewable energy sources only account for about 12 percent of India's power, [17] while 50 percent comes from coal-fired plants and the rest from oil and gas. [18] Therefore, progress on alternative energy sources in India was seen as a victory (or at least a face-saving reason) for Ex-Im Bank's reversing its original decision.

A few of hours before Obama landed in Wisconsin, therefore, Ex-Im Bank announced it would reconsider its rejection of the loan guarantees and would review the application again, taking "into account Reliance's expressed commitment to invest in the renewable energy sector" in its review. [19] In a letter to Reliance chairman Anil Ambani, Hochberg asked Reliance to consider building renewable-energy power plants capable of producing at least 250 megawatts of power, which would be among the largest renewable projects built in India to date. [20] The letter did not, however, make the loan guarantees contingent on a fixed amount of renewable energy nor did it impose a deadline for those projects. [21]

Nonetheless, Reliance's agreement to support renewable energy projects was the key factor in the bank's reversed decision. "If we can encourage India to move faster toward renewable energy as part of this project, and to increase opportunities for U.S. exporters, and to finalize the deal with Bucyrus and save jobs, that's a big victory for everyone," an Ex-Im Bank official said. [22]

Although experts agree that Obama's involvement was vital to the bank's reverse decision, many think Bucyrus would have prevailed in the long run anyway, because the bank's decision would not prevent the plant from being built but merely result in the equipment contract going to a foreign competitor.

Experts said Bucyrus's reaction to the bank's initial decision could be a great example of how a company should behave when a deal is threatened by a government agency. [23] Sullivan may have been lucky with Obama's pending visit to Racine, but he also had courage and knew how to seize the moment, enlisting the help of business leaders, union officials, and elected officials alike. "If you are going to be aggressive, the way Bucyrus was in this case, then you had better have the facts on your side," said a University of Wisconsin–Madison professor. Bucyrus took risks and expended much political capital. "The stakes were big here," the professor said. "To me, this was a case of how to respond to a crisis in our new, more political world." [24]

OPENING CASE EXERCISES

(AACSB: Ethical Reasoning, Multiculturalism, Reflective Thinking, Analytical Skills)

1. How was the deal between Bucyrus and Reliance threatened by a government agency?
2. What do you think of how Bucyrus's CEO handled the situation?
3. Do you think governmental agencies will become more involved in business matters? Why or why not?

[1] Ian Davis and Elizabeth Stephenson, "Ten Trends to Watch in 2006," McKinsey Quarterly, January 2006, accessed July 24, 2010, https://www.mckinseyquarterly.com/Ten_trends_to_watch_in_2006_173 4.
[2] Compiled based on reports in Rick Barrett, "Bucyrus Chief Dug Deep for Support," Milwaukee (WI) Journal Sentinel, July 3, 2010, accessed July 23, 2010,http://www.jsonline.com/business/97745649.html; James R. Hagerty, "U.S. Ex-Im Bank Reconsiders India Coal Project," Wall Street Journal, June 30, 2010, accessed July 23, 2010,http://online.wsj.com/article/SB1000142405274870433460457533879 1530127472.html?mod=WSJ_hps_LEFT_WhatsNews; Rich Rovito, "Bucyrus' Sullivan Wants Vote, and Sleep," Milwaukee (WI) Business Journal, July 6, 2010, accessed July 23, 2010,http://milwaukee.bizjournals.com/milwaukee/blog/2010/07/bucyru s_sullivan_wants_vote_and_some_sleep.html?t=printable; Rick Barrett, "Export-Import Bank May Reconsider Bucyrus Decision," Milwaukee (WI) Journal Sentinel, June 28, 2010, accessed July 23, 2010,http://www.jsonline.com/business/97319564.html.
[3] Bucyrus website, accessed July 23, 2010, http://www.bucyrus.com.

[4] "10 Years Highlight: Financial Highlights," Reliance Industries Limited, accessed July 23,
2010, http://www.ril.com/html/investor/10_yearshighlight.html.
[5] Friends of the Earth, "Landmark Global Warming Lawsuit Settled," press release, February 6, 2009, accessed December 12, 2010, http://action.foe.org/t/6545/pressRelease.jsp?press_release_KEY=486.
[6] "Settlement Agreement: Export-Import Bank of the United States," Friends of the Earth, February 6, 2009, accessed December 12, 2010, http://www.foe.org/pdf/Ex-Im_Settlement.pdf;
"Victory!" ClimateLawsuit.org, accessed December 12, 2010,http://www.foe.org/climate/climatelawsuit/index.htm.
[7] Bob Hague, "Ex-Im Bank Moves Forward on Bucyrus Deal," Wisconsin Radio Network, July 14, 2010, accessed December 12, 2010, http://www.wrn.com/2010/07/ex-im-bank-moves-forward-on-bucyrus-deal.
[8] Mark Drajem, "Reliance Power's India Plan Rejected by U.S. Export-Import Bank," BusinessWeek, June 26, 2010, accessed December 12, 2010, http://www.businessweek.com/news/2010-06-26/reliance-power-s-india-plan-rejected-by-u-s-export-import-bank.html.
[9] James R. Hagerty and Amol Sharma, "Employment, Environment at Odds," Wall Street Journal, June 28, 2010, accessed December 12, 2010, http://online.wsj.com/article/SB10001424052748704846004575332810145193160.html.
[10] Patrick McIlheran, "Reprieve for Bucyrus in Era of Mojo," Milwaukee (WI) Journal Sentinel, June 30, 2010, accessed December 12, 2010, http://www.jsonline.com/news/opinion/97521434.html.
[11] Rick Barrett, "Bucyrus Chief Dug Deep for Support," Milwaukee (WI) Journal Sentinel, July 3, 2010, accessed July 23,
2010, http://www.jsonline.com/business/97745649.html.
[12] Rick Barrett, "Obama Visit to Racine Wednesday May Be Pushing Review," Milwaukee (WI) Journal Sentinel, June 28,
2010, http://www.jsonline.com/business/97319564.htmlaccessed November 28, 2010.
[13] Carter Wood, "Ex-Im Bank: Starting to Get Things Right, Slowly," Shop Floor, July 15, 2010, accessed December 12,
2010, http://shopfloor.org/tag/export-import-bank.
[14] Rick Barrett, "Reversal Revives Bucyrus' Big Deal," Milwaukee (WI) Journal Sentinel, June 30, 2010, accessed December 12, 2010, http://www.jsonline.com/business/97484379.html.
[15] Rick Barrett, "Reversal Revives Bucyrus' Big Deal," Milwaukee (WI) Journal Sentinel, June 30, 2010, accessed December 12, 2010, http://www.jsonline.com/business/97484379.html.
[16] Export-Import Bank of the United States, "Ex-Im Bank Approves Preliminary Review of Export Financing Application for India's Sasan Power Plant," press release, July 14, 2010, accessed December 12, 2010, http://www.exim.gov/pressrelease.cfm/D25FB2CF-D13D-A3B0-A324873AFCC72DC7.
[17] Prashant Bawankule, "Renewable Energy Sources: What Will Work for India?" Chilli Breeze, November 2010, accessed December 12, 2010,http://www.chillibreeze.com/articles_various/Renewable-Energy.asp.
[18] Prashant Bawankule, "Renewable Energy Sources: What Will Work for India?" Chilli Breeze, November 2010, accessed December 12, 2010,http://www.chillibreeze.com/articles_various/Renewable-Energy.asp.
[19] Mark Drajem, "U.S. Export-Import Bank Reconsiders India Coal Financing Deal," BusinessWeek, July 1, 2010, accessed December 12, 2010, http://www.businessweek.com/news/2010-07-01/u-s-export-import-bank-reconsiders-india-coal-financing-deal.html.
[20] Fred P. Hochberg, letter to Anil Ambani, Chairman, Reliance ADAG, June 30, 2010, accessed December 12,
2010, http://media.journalinteractive.com/documents/EI-bank-ltr_062010.pdf.
[21] Rick Barrett, "Reversal Revives Bucyrus' Big Deal," Milwaukee (WI) Journal Sentinel, June 30, 2010, accessed December 12, 2010, http://www.jsonline.com/business/97484379.html.
[22] Rick Barrett, "Reversal Revives Bucyrus' Big Deal," Milwaukee (WI) Journal Sentinel, June 30, 2010, accessed December 12, 2010, http://www.jsonline.com/business/97484379.html.
[23] Rick Barrett, "Bucyrus Chief Dug Deep for Support," Milwaukee (WI) Journal Sentinel, July 3, 2010, accessed July 23,
2010, http://www.jsonline.com/business/97745649.html.
[24] Rick Barrett, "Bucyrus Chief Dug Deep for Support," Milwaukee (WI) Journal Sentinel, July 3, 2010, accessed July 23,
2010, http://www.jsonline.com/business/97745649.html.

15.1 International Accounting Standards
LEARNING OBJECTIVES

1. Learn the value of accounting in international business.
2. Describe the role of accounting standards.
3. Recognize the difficulties caused by countries using different accounting standards.

The Role of Accounting in International Business

The purpose of accounting is to communicate the organization's financial position to company managers, investors, banks, and the government. Accounting standards provide a system of rules and principles that prescribe the format and content of financial statements. Through this consistent reporting, a firm's managers and investors can assess the financial health of the firm. Accounting standards cover topics such as how to account for inventories, depreciation, research and development costs, income taxes, investments, intangible assets, and employee benefits. Investors and banks use these financial statements to determine whether to invest in or loan capital to the firm, while governments use the statements to ensure that the companies are paying their fair share of taxes. As countries developed different cultures, languages, and social and economic traditions, they developed different accounting practices as well. In an increasingly globalized world, however, these differences are not optimal for the smooth functioning of international business.

The Emergence of New International Accounting Standards

The International Accounting Standards Board (IASB) is the major entity proposing international standards of accounting. Originally formed in 1973 as the International Accounting Standards Committee (IASC) and renamed the International Accounting Standards Board in 2001, the IASB is an independent agency that develops accounting standards known sinternational financial reporting standards (IFRS). [1] The IASB is composed of fifteen representatives from professional accounting firms from many countries. [2] These board members formulate the international reporting standards. For a standard to be approved, 75 percent of the board members must agree. Often, getting agreement is difficult given the social, economic, legal, and cultural differences among countries. As a result, most IASB statements provide two acceptable alternatives. Two alternatives aren't as solid or straightforward as one, but it's better than having a dozen different options.

Adherence to the IASB's standards is voluntary, but many countries have mandated use of IFRS. For example, all companies listed on EU stock exchanges are required to use IFRS. [3] The same is true for all companies listed on South Africa's Johannesburg Stock Exchange and Turkey's Istanbul Stock Exchange. In all, over one hundred nations have adopted or permitted companies to use the IASB's standards to report their financial results. [4]

The United States doesn't mandate using the IFRS. Instead, the United States has the Financial Accounting Standards Board (FASB), which issues standards known as generally accepted accounting principles (GAAP). The US currently mandates following GAAP. However, the FASB and IASB are working on harmonizing the accounting standards; many IASB standards are similar to FASB ones. The United States is moving toward adopting the IFRS but hasn't committed to a specific time frame. [5]

The primary reason for adopting one standard internationally is that if different accounting standards are used, it's difficult for investors or lenders to compare the financial health of two companies. In addition, if a single international standard is used, multinational firms won't have to prepare different reports for the different countries in which they operate.

Accounting standards can be complex; and this makes modification of standards difficult. In addition, differing practices among various nations add to the complications of a unified accounting format. For example, in the United States and Great Britain, individual investors provide a substantial source of capital to companies, so accounting rules are designed to help individual investors. [6] In contrast, the tradition in Switzerland, Germany, and Japan is for companies to rely more on banks for funding. Companies in these countries have a tighter relationship with banks. This means that less information is disclosed to the public. It also results in accounting rules that value assets conservatively to protect a bank's investment. In other countries, the government steps in to make loans or invest in companies whose activities are in the "national interest."

Finally, accounting rules in China follow neither IFRS nor GAAP, which makes it hard for investors to gauge the true value of a company. [7] To address this issue, some large Chinese companies report results in both Chinese accounting standards and the IASB's standards. The two accounting standards can show quite different results for the same company, which is why convergence proponents advocate using one global accounting standard.

Characteristics of International Accounting Standards and Their Implications for International Business

On one hand, having to adhere to GAAP rules as well as IFRS rules creates extra labor and paperwork for multinational firms. For example, a US company seeking to raise funds in Germany has to prepare a financial report according to IFRS accounting rules as well as US GAAP rules. Further problems arise when different country accounting rules make the financial statements look different. If the same transaction is accounted for in different ways based on different country accounting rules, the comparability of financial reports is undermined.

In some instances, the differences between US GAAP rules and IFRS are significant. For example, the last-in, first-out (LIFO) accounting method is allowed by GAAP but banned by IFRS. Some firms, such as aluminum company Alcoa, receive a tax benefit from using the LIFO method. [8] If IFRS is mandated for all US companies, firms like Alcoa may need to make significant cash-tax payments. This is why US adoption of IFRS is taking time, and why the FASB and IASB are working hard to harmonize the standards.

On the positive side, other companies, like IBM, may gain greater efficiencies and stronger controls from a move to IFRS. For example, converting to IFRS would make it possible for IBM to create a globally shared service center for accounting, rather than having accounting departments in different regions. [9]

US adoption of the IASB's global accounting standards would be useful to big multinational companies. Tyco International, for example, is the parent of 1,200 legal entities, 900 of them outside the United States. For Tyco, having to follow only IFRS rules would be positive, because it would enable Tyco to prepare financials on the same basis worldwide and to more freely move accounting staff from country to country and business to business. Nonetheless, given Tyco's massive network of information systems, making the switch would still be "a tremendous amount of work," according to John Davidson, the company's controller and chief accounting officer. [10]

Some smaller public companies, however, would see only costs from a move to IFRS. Davey Tree Expert Company, for example, which only does business in the United States and Canada, sees no benefits. Because the company is unlikely to ever list on any national exchange, the argument that unified standards would allow comparability of financials has no value. [11]

An interim step toward the United States adopting IFRS is to permit US firms that operate globally to file only under IFRS, rather than under both GAAP and IFRS, thereby reducing their financial-statement preparation costs.

KEY TAKEAWAYS

- The purpose of accounting is to communicate an organization's financial position to company managers, investors, banks, and the government. Accounting provides a system of rules and principles that prescribe the format and content of financial statements. Through this consistent reporting, a company's managers and investors can assess the financial health of the firm.

- Historically, countries have followed different accounting standards. If different accounting standards are used, however, it's difficult for investors or lenders to compare two companies or determine their financial condition. US firms and any listed on a US stock exchange must prepare financial statements in accordance with the US Financial Accounting Standards Board (FASB) standards, which are known as generally accepted accounting principles (GAAP). Firms based in the European Union (EU) follow standards adopted by the International Accounting Standards Board (IASB) known as international financial reporting standards (IFRS). Over one hundred nations have adopted or permit companies to use IFRS to report their financial results. The United States is moving toward adopting IFRS but hasn't committed to a time frame. The FASB and IASB are working on harmonizing the two accounting standards.

- The three main advantages of a single set of international accounting standards are (1) an increased comparability between firms, which reduces investor risk and facilitates cross-border financing and investment; (2) a reduction in the cost of preparing consolidated financial statements for multinational firms; and (3) the improved reliability and credibility of financial reports.

EXERCISES

(AACSB: Reflective Thinking, Analytical Skills)
1. What is the purpose of accounting?

2. Why do countries have different accounting standards?
3. What are the advantages of a single set of international accounting standards?
4. Which set of accounting standards does the United States follow?
5. Why are some governments reluctant to follow IFRS?

[1] "History," International Accounting Standards Board, accessed November 26, 2010, http://www.ifrs.org/Home.htm.
[2] "About the IFRS Foundation and the IASB," IFRS Foundation, accessed November 25, 2010, http://www.ifrs.org/The+organisation/IASCF+and+IASB.htm.
[3] European Commission, "Report to the European Securities Committee and to the European Parliament," April 6, 2010, accessed November 26, 2010, http://eur-lex.europa.eu/LexUriServ/LexUriServ.do?uri=com:2010:0292:fin:en:html.
[4] Neil Baker, "IFAC Calls for Crucial Reporting Roadmap," Compliance Week, July 27, 2009, accessed November 26, 2010, http://www.complianceweek.com/blog/glimpses/2009/07/27/ifac-calls-for-reporting-roadmap.
[5] Marie Leone, "Harvey Goldschmid Named IASB Trustee," CFO, December 11, 2009, accessed November 26, 2010, http://www.cfo.com/printable/article.cfm/14461503.
[6] CIRCA, "International Accounting Norms: Background and Recent Developments in the EU," accessed November 26, 2010, http://circa.europa.eu/irc/dsis/accstat/info/data/en/accounting%20for%20website.htm.
[7] Doug McIntyre, "Chinese Accounting: Greek to Many," Forbes, June 18, 2007, accessed November 26, 2010, http://www.forbes.com/2007/06/18/china-accounting-gaap-pf-education-in_dm_0618investopedia_inl.html.
[8] Marie Leone, "Unfazed by IFRS," CFO, April 30, 2010, accessed August 10, 2010, http://www.cfo.com/article.cfm/14495043.
[9] Marie Leone, "Unfazed by IFRS," CFO, April 30, 2010, accessed August 10, 2010, http://www.cfo.com/article.cfm/14495043.
[10] David McCann, "IFRS: Jekyll or Hyde?" CFO, November 20, 2009, accessed October 28, 2010, http://www.cfo.com/article.cfm/14456597/c_14457492.
[11] David McCann, "IFRS: Jekyll or Hyde?" CFO, November 20, 2009, accessed October 28, 2010, http://www.cfo.com/article.cfm/14456597/c_14457492.

15.2 Accounting in International Business
LEARNING OBJECTIVES

1. Describe what consolidated financial statements are.
2. Understand the risk of currency fluctuations.
3. Explain two methods that firms use for currency translation.

Financial Statements in International Business

Multinational firms often organize as separate legal entities (i.e., companies) in different countries to gain advantages, such as limiting liability or taking advantage of local corporate tax regulations. Also, many countries mandate that companies that do business in their country set up a separate company in that country. As a result, a multinational company may have numerous foreign subsidiaries, all owned by the parent. A consolidated financial statement brings together all the financial statements of a parent and its subsidiaries into a single financial statement. The consolidated financial statement must reconcile all the investment and capital accounts as well as the assets, liabilities, and operating accounts of the firms. Consolidated financial statements demonstrate that firms—although legally separate from the parent and each other—are in fact economically interdependent. Most of the developed nations require consolidated statements so that losses can't be hidden under an unconsolidated subsidiary. The International Accounting Standards Board (IASB) standards mandate the use of consolidated financial statements.

Consolidating financial statements of subsidiaries located in different countries poses problems because of the different currencies used in different countries. Companies must decide on what basis they will translate those different currencies into the home currency of the parent company.

Currency Risk

Currency values fluctuate from day to day relative to each other, which poses a risk for firms that operate internationally. Currency risk is the risk of a change in the exchange rate that will adversely affect the company. Companies face this risk because they typically price their products and services in the local currency of each country in which they operate, to make it easy for local customers to understand the pricing and make the purchase. This practice exposes companies to currency risk. For example, the US dollar fluctuated from 1.501 dollars per euro in October 2009 to 1.19440 in June 2010. [1] This means that if a US company were selling a product for 1,000 euros, the company would receive $1,501 dollars for it in October 2009 but only $1,194 for it in June 2010. To preserve profits, the company might raise the euro-denominated price of its products, but the company would risk a drop in sales due to the increased price.

In a simple example, currency fluctuations mean that if a US-based company sold its product in Germany at a 10 percent profit and the currency value of the dollar dropped 10 percent relative to the euro, then the profit would be wiped out.

Companies can mitigate currency risk by engaging in hedging. Hedging refers to using financial instruments to reduce adverse price movements by taking an offsetting position. Specifically, a firm can lock in a guaranteed foreign exchange rate through a forward contract. In the forward contract, the firm agrees to pay a specific rate at the beginning of the contract for delivery at a future date.

Thus, the firm will pay the agreed-on exchange rate regardless of what the current exchange rate is at the date of the final settlement. There are costs associated with using these instruments, such as premium pricing, bank fees, and interest payments. But companies often prefer to protect themselves against a potential larger downside loss, even if they have to pay extra to avoid that bigger loss.

Currency Translation

When multinational companies consolidate their subsidiaries' financial statements, they must translate all the currencies into the currency used by the parent company in its home country. There are two methods which a company can use for currency translation—the current-rate method or the temporal method.

Current-Rate Method

The current-rate method is a method of foreign-currency translation in which items in the subsidiaries' financial statements are translated into the currency of the parent corporation at the current exchange rate (i.e., the rate on the date when the statements are prepared). In this case, the current value may be different on the day it's translated than on the date when the assets were originally purchased. Although this difference is only a paper gain or loss, it nonetheless affects the valuation of the firm. This method is the most widely used currency-translation method.

Temporal Method

The temporal method is a method of foreign-currency translation that uses exchange rates based on the rate in place when the assets and liabilities were originally acquired or incurred. The temporal method avoids the paper gains or losses problem of the current-rate method. But because subsidiaries purchase assets at different times throughout the year, the multinational firm's balance sheet may not balance if the temporal method is used.

Currency Fluctuations

When the Chinese government announced in 2010 that it would allow its currency, the yuan, to float more freely in relation to other world currencies, US CFOs knew that the change would affect their currency-risk picture. When the yuan was pegged to the dollar (from 2008 to 2010), China's currency had less value, which gave China an advantage in global trade. China's goods were cheaper in world markets. Once the yuan floats more freely, it's expected to appreciate against the dollar.

The yuan's appreciation against the dollar will most likely bring two results. First, it will bring Chinese consumers' purchasing power closer to parity around the world. Second, manufacturing in China will be more expensive than it was in the past, which brings about two results of its own. Foreign firms may move their manufacturing operations out of China (or not open them there in the first place) as they search for the lowest costs elsewhere, and the yuan's value appreciation in the long term means that Chinese products will become more expensive for other countries to buy, which will force China to move from manufacturing lower-margin products like toys and shoes to higher-end businesses. These higher-end areas will bring China into more direct competition with the United States and Europe. [2]

Forward Exchange Rate

One way to deal with the problem of currency fluctuations is to use the forward-exchange-rate method. The forward exchange rate is the rate at which two parties agree to exchange currency and execute a deal at some specific point in the future, usually 30 days, 60 days, 90 days, or 180 days in the future. The firms agree up front on the rate at which they'll exchange currencies, although the actual delivery of the foreign currency will be at a future specified date. For example, a multinational firm based in Spain might sign a contract with a US bank to buy US dollars for euros 90 days from now at a specified exchange rate. The Spanish corporation would use the forward exchange rate as a way to reduce exchange-rate risk if the value of the euro decreases substantially relative to the US dollar.

If two subsidiaries of the same multinational firm do a currency exchange, then they can use an internal forward rate. The internal forward rate is a company-generated forecast of future spot exchange rates. The internal forward rate may differ from the forward rate quoted by the foreign exchange market. The advantage of this agreement between the parent and foreign subsidiaries is that if the exchange rate changes, the subsidiary will be not be blamed or credited for the change.

KEY TAKEAWAYS

- Multinational firms often organize as separate legal entities (i.e., companies) in different countries to gain advantages such as limiting liability or taking advantage of local corporate tax regulations. A consolidated financial statement brings together all the financial statements of a parent and its subsidiaries into a single financial statement. Consolidating financial statements of subsidiaries located in different countries poses problems because of the different currencies used in different countries.

- Currency values fluctuate from day to day relative to each other. Companies can mitigate currency risk by engaging in hedging. Hedging refers to using financial instruments to reduce adverse price movements by taking an offsetting position. Specifically, a firm can lock in a guaranteed foreign exchange rate through a forward contract. In a forward contract, a firm agrees to pay a specific rate at the beginning of the contract for delivery at a future date.

- Companies must decide what method they'll use to translate different currencies into the home currency of the parent company. Under the current-rate method of currency translation, items in the subsidiaries' financial statements are translated at the current exchange rate (i.e., the rate on the date when the statements are prepared) into the currency of the parent corporation. Under the temporal method, firms use the exchange rate based on the rate in place when the assets and liabilities were originally acquired or incurred.

EXERCISES

(AACSB: Reflective Thinking, Analytical Skills)

1. Why do most developed nations require consolidated financial statements?
2. What does currency risk mean?
3. What are some ways that companies can reduce the currency risk they face?
4. Compare the current-rate method of currency translation with the temporal method.
5. Explain the difference between the foreign exchange rate and the internal forward rate.

[1] "Historical Exchange Rates," OANDA, accessed October 28, 2010, http://www.oanda.com/currency/historical-rates?date_fmt=us&date=10/26/09&date1=02/25/09&exch=EUR&exch2=EUR&expr=USD&expr2=USD&format=HTML&margin_fixed=0.
[2] Kate O'Sullivan, "Freeing the Yuan," CFO, June 23, 2010, accessed October 28, 2010, http://www.cfo.com/article.cfm/14506658.

15.3 Fundamentals of Finance
LEARNING OBJECTIVES

1. Know the various financing options available to international firms.
2. Explain the value of capital budgeting.
3. Understand the role of governments in affecting investment decisions.

Financial Structure and Sources of Financing

As demonstrated in the opening case study, governments, banks, and individuals all play a role in international financing.

Businesses get external capital from these sources—capital that lets them build, expand, and grow.

Financial structure refers to the ways in which a multinational firm's assets are financed—from short-term borrowing to long-term debt and equity. Managing a multinational firm's financial structure involves asking: *What is the ideal mix of debt versus equity to finance international operations? Where should these funds be invested?* Multinational firms engage in both transnational financing (i.e., seeking capital from a foreign sources) and transnational investment (i.e., investing capital in foreign markets).

Sources of financing available to firms include foreign stock exchanges, foreign bond markets, foreign banks, venture-capital firms, and funding from the parent company. Although global equity and debt markets offer firms a new way to get funding—often at lower cost than US markets—they are also complicated by foreign currency and exchange rates.

Equity financing refers to raising capital by selling shares of stock. The stock market refers to the organized trading of securities through exchanges. An individual or entity can purchase partial ownership in a corporation, buying shares of stock in the company. The global equity market refers to all stock exchanges worldwide where firms can buy and sell stock for financing an investment.

The largest exchanges in the world include the New York Stock Exchange (NYSE) Euronext, the Tokyo Stock Exchange, NASDAQ (National Association of Securities Dealers Automated Quotations) stock exchange, and the London Stock Exchange. The advantage of raising capital in equity markets is that the firm doesn't have to repay the money at a specific time or at a specific interest rate, as it does with bank loans. The disadvantage is that each time a firm offers stock, the firm's management loses some control of the company because shareholders can now vote to approve or disallow management actions.

Debt financing refers to raising capital by borrowing the money and agreeing to repay the entire amount plus agreed-on interest at a specific date in the future. Firms can borrow money from banks or by selling bonds. The advantage of raising money through debt financing is that company management doesn't give up any ownership of the firm.

Firms can also obtain funding via intrafirm loans or trade credits. A trade credit lets the customer (in this case, the subsidiary buying the goods or services) defer payment on the good or service for a specified period of time, typically thirty or ninety days. By borrowing capital from a parent, both the subsidiary and the parent eliminate paying transaction costs to an outside entity such as a bank, which would charge fees to make the transaction.

Financing Options Available to Subsidiaries
Subsidiaries can choose between two major ways to finance their operations through external sources: overseas equity markets and overseas debt markets. Let's look at each in turn.

Raising Money in Overseas Equity Markets
Multinational firms choose to raise money in foreign markets for a number of reasons. For example, French luxury beauty products company L'Occitane conducted its initial public offering (IPO) on Hong Kong's stock exchange, rather than on the stock exchange in its home country—the NYSE Euronext in Paris. [1] L'Occitane made this decision because emerging-market consumers are its fastest-growing segment. Listing on Hong Kong's exchange makes the company more visible in these growing markets and lets locals participate in the growth of the firm by buying shares.

Some multinational firms raise money in both their home-country and overseas stock exchanges. One of the reasons for listing on multiple exchanges is a lower cost of capital as shares become available to global investors who might not otherwise be able to purchase shares due to international investment barriers.

Emerging markets are also opening stock exchanges. For example, the Shanghai and Shenzhen Stock Exchanges in China opened in 1990. In July 2010, the Shanghai Stock Exchange became the sixth-largest stock exchange in the world based on market capitalization.

Public share ownership in China remains complex with three classes of shares: A, B, and H. A-shares are local shares denominated in China's local currency for domestic investors. B-shares are denominated in Hong Kong dollars or US dollars and are generally owned by foreigners. H-shares are for China-incorporated companies traded in Hong Kong. Chinese authorities (the China Securities Regulatory Commission, the People's Bank of China, and the State Administration of Foreign Exchange) closely regulate the Shanghai and Shenzhen Stock Exchanges. Indeed, the Chinese government actively intervenes in its capital markets. For example, it didn't allow any new equity funds to be established in 2007. The government also owns a relatively high number of shares in many listed companies. China's low transparency, poor implementation of securities regulations, and restrictions on hedging and risk-management tools are warning signs to foreign investment-fund executives. At the same time, the government lacks many regulations related to educating or protecting investors. A brokerage firm can allow an investor to buy and sell any amount of any security after the investor answers three questions in the following areas: name, health, and risk tolerance. [2]

Raising Money in Overseas Debt Markets

Multinational firms can issue bonds in overseas markets as well as in their home countries. Even China now has an active bond market. Before April 2008, Chinese state-owned enterprises were about the only ones issuing corporate debt in China because corporate bonds were so costly and time-consuming to issue there. Corporate bonds had to be listed on the stock exchange and approved by exchange regulators, making the process subject to political whims. State-owned enterprises raised money in the bond market to finance big infrastructure projects, and the bonds had state guarantees. In 2008, new rules simplified the issuing process, and the Chinese government began letting foreign companies issue yuan-denominated bonds through Hong Kong in 2010. The attraction of the Chinese bond market, according to Chris Zhou, director of debt capital markets at UBS Securities in Beijing, is that "the bond market is a relatively easy and cost-effective way to get money." [3]

McDonald's was the first foreign company to issue yuan-denominated bonds, selling 200 million yuan (or $29 million) of 3 percent notes due in September 2013. As Donald Straszheim, senior managing director and head of China research at the International Strategy & Investment Group observed, "There are hundreds of global companies wanting to do more business in China, and they will want to be involved in the country's evolving credit market." [4]

According to McDonald's spokesperson Lisa Howard, issuing bonds in China "gives us access to new funding to support growth in China. We are very confident in the Chinese market and have a strong plan to grow our business in China." [5] McDonald's will use the money it has raised in the bond market to provide working capital for expansion in China, including opening as many as 175 restaurants in 2010, adding to the 1,000 restaurants it already has there.

Innovation and Entrepreneurship

WaterHealth: Financing for Entrepreneurs in Developing Countries
WaterHealth is a company that sells and leases water purification systems for use in developing countries. The company also sells and leases special sanitary water containers that reduce the spread of waterborne diseases

from contaminated ladles. WaterHealth developed ultraviolet technology to sanitize water. The technology doesn't require large-scale operations or equipment, which enables local entrepreneurs in developing countries to use the technology to open their own water shops to sell water to local customers. The result? Consumers gain access to cheaper, cleaner water, while the local economy gains new businesses. WaterHealth's innovative financing doesn't require high up-front payments for its technology. Instead, the company collects user fees, allowing the repayment of financing costs over time. [6]

Investment Decisions

Capital Budgeting

Capital budgeting refers to the process of financing long-term outlays for major projects such as plant expansion, entry into new markets, or research and development. The process of capital budgeting helps a firm decide which major investment projects will be most economically advantageous for the firm by assessing each project's benefits, costs, and risks. When making capital-investment decisions, firms examine the initial investment that will be required, the cost of capital, and the amount of cash flow or other gains which the project will provide. The cost of capital is the rate of return that a company could earn if it chose a different investment of equivalent risk. The cost of capital comes into play because firms have choices in how to put their capital to use; using the capital for one purpose precludes using it for a different purpose.

Some governments court foreign borrowers by offering low-interest loans or by offering lower corporate income tax to attract investment in their countries. For example, Poland created special tax breaks for companies. These tax breaks make the country attractive for firms such as Hewlett-Packard and IBM to locate operations there. Similarly, Singapore's government has invested heavily in education and training in an effort to attract investment by leading multinational firms. Singapore also offers subsidies to companies locating there. As corporations think about where to invest, build factories, locate offices, and source talent, they explore such opportunities actively. [7]

How Government Actions Affect Investment Decisions

Government policy affects foreign investment and innovation. According to Jeffrey Sachs, a leading international economic advisor and Columbia University professor, the near-term prospects for Brazil are bright, and it's poised to do the best among Latin American countries.

Brazil

For the last fifteen years, Brazil has been investing heavily in education. In particular, Brazil made high school available to all citizens and invested in higher education, science, and technology. The result of these government investments is that not only does Brazil have a more educated workforce, but it has also narrowed off the gap between rich and poor and between ethnically divided segments of Brazilian society. In contrast, countries with deep ethnic and racial inequities aren't unified societies, which leads to mediocre economic performance. Brazil plans to invest another $22 billion in science and technology innovation in 2010 and seeks corporations to join in additional investments in the country. [8]

IBM is one of the companies investing in Brazil. CEO Sam Palmisano met with Brazilian President Luiz Inacio Lula Da Silva to discuss the creation of a "collaboratory" in Brazil. IBM's collaboratories match IBM researchers with local experts from governments, universities and companies. IBM's Palmisano praised Brazil's strategy: "Investments in innovation are critical, especially in a downturn. They can help Brazil and other countries, including the US, realize an economic expansion." Among the BRIC countries (Brazil, Russia, India, and China), Brazil is seeing the highest growth in business partners that IBM works with, averaging 150 percent year over year, according to Claudia Fan Munce, managing director of IBM Venture Capital Group. [9]

As the above example illustrates, Brazil is attracting foreign business. Companies making foreign investments, however, must be aware of the total financial picture, including the tax environment. Brazil has a very complex tax system. "If it's not the most complicated tax system in the world, it's certainly right up there," said Mark Buthman, finance chief at Kimberly-Clark, the consumer packaged goods giant, which has approximately 3,000 people in its Brazilian operation. "It's not uncommon to have disagreements with the taxing authorities that you have to work through over time." [10] What makes doing business in Brazil challenging is that the tax laws have not kept pace with the progress of modern products or services; that is, the categories of taxes do not correspond to modern-day categories of products and services. The lack of parallelism leads to confusion and misinterpretation. To deal with the difficulties, Kimberly-Clark, for example, employs seventy people—most of them native Brazilians—in its finance group in Brazil.

In addition to federal taxes, Brazilian states assess their own taxes as well. Thack Brown, CFO of SAP Latin America, says that any misstep regarding a labor or tax regulation can prove costly. "If you do have an issue, not only can the penalties be large, but you can spend three or four or even 10 years working through the judicial system." [11] Despite the difficulties, Brown says that compared to China, the Brazilian system is still more structured and capable of dealing with issues. [12]

Indonesia

Indonesia is the third-largest democracy in the world and the largest economy in Southeast Asia. The country recently created an investment coordinating board to attract foreign direct investment into Indonesia. How is Indonesia making itself attractive to foreign investors?

1. It's touting its young population—half of the population is under thirty years of age, which bodes well for a skilled workforce and growing consumer base.
2. It's touting its political stability of twelve years after democratization, and monetary stability for the last five to six years.
3. It's investing in infrastructure. "We are committing $50 billion from a budgetary standpoint for the development of infrastructure as part of a $150 billion five-year program," said Gita Wirjawan, Indonesia's chairman of Badan Koordinasi Penamaan Modal (BKPM), the country's newly created investment coordinating board. "That will produce 20,000 kilometers of new roads and an additional 15,000 megawatts of power generation. That is going to create a much higher degree of connectivity than what we have today." [13]

Despite these advances, Indonesia still restricts which industries foreign investors can invest in. For example, investors can't invest in telecommunications towers. Nonetheless, Indonesia has attracted some major investors, such as a large Middle Eastern investor who will build an integrated infrastructure project including a port, a rail track, and new power-generation capability. The total investment will be about $5.2 billion. Indonesia has also convinced the Swiss firm Holcim to expand its cement capabilities in Indonesia. [14]

The Role of Government

The role of government in terms of international business and finance includes:

- passing laws and setting policies (e.g., regulating stock and bond markets and setting tax codes),
- enforcing laws (laws laxly enforced have little value),
- providing infrastructure (e.g., fast communications infrastructure and reliable electricity are important to the smooth functioning of capital markets), and

- providing capital (e.g., providing or guaranteeing loans, as the US government does through the Export-Import Bank of the United States). [15]

KEY TAKEAWAYS

- Multinational firms have a choice in how they finance international operations. Some choose to raise capital through equity markets, issuing stock on domestic or overseas stock exchanges. Others opt for debt financing through banks or bond markets in order to not give up ownership in the firm.

- Capital budgeting is the process by which firms assess the relative merits of different investment choices, weighing the cost of capital and the expected returns of different investment options.

- Governments can play an active role in attracting firms to invest in their countries or enticing foreign borrowers by offering low-interest loans or lower corporate income taxes. When evaluating countries for investment potential, companies consider a government's economic policies (e.g., business environment, trade policy, investment policy, and infrastructure) as well as any cultural issues (e.g., ethnic, religious, and gender inequalities) that may be a barrier.

EXERCISES

(AACSB: Reflective Thinking, Analytical Skills)

1. What sources of financing are available to a company's subsidiaries?
2. What is the advantage of equity financing over debt financing?
3. When might a company choose debt financing?
4. Name two advantages of raising money on a foreign stock exchange.
5. Why is capital budgeting important to a multinational company?

[1] Peter Bisson, Rik Kirkland, and Elizabeth Stephenson, "The Great Rebalancing," McKinsey Quarterly, June 2010, accessed October 28, 2010, http://www.mckinseyquarterly.com/The_great_rebalancing_2627.

[2] Matt Anderson, Daniel Curtis, Derek Lin, and Ian Van Reepinghen, "Coming of Age: A Look at China's New Generation of Investors," in The Lauder Institute, Lauder Global Business Insight Report 2010: First-Hand Perspectives on the Global Economy (Philadelphia: Wharton, University of Pennsylvania, 2010), 69–73, accessed October 28, 2010,http://knowledge.wharton.upenn.edu/papers/download/021710_GlobalBiz_2010.pdf.

[3] Frederik Balfour, "In China, A Burst of Corporate Bonds," BusinessWeek, July 6, 2009, 25.

[4] Patricia Kuo and Shelley Smith, "McDonald's Sets Benchmark for China With Yuan Bond Sale," Bloomberg, August 20, 2010, accessed August 23, 2010, http://www.bloomberg.com/news/2010-08-

19/mcdonald-s-yuan-bonds-set-standard-as-china-promotes-debt-credit-markets.html.

[5] Patricia Kuo and Shelley Smith, "McDonald's Sets Benchmark for China with Yuan Bond Sale," Bloomberg, August 20, 2010, accessed August 23, 2010, http://www.bloomberg.com/news/2010-08-19/mcdonald-s-yuan-bonds-set-standard-as-china-promotes-debt-credit-markets.html.

[6] WaterHealth International, "Frequently Asked Questions," accessed August 14, 2010, http://www.waterhealth.com/.

[7] Peter Bisson, Rik Kirkland, and Elizabeth Stephenson, "The Market State," McKinsey Quarterly, June 2010, accessed October 28, 2010, http://www.mckinseyquarterly.com/The_market_state_2628.

[8] Jeffrey Sachs, "Economics for a Crowded Planet" (webinar, HSM Global, 2009), accessed October 28, 2010, http://us.hsmglobal.com/contenidos/hsm-webinars-sachs.html; Jeffrey Sachs, The End of Poverty: Economic Possibilities for Our Time (New York: Penguin, 2005).

[9] Steve Hamm, "Big Blue's Global Lab," BusinessWeek, August 27, 2009, accessed October 28, 2010, http://www.businessweek.com/magazine/content/09_36/b4145040683083.htm; Spencer E. Ante, "IBM Bets on Brazilian Innovation," BusinessWeek, August 17, 2009, accessed October 28, 2010,http://www.businessweek.com/technology/content/aug2009/tc20090817_998497.htm.

[10] Kate O'Sullivan, "Brazil Is Booming (and Maddening)," CFO, July 15, 2010, accessed October 28, 2010, http://www.cfo.com/printable/article.cfm/14508833.

[11] Kate O'Sullivan, "Brazil Is Booming (and Maddening)," CFO, July 15, 2010, accessed October 28, 2010, http://www.cfo.com/printable/article.cfm/14508833.

[12] Kate O'Sullivan, "Brazil Is Booming (and Maddening)," CFO, July 15, 2010, accessed October 28, 2010, http://www.cfo.com/printable/article.cfm/14508833.

[13] "Why Gita Wirjawan Wants to Open Indonesia to International Investors," Knowledge@Wharton, July 21, 2010, accessed August 9, 2010, http://knowledge.wharton.upenn.edu/article.cfm?articleid=2553.

[14] "Why Gita Wirjawan Wants to Open Indonesia to International Investors," Knowledge@Wharton, July 21, 2010, accessed August 9, 2010, http://knowledge.wharton.upenn.edu/article.cfm?articleid=2553.

[15] Scott Leibs, "A Force to Be Reckoned With," CFO, February 1, 2010, accessed August 7, 2010, http://www.cfo.com/printable/article.cfm/14470883.

15.4 Financial Management in International Business

LEARNING OBJECTIVES

1. Understand the factors that underlie political risk and volatility.
2. Identify two ways in which the financial organization of a multinational firm can be structured.
3. Recognize how religion can influence financial practices in some countries.

Accounting for Political and Economic Risk

Companies that locate operations in foreign countries face a set of unavoidable risks, chief among which are political and economic risks. Political risks arise from decisions that foreign governments make, including changes in government that result from wars and coups. Economic risks are often paired with political risks but can also arise from international money markets. Both risks are exacerbated by increased volatility and changes in laws.

Increased Volatility

In the 2010 *McKinsey Global Survey* of 1,416 executives from around the world, 63 percent of respondents "expect increased overall volatility to become a permanent feature of the global economy." [1] For example, the most important growing economy in the world, China, is a force that must be reckoned with. The volatility arises because this major economy isn't a developed state with commitment to the rule of law and strong institutions. Rather, it's an emerging market where political insecurities are the ultimate driver, according to Ian Bremmer, president of the Eurasia Group and author of *The End of the Free Market*. [2]

To prepare for volatility, multinational companies may want to plan contingencies or at least think through how they might react to events that are currently "unthinkable," such as significant, rapid shifts in currency values (e.g., a 30 percent decline of the dollar versus an emerging-market currency); an exit from the euro by some nations; dramatic, rapid changes in commodity prices (e.g., oil prices spiking to $200 a barrel); or defaults on debt by major nations.[3] These events seem highly improbable now, but, if they come to pass, executives who have thought about how to respond to them will be better positioned to react effectively.

Legal Infrastructure: Challenges of Nascent Laws

Variations in contract law, bankruptcy law, real estate law, intellectual property rights, and liability are just some of the legal issues that companies face when operating or making investments in emerging-market countries. Slow civil judicial processes, corrupt judges, and potential biases against foreigners can affect a company's ability to operate effectively, recover losses, or collect bad debts. For example, General Motors (GM) often uses a contractual structure with suppliers in which GM owns the proprietary tooling used in their supplier's factory. In most countries, if the supplier goes bankrupt, GM can easily take the tooling back. But GM noted that this isn't possible in China due to the nascent state of the country's bankruptcy law, which was created only in 1988. [4] As a result, GM uses contracts to mitigate these risks.

Financial Organizational Structure in International Business

Multinational companies can choose to manage their financial operations centrally or via a decentralized organizational structure.

Centralized Structures

The advantages of a centralized structure are that the company can afford to hire and retain specialized staff with deep expertise who can bring savings to the company through centralized cash management and more efficient capital investment. Centralization can improve control and compliance with corporate policies. This structure enables the firm to gain economies of scale for investment and borrowing activities that can reduce transaction costs and provide the firm with the most competitive pricing.

Decentralized Structures

Alternatively, multinational firms may choose a decentralized financial organization structure due to variations in language, consumers, cultures, business practices, and government rules, laws, and regulations among different countries. A decentralized structure lets multinational firms exploit local knowledge and business conditions to deal with uncertainty. The downsides of a decentralized approach are higher costs (due to having to hire more employees), some unavoidable duplication of effort, and a diminishment of control.

Communication with Headquarters

If a company uses a decentralized financial structure, it's vital for regional chief financial officers (CFOs) in the different countries to keep regular contact with their superiors at headquarters. Rebecca Norton, vice president of finance, Asia-Pacific, at Business Objects (a unit of SAP), makes it a point to participate in global conference calls as often as possible, in order to "wave the Asia-Pacific flag." She notes that this is necessary to ensure that her overseas colleagues understand the conditions under which the Asian business operates. [5] The reason for the frequent communication is to help the home office better understand the opportunities and risks of the foreign country. For example, if headquarters is focused on short-term performance indicators, the head office is more likely to allocate funds to developed markets where returns are quick. But this approach neglects emerging markets, which have more future potential.

According to a 2010 McKinsey study, global economic activity is shifting from developed to developing nations with populations that are young and growing.[6] The growth in the number of consumers in these emerging markets make them not only a focus for rising consumption and production but also major providers of talent, capital, and innovation. This makes it vital for US companies to succeed in these emerging markets. Despite identifying this trend as the most important trend for business in the next five years, only 40 percent of executives are taking action and fully 20 percent are taking no action at all to capture emerging-market growth. [7] This is where communication with headquarters becomes imperative. Regional CFOs must spur actions, such as developing partnerships or joint ventures with local companies, recruiting talent from emerging markets, and developing new business models.

One company taking action is the Luxottica Group, a $6.6 billon eyewear company based in Italy. Although Luxottica sells its products online, it remains solidly committed to brick-and-mortar retail stores and is rapidly expanding its retail presence in China. Describing the role of retail stores, Chris Beer, CEO of Asia Pacific, greater China, and South Africa for Luxoticca, said, "You need to create a connection, create a personal experience, and that's what we've done."[8] On the finance side, Kevin Zhou, retail CFO for Luxottica, closely follows the regulatory environment in China and actively communicates with headquarters to explain evolving legislation and help them understand local financial issues. "You have to always tell them the truth about what's happening in China, and keep updating them," he says. "Keep explaining, and before long, people at headquarters will really understand what's going on in this market." [9]

Hybrid Financial Organization Structures

Finally, multinational companies follow a hybrid of centralized financial operations for some tasks and regional operations for others. Before it was acquired by Hewlett-Packard (HP) in April 2010, network switching and routing solutions company 3Com had centralized specific operations in its North America shared service center (SSC). The North America SSC provided a number of accounting services globally. Although the US-based SSC had a much higher cost of labor than Singapore (where 3Com offshored transaction-based processes), 3Com decided to keep higher-value services in the North America SSC due to 3Com's assessment of the risk and complexity in comparison to the anticipated benefit of moving these from one global center to another. Some of the tasks retained by the North American SSC were worldwide consolidation, worldwide intercompany accounting, and external reporting.

The following processes have been performed in each region (i.e., Europe, the Middle East, and Africa [EMEA]; North America; Latin America; and Asia-Pacific) due to language and local knowledge issues:

- Regional general ledger
- Regional revenue accounting
- Local field finance accounting

- Regional and local payroll
- Regional and local value-added tax (VAT) and good-and-services tax (GST) compliance and reporting [10]

3Com also assigned local field finance managers to be key shared accounting services team members located in the company's higher-risk countries to help ensure compliance with local legal, statutory, tax, and reporting requirements and to help with enforcement and communication of corporate policies locally. Their responsibilities include the following:

- Ensuring all statutory and tax (direct and indirect) filings are completed in accordance with local country requirements
- Liaising with local external auditors, tax authorities, and outsource agencies to ensure the proper execution of payroll and employee disbursements
- Communicating and enforcing corporate accounting policies to local employees
- Ensuring appropriate accounting for local accruals by liaising with local marketing and sales teams to determine if services related to outstanding purchase orders have been provided [11]

Did You Know?

What does the job description for a treasury operations manager look like? The tasks of a manager overseeing international-unit financial management include:

- managing foreign exchange exposures, hedging, accounting compliance, multilateral netting, and multilateral cash pool;
- driving collection, disbursement, concentration and cash accounting, and domestic debt-portfolio management;
- performing cost review and analysis of monthly cash management;
- assisting the treasurer in bank coordination, agreement negotiations, and renewals;
- modeling financial transaction scenarios for capital budgeting and planning analysis (i.e., debt, equity, and other capital market transactions);
- preparing, reviewing, and maintaining Sarbanes-Oxley controls; and
- delivering and coordinating cash forecasts with bank-funding needs and regulatory capital requirements.

The Impact of Religion: Islamic Finance

Companies operating in countries where Islam is the official religion, such as Malaysia, Saudi Arabia, Kuwait, Bahrain, and

Yemen, must adhere to Islamic finance laws. Islamic law prohibits certain financial practices that are common in other countries. For example, Islamic law (called Sharia) prohibits charging interest on money. No interest can be charged, including fixed-rate, floating, simple, or compounded interest, at whatever rate. The Sharia also prohibits financial practices like speculation, conventional insurance, and derivatives, because they're considered gambling in the Islamic tradition. Sharia also prohibits *gharar*, which means "uncertainty" and includes conventional practices like short selling.

To overcome these prohibitions, financial products must be Sharia compliant. There are approved alternatives to interest and speculative investments. For example, instead of lending money and charging interest, banks can lend money and earn profits by charging rentals on the asset leased to the customer. One alternative investment strategy, *musharakah*, allows profit and loss sharing. It's a partnership wherein profits are shared per an agreed-on ratio and losses are shared in proportion to the capital or investment of each partner. A *mudarabah* is an investment partnership, whereby the investor provides capital to another party or entrepreneur in order to undertake a business or investment activity. While profits are shared on an agreed-on ratio, loss of investment is born only by the investor. The entrepreneurs only lose their share of the expected income. [12]

These investment arrangements demonstrate the Sharia's risk-sharing philosophy—the lender must share in the borrower's risk. Since fixed, predetermined interest rates guarantee a return to the lender and fall disproportionately on the borrower, they are seen as exploitative, socially unproductive, and economically wasteful. The preferred mode of financing is profit and loss sharing.

Islamic finance law extends to mutual funds, securities firms, insurance companies, and other nonbanks. A growing number of conventional financial institutions, both inside and outside the Islamic world, have in recent years created Islamic subsidiaries or have been offering Islamic "windows" or products in addition to conventional ones. [13]

KEY TAKEAWAYS

- Political and economic risks arise when a country lacks a long history or commitment to the rule of law. Companies can prepare for volatility by thinking through "unthinkable" scenarios and planning how they would respond if such situations occurred.
- Multinational firms can organize their financial operations in a centralized, decentralized, or hybrid

organization structure. The advantages of a centralized structure are that the company can afford to hire and retain specialized staff who have deep expertise and can bring savings to the company through centralized cash management and more efficient capital investment. Centralization also enables the firm to gain economies of scale for investment and borrowing activities that will reduce transaction costs and get the firm the most competitive pricing. On the other hand, a decentralized financial organization structure allows the firm to recognize the variations in language, customs, cultures, business practices, rules, laws, and regulations among different countries. A decentralized structure lets multinational firms exploit local knowledge and business conditions to deal with uncertainty.

- It's important for regional CFOs to stay in regular contact with corporate headquarters to alert headquarters to opportunities (or warn them of dangers) in their countries.
- Islamic countries practice Sharia—the prohibition of charging interest on money. There are approved, Sharia-compliant alternatives to interest and speculative investments. For example, instead of lending money and charging interest, banks can lend money and earn profits by charging rentals on the asset leased to the customer. One alternative investment strategy, *musharakah*, allows profit and loss sharing. It's a partnership wherein profits are shared per an agreed-on ratio and losses are shared in proportion to the capital or investment of each partner.

EXERCISES

(AACSB: Reflective Thinking, Analytical Skills)

1. Name two ways that companies can prepare or deal with political risk or volatility in a country.
2. What advantages does a decentralized financial organization structure bring to a multinational firm?
3. What advantages does a centralized financial organization structure bring?
4. Why are frequent communications between a regional CFO and headquarters important?
5. How might religion impact financing operations?

[1] Renée Dye and Elizabeth Stephenson, "Five Forces Reshaping the Global Economy: McKinsey Global Survey Results," McKinsey Quarterly, May 2010, accessed November 23, 2010, http://www.mckinseyquarterly.com/Five_forces_reshaping_the_global_ec onomy_McKinsey_Global_Survey_results_2581.
[2] Rik Kirkland, "China's State Capitalism and Multinationals: An Interview with the President of Eurasia Group," McKinsey Quarterly, May 2010, accessed November 23, 2010,

http://www.mckinseyquarterly.com/Chinas_state_capitalism_and_multina
tionals_An_interview_with_the_president_of_Eurasia_Group_2583.

[3] Lowell Bryan, "Globalization's Critical Imbalances," McKinsey
Quarterly, June 2010, accessed October 28, 2010,
http://www.mckinseyquarterly.com/Globalizations_critical_imbalances_2
624.

[4] Harjeet S. Bhabra, Tong Liu, and Dogan Tirtiroglu, "Capital Structure
Choice in a Nascent Market," Financial Management, June 22, 2008,
accessed November 25, 2010, http://www.allbusiness.com/company-
activities-management/company-structures-ownership/11673477-1.html.

[5] Don Durfee, "Local Knowledge," CFO, November 1, 2008, accessed
August 12, 2010, http://www.cfo.com/printable/article.cfm/12465219.

[6] Renée Dye and Elizabeth Stephenson, "Five Forces Reshaping the
Global Economy: McKinsey Global Survey Results," McKinsey Quarterly,
May 2010, accessed November 23, 2010,
http://www.mckinseyquarterly.com/Five_forces_reshaping_the_global_ec
onomy_McKinsey_Global_Survey_results_2581.

[7] Renée Dye and Elizabeth Stephenson, "Five Forces Reshaping the
Global Economy: McKinsey Global Survey Results," McKinsey Quarterly,
May 2010, accessed November 23, 2010,
http://www.mckinseyquarterly.com/Five_forces_reshaping_the_global_ec
onomy_McKinsey_Global_Survey_results_2581.

[8] Sheila Shayon, "Luxottica Envisions Future of Retail," Brand Channel,
July 22, 2010, accessed November 26, 2010,
http://www.brandchannel.com/home/post/2010/07/22/Luxottica-Eye-
Hub-Retail-Concept.aspx

[9] Don Durfee, "Local Knowledge," CFO, November 1, 2008, accessed
August 12, 2010, http://www.cfo.com/printable/article.cfm/12465219.

[10] Phil Searle and Fraser Kirk, "Expanding Geographic Scope and
Setting Up a Truly Global Process Model," Shared Services & Outsourcing
Network 5, no. 9 (January 2004), accessed November 23,
2010, http://www.ssonetwork.co.uk/topic_detail.aspx?id=194&ekfrm=50.

[11] Phil Searle and Fraser Kirk, "Expanding Geographic Scope and
Setting Up a Truly Global Process Model," Shared Services & Outsourcing
Network 5, no. 9 (January 2004), accessed November 23,
2010, http://www.ssonetwork.co.uk/topic_detail.aspx?id=194&ekfrm=50.

[12] "Introduction to Islamic Financing," HSBC Amanah, accessed August
14, 2010,
http://www.assetmanagement.hsbc.com/gam/attachments/mena/amanah
/islamic_invest.pdf.

[13] Ibrahim Warde, Islamic Finance in the Global Economy (Edinburgh,
UK: Edinburgh University Press, 2000).

15.5 Global Money Management: Moving Money across Borders

LEARNING OBJECTIVES

1. Understand the role of global money management in a multinational firm.
2. Know how multilateral netting and transfer pricing can be used to minimize transaction costs and taxes for the firm.
3. Appreciate the efficiencies and savings that result from centralized depositories.

Global Money Management and Centralized Depositories

Global money management involves moving money across borders and managing the firm's financial resources in a way that minimizes taxes and transaction fees while maximizing the firm's returns.

A multinational company can make the most of its cash reserves by holding cash balances at a central location, called a centralized depository. There are two main advantages of centralized depositories:

1. The company earns a higher interest on higher amounts of cash, because cash from across the company is pooled.
2. Pooling cash reserves reduces the total amount of cash that the company needs to hold, because the amount of cash held on hand as a precautionary measure against the unexpected can be pooled and thus reduced—it's unlikely that all the worst cases will happen simultaneously.

Centralized money management also lets a company trade currencies between its subsidiaries and thereby eliminate intermediaries like banks. This practice saves the firm transaction costs. Centralization also means that the company can buy currencies in larger lot sizes, which gives it a better price.

Two facts are important to keep in mind when using the centralized depository technique for global cash management. First, a government can restrict how much capital can flow out of the country (governments do this to preserve foreign exchange reserves). Second, there are transaction costs associated with moving money across borders, and these costs are incurred each time the money is moved.

Cash Management

Companies need to be aware of differences in local cash practices. For example, business customers in Asia often pay their invoices via bank draft—a common method there, but almost unheard of in the United States. This approach typically means a company gets its cash slowly, creating potential working-capital problems. "If you sell to a customer on 30-day terms and on day 29 they give you a bank draft, that's three months more you'll have to wait," said Brian Kenny, CFO of specialty chemicals materials company W. R. Grace's Asia-Pacific division. [1]

Multilateral Netting

Multilateral netting is a technique which companies use to reduce the costs of cross-border payments between subsidiaries. Three or more subsidiaries must participate. (If only two participate, the technique is known as bilateral netting.)

For example, let's say a firm's subsidiary in the Czech Republic owes the Australian subsidiary $4 million, while the Australian subsidiary owes the Czech subsidiary $10 million. Rather than the Czech subsidiary transferring $4 million and the Australian transferring $10 million, the parties agree to one payment in which the Australian subsidiary pays the Czech $6 million. Both payments are thus satisfied. The total funds that flowed between the subsidiaries are reduced from $14 million to $6 million, reducing costs. For example, if the transaction costs (i.e., the foreign exchange commission plus the transfer fees) are 1 percent of the total funds transferred, the transaction costs in this example drop from $140,000 to $60,000. In cases where multiple subsidiaries trade amongst each other, the savings are even more significant. For example, if four subsidiaries each trade with three other subsidiaries, the total number of transactions can be reduced from twelve to three, which reduces transaction costs substantially.

In a real-life example, Colgate-Palmolive operates in 218 countries. Much of its manufacturing operations are centralized rather than being located in numerous countries around the world. As a result, subsidiaries do a lot of business with each other. Colgate headquarters requires that all subsidiaries submit and settle their payments to each other on the same day. By directing all settlements to one day, Colgate maximizes the benefits of multilateral netting and saves on the spread. This reduces the transaction costs as well as the risk of currency fluctuations. [2]

Did You Know?
According to a survey of almost five hundred CFOs and controllers from US-based companies, the following are the top concerns regarding international taxes:

* Cost of complying with international taxes (31 percent of respondents)
* Transfer pricing (28 percent)
* Repatriation of offshore earnings (21 percent)
* Risk management in developing countries (14 percent)
* Mergers and acquisitions transactions (5 percent) [3]

Tax Advantages of Fronting Loans
A fronting loan is a loan made between a parent company and its subsidiary through a financial intermediary such as a bank. The advantage of using fronting loans as a way to lend money, rather than the parent lending the money directly to the subsidiary, is that the parent can gain some tax benefits and bypass local laws that restrict the amount of funds that can be transferred abroad. With a fronting loan, the parent deposits the total amount of the loan in the bank. The bank

then lends the money to the subsidiary. For the bank, the loan is risk free, because the parent has provided the money to the bank. The bank charges the subsidiary a slightly higher interest rate on the loan than it pays to the parent, thus making a profit.

The tax advantages of fronting loans come into play if the loan is made by a subsidiary located in a tax haven. A tax haven is a country that has very advantageous (i.e., low) corporate income taxes. Bermuda is a well-known tax haven. The bank pays interest to the tax-haven subsidiary. The subsidiary doesn't pay taxes on that interest because of the tax-haven laws. At the same time, the interest paid by the subsidiary receiving the loan is tax deductible.

Transfer Pricing
Multinational firms that conduct business among their cross-border subsidiaries can use tax-advantageous transfer pricing. Transfers occur when a company transfers goods or services between its subsidiaries in different countries. For example, a firm might design a product in one country, manufacture it in a second country, assemble it in a third country, and then sell it around the world. Each time the good or service is transferred between subsidiaries, one subsidiary sells it to the other. The question is, what price should be paid? The transfer price is the price that one subsidiary (or subunit of the company) charges another subsidiary (or subunit) for a product or service supplied to that subsidiary.

Since the pricing taking place is between entities owned by the same parent firm, there's an opportunity for pricing an item or service at significantly above or below cost in order to gain advantages for the firm overall. For example, transfer pricing can be a way to bring profits back to the home country from countries that restrict the amount of earnings that multinational firms can take out of the country. In this case, the firm may charge its foreign subsidiary a high price, thus extracting more money out of the country. The firm would use a cost-plus markup method for arriving at the transfer price, rather than using market prices.

Although this practice optimizes results for the company as a whole, it may bring morale problems for the subsidiaries whose profits are impacted negatively from such manipulation. In addition, the pricing makes it harder to determine the actual profit which the favored subsidiary would bring to the company *without* such favored treatment. Finally, all the price manipulations need to remain compliant with local regulations. In fact, to combat such potential losses of income tax revenue, more than forty countries have adopted transfer-pricing rules and requirements. [4]

Generally, compliance with local tax regulations means setting prices such that they satisfy the "arm's length principle." That is, the prices must be consistent with third-party market results. The test of fairness is, "What would an independent company, operating in a competitive market, charge for performing comparable services or selling similar products?" [5]

Nonetheless, even within these guidelines, multinational firms can adjust prices to shift income from a higher-tax country to a lower-tax one. Governments, of course, are instituting or revising legislation to ensure maximum taxes are collected in their own countries. As a result, multinational firms must monitor compliance with local transfer-pricing regulations. [6]

Indirect Taxes

One way that governments respond to budget shortfalls is by imposing or increasing indirect taxes like the value-added tax (VAT) and goods-and-services tax (GST). The reach of these indirect taxes is extending into new areas of the global economy. "The slow economy and falling direct-tax rates are causing many governments worldwide to tighten their existing indirect-tax regimes or introduce new ones," said Frank Sangster, a principal in KPMG's US Indirect Tax practice. "Finance and tax directors must be proactive in considering how their organizations are responding to the global VAT changes, which are already affecting their markets, operations and internal systems." [7]

More countries are coming to rely on VAT as a significant and stable source of tax revenue, so these taxes are unlikely to diminish. China and India are considering introducing national VAT systems for the first time, while European Union (EU) countries might be looking at ways to raise more revenue through VAT. International companies can assess and manage the risks and opportunities of new VAT systems by using merging technologies to increase automation of the indirect tax process, deciding whether to insource or outsource new compliance obligations, and using modeling techniques to assess the impact of local VAT changes. [8]

Manufacturing shoes in China for the Chinese market is subject to a 17 percent VAT, for example, but shoes for export aren't subject to this tax. In some cases, it may be cheaper to make the shoes in China, export them to Hong Kong, reimport them into China, and pay import duties instead of VAT. Local import/export regulations can also impact where companies decide to locate specific functions of the supply chain, such as distribution centers or warehouses. In Fujian province, one can import materials one day and export the output the next day. In Guangdong province, in contrast, the local authorities insist on thirty days' notice for reexported materials. The point is that each emerging-market country and even each region in an emerging-market country can have its own interplay of taxes, duties, and regulatory delays that affect how companies design their operations and the margins they're able achieve.

Did You Know?

Colombia and Indirect Taxes
To attract business process outsourcing (BPO) vendors to Colombia, the country eliminated the VAT tax on BPO service exports. This makes it more attractive to locate offshoring services in Colombia. Local governments also created two free-trade zones in Bogotá and Medellín specifically for BPO, providing state-of-the-art infrastructure and services to companies that settle there. [9]

KEY TAKEAWAYS

- Global money management involves moving money across borders and managing the firm's financial resources in a way that minimizes taxes and transaction fees while maximizing the firm's returns.

- Companies can use multilateral netting as a way to reduce the costs of cross-border payments between subsidiaries. They can also use fronting loans to gain tax advantages.

- The transfer price is the prices at which subsidiaries or affiliates of the same firm sell goods or services to each other. When subsidiaries are located in countries with different tax rates, opportunities exist to move income to a lower-taxing jurisdiction. Firms can manipulate transfer prices to reduce global tax liabilities

- A multinational company can make the most of its cash reserves by holding cash balances at a central location, called a centralized depository, thus earning higher interest and being able to reduce the total amount of cash reserves held on hand. However, the two downsides of centralized depositories are that governments can restrict how much capital flows out of their country and transaction costs are incurred each time money is moved across borders.

EXERCISES

(AACSB: Reflective Thinking, Analytical Skills)
1. How can local cash practices in a country affect a subsidiary's cash flow?

2. What are some advantages that multinational firms gain from centralized depositories?

3. Explain multilateral netting and how it can reduce transaction costs.

4. Why would a company choose to do a fronting loan?

5. What are the challenges of transfer pricing?

[1] Don Durfee, "Local Knowledge," CFO, November 1, 2008, accessed August 12, 2010, http://www.cfo.com/printable/article.cfm/12465219.

[2] Kabir Masson, "'Managing International Financial Risk': A Presentation by Hans L. Pohlschroeder," Columbia Business School Chazen Web Journal of International Business, February 24, 2009, accessed November 23, 2010, http://www1.gsb.columbia.edu/mygsb/faculty/research/pubfiles/3386/Managing%20International%20Financial%20Risk%2Epdf.

[3] Marie Leone, "Tax Sticklers, Not Schemers," CFO, May 26, 2010, accessed October 28, 2010, http://www.cfo.com/printable/article.cfm/14501223.

15.6 End-of-Chapter Questions and Exercises

These exercises are designed to ensure that the knowledge you gain from this book about international business meets the learning standards set out by the international Association to Advance Collegiate Schools of Business (AACSB International). [1] AACSB is the premier accrediting agency of collegiate business schools and accounting programs worldwide. It expects that you will gain knowledge in the areas of communication, ethical reasoning, analytical skills, use of information technology, multiculturalism and diversity, and reflective thinking.

EXPERIENTIAL EXERCISES

(AACSB: Communication, Use of Information Technology, Analytical Skills)

1. You've been tasked with obtaining financing for your subsidiary in Brazil. Of all the sources of financing you've learned about in this chapter, which sources of financing would you explore? Would you consider equity financing in the Brazilian stock exchange? What factors would you research before making this financing decision?

2. Go to http://www.oanda.com to check the current value of the US dollar relative to the euro. Compare this exchange rate to the exchange rate one year ago. Imagine that you are an executive in a multinational firm that will be manufacturing components at a Chinese subsidiary and selling those components to a US subsidiary that will assemble the components into finished goods and then sell them to a Portuguese subsidiary to sell to European markets. What actions would you take to mitigate currency risk?

3. You are the treasury operations manager for a multinational company. You've been tasked with recommending a cash-investment strategy that will maximize a return on the cash and maintain the liquidity needed for emergencies. Using what you've learned about centralized depositories, multilateral netting, fronting loans, tax havens, and transnational investment, what recommendations would you make?

Ethical Dilemmas

(AACSB: Ethical Reasoning, Multiculturalism, Reflective Thinking, Analytical Skills)

1. Coca-Cola operates thirty-nine bottling plants in China. [2] China is an important market for Coca-Cola. The company's sales in volume grew 19 percent in China in 2009 while declining 1 percent in the United States. Coca-Cola also hopes to expand its business into the juice, dairy, and ready-to-drink markets. It had offered $2.3 billion to buy Chinese company China Huiyuan Juice to get a strong (20 percent) share in China's juice market. Chinese regulators, however, rejected the deal. In 2004, Coca-Cola was forced to shut down one of its bottling plants in south India after community organizers blamed it for causing water shortages there. (A year earlier PepsiCo's plant in the same state also lost its operating license for similar reasons.) Coca-Cola is now partnered with the World Wildlife Fund (WWF) to improve the water quality of the Yangtze River, which is the longest river in Asia and supplies 35 percent of China's water but is now the most threatened river in the world due to pollution. Coca-Cola is working with rural farmers, for example, to reduce runoff from animal waste into the river by turning it into biogas for cooking and heating instead. The company has pledged $24 million over seven years to support fresh-water programs globally. It's also striving to be "water neutral" by making its "waste" water pure enough for agricultural irrigation and completely offsetting the amount of water it uses in its soft-drink products by funding clean-water projects and watershed preservation efforts around the world. What do you think of these moves by Coca-Cola? On the one hand, as the world's largest beverage company, its water-neutral plan could make a big difference, and its clout brings attention to the world water issue. On the other hand, bringing attention to the issue could put the spotlight on the company itself, which uses 2.5 liters of water to make a liter of Coke. In fact, when looking across the whole supply chain, 200 liters of water go into making a single liter of Coke (due to water-intensive sugar cane crops). However, looked at from an entire-chain perspective, it takes 140 liters of water to make a cup of coffee and 800 to 1,000 gallons of water to get a single gallon of milk. [3] If you were a

Chinese consumer, would you be more likely to buy Coca-Cola products given the company's efforts to clean up the Yangtze River? If you were an executive at Coca-Cola, what actions or programs would you recommend or support?

2. Transfer pricing is legal, and firms can manipulate transfer prices to avoid taxes. The practice, however, violates the spirit of the law in some countries. Should firms engage in this practice? On the other hand, by not taking advantage of these opportunities, would firms be shortchanging their investors?

[1] Association to Advance Collegiate Schools of Business website, accessed January 26, 2010, http://www.aacsb.edu.
[2] "Coca-Cola on the Yangtze: A Corporate Campaign for Clean Water in China," Knowledge@Wharton, August 18, 2010, accessed August 25, 2010, http://knowledge.wharton.upenn.edu/article.cfm?articleid=2568.
[3] Peter M. Senge, The Necessary Revolution (New York: Doubleday, 2008), 77–92.

NOTES:

www.ingramcontent.com/pod-product-compliance
Lightning Source LLC
Chambersburg PA
CBHW051406200326
41520CB00023B/7136